500 PASTRY RECIPES

500 PASTRY RECIPES

A FABULOUS COLLECTION OF EVERY KIND OF PASTRY FROM PIES AND TARTS TO MOUTHWATERING PUFFS AND PARCELS, SHOWN IN 500 PHOTOGRAPHS

MARTHA DAY

LORENZ BOOKS

This edition is published by Lorenz Books, an imprint of Anness Publishing Ltd,
108 Great Russell Street, London WC1B 3NA; info@anness.com

www.lorenzbooks.com; www.annesspublishing.com

If you like the images in this book and would like to investigate using them for publishing, promotions or advertising, please visit our website www.practicalpictures.com for more information.

Publisher: Joanna Lorenz
Executive Editor: Joanne Rippin
Designer: Adelle Morris

A CIP catalogue record for this book is available from the British Library.

NOTES

Bracketed terms are intended for American readers.

For all recipes, quantities are given in both metric and imperial measures and, where appropriate, in standard cups and spoons. Follow one set of measures, but not a mixture, because they are not interchangeable.

Standard spoon and cup measures are level. 1 tsp = 5ml, 1 tbsp = 15ml, 1 cup = 250ml/8fl oz.

Australian standard tablespoons are 20ml. Australian readers should use 3 tsp in place of 1 tbsp for measuring small quantities.

American pints are 16fl oz/2 cups. American readers should use 20fl oz/2.5 cups in place of 1 pint when measuring liquids.

Electric oven temperatures in this book are for conventional ovens. When using a fan oven, the temperature will probably need to be reduced by about 10–20°C/20–40°F. Since ovens vary, you should check with your manufacturer's instruction book for guidance.

The nutritional analysis given for each recipe is calculated per portion (i.e. serving or item), unless otherwise stated. If the recipe gives a range, such as Serves 4–6, then the nutritional analysis will be for the smaller portion size, i.e. 6 servings.

The analysis does not include optional ingredients, such as salt added to taste.

Medium (US large) eggs are used unless otherwise stated.

PUBLISHER'S NOTE

Although the advice and information in this book are believed to be accurate and true at the time of going to press, neither the authors nor the publisher can accept any legal responsibility or liability for any errors or omissions that may have been made nor for any inaccuracies nor for any loss, harm or injury that comes about from following instructions or advice in this book.

Contents

Introduction 6

Savoury Bites and Mini Pastries 12

Tartlets and Mini Pies 38

Dumplings and Dim Sum 48

Turnovers and Pastry Packages 58

Savoury Tarts and Flans 80

Single and Double Crust Savoury Pies 96

Sweet Little Pastries 122

Strudels and Choux Puffs 168

Sweet Tarts and Fruit Flans 176

Chocolate Pastry Confections 208

Sweet Pies and Desserts 224

Pastry Accompaniments and Fillings 244

Index 254

Introduction

Few can resist the display in the window of a good quality pâtisserie, and many of us have fond memories of the savoury pies and rich, fruit-laden tarts served up by our mothers at dinnertime. Be it a humble apple pie or a hearty chicken and mushroom pie, there is something irresistible about well-made pastry that makes it popular with people of all ages.

Pastries were made as long ago as the 5th century BC and, in ancient Greece, pastry cooks were considered to be a separate trade to bakers. As the ancient Romans and Greeks used oil, not butter, in their cooking, it would not have been possible to shape the pastry as we do today. Consequently, pastry was used primarily as a container.

For some time, pastry was used chiefly as a means of enclosing food, to protect it from the heat of the fire. These pastry cases or 'coffers' were often simply a mixture of flour and water, that was broken off and discarded. However, as ovens improved and the temperature became more controllable and less fierce, it was possible to release pastry from its original role as fire-retardant and explore ways of making it more edible.

Below: *Earliest pies had a simple flour and water crust that was there to keep the food from burning.*

Above: *Spicy little samosas, made from filo pastry, have a variety of tempting savoury fillings.*

In Northern Europe, hard fats such as butter and especially lard were used in cooking, and it was this important addition to the basic pastry recipe that made stiffer, more pliable pastries, such as raised pies, possible. As the art of pastry-making developed, there was little distinction made between sweet and savoury, and the two flavours were often combined. It was not uncommon, for example, for a meat or fish pie to be topped with a sweet pastry. Right up until Victorian times in England, mince pies, often served at Christmas time, contained pieces of minced (ground) meat and shredded suet combined with chopped dried fruits, mixed nuts, spices and sugar, all encased in a rich, sweet pastry. Eventually, the meat was dropped from most recipes, but the name 'mince pie' is still used today.

As chefs experimented with different ingredients and techniques, pastry-making became simpler and less time-consuming, and a number of shortcut recipes such as rough puff pastry came into being. For the average cook, this was a welcome development as the exquisitely decorated pies typical of Victorian

Above: *Traditional recipes can be adapted according to taste, such as this pear tarte tatin.*

times were really possible only with a large household staff. As staff numbers fell and working conditions and hours improved, the fashion for making ornate pies declined.

Time-saving machines such as food processors and refrigeration have further simplified pastry-making. Trends have come and gone, but at heart all sweet and savoury pastries still rely on a well-made pastry. Indeed, the rules of making it have not changed much since the 1800s and still apply to classic and contemporary recipes.

Making pastry isn't difficult if you follow a few simple rules and master the basic techniques. Any good pastry cook knows that practice really does make perfect. You don't need fancy equipment: a bowl, a set of scales or measuring cups and a rolling pin are all you need to begin with, plus one or two pie plates or dishes in sizes to suit your style of cooking. As you become more proficient and discover how satisfying and creative making pastry can be, you may want to expand your range of utensils, but remember, when it comes to good pastry-making, cool hands are the cook's most valuable assets.

This book contains a comprehensive selection of wonderful recipes, covering every kind of pastry and pastry dish. It also ranges the world, presenting not only familiar meat or fruit pies, but also delicious honey-soaked baklava, spicy samosas, delicate dim sum and tempting strudels and tarts from all corners of the globe. The chapters are laid out to help you find the type of dish you want to make, from savoury tarts, sweet filled little pastries to fruit pies.

The recipes cover all the major types of pastry; shortcrust, puff, rough puff, choux and filo, and the essential techniques for each dish are explained, from rolling out and lining to decorating and shaping pastry, so that you can feel confident about every aspect. Less common pastries such as hot water crust, olive oil pastry, and a wide variety of flavoured or spiced sweet pastries are also included. Many of these pastry treats are delightfully simple to make, such as a rustic Mediterranean One-crust Pie, a Tomato Tart made from store-bought puff pastry, or sweet little Almond Cream Puffs, while others are sumptuous indeed – for example the classic pastry gâteau, Saint-Honoré. Whatever the filling, pastry type or technique, each recipe is a delicious example of the pleasure to be had from pastry-making.

Below: *Every classic pastry recipe is included in the book, such as this wonderful apple pie.*

Making Pastry

Making your own pastry may seem daunting at first, but if you follow a few basic rules and stick to the right quantities, you will soon find the technique easy. The key is not to hurry and to keep your hands cool when handling the dough. The crisp, light results are always worth the effort and the popularity of your home-made tarts and pies will be truly satisfying.

SHORTCRUST PASTRY

This crumbly pastry is the best known and most frequently used type. Although the simplest of all pastries, perfect shortcrust needs a cool light hand, as over-handling the dough makes it heavy and hard. The following makes enough for a 25cm/10in flan tin (pan) or ten 7.5cm/3in tartlet tins (mini quiche pans).

Makes about 375g/13oz

225g/8oz/2 cups plain (all-purpose) flour
pinch of salt
115g/4oz/½ cup chilled butter, diced, or half butter and half lard or white vegetable fat
45–60ml/3–4 tbsp chilled water

1 Sift the flour and salt together into a mixing bowl. Cut the fat into the flour using a pastry blender or use your fingertips to rub it in. Shake the bowl occasionally to bring any large pieces of fat to the top. Blend until the mixture resembles fine breadcrumbs.

2 Sprinkle 45ml/3 tbsp of the water evenly over the mixture and mix lightly with a round-bladed knife or fork until the dough comes together. Add a little more water if the mixture is still too dry; it should just begin to hold together.

3 Using one hand, gather the dough together to form a ball. Incorporate any loose pieces of the rubbed-in mixture. Knead on a lightly floured surface for just a few seconds until smooth.

4 Wrap the dough in clear film (plastic wrap), and chill in the refrigerator for about 30 minutes, or until firm but not too stiff to roll. The shortcrust pastry is now ready to use.

MAKING SHORTCRUST PASTRY IN A FOOD PROCESSOR

This method of making pastry is good for rich shortcrust, especially where the higher proportion of fat and sugar may make it harder to handle. It also helps to keep the dough cool in hot weather.

1 Put the sifted flour, salt and sugar, if using, into the food processor. Process for 4–5 seconds. Sprinkle the cubes of fat over the dry ingredients. Process for 10–12 seconds only, or until the mixture resembles fine breadcrumbs.

2 Sprinkle the water or other liquid (such as egg and water) over the flour mixture and, using the pulse button, process until it starts to hold together. Pinch a little of the mixture between your finger and thumb; if the dough is too dry and crumbly, add a little more water and process for just 1–2 seconds more. Do not allow the pastry to form a ball in the food processor.

3 Remove the mixture and form into a ball. Lightly knead on a floured surface for just a few seconds until smooth, then wrap in clear film (plastic wrap) and chill for 30 minutes.

RICH SHORTCRUST PASTRY

Also known as pâte brisée, this is a richer version of shortcrust pastry that contains a higher proportion of fat. It is usually made with an egg yolk and chilled water, but a whole egg may be used. This quantity is enough for a 25cm/10in flan tin (pan) or ten 7.5cm/3in tartlet tins (mini quiche pans).

Makes about 400g/14oz

225g/8oz/2 cups plain (all-purpose) flour
pinch of salt
150g/5oz/10 tbsp chilled butter, diced
1 egg yolk
30ml/2 tbsp chilled water

1 Sift the flour and salt into a large mixing bowl. Rub with your fingertips or cut in the butter until the mixture resembles fine breadcrumbs.

2 Mix the egg yolk and water together. Sprinkle over the dry ingredients and mix in lightly to form a soft dough.

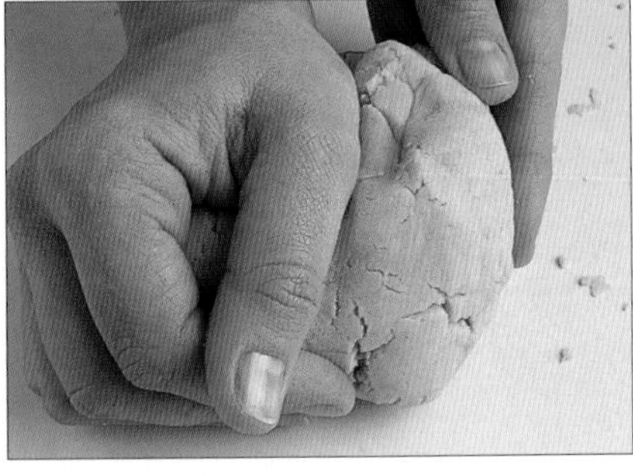

3 Gather the dough together into a ball. Knead on a floured surface until smooth. Wrap in clear film (plastic wrap) and chill in the refrigerator for 30 minutes before using.

PÂTE SUCRÉE

This rich and crisp-textured sweet pastry, also known as biscuit pastry, is used mainly for making flan and tartlet cases. Because it has a high proportion of sugar, it has a crumblier consistency than shortcrust and needs to be chilled for about 1 hour before using. Mix the pastry either in a bowl or on a cold surface. This quantity is enough to make a 23cm/9in flan tin (pan) or eight 7.5cm/3in tartlet tins (mini quiche pans).

Makes about 275g/10oz

150g/5oz/1¼ cups plain (all-purpose) flour
pinch of salt
75g/3oz/6 tbsp chilled butter, diced
25g/1oz/¼ cup icing (confectioners') sugar, sifted
2 egg yolks

1 Sift the flour and salt together to make a mound on a marble slab, pastry board or cold work surface. Make a well in the centre and put in the butter and sugar, then place the egg yolks on top.

2 Using your fingertips only, with a pecking action, work the butter, yolks and sugar together. As you do this, pull in a little of the surrounding flour to prevent the mixture from becoming too sticky.

3 When the mixture begins to form a smooth paste, gradually pull in the rest of the flour to make a rough dough. Lightly knead the dough with just the heel of your hand for about 1 minute, form into a flat disc, wrap and chill for up to 1 hour.

Top Tips for Making and Baking Pâte Sucrée

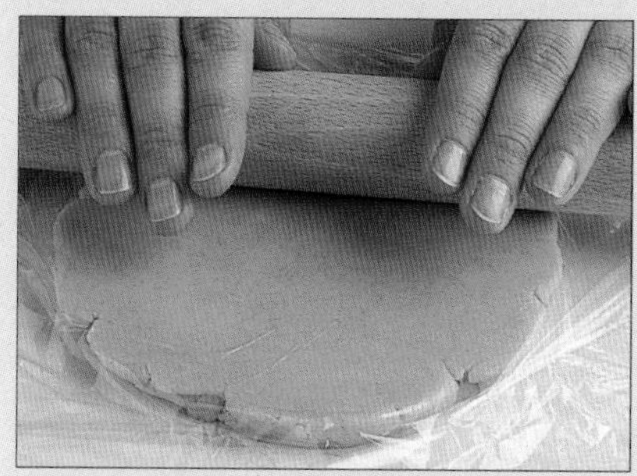

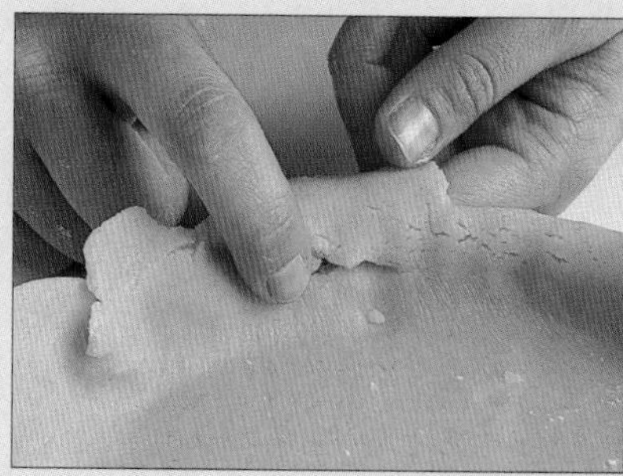

- *Allow plenty of time for the pastry to chill and relax in the refrigerator.*
- *If the pastry has been chilled for more than 1 hour, allow it to soften at room temperature before rolling, or it may crack.*
- *If you find sweet pastry difficult to handle, roll it between sheets of clear film (plastic wrap) or press into the tin with your fingers without rolling it out first.*
- *Pies made using sweet pastry should be taken out of the oven as soon as the pastry is golden brown and crisp. Once it reaches this stage the pastry will burn very quickly because of the sugar content.*

Baking Blind

This process is used for a number of reasons. It is used to partly cook an empty pastry case so that it does not become soggy when the filling is added and the final baking is done. It is also used to completely bake a pastry case when the filling cooks in a relatively short time and you need to ensure that the pastry is fully cooked through. The process is also required when the pastry case is to contain a precooked mixture or an uncooked filling. Lining the pastry case with baking parchment or foil and filling it with baking beans stops the pastry from rising up during cooking.

1 Cut out a round of baking parchment or foil about 7.5cm/3in larger than the flan tin (pan). Prick the base all over with a fork. Lay the baking parchment or foil in the pastry case (pie shell) and press it smoothly over the base and up the side.

2 Put either the commercially made ceramic baking beans, or dried beans or peas, in the case, spreading them out evenly to cover the base. Whichever kind you choose, they can be used over and over again.

3 To partially bake the pastry, bake in an oven preheated to 200°C/400°F/Gas 6 for 15 minutes, or until the pastry is set and the rim is dry and golden. Remove from the oven and lift out the paper and beans. Return the case to the oven for a further 5 minutes until the base is completely dry. If time, allow to cool completely on a wire try before filling and finishing the recipe.

PUFF PASTRY

This pastry forms light flaky layers. The recipe uses a mixture of half butter, for flavour, and half white vegetable fat or lard, to give it a crisper texture. This is enough for two single-crusts in 1.5 litre/ 2½ pint/5 cup pie dishes.

Makes about 500g/1lb

115g/4oz/½ cup butter
115g/4oz/½ cup white vegetable fat or lard
225g/8oz/2 cups plain (all-purpose) flour
pinch of salt
10ml/2 tsp lemon juice
150ml/¼ pint/⅔ cup chilled water

1 Dice the butter and fat. Spread out on a plate and freeze for 10 minutes. Sift the flour and salt into a mixing bowl. Add the diced fat and stir to coat in the flour.

2 Make a well in the centre. Stir the lemon juice into the water and add to the dry ingredients. Mix together with a round-bladed knife to make a dough.

3 Put the dough on to a pastry board or work surface, along with any loose flour left in the bowl. Gently shape to a block and seal the edges with the rolling pin.

4 Roll out the pastry to a 35 x 20cm/14 x 8in rectangle. Fold the lower third of the pastry over the centre third, then fold the top third over that.

5 Press the edges firmly with the rolling pin to seal. Wrap in clear film (plastic wrap) and chill for 10 minutes

6 Roll out the pastry to the same size again, with the sealed edges at the top and bottom. Fold up and chill as before.

7 Repeat the rolling, folding and chilling process three more times. Wrap in clear film. Chill for at least 3 hours, but preferably overnight, before using.

FLAKY PASTRY

It is convenient to buy ready-made puff pastry, but if you want to make it yourself flaky is an easier method than puff pastry. When baked, it looks and tastes very similar. The fat, in this case butter, is incorporated by dotting it over the rolled-out dough, which creates pockets of air that separate the layers. This makes enough for two single-crusts in 1.2 litre/ 2 pint/5 cup tin (pan).

Makes about 450g/1lb

225g/8oz/2 cups strong white bread flour
pinch of salt
175g/6oz/¾ cup chilled butter
150ml/¼ pint/⅔ cup chilled water

1 Sift the flour and salt into a mixing bowl. Rub or cut in 40g/½oz/3 tbsp of the butter until the mixture resembles fine breadcrumbs.

2 Pour over 120ml/4fl oz/½ cup of the water and, using a round-bladed knife, mix to a soft dough, adding a little more water if needed.

3 Put on a lightly floured surface and knead until smooth. Wrap in clear film (plastic wrap) and chill for 15 minutes.

4 Roll the dough out to a 30 x 10cm/12 x 4in rectangle. Cut another 40g/1½oz/ 3 tbsp of the remaining butter into small pieces and dot evenly all over the top two-thirds of the pastry, leaving a 1cm/½in margin at the edge.

5 Fold the lower third of the pastry over the centre third, then fold the top third over that. Press the edges firmly with the rolling pin to seal.

6 Wrap in clear film and chill for 10 minutes. Repeat the rolling and folding process once more.

7 Roll out two more times, with the folded edges at the sides, using 40g/ 1½oz/3 tbsp of the butter each time.

8 Roll out and fold once again (without fat). Chill for at least 1 hour before using.

Ready-made pastry

If you buy ready-made puff pastry use one that has a high butter content as this will have a much better flavour.

Gluten-free pastry

The recipes in this book can be made with gluten-free pastry by replacing the wheat flour with a gluten-free substitute. You may also be able to find quinoa flour or chestnut flour, which are also gluten free and are suitable for making pastry. Other flours, such as oat flour or rice flour may not be suitable, so check the information on the packet before using.

Pastry that is made with gluten-free flour often needs a little more water than wheat flour when mixing to a dough.

CHOUX PASTRY

Elegantly light and crisp, choux pastry puffs up during baking to create a hollow centre, perfect for fillings. This quantity is sufficient for 20 small puffs.

Makes about 150g/5oz
65g/2½oz/9 tbsp plain (all-purpose) flour
pinch of salt
50g/2oz/¼ cup butter, diced
150ml/¼ pint/⅔ cup water
2 eggs, lightly beaten

1 Preheat the oven to 200°C/400°F/Gas 6. Sift the flour and salt on to a small sheet of baking parchment. Put the butter and water in a pan and heat very gently until the butter has melted.

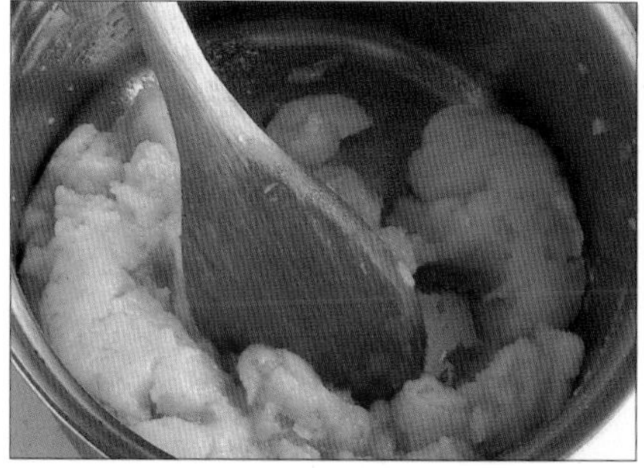

2 Increase the heat and bring to a rolling boil. Remove the pan from the heat, tip in all the flour and beat vigorously until the flour is mixed into the liquid.

3 Return the pan to a low heat and beat until it begins to form a ball. This will take about 1 minute. Remove the pan from the heat again and allow to cool for 2–3 minutes. Add the beaten eggs a little at a time, beating all the time, until you have a smooth shiny paste, that can hold its shape. You may not need all the egg.

4 Shape or pipe, following your recipe, on to a baking tray that is lined with baking parchment and sprinkled with water.

ALMOND PASTRY

This dough resembles pâte sucrée and can be used as an alternative in most sweet tart recipes for added nutty texture and richness. The addition of ground almonds makes it fairly soft, so it must be well chilled, for up to an hour, before using. This quantity is sufficient for a 23cm/9in flan tin (pan).

Makes about 350g/12oz
150g/5oz/1¼ cups plain (all-purpose) flour
pinch of salt
25g/1oz/2 tbsp caster (superfine) sugar
50g/2oz/½ cup ground almonds
90g/3½oz/7 tbsp chilled butter, diced
1 egg
1–2 drops almond extract

1 Sift the plain flour and salt into a large mixing bowl. Stir in the caster sugar and ground almonds. Rub in the butter with your fingertips until the mixture resembles fine breadcrumbs.

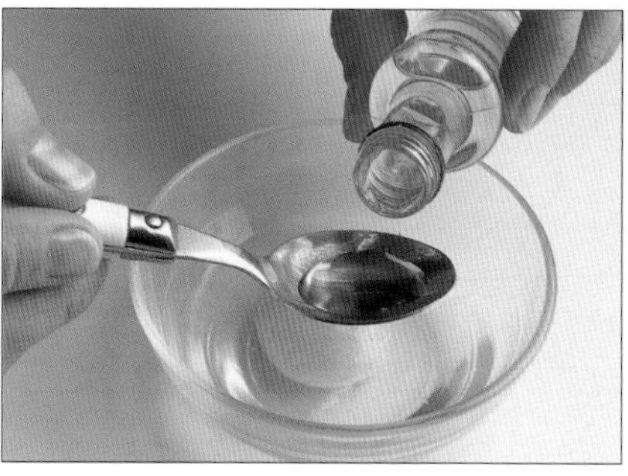

2 Beat the egg and almond extract together in a bowl. Stir into the dry ingredients to make a soft dough. Wrap in clear film (plastic wrap) and chill for 40 minutes until firm, before using in your chosen recipe.

Variation
Make a slightly spiced almond pastry by adding 5ml/1 tsp cinnamon and some grated nutmeg to the flour.

SPICED ORANGE PASTRY

This spicy pastry works perfectly with winter fruit fillings as an alternative to a sweet shortcrust pastry. Use it for Christmas mince pies, for example. The following quantity is enough to line a 23cm/9in flan tin (pan).

Makes about 275g/10oz
175g/6oz/1½ cups plain (all-purpose) flour
pinch of salt
75g/3oz/6 tbsp chilled butter, diced
4 green cardamom pods
pinch of ground cloves
finely grated rind of 1 orange
25g/1oz/2 tbsp caster (superfine) sugar
2 egg yolks
10ml/2 tsp fresh orange juice

1 Sift the flour and salt into a mixing bowl. Rub or cut in the butter until the mixture resembles fine breadcrumbs.

2 Smash the cardamom pods and extract the seeds, discard the pod shells. Using a pestle and mortar, crush the cardmom seeds to a powder.

3 Stir the crushed cardamom seeds into the flour together with the ground cloves, orange rind and sugar.

4 Mix the egg yolks with the orange juice. Add to the bowl and mix to a dough.

5 Knead the pastry briefly until smooth, then wrap in cling film (plastic wrap) and chill for 40 minutes before using in your chosen recipe..

Cheese Straws

Cheese-flavoured pastries are ideal as an appetizer with pre-dinner drinks or as a party snack.

Makes about 10

75g/3oz/¾ cup plain (all-purpose) flour, plus extra for dusting
40g/1½oz/3 tbsp butter, diced
40g/1½oz mature (sharp) hard cheese, such as Cheddar, finely grated
1 egg
5ml/1 tsp ready-made mustard
salt and ground black pepper

1 Preheat the oven to 180°C/350°F/Gas 4. Line a baking sheet with baking parchment. Sift together the flour and seasoning into a bowl and add the butter. Rub in with your fingertips until the mixture resembles fine breadcrumbs. Stir in the grated cheese until thoroughly combined.

2 Crack the egg into another bowl, add the mustard and lightly whisk together with a fork. Add half the egg mixture to the flour and stir gently until the mixture can be gathered together into a smooth ball of dough.

3 Roll out the dough on a lightly floured surface to a square measuring about 15cm/6in. Cut into ten lengths with a sharp knife. Place on the baking sheet and brush with the remaining egg mixture. Bake for 12 minutes, until golden brown. Transfer the straws to a wire rack to cool slightly. Serve warm.

Super Speedy Cheese Straws

Cheese straws are a great standbys when you have unexpected guests. Keep some ready-made all-butter rolled puff pastry in the refrigerator so that you can quickly make this super-fast version. Place the rolled pastry on a floured board and sprinkle half of it with a couple of handfuls of grated Parmesan. Fold over the uncovered half to make a sandwich, then gently roll with a rolling pin so that it sticks together. Trim the edges to make straight sides, brush with beaten egg or a little milk, and sprinkle again with a little Parmesan. Cut the pastry into straws, place on a baking tray and bake as above.

Deep-Fried Pastry with Cheese

These crisp little cheesy parcels come from Brazil, and are simple but delicious. Their famous spirit, cachaça, is used to make the pastry.

Serves 6

For the pastry
260g/9½oz/scant 2¾ cups plain (all-purpose) flour
5ml/1 tsp salt
30ml/2 tbsp lard or white cooking fat, diced
5ml/1 tsp cachaça or vodka
15ml/1 tbsp white vinegar
120ml/4fl oz/½ cup warm water

For the filling
200g/7oz/2 cups grated mozzarella
salsa, hot pepper sauce or ketchup, to serve

1 To make the pastry, sift the flour and salt into a large bowl. Rub in the lard with your fingertips until the mixture resembles fine breadcrumbs. Stir in the cachaça and white vinegar, then gradually mix in the warm water; you may not need it all, so add a little at a time until the mixture forms a ball.

2 Transfer to a floured surface and knead for 3–4 minutes until you have a smooth but stiff dough. Shape into a roll with a diameter of about 5cm/2in. Wrap in clear film (plastic wrap) and leave at room temperature for at least 4 hours.

3 Cut the dough into six pieces. Using a rolling pin or pasta machine, roll each piece until a little thinner than 3mm/⅛in, then trim into a 10 x 20cm/4 x 8in rectangle. Place six rectangles on a floured surface and brush the edges with water.

4 Put a heaped tablespoonful of grated cheese in the centre of one half of each rectangle, and fold the other half over it. Firmly press the edges together, then, using a fork, mark a pattern all around the edges.

5 Heat a 7.5cm/3in depth of vegetable oil in a deep pan to 190°C/375°F on a sugar thermometer. Fry the pastries, one at a time until golden and crisp. Use metal slotted spoons to turn them over every 30 seconds, so that they brown on both sides.

6 Serve hot with salsa, hot pepper sauce or ketchup.

Cheese Straws Energy 49kcal/206kJ; Protein 1.5g; Carbohydrate 3.9g, of which sugars 0.1g; Fat 3.1g, of which saturates 1.9g; Cholesterol 13mg; Calcium 32mg; Fibre 0.2g; Sodium 39mg.
Deep-fried Pastry Energy 278kcal/1167kJ; Protein 10.3g; Carbohydrate 33.7g, of which sugars 0.7g; Fat 12.3g, of which saturates 6.7g; Cholesterol 24mg; Calcium 181mg; Fibre 1.6g; Sodium 461mg.

Tiny Cheese Puffs

These choux pastry bites go perfectly with chilled white wine. They are delicious on their own, but are also good filled with garlic-flavoured cheese.

Makes about 45

115g/4oz/1 cup plain (all-purpose) flour
pinch of salt
5ml/1 tsp mustard powder
pinch of cayenne pepper
250ml/8fl oz/1 cup water
115g/4oz/½ cup butter, diced
4 eggs
75g/3oz Gruyère cheese, diced
15ml/1 tbsp fresh chives, chopped

1 Preheat the oven to 200°C/400°F/Gas 6. Lightly grease two large baking sheets.

2 Sift together the flour, salt, mustard powder and cayenne pepper into a large mixing bowl.

3 In a pan, bring the water and butter to the boil over a medium heat. Remove from the heat. Add the flour mixture all at once, beating with a wooden spoon until a dough ball forms. Return the pan to the heat and beat constantly for 2 minutes. Remove from the heat and cool for 5 minutes.

4 Beat three of the eggs into the dough, one at a time, beating well after each addition.

5 Beat the fourth egg in a small bowl, then add a little at a time, beating until the dough is smooth and falls slowly when dropped from a spoon. (You may not need all of it.)

6 Stir the diced cheese and chives into the dough.

7 Drop small mounds of dough, spaced about 5cm/2in apart, on to the prepared baking sheets. Beat any remaining egg with 15ml/1 tbsp water and brush the tops with the glaze.

8 Bake for 8 minutes, then reduce the temperature to 180°C/350°F/Gas 4 and bake for another 7–8 minutes, until puffed and golden. Transfer to a wire rack to cool. Serve warm.

Gouda-filled Puffs

To give your guests a special surprise at a dinner party, or simply for a light snack, try making these elegant cheese puffs.

Makes about 50

100g/3¾oz/3 tbsp butter
250ml/8fl oz/1 cup water
150g/5oz/1¼ cups plain (all-purpose) flour
4 eggs
150g/5oz/1¼ cups grated extra-mature (sharp) Gouda cheese
freshly grated nutmeg
salt and ground black pepper, to taste

1 Preheat the oven to 220°C/425°F/Gas 7. Line two baking sheets with baking parchment if they aren't non-stick.

2 Heat the butter, water and salt to taste in a small covered pan over low heat until the butter has melted. Bring to the boil, remove from the heat and add in all the flour immediately.

3 Return the pan to the heat and cook, stirring constantly, until the mixture comes away from side of the pan and forms a ball. This may take a few minutes.

4 Transfer the dough to a large bowl and beat in the eggs, one at a time, with a hand-held mixer fitted with dough hooks. Continue beating until the dough is smooth and glossy.

5 Add 50g/2oz/½ cup of the cheese and season with nutmeg, salt and pepper to taste. Stir to mix.

6 Using two teaspoons, place 25 walnut-size mounds of the mixture on the prepared baking sheets, spacing them about 5cm/2in apart. Bake for about 20 minutes, until puffed up and light golden brown.

7 Remove from the oven and leave to cool. Cut the puffs open with scissors and fill with the remaining cheese using a teaspoon.

8 Just before serving, heat through in a hot oven for a few minutes. Cheese puffs also freeze well. Reheat from frozen in a preheated oven at 220°C/425°F/Gas 7 for 10 minutes.

Tiny Cheese Puffs Energy 41kcal/172kJ; Protein 1.2g; Carbohydrate 2g, of which sugars 0.1g; Fat 3.2g, of which saturates 1.8g; Cholesterol 24mg; Calcium 20mg; Fibre 0.1g; Sodium 34mg.
Gouda Puffs Energy 43kcal/181kJ; Protein 1.6g; Carbohydrate 2.3g, of which sugars 0.1g; Fat 3.1g, of which saturates 1.8g; Cholesterol 22mg; Calcium 29mg; Fibre 0.1g; Sodium 40mg.

Cheese Filo Scrolls

These delicious Bulgarian savouries are traditionally served warm as a first course, or else as a snack in cafés, restaurants and homes at any time of the day.

Serves 4–6

450g/1lb/2 cups feta cheese, well drained and finely crumbled
90ml/6 tbsp natural Greek (US strained plain) yogurt
2 eggs, beaten
14–16 sheets 40 x 30cm/16 x 12in ready-made filo pastry, thawed if frozen
225g/8oz/1 cup unsalted (sweet) butter, melted
sea salt and chopped spring onions (scallions), to garnish

1 Preheat the oven to 200°C/400°F/Gas 6. In a large bowl, mix together the feta cheese, yogurt and eggs, beating well until the mixture is smooth.

2 Fit a piping (pastry) bag with a large 1cm/½in plain round nozzle and fill with half of the cheese mixture.

3 Lay out one sheet of pastry, fold into a 30 x 20cm/12 x 8in rectangle and brush with a little melted butter. Along one long edge pipe the cheese mixture 5mm/¼in away from the edge.

4 Roll up the pastry to form a sausage shape and tuck in each end, to prevent the filling escaping. Brush with more melted butter.

5 Form the 'sausage' into a tight 'S' or a crescent shape. Repeat with the remaining ingredients, refilling the piping bag as necessary.

6 Place the scrolls on a greased baking sheet and sprinkle with a little salt and chopped spring onion. Bake for 20 minutes, or until golden brown and crispy. Cool on a wire rack, before serving.

Cook's Tip
If possible, use the locally made sheep's cheese, bryndza. Made throughout Eastern Europe, it is a subtly flavoured, crumbly and moist cheese that resembles feta, but it is not as salty. It is increasingly available in Middle Eastern or Cypriot delicatessens.

Cheese Aigrettes

Choux pastry is often used to make sweet pastries, such as profiteroles, but these little savoury buns, flavoured with Gruyère and dusted with grated Parmesan, are just delicious. They make a wonderful party snack and are best made ahead of time and deep fried to serve.

Makes 30

100g/3¾oz/scant 1 cup plain (all-purpose) flour
2.5ml/½ tsp paprika
2.5ml/½ tsp salt
75g/3oz/6 tbsp butter, diced
3 eggs, beaten
75g/3oz mature (sharp) Gruyère cheese, coarsely grated
corn or vegetable oil, for deep-frying
50g/2oz/⅔ cup freshly grated Parmesan cheese
ground black pepper

1 Mix together the flour, paprika and salt by sifting them on to a sheet of baking parchment. Add a grinding of black pepper.

2 Put the butter and 200ml/7fl oz/scant 1 cup water into a pan and heat gently. As soon as the butter has melted and the liquid starts to boil, add in all the seasoned flour and beat hard with a wooden spoon until the mixture forms a stiff paste and comes away from the sides of the pan in a ball.

3 Remove the pan from the heat and cool the paste for 5 minutes. This is important if the aigrettes are to rise well. Gradually beat in enough of the beaten egg to give a stiff dropping consistency that still holds a shape on the spoon. Mix in the Gruyère cheese.

4 Heat the oil for deep-frying to 180°C/350°F or until it is hot enough to turn a cube of bread brown in 1 minute. Take a teaspoonful of the choux paste and use a second spoon to carefully slide it into the oil.

5 Make more aigrettes in the same way. Fry for 3–4 minutes until golden brown. Drain on kitchen paper and keep warm while cooking successive batches. To serve, pile the aigrettes on a warmed serving dish and sprinkle with Parmesan.

Cheese Scrolls Energy 586kcal/2425kJ; Protein 17.1g; Carbohydrate 15.1g, of which sugars 2g; Fat 51.4g, of which saturates 32.3g; Cholesterol 203mg; Calcium 344mg; Fibre 0.5g; Sodium 1390mg.
Cheese Aigrettes Energy 84kcal/348kJ; Protein 2.2g; Carbohydrate 2.4g, of which sugars 0.1g; Fat 7.3g, of which saturates 2.7g; Cholesterol 28mg; Calcium 46mg; Fibre 0.1g; Sodium 58mg.

Filo Cigars Filled with Feta

These classic cigar-shaped Turkish pastries are popular snack and meze food, and they are also good as nibbles with drinks. In this version they are filled with cheese and herbs, but other popular fillings include aromatic minced meat, baked aubergine and cheese, or pumpkin, cheese and dill. The filo pastry can be folded into triangles, but cigars are the most traditional shape. They can be prepared in advance and kept under a damp dish towel in the refrigerator until you are ready to fry them at the last minute.

Serves 3–4

225g/8oz feta cheese
1 egg, lightly beaten
1 small bunch each of fresh flat leaf parsley, mint and dill, finely chopped
4–5 sheets of filo pastry
sunflower oil, for deep-frying
dill fronds, to garnish (optional)

1 In a large mixing bowl, mash the feta with a fork. Beat in the egg and fold in the herbs.

2 Working with one sheet at a time, cut the filo into strips about 10–13cm/4–5in wide, and pile them on top of each other. Keep the strips covered with a damp dish towel.

3 Place a heaped teaspoon of the cheese filling along one of the short ends of a strip. Roll the end over the filling, quite tightly to keep it in place, then tuck in the sides to seal in the filling and continue to roll until you get to the other end.

4 Brush the tip with a little water to help seal the roll. Place the filled cigar, join side down, on a plate and cover with a damp dish towel to keep it moist. Continue with the remaining sheets of filo and filling.

5 Heat enough oil for deep-frying in a wok or other heavy, deep-sided pan, and deep-fry the filo cigars in batches for about 5–6 minutes until crisp and golden brown.

6 Lift out of the oil with a slotted spoon and drain on kitchen paper. Serve immediately, garnished with dill fronds, if you like.

Tomato and Cheese Cups

These crisp little tartlets look really impressive but are actually incredibly easy to make. They are at their best when eaten fresh from the oven and they make ideal snacks when served with drinks. Filo pastry is usually brushed with butter to prevent it sticking while it cooks, but here egg white and cornflour serves the same purpose.

Serves 4

2 sheets filo pastry
cornflour (cornstarch), for dusting
1 egg white
115g/4oz/1½ cup cream cheese
a handful of fresh basil leaves
4 tomatoes, sliced
salt and ground black pepper

1 Preheat the oven to 200°C/400°F/Gas 6. Lay out the filo pastry on a board dusted with cornflour (cornstarch). Brush the sheets of filo pastry lightly with egg white and cut into 16 10cm/4in squares.

2 Layer the squares in twos, in a tartlet tin (muffin pan). Divide the cheese among the pastry cases (pie shells). Season with black pepper and top with a few basil leaves.

3 Arrange the tomato slices on the cheese, season and bake for 10–12 minutes, until golden and crisp. Serve warm.

Variation

To add a Mediterranean flavour to these pastry cups, try adding a few thinly sliced black olives, if you wish, or a few baby capers, together with some fine strips of anchovy.

Cook's Tip

This recipe comes from Eastern Europe where a subtly flavoured goat's cheese, which resembles feta but is less salty, would be used. Cream cheese makes a good substitute, but you can also use a mild creamy soft goat's cheese if you wish.

Filo Cigars Energy 311kcal/1291kJ; Protein 12.4g; Carbohydrate 11.2g, of which sugars 1.6g; Fat 24.4g, of which saturates 9.5g; Cholesterol 92mg; Calcium 278mg; Fibre 1.7g; Sodium 838mg.
Tomato & Cheese Cups Energy 67kcal/283kJ; Protein 2.6g; Carbohydrate 12.6g, of which sugars 3g; Fat 1g, of which saturates 0.5g; Cholesterol 1mg; Calcium 31mg; Fibre 1.7g; Sodium 28mg.

Corn and Cheese Pastries

These tasty pastries are really simple to make and extremely moreish – why not make double the amount – they'll go like hot cakes.

Serves 4

250g/9oz corn, fresh or canned
115g/4oz feta cheese
1 egg, beaten
30ml/2 tbsp whipping cream
15g/½oz Parmesan cheese, grated
3 spring onions (scallions), chopped
8–10 small sheets filo pastry
115g/4oz butter, melted
ground black pepper

1 Preheat the oven to 190°C/375°F/Gas 5 and butter two patty tins (muffin pans).

2 If using fresh corn, strip the kernels from the cob using a sharp knife and simmer in water for 3–5 minutes until tender. For canned corn, drain and rinse under cold running water.

3 Crumble the feta cheese into a bowl and stir in the corn. Add the egg, cream, Parmesan cheese, spring onions and ground black pepper, and stir well.

4 Take one sheet of pastry and cut it in half to make a square. (Keep the remaining pastry covered with a damp cloth to prevent it drying out.) Brush with melted butter and then fold into four, to make a smaller square (about 7.5cm/3in).

5 Place a heaped teaspoon of mixture in the centre of each pastry square and then squeeze the pastry around the filling to make a 'money bag' casing.

6 Continue making pastries until all the mixture is used up. Brush the outside of each with any remaining butter and then bake in the oven for about 15 minutes until golden. Serve hot.

Cook's Tip
To peel the tomatoes easily, plunge them into boiling water for 30 seconds, then refresh in cold water. Peel away the skins.

Cheese and Pesto Triangles

These pastries can be made ahead and frozen uncooked. Freeze them in a single layer and then transfer them to a freezer-proof container. To serve, arrange the triangles on baking trays, brush them with oil and bake from frozen for 5–10 minues longer than the recommended time. Serve warm as an appetizer.

Serves 8

225g/8oz frozen chopped spinach
30ml/2 tbsp pesto sauce
115g/4oz Gruyère cheese
50g/2oz/½ cup grated Parmesan cheese
2 x 275g/10oz packet of frozen filo pastry, thawed
30ml/2 tbsp olive oil
salt and ground black pepper

1 Preheat the oven to 190°C/375°F/Gas 5.

2 Prepare the filling. Put the frozen spinach into a pan, and heat gently to defrost, breaking it up as it softens. Increase the heat to drive off any excess moisture. Transfer to a bowl and cool.

3 Put the pine nuts into a frying pan and stir over very low heat until they are lightly toasted. Chop them and add them to the spinach, with the pesto and Gruyère and Parmesan cheeses. Season to taste with salt and pepper.

4 Unwrap the filo pastry and cover it with clear film (plastic wrap) and a damp tea towel (to prevent it from drying out). Take one sheet at a time and cut it into 5cm/2in wide strips. Brush each strip with oil.

5 Put a teaspoon of filling on one end of each strip of pastry. Fold the end over in a triangle, enclosing the filling.

6 Continue to fold the triangle over and over again until the end of the strip is reached. Repeat with the other strips, until all the fillng has been used up.

7 Place the triangles on baking trays, brush them with oil and bake for 20–25 minutes, or until golden brown. Cool on a wire rack. Serve warm.

Corn Pastries Energy 475kcal/1970kJ; Protein 11.5g; Carbohydrate 19.7g, of which sugars 2.7g; Fat 39.5g, of which saturates 24g; Cholesterol 158mg; Calcium 197mg; Fibre 2g; Sodium 645mg.
Cheese Triangles Energy 484Kcal/2037kJ; Protein 3.7g; Carbohydrate 64.1g, of which sugars 64.1g; Fat 16.3g, of which saturates 10.3g; Cholesterol 48mg; Calcium 125mg; Fibre 1g; Sodium 53mg.

Filo Baskets with Ginger and Dill

Make up some elegant filo baskets, then fill with some crisply steamed vegetables tossed in a tasty and creamy sauce. The mushroom filling has a lovely warm flavour from the fresh ginger and dill. If you are unable to find oyster mushrooms add extra chestnut or brown mushrooms to make up to the correct weight.

Serves 4

4 sheets of filo pastry
40g/1½oz/3 tbsp butter, melted

For the filling
30ml/2 tbsp olive oil
15ml/1 tbsp fresh root ginger, grated
2 garlic cloves, crushed
2 shallots, sliced
225g/8oz mushrooms, chestnut or brown, sliced
115g/4oz oyster mushrooms, sliced
1 courgette (zucchini), sliced
220g/7oz crème fraîche
30ml/2 tbsp fresh dill, chopped
salt and ground black pepper
dill and parsley sprigs, to serve

1 Cut the filo sheets into four. Line four large tartlet tins (muffin pans), angling the layers so that the corners form a pretty star shape. Brush between each layer with butter. Set aside.

2 Preheat the oven to 190°C/375°F/Gas 5. Bake the cases for about 10 minutes until golden brown and crisp. Remove set aside to cool.

3 For the filling, heat the oil and sauté the ginger, garlic and shallots for 2 minutes, then add the mushrooms and courgette. Cook for another 3 minutes.

4 Mix in the crème fraîche, chopped dil and seasoning. Heat until just bubbling then spoon into the filo cases. Garnish with the dill and parsley and serve.

Cook's Tip

If the mushrooms release a lot of water while cooking, keep them on the heat, stirring, until it evaporates, otherwise the liquid will thin the sauce.

Filo Purses with Creamy Leeks

These elegant pastry purses offer a delightful combination of textures and tastes, with the crisp buttery filo exterior contrasting nicely with the smooth, tender leek and tangy cream cheese filling.

Serves 4

115g/4oz/½ cup butter
225g/8oz/2 cups leeks, trimmed and finely chopped
225g/8oz/1 cup cream cheese
15ml/1 tbsp finely chopped fresh dill
15ml/1 tbsp finely chopped fresh parsley
2 spring onions (scallions), finely chopped
pinch of cayenne pepper
1 garlic clove, finely chopped
2.5ml/½ tsp salt
1.5ml/¼ tsp ground black pepper
1 egg yolk
9 sheets filo pastry, thawed if frozen
lightly cooked leeks, to serve

1 Preheat the oven to 200°C/400°F/Gas 6. Melt 25g/1oz/2 tbsp of the butter in a frying pan and fry the leeks for 4–5 minutes until soft. Drain off any liquid.

2 Put the cream cheese in a bowl and stir in the dill, parsley, spring onions, cayenne, garlic and seasoning.

3 Add the egg yolk and leeks to the cheese mixture and stir well. Melt the remaining butter.

4 Place one sheet of filo pastry on a board, brush with a little of the melted butter and place another sheet on top. Brush again with butter and top with a third sheet of filo.

5 Cut the layered filo into four squares and place 20ml/4 tsp of the cheese mixture in the centre of each square. Gather up the edges into a purse, twisting around to seal.

6 Repeat with the other six sheets of filo to make a total of 12 purses. Brush each one with a little more butter.

7 Place the purses on a greased baking sheet and bake in the oven for 20–25 minutes until they are golden brown. Serve on a bed of lightly cooked leeks.

Filo Baskets Energy 389kcal/1607kJ; Protein 4.8g; Carbohydrate 11g, of which sugars 2.7g; Fat 36.5g, of which saturates 21.1g; Cholesterol 83mg; Calcium 79mg; Fibre 2.4g; Sodium 79mg.
Filo Purses Energy 578kcal/2389kJ; Protein 6.2g; Carbohydrate 21.6g, of which sugars 2.1g; Fat 52.4g, of which saturates 32.2g; Cholesterol 165mg; Calcium 132mg; Fibre 3.3g; Sodium 350mg.

Red Pepper and Watercress Parcels

Peppery watercress combines well with sweet red pepper in these crisp little tasty parcels. Serve with a mixed salad and mustard dressing.

Makes 8

3 red (bell) peppers
175g/6oz/1 bunch watercress
225g/8oz/1 cup ricotta cheese
50g/2oz/¼ cup blanched almonds, toasted and chopped
8 sheets filo pastry
30ml/2 tbsp olive oil
salt and ground black pepper

1 Preheat the oven to 190°C/375°/Gas 5. Place the peppers under a hot grill (broiler) until blistered and charred. Place in a plastic bag. When cool enough to handle, peel, seed and pat dry on kitchen paper.

2 Place the peppers and watercress in a food processor and blend until coarsely chopped. Spoon into a bowl. Mix in the ricotta and almonds, and season to taste.

3 Working with one sheet of filo pastry at a time, cut out two 8cm/7in and two 5cm/2in squares from each sheet. Brush one large square with a little olive oil and place a second large square at an angle of 90 degrees to form a star shape.

4 Place one of the small squares in the centre of the star shape. Brush lightly with oil and top with a second small square.

5 Top with one-eighth of the red pepper mixture. Bring the edges together to form a purse shape and twist to seal. Repeat with the other parcels, then place on a lightly greased baking sheet and cook for 25–30 minutes until golden. Serve warm.

Cook's Tip
These little parcels, with nutrient-rich watercress, red (bell) peppers and almonds, are packed with goodness. Try adding them to lunch boxes for a healthy meal.

Cheese and Dill Pastries

These little cheese pastries are best served hot so that the cheese is still soft and light and the pastry melts in the mouth. They make ideal snacks for parties, or a meze spread.

Serves 4–6

225g/8oz feta cheese, rinsed and drained
225g/8oz mozzarella or halloumi cheese
small bunch of fresh dill, chopped
2 eggs, lightly beaten
flour, for dusting
450g/1lb ready-prepared puff pastry
2 egg yolks, mixed with a little oil or water, for brushing
sea salt and ground black pepper

1 Preheat the oven to 200°C/400°F/Gas 6. In a bowl, mash the feta with a fork. Grate the mozzarella or halloumi, or whizz to a paste in a blender or food processor, and add it to the feta.

2 Mix in the dill and beaten eggs, season with salt and pepper and mix together. Set aside while you prepare the pastry.

3 Dust the work surface with flour and roll out the pastry thinly. Using a round pastry (cookie) cutter, or the rim of a cup, cut out as many 10cm/4in rounds as you can, then gather up the trimmings, reroll and cut out further rounds. Dust the pastry circles lightly with flour before stacking them.

4 Place 10ml/2 tsp of the cheese mixture just off centre on each pastry round. Lift the other side and bring it up over the filling until the edges touch each other to make a half-moon shape. Use your finger to dampen the edges with a little water and pinch them together to seal. You can press along the edges with the back of a fork to make a pattern.

5 Line several baking trays with baking parchment and arrange the pastries on them. Brush the top of each pastry with a little of the beaten egg yolk mixture.

6 Bake for about 20 minutes, until the pastries are puffed up and golden brown. Serve immediately, while the cheese filling is still warm.

Red Pepper Parcels Energy 165kcal/690kJ; Protein 6.3g; Carbohydrate 13.5g, of which sugars 5.5g; Fat 10g, of which saturates 2.8g; Cholesterol 14mg; Calcium 140mg; Fibre 2.4g; Sodium 43mg.
Cheese Pastries Energy 526kcal/2192kJ; Protein 20.6g; Carbohydrate 30.5g, of which sugars 1.8g; Fat 37.4g, of which saturates 11.3g; Cholesterol 179mg; Calcium 352mg; Fibre 0.5g; Sodium 950mg.

Half-Moon Cheese Pies

These delicious small Greek pies, which are called *skaltsounakia*, always dazzle people and are a favourite at every meze table. In Crete, where they are very popular, there are several variations, including one with a filling of sautéed wild greens. Serve them freshly baked, hot from the oven or while still warm.

Makes 12–14

1 egg, plus 1 egg yolk, mixed with a little water for glazing
150g/5oz feta cheese, chopped and crumbled
30ml/2 tbsp milk
30ml/2 tbsp chopped fresh mint leaves
15ml/1 tbsp raisins
15ml/1 tbsp pine nuts, lightly toasted
a little vegetable oil, for greasing
a few sprigs of fresh mint, to garnish

For the pastry

225g/8oz/2 cups self-raising (self-rising) flour
45ml/3 tbsp extra virgin olive oil
15g/½oz/1 tbsp butter, melted
90g/3½oz/scant ½ cup Greek (US strained plain) yogurt

1 To make the pastry, put the flour in a large bowl and mix in the oil, butter and yogurt by hand. Cover and rest in the refrigerator for 15 minutes.

2 Meanwhile, make the filling. Beat the egg lightly in a bowl. Crumble in the feta cheese, then mix in the milk, mint, raisins and toasted pine nuts.

3 Preheat the oven to 190°C/375°F/Gas 5. Cut the pastry into two pieces and cover one with clear film (plastic wrap) or a dish towel. Thinly roll out the remaining piece of pastry and cut out 7.5cm/3in rounds.

4 Place a heaped teaspoonful of filling on each round and fold the pastry over to make a half-moon shape. Press the edges to seal, then place the pies on a greased baking sheet. Repeat with the remaining pastry.

5 Brush the pies with the egg yolk and water mix and bake in the preheated oven for about 20 minutes, or until golden brown. Serve immediately.

Baked Vegetable Samosas

Potatoes and peas are the most common samosa fillings, but other vegetables such as carrots are also used

Makes 12

60ml/4 tbsp vegetable oil
1.5ml/¼ tsp asafoetida
2.5ml/½ tsp black mustard seeds
5ml/1 tsp cumin seeds
2.5ml/½ tsp nigella seeds
1 medium onion, finely chopped
2 green chillies, finely chopped
2.5ml/½ tsp ground turmeric
5ml/1 tsp ground cumin
350g/12oz boiled potatoes, finely diced
115g/4oz/1 cup peas
50g/2oz/½ cup carrots, grated
5ml/1 tsp salt or to taste
2.5ml/½ tsp garam masala
30ml/2 tbsp fresh coriander (cilantro) leaves, chopped
12 sheets filo pastry
75g/3oz/6 tbsp butter, melted

1 Heat the oil over a medium heat. Add the asafoetida, followed by the mustard, cumin, and nigella seeds. Add the onion and chillies and fry until the onion is browning.

2 Add the turmeric and cumin, cook for about a minute, then add the potatoes, peas, carrots and salt. Stir them around until the vegetables are thoroughly coated with the spices. Stir in the coriander leaves and remove from the heat. Allow the mixture to cool completely. Preheat the oven to 180°C/350°F/Gas 4 and line a baking sheet with baking parchment.

3 Remove the filo pastry from its packaging and cover with a moist cloth or clear film (plastic wrap). Place one sheet of filo pastry on a board and brush generously with melted butter. Fold the buttered pastry sheet in half lengthways, brush with some more butter and fold lengthways again.

4 Place about 15ml/1 tbsp of the filling on the bottom right-hand corner of the pastry sheet and fold over to form a triangle. Continue to fold to the top of the sheet, maintaining the triangular shape. Moisten the ends and seal the edges.

5 Place on the baking sheet and brush with some melted butter. Make the rest of the samosas in the same way. Bake in the oven for 20 minutes or until browned. Serve warm.

Half-Moon Pies Energy 160Kcal/669kJ; Protein 5g; Carbohydrate 16.4g, of which sugars 2.5g; Fat 8.8g, of which saturates 3.4g; Cholesterol 31mg; Calcium 129mg; Fibre 0.7g; Sodium 270mg.
Baked Samosas Energy 180kcal/752kJ; Protein 3.6g; Carbohydrate 19.6g, of which sugars 2.5g; Fat 10.4g, of which saturates 4.1g; Cholesterol 26mg; Calcium 38mg; Fibre 1.6g; Sodium 58mg.

Potato, Shallot and Garlic Samosas

Most samosas are deep-fried, but these are baked, making them a healthier option. They are also perfect for parties as no deep-frying is involved.

Makes 25

1 large potato, about 250g/9oz, diced
15ml/1 tbsp groundnut (peanut) oil
2 shallots, finely chopped
1 garlic clove, finely chopped
60ml/4 tbsp coconut milk
5ml/1 tsp Thai red or green curry paste
75g/3oz/¾ cup peas
juice of ½ lime
25 samosa wrappers or 10 x 5cm/4 x 2in strips of filo pastry
salt and ground black pepper
oil, for brushing

1 Preheat the oven to 220°C/425°F/Gas 7. Bring a small pan of water to the boil, add the diced potato, cover and cook for 10–15 minutes, until tender. Drain and set aside.

2 Meanwhile, heat the groundnut oil in a large frying pan and cook the shallots and garlic over a medium heat, stirring occasionally, for 4–5 minutes, until softened and golden.

3 Add the drained potato, coconut milk, red or green curry paste, peas and lime juice to the frying pan. Mash coarsely with a wooden spoon. Season to taste with salt and pepper and cook over a low heat for 2–3 minutes, then remove the pan from the heat and set aside until the mixture has cooled a little.

4 Lay a samosa wrapper or filo strip flat on the work surface. Brush with a little oil, then place a generous teaspoonful of the mixture in the middle of one end. Turn one corner diagonally over the filling to meet the long edge.

5 Continue folding over the filling, keeping the triangular shape as you work down the strip. Brush with a little more oil if necessary and place on a baking sheet. Prepare all the other samosas in the same way.

6 Bake for 15 minutes, or until the pastry is golden and crisp. Leave to cool slightly before serving.

Spicy Chickpea Samosas

A blend of crushed chickpeas and coriander sauce makes an interesting alternative to the more familiar meat or vegetable fillings in these little pastries. Garnish with coriander leaves and finely sliced onion and serve with a yogurt and mint dip.

Makes 18

2 x 400g/14oz cans chickpeas, drained and rinsed
120ml/4fl oz/½ cup hara masala or coriander sauce
275g/10oz filo pastry
60ml/4 tbsp chilli-and-garlic flavoured oil
salt and ground black pepper

1 Preheat the oven to 220°C/425°F/Gas 7. Process half the chickpeas to a paste in a food processor.

2 Put the paste into a bowl and add the whole chickpeas, the hara masala or coriander sauce, and a little salt. Mix until the ingredients are well combined.

3 Lay a sheet of filo pastry on a work surface and cut into three strips. Brush the strips with a little of the oil. Place a dessertspoon of the filling at one end of a strip. Turn one corner diagonally over the filling to meet the long edge.

4 Continue folding the filling and the pastry along the length of the strip, keeping the triangular shape. Transfer to a baking sheet and repeat with the remaining filling and pastry.

5 Brush the pastries with any remaining oil and bake for 15 minutes, until the pastry is golden. Cool before serving.

Cook's Tip

To make chilli oil, add several dried chillis to a bottle of olive oil and leave to infuse (steep) for about 2 weeks before tasting. If the flavour hasn't infused sufficiently, leave for a further week before using. The chillies can be left in the bottle as they give a decorative effect. Garlic oil is made in the same way with peeled garlic cloves, but remove the cloves once infused.

Potato Samosas Energy 42kcal/178kJ; Protein 1.2g; Carbohydrate 8.5g, of which sugars 0.6g; Fat 0.6g, of which saturates 0.1g; Cholesterol 0mg; Calcium 14mg; Fibre 0.5g; Sodium 4mg.
Chickpea Samosas Energy 119kcal/499kJ; Protein 4.1g; Carbohydrate 13.7g, of which sugars 0.4g; Fat 5.7g, of which saturates 0.8g; Cholesterol 0mg; Calcium 36mg; Fibre 2.2g; Sodium 99mg.

Spinach Pastries with Pine Nuts

Variations of these pastries are found throughout the eastern Mediterranean. In Lebanon they are often prepared by the Christian communities for Lent.

Serves 6

500g/1¼lb fresh spinach, trimmed, washed and drained
30ml/2 tbsp olive oil, plus extra for brushing
15ml/1 tbsp butter
2 onions, chopped
45ml/3 tbsp pine nuts
15ml/1 tbsp ground sumac, or the juice of 1 lemon
5ml/1 tsp ground allspice
450g/1lb ready-rolled puff pastry
salt and ground black pepper

1 Steam the spinach until wilted, then drain, refresh under running cold water and squeeze out the excess liquid with your hands. Chop the spinach coarsely.

2 Heat the oil and butter in a heavy pan and stir in the onion to soften. Add the pine nuts and cook for 2–3 minutes until the onions and pine nuts begin to turn golden. Stir in the spinach, sumac or lemon juice, and allspice and season well. Remove the pan from the heat.

3 Preheat the oven to 180°C/350°F/Gas 4. Roll out the pastry on a lightly floured surface and cut into 10cm/14in rounds.

4 Spoon a little spinach mixture in the middle of each round and pull up the sides to make a pyramid.

5 Line several baking trays with baking parchment and place the pastries on top. Brush the pastries with a little oil and bake for about 30 minutes, until golden brown. Serve warm.

Variations

Instead of spinach you can use the finely shredded leaves of Swiss chard instead. You may need a smaller amount, as chard does not reduce as dramatically as spinach does when it is cooked. Make sure you shred it very finely, however, as it also retains its shape more than spinach.

Spinach Empanadillas

The Arabs brought spinach to Europe and little pies like these are part of the Moorish tradition in Spain. The addition of sweet dried fruit to savoury fillings is common.

Makes 20

25g/1oz/¼ cup raisins
25ml/1½ tbsp olive oil
450g/1lb fresh spinach leaves, washed, drained and chopped
6 canned anchovies, drained and chopped
2 garlic cloves, finely chopped
25g/1oz/¼ cup pine nuts, roughly chopped
350g/12oz puff pastry
1 egg, beaten
salt and ground black pepper

1 To make the filling, soak the raisins in a little warm water for 10 minutes. Drain well, then chop roughly.

2 Heat the olive oil in a large pan, add the spinach, stir, then cover and cook over a low heat for about 2 minutes until the spinach starts to wilt. Remove the lid, turn up the heat and cook until any liquid has evaporated.

3 Add the chopped anchovies, garlic and seasoning to the spinach and cook, stirring, for about 1 minute. Remove the pan from the heat, then stir in the soaked raisins and pine nuts, and set aside to cool.

4 Meanwhile, preheat the oven to 180°C/350°F/Gas 4. Roll out the pastry on a lightly floured surface to a 3mm/⅛ in thickness.

5 Using a 7.5cm/3in pastry (cookie) cutter, cut the pastry into 20 rounds, re-rolling any scraps if necessary. Place about 10ml/2 tsp filling in the middle of each round, then brush the edges with a little water.

6 Bring up the sides of the pastry and seal well. Press the edges together with the back of a fork. Brush with egg.

7 Place the pies, slightly apart, on a lightly greased baking sheet and bake for about 15 minutes, until puffed and golden brown. Transfer to a wire rack to cool and serve warm.

Spinach Pastries Energy 441kcal/1834kJ; Protein 9g; Carbohydrate 36.8g, of which sugars 7.2g; Fat 30.4g, of which saturates 2.3g; Cholesterol 6mg; Calcium 212mg; Fibre 3.1g; Sodium 371mg.
Spinach Empanadillas Energy 95kcal/396kJ; Protein 2.4g; Carbohydrate 7.8g, of which sugars 1.5g; Fat 6.4g, of which saturates 0.3g; Cholesterol 10mg; Calcium 53mg; Fibre 0.5g; Sodium 125mg.

Spiced Sweet Potato Turnovers

The subtle sweetness of the potatoes makes a great filling flavoured with spices.

Makes 8

1 sweet potato, about 225g/8oz
30ml/2 tbsp vegetable oil
2 shallots, finely chopped
10ml/2 tsp coriander seeds, crushed
5ml/1 tsp ground cumin
5ml/1 tsp garam masala
115g/4oz/1 cup frozen peas
15ml/1 tbsp chopped fresh mint
salt and ground black pepper

For the pastry

15ml/1 tbsp olive oil
1 small egg
150ml/¼ pint/⅔ cup natural (plain) yogurt
115g/4oz/8 tbsp butter, melted
275g/10oz/2½ cups plain (all-purpose) flour
1.5ml/¼ tsp bicarbonate of soda (baking soda)
10ml/2 tsp paprika
5ml/1 tsp salt
beaten egg, to glaze

1 Cook the sweet potato in boiling salted water for about 15–20 minutes, until tender. Drain and leave to cool. When cool enough to handle, peel the potato and cut into 1cm/½in cubes.

2 Heat the oil in a frying pan, add the shallots and cook until softened. Add the sweet potato and fry until it browns at the edges. Add the spices and fry, for a few seconds. Remove from the heat and add the peas, mint and seasoning. Leave to cool.

3 Preheat the oven to 200°C/400°F/Gas 6. Grease a baking sheet. To make the pastry, whisk together the oil and egg, stir in the yogurt, then add the melted butter. Sift the flour, bicarbonate of soda, paprika and salt into a bowl, then stir into the yogurt mixture to form a soft dough. Turn out the dough, and knead gently. Roll it out, then stamp it out into rounds.

4 Spoon about 10ml/2 tsp of the filling on to one side of each round, then fold over and seal the edges. Re-roll the trimmings and stamp out more rounds until the filling is used up.

5 Arrange the turnovers on the prepared baking sheet and brush the tops with beaten egg. Bake in the oven for about 20 minutes until crisp and golden brown. Serve hot.

Rice Pudding Pastries

These unusual pastries, with some of the filling left exposed, are from Finland. They are served warm as part of a coffee-time treat.

Makes 8

15g/½oz/1 tbsp butter
100g/3¾oz/¾ cup rye flour
75g/3oz/⅔ cup plain (all-purpose) flour
2.5ml/½ tsp salt
100ml/3½fl oz/scant ½ cup cold water
100g/3¾oz/½ cup rice
15ml/1 tbsp salt
300ml/½ pint/1¼ cups water
600ml/1 pint/2½ cups milk
25g/1oz/2 tbsp butter
75ml/5 tbsp milk

For the garnish

6 hard-boiled eggs
25g/1oz/2 tbsp butter, softened

1 To make the dough, melt the butter and place in a large bowl. Leave to cool, then add the rye and plain flours, the salt and water and mix together to form a dough. Divide the dough into eight small balls and roll out each ball on a lightly floured surface into a 12–15cm/4½–6in round.

2 Prepare the filling by putting the rice, salt and water in a pan. Bring to the boil, then boil for about 20 minutes until the water has almost evaporated. Add the milk, reduce the heat, cover and simmer, stirring frequently to prevent the rice from sticking, for about 15 minutes, until the rice is tender. Leave to cool.

3 Preheat the oven to 200°C/400°F/Gas 6. When the rice is cool, place a heap in the centre of each round of dough. Fold the sides of the dough into the centre so that they do not quite reach each other and some of the filling is left exposed. Crimp the edges and place the pastries on a baking tray. Bake in the oven for 10–15 minutes, until brown.

4 Meanwhile, make the glaze. Melt the butter and stir in the milk. As the pastries are taken out of the oven, dunk them in the glaze, then leave, covered with a dish towel, to soften.

5 To prepare the garnish, chop the hard-boiled eggs and put in a bowl. Add the butter and mix together. Serve the pastries with a spoonful of the garnish in the centre of each.

Sweet Potato Energy 660kcal/2760kJ; Protein 13.9g; Carbohydrate 75.8g, of which sugars 9.3g; Fat 35.9g, of which saturates 17g; Cholesterol 105mg; Calcium 216mg; Fibre 5.2g; Sodium 740mg.
Rice Pudding Pastries Energy 195kcal/820kJ; Protein 5.7g; Carbohydrate 30.7g, of which sugars 4.1g; Fat 6g, of which saturates 3.6g; Cholesterol 16mg; Calcium 122mg; Fibre 2.3g; Sodium 804mg.

Spiced Pea Samosas

These simple and tasty treats from India are the perfect accompaniment to all types of curried dishes.

Makes 8

60ml/4 tbsp sunflower oil
1 small onion, finely chopped
175g/6oz/1½ cups peas
15ml/1 tbsp grated fresh root ginger
1 green chilli, seeded and finely chopped
45ml/3 tbsp water
350g/12oz cooked potatoes, finely diced
7.5ml/1½ tsp ground coriander
5ml/1 tsp garam masala
7.5ml/1½ tsp ground cumin
1.5ml/¼ tsp cayenne pepper
10ml/2 tsp lemon juice
30ml/2 tbsp chopped fresh coriander (cilantro)
vegetable oil, for deep frying

For the samosa dough

275g/10oz/2½ cups plain (all-purpose) flour
1.5ml/¼ tsp salt
30ml/2 tbsp sunflower oil
150ml/¼ pint/⅔ cup warm water

1 For the dough, mix the flour and salt in a bowl. Add the oil and water and mix to a soft dough. Knead briefly. Wrap in clear film (plastic wrap) and chill for 30 minutes.

2 To make the filling, heat the oil in a frying pan and add the onion. Cook for 6–7 minutes until golden. Add the peas, ginger, chilli and water. Cover and simmer for 5–6 minutes, until the peas are cooked. Add the potatoes, spices and lemon juice. Cook over a low heat for 2–3 minutes, then stir in the chopped fresh coriander. Season well and leave to cool.

3 Divide the dough into eight. On a floured surface, roll out one piece into an 18cm/7in round. Keep the remaining dough covered. Cut the round in half and place 30ml/2 tbsp of the filling on each half towards one corner. Dampen the edges and fold the dough to make a triangle. Pinch the edges together to seal. Repeat with the remaining dough and filling.

4 Heat the oil for deep-frying to 190°C/375°F, or until a cube of bread rises and sizzles in 30 seconds. Fry the samosas for 4–5 minutes, turning once. Drain on kitchen paper. Serve the samosas warm, as an appetizer or an accompaniment.

Spiced Lentil-Filled Pasties

These pasties, from India, are wholesome and healthy, and taste delicious. Serve as an appetizer or snack.

Makes 12

225g/8oz/1 cup skinless split chickpeas, soaked overnight
2 large garlic cloves, chopped
2.5cm/1in piece of fresh root ginger, peeled and chopped
2 dried red chillies, chopped
1 green chilli, chopped
2.5ml/½ tsp ground turmeric
2.5ml/½ tsp asafoetida
50g/2oz/¼ cup natural (plain) yogurt
30ml/2 tbsp coriander (cilantro), chopped
5ml/1 tsp salt or to taste

For the pastry

150g/5oz/1¼ cups wholemeal (whole-wheat) flour
150g/5oz/1¼ cups plain (all-purpose) flour
2.5ml/½ tsp salt
200ml/7fl oz/¾ cup water

1 Drain the chickpeas and put into a food processor with the garlic, ginger and both types of chillies. Blend to a fine paste, adding 2–3 tbsp water if necessary.

2 Put the paste into a non-stick pan with the turmeric and asafoetida. Cook, stirring, until the mixture is dry and crumbly. Remove from the heat and transfer to a mixing bowl. Mix in the yogurt, coriander leaves and salt. If the mixture is still slightly crumbly, add a little water to make a paste. Set aside to cool.

3 To make the pastry, mix both types of flour and the salt in a bowl, then gradually add the water (the amount needed will depend on the absorbency of the flour). When a soft dough has formed, transfer it to a flat surface and knead briefly.

4 Wrap the dough in clear film (plastic wrap) and allow to rest for 30 minutes, then divide into 12 portions. Make each portion into a flat cake, while keeping the remaining dough covered with a damp cloth. Roll out each cake into a 10cm/4in circle.

5 Place a portion of filling on half of each circle. Moisten the edges and fold over the other half, making a half-moon shape. Press to seal and crimp the edges with the back of a fork. Cook the pasties in a steamer for 25 minutes.

Pea Samosas Energy 260kcal/1093kJ; Protein 6.1g; Carbohydrate 36g, of which sugars 3.2g; Fat 11.2g, of which saturates 1.3g; Cholesterol 1mg; Calcium 78mg; Fibre 4g; Sodium 468mg.
Lentil-filled Pasties Energy 148kcal/630kJ; Protein 7.7g; Carbohydrate 29.2g, of which sugars 1.2g; Fat 0.9g, of which saturates 0.2g; Cholesterol 0mg; Calcium 43mg; Fibre 2.4g; Sodium 12mg.

Jewish Tuna and Egg Pasties

These pastries are sold in the marketplaces of Israel, often by men carrying large trays full of them at lunchtimes.

Makes 4

1 onion, finely chopped
30–45ml/2–3 tbsp chopped fresh parsley or coriander (cilantro), or a mixture of both
a pinch of chopped fresh chilli (optional)
4 filo pastry sheets
90–115g/3½–4oz can tuna, well drained
vegetable oil, for deep-frying
4 eggs
tomato and chilli salsa or Tabasco, to serve

1 In a bowl, combine the onion, herbs and chilli, if using. Lay a sheet of pastry on some baking parchment.

2 Put one-quarter of the onion mixture at one corner of the pastry square, then add one-quarter of the tuna.

3 Preheat the oven to 200°C/400°F/Gas 6. Heat the oil in a pan until it browns a cube of bread in 30 seconds.

4 Working quickly, break an egg into a small bowl or cup, then carefully pour it into the corner of the pastry sheet with the onion. Quickly fold over the pastry to form a triangle and enclose the egg completely.

5 Carefully slide the parcel into the oil and fry until sealed and a pale golden brown colour. (The egg inside should be lightly cooked and still soft.)

6 Remove the parcel from the pan with a slotted spoon, drain on kitchen paper, then transfer to a baking sheet. Make three more pastries in the same way.

7 Bake the pastries in the oven for 5 minutes, or until crisp and golden brown. Do not overcook, as the egg yolk must be served runny. Serve immediately, accompanied by Tabasco for dipping or drizzling over.

Fish and Prawn Vol-au-vents

These are great little fish-shaped pastry treats, stuffed with a creamy cod and prawn mixture, and perfect for the children's party,

Makes 4

150g/5oz ready-rolled all-butter puff pastry
beaten egg, to glaze
175g/6oz cod fillet
100ml/3½fl oz/scant ½ cup milk
½ leek, trimmed and washed
15ml/1 tbsp butter
15ml/1 tbsp plain (all-purpose) flour
25g/1oz fresh cooked prawns (shrimp)
salt and ground black pepper
steamed vegetable, to serve

1 Preheat the oven to 220°C/425°F/Gas 7. Roll out the pastry on a lightly floured surface to make a rectangle. Cut into fish shapes with a sharp knife. Knock up the edges with a knife and cut an oval shape just in from the edge without cutting through.

2 Brush the edges of the fish shapes with beaten egg and cook in the oven for 10 minutes until well risen and golden brown.

3 Meanwhile make the filling. Cut the fish in two and put in a large pan with the milk. Slice the leek thinly and add to the pan. Heat to a simmer and cook gently for 6–8 minutes or until the fish flakes easily. Lift out of the pan, and flake with your fingers, discarding any bones or skin.

4 In a clean pan melt the butter and add the flour, then gradually add the milk and leeks, stirring, until thickened. Add the fish and the prawns to the sauce. Season to taste, but don't add too much salt.

5 Carefully lift away the centres of the pastry fish shapes to leave a hole. Into this, scoop a spoonful or two of the fish filling, and pile it up. Add a pea for an eye, if you wish, and serve with steamed vegetables.

Variation
For older children you can try smoked haddock instead of cod.

Tuna and Egg Energy 267kcal/1111kJ; Protein 14.1g; Carbohydrate 11.2g, of which sugars 1.3g; Fat 18.9g, of which saturates 3.2g; Cholesterol 202mg; Calcium 75mg; Fibre 1.2g; Sodium 140mg.
Fish Vol-au-vents Energy 204kcal/853kJ; Protein 10.2g; Carbohydrate 16.4g, of which sugars 2.2g; Fat 11.3g, of which saturates 5.8g; Cholesterol 54mg; Calcium 68mg; Fibre 0.9g; Sodium 162mg.

Moroccan Prawn Packages

These tasty little packages have the typically Moroccan-influenced mixture of sweet and savoury, they are delicious and very moreish.

Makes about 24

175g/6oz filo pastry sheets
40g/1½oz/3 tbsp butter, melted
sunflower oil, for frying
1 spring onion (scallion) and fresh coriander (cilantro) leaves, to garnish
ground cinnamon and icing (confectioners') sugar, to serve

For the filling
15ml/1 tbsp olive oil
15g/½oz/1 tbsp butter
2–3 spring onions (scallions), finely chopped
15g/½oz/2 tbsp plain (all-purpose) flour
300ml/½ pint/1¼ cups milk
2.5ml/½ tsp paprika
350g/12oz cooked peeled prawns (shrimp), chopped
salt and white pepper

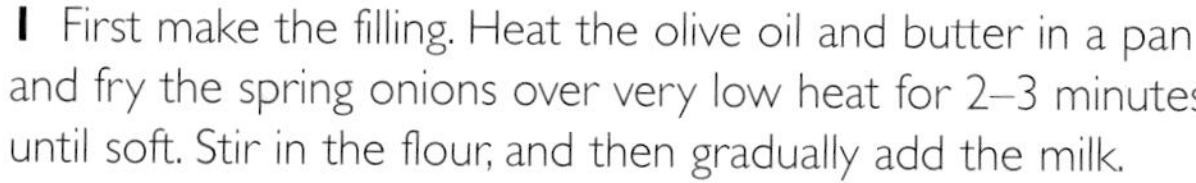

1 First make the filling. Heat the olive oil and butter in a pan and fry the spring onions over very low heat for 2–3 minutes until soft. Stir in the flour, and then gradually add the milk.

2 Heat gently, stirring constantly, until the sauce is thickened and smooth. Simmer gently for 2–3 minutes, stirring. Season the sauce with paprika, salt and pepper and stir in the prawns.

3 Halve a sheet of filo pastry widthways, to make a rectangle about 18 x 14cm/7 x 5½in. Cover the remaining pastry with clear film (plastic wrap) to prevent it drying out.

4 Brush the pastry with melted butter and place a heaped teaspoon of filling at one end. Roll up, tucking in the sides as you go. Continue until you have used all the pastry and filling.

5 Heat about 1cm/½in oil in a heavy pan and fry the cigars, in batches if necessary, for 2–3 minutes until golden, turning occasionally. Drain on kitchen paper.

6 Arrange the cigars on a serving plate. Serve garnished with spring onion and coriander leaves, and sprinkled with, or dipped in, cinnamon and icing sugar.

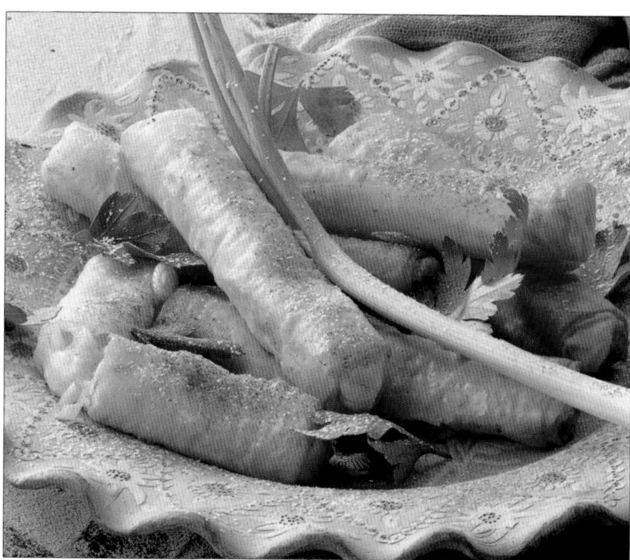

Firecrackers

It's easy to see how these pastry-wrapped prawn snacks got their name – they explode with flavour.

Makes 16

16 large, raw king prawns (jumbo shrimp), heads and shells removed but tails left on
5ml/1 tsp red curry paste
15ml/1 tbsp Thai fish sauce
16 small wonton wrappers, about 8cm/3¼in square, thawed if frozen
16 fine egg noodles, for tying
oil, for deep-frying

1 Place the prawns on their sides and cut two slits through the underbelly of each, one about 1cm/½in from the head end and the other about 1cm/½in from the first cut, across the prawn. This will prevent the prawns from curling up as they cook.

2 Mix the curry paste with the fish sauce in a shallow dish. Add the prawns and turn them in the mixture until they are well coated. Cover and leave to marinate for 10 minutes.

3 Soak the fine egg noodles for ties in a bowl of boiling water for 2–3 minutes, until softened, then drain.

4 Place a wonton wrapper on the work surface at an angle so that it forms a diamond shape, then fold the top corner over so that the point is in the centre. Place a prawn, slit side down, on the wrapper, with the tail projecting from the folded end, then fold the bottom corner over the other end of the prawn.

5 Fold each side of the wrapper over in turn to make a tightly folded roll. Tie a noodle in a bow around the roll and set it aside. Repeat with the remaining prawns,wrappers and noodles.

6 Heat the oil in a deep-fryer or wok to 190°C/375°F or until a cube of bread, added to the oil, browns in 45 seconds. Fry the prawns, a few at a time, for 5–8 minutes, until golden brown and cooked through.

7 Drain the prawns well on kitchen paper and keep hot while you cook the remaining batches. Serve warm.

Prawn Packages Energy 77kcal/320kJ; Protein 4.3g; Carbohydrate 5.5g, of which sugars 0.7g; Fat 4.3g, of which saturates 1.6g; Cholesterol 17mg; Calcium 47mg; Fibre 0.2g; Sodium 251mg.
Firecrackers Energy 71kcal/298kJ; Protein 3.2g; Carbohydrate 7.1g, of which sugars 0.2g; Fat 3.5g, of which saturates 0.5g; Cholesterol 25mg; Calcium 20mg; Fibre 0.3g; Sodium 30mg.

Thai Tung Tong

Called 'gold bags' in Thailand, these crisp pastry purses are the perfect snack.

Makes 18

18 spring roll wrappers, about 8cm/3¼in square, thawed if frozen
oil, for deep-frying
salt and pepper
sweet chilli sauce, to serve

For the filling

4 baby corn cobs
130g/4½oz can water chestnuts, drained and chopped
1 shallot, coarsely chopped
5ml/1 tsp Thai fish sauce
1 egg, separated
30ml/2 tbsp cornflour (cornstarch)
60ml/4 tbsp water
small bunch fresh coriander (cilantro), chopped

1 Make the filling. Place the baby corn, water chestnuts, shallot, Thai fish sauce and egg yolk in a food processor or blender. Process to a coarse paste. Place the egg white in a cup and whisk it lightly with a fork.

2 Put the cornflour in a small pan and stir in the water until smooth. Add the corn mixture and chopped coriander and season with salt and pepper to taste. Cook over a low heat, stirring constantly, until thickened.

3 Leave the filling to cool slightly, then place 5ml/1 tsp in the centre of a spring roll wrapper. Brush the edges with the beaten egg white, then gather up the points and press them firmly together to make a pouch or bag.

4 Repeat with remaining wrappers and filling. Heat the oil in a deep-fryer or wok to 190°C/375°F or until a cube of bread, added to the oil, browns in about 45 seconds.

5 Fry in batches, for about 5 minutes, until golden brown. Drain on kitchen paper and serve hot, with the chilli sauce.

Cook's Tip
If you wish you could add a few dried shrimp, or fresh prawns (shrimp) to the filling.

Fish and Chermoula Mini Pies

The filling of these pies is flavoured with chermoula, a mixture of spices and fresh coriander and parsley.

Makes 8

500g/1¼lb firm white fish fillets
225g/8oz uncooked king prawns (jumbo shrimp)
16 sheets filo pastry
60–75ml/4–5 tbsp sunflower oil
1 egg yolk, mixed with a few drops of water
salt

For the chermoula

75ml/5 tbsp olive oil
juice of 1 lemon
5ml/1 tsp ground cumin
5–10ml/1–2 tsp paprika
2–3 garlic cloves, crushed
1 red chilli, seeded and chopped
large bunch of fresh flat leaf parsley, chopped
large bunch of fresh coriander (cilantro), chopped

1 Prepare the chermoula. Combine all the ingredients in a bowl and set aside.

2 Place the fish in a frying pan and add just enough water to cover. Season with a little salt and heat until just simmering, then cook gently for 3 minutes, until the fish begins to flake. Take the fish from the pan and break it up, removing any bones.

3 Poach the prawns in the fish liquor for 10 minutes, then drain and shell. Toss the prawns and fish in the chermoula, cover and set aside for 1 hour. Preheat the oven to 180°C/350°F/Gas 4. Grease two baking sheets.

4 To make the pies, lay the filo pastry under a damp cloth. Take two sheets of filo: brush one with oil, lay the second one on top, then brush it with oil. Place some filling in the middle of the length of the sheet but to one side. Fold the edge of the pastry over the filling, then fold the long side over to cover the filling. Wrap the ends around the filling like a collar to make a neat package with the edges tucked in, then brush with egg yolk.

5 Continue as before with the rest of the fish and chermoula mixture. Bake the pies for about 20 minutes, until the pastry is crisp and golden brown. Serve hot or warm.

Tung Tong Energy 55kcal/229kJ; Protein 1.2g; Carbohydrate 6.3g, of which sugars 0.4g; Fat 2.9g, of which saturates 0.4g; Cholesterol 12mg; Calcium 19mg; Fibre 0.5g; Sodium 42mg.
Fish Mini Pies Energy 236kcal/984kJ; Protein 18.2g; Carbohydrate 10g, of which sugars 0.4g; Fat 13.9g, of which saturates 2g; Cholesterol 109mg; Calcium 67mg; Fibre 0.9g; Sodium 96mg.

Salmon Parcels

Serve these little savoury parcels just as they are for a snack, or with a pool of fresh tomato sauce for a special first course. Using canned salmon makes it a very quick and easy recipe, and tasty too.

Makes 12

90g/3½ oz can red or pink salmon
15ml/1 tbsp chopped fresh coriander (cilantro)
4 spring onions (scallions), finely chopped
4 sheets filo pastry, thawed if frozen
sunflower oil, for brushing
spring onions (scallions), shredded and mixed salad leaves, to serve

1 Preheat the oven to 200°C/400°F/Gas 6. Lightly oil a baking sheet. Drain the salmon, discarding any skin and bones, then place the flesh in a large bowl.

2 Flake the salmon with a fork and mix with the fresh coriander and spring onions.

3 Place a single sheet of filo pastry on a work surface and brush lightly with oil. Place another sheet on top. Cover the remaining sheets of filo with a clean, damp tea towel to prevent them from drying out.

4 Cut the double sheet of pastry into six squares, about 10cm/4in. Repeat with the remaining pastry, to make 12 squares.

5 Place a spoonful of the salmon mixture on to each square. Brush the edges of the pastry with oil, then draw together, pressing to seal. Place the pastries on a baking sheet and bake for 12–15 minutes, until golden. Serve the parcels warm, with a fresh green salad and shredded spring onions.

Variation
Replace the canned salmon with canned tuna, if you wish, and add a few mini capers if you have some.

Tunisian Brik

The eggs in these little parcels need to be enclosed completely to prevent it from running out.

Serves 6

40g/1½oz/3 tbsp butter, melted
1 small red onion, finely chopped
150g/5oz skinless, boneless chicken or turkey, minced (ground)
1 large garlic clove, crushed
juice of ½ lemon
30ml/2 tbsp chopped fresh parsley
12 sheets of filo pastry, each measuring 25 x 15cm/10 x 6in, thawed if frozen
6 small eggs, such as bantam, or quail
oil, for deep-frying
salt and ground black pepper

1 Heat half the butter in a pan. Sauté the onion for about 3 minutes until soft. Add the minced meat, garlic, lemon juice, parsley and seasoning. Cook, stirring with chopsticks, for 2–3 minutes until the meat is just cooked. Set aside to cool.

2 Place one sheet of pastry lengthways on the work surface and brush with melted butter; top with a second sheet. Brush the edges with butter and place one-sixth of the meat mixture on the lower left side of the pastry sheet, about 2.5cm/1in from the base. Flatten the filling, making a slight hollow in it.

3 Carefully crack an egg into the hollow and be ready to fold up the pastry immediately so that the egg white does not run out. Lift the right-hand edge of the pastry and fold it over to the left edge to enclose the filling.

4 Seal the parcel quickly, folding the bottom edge straight up to seal, then folding the bottom left corner across to the right corner, forming a triangle.

5 Use the remaining pastry sheets and filling to make another five parcels in the same way. Heat the oil in a wok until a cube of bread added to it turns golden in about 1½ minutes.

6 Cook the pastries, two or three at a time until golden. Lift them out of the pan with a slotted spoon and drain on kitchen paper. Serve the pastries hot or cold.

Salmon Parcels Energy 67kcal/279kJ; Protein 2.5g; Carbohydrate 6.6g, of which sugars 0.2g; Fat 3.6g, of which saturates 0.5g; Cholesterol 3mg; Calcium 21mg; Fibre 0.4g; Sodium 33mg.
Tunisian Brik Energy 316kcal/1321kJ; Protein 15g; Carbohydrate 24g, of which sugars 2g; Fat 18g, of which saturates 6g; Cholesterol 210mg; Calcium 36mg; Fibre 1g; Sodium 225mg.

Chicken and Onion Turnovers

In Poland these little turnovers, called pirozhki, are great favourites with old and young alike. They are often made at home for parties and family meals and look splendid piled high and golden brown.

Makes 35

225g/8oz/2 cups strong white bread flour
2.5ml/½ tsp salt
2.5ml/½ tsp caster (superfine) sugar
5ml/1 tsp easy-blend (rapid-rise) dried yeast
25g/1oz/2 tbsp butter, softened
1 egg, beaten, plus a little extra
90ml/6 tbsp warm milk

For the filling

1 small onion, finely chopped
175g/6oz minced (ground) chicken
15ml/1 tbsp sunflower oil
75ml/5 tbsp chicken stock
30ml/2 tbsp chopped fresh parsley
pinch of grated nutmeg
salt and ground black pepper

1 Sift the flour, salt and sugar into a large bowl. Stir in the dried yeast, then make a well in the centre. Add the butter, egg and milk and mix to a soft dough. Turn on to a lightly floured surface and knead for 10 minutes, until smooth and elastic.

2 Put the dough in a clean bowl, cover with clear film (plastic wrap) and leave in a warm place to rise for 1 hour, or until the dough has doubled in size.

3 Meanwhile, fry the onion and chicken in the oil for about 10 minutes. Add the stock and simmer for 5 minutes. Stir in the parsley, nutmeg and salt and pepper. Leave to cool.

4 Preheat the oven to 220°C/425°F/Gas 7. Knead the dough, then roll out until 3mm/⅛in thick. Stamp out rounds with a 7.5cm/3in pastry (cookie) cutter.

5 Brush the edges with beaten egg. Put a little filling in the middle, then press the edges together. Leave to rise on oiled baking sheets, covered with oiled clear film, for 15 minutes.

6 Brush the turnovers with a little more egg. Bake for about 5 minutes, then for about 10 minutes at 190°C/375°F/Gas 5, until well risen and golden brown.

Prosciutto and Mozzarella Parcels

Italian prosciutto crudo is a delicious raw smoked ham. Here it is baked with melting mozzarella in a pastry case. These little parcels may be a little fiddly to make, but can be done in advance and make a lovely party snack or appetizer. If you wish to freeze them, do so spaced out on a baking tray before they are cooked. Once frozen, transfer to a freezer bag. Cook from frozen, but increase the cooking time by about 5 minutes.

Serves 6

a little hot chilli sauce
6 prosciutto crudo slices
200g/7oz mozzarella cheese, cut into 6 slices
6 sheets filo pastry, each measuring 45 x 28cm/18 x 11in, thawed if frozen
50g/2oz/¼ cup butter, melted
150g/5oz frisée lettuce, to serve

1 Preheat the oven to 200°C/400°F/Gas 6. Sprinkle a little chilli sauce over the slices of prosciutto. Line a large baking tray with a piece of baking parchment.

2 Place a slice of mozzarella on top of the ham, then fold it around the cheese so the cheese is enclosed by the ham.

3 Brush a filo pastry sheet with melted butter and fold it in half. Place a ham and mozzarella parcel in the middle of the pastry.

4 Brush the pastry around the ham and cheese with butter, then fold it to make a neat parcel. Repeat with the remaining parcels and sheets.

5 Brush all the parcels with melted butter and place on the prepared baking tray. Bake for 15 minutes, until the pastry is golden. Serve immediately. You can prepare in advance and reheat if necessary.

Cook's Tip

Parma ham, or the Spanish equivalent – Serrano ham – can be used in place of prosciutto, if you like.

Chicken Turnovers Energy 42kcal/175kJ; Protein 2.2g; Carbohydrate 5.6g, of which sugars 0.6g; Fat 1.3g, of which saturates 0.5g; Cholesterol 12mg; Calcium 16mg; Fibre 0.4g; Sodium 42mg.
Prosciutto Parcels Energy 136kcal/566kJ; Protein 3g; Carbohydrate 10g, of which sugars 1g; Fat 9g, of which saturates 5g; Cholesterol 23mg; Calcium 9mg; Fibre 1g; Sodium 268mg.

Smoked Chicken with Peach Mayonnaise in Filo Tartlets

The filling for these tartlets can be prepared a day in advance and chilled, but only fill the pastry cases when you are ready to serve.

Makes 12

25g/1oz/2 tbsp butter
3 sheets of filo pastry, each measuring 45 x 28cm/18 x 11in, thawed if frozen
2 skinless, boneless smoked chicken breast portions, finely sliced
150ml/¼ pint/⅔ cup mayonnaise
grated rind of 1 lime
30ml/2 tbsp lime juice
2 ripe peaches, peeled, stoned (pitted) and chopped
salt and ground black pepper
fresh tarragon sprigs, lime slices and salad leaves, to garnish

1 Preheat the oven to 200°C/400°F/Gas 6. Place the butter in a small pan and heat gently until melted. Lightly brush 12 mini flan rings with a little melted butter.

2 Cut each sheet of filo pastry into 12 equal rounds large enough to line the tins and stand above the rims. Place a round of pastry in each tin and brush with a little butter, then add another round of pastry. Brush each with more butter and add a third round of pastry.

3 Bake the tartlets for 5 minutes. Leave in the tins for a few moments before transferring to a wire rack to cool. Once cool, store in a tin until ready to use.

4 Mix together the chicken, mayonnaise, lime rind and peaches and season with salt and pepper. Chill for at least 30 minutes, preferably overnight. Just before serving, spoon the chicken mixture into the filo pastry cases and garnish with tarragon, lime slices and salad leaves.

Cook's Tip

You can use small tartlet tins (muffin pans) if you do not have any mini flan rings.

Turkey and Cranberry Purses

After the traditional Christmas or Thanksgiving meal, it is easy to end up with lots of turkey left-overs. These delicious filo pastry parcels are a marvellous way to use up the small pieces of cooked turkey.

Serves 6

450g/1lb cooked turkey, cut into chunks
115g/4oz/1 cup Brie, diced
30ml/2 tbsp cranberry sauce
30ml/2 tbsp chopped fresh parsley
9 sheets filo pastry, 45 x 28cm/18 x 11in each, thawed if frozen
50g/2oz/¼ cup butter, melted
salt and ground black pepper
green salad, to serve

1 Preheat the oven to 200°C/400°F/Gas 6. Mix the turkey, diced Brie, cranberry sauce and chopped parsley. Season with salt and ground black pepper.

2 Cut the filo sheets in half widthways and trim to make 18 squares. Layer three pieces of pastry together, brushing them with a little melted butter so that they stick together. Repeat with the remaining filo squares to give six pieces.

3 Divide the turkey mixture among the pastry, making neat piles on each piece. Gather up the pastry to enclose the filling in neat bundles. Place on a baking sheet, brush with a little melted butter and bake for 20 minutes, or until the pastry is crisp and golden. Serve hot or warm with a green salad.

Variation

These little parcels can be made with a variety of fillings and are great for using up left-over cooked meats. To make Ham and Cheddar Purses, replace the turkey with ham and use Cheddar in place of the Brie. A fruit-flavoured chutney would make a good alternative to the cranberry sauce. Alternatively, to make Chicken and Stilton Purses, use cooked chicken in place of the turkey and white Stilton instead of Brie. Replace the cranberry sauce with mango chutney.

Chicken Filo Tartlets Energy 164kcal/682kJ; Protein 10g; Carbohydrate 5g, of which sugars 2g; Fat 12g, of which saturates 3g; Cholesterol 40mg; Calcium 5mg; Fibre 1g; Sodium 92mg.
Turkey Purses Energy 285kcal/1192kJ; Protein 25.5g; Carbohydrate 15.5g, of which sugars 3.6g; Fat 13.4g, of which saturates 8g; Cholesterol 89mg; Calcium 85mg; Fibre 0.7g; Sodium 190mg.

Haggis Cups with Neeps and Tatties

Haggis is the Scottish sausage of spiced lamb's offal bound with oatmeal, packed into a lamb's stomach ready for gentle poaching. The casing is not eaten, but split open so that the filling can be scooped out. These days synthetic casings are used. Haggis, neeps (swede) and tatties (mashed potato) is the traditional meal eaten at Hogmanay, the Scottish New Year. Here the haggis is served in filo cups.

Serves 8

450g/1lb haggis
3 filo pastry sheets, each about 30 x 20cm/12 x 8in
25g/1oz/2 tbsp butter, melted
90ml/6 tbsp whiskey, to serve
salt and ground black pepper

For the bashed neeps

1 large swede (rutabaga), cut into chunks
45ml/3 tbsp double (heavy) cream
50g/2oz/¼ cup butter

For the tatties

900g/2lb potatoes, cut into chunks
60ml/4 tbsp double (heavy) cream
50g/2oz/¼ cup butter
large pinch of grated nutmeg

1 Cook or reheat the haggis according to the packet instructions. Preheat the oven to 190°C/375°F/Gas 5.

2 Cut each sheet of filo pastry into six 15cm/6in squares. Brush eight sections of a deep tartlet tin (muffin pan) with melted butter and line each with a filo square. Brush with butter and place a second piece of pastry on top. Bake for 5–7 minutes, or until crisp and pale golden.

3 To make the neeps and tatties, cook the swede and potato in separate pans of boiling salted water for 20 minutes, until tender.

4 Drain and mash the swede and potato separately with cream and butter. Season and add a little nutmeg to the potatoes.

5 Split the cooked haggis open and use a teaspoon to scoop out the mixture, dividing it among the filo tartlet cases.

6 Moisten each tartlet with a generous amount of whiskey and serve immediately with the bashed neeps and tatties.

Sausage Rolls

Small sausage rolls rank high in the league of popular teatime and party foods. They are delicious when homemade, particularly if good quality butcher's sausage meat is used to fill them. Serve them hot or cold. They also make an ideal addition to a picnic or packed lunch.

Makes about 16

175g/6oz/1½ cups plain (all-purpose) flour
pinch of salt
40g/1½ oz/3 tbsp lard or white cooking fat, diced
40g/1½ oz/3 tbsp butter, diced
250g/9oz pork sausage meat (bulk sausage)
beaten egg, to glaze

1 To make the pastry, sift the flour and salt and add the lard and butter. Rub the fats into the flour until the mixture resembles fine crumbs. Stir in about 45ml/3 tbsp ice cold water until the mixture can be gathered into a smooth ball of dough. Wrap in clear film (plastic wrap) and chill for 30 minutes.

2 Preheat the oven to 190°C/375°F/Gas 5. Roll out the pastry on a lightly floured surface to make a rectangle about 30cm/12in long. Cut lengthways into two long strips.

3 Divide the sausage meat into two pieces and, on a lightly floured surface, shape each into a long roll the same length as the pastry. Lay a roll on each strip of pastry. Brush the pastry edges with water and fold them over the meat, pressing the edges together to seal them well.

4 Turn the rolls over and, with the seam side down, brush with beaten egg. Cut each roll into eight and place on a baking sheet. Bake in the hot oven for 30 minutes until crisp and golden brown. Cool on a wire rack.

Variation

Add 2.5ml/½ tsp English (hot) mustard powder to the dough mix for an extra little bite to your sausage rolls. Sift it into the bowl along with the flour.

Haggis Cups Energy 519kcal/2166kJ; Protein 10.4g; Carbohydrate 42.7g, of which sugars 3.7g; Fat 33.4g, of which saturates 17g; Cholesterol 117mg; Calcium 73mg; Fibre 2.5g; Sodium 578mg.
Sausage Rolls Energy 125kcal/521kJ; Protein 2.5g; Carbohydrate 10.3g, of which sugars 0.5g; Fat 8.4g, of which saturates 3.9g; Cholesterol 14mg; Calcium 23mg; Fibre 0.4g; Sodium 142mg.

Savoury Cigars

These little pastries, known as briouats in Morocco, are filled with meat or cheese.

Makes about 32
8 sheets of filo pastry
sunflower oil, for deep-frying
salt and ground black pepper

For the cheese filling
450g/1lb ricotta cheese
4 eggs
bunch of fresh coriander (cilantro), finely chopped
bunch of flat leaf parsley, chopped
bunch of mint, finely chopped

For the beef filling
15–30ml/1–2 tbsp olive oil
1 onion, finely chopped
30ml/2 tbsp pine nuts
5ml/1 tsp ras el hanout
225g/8oz minced (ground) beef

For the spinach filling
50g/2oz/¼ cup butter
1 onion, finely chopped
275g/10oz fresh spinach, cooked, drained and chopped
small bunch of fresh coriander (cilantro), finely chopped
pinch of grated nutmeg

1 To make the cheese filling, place the cheese in a bowl and mash with a fork, then beat in the eggs and chopped herbs.

2 To make the beef filling, heat the olive oil in a frying pan. Add the onion and pine nuts; cook, stirring, until coloured, then stir in the ras el hanout. Add the beef and cook for about 15 minutes, stirring, until browned. Season and cool.

3 To make the spinach filling, melt the butter in a small pan. Add the onion and cook for 15 minutes until soft. Stir in the spinach and coriander. Season with nutmeg, salt and pepper, and cool.

4 Lay a sheet of filo pastry on a work surface. Cut it widthways into four strips. Spoon a little filling mixture on end of one strip, Fold the corners of the pastry over the mixture to seal it, then roll up the pastry and filling into a tight cigar. As you roll, brush the edges with a little water. Repeat, placing the finished cigars under a damp cloth.

5 Heat the sunflower oil for deep-frying to 180°C/350°F. Fry the cigars in batches until golden brown. Drain on kitchen paper and serve warm.

Minced Pork and Taro Puffs

A dim sum favourite, these are called wu kok in Cantonese and they make very savoury snacks. Taro, otherwise known as yam, is sold in most Chinese supermarkets. Look for the type that has light purple flesh with dark specks, as it has the best flavour and is starchy enough to make a stiff dough.

Serves 4
cornflour (cornstarch), for dusting
oil, for deep-frying

For the pastry
500g/1¼lb taro or yam
30ml/2 tbsp plain (all-purpose) flour
15ml/1 tbsp lard or white cooking fat
pinch of bicarbonate of soda (baking soda)
15ml/1 tbsp sesame oil
5ml/1 tsp sugar
salt and ground black pepper

For the filling
150g/5oz minced (ground) pork
5ml/1 tsp cornflour (cornstarch)
30ml/2 tbsp vegetable oil
30ml/2 tbsp frozen peas
5g/1 tsp sugar
15ml/1 tbsp sesame oil
salt and ground black pepper

1 To make the pastry, peel the taro and cut it into chunks. Steam for about 15 minutes until soft. Mash while still warm and mix with the remaining pastry ingredients to form a dough.

2 Turn out on to a lightly floured board and knead until the dough is soft and pliable. Set it aside while you make the filling, covered with a damp dish towel to prevent it drying out.

3 Mix the pork with the cornflour and moisten the mixture with a little water. Heat the vegetable oil in a pan and fry the pork until nearly cooked. Stir in all other filling ingredients.

4 Remove from the heat and leave to cool a little. Meanwhile, divide the dough into four portions and roll out into flat rounds.

5 Fill each round with 15ml/1 tbsp of the pork mixture. Shape into an oval pasty, pinching the edges of the pastry well around the filling to seal. Dust with cornflour and deep-fry until golden brown. Serve the puffs warm.

Savoury Cigars Energy 41kcal/171kJ; Protein 0.6g; Carbohydrate 2.8g, of which sugars 0.3g; Fat 3.1g, of which saturates 1g; Cholesterol 3mg; Calcium 23mg; Fibre 0.4g; Sodium 22mg.
Pork Puffs Energy 367Kcal/1541kJ; Protein 11.2g; Carbohydrate 45.7g, of which sugars 3.8g; Fat 16.8g, of which saturates 3.7g; Cholesterol 27mg; Calcium 36mg; Fibre 2.2g; Sodium 30mg.

Curried Lamb Samosas

Filo pastry is perfect for making samosas. Once you've mastered folding them, you'll be amazed at how quick they are to make. These lamb samosas have a simple filling that is tasty and quick to make – perfect for appetizers or party fare.

Serves 4

25g/1oz/2 tbsp butter
225g/8oz/1 cup minced (ground) lamb
30ml/2 tbsp mild curry paste
12 sheets of filo pastry, thawed and wrapped in a damp dish towel
salt and ground black pepper

1 Heat a little of the butter in a large pan and add the lamb. Fry for 5–6 minutes, stirring occasionally until browned.

2 Stir the curry paste into the lamb and cook for 1–2 minutes. Season and set aside. Preheat the oven to 200°C/400°F/Gas 6.

3 Melt the remaining butter in a pan. Cut the pastry sheets in half lengthways. Brush one strip of pastry with butter, then lay another strip on top and brush with more butter.

4 Place a spoonful of lamb in the corner of the strip and fold over to form a triangle at one end. Keep folding over in the same way to form a triangular shape.

5 Brush with butter and place on a baking sheet. Repeat using the remaining pastry and filling. Bake for 10–15 minutes until golden. Serve hot.

Variation

For Cashew Nut Samosas, mix together 225g/8oz cooked and mashed potato, 15ml/1 tbsp chopped cashew nuts, 5ml/1 tsp coconut milk powder, ½ chopped green chilli, 5ml/1 tsp mustard seeds, 5ml/1 tsp cumin seeds, 15ml/1 tbsp chopped fresh coriander (cilantro) and 5ml/1 tsp soft light brown sugar. Use to fill the samosas in place of the lamb filling. If you like, the mustard and cumin seeds can be dry-roasted first.

Turkish Lamb Kebab Puffs

Kebabs in pastry are a more recent addition to the food of Turkey, and reflects a French influence. You can make your own buttery puff pastry for this kebab, or use the ready-prepared packs, which make life easier.

Serves 6–8

25g/1oz/2 tbsp butter
2 onions, cut into four and sliced
450g/1lb lean shoulder of lamb, cut into thin strips
7.5ml/1½ tsp tomato purée (paste)
10ml/2 tsp sugar
5ml/1 tsp dried mint
500g/1¼lb puff pastry, thawed if frozen
1 egg yolk, beaten
salt and ground black pepper

1 Melt the butter in a heavy pan, add the onions and cook until they have softened. Add the strips of lamb and cook for 3–4 minutes, or until most of the liquid has evaporated.

2 Stir in the tomato purée and sugar, and pour in about 250ml/8fl oz/1 cup water. Reduce the heat, cover the pan and cook gently for about 40 minutes, or until the meat is tender. Meanwhile, preheat the oven to 180°C/350°F/Gas 4 and lightly grease a baking tray.

3 Drain the meat over a pan to catch the cooking liquid. Reserve the cooking liquid and place the meat in a dish. Sprinkle the meat with a little salt and the dried mint. Leave to cool.

4 On a lightly floured board, roll out the puff pastry into a rectangle. Cut out squares, about 10 x 10cm/4 x 4in square. Place a little of the cooked lamb in the centre of each square and fold over the edges to form a neat packet.

5 Place the packets, seam side down, in the baking tray. Brush the egg yolk over the pastry packets. Put the pastries in the oven and bake them for about 35 minutes, or until puffed up and golden brown.

6 Heat up the reserved cooking liquid, season it and serve as a gravy with the kebabs.

Lamb Samosas Energy 101kcal/423kJ; Protein 5g; Carbohydrate 10.4g, of which sugars 0.2g; Fat 4.6g, of which saturates 2.3g; Cholesterol 19mg; Calcium 37mg; Fibre 1g; Sodium 37mg.
Lamb Puffs Energy 388kcal/1621kJ; Protein 15.6g; Carbohydrate 28.5g, of which sugars 5.1g; Fat 25g, of which saturates 4.8g; Cholesterol 75mg; Calcium 58mg; Fibre 0.7g; Sodium 266mg.

Lebanese Meat Pastries

Little meat pastries are popular throughout the eastern Mediterranean region, varying only in the spices and herbs employed or in the shape of the pastry, which may be shaped like a crescent moon, a triangle or cigar-shaped. Perhaps the most popular of all the pastries, these meat-filled ones grace many mezze tables in Lebanon and are prepared for celebratory feasts and parties.

Serves 6
30ml/2 tbsp olive oil
1 onion, finely chopped
30ml/2 tbsp pine nuts
250g/9oz lean lamb, finely minced (ground)
10ml/2 tsp ground cinnamon
30ml/2 tbsp thick, strained yogurt
small bunch of flat leaf parsley, finely chopped
plain (all-purpose) flour, for dusting
450g/1lb ready-prepared puff pastry
sunflower oil, for frying
sea salt and ground black pepper

1 Heat the olive oil in a heavy pan, stir in the chopped onion and cook until transparent but not browned. Add the pine nuts and just as they begin to colour, stir in the minced lamb.

2 Cook the lamb mixture for 4–5 minutes until all the meat is browned, stirring constantly. Stir in the cinnamon and season well with salt and pepper. Transfer the mixture to a large bowl to cool, then beat in the strained yogurt and chopped parsley.

3 Dust the work surface with a little flour and roll out the puff pastry thinly. Cut into 10cm/4in rounds or squares, depending on whether you want to create half-moon shapes or triangles. Place 10ml/2 tsp of the meat mixture just off centre, then pull the other side of the pastry over the filling.

4 Using your finger, dampen the edges with water and pinch the parcels together to seal. You can create a pattern along the edge with a fork, if you like.

5 Heat enough oil in a pan for deep-frying. When the oil is hot, fry the pastries in batches for 5–6 minutes, until they are golden brown. Drain on kitchen paper and serve the pastries warm or at room temperature.

Golden Beef Samosas

A variation on a popular Indian appetizer, these golden samosas have a spicy meat and vegetable filling. Delicious served with traditional accompaniments or just as a snack.

Serves 4
15ml/1 tbsp oil
115g/4oz/1 cup minced (ground) beef
3 spring onions (scallions), sliced
50g/2oz baby corn, chopped
1 carrot, diced
2.5ml/½ tsp ground cumin
2.5ml/½ tsp ground coriander
5ml/1 tsp curry paste
50ml/2fl oz/¼ cup beef stock
6 sheets filo pastry
25g/1oz/2 tbsp melted butter
oil for deep-frying
fresh coriander (cilantro), to garnish
lime pickle and poppadums, to serve

1 Heat the oil in a frying pan. Fry the minced beef for about 5 minutes, or until browned and sealed.

2 Add the spring onions, corn, carrot, cumin, coriander and the curry paste. Cook for a further 5 minutes. Add the beef stock and bring the mixture to the boil.

3 Cut each filo sheet into eight. Brush one sheet with melted butter, place another on top. Brush with butter and repeat to make eight stacks of pastry. Put one-eighth of the filling in the centre of each sheet, brush the edges with butter. Fold into a triangle. Brush with butter.

4 Heat the oil for deep-frying in a large heavy pan to 180°C/350°F. Cook the samosas for 5 minutes until golden brown. Drain well and garnish with fresh coriander. Serve with lime pickle and poppadums.

Cook's Tip
Instead of deep-frying the samosas they can be baked in a preheated oven at 200°C/400°F/Gas 6. Arrange them on several baking trays lined with baking parchment. Bake for 15–20 minutes, until golden brown.

Lamb Pastries Energy 555kcal/2308kJ; Protein 14.5g; Carbohydrate 34.8g, of which sugars 4.4g; Fat 41.5g, of which saturates 4.3g; Cholesterol 32mg; Calcium 76mg; Fibre 0.9g; Sodium 275mg.
Beef Samosas Energy 101kcal/423kJ; Protein 5g; Carbohydrate 10.4g, of which sugars 0.2g; Fat 4.6g, of which saturates 2.3g; Cholesterol 19mg; Calcium 37mg; Fibre 1g; Sodium 37mg.

Brazilian Beef Pasties

The secret of this crisp and flaky pastry is the addition of cachaça, Brazil's favourite spirit.

Makes about 6

For the pastry

260g/9½oz/scant 2¾ cups plain (all-purpose) flour
5ml/1 tsp salt
30ml/2 tbsp lard, diced
5ml/1 tsp cachaça or vodka
15ml/1 tbsp white vinegar

For the filling

¼ onion, finely chopped
400g/14oz minced (ground) beef
2 cloves garlic, crushed
40g/1½oz/¼ cup olives, sliced
15ml/1 tbsp parsley, chopped
15ml/1 tbsp finely chopped spring onions (scallions)
ground black pepper
hot pepper sauce, to serve

1 To make the pastry, sift the flour and salt into a large bowl. Rub in the lard with your fingertips until the mixture resembles fine breadcrumbs. Stir in the cachaça and white vinegar, then gradually mix in warm water until a rough, dry dough forms.

2 Transfer to a lightly floured surface and knead for 3–4 minutes until you have a smooth but fairly stiff dough. Shape into a roll with a diameter of about 5cm/2in. Wrap in clear film (plastic wrap) and leave at room temperature for at least 4 hours.

3 Cut the dough into six pieces. Roll each piece until a little thinner than 3mm/⅛in, then trim into a 10 x 20cm/4 x 8in rectangle. Tightly cover the whole stack with clear film and refrigerate until needed. It will keep for up to four days.

4 To make the filling, heat 30ml/2 tbsp vegetable oil in a frying pan and fry the onion until soft. Add the beef and garlic, and cook until the liquid has evaporated. Stir in the olives, parsley and spring onions, and season to taste. Leave to cool.

5 Place six pastry rectangles on a floured surface and brush the edges with water. Add a tablespoon of cold filling to one half and fold the other half over it. Press the edges together firmly.

6 Heat a 7.5cm/3in depth of vegetable oil in a deep pan to 190°C/375°F. Fry the pastries, until golden and crisp. Serve hot.

Crackling Flat Cakes

These tasty little savoury cakes are especially popular in the north-eastern region of Slovenia, where they are commonly served as a snack with drinks, usually white wine. They are delicious eaten warm from the oven.

Makes about 20

300g/11oz/2¾ cups self-raising (self-rising) flour
250g/9oz pork crackling, chopped
2 egg yolks
45ml/3 tbsp white wine
1 egg yolk, to glaze
salt

1 Preheat the oven to 180°C/350°F/Gas 4. Grease two baking trays with vegetable oil. Place the flour in a bowl and stir in the pork crackling with a pinch of salt. Make a well in the middle of the mixture and then add the egg yolks and wine.

2 Stir the yolks and wine together with a fork, then mix all the ingredients together, using the fork at first and then bringing the mixture together gently with your hands to make a dough.

3 Place the dough on a floured surface and roll it out lightly until it is about 5mm/¼in thick. Use a biscuit (cookie) cutter to stamp out 3–5cm/1¼–2in circles. Re-roll and cut out more cakes. Transfer to the baking trays, spacing them 2.5cm/1in or so apart to allow room for them to spread and rise.

4 Use a small sharp knife to lightly score the surface of the cakes. Mix the egg yolk with a little water, brush over the cakes, then bake in the preheated oven for about 15 minutes, until lightly browned, risen and just firm.

5 Leave on the baking trays for a couple of minutes, then lift them on to a wire rack. Serve while still warm.

Cook's Tip

Ocvirki, the crisp brown residue of rendered pork, or crackling, feature in many savoury Slovene recipes. If you haven't the time or inclination to prepare them yourself, packets of pork scratchings are the perfect alternative.

Brazilian Pasties Energy 342kcal/1433kJ; Protein 18.9g; Carbohydrate 34.5g, of which sugars 1.2g; Fat 15.1g, of which saturates 4.4g; Cholesterol 47mg; Calcium 75mg; Fibre 2.1g; Sodium 286mg.
Crackling Cakes Energy 129kcal/540kJ; Protein 6.3g; Carbohydrate 11.4g, of which sugars 0.2g; Fat 6.6g, of which saturates 2.2g; Cholesterol 43mg; Calcium 56mg; Fibre 0.5g; Sodium 55mg.

Little Russian Beef Pies

These golden pastries are often served with soup.

Makes 24 little pies

1 large onion, finely chopped
30–45ml/2–3 tbsp vegetable oil
400g/14oz minced (ground) beef
100ml/3½fl oz/½ cup beef stock
30ml/2 tbsp crème fraîche
1 egg, hardboiled and chopped
salt and ground black pepper
a little milk, for glazing

For the dough

50g/2oz/¼ cup butter
200ml/7fl oz/scant 1 cup milk
45ml/3 tbsp water
1 egg
2.5ml/½ tsp salt
7.5ml/1½ tsp caster (superfine) sugar
5g/⅛oz easy-blend (rapid-rise) dried yeast
400g/14oz/3½ cups plain (all-purpose) flour

1 To make the filling, heat the oil in a frying pan, add the onion and fry until soft. Add the beef and fry, stirring, for 10 minutes, until browned, then add the stock and crème fraîche. Cover and simmer, stirring occasionally, for 10–15 minutes. Leave to cool then stir in the chopped egg. Season with salt and pepper to taste. Set aside while you make the dough.

2 To make the dough, melt the butter in a pan. Add the milk and water and heat it to 45°C/110°F. Remove from the heat. Whisk the whole egg in a large bowl with the salt and sugar. Pour in the warm milk mixture.

3 Mix the yeast with the flour and stir, a little at a time, into the warm egg mixture. Knead the dough for 5 minutes. Cover and leave to rise for 30 minutes, until doubled in size. Turn the dough on to a lightly floured surface and knead for 2–3 minutes.

4 Cut the dough into 24 pieces and form into balls. Rest for 5–10 minutes. Flatten each ball to a round measuring 10cm/4in in diameter. Spread 25ml/1½ tbsp of the beef filling in the centre of each round. Fold together and seal the edges. Place on a lined baking sheet, edge down, and rest for 20 minutes.

5 Preheat the oven to 230°C/450°F/Gas 8. Brush the pies with a little milk, then bake in the oven for 12–13 minutes, until golden. Transfer to a wire rack and leave to cool.

Golden Beef and Potato Puffs

These crisp, golden pillows of pastry filled with spiced beef and potatoes are delicious served straight from the wok. The light pastry puffs up in the hot oil and contrasts enticingly with the fragrant spiced beef.

Serves 4

15ml/1 tbsp sunflower oil
½ small onion, finely chopped
3 garlic cloves, crushed
5ml/1 tsp fresh root ginger, grated
1 red chilli, seeded and chopped
30ml/2 tbsp hot curry powder
75g/3oz minced (ground) beef
115g/4oz mashed potato
60ml/4 tbsp chopped fresh coriander (cilantro)
2 sheets ready-rolled, fresh puff pastry
1 egg, lightly beaten
vegetable oil, for frying
salt and ground black pepper
fresh coriander (cilantro) leaves, to garnish
tomato ketchup, to serve

1 Heat the oil in a wok, then add the onion, garlic, ginger and chilli. Stir-fry over medium heat for 2–3 minutes. Add the curry powder and beef and stir-fry over high heat for a further 4–5 minutes, or until the beef is browned and just cooked through, then remove from the heat.

2 Transfer the beef mixture to a large bowl and add the mashed potato and chopped fresh coriander. Stir well, then season and set aside.

3 Lay the pastry sheets on a clean, dry surface and cut out eight rounds, using a 7.5cm/3in pastry (cookie) cutter. Place a large spoonful of the beef mixture in the centre of each pastry round. Brush the edges of the pastry with the beaten egg and fold each round in half to enclose the filling. Press and crimp the edges with the tines of a fork to seal.

4 Fill a wok one-third full of oil and heat to 180°C/350°F (or until a cube of bread, dropped into the oil, browns in 15 seconds).

5 Deep-fry the puffs, in batches, for about 2–3 minutes until they turn a golden brown colour. Drain on kitchen paper and serve garnished with fresh coriander leaves. Offer tomato ketchup to diners for dipping.

Little Beef Pies Energy 411kcal/1719kJ; Protein 17.4g; Carbohydrate 41.7g, of which sugars 3.4g; Fat 20.5g, of which saturates 9g; Cholesterol 117mg; Calcium 120mg; Fibre 1.7g; Sodium 108mg.
Golden Beef Puffs Energy 408kcal/1695kJ; Protein 9g; Carbohydrate 24.2g, of which sugars 1.8g; Fat 31.8g, of which saturates 4.2g; Cholesterol 67mg; Calcium 46mg; Fibre 0.5g; Sodium 202mg.

Caraway and Beef Pastries

These pastries are similar to Polish pirozhki. The pastry encloses a stuffing of beef with dill.

Makes 12–15

5ml/1 tsp caraway seeds
225g/8oz/2 cups plain (all-purpose) flour
2.5ml/½ tsp salt
2.5ml/½ tsp baking powder
115g/4oz/½ cup butter, diced
2 egg yolks, beaten
120ml/4fl oz/½ cup sour cream
a little milk, for glazing

For the filling

60ml/4 tbsp vegetable oil
1 onion, finely chopped
200g/7oz/scant 1 cup minced (ground) beef
1 bunch dill, finely chopped
2 egg yolks, beaten
salt and ground black pepper

1 Put the caraway seeds in a dry pan over a medium-high heat and toast for 1 minute, to release their aroma. Set aside.

2 To make the filling, heat the oil in a heavy frying pan and cook the onion for 3 minutes, until soft. Add the beef and cook, stirring frequently, for 10 more minutes. Stir in the dill and egg yolks and season with salt and pepper. Cool until ready to use.

3 Put the flour, salt and baking powder into a large bowl. Rub the butter into the flour by hand to resemble fine crumbs. Add the caraway seeds. Stir in the beaten egg yolks and sour cream, a little at a time, working it all together to achieve a smooth and elastic dough. Knead for 2–3 minutes, then wrap in clear film (plastic wrap) and chill for 1 hour.

4 Preheat the oven to 190°C/375°F/Gas 5 and grease a baking sheet. Roll out the dough to about 5mm/¼in thick. Using a pastry (cookie) cutter or a glass about 7.5cm/3in in diameter, stamp out as many rounds as you can.

5 Brush the edges of the rounds with water, and put a spoonful of filling in the centre of each round. Press the edges gently together with your fingers to make a half-circle shape. Repeat with the remaining dough and filling. Put the pastries on the baking sheet, brush the tops with a little milk, and bake for 25 minutes. Serve immediately.

Peruvian Beef Pies

Known as empanadas, these pastries have been part of Peru's culinary history since the first days of Spanish rule. The little pies make very popular mid-morning snacks.

Makes 20 small pies

For the filling

75ml/5 tbsp vegetable oil
450g/1lb/2 cups minced (ground) beef
1 large red onion, finely chopped
150g/5oz/1 cup raisins, chopped
150g/5oz/1 cup kalamata olives, pitted and chopped
250ml/8fl oz/1 cup water
3 hard-boiled eggs, diced
salt

For the pastry

450g/1lb/4 cups self-raising (self-rising) flour
1.5ml/¼ tsp salt
150g/5oz margarine
60ml/4 tbsp water
150g/5oz/1¼ cups icing (confectioners') sugar

1 To make the filling, heat the oil in a large frying pan and fry the beef for 5–10 minutes, stirring, until browned. Stir in the onion and fry until it is starting to caramelize, then add the raisins and olives. Add the water and season to taste with salt. Cover and simmer for 10 minutes, then remove from the heat and leave to cool while you make the pastry.

2 Sift the flour into a large mixing bowl and add the salt. Blend in the margarine using two forks or rub it in with your fingers. Add the water and knead until the dough is smooth and not sticky. Cover the bowl with a clean dish towel and leave it to rest for 15 minutes. Preheat the oven to 200°C/400°F/Gas 6.

3 Roll out the dough thinly on a floured surface and cut out 6cm/2½in circles using a plain pastry (cookie) cutter. Spoon a little of the cooled filling, minimizing any liquid, on to each circle and add a piece of hard-boiled egg.

4 Fold the dough circle in half over the stuffing, wet the rim with a little water and pinch the edges together with your fingers. Place on an oiled baking tray, well spaced so the pies have room to spread. Bake for 15 minutes or until they are golden. Leave the pastries on the tray to cool a little. Dust with sifted icing sugar before serving.

Caraway Pastries Energy 206kcal/858kJ; Protein 5.3g; Carbohydrate 14.1g, of which sugars 2.1g; Fat 14.7g, of which saturates 6.8g; Cholesterol 85mg; Calcium 47mg; Fibre 0.9g; Sodium 76mg.
Peruvian Beef Pies Energy 223kcal/930kJ; Protein 8g; Carbohydrate 15.3g, of which sugars 0.9g; Fat 14.9g, of which saturates 4.8g; Cholesterol 27mg; Calcium 26mg; Fibre 0.8g; Sodium 61mg.

Chorizo Pastry Puffs

These flaky pastry puffs make a really superb accompaniment to a glass of cold sherry or beer. For best results, choose a mild cheese, as the chorizo has plenty of flavour. By using ready-made puff pastry and ingredients from the storecupboard, these are a quick and easy snack to make for those times when unexpected visitors call.

Makes 16

225g/8oz puff pastry, thawed if frozen
115g/4oz cured chorizo sausage, finely chopped
50g/2oz/½ cup grated cheese
1 small (US medium) egg, beaten
5ml/1 tsp paprika

1 Roll out the pastry thinly on a floured work surface. Using a 7.5cm/3in cutter, stamp out 16 rounds.

2 Preheat the oven to 230°C/450°F/Gas 8. Put the chopped chorizo sausage and grated cheese in a bowl and toss together lightly until combined.

3 Lay one of the pastry rounds in the palm of your hand and place a little of the chorizo mixture across the centre. Using your other hand, pinch the edges of the pastry together along the top to seal. Repeat the process with the remaining rounds to make 16 puffs in all.

4 Place the pastries on a non-stick baking sheet and brush lightly with the beaten egg. Dust the tops of the pastries lightly with a little paprika.

5 Bake the pastries in the preheated oven for about 10–12 minutes, until puffed up and golden all over. Serve the puffs immediately while warm.

Cook's Tip
Chorizo is a spicy pork sausage flavoured with garlic, chilli and other spices. It is popular in Mexican and Spanish cuisine. Remove the casing on the sausage before cooking.

Onion Tarts with Goats Cheese

Crisp and savoury, these attractive little tarts are delicious served with a few mixed salad leaves.

Serves 6

60ml/4 tbsp olive oil
25g/1oz/2 tbsp butter
4 red onions, thinly sliced
5ml/1 tsp soft brown sugar
15ml/1 tbsp balsamic vinegar
15ml/1 tbsp soy sauce
200g/7oz button (white) mushrooms, thinly sliced
1 garlic clove, finely chopped
2.5ml/½ tsp chopped tarragon
30ml/2 tbsp chopped parsley
250g/9oz roll of goat's cheese
225g/8oz puff pastry, thawed if frozen
salt and ground black pepper
mixed salad leaves, to serve

1 Heat 15ml/1 tbsp of the oil and half the butter in a frying pan, add the onions, cover and cook for 15 minutes, stirring occasionally. Uncover the pan, increase the heat slightly and sprinkle in the brown sugar. Cook, stirring, until the onions begin to caramelize. Add the vinegar and soy sauce and cook briskly until the liquid evaporates. Season to taste then set aside.

2 Heat another 30ml/2 tbsp of the oil and the remaining butter in a pan, add the mushrooms and garlic and cook fairly briskly for 5–6 minutes, until the mushrooms are browned. Stir the mushrooms into the onions with the tarragon and parsley. Season to taste. Preheat the oven to 190°C/375°F/Gas 5.

3 Roll out the pastry and use to line 6 x 10cm/4in tartlet tins (muffin pans). Prick the bases with a fork and line with foil. Bake for 10 minutes, remove the foil and bake for another 5–7 minutes until cooked. Remove from the oven and increase the temperature to 200°C/400°F/Gas 6.

4 Remove the pastry shells from the tins and arrange on a baking sheet. Distribute the onion mixture equally among the pastry shells. Cut the goat's cheese into six slices and place one slice on each tartlet, drizzle with oil and season with pepper.

5 Return the tartlets to the oven and bake for 5–8 minutes, or until the goat's cheese is just beginning to turn brown. Serve with mixed salad leaves.

Chorizo Puffs Energy 183kcal/763kJ; Protein 5.4g; Carbohydrate 12.1g, of which sugars 0.6g; Fat 13.1g, of which saturates 3g; Cholesterol 36mg; Calcium 73mg; Fibre 0.1g; Sodium 258mg.
Onion Tarts Energy 251kcal/1048kJ; Protein 8g; Carbohydrate 23g, of which sugars 5g; Fat 15g, of which saturates 8g; Cholesterol 88mg; Calcium 149mg; Fibre 2g; Sodium 151mg.

Herbed Mini Tarts

These little tarts, cooked in tart tins, are ideal for picnics.

Makes 8

45–60ml/3–4 tbsp tapenade or sun-dried tomato paste
1 large egg
100g/3¾oz/scant ½ cup thick Greek (US strained plain) yogurt
90ml/6 tbsp milk
1 garlic clove, crushed
30ml/2 tbsp chopped mixed herbs, such as thyme, marjoram, basil and parsley
salt and ground black pepper

For the pastry

115g/4oz/1 cup plain (all-purpose) flour
pinch of salt
50g/2oz/¼ cup butter, diced
30ml/2 tbsp chilled water

1 To make the pastry, sift the flour and salt into a large bowl. Rub or cut in the butter until the mixture resembles fine breadcrumbs. Sprinkle over the water and mix to a dough. Knead briefly, then wrap and chill for 20 minutes.

2 Roll out the pastry and cut out eight rounds. Use to line deep tartlet tins (muffin pans). Chill the pastry cases (pie shells) for 30 minutes. Preheat the oven to 190°C/375°F/Gas 5.

3 Line each pastry case with a small piece of foil. Bake for about 15 minutes. Remove the foil and bake for a further 5 minutes, until crisp. Set aside to cool.

4 Spread a little tapenade or tomato paste in the base of each pastry case. Whisk together the egg, yogurt, milk, garlic, herbs and seasoning and spoon into the pastry cases.

5 Bake for about 30 minutes, or until the filling is just firm to the touch and the pastry golden. Allow the pies to cool slightly before carefully removing them from the tins and serving with a crisp salad tossed in extra virgin olive oil.

Variation
A few chopped green or black olives would be a tasty addition to the filling for these pies.

Creamy Roquefort Tartlets

These festive treats can be made in shallow tartlet tins to serve hot as a first course. You could also make them in tiny cocktail tins to serve warm as bitesize snacks with a Christmas drink before a meal.

Makes 12

175g/6oz/1½ cups plain (all-purpose) flour
large pinch of salt
115g/4oz/½ cup butter
1 egg yolk
30ml/2 tbsp cold water

For the filling

15g/½oz/1 tbsp butter
15g/½oz/1 tbsp flour
150ml/¼ pint/⅔ cup milk
115g/4oz Roquefort cheese, crumbled
150ml/¼ pint/⅔ cup double (heavy) cream
2.5ml/½ tsp dried mixed herbs
3 egg yolks
salt and ground black pepper

1 To make the pastry, sift the flour and salt into a bowl and rub the butter into the flour until it resembles breadcrumbs. Mix the egg yolk with the water and stir into the flour to make a soft dough. Knead until smooth, wrap in clear film (plastic wrap) and chill for 30 minutes. (You can also make the dough in a food processor, if you prefer.)

2 Melt the butter in a pan, stir in the flour and then the milk. Boil to thicken slightly, stirring constantly. Off the heat, beat in the cheese and season with salt and pepper. Set aside.

3 In a separate pan, bring the cream and mixed herbs to the boil. Reduce the liquid to about 30ml/2 tbsp. Beat the herby cream into the cheese sauce together with the egg yolks.

4 Preheat the oven to 190°C/375°F/Gas 5. On a lightly floured work surface, roll out the pastry 3mm/⅛in thick. Stamp out rounds with a fluted pastry (cookie) cutter and use to line your chosen tartlet tins (muffin pans).

5 Divide the filling between the tartlets; they should be filled only two-thirds full. Stamp out smaller fluted rounds or star shapes for the tops and lay on top of each tartlet. Bake for 20–25 minutes, or until puffed and golden brown.

Herbed Mini Tarts Energy 133Kcal/555kJ; Protein 4g; Carbohydrate 13g, of which sugars 2g; Fat 7.7g, of which saturates 4.3g; Cholesterol 43mg; Calcium 74mg; Fibre 1g; Sodium 78mg.
Roquefort Tartlets Energy 252kcal/1045kJ; Protein 5.1g; Carbohydrate 13.2g, of which sugars 1.2g; Fat 20.9g, of which saturates 12.2g; Cholesterol 117mg; Calcium 100mg; Fibre 0.5g; Sodium 217mg.

Leek, Saffron and Mussel Tartlets

Serve these vividly coloured little tarts with cherry tomatoes and salad leaves.

Makes 12

4 large yellow (bell) peppers, halved
large pinch of saffron threads
30ml/2 tbsp hot water
4 large leeks, sliced
60ml/4 tbsp olive oil
2kg/4½lb mussels, scrubbed and beards removed
4 large (US extra large) eggs
600ml/1 pint/2½ cups single (light) cream
60ml/4 tbsp chopped fresh parsley
salt and ground black pepper

For the pastry

450g/1lb/4 cups plain (all-purpose) flour
5ml/1 tsp salt
250g/8oz/1 cup butter, diced
30–45ml/2–3 tbsp water

1 To make the pastry, mix together the flour and salt and rub in the butter. Mix in the water and knead lightly. Wrap the dough in clear film (plastic wrap) and chill for 30 minutes.

2 Grill (broil) the pepper halves, skin sides uppermost, until blackened. Place them in a plastic bag and leave for 10 minutes, then peel and cut the flesh into thin strips.

3 Preheat the oven to 190°C/375°F/Gas 5. Use the pastry to line twelve 10cm/4in tartlet tins (muffin pans), 2.5cm/1in deep. Prick the bases and line with foil. Bake for 10 minutes. Remove the foil and bake for another 5–8 minutes, or until lightly coloured. Reduce the oven temperature to 180°C/350°F/Gas 4.

4 Soak the saffron in the hot water for 10 minutes. Fry the leeks in the oil for 6–8 minutes until beginning to brown. Add the pepper strips and cook for another 2 minutes.

5 Put the mussels in a large pan and discard any open mussels that do not shut when tapped sharply. Cover and cook, shaking the pan occasionally, for 3–4 minutes, or until the mussels open. Discard any mussels that do not open. Shell the remainder. Beat the eggs, cream, saffron liquid and parsley together and season. Arrange the leeks, peppers and mussels in the pastry, add the egg mixture and bake for 20–25 minutes, until just firm.

Mushroom Tarts with Walnut Pastry

Fontina cheese gives these tarts a creamy, nutty flavour. Serve warm with a lemon-dressed rocket salad.

Serves 4

25g/1oz/½ cup dried wild mushrooms
30ml/2 tbsp olive oil
1 red onion, chopped
2 garlic cloves, chopped
30ml/2 tbsp medium-dry sherry
1 egg
120ml/4fl oz/½ cup single (light) cream
25g/1oz Fontina cheese, sliced
salt and ground black pepper
rocket (arugula) leaves, to serve

For the pastry

115g/4oz/1 cup wholemeal (whole-wheat) flour
50g/2oz/4 tbsp unsalted butter
25g/1oz/¼ cup walnuts, roasted and ground
1 egg, lightly beaten

1 To make the pastry, rub the flour and butter together until the mixture resembles fine breadcrumbs, then stir in the walnuts. Add the egg and mix to form a soft dough. Wrap in clear film (plastic wrap) and chill for about 30 minutes.

2 Meanwhile, soak the dried mushrooms in 300ml/½ pint/1¼ cups boiling water for 30 minutes. Drain and reserve the liquid. Heat the oil in a frying pan. Add the onion and fry for 5 minutes, then add the garlic and fry for 2 minutes, stirring.

3 Add the mushrooms and cook over high heat until the edges become crisp. Add the sherry and the reserved liquid. Cook for 10 minutes until the liquid evaporates. Season and leave to cool.

4 Preheat the oven to 200°C/400°F/Gas 6. Lightly grease four 10cm/4in tart tins (pans). Roll out the pastry on a lightly floured work surface and use to line the tart tins.

5 Prick the pastry, line with baking parchment and baking beans and bake blind for 10 minutes. Remove the paper and beans.

6 Whisk the egg and cream to mix, add to the mushroom mixture, then season to taste. Spoon into the pastry cases (pie shells), top with cheese slices and bake for 18 minutes until the filling is set. Serve warm with rocket.

Leek Tartlets Energy 506kcal/2112kJ; Protein 17.2g; Carbohydrate 35.1g, of which sugars 6.1g; Fat 34.1g, of which saturates 18.3g; Cholesterol 155mg; Calcium 221mg; Fibre 2.8g; Sodium 273mg.
Mushroom Tarts Energy 409kcal/1701kJ; Protein 10.2g; Carbohydrate 21.9g, of which sugars 2.3g; Fat 31g, of which saturates 13.4g; Cholesterol 143mg; Calcium 121mg; Fibre 2.3g; Sodium 199mg.

Feta and Olive Tartlets

These upside-down tartlets are filled with vegetables and chunks of feta cheese. They are a perfect meal and make a favourite for outdoor eating and at picnics.

Serves 4

25g/1oz sun-dried aubergine (eggplant) slices
300ml/½ pint boiling water
45ml/3 tbsp sunflower oil
1 onion, thinly sliced
150g/5oz/2 cups button (white) mushrooms, sliced
1 garlic clove, crushed
12–16 cherry tomatoes, halved
8 black or green olives, pitted and chopped
115g/4oz feta cheese, sliced and then crumbled
350g/12oz ready-made puff pastry, thawed if frozen
salt and ground black pepper

1 Preheat the oven to 200°C/400°F/Gas 6. Place the aubergine slices in a shallow dish. Pour over the boiling water and leave to soak for 10 minutes. Rinse in cold water, and then drain on kitchen paper. Cut the aubergine slices in half or quarters, depending on size.

2 Heat 30ml/2 tbsp of the oil in a frying pan and fry the onion over a medium heat for 5 minutes. Add the mushrooms and cook for 3–4 minutes, or until the onions are golden. Set aside.

3 Heat the remaining oil in the frying pan, add the aubergine slices and garlic and lightly fry for 1–2 minutes. Lightly oil four individual dishes.

4 Mix the tomatoes with the onions, mushrooms, aubergines, olives and feta cheese, divide among the dishes and season.

5 Roll out the pastry thinly, then cut out four rounds, each slightly larger than the diameter of the dishes.

6 Place the pastry on top of the vegetable and cheese mixture, tucking the overlap down inside the dish.

7 Bake for 20 minutes, or until the pastry is risen and golden. Cool slightly then invert on to individual warmed serving plates to serve immediately.

Leek and Onion Tartlets

These winter tartlets are popular snacks in the Alsace region of France. They make a great appetizer or addition to a celebratory buffet.

Serves 6

25g/1oz/2 tbsp butter
1 onion, thinly sliced
2.5ml/½ tsp dried thyme
450g/1lb leeks, thinly sliced
50g/2oz Gruyère cheese, grated
3 eggs
300ml/½ pint/1¼ cups single (light) cream
pinch of freshly grated nutmeg
salt and ground black pepper
mixed salad leaves, to serve

For the pastry

175g/6oz/1⅓ cup plain (all-purpose) flour
75g/3oz/6 tbsp cold butter
1 egg yolk
30–45ml/2–3 tbsp cold water
2.5ml/½ tsp salt

1 Make the pastry. Sift the flour into a bowl and add the butter. Rub the butter into the flour until it resembles breadcrumbs. Beat together the egg yolk, water and salt, pour into a well in the flour mixture. Combine the flour and liquid until it begins to stick together. Form into a ball. Wrap and chill for 30 minutes.

2 Butter six 10cm/4in tartlet tins (muffin pans). Roll out the pastry until 3mm/⅛in thick, then cut out rounds with a 12.5cm/5in cutter. Press the rounds into the tins. Re-roll the trimmings and line the remaining tins. Prick the bases and chill.

3 Preheat the oven to 190°C/375°F/Gas 5. Line the cases with foil and fill with baking beans. Place on a baking sheet and bake for 6–8 minutes until golden. Remove the foil and beans and bake for 2 minutes. Transfer to a wire rack to cool. Reduce the oven temperature to 180°C/350°F/Gas 4.

4 In a large pan, melt the butter. Cook the onion and thyme for 3–5 minutes, then add the leeks for 10–12 minutes. Divide the mixture among the cases and sprinkle each with cheese.

5 Beat together the eggs, cream, nutmeg and seasoning. Place the cases on a baking sheet and pour in the mixture. Bake for 15–20 minutes until golden. Cool on a wire rack slightly, then serve warm or at room temperature with salad leaves.

Feta and Olive Energy 520Kcal/2,167kJ; Protein 12g; Carbohydrate 38.8g, of which sugars 6.9g; Fat 37.2g, of which saturates 5.3g; Cholesterol 20mg; Calcium 182mg; Fibre 4g; Sodium 865mg.
Leek Tartlets Energy 422kcal/1755kJ; Protein 11.5g; Carbohydrate 26.8g, of which sugars 3.9g; Fat 30.4g, of which saturates 17.7g; Cholesterol 200mg; Calcium 189mg; Fibre 2.7g; Sodium 215mg.

Grilled Pepper Tartlets

These pretty Spanish tartlets are filled with strips of roasted sweet peppers and a creamy, cheesy custard. They make a perfect snack to serve with a glass of sherry or a cold beer.

Serves 4

1 red (bell) pepper
1 yellow (bell) pepper
175g/6oz/1½ cups plain (all-purpose) flour
75g/3oz/6 tbsp chilled butter, diced
30–45ml/2–3 tbsp cold water
60ml/4 tbsp double (heavy) cream
1 egg
15ml/1 tbsp grated Parmesan cheese
salt and ground black pepper

1 Preheat the oven to 200°C/400°F/Gas 6, and heat the grill (broiler). Place the peppers on a baking sheet and grill (broil) for 10 minutes, turning occasionally, until blackened. Cover with a dish towel and leave for 5 minutes. Peel away the skin, then discard the seeds and cut the flesh into very thin strips.

2 Sift the flour and a pinch of salt into a mixing bowl. Add the butter and rub it in with your fingertips until the mixture resembles fine breadcrumbs. Stir in enough of the water to make a firm, not sticky, dough.

3 Roll the dough out thinly on a lightly floured surface and line 12 individual moulds or a 12-hole tartlet tin (muffin pan). Prick the bases with a fork and fill the pastry cases (pie shells) with crumpled foil. Bake for 10 minutes, then remove the foil and divide the pepper strips among the pastry cases.

4 Whisk the cream and egg in a bowl. Season and pour over the peppers. Sprinkle each tartlet with Parmesan and bake for 15–20 minutes until firm. Cool for 2 minutes, then remove from the moulds and transfer to a wire rack. Serve warm or cold.

Variation
Use strips of grilled aubergine (eggplant) mixed with sun-dried tomatoes in place of the roasted (bell) peppers.

Quail's Egg and Vermouth Tartlets

Eggs hard-boiled in this way have an attractive marbled surface rather like Chinese hundred-year-old eggs.

Serves 4

10 quail's eggs
30ml/2 tbsp soy sauce
30ml/2 tbsp mustard seeds
15ml/1 tbsp green tea leaves
6 filo pastry sheets
50g/2oz/¼ cup butter, melted
1 small avocado
45ml/3 tbsp dry white vermouth
30ml/2 tbsp mayonnaise
10ml/2 tsp fresh lime juice
salt and ground black pepper
paprika, for dusting

1 Put the quail's eggs into a pan. Pour over cold water to cover. Add the soy sauce, mustard seeds and tea leaves. Bring to the boil, then lower the heat and simmer for 3 minutes.

2 Remove the pan from the heat and lift out the eggs with a slotted spoon. Gently tap them on a firm surface so that the shells crack all over. Put the eggs back into the liquid and leave in a cool place for 8 hours or overnight.

3 Line the tartlet cases with the pastry and frill the edge of each. Put a crumpled piece of foil in each filo case and bake for 12–15 minutes until cooked and golden. Remove the foil and leave to cool.

4 Cut the avocado in half, remove the stone (pit) and scoop the flesh into a blender or food processor. Add the vermouth, mayonnaise and lime juice, and season to taste with salt and pepper. Process until smooth.

5 Shell the quail's eggs and cut them in half. Pipe or spoon the avocado mixture into the pastry cases (pie shells) and arrange the halved eggs on top. Dust with a little paprika and serve.

Cook's Tip
Pack cooked shelled eggs into wide-necked sterilized jars and cover with dry sherry or vermouth. Seal, label, store in a cool place, and use within six weeks.

Pepper Tartlets Energy 427kcal/1778kJ; Protein 8.4g; Carbohydrate 40g, of which sugars 6.4g; Fat 27g, of which saturates 16.1g; Cholesterol 112mg; Calcium 131mg; Fibre 2.8g; Sodium 180mg.
Quail's Egg Tartlet Energy 336kcal/1399kJ; Protein 5.4g; Carbohydrate 24.8g, of which sugars 1.6g; Fat 23.4g, of which saturates 9g; Cholesterol 150mg; Calcium 59mg; Fibre 2.4g; Sodium 640mg.

Brandied Roquefort Tarts

These light puff pastry rounds are topped with the irresistible combination of brandy and Roquefort cheese. They are rich and delicious and make a very good appetizer for a sophisticated supper party.

Makes 6

150g/5oz Roquefort cheese
30ml/2 tbsp brandy
30ml/2 tbsp olive oil
2 red onions (about 225g/8oz total weight), thinly sliced
225g/8oz puff pastry, thawed if frozen
beaten egg or milk, to glaze
6 walnut halves, chopped
30ml/2 tbsp chopped fresh chives
salt and ground black pepper
chive knots, to garnish
salad leaves, diced cucumber and thin tomato wedges, to serve

1 Crumble the Roquefort into a small bowl, pour the brandy over and leave to marinate for 1 hour. Meanwhile, heat the oil in a frying pan and gently fry the onions for 20 minutes, stirring occasionally. Set the pan aside.

2 Preheat the oven to 220°C/425°F/Gas 7. Grease a baking sheet. Roll out the pastry on a floured surface and stamp out six rounds with a 10cm/4in fluted cutter. Put the rounds on the baking sheet and prick them with a fork.

3 Brush the edges of the pastry with a little beaten egg or milk. Add the walnuts and chives to the onion mixture, with salt and pepper to taste. Divide the mixture among the pastry shapes, leaving the edges clear.

4 Spoon the brandied cheese mixture on top of the pastries and bake for 12–15 minutes until golden. Serve warm, garnished with chive knots, on a bed of salad leaves, diced cucumber and thin tomato wedges.

Cook's Tip
To make the chive knots, simply tie chives together in threes, with a central knot. Blanch the chives briefly in just-boiled water if they are not very pliable.

Crab and Ricotta Tartlets

Use the meat from a freshly cooked crab, weighing about 450g/1lb, if you can. Otherwise, look out for frozen brown and white crab meat as an alternative.

Serves 4

225g/8oz/2 cups plain (all-purpose) flour
pinch of salt
115g/4oz/½ cup butter, diced
225g/8oz/1 cup ricotta cheese
15ml/1 tbsp grated onion
30ml/2 tbsp grated Parmesan cheese
2.5ml/½ tsp mustard powder
2 eggs, plus 1 egg yolk
225g/8oz crab meat
30ml/2 tbsp chopped fresh parsley
2.5–5ml/½–1 tsp anchovy essence (paste)
5–10ml/1–2 tsp lemon juice
salt and cayenne pepper
salad leaves, to garnish

1 Preheat the oven to 200°C/400°F/Gas 6. Sift the flour and salt into a bowl, add the butter and rub it in until it resembles fine breadcrumbs. Stir in about 60ml/4 tbsp cold water.

2 Turn the dough on to a floured surface and knead lightly. Roll out and line four 10cm/4in tartlet tins (muffin pans). Prick the bases with a fork, then chill for 30 minutes.

3 Line the bases with baking parchment and fill with baking beans. Bake for 10 minutes, remove the paper and beans and bake for another 10 minutes.

4 Place the ricotta cheese, onion, Parmesan and mustard powder in a bowl and beat until soft. Gradually beat in the eggs and egg yolk.

5 Stir in the crab meat and chopped fresh parsley, then add the anchovy essence and lemon juice. Season to taste with salt and cayenne pepper.

6 Remove the tartlet cases from the oven and reduce the temperature to 180°C/350°F/Gas 4.

7 Spoon the filling into the cases and bake for 20 minutes, until set and golden. Serve hot, garnished with salad leaves.

Roquefort Tarts Energy 340kcal/1411kJ; Protein 8.6g; Carbohydrate 17.1g, of which sugars 2.8g; Fat 25.6g, of which saturates 10.4g; Cholesterol 44mg; Calcium 172mg; Fibre 1.1g; Sodium 536mg.
Crab Tartlets Energy 644kcal/2685kJ; Protein 28.1g; Carbohydrate 46.3g, of which sugars 3.3g; Fat 39.8g, of which saturates 23g; Cholesterol 278mg; Calcium 288mg; Fibre 2.4g; Sodium 609mg.

Smoked Trout Tartlets

Crisp, golden filo pastry contrasts with a creamy trout and three-cheese filling in these pretty little tartlets. Emmenthal or Jarlsberg cheese can be used instead of Gruyère, if you prefer.

Serves 8

8 x 15cm/6in squares filo pastry
50g/2oz/¼ cup butter, melted
50g/2oz Gruyère cheese, grated
115g/4oz/ cup mascarpone cheese
50g/2oz Parmesan cheese, grated
45ml/3 tbsp milk
75g/3oz smoked trout
8 cherry tomatoes, halved
salt and ground black pepper
fresh flat leaf parsley and salad leaves, to garnish

1 Preheat the oven to 180°C/350°F/Gas 4. For each tartlet, place two squares of filo pastry on top of each other at angles to form a star shape.

2 Brush the pastry with melted butter and place, buttered side down, in an individual Yorkshire pudding pan or 10cm/4in tartlet pan. Repeat with the remaining filo. and pans.

3 Support the pans on a baking sheet and brush the pastry with a little more butter. Bake for 5 minutes or until the tartlets are crisp and light golden brown in colour. Remove the tartlets from the oven but leave the oven on.

4 In a large bowl, combine the three cheeses and milk. Season generously with salt and pepper and mix well.

5 Cut the smoked trout into bitesize pieces using kitchen scissors or a knife. Arrange the halved tomatoes and trout in the pastry cases.

6 Spoon the cheese mixture into the cooked pastry cases, gently pressing it down with the back of a spoon. Return the tartlets to the oven and bake for 10–15 minutes more, until the cheese is bubbling and golden brown.

7 Serve warm on individual plates, garnished with the parsley and a few salad leaves.

Prawn Tartlets

These little tartlets are made with delicious, buttery shortcrust pastry. The pastry is cooked completely before the filling goes inside, as the tarts are not cooked twice.

Makes 8

200g/7oz/1¾ cups plain (all-purpose) flour
125g/4¼oz/9 tbsp butter
150ml/¼ pint/⅔ cup cold water, or enough to bind

For the filling
45g/1½oz/scant ¼ cup butter
20g/¾oz/scant ¼ cup plain (all-purpose) flour
475ml/16fl oz/2 cups single (light) cream
275g/10oz cooked prawns (shrimp)
salt and ground white pepper
25ml/1½ tbsp chopped fresh dill sprigs, to garnish

1 Sift the flour into a large bowl. Cut the butter into small pieces, add to the flour and rub in until the mixture resembles fine breadcrumbs. Gradually add the cold water and mix well to form a dough.

2 On a lightly floured surface, roll out the pastry and cut circles to fit 7cm/2¾in diameter fluted tart tins (pans). Cut a 13cm/5in square of foil to line each pastry case (pie shell) and fill with a handful of dried peas or beans to help the pastry keep its shape.

3 Chill for at least 30 minutes to rest the pastry. Preheat the oven to 200°C/400°F/Gas 6. Bake the shells for 10–15 minutes until crisp and golden. Remove the beans and foil for the final 5 minutes so that the pastry base is crisp and dry. Cool on a wire tray, then remove the pastry cases from the tins.

4 To make the filling, melt the butter in a pan over a medium heat, and stir in the flour. Cook the roux for 3–5 minutes until pale beige. Slowly stir in the cream and cook, stirring constantly, for about 5 minutes, until thickened. Stir the prawns into the sauce and heat gently for 3–4 minutes. Season well.

5 Fill the baked pastry cases with the creamed prawns, and sprinkle with fresh dill. Serve immediately while the pastry is still crisp and the filling is soft and warm.

Smoked Trout Tartlets Energy 469kcal/1953kJ; Protein 17g; Carbohydrate 25g, of which sugars 4g; Fat 33g, of which saturates 21g; Cholesterol 94mg; Calcium 298mg; Fibre 0g; Sodium 515mg.
Prawn Tartlets Energy 274kcal/1138kJ; Protein 9g; Carbohydrate 11g, of which sugars 1.7g; Fat 21.9g, of which saturates 13.4g; Cholesterol 95mg; Calcium 83mg; Fibre 0.6g; Sodium 131mg.

Small Chicken Pies

These little pies make a tempting snack or you could have two or three of them with a salad for a light lunch.

Makes about 12

1 chicken, weighing 1.6–2kg/3½–4½lb, jointed
45ml/3 tbsp olive oil
1 sausage
150g/5oz bacon
1 garlic clove
10 black peppercorns
1 onion stuck with 2 cloves
1 bunch of parsley, chopped
4 thyme or marjoram sprigs
juice of 1 lemon
butter, for greasing
500g/1¼lb puff pastry
2 egg yolks, lightly beaten
salt
plain (all-purpose) flour, for dusting

1 Heat the oil in a large pan. Add the chicken pieces and cook over a medium-low heat, turning occasionally, for 10 minutes, until golden brown on all sides. Add the sausage, bacon, garlic, peppercorns, onion, parsley, thyme and lemon juice.

2 Pour in enough water to cover and bring to the boil. Lower the heat, cover and simmer for 1–1½ hours, until tender.

3 Remove all the meat from the stock with a slotted spoon. Then return the stock to the heat and cook, uncovered, until reduced. Strain into a bowl and season with salt to taste.

4 Remove and discard the chicken skin and bones and cut the meat into small pieces. Cut the sausage and bacon into small pieces and mix with the chicken. Preheat the oven to 200°C/400°F/Gas 6. Grease a 12-cup muffin tin (pan) with butter.

5 Roll out the pastry thinly on a floured surface and stamp out 12 rounds with a 7.5cm/3in cutter. Gather the trimmings, re-roll, and stamp out 12 rounds with a 6cm/2½in cutter.

6 Place the larger rounds in the cups of the prepared tin, and divide the meat among them. Spoon in a little of the stock, then brush the edges with beaten egg yolk and cover with the smaller rounds, pinching to seal. Brush the remaining egg yolk, and make a small hole in the centre of each pie. Bake for 15–25 minutes, and leave to cool slightly before serving.

Chicken and Mushroom Vol-au-Vents

These mini pastries can be packed with a range of fillings, such as chicken and mushrooms.

Serves 4–6

1 carrot, halved
1 onion, quartered
1 leek, thickly sliced
1 chicken, 1.3–1.8kg/3–4lb
2 bay leaves
1.5 litres/2½ pints/6¼ cups water
50g/2oz/¼ cup butter
50g/2oz/½ cup plain (all-purpose) flour
200ml/7fl oz/scant 1 cup milk
1 egg yolk
juice of 1 lemon
8 ready-made vol-au-vent cases
sprigs of parsley, to garnish

For the mushrooms

15g/½oz/1 tbsp butter
1 garlic clove, finely chopped
250g/9oz/3½ cups mushrooms, sliced

1 Put the carrot, onion, leek and bay leaves in a large pan. Place the chicken on top, pour over the water and bring to a gentle boil. Reduce the heat and simmer for about 1 hour. Lift the chicken out and leave to cool. Save the pan of stock.

2 When the chicken is cool enough to handle, remove the skin and shred the meat from the bones in bitesize pieces.

3 Preheat the oven to the temperature given on the packet of vol-au-vents or to 220°C/425°F/Gas 7 if using home-made.

4 To cook the mushrooms, melt the butter in a frying pan over medium-high heat. Add the garlic and cook for 1 minute. Add the mushrooms and cook for 5 minutes more. Season, cover and keep warm. Cook the vol-au-vents for 15–18 minutes.

5 Melt the butter in a heavy pan. Add the flour and cook, stirring, for 1 minute. Gradually stir in the chicken stock, then add the milk. Stir for about 8 minutes to make a thick and creamy sauce. Remove from the heat and stir in the egg yolk.

6 Add the mushrooms and the chicken with the lemon juice to the sauce. Adjust the seasoning. Place two vol-au-vent cases on each plate and fill with the warm filling. Garnish with parsley or chervil sprigs and serve.

Chicken Pies Energy 368kcal/1534kJ; Protein 24.5g; Carbohydrate 18.3g, of which sugars 1.2g; Fat 22.8g, of which saturates 4.3g; Cholesterol 109mg; Calcium 44mg; Fibre 0.2g; Sodium 547mg.
Vol-au-vents Energy 648kcal/2695kJ; Protein 37.8g; Carbohydrate 22.6g, of which sugars 2.3g; Fat 46.1g, of which saturates 14.7g; Cholesterol 244mg; Calcium 100mg; Fibre 0.8g; Sodium 345mg.

Chicken and Asparagus Tartlets

These crispy pastry cases and the creamy filling are cooked separately.

Makes 8

200g/7oz/1¾ cups plain (all-purpose) flour
125g/4¼oz/9 tbsp butter
150ml/¼ pint/⅔ cup cold water, or enough to bind

For the filling

65g/2½oz/5 tbsp butter, diced
225g/8oz fresh asparagus, cut into 2cm/¾in pieces
15ml/1 tbsp cooking oil
225g/8oz chicken fillets, cut into 2cm/¾in cubes
20g/¾oz/scant ¼ cup plain (all-purpose) flour
475ml/16fl oz/2 cups single (light) cream
salt and ground white pepper
45ml/3 tbsp chopped fresh parsley, to garnish

1 Sift the flour into a large bowl, rub the butter in until the mixture resembles fine breadcrumbs. Gradually add the water and mix to form a dough. On a lightly floured surface, roll out the pastry and cut circles to fit 7cm/2¾in diameter fluted tart tins (pans). Line each shell with foil and fill with a handful of dried peas or beans to help the pastry keep its shape.

2 Chill for at least 30 minutes to rest the pastry. Preheat the oven to 200°C/400°F/Gas 6. Bake the shells for 10–15 minutes until crisp. Remove the beans and foil for the final 5 minutes so that the pastry cooks and the base is crisp and dry. Cool on a wire tray, then remove the pastry cases (pie shells) from the tins.

3 To make the filling, melt half the butter in a pan over a medium heat. Add the asparagus and cook, stirring, for about 4 minutes, until tender. Remove and set aside. In the same pan, heat the oil. Add the chicken and cook for about 5 minutes, stirring, until it is no longer pink. Set aside.

4 Melt the remaining butter in a pan over a medium heat and stir in the flour. Cook the roux for 3–5 minutes, then slowly stir in the cream and cook, stirring constantly, for about 5 minutes until thickened. Add the asparagus and season well. Transfer into the pastry cases, garnish with parsley, and serve immediately while the filling is still warm.

Mini Pork and Bacon Pies

These little pies can be made in advance. They are a good choice for a summer picnic.

Makes 12

10ml/2 tsp sunflower oil
1 onion, chopped
225g/8oz pork, coarsely chopped
115g/4oz cooked bacon, diced
45ml/3 tbsp chopped fresh herbs, such as sage and parsley
6 eggs, hard-boiled and halved
1 egg yolk, beaten
20g/¾oz packet powdered aspic
300ml/½ pint/1¼ cups boiling water
salt and ground black pepper

For the pastry

450g/1lb/4 cups plain (all-purpose) flour
115g/4oz/½ cup white vegetable fat
275ml/9fl oz/generous 1 cup water

1 To make the pastry, sift the flour into a bowl and add salt and pepper. Gently heat the fat and water in a large pan until the fat has melted. Increase the heat and bring the mixture to the boil. Pour the hot liquid into the flour, stirring constantly. Press the mixture into a ball of dough using a spoon. When the dough is smooth, cover the bowl and set aside.

2 Preheat the oven to 200°C/400°F/Gas 6. Heat the oil in a pan, add the onion and cook until soft. Stir in the pork and bacon and cook until just brown. Stir in the herbs and season.

3 Roll out two-thirds of the pastry on a floured surface. Use a 12cm/4½in fluted cutter to stamp out rounds. Line 12 tartlet tins (muffin pans) with the rounds and place some meat mixture in each. Add half an egg and top with the remaining mix.

4 Roll out the remaining pastry and use a 7.5cm/3in fluted cutter to stamp out lids. Dampen the rim of each pastry base and press a lid in place. Brush with egg yolk and make a small steam hole in the top of each pie. Bake for 30–35 minutes. Cool for 15 minutes, then place on a wire rack to cool completely.

5 Meanwhile, stir the aspic powder into the boiling water until dissolved. Shape a piece of foil into a small funnel and use this to guide a little aspic through the hole in the top of each pie. Chill for up to 24 hours before serving at room temperature.

Chicken Tartlets Energy 274kcal/1138kJ; Protein 9g; Carbohydrate 11g, of which sugars 1.7g; Fat 21.9g, of which saturates 13.4g; Cholesterol 95mg; Calcium 83mg; Fibre 0.6g; Sodium 131mg.
Mini Pies Energy 209kcal/868kJ; Protein 4.2g; Carbohydrate 14.2g, of which sugars 0.7g; Fat 15.4g, of which saturates 3.8g; Cholesterol 26mg; Calcium 38mg; Fibre 0.9g; Sodium 131mg.

Beef, Leek and Cheese Tartlets

The minced beef in these mouthwatering little tartlets is seasoned with thyme and leeks, and topped with a tangy cheese sauce to whet the appetite.

Serves 4

225g/8oz prepared shortcrust pastry

For the filling

7.5ml/1½ tsp oil
115g/4oz/1 cup lean minced (ground) beef
7.5ml/1½ tsp chopped fresh thyme
1 small leek, trimmed, washed and thinly sliced
salt and ground black pepper
sliced cherry tomatoes, to garnish
crisp salad, to serve

For the cheese sauce

15g/½oz/1 tbsp butter
15g/½ oz/1 tbsp flour
120ml/4fl oz/½ cup milk
25g/1oz/¼ cup freshly grated mature (strong) Cheddar cheese
2.5ml/½ tsp mustard

1 Preheat the oven to 190°C/375°F/Gas 5. Roll out the prepared pastry on a floured surface and use it to line four 7.5cm/3in tartlet tins (muffin pans).

2 Place foil or baking parchment inside the pastry cases (pie shells), weigh down with baking beans, and bake blind in the oven for about 15 minutes. Remove the tins from the oven and leave the cases to cool completely on a wire rack.

3 Heat the oil and fry the beef, thyme and sliced leek for about 10 minutes, stirring, until the meat is browned. Season with salt and black pepper.

4 For the cheese sauce, melt the butter in a pan. Add the flour and cook, stirring, for 1 minute. Gradually stir in the milk until it is all incorporated, and then add the grated cheese. Bring slowly to the boil, stirring constantly, until thickened. Add the mustard and season well.

5 Divide the beef mixture between the cooled tartlet cases, top with the cheese sauce and cook for 10–15 minutes in the preheated oven until the tops are golden and bubbling. Serve the tartlets hot with a crisp green salad.

Mutton Pies

Small savoury pies were one of England's first fast foods, sold as street food from the Middle Ages. Mutton was a favourite filling, and pies like these were served in Victorian times as appetizers at Buckingham Palace.

Makes 6

450g/1lb minced (ground) mutton or lamb, such as shoulder
3 spring onions (scallions), chopped
1.5ml/¼ tsp freshly grated nutmeg
90ml/6 tbsp meat stock
salt and ground black pepper

For the pastry

250g/9oz/2¼ cups plain (all-purpose) flour
generous pinch of salt
50g/2oz/4 tbsp lard
60ml/4 tbsp milk
beaten egg, to glaze

1 Preheat the oven to 190°C/375°F/Gas 5. Combine the meat with the spring onions and seasoning. Mix well then stir in the stock and set aside.

2 To make the pastry, sift the flour and salt into a bowl and make a well in the centre. Heat the lard, milk and 75ml/5 tbsp water until just boiling. Immediately pour it into the flour and beat quickly to make a soft dough.

3 Knead the dough lightly on a floured surface until smooth, adding a little more boiling water if necessary. Working quickly, divide two-thirds of the pastry into six pieces.

4 Press each into a hole in a non-stick muffin tin (pan), with the pastry slightly above the rim. Divide the meat mixture equally between the pastry cases.

5 Use the remaining pastry to make lids for the pies. Moisten the pastry edges with water and top each with a pastry lid, pressing the edges together to seal them well. Make a small slit in the centre of each lid and brush with beaten egg.

6 Put the pies into the hot oven and cook for about 35 minutes until the pastry is crisp and golden brown. Leave to cool in the tin for 5 minutes then transfer to a wire rack. Serve warm or cold.

Beef Tartlets Energy 404kcal/1687kJ; Protein 12.3g; Carbohydrate 31.4g, of which sugars 2.6g; Fat 26.4g, of which saturates 10.6g; Cholesterol 41mg; Calcium 145mg; Fibre 2.3g; Sodium 330mg.
Mutton Pies Energy 369kcal/1547kJ; Protein 18.7g; Carbohydrate 33g, of which sugars 1.2g; Fat 19g, of which saturates 8.2g; Cholesterol 66mg; Calcium 85mg; Fibre 1.4g; Sodium 58mg.

Mushroom and Meat Fritters

This recipe is from Sardinia, and is an Italian version of empanadas. The fritters can be made in a variety of different sizes, using all kinds of ingredients, including grated Pecorino cheese, cured meats, or fresh fish.

Serves 6

200g/7oz/scant 1 cup butter, cubed
400g/14oz plain (all-purpose) flour, plus extra for dusting
50g/2oz/1 cup dried porcini mushrooms
25g/1oz/2 tbsp unsalted butter
1 large onion, finely chopped
3 garlic cloves, finely chopped
45ml/3 tbsp fresh or frozen peas, thawed if frozen
5 sun-dried tomatoes, chopped
200g/7oz cooked meat (beef, lamb, pork or veal), finely chopped
1 small egg, beaten
vegetable oil, for deep-frying
sea salt and ground black pepper

1 First, make the pastry. Rub the butter into the flour, with 1.5ml/¼ tsp salt, until it resembles fine breadcrumbs. Sprinkle over 45ml/3 tbsp cold water. Stir to bind the dough together, adding water as necessary, a little at a time. Using your hands, gather it together into a ball and put into a plastic bag or wrap it in clear film (plastic wrap). Chill the pastry for 30 minutes.

2 Place the porcini mushrooms in a small bowl and add warm water to cover. Leave to soak for 30 minutes, then drain and rinse them well.

3 Melt the butter in a large pan and add the chopped onion, garlic, drained mushrooms, peas and sun-dried tomatoes. Cook for 10 minutes over a medium heat, or until the peas are tender. Stir in the chopped meat. Season, and allow to cool.

4 Roll out the pastry thinly on a floured surface and cut into circles using a 10cm/4in pastry (cookie) cutter. Put a spoonful of filling in the centre of half the rounds. Use the other half of the rounds to form a lid. Seal the edges with a little beaten egg.

5 Heat the oil until a small piece of the pastry, dropped into the oil, sizzles instantly. Fry the fritters in batches until crisp and golden. Drain on kitchen paper and serve them piping hot.

Kasha and Mushroom Knishes

Usually made in tiny, one-bite pastries, knishes are a delicious Russian appetizer. They can be served as a snack, or as the perfect accompaniment to a large bowl of borscht.

Makes about 15

40g/1½oz/3 tbsp butter, or 45ml/3 tbsp rendered chicken or duck fat, or vegetable oil
2 onions, finely chopped
200g/7oz/scant 3 cups mushrooms, diced (optional)
200–250g/7–9oz/1–1¼ cups buckwheat, cooked
handful of dried mushrooms, broken into small pieces
200ml/7fl oz/scant 1 cup hot stock, preferably mushroom
1 egg, lightly beaten
salt and ground black pepper

For the sour cream pastry

250g/9oz/2¼ cups plain (all-purpose) flour
5ml/1 tsp baking powder
2.5ml/½ tsp salt
2.5ml/½ tsp sugar
130g/4½oz/generous ½ cup plus 15ml/1 tbsp butter, diced
75g/3oz sour cream or Greek (US strained plain) yogurt

1 To make the pastry, sift together the flour, baking powder, salt and sugar, then rub in the butter until the mixture resembles fine breadcrumbs. Add the sour cream or yogurt and mix together to form a dough. Add 5ml/1 tsp water if necessary. Wrap the dough in a plastic bag and chill for about 2 hours.

2 To make the filling, heat the butter, fat or oil in a pan, add the onions and fresh mushrooms, if using, and fry until soft and browned. Add the buckwheat and cook until slightly browned. Add the dried mushrooms and stock and cook over a medium-high heat until the liquid has been absorbed. Leave to cool, then stir in the egg and season well.

3 Preheat the oven to 200°C/400°F/Gas 6. Roll out the pastry on a lightly floured surface to about 3mm/⅛in thickness, then cut into rectangles (about 7.5 x 16cm/3 x 6¼in).

4 Place 2–3 spoonfuls of the filling in the middle of each piece of pastry and brush the edges with water, fold up and pinch together to seal. Bake for 15 minutes. Serve hot or warm, with drinks as an apperitif, or with soup for a hearty lunch.

Meat Fritters Energy 672kcal/2795kJ; Protein 15.2g; Carbohydrate 49.2g, of which sugars 3.5g; Fat 47.4g, of which saturates 5.2g; Cholesterol 61mg; Calcium 101mg; Fibre 2.8g; Sodium 467mg.
Kasha Knishes Energy 728kcal/3034kJ; Protein 48.2g; Carbohydrate 27.5g, of which sugars 9.8g; Fat 48g, of which saturates 14.3g; Cholesterol 193mg; Calcium 129mg; Fibre 1.8g; Sodium 398mg.

Braised Beancurd Skin Parcels

Beancurd skins are a healthier option than wheat flour-based spring roll wrappers and taste much better, especially when they have a delicious chicken, mushroom and bean sauce filling. These little parcels do not take long to steam, and make an excellent addition to a selection of dim sum.

Serves 4

4 dried Chinese black mushrooms
300g/11oz chicken breast fillet
30ml/2 tbsp vegetable oil
30ml/2 tbsp black bean sauce
2.5ml/½ tsp ground black pepper
2.5ml/½ tsp sugar
30ml/2 tbsp sesame oil
100ml/3½fl oz/scant ½ cup water
1–2 sheets of beancurd skins

1 Soak the mushrooms in a bowl of boiling water for about 20–30 minutes, until soft. Drain and slice into thin strips, discarding the stems. Slice the chicken into 1cm/½in thick strips.

2 Heat the vegetable oil in a wok or frying pan. Add the chicken and mushroom strips and stir-fry for 3 minutes. Add the black bean sauce, pepper, sugar and sesame oil and stir-fry for 2 minutes more.

3 Pour in the water. Cook over high heat until most of the liquid has been driven off and the mixture is thick and almost dry. Transfer to a bowl and leave to cool.

4 Place a beancurd skin on a clean, flat surface or chopping board and cut into pieces about 10cm/4in wide. Top with two or three pieces each of chicken and mushroom, tuck in the edges and roll up to make a parcel about 6cm/2½in long. Fill the other skins in the same way.

5 Place the beancurd skin parcels on a large plate and steam over a wok of rapidly boiling water for 10 minutes. Serve hot.

Variations
Add a few pieces of finely shredded fresh root ginger to the filling for an extra spicy touch.

Crystal Dumplings

A much-loved street food in South China, these dumplings are served with a chilli dip.

Serves 6–8

200g/7oz/1¾ cups sweet potato flour
400ml/14fl oz/1⅔ cups water
30ml/2 tbsp vegetable oil
115g/4oz/1 cup tapioca flour

For the filling

400g/14oz can bamboo shoots, drained
45ml/3 tbsp vegetable oil
3 garlic cloves, crushed
30ml/2 tbsp dark soy sauce
30ml/2 tbsp oyster sauce
5ml/1 tsp ground black pepper
200ml/7fl oz/scant 1 cup water

For the dipping sauce

45ml/3 tbsp dark soy sauce
15ml/1 tbsp ginger purée (paste)
15ml/1 tbsp rice vinegar
15ml/1 tbsp sesame oil
5ml/1 tsp sugar
5ml/1 tsp chilli bean paste

1 Put the sweet potato flour in a non-stick pan. Add the water and oil and cook over low heat, stirring occasionally, until thick. Remove from the heat and leave to cool for 15 minutes. Shred the bamboo shoots for the filling until they are the shape and size of beansprouts. Rinse thoroughly and drain.

2 Heat the oil in a wok and fry the garlic over low heat for a few seconds. Do not let it burn. Add the bamboo shoots, soy sauce, oyster sauce, pepper and water. Cook over medium heat for 10 minutes, until almost dry. Set aside to cool.

3 Stir the tapioca flour into the cool sweet potato flour mixture. Mix well, then transfer to a floured board. Knead for at least 5 minutes, punching the dough as you roll and fold. Shape into a long roll, about 5cm/2in in diameter. Cut slices 9mm/⅜in thick and flatten each with a rolling pin to form very thin circles.

4 Place about 30ml/2 tbsp bamboo shoots on each dough circle, fold over into a half-moon shape and seal the edges. Fold and pinch to get a serrated edge on each dumpling.

5 Place the dumplings on a lightly oiled plate and steam over a wok of rapidly boiling water for 30 minutes. Mix together the ingredients for the dip. Serve the dumplings warm with the dip.

Beancurd Parcels Energy 188kcal/785kJ; Protein 18.6g; Carbohydrate 1.9g, of which sugars 0.6g; Fat 11.9g, of which saturates 1.7g; Cholesterol 53mg; Calcium 7mg; Fibre 0.2g; Sodium 46mg.
Crystal Dumplings Energy 244kcal/1022kJ; Protein 3.6g; Carbohydrate 38.2g, of which sugars 5.2g; Fat 8.7g, of which saturates 1.1g; Cholesterol 0mg; Calcium 21mg; Fibre 1.3g; Sodium 1134mg.

Chive Dumplings

These dumplings are lovely and light, thanks to the wheat starch flour used for the wrappers. Although there is an art to making them, the end result is well worth the effort. Some versions feature a filling of bamboo shoots or sweet Chinese turnips, but the Chinese chives used in this recipe add crunch and flavour. These are different from regular chives, being flatter and broader and with a distinctive, fresh aroma.

Serves 6–8
150g/5oz/1 ¼ cups wheat starch
200ml/7fl oz/scant 1 cup water
15ml/1 tbsp vegetable oil
50g/2oz/½ cup tapioca flour
pinch of salt
sesame oil, for brushing
chilli sauce, for dipping

For the filling
200g/7oz Chinese chives
30ml/2 tbsp light soy sauce
15ml/1 tbsp sesame oil
2.5ml/½ tsp ground black pepper
15ml/1 tbsp cornflour (cornstarch)

1 Put the wheat starch in a non-stick pan. Add the water and oil and cook over low heat, stirring occasionally, until very thick. Remove from the heat and leave to cool for 15 minutes.

2 Meanwhile, for the filling, chop the chives finely. Put them in a bowl and stir in the soy sauce, sesame oil, pepper and cornflour.

3 Heat a wok, add the mixture and toss over low heat for about 5 minutes. Stir in the lightly beaten egg to bind the mixture, then set it aside.

4 Stir the tapioca flour and salt into the cool wheat starch mixture. Mix well, then transfer to a floured board. Knead for at least 5 minutes. Roll out the dough and stamp out into 12 circles, 7.5cm/3in in diameter.

5 Place 1 heaped tablespoon of the filling on each dough circle and fold to make half-moon shapes. Seal the edges with a little water. Brush each dumpling with a little sesame oil to prevent them from sticking together when being steamed.

6 Place the dumplings on a plate and steam over rapidly boiling water for 10 minutes. Serve immediately, with a chilli sauce dip.

Pork and Nut Dumplings

These dainty little bites use basically the same dough as for chive dumplings, but their taste and texture is totally different, thanks to the unusual filling.

Serves 6–8
150g/5oz/1 ¼ cups wheat starch
200ml/7fl oz/scant 1 cup water
15ml/1 tbsp vegetable oil
50g/2oz/½ cup tapioca flour or cornflour (cornstarch)
salt

For the filling
30ml/2 tbsp vegetable oil
200g/7oz/scant 1 cup minced (ground) pork
90ml/6 tbsp water
50g/2oz/½ cup peanuts, chopped
30ml/2 tbsp light soy sauce
15ml/1 tbsp sesame oil
2.5ml/½ tsp black pepper

For the dip
45ml/3 tbsp black vinegar
5ml/1 tbsp finely shredded fresh root ginger

1 Put the wheat starch in a non-stick pan. Add the water and oil and cook over low heat, stirring occasionally, until very thick. Remove from the heat and leave to cool for 15 minutes.

2 Meanwhile, make the filling. Heat the oil in a small pan and fry the pork for 2 minutes. Add the water, chopped peanuts, soy sauce, sesame oil and ground black pepper. Stir for 3 minutes until the pork is cooked through and there is the barest hint of sauce. Set aside to cool.

3 Stir the tapioca flour and salt into the cool wheat starch mixture. Mix well, then transfer to a floured board. Knead for at least 5 minutes. Divide into 12 portions. Flatten each piece of dough and roll them into 7.5cm/3in circles.

4 Place 1 heaped tablespoon of the filling on each dough circle and fold to make half-moon shapes. Seal the edges with a little water. Brush each dumpling with a little sesame oil to prevent them from sticking together when being steamed.

5 Place the dumplings on a large plate and steam over a wok of rapidly boiling water for 10 minutes. Meanwhile, mix the vinegar and ginger for the dip in a small bowl together with a pinch of salt. Serve the dumplings hot, with the dipping sauce.

Chive Dumplings Energy 140kcal/589kJ; Protein 1.8g; Carbohydrate 25.9g, of which sugars 0.9g; Fat 3.9g, of which saturates 0.6g; Cholesterol 24mg; Calcium 58mg; Fibre 1.3g; Sodium 295mg.
Pork Dumplings Energy 216kcal/906kJ; Protein 6.7g; Carbohydrate 24.3g, of which sugars 0.7g; Fat 10.9g, of which saturates 2.1g; Cholesterol 17mg; Calcium 10mg; Fibre 0.4g; Sodium 294mg.

Pork and Peanut Wontons

These crispy filled wontons are delicious served with a sweet plum sauce. The wontons can be filled and set aside for up to eight hours before they are cooked.

Makes 40–50 wontons

175g/6oz/1½ cups minced (ground) pork or 175g/6oz pork sausages, skinned
2 spring onions (scallions), finely chopped
30ml/2 tbsp peanut butter
10ml/2 tsp oyster sauce (optional)
40–50 wonton skins
30ml/2 tbsp flour paste
vegetable oil, for deep-frying
salt and ground black pepper
lettuce and radishes, to garnish

For the plum sauce

225g/8oz/generous ¾ cup dark plum jam
15ml/1 tbsp rice or white wine vinegar
15ml/1 tbsp dark soy sauce
2.5ml/½ tsp chilli sauce

1 Combine the minced pork or skinned sausages with the spring onions, peanut butter, oyster sauce, if using, and seasoning in a large bowl, and set aside.

2 For the sauce, combine the plum jam, vinegar, soy and chilli sauces in a serving bowl and set aside.

3 To fill the wonton skins, place eight wrappers at a time on a work surface, moisten the edges with the flour paste and place 2.5ml/½ tsp of the filling on each one. Fold in half, corner to corner, and twist.

4 Fill a wok or deep frying pan one-third with vegetable oil and heat to 190°C/375°F. Have ready a wire strainer or frying basket and a tray lined with kitchen paper.

5 Drop the wontons, eight at a time, into the hot fat and then fry until they are golden all over, for about 1–2 minutes. Lift out the cooked wontons on to the paper-lined tray, using a slotted spoon and sprinkle with fine salt.

6 Serve the wontons immediately with the plum sauce, garnished with the lettuce and radishes.

Roast Pork Dumplings

These Cantonese dumplings are made with a low gluten flour that makes them light, white and fluffy. It is available in Chinese food stores.

Makes 12

200g/7oz/1¾ cups low gluten flour (dai garn fun)
pinch of salt
5ml/1 tsp easy-blend (rapid-rise) dried yeast
120ml/4fl oz/½ cup warm water
5ml/1 tsp vinegar

For the filling

115g/4oz roast pork, finely diced
30ml/2 tbsp hoisin sauce
1 spring onion (scallion), finely chopped

1 Put the flour and salt in a large mixing bowl and sprinkle in the yeast. Make a well in the centre and pour in the warm water and vinegar. Mix to a dough.

2 Place the dough on a floured board and knead for 10 minutes. Return it to the bowl, cover and set aside in a warm place to rise for 20 minutes or until it has doubled in bulk.

3 Knock back (punch down) the dough, knead it again, return it to the bowl and set aside in a warm place for 15 minutes.

4 Meanwhile, make the filling. Put the diced pork in a bowl. Stir in the hoisin sauce to moisten it, then add the spring onion.

5 Roll out the pastry on a floured board and shape it into a 30cm/12in long roll, about 5cm/2in in diameter. Cut the roll into 2.5cm/1in slices and flatten each of these with a rolling pin to a thin round, about 9cm/3½in across.

6 Holding a pastry round on the palm of one hand, spoon a heaped teaspoon of the filling into the centre. Cup your hand so that the dough enfolds the filling, pleating and pinching it where necessary. Pinch off the excess dough at the top and seal with a twist. Fill the remaining dumplings in the same way.

7 Cut 5cm/2in squares of baking parchment. Stand a dumpling on each piece of paper in a steamer. Steam for 15 minutes. Serve immediately.

Pork Wontons: Energy 56kcal/236kJ; Protein 1.5g; Carbohydrate 7.9g, of which sugars 4.1g; Fat 2.3g, of which saturates 0.4g; Cholesterol 3mg; Calcium 8mg; Fibre 0.2g; Sodium 35mg.
Roast Pork Dumplings Energy 73kcal/309kJ; Protein 2.4g; Carbohydrate 15.6g, of which sugars 0.2g; Fat 0.5g, of which saturates 0.2g; Cholesterol 6mg; Calcium 4mg; Fibre 0g; Sodium 194mg.

Pork and Prawn Dumplings

While dim sum are generally attributed to southern China, these bitesize morsels are enjoyed throughout the country. Pork is the main filling ingredient here, along with prawns, but there are also seafood versions.

Serves 4

100g/3¾oz raw prawns (shrimp), peeled and deveined
2 spring onions (scallions)
225g/8oz/1 cup minced (ground) pork
30ml/2 tbsp light soy sauce
15ml/1 tbsp sesame oil
2.5ml/½ tsp ground black pepper
15ml/1 tbsp cornflour (cornstarch)
16 round wonton wrappers
16 large garden peas, thawed if frozen
sweet chilli sauce, for dipping

1 Chop the prawns finely to make a coarse paste. This can be done using a sharp knife or in a food processor, but if you use a food processor use the pulse button and go slowly, or the prawns will become rubbery. Scrape into a bowl.

2 Chop the spring onions very finely. Add them to the puréed prawns, with the pork, soy sauce, sesame oil, pepper and cornflour. Mix well.

3 Holding a wonton wrapper on the palm of one hand, spoon a heaped teaspoon of the filling into the centre. Cup your hand so that the wrapper enfolds the filling to make the classic dumpling shape. Squeeze the edges together but leave the top slightly open. Top each gap with a pea. Fill the remaining wonton wrappers in the same way.

4 Tap the dumplings gently to flatten the base, then place the dumplings on a lightly oiled plate and steam over a wok of rapidly boiling water for 10 minutes. Serve immediately with a sweet chilli dipping sauce.

Cook's Tip
If you can only find square wonton wrappers, trim off the corners to make a rough circle before filling them.

Deep-fried Wontons

These are a close cousin of pork dumplings. They have much the same ingredients but are fried rather than steamed. Crisp on the outside, with a tender filling, it may be an idea to make double the quantity of these delicious snacks as they will soon disappear.

Serves 4

300g/11oz/1½ cups minced (ground) pork
15ml/1 tbsp light soy sauce
15ml/1 tbsp sesame oil
2.5ml/½ tsp ground black pepper
15ml/1 tbsp cornflour (cornstarch)
16 wonton wrappers
vegetable oil for deep-frying
chilli dipping sauce, to serve

1 Put the minced pork in a bowl. Add the light soy sauce, sesame oil, ground black pepper and cornflour. Mix well.

2 Place about 5ml/1 tsp of the mixture in the centre of a wonton wrapper, bring the corners together so that they meet at the top, and pinch the neck to seal. Fill the remaining wontons in the same way.

3 Heat the oil in a wok or deep-fryer. Carefully add the filled wontons, about four or five at a time, and deep-fry until golden.

4 Carefully lift out the cooked wontons with a slotted spoon, drain on kitchen paper and keep hot while frying the rest. Serve the wontons hot with chilli dipping sauce.

Variation
For seafood wontons, use finely chopped crab, scallops or prawns (shrimp) in place of the pork.

Cook's Tips
- *If the wonton skins are brittle, wipe them with a damp towel or they will be difficult to shape without cracking.*
- *Filled wontons take very little time to cook. Make sure your oil is not too hot as they scorch very quickly.*

Pork Dumplings Energy 228kcal/957kJ; Protein 18.2g; Carbohydrate 20.2g, of which sugars 1.3g; Fat 8.8g, of which saturates 2.5g; Cholesterol 86mg; Calcium 57mg; Fibre 1.3g; Sodium 622mg.
Deep-fried Wontons Energy 326kcal/1357kJ; Protein 16.3g; Carbohydrate 18.3g, of which sugars 0.6g; Fat 21.3g, of which saturates 4.4g; Cholesterol 50mg; Calcium 33mg; Fibre 0.6g; Sodium 319mg.

Duck Wontons

These Chinese-style wontons are easy to make using ready-cooked smoked duck or chicken.

Makes about 40

15ml/1 tbsp light soy sauce
5ml/1 tsp sesame oil
2 spring onions (scallions), finely chopped
grated rind of ½ orange
5ml/1 tsp brown sugar
275g/10oz/1½ cups chopped smoked duck
about 40 small wonton wrappers
15ml/1 tbsp vegetable oil
whole fresh chives, to garnish (optional)

For the mango sauce

30ml/2 tbsp vegetable oil
5ml/1 tsp ground cumin
2.5ml/½ tsp ground cardamom
1.5ml/¼ tsp ground cinnamon
250ml/8fl oz/1 cup mango purée (made from 1 large mango)
15ml/1 tbsp clear honey
2.5ml/½ tsp Chinese chilli sauce (or to taste)
15ml/1 tbsp cider vinegar
chopped fresh chives, to garnish

1 First prepare the sauce. In a medium pan, heat the oil over a medium-low heat. Add the ground cumin, cardamom and cinnamon and cook for about 3 minutes, stirring constantly.

2 Stir in the mango purée, honey, chilli sauce and vinegar. Remove from the heat and leave to cool. Pour into a bowl and cover until ready to serve.

3 Prepare the wonton filling. In a large bowl, mix together the soy sauce, sesame oil, spring onions, orange rind and brown sugar until well blended. Add the duck and toss to coat well.

4 Place a teaspoonful of the duck mixture in the centre of each wonton wrapper. Brush the edges with water and then draw them up to the centre, twisting to seal and form a pouch shape.

5 Preheat the oven to 190°F/375°C/Gas 5. Line a large baking sheet with foil and brush lightly with oil. Arrange the wontons on the baking sheet and bake for 10–12 minutes until crisp and golden. Serve with the mango sauce garnished with chopped fresh chives. If you wish, tie each wonton with a fresh chive, wilted briefly in boiled water to make it pliable.

Crispy Mango Wontons with Raspberry Drizzle Sauce

These crisp, golden parcels filled with meltingly sweet, hot mango are perfect for a casual supper or a sophisticated dinner. The raspberry sauce looks great drizzled over the wontons and is a delicious addition.

Serves 4

2 firm, ripe mangoes
24 fresh wonton wrappers (about 7.5cm/3in square)
oil, for frying
icing (confectioners') sugar, for dusting

For the sauce

400g/14oz/3½ cups raspberries
45ml/3 tbsp icing (confectioners') sugar
a squeeze of lemon juice

1 First make the sauce. Place the raspberries and icing sugar in a food processor and blend until smooth. Press the raspberry purée through a sieve (strainer) to remove the seeds, then stir a squeeze of lemon juice into the sauce. Cover and place in the refrigerator until ready to serve.

2 Peel the mango, then carefully slice the flesh away from one side of the flat stone (pit). Repeat on the second side, then trim off any remaining flesh from around the stone. Cut the mango flesh into 1cm/½in dice.

3 Lay 12 wonton wrappers on a clean work surface and place 10ml/2 tsp of the chopped mango in the centre of each one. Brush the edges with water and top with the remaining wonton wrappers. Press the edges to seal.

4 Heat the oil in a wok to 180°C/350°F (or until a cube of bread, dropped into the oil, browns in 15 seconds). Deep-fry the wontons, two or three at a time, for about 2 minutes, or until crisp and golden. Remove from the oil using a slotted spoon and drain on kitchen paper.

5 Dust the wontons with icing sugar and serve immediately on individual plates drizzled with the raspberry sauce, if you like. Serve the remaining sauce in bowls for diners to help themselves.

Duck Wontons: Energy 95kcal/404kJ; Protein 6.8g; Carbohydrate 14.7g, of which sugars 0.4g; Fat 1.9g, of which saturates 0.4g; Cholesterol 28mg; Calcium 35mg; Fibre 0.7g; Sodium 36mg.
Mango Wontons Energy 314Kcal/1331kJ; Protein 5.5g; Carbohydrate 56.1g, of which sugars 27.3g; Fat 9.2g, of which saturates 1.2g; Cholesterol 0mg; Calcium 93mg; Fibre 5.6g; Sodium 6mg.

Crispy Vegetable Spring Rolls

These small and dainty spring rolls are ideal served as appetizers or as cocktail snacks. You could replace the mushrooms with chicken or pork, and the carrots with prawns.

Makes 40 rolls

225g/8oz fresh beansprouts
115g/4oz small leeks
115g/4oz carrots
115g/4oz bamboo shoots, sliced
115g/4oz mushrooms
45–60ml/3–4 tbsp vegetable oil
5ml/1 tsp salt
5ml/1 tsp light brown sugar
15ml/1 tbsp light soy sauce
15ml/1 tbsp Chinese rice wine or dry sherry
20 frozen spring roll skins, defrosted
15ml/1 tbsp cornflour (cornstarch) paste
flour, for dusting
oil, for deep-frying

1 Cut all the vegetables into thin shreds, roughly the same size and shape as the beansprouts.

2 Heat the vegetable oil in a wok and stir-fry the vegetables for about 1 minute. Add the salt, sugar, soy sauce and wine or sherry and continue stirring the vegetables for 1½–2 minutes. Remove and drain away the excess liquid, then leave to cool.

3 To make the spring rolls, cut each spring roll skin in half diagonally, then place about a tablespoonful of the vegetable mixture one-third of the way down on the skin, with the triangle pointing away from you.

4 Lift the lower edge over the filling and roll once. Fold in both ends and roll once more, then brush the upper pointed edge with a little cornflour paste (made by mixing together 4 parts cornflour with about 5 parts cold water until smooth) and roll into a neat package. Lightly dust a tray with flour and place the spring rolls on the tray with the flap side underneath.

5 To cook, heat the oil in a wok or deep-fryer until hot, then reduce the heat to low. Deep-fry the spring rolls in batches (about eight to ten at a time) for 2–3 minutes or until golden and crispy, then remove and drain. Serve hot with a dipping sauce, such as soy sauce, or mixed salt and pepper.

Pork and Crab Spring Rolls

Chinese spring roll wrappers are easily obtainable from Asian stores. The vegetable content of the filling can be varied as long as the flavours are complementary.

Makes 15

25g/1oz cellophane noodles soaked for 10 minutes in hot water to cover
6–8 dried cloud ear (wood ear) mushrooms, soaked for 30 minutes in warm water
225g/8oz minced (ground) pork
225g/8oz fresh or canned crab meat
4 spring onions (scallions), trimmed and finely chopped
5ml/1 tsp fish sauce
flour and water paste, to seal
250g/9oz packet spring roll wrappers
vegetable oil, for deep frying
salt and ground black pepper

For the nuoc cham sauce

2 fresh red chillies, seeded and pounded to a paste
2 garlic cloves, crushed
15ml/1 tbsp sugar
45ml/3 tbsp fish sauce
juice of 1 lime or ½ lemon

1 Make the nuoc cham sauce by mixing the chillies, garlic, sugar and fish sauce in a bowl and stirring in lime or lemon juice to taste. Drain the noodles and snip into 2.5cm/1in lengths. Drain the cloud ears, trim away any rough stems and slice finely.

2 Mix the noodles and the cloud ears with the pork and set aside. Remove any cartilage from the crab meat and add to the pork mixture with the spring onions and fish sauce. Season to taste, mixing well.

3 Place a spring roll wrapper in front of you, diamond-fashion. Spoon some mixture just below the centre, fold over the nearest point and roll once.

4 Fold in the sides to enclose, then brush the edges with flour paste and roll up to seal. Repeat with the remaining wrappers and filling. Heat the oil in a wok or deep-fryer to 190°C/375°F.

5 Deep-fry the rolls in batches for 8–10 minutes or until they are cooked through. Drain them well on kitchen paper and serve hot. To eat, dip the rolls in the nuoc cham sauce.

Crispy Spring Rolls Energy 38kcal/161kJ; Protein 1.1g; Carbohydrate 6.6g, of which sugars 0.6g; Fat 1g, of which saturates 0.1g; Cholesterol 0mg; Calcium 15mg; Fibre 0.5g; Sodium 88mg.
Pork and Crab Rolls Energy 55kcal/232kJ; Protein 4.5g; Carbohydrate 7g, of which sugars 0.3g; Fat 0.9g, of which saturates 0.3g; Cholesterol 31mg; Calcium 10mg; Fibre 0.1g; Sodium 24mg.

Green Curry Puffs

Shrimp paste and green curry sauce, used judiciously, give these puffs their distinctive, spicy, savoury flavour, and the addition of chilli steps up the heat.

Makes 24

24 small wonton wrappers, about 8cm/3¼in square, thawed if frozen
15ml/1 tbsp cornflour (cornstarch), mixed to a paste with 30ml/2 tbsp water
oil, for deep-frying

For the filling

1 small potato, about 115g/4oz, boiled and mashed
25g/1oz/3 tbsp cooked petits pois (baby peas)
25g/1oz/3 tbsp cooked corn
few sprigs fresh coriander (cilantro), chopped
1 small fresh red chilli, seeded and finely chopped
½ lemon grass stalk, finely chopped
15ml/1 tbsp soy sauce
5ml/1 tsp shrimp paste or fish sauce
5ml/1 tsp Thai green curry paste

1 Combine the filling ingredients. Lay out one wonton wrapper and place a teaspoon of the filling in the centre.

2 Brush a little of the cornflour paste along two sides of the square. Fold the other two sides over to meet them, then press together to make a triangular pastry and seal in the filling. Make more pastries in the same way.

3 Heat the oil in a deep-fryer or wok to 190°C/375°F or until a cube of bread, added to the oil, browns in about 45 seconds. Add the pastries to the oil, a few at a time, and fry them for about 5 minutes, until golden brown.

4 Remove the cooked pastries from the fryer or wok and drain on kitchen paper. If you intend serving the puffs hot, place them in a low oven while cooking successive batches. The puffs also taste good cold.

Cook's Tip
Wonton wrappers dry out quickly, so keep them covered, using clear film (plastic wrap), until you are ready to use them.

Siberian Beef Dumplings

In Russia these dumplings, or pelmeni, are so small they are more like ravioli.

Serves 4–6

2 eggs
150ml/¼ pint/⅔ cup water
15ml/1 tbsp rapeseed (canola) oil
2.5ml/½ tsp salt
360g/12½oz/3⅛ cups plain (all-purpose) flour, plus extra for dusting

For the filling

1 onion, total weight 100g/3¾oz
200g/7oz minced (ground) beef
200g/7oz minced (ground) pork
7.5ml/1½ tsp salt
2–2.5ml/⅓–½ tsp ground black pepper
red wine vinegar, melted butter, salt and ground black pepper, and smetana (optional), to serve

1 To make the pastry, put the eggs, water, oil, salt and half of the flour in a food processor and process until blended. Add the remaining flour, in batches, to form a smooth dough.

2 Turn the dough on to a floured surface and knead for 5 minutes. Put in a plastic bag and chill for 30 minutes.

3 To make the filling, finely grate the onion and put in a bowl. Mix in the beef and pork, salt and pepper and set aside.

4 To make the dumplings, cut the dough into eight pieces. Work with one piece at a time, keeping the rest in the plastic bag so they don't dry out.

5 On a floured surface, shape the piece of dough into a roll, the thickness of a finger. Cut the roll into 10–12 small pieces. Flatten each piece to a round, about 3cm/1¼in in diameter, and then roll out to 5–6cm/2–2½in in diameter. Spread each round with 5m/1 tsp of the meat mixture, leaving a small edge. Fold and pinch into to a half-moon shape.

6 Put in a pan of lightly salted boiling water. Simmer until the dumplings float to the surface then simmer for a further 1 minute. Using a slotted spoon, scoop the dumplings out of the water and serve immediately, sprinkled with vinegar, melted butter, salt and pepper.

Green Curry Puffs Energy 32kcal/134kJ; Protein 1g; Carbohydrate 6.7g, of which sugars 0.4g; Fat 0.3g, of which saturates 0g; Cholesterol 1mg; Calcium 16mg; Fibre 0.4g; Sodium 58mg
Beef Dumplings Energy 381kcal/1605kJ; Protein 20.9g; Carbohydrate 47.9g, of which sugars 1.8g; Fat 13.1g, of which saturates 4.4g; Cholesterol 105mg; Calcium 103mg; Fibre 2.1g; Sodium 74mg.

Steamed Tofu Dumplings

These Korean style dumplings are flavoured with chives and dipped into a spicy sauce to serve.

Makes 8

3 spring onions (scallions), finely chopped
3 garlic cloves, crushed
5ml/1 tsp finely grated root ginger
5ml/1 tsp mirin or rice wine
90g/3½oz/scant ½ cup minced (ground) beef
90g/3½oz firm tofu
90g/3½oz chives, finely chopped
½ onion, finely chopped
30ml/2 tbsp soy sauce
30ml/2 tbsp sesame oil
15ml/1 tbsp sugar
15ml/1 tbsp salt
10ml/2 tsp ground black pepper
8 dumpling wrappers
beaten egg, for brushing

For the dipping sauce
60ml/4 tbsp dark soy sauce
30ml/2 tbsp rice vinegar
5ml/1 tsp Korean chilli powder

1 To make the dipping sauce, mix the soy sauce, rice vinegar and chilli powder in a small serving bowl. To make the filling, put the chopped spring onions, garlic, grated ginger, mirin or rice wine and minced beef into a large bowl and mix well. Leave to marinate for 15 minutes.

2 Meanwhile, drain off any excess liquid from the tofu then crumble it into a bowl. Add the chopped chives to the seasoned beef, with the tofu and remaining filling ingredients. Mix together.

3 Take a dumpling wrapper and brush with a little beaten egg. Place a spoonful of the stuffing in the middle and fold into a half-moon shape, crimping the edges firmly to seal. Repeat with the other wrappers. Place in a steamer over a pan of boiling water and cook for 6 minutes, or in boiling water for 3 minutes.

4 Arrange the dumplings on a serving dish and serve, garnished with chives together with the soy dipping sauce.

Cook's Tip
These dumplings can also be shallow fried in a little oil, then steamed in a splash of water, with the pan covered.

Steamed Crab Dim Sum

These delectable Chinese-style dumplings have a wonderfully sticky texture. You can make them in advance, storing them in the refrigerator until ready to cook. Steam just before serving, then enjoy the sensation as your teeth sink through the soft wrapper into the filling. It is easy to make the dumpling pastry, but not so easy to roll it as thinly as needed, so use ready made if available.

Serves 4

150g/5oz fresh white crab meat
115g/4oz/½ cup minced (ground) pork
30ml/2 tbsp chopped Chinese chives
15ml/1 tbsp finely chopped red (bell) pepper
30ml/2 tbsp sweet chilli sauce
30ml/2 tbsp hoisin sauce
24 fresh dumpling wrappers (available from Asian stores)
Chinese chives, to garnish
chilli oil and soy sauce, to serve

1 Place the crab meat, pork and chopped chives in a large bowl. Add the red pepper, sweet chilli and hoisin sauces and mix well to combine.

2 Working with two or three wrappers at a time, put a small spoonful of the mixture into the centre of each wrapper.

3 Brush the edges of each wrapper with water and fold over to form a half-moon shape. Press and pleat the edges to seal, and tap the base of each dumpling to flatten. Cover with a clean, damp cloth and make the remaining dumplings½ *cup*.

4 Arrange the dumplings on one to three lightly oiled plates and fit inside the same number of tiers of a bamboo steamer.

5 Cover the steamer and place over a wok of simmering water (making sure the water does not touch the steamer). Steam for 8–10 minutes, or until the dumplings are cooked through and become slightly translucent.

6 Divide the dumplings among four plates. Garnish with Chinese chives and serve immediately with chilli oil and soy sauce for dipping.

Tofu Dumplings Energy 140kcal/589kJ; Protein 1.8g; Carbohydrate 25.9g, of which sugars 0.9g; Fat 3.9g, of which saturates 0.6g; Cholesterol 24mg; Calcium 58mg; Fibre 1.3g; Sodium 295mg
Crab Dim Sum Energy 166kcal/700kJ; Protein 14.7g; Carbohydrate 20.5g, of which sugars 1.4g; Fat 3.3g, of which saturates 1.1g; Cholesterol 46mg; Calcium 83mg; Fibre 0.8g; Sodium 287mg.

Potato and Cheese Pirozhki

These Polish dumplings can be served after they are cooked, or allowed to cool and then fried in butter.

Serves 4–6

500g/1¼ lb plain (all-purpose) flour, plus extra for dusting
2.5ml/½ tsp salt
2 eggs, beaten
45ml/3 tbsp vegetable oil
250ml/8fl oz/1 cup warm water
chopped fresh parsley, to garnish
thick sour cream, to serve

For the filling

15g/½oz/1 tbsp butter
½ large onion, finely chopped
250g/9oz peeled, cooked potatoes
250g/9oz/1¼ cups cream cheese
1 egg, beaten
salt and ground black pepper

1 To make the filling, heat the butter in a small pan, add the onion and cook for about 5 minutes, or until softened.

2 Push the cooked potatoes through a ricer, or mash in a large bowl. Stir in the cheese. Add the egg, onion and seasoning to taste to the potato mixture and mix well.

3 To make the dough, sift the flour into a large bowl, then add the salt and the two eggs. Pour in the oil and water, and mix to form a loose dough. Turn out on to a floured surface and knead well for about 10 minutes, or until the dough is pliant.

4 Divide the dough into four equal pieces, then roll each one out thinly with a floured rolling pin. (Cover the portions you are not working with to prevent them from drying out.) Cut the dough into 5–6cm/2–2½in circles.

5 Place a heaped teaspoonful of the cheese filling mixture in the centre of each of the circles of dough, then fold over the dough and press firmly to seal the edges. The dumplings should be neat and well filled, but not bursting.

6 Bring a large pan of lightly salted water to the boil, add the dumplings and cook for about 4–5 minutes, or until they rise to the surface. Cook for a further 2 minutes, once they have risen, then remove with a slotted spoon and place in a warmed serving dish. Garnish with parsley and serve with sour cream.

Polish Mushroom Dumplings

The Polish name for these dumplings, 'uszka', means little ears. These dumplings are often served with borscht or clear soup.

Serves 4

225g/8oz/2 cups plain (all-purpose) flour
2.5ml/½ tsp salt
1 egg, beaten
30–45ml/2–3 tbsp warm water

For the filling

115g/4oz/2 cups dried mushrooms, rinsed and soaked in warm water for 30 minutes
25g/1oz/2 tbsp butter
1 onion, very finely chopped
15ml/1 tbsp fresh white breadcrumbs
30ml/2 tbsp chopped parsley
1 egg, beaten
salt and ground black pepper

1 To make the filling, drain the soaked mushrooms and chop finely. Gently heat the butter in a large frying pan, add the onion and sauté for 5 minutes. Add the mushrooms and cook for 10 minutes, or until the liquid has evaporated.

2 Turn the mushroom mixture into a large bowl, then add the breadcrumbs, chopped parsley and egg. Season to taste and mix together to form a firm paste, then set aside to cool.

3 Sift the flour into a large bowl, mix in the salt, then make a dip in the middle with the back of a wooden spoon. Put the egg in the dip and stir in enough warm water to form a stiff dough.

4 Turn the dough out on to a lightly floured surface and knead until the dough is pliant but fairly stiff. Rest for 30 minutes. Roll out the dough thinly, to a thickness of about 3mm/⅛in, then cut into 5cm/2in squares.

5 Place a small amount of the filling in the centre of each square. Fold one corner over the filling diagonally and press the edges together. Fold the two bottom corners of the triangle to the middle and press together to form a 'pig's ear' shape.

6 Bring a large pan of lightly salted water to the boil. Drop in the dumplings and cook for about 3–5 minutes until they float to the surface. Lift out the dumplings with a slotted spoon and place on a warmed serving dish. Serve immediately.

Potato Pirozhki Energy 419kcal/1768kJ; Protein 11.7g; Carbohydrate 71.6g, of which sugars 2.3g; Fat 11.5g, of which saturates 2.9g; Cholesterol 100mg; Calcium 136mg; Fibre 3.1g; Sodium 57mg.
Mushroom Dumplings Energy 198kcal/835kJ; Protein 6.4g; Carbohydrate 32g, of which sugars 1.3g; Fat 5.9g, of which saturates 2.8g; Cholesterol 72mg; Calcium 70mg; Fibre 1.5g; Sodium 70mg.

Cottage Cheese Dumplings

These Polish dumplings can be served after they are cooked, or allowed to cool and then fried in butter.

Serves 6

300g/11oz/scant 3 cups plain (all-purpose) flour, plus extra for dusting
2 eggs
salt and ground black pepper
75g/3oz/6 tbsp butter, melted, to serve

For the filling
300g/11oz swede (rutabaga) or turnips, diced
200g/7oz/scant 1 cup cottage cheese
1 bunch spring onions (scallions), finely chopped
1 bunch fresh dill, finely chopped

1 Cook the swede or turnips for the filling in a pan of boiling water until tender. Drain and mash, then set aside to cool.

2 In a food processor mix the flour, eggs, a pinch of salt and 60–75ml/4–5 tbsp water to make a smooth dough. (Or, put the flour and salt in a bowl and stir in the eggs and water using a wooden spoon, then use your hands to make the dough.) Work the dough on a board until it is smooth and elastic.

3 Divide the dough in half and roll each half into a very thin sheet on a floured surface. (Use a pasta machine, if you have one.) Cut into small rounds, 13–15cm/5–6in in diameter with a pastry (cookie) cutter.

4 To make the filling, add the cottage cheese to the mashed swede, with the spring onions and dill, reserving a little to garnish. Mix well and season with salt and pepper.

5 Arrange a spoonful of the filling a little in from one edge of each round, and dampen the dough edges with a little water. Fold over and press the edges of the dough together to make a half-circle. Repeat until all the ingredients are used up.

6 Boil a large pan of water, then drop in the dumplings a few at a time. When the dumplings rise to the top, they are cooked. Serve with a little melted butter poured over the top, and garnished with the reserved dill.

Potato Dumplings

These Lithuanian dumplings are called Zeppelins. Delicious and filling, they have a pork and herb filling, served with crispy bacon and sour cream.

Serves 4

3 large potatoes, peeled and cut into large pieces
1kg/2½lb potatoes, peeled and grated
salt and ground black pepper
bacon rashers (strips), diced
chopped marjoram and sour cream, to serve

For the filling
5ml/1 tsp butter
1 large onion, grated
300g/11oz minced (ground) pork
5ml/1 tsp chopped marjoram
5ml/1 tsp finely chopped thyme

1 Cook the large potatoes in a pan of boiling water until soft. Drain and mash. Wrap the grated potatoes in a piece of muslin (cheesecloth) and squeeze out as much water as possible into a bowl. Put the grated potato into a large bowl. Save the potato liquid and allow it to settle, then discard the thin liquid at the top and keep the starch at the bottom. Mix the starch with the squeeze-dried grated potatoes.

2 Stir the boiled potatoes into the grated potatoes, mixing to combine well. Season well with salt and pepper.

3 For the filling, melt the butter in a frying pan over a medium heat and then add the onion. Cook, stirring, for 2 minutes. Add the pork and cook, stirring, for 5–7 minutes, until no pink remains, then add the marjoram and thyme. Season and mix.

4 Scoop up about 30ml/2 tbsp of the potato mixture and flatten it into a large round. Put a generous amount of the filling in the middle and seal it in by folding the edges over to overlap in the centre, then roll it in your hands to make a long cylindrical shape. Repeat with the remaining potato mixture.

5 Bring a large pan of water to the boil and gently drop in the dumplings. Cook for 30 minutes, stirring very gently from time to time. When they float to the surface, lift out the dumplings and put on a serving platter. Fry the bacon until crisp. Serve the dumplings topped with the crispy bacon and sour cream.

Cheese Dumplings Energy 336kcal/1410kJ; Protein 12.1g; Carbohydrate 42.6g, of which sugars 4.4g; Fat 14.3g, of which saturates 8.2g; Cholesterol 97mg; Calcium 139mg; Fibre 2.8g; Sodium 254mg.
Potato Dumplings Energy 344kcal/1451kJ; Protein 19.9g; Carbohydrate 48.4g, of which sugars 8.9g; Fat 9.3g, of which saturates 3.6g; Cholesterol 52mg; Calcium 46mg; Fibre 3.9g; Sodium 90mg.

Wild Mushroom and Cockle Puff

Oyster mushrooms, ceps and cockles or mussels combine in a rich herb broth and covered with pastry. When baked, the broth steams and the pastry puffs in a dome.

Serves 4
350g/12oz puff pastry, thawed, if frozen
1 egg beaten, to glaze
45ml/3 tbsp sesame seeds

For the soup
25g/1oz/2 tbsp unsalted butter
4 spring onions (scallions), trimmed and chopped
1 celery stick, sliced
1 small carrot, peeled, halved and sliced
115g/4oz/1¼ cups fresh young ceps or bay boletus, sliced
175g/6oz/1¾ cups oyster mushrooms
450ml/¾ pint/scant 2 cups milk
275g/10oz shelled fresh cockles or mussels, cooked
50g/2oz samphire or glasswort, trimmed (optional)
115g/4oz cooked potato, diced
4 sprigs thyme

1 Roll out the pastry on a floured surface and cut into four 18cm/7in rounds. Rest in a cool place for 1 hour. Preheat the oven to 190°C/375°F/Gas 5.

2 Melt the butter in a frying pan and fry the spring onions, celery and carrot for 2–3 minutes. Add the mushrooms and cook until the juices begin to flow. Transfer to a large pan.

3 Pour the milk over the mushrooms. Bring to a simmer. Add the shellfish, samphire or glasswort, and potato. Heat through the contents of the pan and then ladle into four deep ovenproof soup bowls. Add a sprig of thyme to each.

4 Moisten the edges of the bowls with beaten egg, cover with the pastry rounds and press the edges to seal. Brush with more egg, sprinkle with sesame seeds, and bake in the oven for 35–40 minutes until the pastry top is puffed and golden.

Cook's Tip
Closed button (white) or Paris mushrooms can be substituted.

Mushroom Börek

A börek is a rich pastry parcel from Turkey, with various savoury fillings, such as the following.

Serves 4
50g/2oz/⅓ cup couscous
45ml/3 tbsp olive oil
1 medium onion, chopped
225g/8oz/2½ cups assorted wild and cultivated mushrooms, trimmed and sliced
1 garlic clove, crushed
60ml/4 tbsp chopped fresh parsley
5ml/1 tsp chopped fresh thyme
1 egg, hard-boiled, peeled and chopped
salt and ground black pepper

For the börek pastry
400g/14oz/3½ cups self-raising (self-rising) flour
5ml/1 tsp salt
1 egg, plus extra for glazing
150ml/¼ pint/⅔ cup natural (plain) yogurt
150ml/¼ pint/⅔ cup olive oil
grated rind of ½ lemon

For the yogurt sauce
200ml/7fl oz/scant 1 cup natural (plain) yogurt
45ml/3 tbsp chopped fresh mint
2.5ml/½ tsp caster (superfine) sugar
1.5ml/¼ tsp cayenne pepper
1.5ml/¼ tsp celery salt
a little milk or water

1 Preheat the oven to 190°C/375°F/Gas 5. Just cover the couscous with boiling water and soak for 10 minutes.

2 Heat the oil in a frying pan and sauté the onion until soft. Add the mushrooms and garlic and cook until the juices begin to run, then increase the heat to evaporate the liquid. Transfer the mixture to a bowl, add the parsley, thyme, couscous, and chopped hard-boiled egg, season and combine.

3 To make the pastry, sift the flour and salt into a bowl. Make a well in the centre, then add the egg, yogurt, olive oil and lemon rind and combine with a fork. Turn out on to a floured surface and roll into a 30cm/12in circle. Pile the mixture into the centre of the pastry, then bring the edges over to enclose. Turn upside down on to a baking sheet. Press the börek out flat with your hand, glaze with beaten egg and bake for 25 minutes.

4 To make the sauce, blend the yogurt with the mint, sugar, cayenne pepper and celery salt, adjusting the consistency with milk or water. Serve the börek warm with the sauce.

Mushroom Puff Energy 557kcal/2328kJ; Protein 21g; Carbohydrate 42.7g, of which sugars 7.2g; Fat 34.8g, of which saturates 15.6g; Cholesterol 116mg; Calcium 352mg; Fibre 1.8g; Sodium 756mg.
Mushroom Börek Energy 745kcal/3127kJ; Protein 17.5g; Carbohydrate 89.7g, of which sugars 8.3g; Fat 37.6g, of which saturates 6.1g; Cholesterol 59mg; Calcium 555mg; Fibre 5.8g; Sodium 445mg.

Aubergine and Bean One-crust Pie

If your pastry cracks when making this free-form pie, just patch it up – it adds to its rustic character.

Serves 4

500g/1¼lb aubergine (eggplant), cubed
1 red (bell) pepper
30ml/2 tbsp olive oil
1 large onion, finely chopped
1 courgette (zucchini), sliced
2 garlic cloves, crushed
15ml/1 tbsp chopped fresh oregano plus extra to garnish
200g/7oz can red kidney beans, rinsed and drained
115g/4oz/1 cup pitted black olives, rinsed
350ml/12fl oz/1½ cups passata (bottled strained tomatoes)
1 egg, beaten
30ml/2 tbsp semolina
salt and ground black pepper

For the pastry

75g/3oz/¾ cup plain (all-purpose) flour
75g/3oz/¾ cup wholemeal (whole-wheat) flour
75g/3oz/6 tbsp margarine
50g/2oz/⅔ cup freshly grated Parmesan cheese

1 Preheat the oven to 220°C/425°F/Gas 7. To make the pastry, sift the flours into a bowl. Rub in the margarine then stir in the Parmesan. Mix in enough cold water to form a dough. Wrap in clear film (plastic wrap) and chill for 30 minutes.

2 Place the aubergine in a colander and sprinkle with salt, then leave for about 30 minutes. Rinse and pat dry. Meanwhile, place the pepper on a baking sheet and roast for 20 minutes. Put in a plastic bag and leave for 5 minutes then peel and dice.

3 Heat the oil in a large pan. Fry the onion for 5 minutes until softened, then add the aubergine and fry for 5 minutes. Add the courgette, garlic and oregano, and cook for a further 5 minutes, stirring. Add the kidney beans and olives, then the passata and red pepper. Cook for 5 minutes, then leave to cool.

4 Roll out the pastry to a rough round and place on a lightly oiled baking sheet. Brush with beaten egg, sprinkle over the semolina, leaving a 4cm/1½in border, then spoon over the filling. Gather up the edges to partly cover the filling. Brush with egg and bake for 30–35 minutes until golden. Garnish with oregano.

Mushroom, Nut and Prune Jalousie

This pie has a rich, nutty filling and, served with crisp roast potatoes and steamed vegetables, makes a great alternative to a festive roast.

Serves 6

75g/3oz/⅓ cup green lentils, rinsed
5ml/1 tsp vegetable bouillon powder
15ml/1 tbsp sunflower oil
2 large leeks, sliced
2 garlic cloves, chopped
200g/7oz/2¾ cups field (portabello) mushrooms, chopped
10ml/2 tsp dried mixed herbs
75g/3oz/¾ cup chopped mixed nuts
15ml/1 tbsp pine nuts (optional)
75g/3oz/⅓ cup pitted prunes
25g/1oz/½ cup fresh breadcrumbs
2 eggs, beaten
2 sheets ready-rolled puff pastry, total weight about 425g/15oz
salt and ground black pepper
flour, for dusting

1 Put the lentils in a pan and cover with water. Bring to the boil, then reduce the heat and add the bouillon powder. Partly cover and simmer for 20 minutes until the lentils are tender. Set aside.

2 Heat the oil in a frying pan, and cook the leeks and garlic for 5 minutes or until softened. Add the mushrooms and herbs and cook for 5 minutes. Transfer the mixture to a bowl. Stir in the nuts, pine nuts, if using, prunes, breadcrumbs and lentils.

3 Preheat the oven to 220°C/425°F/Gas 7. Add two-thirds of the beaten egg to the mixture and season. Set aside to cool.

4 Meanwhile, unroll one of the pastry sheets. Cut off 2.5cm/1in from its width and length, then lay it on a dampened baking sheet. Unroll the second pastry sheet, dust with flour, then fold in half lengthways. Make a series of cuts across the fold, 1cm/½in apart, leaving a 2.5cm/1in border around the edge of the pastry.

5 Spoon the filling over the pastry base, leaving a 2.5cm/1in border. Dampen the edges with water. Open out the folded piece and carefully lay it over the top. Trim the edges, then press the edges of the pastry together to seal and crimp.

6 Brush the top of the pastry with the remaining beaten egg and bake for 25–30 minutes until golden. Serve hot.

One-Crust Pie Energy 554kcal/2318kJ; Protein 17.7g; Carbohydrate 56.6g, of which sugars 15.7g; Fat 30.2g, of which saturates 4.2g; Cholesterol 13mg; Calcium 295mg; Fibre 11.6g; Sodium 1353mg.
Mushroom Jalousie Energy 480kcal/2004kJ; Protein 13.5g; Carbohydrate 42.3g, of which sugars 7.3g; Fat 30.5g, of which saturates 1.6g; Cholesterol 63mg; Calcium 99mg; Fibre 4.2g; Sodium 281mg.

Cheese, Rice and Vegetable Strudel

This dish makes a perfect vegetarian main course or a side dish to cold roast meat.

Serves 8

175g/6oz/⅞ cup long grain rice
25g/1oz/2 tbsp butter
1–2 leeks, thinly sliced
350g/12oz mushrooms, sliced
225g/8oz Gruyère cheese, grated
225g/8oz feta cheese, cubed
30ml/2 tbsp currants
50g/2oz/½ cup chopped almonds or hazelnuts, toasted
30ml/2 tbsp chopped fresh parsley
275g/10oz packet frozen filo pastry, thawed
30ml/2 tbsp olive oil
salt and ground black pepper

1 Cook the rice in boiling, salted water for 10–12 minutes, until tender. Drain, rinse under cold running water and set aside. Melt the butter and cook the leeks and mushrooms for 5 minutes.

2 Transfer to a bowl and leave to cool. Add the well-drained rice, the cheeses, currants, toasted almonds or hazelnuts, chopped fresh parsley and seasoning.

3 Preheat the oven to 190°C/375°F/Gas 5. Unwrap the filo pastry. Cover it with a piece of clear film (plastic wrap) and a clean damp cloth. Lay a sheet of pastry on a large piece of baking parchment and brush with oil. Lay a second sheet on top, overlapping the first by 2.5cm/1in. Put another sheet with its long side running at right angles to the first two. Lay a fourth sheet in the same way, overlapping by 2.5cm/1in. Continue in this way, alternating the layers of two sheets so that the join between the two runs in the opposite direction for each layer.

4 Place the filling mixture along the centre of the pastry sheet and shape it into a rectangle, measuring 10 x 30cm/4 x 12in. Fold the layers of filo pastry over the filling and carefully roll it over, with the help of the baking parchment, so that the join ends up being hidden on the underside of the strudel.

5 Lift the strudel on to a greased baking tray and tuck the edges under, so that the filling does not escape. Brush with oil and bake for 30–40 minutes, until golden and crisp. Leave to stand for 5 minutes before cutting into thick slices and serving.

Ratatouille and Fontina Strudel

Mix a jumble of ratatouille vegetables with chunks of creamy fontina cheese, then wrap in sheets of filo and bake for a delicious, summery party pastry.

Serves 6

1 small aubergine (eggplant), diced
45ml/3 tbsp extra virgin olive oil
1 onion, sliced
2 garlic cloves, crushed
1 red and 1 yellow (bell) pepper, cored and sliced
2 courgettes (zucchini), diced
generous pinch of dried mixed herbs
30ml/2 tbsp pine nuts
30ml/2 tbsp raisins
8 sheets of filo pastry, each measuring 30 x 18cm/12 x 7in, thawed if frozen
50g/2oz/¼ cup butter, melted
130g/4½oz/generous 1 cup diced Fontina cheese
salt and ground black pepper
dressed mixed salad, to serve

1 Layer all the diced aubergine in a colander, sprinkling each layer with salt. Drain over the sink for 20 minutes, then rinse well and pat dry.

2 Heat the oil in a large, heavy frying pan, add the onion, garlic, peppers and aubergine and gently fry over a low heat, stirring occasionally, for about 10 minutes until soft and golden.

3 Add the courgettes, herbs and salt and pepper. Cook for 5 minutes until softened. Cool to room temperature, then stir in the pine nuts and raisins.

4 Preheat the oven to 180°C/350°F/Gas 4. Brush two sheets of filo pastry with a little of the melted butter. Lay the filo sheets side by side, overlapping them slightly by about 5cm/2in, to make a large rectangle. Cover with the remaining filo sheets, brushing each layer with melted butter.

5 Spoon the vegetable mixture down one long side of the filo. Sprinkle the cheese on top, then roll up and transfer to a non-stick baking sheet, curling the roll round in a circle.

6 Brush with the remaining butter. Bake for 30 minutes, cool for 10 minutes, then slice and serve with mixed salad.

Vegetable Strudel Energy 487kcal/2031kJ; Protein 19.4g; Carbohydrate 43.7g, of which sugars 4.7g; Fat 26g, of which saturates 12.7g; Cholesterol 77mg; Calcium 387mg; Fibre 2.8g; Sodium 646mg.
Ratatouille Strudel Energy 327kcal/1359kJ; Protein 8.7g; Carbohydrate 22.8g, of which sugars 9.6g; Fat 22.4g, of which saturates 9.5g; Cholesterol 38mg; Calcium 106mg; Fibre 2.9g; Sodium 178mg.

Spicy Potato Strudel

Wrap up this tasty mixture of vegetables in a spicy, creamy sauce with crisp filo pastry. Serve with a good selection of chutneys or a spicy yogurt sauce.

Serves 4

1 onion, chopped
2 carrots, coarsely grated
1 courgette (zucchini), chopped
350g/12oz firm potatoes, finely chopped
65g/2½oz/5 tbsp butter
10ml/2 tsp mild curry paste
2.5ml/½ tsp dried thyme
150ml/¼ pint/⅔ cup water
1 egg, beaten
30ml/2 tbsp single (light) cream
50g/2oz/¼ cup Cheddar cheese, grated
8 sheets filo pastry, thawed if frozen
sesame seeds, for sprinkling
salt and ground black pepper

1 In a large frying pan, cook the onion, carrots, courgette and potatoes in about 25g/1oz/2 tbsp of the butter for 5 minutes, tossing frequently so they cook evenly. Add the curry paste and stir in. Continue to cook the vegetables for a further minute.

2 Add the thyme, water and seasoning. Gradually bring to the boil, then reduce the heat and simmer for about 10 minutes until tender, stirring occasionally.

3 Remove from the heat and leave to cool. Transfer the mixture into a large bowl and then mix in the egg, cream and cheese. Chill until ready to fill the filo pastry.

4 Melt the remaining butter and lay out four sheets of filo pastry, slightly overlapping them to form a fairly large rectangle. Brush the pastry with some melted butter and fit the other sheets on top. Brush again with butter.

5 Preheat the oven to 190°C/375°F/Gas 5. Spoon the filling along one long side, then roll up the pastry. Form it into a circle and set on a baking sheet. Brush again with the last of the butter and sprinkle over the sesame seeds.

6 Bake the strudel in the oven for about 25 minutes until golden and crisp. Leave to stand for 5 minutes before serving.

Puff Pastry Cabbage Pie

Crisp puff pastry with a very soft cabbage filling, is a favourite dish for Russians to eat on a Saturday night when the whole family is gathered.

Serves 4–6

300–400g/11–14oz cabbage
40–50g/1½–2oz/3–4 tbsp butter
3 eggs, hardboiled
1 sheet ready-made chilled puff pastry, measuring about 40x20cm/16x8in
salt

For the glaze

1 egg yolk
5ml/1 tsp water
15ml/1 tbsp fresh white breadcrumbs

1 Discard the outer leaves and hard stalk of the cabbage, cut in half and chop finely. Heat the butter in a medium frying pan over a low heat, add the cabbage and stir-fry for 25 minutes until softened, don't allow it to brown. Season and leave to cool.

2 Remove the shells from the eggs then chop and put in a large bowl. Add the cabbage to the bowl and mix.

3 Preheat the oven to 220°C/425°F/Gas 7. Put the sheet of pastry on a dampened baking tray. Spread the cabbage and egg mixture lengthways on one half of the pastry sheet. Brush the edges with water and fold the other side over to enclose. Seal together by pressing with a fork along the join. It should look like a tightly packed loaf.

4 To make the glaze, whisk together the egg yolk and water. Brush the pastry with the mixture and make some small holes in the top with a fork. Sprinkle the top with the breadcrumbs.

5 Bake for 12–15 minutes, until the pastry is crisp and golden brown. Leave to rest for 5–10 minutes before serving.

Cook's Tip
This pie is made with one large sheet of ready-made puff pastry, which can be bought chilled in one roll. The size should be about 40 x 20cm/16 x 8in.

Spicy Potato Strudel Energy 362kcal/1512kJ; Protein 9.8g; Carbohydrate 34.8g, of which sugars 6.5g; Fat 21.1g, of which saturates 12.7g; Cholesterol 98mg; Calcium 169mg; Fibre 3g; Sodium 227mg.
Cabbage Pie Energy 333kcal/1388kJ; Protein 7.9g; Carbohydrate 25.3g, of which sugars 3.3g; Fat 23.6g, of which saturates 4.5g; Cholesterol 143mg; Calcium 80mg; Fibre 1.2g; Sodium 276mg.

Tomato and Tapenade Tartlets

These delicious individual tarts look and taste fantastic, despite the fact that they demand very little time or effort. The mascarpone cheese topping melts as it cooks to make a smooth, creamy sauce. Cherry tomatoes have a delicious sweet flavour with a low acidity, but plum tomatoes or the vine-ripened variety are also suitable for these tarts and will give delicious results. Red pesto can be used instead of the tapenade if you prefer a subtler flavour.

Serves 4

500g/1¼lb puff pastry, thawed if frozen
60ml/4 tbsp black or green olive tapenade
500g/1¼lb cherry tomatoes
90g/3½oz/scant ½ cup mascarpone

1 Preheat the oven to 220°C/425°F/Gas 7. Lightly grease a large baking sheet and sprinkle it with water.

2 Roll out the pastry on a lightly floured surface and cut out four 16cm/6¼in rounds, using a bowl or small plate as a guide.

3 Transfer the pastry rounds to the prepared baking sheet. Using the tip of a sharp knife, mark a shallow cut 1cm/½in in from the edge of each round to form a rim.

4 Reserve half the tapenade and spread the rest over the pastry rounds, keeping the paste inside the marked rim.

5 Cut half the tomatoes in half. Pile all the tomatoes, whole and halved, on the pastry, again keeping them inside the rim. Season lightly with salt and pepper.

6 Place the baking sheet in the oven and bake the tarts for 20 minutes, until the pastry is well risen and golden.

7 Dot with the remaining tapenade. Spoon a little mascarpone on the centre of the tomatoes and season with black pepper. Bake for a further 10 minutes, until the mascarpone has melted to make a sauce. Serve the tarts warm.

Mushroom and Quail's Egg Gougère

This is a choux pastry from the Burgundy area of France.

Serves 4–6

25g/1oz/¼ cup cornflour (cornstarch)
150ml/¼ pint/⅔ cup mixed red wine and water
25g/1oz/2 tbsp butter
1 onion, chopped
2 celery sticks, sliced
350g/12oz/4–5 cups mushrooms, halved or quartered
150ml/¼ pint/⅔ cup stock
dash of Worcestershire sauce
15ml/1 tbsp chopped parsley
12 quail's eggs, boiled for 1 minute, and peeled

For the pastry

75g/3oz/6 tbsp butter, diced
2.5ml/½ tsp salt
175ml/6fl oz/¾ cup water
100g/3¾oz/scant 1 cup plain (all-purpose) flour, sifted
4 eggs
115g/4oz/1 cup grated Gruyère cheese

1 Preheat the oven to 220°F/425°C/Gas 7. To make the pastry, melt the butter in a pan with the salt and water, and bring to the boil. Remove from the heat, add all the flour and beat with a wooden spoon until it forms a ball. Return the pan to the heat and cook, beating hard, for 1–2 minutes. Leave to cool slightly. Add two eggs, beating until the mixture becomes glossy. Beat in the third egg, then beat in as much of the fourth egg as you need to create glossy, soft pastry. Beat in half the cheese.

2 Line a baking sheet and place spoonfuls of the dough close together in a 20cm/8in circle. Bake for 30 minutes until well risen and golden all over. Remove from the oven, cut a few slits in the side to release the steam and set aside to cool slightly.

3 Mix the cornflour and wine and water in a bowl. Meanwhile, melt the butter in a pan, add the onion and celery and fry until soft. Add the mushrooms and cook gently, then add the wine mixture. Add the stock to the mushrooms and gradually stir in the cornflour mixture. Cook gently until it is starting to thicken. Add the Worcestershire sauce and parsley, and cook until thick.

4 Slice the gougère in half horizontally. Fill with the mushroom mixture and top with the eggs. Replace the lid, sprinkle over the remaining cheese and return to the oven until the cheese melts.

Tomato Tartlets Energy 543kcal/2269kJ; Protein 10.2g; Carbohydrate 50.8g, of which sugars 6.2g; Fat 35.9g, of which saturates 2.4g; Cholesterol 9mg; Calcium 91mg; Fibre 1.7g; Sodium 736mg.
Mushroom Gougère Energy 364kcal/1513kJ; Protein 14.7g; Carbohydrate 17.4g, of which sugars 4.5g; Fat 26.1g, of which saturates 14.1g; Cholesterol 150mg; Calcium 283mg; Fibre 2.4g; Sodium 327mg.

Tuna and Egg Galette

This flaky pastry tart combines soft-centred eggs and a slightly piquant fish filling. It makes a wonderful dish for a summer supper.

Serves 4

2 sheets of ready-rolled puff pastry
flour, for rolling
beaten egg, to glaze
60ml/4 tbsp olive oil
175g/6oz tuna steak
2 onions, sliced
1 red (bell) pepper, chopped
2 garlic cloves, crushed
45ml/3 tbsp capers, drained
5ml/1 tsp grated lemon rind
30ml/2 tbsp lemon juice
5 eggs
salt and ground black pepper
30ml/2 tbsp chopped flat leaf parsley, to garnish

1 Preheat the oven to 190°C/375°F/Gas 5. Lay one sheet of puff pastry on a lightly floured baking tray and cut it to a 28 x 18cm/11 x 7in rectangle. Brush the whole sheet with beaten egg.

2 Cut the second sheet of pastry to the same size. Cut out a rectangle from the centre and discard, leaving a 2.5cm/1in border. Carefully lift the border on to the first sheet. Brush the border with beaten egg and prick the base. Bake the pastry case (pie shell) for about 15 minutes until golden and well risen.

3 Heat 30ml/2 tbsp of the oil in a frying pan and fry the tuna steak for 2–3 minutes on each side until golden but still pale pink in the middle. Transfer the steak to a plate and flake into small pieces.

4 Add the remaining oil to the pan and fry the onions, red pepper and garlic for about 6–8 minutes until softened, stirring occasionally. Remove the pan from the heat and stir in the flaked tuna, capers and lemon rind and juice. Season well with salt and black pepper.

5 Spoon the filling into the pastry case and level the surface with the back of a spoon. Break the eggs into the filling and return the galette to the oven for about 10 minutes, or until the eggs have just cooked through. Garnish with chopped parsley and serve immediately.

Sardine and Spinach Parcels

Not often used as a pastry filling, as it's an oily fish, the sardine in these parcels will offer you plenty of encouragement to eat more oily fish. The additional tomatoes, leeks and spinach make a beautifully balanced, and very healthy, filling.

Serves 6

2 x 120g/4¼oz cans large sardines in oil
3 leeks, finely chopped
300g/11oz fresh spinach leaves, finely shredded
2 tomatoes, peeled, seeded and finely chopped
lemon juice
24 sheets of filo pastry, about 20cm/8in square, thawed if frozen
30ml/2 tbsp olive oil, for brushing the filo pastry
sea salt and ground black pepper
salad leaves, to garnish

1 Preheat the oven to 180°C/350°F/Gas 4. Drain the oil from one of the cans of sardines into a frying pan. Set six sardines aside. Heat the oil in the pan and fry the leeks for 5 minutes. Add the spinach and tomatoes to the pan and cook over a low heat for 5 minutes, stirring occasionally, until soft. Add salt, pepper and lemon juice to taste.

2 Stack four sheets of filo, brushing each sheet with olive oil and laying each sheet at an angle of 45 degrees to the one below. Spoon a sixth of the vegetable mixture into the centre of the top sheet. Press a whole sardine into the middle of the vegetable mixture.

3 Fold over the filo to make a parcel, brushing each fold with olive oil. Brush the top of the parcel with oil and place it on a baking sheet. Make five more parcels.

4 Bake the filo parcels for 20 minutes, or until the filo is crisp and brown. Garnish with salad leaves.

Cook's Tip

Delicious served warm, these parcels can also be eaten cold, and are good for packed lunches.

Tuna Galette Energy 544kcal/2263kJ; Protein 21.7g; Carbohydrate 27.7g, of which sugars 4.6g; Fat 39.5g, of which saturates 10.1g; Cholesterol 260mg; Calcium 102mg; Fibre 1.9g; Sodium 320mg.
Sardine Parcels Energy 252kcal/1060kJ; Protein 15.4g; Carbohydrate 29.5g, of which sugars 4g; Fat 8.8g, of which saturates 1.7g; Cholesterol 26mg; Calcium 354mg; Fibre 5.7g; Sodium 255mg.

Fillets of Sea Bream in Filo Pastry

Each of these little parcels is a meal in itself and can be prepared several hours in advance, which makes the recipe ideal for entertaining. Serve the pastries with fennel braised with orange juice or a mixed leaf salad.

Serves 4

8 small waxy salad potatoes, preferably red-skinned
200g/7oz sorrel, stalks removed
30ml/2 tbsp extra virgin olive oil
16 filo pastry sheets, thawed if frozen
4 sea bream fillets, about 175g/6oz each, scaled but not skinned
50g/2oz/¼ cup butter, melted
120ml/4fl oz/½ cup fish stock
250ml/8fl oz/1 cup whipping cream
salt and ground black pepper
finely diced red (bell) pepper, to garnish

1 Preheat the oven to 200°C/400°F/Gas 6. Cook the potatoes in a pan of lightly salted boiling water for about 15–20 minutes, or until just tender. Drain and leave to cool. Set about half the sorrel leaves aside. Shred the remaining leaves by piling up six or eight at a time, rolling them up like a fat cigar and slicing them with a sharp knife. Thinly slice the potatoes lengthways.

2 Brush a baking sheet with a little of the oil. Lay a sheet of filo pastry on the sheet, brush it with oil, then lay a second sheet crossways over the first. Repeat with two more sheets. Arrange a quarter of the sliced potatoes in the centre, season and add a quarter of the shredded sorrel. Lay a bream fillet on top, skin side up. Season with salt and ground black pepper.

3 Loosely fold the filo pastry up and over to make a neat parcel, them repeat to make three more. Place the parcels on the baking sheet and brush with half the butter. Bake for about 20 minutes, or until the filo is puffed up and golden brown.

4 Meanwhile, make the sorrel sauce. Heat the remaining butter in a pan, add the reserved sorrel and cook gently for 3 minutes, stirring, until it wilts. Stir in the stock and cream. Heat almost to boiling point, stirring so that the sorrel breaks down. Season to taste and keep hot until the fish parcels are ready. Serve garnished with red pepper. Pass round the sauce separately.

Filo-Wrapped Cod

The choice of fish can be varied according to what is freshest on the day of purchase. When working with filo pastry, keep it covered with clear film (plastic wrap) or a damp dish towel as much as possible. Once exposed to the air it dries out quickly, making it difficult to handle.

Serves 3–4

about 130g/4½oz filo pastry (6–8 large sheets), thawed if frozen
about 30ml/2 tbsp olive oil, for brushing
450g/1lb salmon or cod steaks or fillets
550ml/18fl oz/2½ cups fresh tomato sauce (see Cook's Tip)

1 Preheat the oven to 200°C/400°F/Gas 6. Take a sheet of filo pastry, brush with a little olive oil and cover with a second sheet of pastry. Place a piece of fish on top of the pastry, towards the bottom edge, then top with 1–2 spoonfuls of the tomato sauce, spreading it in an even layer.

2 Roll the fish in the pastry, taking care to enclose the filling completely. Brush with a little olive oil. Arrange the pastry parcel on a baking sheet and repeat with the remaining fish and pastry. You should have about half the sauce remaining, to serve alongside the fish.

3 Bake for 10–15 minutes, or until golden. Avoid opening the oven door before 10 minutes as the drop in temperature can stop the filo pastry from rising. Meanwhile, reheat the remaining sauce gently in a small pan. Serve the wrapped fish immediately with the remaining heated tomato sauce and a lightly dressed green or mixed salad.

Cook's Tip

To make the tomato sauce, fry 1 chopped onion and a crushed garlic clove in 15ml/1 tbsp oil until softened. Add a 400g/14oz can chopped tomatoes, 15ml/1 tbsp tomato purée (paste) and 15ml/1 tbsp chopped fresh herbs. Add a pinch of sugar and season to taste. Simmer for 20 minutes.

Sea Bream Pastry Energy 651kcal/2710kJ; Protein 35.8g; Carbohydrate 23.2g, of which sugars 3.3g; Fat 46.8g, of which saturates 23.2g; Cholesterol 159mg; Calcium 222mg; Fibre 2g; Sodium 359mg.
Filo-Wrapped Cod Energy 382kcal/1601kJ; Protein 27.1g; Carbohydrate 27.9g, of which sugars 7.8g; Fat 18.8g, of which saturates 3.1g; Cholesterol 56mg; Calcium 103mg; Fibre 3.7g; Sodium 144mg.

Trout with Pastry and Almond Crust

Beautiful presentation is a real plus when it comes to serving fish, and this trout is as pretty as a picture with its filo wrapping dusted with almonds. The delicious stuffing helps make this a tasty and filling main course.

Serves 4

4 whole trout, about 175g/6oz each, cleaned
40g/1½oz/3 tbsp butter
1 small onion, finely chopped
115g/4oz/1 cup ground almonds
30ml/2 tbsp chopped fresh parsley
finely grated rind of 1 lemon
12 sheets filo pastry
salt and ground black pepper
lemon slices and parsley sprigs, to garnish

1 Preheat the oven to 200°C/400°F/Gas 6. Season the trout generously with salt and black pepper.

2 Melt 25g/1oz/2 tbsp of the butter in a large pan and cook the onion for 1–2 minutes until soft and translucent. Do not allow the onion to brown.

3 Stir 75g/3oz/¾ cup of the ground almonds into the onions in the pan, then add the chopped parsley and the lemon rind. Stir well to combine.

4 Gently stuff the cavity of each trout with one-quarter of the mixture. Press the mixture down firmly to mould it to the shape of the cavity.

5 Melt the remaining butter in small pan. Cut three sheets of filo pastry into long strips and brush with the melted butter. Wrap the strips around one fish, with the buttered side inside. Leave the head and the tail free. Place the fish on a baking sheet. Wrap the other trout.

6 Brush the top of the pastry casing with melted butter and sprinkle the remaining ground almonds over the fish. Bake for 20–25 minutes until the pastry is golden brown. Place on warmed individual serving dishes, garnish with the lemon slices and parsley sprigs and serve.

Salmon and Quinoa Pie

Quinoa is a wonder grain that comes in three colours, red gives a great contrast but if unavailable use you can use white instead.

Serves 4

400g/14oz salmon fillet
15ml/1 tbsp olive oil
1 medium onion, finely chopped
75g/3oz/scant 1 cup mushrooms, finely chopped
1 clove garlic, crushed
115g/4oz/⅔ cup red quinoa, rinsed
350ml/12fl oz/1½ cups fish stock
2 eggs
120ml/4fl oz/½ cup white wine
a good handful of parsley, chopped
juice and zest of 1 lemon
350g/12oz all-butter puff pastry
30ml/2 tbsp mix of milk/melted butter, to glaze
salt and ground black pepper

1 Place the salmon fillets on a baking tray and part-cook under a moderate grill (broiler) for 5 minutes on each side. Remove the skin. Flake the flesh, removing any bones, and set aside.

2 Heat the olive oil in a pan, add the onion, mushrooms, garlic and rinsed quinoa and cook for 2–3 minutes until the onions start to brown. Add the fish stock, then the whole eggs in their shells, cover and simmer for 8 minutes to hard-boil the eggs. Remove the eggs with a slotted spoon and place in cold water. Add the wine to the quinoa broth and continue cooking until most of the liquid has been absorbed.

3 Add the chopped parsley, grated lemon zest and juice to the quinoa mixture, season and set aside to cool. Heat the oven to 200°C/400°F/Gas 6. Peel and roughly chop the cooked eggs.

4 Roll out the pastry into a large rectangle, and cut lengthways into two halves, one slightly wider than the other. Move the larger half on to a baking tray, and spread the salmon down the middle, leaving a margin on all sides. Pile the quinoa mix on top, shaping into a rounded shape. Top with the chopped eggs.

5 Moisten the edge of the pastry, then lift the other piece of pastry over the top. Press the edges together to seal.
Glaze the coulibiac with the milk/butter mixture, cut a slit on the top and bake for 25–30 minutes, until golden. Serve hot.

Trout with Pastry Energy 475kcal/1978kJ; Protein 39.2g; Carbohydrate 7.6g, of which sugars 0.8g; Fat 32.2g, of which saturates 12.4g; Cholesterol 187mg; Calcium 101mg; Fibre 1.2g; Sodium 249mg.
Salmon & Quinoa Pie Energy 797kcal/2994kJ; Protein 32g; Carbohydrate 57g, of which sugars 7g; Fat 39g, of which saturates 3g; Cholesterol 114mg; Calcium 134mg; Fibre 5g; Sodium 519mg.

Salmon Coulibiac

This wonderful and impressive pie is from the imperial era of Russia.

Serves 4

50g/2oz/¼ cup butter
1 small onion, finely chopped
175g/6oz/scant 1 cup rice
350ml/12fl oz/1½ cups fish stock
1 bay leaf
olive oil
175g/6oz mushrooms, finely sliced
450g/1lb ready-made puff pastry
2 salmon fillets, about 2.25kg/5lb in total
dash of dry white wine
chopped fresh fennel
3 eggs, boiled until firm and sliced
egg wash, made by whisking 1 egg with a little milk
salt and ground black pepper

1 Melt half the butter in a pan and cook the onion until soft. Add the rice, stock, bayleaf and a pinch of salt. Bring to the boil, cover and cook on a low heat until all the liquid is absorbed.

2 Heat the remaining butter with a little olive oil in a second pan and quickly fry the mushrooms. Set aside to cool.

3 Roll out the puff pastry into a square, long enough for a fillet and leaving 2.5cm/1in at each end. Place half the rice in a strip across the centre of the pastry. Cover with one salmon fillet, moisten with a little wine, season, and sprinkle with fennel.

4 Cover the salmon with half the sliced egg and half the cooked mushrooms and a few spoonfuls of the rice. Then lay the second salmon fillet on top, adding another splash of wine and seasoning. Add another layer of sliced egg, the rest of the mushrooms, and finally the remaining rice.

5 Brush the edges of the pastry with the egg wash, fold the pastry over and press to seal. Brush egg wash all over. Rest in a cool place for an hour. Meanwhile preheat the oven to 220°C/425°F/Gas 7.

6 Bake the coulibiac for about 40 minutes. Allow to rest for 10 minutes before serving. Use a serrated bread knife to cut the coulibiac and slice across its width. It is delicious served hot with a green vegetable. It is also excellent cold with a fresh salad.

Salmon Puffs

The flavour and texture of canned salmon works well in these little puffs.

Serves 6–8

65g/2½oz/9 tbsp plain (all-purpose) flour
50g/2oz/¼ cup butter
150ml/¼ pint/⅔ cup water
2 eggs, beaten

For the filling
200g/7oz can red salmon, drained,
60ml/4 tbsp mayonnaise
50g/2oz/⅓ cup sun-dried tomatoes in oil, drained and finely chopped
grated rind and juice of ½ lemon
chopped parsley
salt and ground black pepper
salad leaves and halved cherry tomatoes, to serve

1 Sift the flour on to a sheet of baking parchment. Put the butter and water in a pan and heat until the butter melts. Bring to the boil and remove from the heat. Add in all the flour and beat with a wooden spoon until the mixture forms a smooth, glossy paste. Set aside to cool slightly for 5 minutes.

2 Meanwhile, make the filling. Flake the salmon finely and put it in a bowl. Add the mayonnaise, sun-dried tomatoes, lemon rind and juice. Stir in the parsley, with salt and pepper to taste. Cover and chill until ready to serve.

3 Add the beaten egg gradually to the cooled paste, beating after each addition. It may not be necessary to add all the egg; stir in enough to produce a smooth, shiny mixture. Set aside.

4 Preheat the oven to 190°C/375°F/Gas 5. Grease a large baking sheet. Spoon the pastry into a piping (pastry) bag fitted with a 1cm/½in plain round nozzle. Pipe the pastry on to the baking sheet to make about 24 small rounds, spaced well apart. Bake for 20–25 minutes until the puffs are browned.

5 Remove the puffs from the oven and split them horizontally in half to release the steam. Leave to cool on a wire rack.

6 Just before serving, use a teaspoon to fill each puff with the salmon mixture. Serve with salad leaves and tomatoes.

Salmon Coulibiac Energy 1005kcal/4190kJ; Protein 50.7g; Carbohydrate 77.9g, of which sugars 2.4g; Fat 56.6g, of which saturates 7.8g; Cholesterol 244mg; Calcium 139mg; Fibre 0.7g; Sodium 521mg.
Salmon Puffs Energy 206kcal/855kJ; Protein 8g; Carbohydrate 7g, of which sugars 0g; Fat 16g, of which saturates 5g; Cholesterol 86mg; Calcium 46mg; Fibre 0g; Sodium 232mg

Egg and Salmon Puff Parcels

These crisp elegant parcels hide a mouthwatering collection of flavours and textures and make a delicious appetizer or lunch dish.

Serves 6

75g/3oz/scant ½ cup long grain rice
300ml/½ pint/1¼ cups fish stock
350g/12oz piece salmon tail
juice of ½ lemon
15ml/1 tbsp chopped fresh dill
15ml/1 tbsp chopped fresh parsley
10ml/2 tsp mild curry powder
6 small (US medium) eggs, soft-boiled and cooled
425g/15oz flaky pastry, thawed if frozen
1 small (US medium) egg, beaten
salt and ground black pepper

1 Cook the rice in boiling fish stock for 15 minutes. Drain and set aside to cool. Preheat the oven to 220°C/425°F/Gas 7.

2 Poach the salmon, then remove the bones and skin and flake the fish into the rice. Add the lemon juice, herbs, curry powder and seasoning and mix well. Peel the soft-boiled eggs.

3 Roll out the pastry and cut into six 14–15cm/5½–6in squares. Brush the edges with the beaten egg. Place a spoonful of rice in the middle of each square, push an egg into the middle and top with a little more rice.

4 Pull over the pastry corners to the middle to form a square parcel, squeezing the joins together well to seal. Brush with more egg, place on a baking sheet and bake the puffs in the oven for 20 minutes, then reduce the oven temperature to 190°C/375°F/Gas 5 and cook the puffs for a further 10 minutes, or until golden and crisp underneath.

5 Cool slightly before serving with a curry-flavoured mayonnaise or hollandaise sauce, if you like.

Variation
You can also add a spoonful of cooked chopped fresh or frozen spinach to each parcel.

Egg and Anchovy Pies

If you can, use large muffin tins to make these little pies. They provide a deep case to hold plenty of the deliciously tangy yogurt filling. Eat warm or wrap them up and take them outside for a tasty summer picnic.

Makes 8

175g/6oz shortcrust pastry
45–60ml/3–4 tbsp tapenade or sun-dried tomato paste
4 anchovy fillets, drained and snipped into pieces
1 large egg
100g/3¾oz/scant ½ cup thick Greek (US strained plain) yogurt
90ml/6 tbsp milk
1 garlic clove, crushed
30ml/2 tbsp chopped mixed herbs, such as thyme, marjoram, basil and parsley
salt and ground black pepper

1 Preheat the oven to 190°C/375°F/Gas 5. Roll out the pastry thinly and cut out eight rounds using a 7.5cm/3in cutter.

2 Line deep patty or muffin tins with the pastry rounds, then line each one with a small piece of baking parchment.

3 Bake the pastry cases (pie shells)for 15 minutes. Remove the paper and cook for a further 5 minutes or until the cases are crisp. Spread a little tapenade or tomato paste in the base of each pastry case. Sprinkle the chopped anchovies over the top.

4 Whisk together the egg, yogurt, milk, garlic, herbs and seasoning. Spoon carefully into the pastry cases.

5 Bake in the oven for 15–20 minutes or until the filling is just firm and the pastry golden. Allow the pies to cool slightly before carefully removing from the tins and serving.

Variations
• *You can make mini tartlets from this recipe, which are ideal for parties. Bake for only 15 minutes with the filling.*
• *For a vegetarian version of these pies, simply omit the anchovy fillets.*

Salmon and Egg Parcels Energy 540kcal/2252kJ; Protein 36g; Carbohydrate 36g, of which sugars 1g; Fat 35g, of which saturates 10g; Cholesterol 255mg; Calcium 104mg; Fibre 1g; Sodium 433mg.
Egg and Anchovy Pies Energy 193kcal/806kJ; Protein 5.2g; Carbohydrate 18.8g, of which sugars 3.7g; Fat 11.4g, of which saturates 3.8g; Cholesterol 50mg; Calcium 93mg; Fibre 0.9g; Sodium 190mg.

Fish in a Dough Jacket

In this traditional rustic recipe, the whole fish is encased in a dough, which traps the juices and flavour.

Serves 4–6

about 1kg/2¼lb whole fish, such as mullet, skinned and cleaned
flaked sea salt
sprigs of fennel, to garnish
lemon wedges, to serve

For the dough

225g/8oz/2 cups strong white flour, sifted
1.5ml/¼ tsp salt
7g/¼oz sachet easy-blend dried yeast
1 egg, beaten
100–120ml/3½–4fl oz/⅓–½ cup milk and warm water mixed together

1 Preheat the oven to 180°C/350°F/Gas 4. Pat the fish dry with kitchen paper and sprinkle inside and out with salt.

2 For the dough, put the flour and salt into a large bowl and stir in the yeast. Make a well in the centre. Whisk together the egg, milk and water, then pour half into the centre of the flour. Form into a soft dough. Knead the dough until smooth on a very lightly floured surface. Divide the dough into two pieces, making one portion slightly larger than the other.

3 Carefully roll out the smaller piece of dough on a lightly floured surface to the shape of your fish, allowing a 5cm/2in border. Lay the dough on a large greased shallow baking sheet. Place the fish on top.

4 Roll out the remaining piece of dough until large enough to cover the fish, again allowing for a 5cm/2in border. Brush the edges of the pastry with water and seal well. Make criss-cross patterns across the top. Leave to rise for 30 minutes.

5 Glaze the dough with the remaining egg mixture. Make a small hole in the top of the pastry to allow steam to escape.

6 Bake the fish for 25–30 minutes or until golden brown and well risen. Garnish with sprigs of fennel and serve with wedges of lemon and a salad of finely sliced courgette, tossed in melted butter and sprinkled with dill seeds.

Sweet Pepper Choux with Anchovies

The ratatouille vegetables in this dish are roasted instead of stewed, and have a wonderful flavour.

Serves 6

300ml/½ pint/1¼ cups water
115g/4oz/½ cup butter or margarine
150g/5oz/1¼ cups plain (all-purpose) flour
4 eggs
115g/4oz Gruyère or Cheddar cheese, finely diced
5ml/1 tsp Dijon mustard
salt

For the filling

3 red or yellow (bell) peppers, seeded and cut into chunks
1 large onion, sliced
3 tomatoes, peeled and quartered
1 courgette (zucchini), sliced
6 basil leaves, torn in strips
1 garlic clove, crushed
30ml/2 tbsp olive oil
about 18 black olives, pitted
45ml/3 tbsp red wine
175ml/6fl oz/¾ cup passata (bottled strained tomatoes) or puréed canned tomatoes
50g/2oz can anchovy fillets
salt and ground black pepper

1 Preheat the oven to 240°C/475°F/Gas 9. Halve the peppers, seed and core and cut into 2.5cm/1in chunks. Place the peppers, onion, tomatoes and courgette in a roasting pan. Mix in the basil, garlic and olive oil. Sprinkle with salt and pepper and roast for about 25–30 minutes until the vegetables are tender. Reduce the oven temperature to 200°C/400°F/Gas 6.

2 To make the choux pastry, put the water and butter together in a large pan and heat until the butter melts. Remove from the heat and add all the flour in one go. Beat well with a wooden spoon for about 30 seconds until smooth. Allow to cool slightly.

3 Beat in the eggs, one at a time, and then continue beating until the mixture is thick and glossy. Stir in the cheese and mustard, then season with salt and pepper. Spoon the mixture around the sides of six greased ovenproof dishes.

4 Mix the vegetables with the olives, wine and passata. Divide the pepper mixture between the dishes and arrange the drained anchovy fillets on top. Bake for about 25–35 minutes until the choux pastry is puffy and golden. Serve hot from the oven with a fresh green salad.

Fish in Dough Jacket Energy 224kcal/950kJ; Protein 19.8g; Carbohydrate 29.2g, of which sugars 0.6g; Fat 4g, of which saturates 0.1g; Cholesterol 0mg; Calcium 113mg; Fibre 1.6g; Sodium 85mg.
Sweet Pepper Choux Energy 484kcal/2015kJ; Protein 17g; Carbohydrate 30g, of which sugars 9g; Fat 34g, of which saturates 16g; Cholesterol 222mg; Calcium 294mg; Fibre 4g; Sodium 739mg.

Scallops with Wild Mushrooooms

Mushrooms perfectly complement scallops in this smooth creamy sauce. Crisp pastry completes the dish.

Serves 4

350g/12oz puff pastry
1 egg, beaten
75g/3oz/6 tbsp butter
12 scallops, trimmed and sliced
2 shallots, chopped
½ celery stick, cut into strips
½ carrot, cut into strips
225g/8oz/3 cups assorted wild mushrooms, trimmed and sliced
60ml/4 tbsp dry vermouth
150ml/¼ pint/⅔ cup crème fraîche
4 egg yolks
15ml/1 tbsp lemon juice
salt, ground black pepper, celery salt and cayenne pepper

1 Roll out the puff pastry on a floured surface, then cut out four 13cm/5in shell shapes. Mark a shell pattern on each with a small knife then brush with a little beaten egg. Place on a baking sheet, then chill. Preheat the oven to 200°C/400°F/Gas 6.

2 Melt 25g/1oz/2 tbsp of the butter in a pan. Season the scallops with salt and black pepper, add them to the pan and cook for 30 seconds over a high heat. Transfer to a plate.

3 Score an inner shell 2.5cm/1in from the outer edge of each pastry shape. Bake for 20–25 minutes until golden.

4 Fry the shallots, celery and carrot gently in the remaining butter. Add the mushrooms and cook until the juices begin to run. Pour in the vermouth and then increase the heat to evaporate the pan juices. Add the crème fraîche and cooked scallops and bring to a simmer (do not boil).

5 Remove the pan from the heat and blend in the egg yolks. Return the pan to a gentle heat and cook for a moment or two until the sauce has thickened to the consistency of thin cream, then remove the pan from the heat. Season with celery salt and cayenne pepper, and add the lemon juice.

6 Gently split the pastry shapes open and place the bases on four plates. Spoon in the filling and arrange the lids on top. Serve with potatoes and salad, if you like.

Seafood Gougère

This is an easy-to-prepare yet impressive supper dish.

Serves 4

130g/4½oz/1 cup plus 30ml/2 tbsp plain (all-purpose) flour
1.5ml/¼ tsp salt
130g/4½oz/9 tbsp butter
200ml/7fl oz/scant 1 cup water
3 eggs, beaten
150g/5oz Gruyère cheese, grated
250g/9oz smoked haddock fillet
1 bay leaf
250ml/8fl oz/1 cup milk
1 small red onion, chopped
150g/5oz/2–2½ cups white (button) mushrooms, sliced
fresh lemon juice
30ml/2 tbsp chopped parsley
salt and ground black pepper

1 Lightly grease a shallow ovenproof dish. Sift 100g/3¾oz/scant 1 cup of the flour on to a sheet of baking parchment and add the salt. Place 75g/3oz/6 tbsp of the butter in a pan. Add the water and heat gently. As soon as the butter has melted, bring the water to the boil. Tip in the flour mixture and beat well. When the mixture forms a soft, smooth paste, remove the pan from the heat and leave to cool for 5 minutes.

2 Gradually beat the eggs into the dough, beating well, until the mixture has the consistency of creamy mashed potato. You may not need all the egg. Stir in two-thirds of the grated cheese. Spoon the choux pastry around the edge of the prepared dish, making sure it comes well up the sides. Set aside.

3 Preheat the oven to 180°C/350°F/Gas 4. Poach the haddock in the milk until just cooked. Lift out the fish and set aside reserving the milk. Melt the remaining butter in a frying pan. Add the onion and mushrooms and sauté for about 5 minutes, then add the remaining flour. Gradually stir in the hot milk. Heat, stirring continuously, until the sauce is a smooth consistency. Simmer for 2–3 minutes, then add the lemon juice, parsley, and salt and pepper to taste.

4 Increase the oven temperature to 200°C/400°F/Gas 6. Skin and flake the fish and place in the centre of the choux-lined dish, along with the mushroom mixture. Sprinkle over the rest of the cheese. Bake for 35–40 minutes until the gougère has risen and is golden brown. Serve immediately.

Scallops with Mushrooms Energy 335kcal/1402kJ; Protein 24g; Carbohydrate 19g, of which sugars 2g; Fat 19g, of which saturates 11g; Cholesterol 86mg; Calcium 70mg; Fibre 2g; Sodium 284mg.
Seafood Gougère Energy 597kcal/2485kJ; Protein 30.7g; Carbohydrate 26.8g, of which sugars 1.6g; Fat 41.1g, of which saturates 24.2g; Cholesterol 261mg; Calcium 391mg; Fibre 1.6g; Sodium 1101mg.

Trout Gougère

This gougère, a choux pastry ring flavoured with cheese, uses the same recipe for the dough as for the Seafood Gougère recipe on page 69. This variation is piped into a ring shape and contains a rich, creamy trout and watercress filling.

Serves 4

For the gougère

1 quantity of choux pastry from Seafood Gougère on page 69, made up to the end of step 2

For the filling

350g/12oz trout fillet
150ml/¼ pint/⅔ cup white wine
4 fresh parsley sprigs
½ lemon, sliced
1 bay leaf
25g/1oz/2 tbsp butter
1 small onion, chopped
25g/1oz/¼ cup plain (all-purpose) flour
150ml/¼ pint/⅔ cup milk
60ml/4 tbsp double (heavy) cream
50g/2oz Gruyère cheese, grated
50g/2oz watercress, chopped
salt and ground black pepper

1 Spoon the choux paste into a piping (pastry) bag fitted with a 1cm/½in plain round nozzle and pipe just inside the circle to form a ring. Sprinkle with the remaining cheese. Bake in the oven for 20–25 minutes or until golden brown and crisp.

2 Meanwhile, make the filling. Place the trout fillet, wine, parsley, lemon slices and bay leaf in a large frying pan. Gently poach the fish for 4–6 minutes, until just cooked. Remove the fish from the pan. Strain the cooking liquid and reserve. Skin the fish, remove any bones and flake it into bitesize pieces.

3 Heat the butter in a pan, add the onion and fry gently for about 5 minutes until softened. Stir the flour into the pan and cook for 1 minute, stirring. Gradually add the reserved cooking liquid and the milk, stirring constantly to form a thick sauce.

4 Add the flaked trout, cream, cheese and watercress to the sauce and season well. Heat gently until piping hot.

5 When the choux ring is cooked, remove it from the oven and place on a warmed serving plate. Slice the gougère in half horizontally and spoon in the hot trout and watercress filling. Replace the pastry lid on the ring and serve immediately.

Shellfish in Puff Pastry

A classic combination of seafood in a creamy sauce served in a puff pastry case.

Serves 6

350g/12oz ready rolled puff pastry
1 egg beaten with a little water
60ml/4 tbsp dry white wine
2 shallots, finely chopped
450g/1lb mussels, cleaned
15g/½oz/1 tbsp butter
450g/1lb shelled scallops, halved
450g/1lb peeled prawns (shrimp)
175g/6oz cooked lobster, sliced

For the sauce

225g/8oz/1 cup unsalted (sweet) butter, diced
2 shallots, finely chopped
250ml/8fl oz/1 cup fish stock
90ml/6 tbsp dry white wine
15–30ml/1–2 tbsp cream
lemon juice
salt and white pepper

1 Cut the pastry into six diamond shapes. Place on baking sheets and brush with egg glaze. Score a line 1.2cm/½in from the edge of each case, then chill for 30 minutes. Preheat the oven to 220°C/425°F/Gas 7. Bake for 20 minutes until puffed and brown. Transfer to a wire rack and remove and retain each lid. Scoop out and discard any uncooked dough.

2 In a large pan, bring the wine and shallots to the boil over a high heat. Add the mussels and cook, covered, for 4–6 minutes until the shells open. Discard any mussels that do not open and remove the rest from their shells. Strain and reserve the stock. In a frying pan, melt the butter over a medium heat. Add the scallops and prawns, and cook for 3–4 minutes.

3 To make the sauce, melt 30g/1oz/2 tbsp of the butter in a heavy pan. Add the shallots and cook for 2 minutes. Add the fish stock and boil for 15 minutes until reduced by three-quarters. Add the wine and mussel liquid and boil again until reduced by half. Lower the heat to medium and whisk in the remaining butter, a little at a time, to make a smooth sauce (don't let it boil). Whisk in the cream and lemon juice. Keep warm, covered.

4 Warm the pastry cases (pie shells) in a low oven. Put the mussels, scallops and prawns in a pan. Add a quarter of the sauce, heat gently, then stir in the lobster. Divide among the cases and top with the lids. Serve with the remaining sauce.

Trout Gougère Energy 450kcal/1872kJ; Protein 25.9g; Carbohydrate 18.1g, of which sugars 3.5g; Fat 28.3g, of which saturates 12.8g; Cholesterol 97mg; Calcium 242mg; Fibre 1.3g; Sodium 320mg.
Shellfish in Pastry Energy 793kcal/3303kJ; Protein 44.4g; Carbohydrate 25.6g, of which sugars 1.5g; Fat 56g, of which saturates 33.2g; Cholesterol 371mg; Calcium 159mg; Fibre 0.3g; Sodium 815mg.

Seafood Puff Ring

The freshest fish and wild mushrooms are combined here in a delicious sauce.

Serves 4

350g/12oz puff pastry
1 egg, beaten with a little water
200ml/7fl oz/scant 1 cup white wine
200ml/7fl oz/scant 1 cup chicken or vegetable stock
350g/12oz/3½ cups assorted wild and cultivated mushrooms, trimmed and sliced thinly
12 mussels, scrubbed
115g/4oz monkfish, boned and cut into large pieces
225g/8oz salmon fillet, skinned and cut into bitesize pieces
12 large peeled prawns (shrimp)
6 scallops, halved
50g/2oz/4 tbsp unsalted butter
2 shallots, finely chopped
50g/2oz/4 tbsp plain (all-purpose) flour
75ml/5 tbsp crème fraîche
10ml/2 tsp lemon juice
salt and cayenne pepper

1 Roll out the pastry on a floured surface to form a rectangle 30 x 38cm/12 x 15in. Cut out a 23cm/9in circle and place on a baking sheet. Prick all over with a fork and brush the surface with beaten egg. Cut out 4cm/1½in circles with a fluted pastry (cookie) cutter. Overlap these shapes around the edge of the large circle, brush again with egg and chill for 1 hour. Preheat the oven to 200°C/400°F/Gas 6.

2 Bring the wine and stock to a simmer, add the mushrooms and cook gently for 3–4 minutes. Remove with a slotted spoon and transfer to a large bowl.

3 Tap the mussels sharply and discard any that do not close. Bring the stock to a simmer and add the monkfish, mussels, salmon, prawns and scallops. Cook for 6 minutes. Remove with a slotted spoon and add to the bowl with the mushrooms. Discard any mussels which do not open. Strain the cooking liquid and make up to 350ml/12fl oz/1½ cups with water, if necessary. Bake the pastry for 25–30 minutes until golden.

4 Add the crème fraîche to the stock and then stir in the mushrooms and fish. Add the lemon juice, and season to taste with salt and pepper. Spoon the mixture into the cooked pastry case (pie shell) and serve.

Snails with Ceps

An unusual and delicious mushroom and snail filling goes into shell-shaped pastry cases.

Serves 4

350g/12oz puff pastry
1 egg, beaten, to glaze
25g/1oz/½ cup grated Parmesan cheese
50g/2oz/4 tbsp unsalted butter
2 shallots, finely chopped
50g/2oz fennel, finely chopped
50g/2oz fine green beans, cut in three
115g/4oz/1¼ cups fresh ceps, sliced, or 15g/½oz/¼ cup dried ceps, soaked in warm water for 20 minutes and chopped
1 garlic clove, crushed
75ml/5 tbsp dry sherry
150ml/¼ pint/⅔ cup beef stock
10ml/2 tsp cornflour (cornstarch)
5ml/1 tsp Dijon mustard
2 x 200g/7oz cans snails, drained
2.5ml/½ tsp black olive paste
5ml/1 tsp balsamic or wine vinegar
salt and ground black pepper
45ml/3 tbsp chopped parsley, to garnish

1 Roll out the pastry on a floured surface to a 30cm/12in square. Cut out eight 10cm/4in fluted rings, then cut four circles with a 7.5cm/3in plain (cookie) cutter. Place on a baking sheet, top each with two pastry rings and brush with beaten egg.

2 Roll out the trimmings in a dusting of Parmesan cheese, cut into 2cm/¾in wide strips and wind around four cream horn moulds. Chill all the pastry shapes for about 1 hour.

3 Preheat the oven to 200°C/400°F/Gas 6. Melt the butter in a large non-stick frying pan, and gently fry the shallots, fennel and beans until soft but not brown. Add the ceps and garlic and sauté for another 6 minutes. Add the sherry and beef stock to the pan and simmer briefly. Bake the pastry shapes for about 25 minutes until crisp.

4 Place the cornflour and mustard in a cup and blend with 15ml/1 tbsp cold water. Stir the cornflour mixture into the pan and simmer to thicken. Add the snails and the olive paste and simmer to heat through, then add the vinegar. Season to taste.

5 Spoon the mixture into the pastry shapes and sprinkle with chopped parsley. Serve with creamed potatoes and cabbage.

Seafood Ring Energy 771kcal/3218kJ; Protein 33.7g; Carbohydrate 45.2g, of which sugars 2.6g; Fat 48.4g, of which saturates 24.5g; Cholesterol 162mg; Calcium 127mg; Fibre 2g; Sodium 498mg.
Snails with Ceps Energy 556kcal/2319kJ; Protein 19.4g; Carbohydrate 38.8g, of which sugars 2.8g; Fat 34.7g, of which saturates 17.9g; Cholesterol 118mg; Calcium 187mg; Fibre 2.2g; Sodium 674mg.

Chicken Parcels with Herb Butter

These chicken parcels are flavoured with parsley and nutmeg, and will be an instant success with your dinner guests.

Makes 35

225g/8oz/2 cups strong white bread flour, plus extra for dusting
2.5ml/½ tsp salt
2.5ml/½ tsp caster (superfine) sugar
5ml/1 tsp easy-blend (rapid-rise) dried yeast
25g/1oz/2 tbsp butter, softened
1 egg, beaten, plus a little extra
90ml/6 tbsp warm milk
lemon wedges, to serve
flat leaf parsley, to garnish

For the filling

1 small onion, finely chopped
175g/6oz/1½ cups minced (ground) chicken
15ml/1 tbsp sunflower oil
75ml/5 tbsp chicken stock
30ml/2 tbsp chopped fresh parsley
pinch of grated nutmeg
salt and ground black pepper

1 Sift the flour, salt and sugar into a large bowl. Stir in the dried yeast, then make a well in the centre of the flour. Add the butter, egg and milk and mix to a soft dough. Turn on to a lightly floured surface and knead for 10 minutes, until the dough is smooth and elastic. Put the dough in a clean bowl, cover with clear film (plastic wrap) and then leave in a warm place to rise for 1 hour, or until the dough has doubled in size.

2 Meanwhile, fry the onion and chicken in the oil for about 10 minutes. Add the stock and simmer for 5 minutes. Stir in the parsley, grated nutmeg and seasoning. Leave to cool.

3 Preheat the oven to 220°C/425°F/Gas 7. Knead the dough, then roll it out until it is 3mm/⅛in thick. Stamp out rounds with a 7.5cm/3in cutter. Brush the edges with beaten egg. Put a little filling in the middle, then press the edges together. Leave to rise on oiled baking sheets, covered with oiled clear film (plastic wrap), for 15 minutes.

4 Brush the pastry with more egg. Bake for 5 minutes, then for 10 minutes at 190°C/375°F/Gas 5, until well risen. Serve with lemon wedges and garnish with flat leaf parsley.

Chicken and Couscous Turnover

This is a version of the Turkish börek, a rich pastry parcel with a savoury filling. Serve with a minty yogurt.

Serves 4

50g/2oz/⅓ cup couscous
45ml/3 tbsp olive oil
1 onion, chopped
115g/4oz/1⅔ cups mushrooms
1 garlic clove, crushed
115g/4oz cooked chicken, diced
30ml/2 tbsp walnuts, chopped
30ml/2 tbsp raisins
5ml/1 tsp chopped fresh thyme
2 eggs, hard-boiled and peeled
salt and ground black pepper

For the pastry

400g/14oz/3½ cups self-raising (self-rising) flour
5ml/1 tsp salt
1 egg, plus extra for glazing
150ml/¼ pint/⅔ cup yogurt
150ml/¼ pint/⅔ cup olive oil
grated rind of ½ lemon
plain (all-purpose) flour, for rolling

For the yogurt sauce

200ml/7fl oz/scant 1 cup natural (plain) yogurt
45ml/3 tbsp chopped fresh mint
2.5ml/½ tsp caster (superfine) sugar
1.5ml/¼ tsp cayenne pepper
1.5ml/¼ tsp celery salt

1 Preheat the oven to 190°C/375°F/Gas 5. Just cover the couscous with boiling water and soak for 10 minutes or until all the liquid is absorbed.

2 Heat the oil in a pan and cook the chopped onion without letting it colour. Add the mushrooms and garlic, and cook until the juices begin to run. Increase the heat to boil off the juices. Transfer the mushroom and onion mixture to a bowl, mix in the chicken, walnuts, raisins, thyme and couscous. Chop the eggs and stir them into the mixture with seasoning to taste.

3 To make the pastry, sift the flour and salt into a bowl. Make a well in the centre, add the egg, yogurt, olive oil and lemon rind, and mix together with a round-bladed knife. Turn out onto a floured surface and roll into a 30cm/12in round.

4 Pile the filling into the centre and bring the edges over to enclose the filling. Turn upside down on to a baking sheet and press flat. Glaze with beaten egg and bake for 25 minutes. Blend together all the ingredients for the sauce. Serve the pie warm, with the sauce spooned over the top.

Parcels with Butter Energy 885kcal/3707kJ; Protein 28.3g; Carbohydrate 97.2g, of which sugars 14.5g; Fat 45.5g, of which saturates 7.1g; Cholesterol 164mg; Calcium 369mg; Fibre 4.5g; Sodium 156mg.
Chicken Turnover Energy 554kcal/2310kJ; Protein 42.5g; Carbohydrate 14.8g, of which sugars 0.5g; Fat 36.6g, of which saturates 22g; Cholesterol 240mg; Calcium 138mg; Fibre 0.6g; Sodium 417mg.

Pork Sausage Plait

Local butchers often sell a wonderful variety of their own sausages, including venison, pork and apple, and herb. All taste delicious when wrapped around a wild mushroom filling and baked in pastry.

Serves 4

50g/2oz/4 tbsp butter
½ garlic clove, crushed
15ml/1 tbsp chopped fresh thyme
450g/1lb assorted wild and cultivated mushrooms, sliced
50g/2oz/1 cup fresh white breadcrumbs
75ml/5 tbsp chopped fresh parsley
350g/12oz puff pastry
675g/1½lb best pork sausages
1 egg, beaten with a pinch of salt
salt and ground black pepper

1 Melt the butter in a large frying pan and soften the garlic, thyme and mushrooms gently for 5–6 minutes.

2 When the mushroom juices begin to run, increase the heat to drive off the liquid, then stir in the breadcrumbs, parsley and salt and black pepper.

3 Roll out the pastry on a floured surface to a 36 x 25cm/14 x 10in rectangle. Place on a large baking sheet.

4 Skin the sausages. Place half of the sausagemeat in a 13cm/5in strip along the centre of the pastry. Cover the sausage layer with the mushroom mixture, then top this with the rest of the sausagemeat.

5 Make a series of slanting 2.5cm/1in cuts in the pastry on either side of the filling, leaving an uncut margin down the sides of the filling. Fold each end of the pastry over the filling, moisten the pastry with beaten egg and then cross the top with alternate strips of pastry from each side.

6 Allow the plait to rest for 40 minutes. Preheat the oven to 180°C/350°F/Gas 4. Brush the plait with a little more egg and bake for 1 hour. Leave the plait to rest for about 5–10 minutes before serving and slicing, or leave it to cool completely for eating cold.

Chicken, Cheese and Leek Plait

Strips of puff pastry are cleverly crossed over a creamy chicken filling to make this attractive family-size pie, which tastes good either warm or cold.

Serves 6

1 roast chicken, about 1.6kg/3½lb
40g/1½oz/3 tbsp butter
2 large leeks, thinly sliced
2 garlic cloves, crushed
115g/4oz/1 cup button (white) mushrooms, sliced
200g/7oz/scant 1 cup low-fat cream cheese
grated rind of 1 small lemon
45ml/3 tbsp chopped fresh flat leaf parsley
500g/1¼lb puff pastry
1 egg, beaten
salt and ground black pepper
fresh herbs, to garnish

1 Strip the meat from the chicken, discarding the skin and bones. Chop or shred the meat and set it aside.

2 Melt the butter in a pan, add the leeks and garlic and cook for 10 minutes. Stir in the mushrooms and cook for 5 minutes. Leave to cool, then add the cream cheese, lemon rind, parsley and seasoning. Stir in the chicken.

3 Roll out the pastry on a lightly floured work surface to a large rectangle, about 35 x 25cm/14 x 10in. Using a rolling pin to help you, lift the pastry onto a non-stick baking sheet.

4 Spoon the filling on to the pastry, leaving a margin at each end, and about 10cm/4in on each long side. Use a sharp knife to cut the pastry sides diagonally in strips, cutting up to the filling at 2cm/¾in intervals. Preheat the oven to 200°C/400°F/Gas 6.

5 Brush the edges of the pastry with a little of the beaten egg. Cross the pastry strips over each other alternately to enclose the filling. Seal the edges. Glaze with beaten egg.

6 Bake for about 15 minutes, then lower the oven temperature to 190°C/375°F/Gas 5 and bake for a further 15 minutes, or until the pastry is golden brown and crisp. Allow to stand for 10 minutes before sliding the parcel on to a board or platter to serve. Garnish with herbs.

Pork Sausage Plait Energy 822kcal/3424kJ; Protein 26g; Carbohydrate 55g, of which sugars 4g; Fat 58g, of which saturates 17g; Cholesterol 1350mg; Calcium 189mg; Fibre 6.2g; Sodium 2076mg.
Chicken Plait Energy 667kcal/2788kJ; Protein 48g; Carbohydrate 33.9g, of which sugars 3.7g; Fat 38.6g, of which saturates 17.5g; Cholesterol 226mg; Calcium 125mg; Fibre 2.2g; Sodium 560mg.

Lamb Roll with Pear Stuffing

Cooking lamb with fruit is an idea taken from traditional Persian cuisine. You'll need skewers and string for tying.

Serves 6
1 boned mid-loin of lamb, 1kg/2lb
8 large sheets filo pastry
25g/1oz/ 2 tbsp butter, melted
salt and ground black pepper

For the stuffing
15ml/1 tbsp butter
1 small onion, chopped
115g/4oz/2 cups wholemeal (whole-wheat) breadcrumbs
grated rind of 1 lemon
175g/6oz drained canned pears from a 400g/14oz can
1.5ml/¼ tsp ground ginger
1 small egg, beaten

1 Preheat the oven to 180°C/350°F/Gas Mark 4. Prepare the stuffing. Melt the butter in a pan and add the onion, cooking until soft. Put the butter and onion into a mixing bowl and add the breadcrumbs, lemon rind, pears and ginger. Season lightly and add enough beaten egg to bind.

2 Spread the loin out flat, fat side down, and season. Place the stuffing along the middle of the loin and roll carefully, holding with skewers while you sew it together with string.

3 Heat a large roasting pan in the oven and brown the loin slowly on all sides. This will take 20–30 minutes. Leave to cool completely, then store in the refrigerator until needed.

4 Preheat the oven to 200°C/400°F/Gas 6. Take two sheets of filo pastry and brush with melted butter. Overlap by about 13cm/5in to make a square. Place the next two sheets on top and brush with more of the butter. Continue this process until all the pastry is used up.

5 Place the roll of lamb diagonally across one corner of the pastry, without overlapping the sides. Fold the corner over the lamb, fold in the sides, and brush the pastry well with melted butter. Roll to the far corner of the sheet.

6 Place join side down on a buttered baking sheet and brush all over with the rest of the melted butter. Bake for 30 minutes or until golden brown. Serve warm, in slices.

Beef Wellington

This dish, a dinner party favourite, is derived from the classic French boeuf en croûte. The English name was applied to it in honour of the Duke of Wellington, following his victory at the Battle of Waterloo in 1815. Begin preparing the dish well in advance to allow time for the meat to cool before it is wrapped in pastry.

Serves 6
1.5kg/3lb 6oz fillet of beef
45ml/3 tbsp oil
115g/4oz mushrooms, chopped
2 garlic cloves, crushed
175g/6oz smooth liver pâté
30ml/2 tbsp chopped fresh parsley
400g/14oz puff pastry
beaten egg, to glaze
salt and ground black pepper

1 Tie the fillet at intervals with string. Heat 30ml/2 tbsp of the oil, and brown on all sides over a high heat. Transfer to a roasting pan and cook in the oven for 20 minutes. Leave to cool.

2 Heat the remaining oil and cook the mushrooms and garlic for 5 minutes. Beat the mushrooms into the pâté. Add the parsley, season and leave to cool.

3 Roll out the pastry, reserving a small amount, into a rectangle large enough to enclose the beef. Spread the pâté mixture down the middle, untie the beef and lay it on the pâté.

4 Preheat the oven to 220°C/425°F/Gas 7. Brush the pastry edges with beaten egg and fold it over the meat. Place, seam down, on a baking sheet. Cut leaves from the reserved pastry and decorate the top. Brush the parcel with beaten egg. Chill for 10 minutes or until the oven is hot.

5 Cook for 50–60 minutes, covering loosely with foil after about 30 minutes to prevent the pastry from burning. Once done, let it rest for 5–10 minutes then cut into thick slices.

Cook's Tip
Use the best beef and a very good quality pâté for this recipe.

Lamb Roll Energy 440kcal/1850kJ; Protein 57g; Carbohydrate 21g, of which sugars 10g; Fat 16g, of which saturates 6g; Cholesterol 179mg; Calcium 69mg; Fibre 3.2g; Sodium 358mg.
Beef Wellington Energy 849kcal/3532kJ; Protein 34.1g; Carbohydrate 45.3g, of which sugars 3g; Fat 61.1g, of which saturates 33.6g; Cholesterol 348mg; Calcium 162mg; Fibre 1.5g; Sodium 602mg.

Leg of Lamb in Pastry

This is an impressive dish to serve on special occasions. Skim the meat juices, bring them back to the boil and serve as a gravy. You will need plenty of time to make this, as the meat must cool before wrapping in pastry, otherwise it will make the pastry soggy.

Serves 4

1.5kg/3½lb leg of lamb, boned
40g/1½oz/3 tbsp butter
2.5ml/½ tsp each dried thyme, basil and oregano
2 garlic cloves, crushed
45ml/3 tbsp lemon juice
salt, for sprinkling
1 egg, beaten

For the pastry

450g/1lb/4 cups plain (all-purpose) flour, sifted
250g/9oz/generous 1 cup chilled butter, diced
150–250ml/¼–½ pint/⅔–1 cup iced water

1 Preheat the oven to 190°/375°F/Gas 5. To make the pastry, place the flour and butter in a food processor or blender and process until the mixture resembles fine breadcrumbs. Add enough iced water to make a soft dough. Form into a ball. Wrap in clear film (plastic wrap) and refrigerate for 1–2 hours.

2 Meanwhile, tie the joint with string so it keeps its shape, and cut 20 small holes in the meat, with a sharp, narrow knife. Put the lamb in a roasting pan.

3 Cream together the butter, dried herbs, garlic and lemon juice and use to fill the small cuts in the lamb. Sprinkle with salt. Cook the lamb for about 1 hour, then allow to cool. Remove the string and retain the meat juices in the pan.

4 Preheat the oven to 190°/375°F/Gas 5. Roll out the pastry on a lightly floured surface until large enough to enclose the meat. Place the cooled lamb in one half of the pastry and fold the other half over. Seal the pastry edges with a little of the egg and place in a clean pan. Brush with the rest of the egg.

5 Bake in the oven for 30–45 minutes until golden. Serve hot, in thin slices, accompanied by the reheated meat juices and some fresh seasonal vegetables.

Chard and Bacon Pasties

Unlike some green vegetables, chard can survive a little extra cooking and is substantial enough to be the principal ingredient. For a more savoury pastry, add a handful of grated cheese.

Serves 4

675g/1½lb Swiss chard
25g/1oz/2 tbsp butter
1 onion, finely chopped
75g/3oz/½ cup chopped streaky (fatty) bacon
50g/2oz/½ cup grated Gruyère cheese
25g/1oz/½ cup fresh breadcrumbs
90ml/6 tbsp single (light) cream
salt and black pepper

For the pastry

275g/10oz/2½ cups plain (all-purpose) flour
150g/5oz/10 tbsp butter
a pinch of salt
beaten egg for glazing

1 To make the pastry, place the flour and salt in a bowl and rub in the fat. Add a little cold water and mix to a soft dough. Knead on a floured surface. Wrap and chill for 30 minutes.

2 Trim the stalks of the chard and then chop both the leaves and stalk. Place in a heavy pan, cover and cook over a low heat for 6–8 minutes until the stalks are tender and the leaves wilted. Shake the pan occasionally. Strain and press out the excess liquid using the back of a spoon, then place in a mixing bowl and leave to cool.

3 Melt the butter in a small frying pan and fry the onion and bacon for about 4–5 minutes, until the onion is lightly golden and the bacon is browned.

4 Add the onion and bacon to the chard and stir in the cheese, breadcrumbs, cream and seasoning to taste. Preheat the oven to 200°C/400°F/Gas 6.

5 Divide the pastry into four and roll out into rounds. Spoon the filling on to the centre of each and dampen the edges with water. Bring the sides together over the filling and press together to seal. Brush with beaten egg and then put on an oiled baking sheet. Bake for 15–20 minutes, until golden.

Lamb in Pastry Energy 768kcal/3201kJ; Protein 33.8g; Carbohydrate 44.1g, of which sugars 1.2g; Fat 51.9g, of which saturates 26.3g; Cholesterol 187mg; Calcium 104mg; Fibre 2.1g; Sodium 310mg.
Chard Pasties Energy 752kcal/3136kJ; Protein 18g; Carbohydrate 62g, of which sugars 3g; Fat 50g, of which saturates 30g; Cholesterol 132mg; Calcium 337mg; Fibre 3g; Sodium 996mg.

Beef and Curd Cheese Pasties

This recipe from Finland uses a rich pastry, that is flavoured with curd cheese, and a flavoursome egg and beef filling.

Serves 6

25g/1oz/2 tbsp butter
1 onion, chopped
1 small celery stick, thinly sliced
500g/1¼lb minced (ground) beef
6 hard-boiled eggs, chopped
200g/7oz cooked rice
5ml/1 tsp ground allspice
pinch salt
2.5ml/½ tsp ground white pepper
1 egg
beaten egg, to glaze

For the pastry
250g/9oz/2¼ cups plain (all-purpose) flour
250g/9oz/1 cup butter
250g/9oz/generous 1 cup curd (farmers') cheese

1 To make the pastry, put the flour in a bowl. Cut the butter into small pieces, add to the flour and rub in until the mixture resembles fine breadcrumbs. Alternatively put the flour in a food processor, add the butter and, using a pulsating action, blend to form fine breadcrumbs.

2 Mix the curd cheese into the flour mixture and use your hands to form the dough into a ball. Leave to rest.

3 Melt the butter in a pan, add the onion and celery and fry for about 5 minutes, until softened. Add the beef and fry, stirring occasionally, for 8–10 minutes until browned.

4 Turn the mince mixture into a bowl. Stir in the hard-boiled eggs, rice, allspice, salt and pepper. Add the raw egg and mix to bind the mixture together.

5 Preheat the oven to 200°C/400°F/Gas 6. On a lightly floured surface, roll out the pastry into six 10cm/4in rounds. Brush the edges with water and place a tablespoonful of the filling in the centre of each round. Fold the pastry over the filling to make a pasty shape and crimp the edges to seal in the filling.

6 Place the pasties on a baking tray and brush with beaten egg. Bake in the oven for 30 minutes, until golden. Serve warm.

Pheasant Pasty

This game pasty is packed with a little of everything and can be served on its own or accompanied by mashed potatoes and gravy.

Makes 10

30ml/2 tbsp vegetable oil
1 small onion, finely diced
450g/1lb pheasant breast, minced (ground)
450g/1lb minced (ground) pork
115g/4oz smoked streaky (fatty) bacon very finely diced
pinch of ground cinnamon
pinch of ground ginger
5ml/1 tsp dried thyme
45ml/3 tbsp apple juice
50g/2oz/1 cup fresh breadcrumbs
1 crisp eating apple, grated
30ml/2 tbsp parsley, chopped
15ml/1 tbsp sage, chopped
675g/1½lb/6 cups plain (all-purpose) flour, plus extra for rolling
350g/12oz lard, diced
2 eggs, beaten
sea salt and ground black pepper

1 Heat the oil in a large pan over medium heat. Place the onion, pheasant, pork, bacon, spices and thyme in the pan and cook, stirring occasionally, for 15 minutes. Add the apple juice, breadcrumbs, apple, parsley and sage and season. Stir to fully incorporate all the ingredients and cook for 5 minutes.

2 Reduce the heat to low and continue to cook for about 10–15 minutes, stirring regularly to prevent the ingredients sticking to the pan. Transfer to a tray and leave to cool.

3 While the filling is cooling, make the pastry. Place the flour, lard and a generous pinch of salt in a bowl and rub the fat into the flour with your fingers. Add sufficient cold water (approximately 60ml/4 tbsp) to make a soft, pliable dough. Form the dough into a ball, wrap in clear film (plastic wrap) and chill for at least 30 minutes. Preheat oven to 200°C/400°F/Gas 6.

4 Once the pastry has rested, roll out to a thickness of 3mm/⅛in. Cut 10 circles out of the rolled pastry using a 15cm/6in bowl as a template. Divide the filling evenly among the cases, spooning it into the centre; brush half the edge of each case with beaten egg and fold up over the filling and seal. Transfer to a baking sheet, brush with the remaining egg and bake for 15 minutes, until golden.

Beef Pasties Energy 511kcal/2131kJ; Protein 41.7g; Carbohydrate 19.3g, of which sugars 1.2g; Fat 30.6g, of which saturates 7.2g; Cholesterol 128mg; Calcium 41mg; Fibre 0.4g; Sodium 320mg.
Pheasant Pasty Energy 751kcal/3137kJ; Protein 32.4g; Carbohydrate 57.8g, of which sugars 2.5g; Fat 42.2g, of which saturates 17.1g; Cholesterol 99mg; Calcium 134mg; Fibre 2.4g; Sodium 132mg.

Steak and Onion Pasties

Best quality beef steak is the traditional filling for pasties, although you can also use lamb. These pasties don't have any vegetables other than onion, and are perfect served either cold or warmed for lunch.

Makes 10

For the pastry

900g/2lb/8 cups plain (all-purpose) flour
225g/8oz/1 cup butter
225g/8oz/1 cup lard or white cooking fat
pinch of salt
a little milk, for glazing

For the filling

1.2kg/2½lb rump (round) steak
225g/8oz/1¾ cups beef suet (US chilled, grated shortening)
5 onions, finely chopped
salt and ground black pepper

1 Preheat the oven to 200°C/400°F/Gas 6. Using a mixer, place the flour in the mixing bowl and blend in the butter and lard or white cooking fat using the dough hook.

2 Add salt to the bowl and mix to a stiff dough, adding water gradually as needed. Leave the pastry ball to rest in clear film (plastic wrap) for 30 minutes.

3 Meanwhile, trim the meat of any excess fat and cut into 1cm/½in squares. Chop the suet finely then mix with the meat and onions. Season with salt and pepper.

4 Divide the pastry into ten equal pieces. Roll out each piece into an oval, not too thinly, and divide the meat mixture among them at one end, leaving an edge for sealing.

5 Dampen the edges of each pastry oval with cold water and fold the pastry over the filling. Press the edges down to seal – then use a fork to make sure the edges are stuck together securely and make a pattern around the edges.

6 Make a hole in the top of each pasty, then place on a greased baking sheet. Brush the tops with a little milk, then bake in the preheated oven for 45 minutes. Serve warm, or cool on a wire rack for lunch boxes the next day.

Cornish Pasties

These traditional pastries are made with potato and swede to bulk out the beef. The filling is raw when enclosed in the pastry, so they must be cooked thoroughly.

Makes 6

450g/1lb chuck steak, diced
1 potato, about 175g/6oz, diced
175g/6oz swede (rutabaga), diced
1 onion, chopped
2.5ml/½ tsp dried mixed herbs
1 egg, beaten
salt and ground black pepper
salad, to garnish

For the pastry

350g/12oz/3 cups plain (all-purpose) flour
pinch of salt
115g/4oz/½ cup butter, diced
50g/2oz/¼ cup lard or white vegetable fat
75–90ml/5–6 tbsp chilled water

1 To make the pastry, sift the flour and salt into a bowl. Using your fingertips or a pastry blender, lightly rub or cut in the butter and lard or vegetable fat, then sprinkle over most of the chilled water and mix to a soft dough, adding more water if necessary. Knead the pastry on a lightly floured surface for a few seconds until smooth. Wrap in clear film (plastic wrap) and chill for 30 minutes.

2 Preheat the oven to 220°C/425°F/Gas 7. Divide the pastry into six pieces, then roll out each piece on a lightly floured surface to a 20cm/8in round.

3 Mix together the steak, vegetables, herbs and seasoning in a large bowl, then spoon an equal amount of the filling on to one half of each pastry round.

4 Brush the pastry edges with water, then fold the free half of each round over the filling. Press the edges firmly together to seal, then use your fingertips to crimp the edges.

5 Brush the pasties with the egg. Bake for 15 minutes, reduce the oven to 160°C/325°F/Gas 3 and bake for 1 hour more.

6 Serve the pasties immediately while hot or leave to cool and eat cold as part of a picnic or light lunch.

Steak Pasties Energy 1131kcal/4714kJ; Protein 37.7g; Carbohydrate 84.8g, of which sugars 4.5g; Fat 74.5g, of which saturates 37.9g; Cholesterol 171mg; Calcium 162mg; Fibre 3.9g; Sodium 232mg.
Cornish Pasties Energy 414kcal/1731kJ; Protein 10.4g; Carbohydrate 38.8g, of which sugars 1.4g; Fat 25.3g, of which saturates 9.2g; Cholesterol 51mg; Calcium 93mg; Fibre 1.4g; Sodium 620mg.

Beef Turnovers

A tasty layer of rice and juicy wild mushrooms tops each fillet steak before it is wrapped in puff pastry.

Serves 4

20g/¾oz/¼ cup dried wild mushrooms, soaked for 10 minutes in warm water to cover
115g/4oz/1½–1¾ cups morel mushrooms, trimmed and sliced
about 45ml/3 tbsp olive oil
4 shallots, finely chopped
1 garlic clove, crushed
20g/¾oz/1½ tbsp butter
175g/6oz/1½ cups cooked white long grain rice
10ml/2 tsp chopped marjoram
15ml/1 tbsp finely chopped parsley
4 fillet steaks, each about 90g/3½oz and 2.5cm/1in thick
275g/10oz puff pastry
10ml/2 tsp Dijon mustard
1 egg, mixed with a little water
salt and ground black pepper
roast potatoes and patty pan squash, to serve (optional)

1 Preheat the oven to 220°C/425°F/Gas 7. Drain the dried mushrooms, reserving the liquid, and chop finely.

2 Heat 15ml/1 tbsp of the olive oil in a frying pan and fry the shallots and garlic for 2–3 minutes until soft, stirring occasionally. Add the butter to the pan. When it foams, add the mushrooms and cook for 3–4 minutes more, stirring occasionally. Scrape the mixture into a large bowl. Add the rice and stir in the marjoram and parsley. Season to taste.

3 Heat the remaining olive oil in the pan and fry the steaks for about 30 seconds on each side until browned. Remove from the pan and set aside to cool.

4 Cut the pastry into four and roll out each piece into an 18cm/7in circle. Trim the top and bottom edges. Spread a little mustard over each steak then place on one side of each piece of pastry. Spoon a quarter of the mushroom and rice mixture on top of each steak.

5 Fold the pastry over to make a pasty, sealing the join with a little of the egg wash. Place them on an oiled baking sheet. Slit the top of each pasty, dand glaze with more egg wash. Bake in the oven for about 15 minutes, until the pastry is golden.

Meat Briouates

The Moroccans, who enjoy the taste of sweet and savoury together, sprinkle these little pastry snacks with ground cinnamon and icing sugar.

Makes about 24

175g/6oz filo pastry
40g/1½oz/3 tbsp butter, melted
sunflower oil, for frying
fresh flat leaf parsley, to garnish
ground cinnamon and icing (confectioners') sugar, to serve

For the meat filling
30ml/2 tbsp sunflower oil
1 onion, finely chopped
1 small bunch fresh coriander (cilantro), chopped
1 small bunch fresh parsley, chopped
375g/12oz lean minced (ground) beef or lamb
2.5ml/½ tsp paprika
5ml/1 tsp ground coriander
good pinch of ground ginger
2 eggs, beaten

1 First make the filling. Heat the oil in a frying pan and fry the onion and herbs over a low heat for about 4 minutes until softened. Add the meat and cook for about 5 minutes, stirring frequently, until the meat is browned.

2 Drain away any excess fat, stir in the spices and fry for a minute. Remove the pan from the heat and stir in the beaten eggs until they begin to set. Set aside.

3 Cut a sheet of filo pastry into 8.5cm/3½in strips. Cover the remaining pastry with clear film (plastic wrap) to prevent it drying out. Brush the strip with melted butter, then place a heaped teaspoon of the meat filling at one end of the strip, about 1cm/½in from the end. Fold one corner over the filling to make a triangular shape.

4 Fold the triangle over itself and then continue to fold, keeping the triangle shape, until you reach the end of the strip. Continue in this way until all the mixture has been used up.

5 Heat about 1cm/½in oil in a heavy pan and fry the briouates in batches for 2–3 minutes until golden, turning once. Drain on kitchen paper and arrange on a plate. Serve garnished with parsley and sprinkled with cinnamon and icing sugar.

Beef Turnovers Energy 576kcal/2401kJ; Protein 26.3g; Carbohydrate 50.2g, of which sugars 2.2g; Fat 31.2g, of which saturates 3.8g; Cholesterol 55mg; Calcium 72mg; Fibre 1g; Sodium 331mg.
Meat Briouates Energy 136kcal/565kJ; Protein 4.6g; Carbohydrate 6.1g, of which sugars 0.4g; Fat 10.5g, of which saturates 2.5g; Cholesterol 24mg; Calcium 21mg; Fibre 0.6g; Sodium 30mg.

Beef and Mushroom Pudding

Based on a great British classic, this steamed pudding has a light herb pastry crust.

Serves 4

60ml/4 tbsp flour
675g/1½lb braising steak, diced
45ml/3 tbsp sunflower oil
1 large onion, finely chopped
225g/8oz mushrooms, sliced
1 bay leaf
15ml/1 tbsp Worcestershire sauce
75ml/2½fl oz/⅓ cup red wine
475ml/16fl oz/2 cups beef stock
salt and ground black pepper

For the pastry

275g/10oz/2½ cups self-raising (self-rising) flour
2.5ml/½ tsp baking powder
2.5ml/½ tsp salt
15ml/1 tbsp each chopped parsley and fresh thyme
75g/3oz/1½ cups beef suet (US chilled, grated shortening)
50g/2oz/¼ cup butter, frozen and grated
1 egg, lightly beaten
about 150ml/¼ pint/⅔ cup cold water

1 Place the flour in a bowl, season, then add the meat and toss to coat. Heat the oil in a frying pan and fry the meat in batches until browned on all sides. Transfer to a large casserole. Preheat the oven to 160°C/325°F/Gas 3.

2 Add the onion to the pan and cook gently for 10 minutes. Transfer to the casserole with the mushrooms, bay leaf, Worcestershire sauce, wine and stock into the pot. Cook in the oven for 2 hours until the meat is very tender. Cool completely.

3 Butter a deep 1.75 litre/3 pint/7½ cup heatproof bowl. Sift the flour, baking powder and salt into a mixing bowl and stir in the herbs followed by the suet and butter. Make a well in the centre, add the egg and enough cold water to mix, and gather into a soft dough. Use three-quarters of the pastry to line the heatproof bowl, allowing the excess to fall over the sides, and then spoon in the filling, reserving the gravy to serve.

4 Roll out the reserved pastry to make a round large enough to use as a lid for the pudding and place on top of the pudding, pressing the edges together to seal. Cover with pleated, double thick layer of baking parchment, and then foil. Steam for 3 hours. Invert the pudding onto a plate and serve with the gravy.

Steak and Kidney Pudding

This classic dish is a 19th-century invention that has, in a relatively short time, become one of England's most famous dishes.

Serves 6

500g/1¼lb stewing steak, cubed
225g/8oz beef kidney or lamb's kidneys, skin and core removed and cut into small cubes
1 medium onion, finely chopped
30ml/2 tbsp finely chopped fresh parsley and thyme
30ml/2 tbsp plain (all-purpose) flour
275g/10oz/2½ cups self-raising (self-rising) flour
150g/5oz/1 cup shredded suet (US chilled, grated shortening)
finely grated rind of 1 small lemon
about 120ml/4fl oz/½ cup beef stock or water
salt and ground black pepper

1 Put the stewing steak into a large mixing bowl and add the kidneys, onion and chopped herbs. Sprinkle the plain flour and seasoning over the top and mix well.

2 To make the pastry, sift the self-raising flour into another large bowl. Stir in the suet and lemon rind. Add sufficient cold water to bind the ingredients and gather into a soft dough. On a lightly floured surface knead the dough gently, and then roll out to make a circle measuring about 35cm/14in across. Cut out one-quarter of the circle, roll up and put aside.

3 Lightly butter a 1.75 litre/3 pint/7½ cup heatproof bowl. Line the bowl with the rolled out dough, pressing the cut edges together and allowing the pastry to overlap the top of the bowl slightly. Carefully spoon the steak mixture into the lined bowl.

4 Pour in sufficient stock to reach no more than three-quarters of the way up the filling. (Any stock remaining can be heated and poured into the cooked pudding to thin the gravy if desired.)

5 Roll out the reserved pastry into a circle to form a lid and lay it over the filling, pinching the edges together to seal them well. Cover with greaseproof paper or baking parchment, pleated in the centre to allow the pudding to rise, and then with a large sheet of foil (again pleated at the centre). Steam for 5 hours. Invert the pudding onto a plate and serve.

Beef Pudding: Energy 1061Kcal/4444kJ; Protein 70g; Carbohydrate 75.1g, of which sugars 4.8g; Fat 54.3g, of which saturates 24.5g; Cholesterol 265mg; Calcium 319mg; Fibre 4.4g; Sodium 941mg.
Steak and Kidney Energy 436kcal/1835kJ; Protein 31.1g; Carbohydrate 49.5g, of which sugars 4.8g; Fat 13.9g, of which saturates 3.6g; Cholesterol 166mg; Calcium 201mg; Fibre 1.9g; Sodium 380mg.

Red Onion Tart

Red onions are wonderfully mild and sweet when cooked and they go well with fontina cheese and thyme in this wintery tart.

Serves 5–6

60ml/4 tbsp olive oil
1kg/2¼lb red onions, thinly sliced
2–3 garlic cloves, thinly sliced
5ml/1 tsp chopped fresh thyme, plus a few whole sprigs
5ml/1 tsp soft dark brown sugar
10ml/2 tsp sherry vinegar
225g/8oz fontina cheese, sliced
salt and ground black pepper

For the pastry

115g/4oz/1 cup plain (all-purpose) flour
75g/3oz/¾ cup fine yellow cornmeal
5ml/1 tsp soft dark brown sugar
5ml/1 tsp chopped fresh thyme
90g/3½oz/7 tbsp butter
1 egg yolk

1 For the pastry, sift the flour and cornmeal into a bowl with 5ml/1 tsp salt. Add black pepper and stir in the sugar and thyme. Rub in the butter until it looks like breadcrumbs. Beat the egg yolk with 30ml/2 tbsp iced water and use to bind the pastry. Gather the dough into a ball, wrap and chill for 40 minutes.

2 Heat 45ml/3 tbsp of the oil in a large, deep frying pan and add the onions. Cover and cook slowly, stirring occasionally, for 20–30 minutes. They should collapse but not brown.

3 Add the garlic and thyme, then cook for another 10 minutes. Increase the heat slightly, then add the sugar and sherry vinegar. Cook, uncovered, for 5–6 minutes, until the onions start to caramelize slightly. Season to taste with salt and pepper. Cool.

4 Preheat the oven to 190°C/375°F/Gas 5. Roll out the pastry thinly and use to line a 25cm/10in loose-based metal flan tin (pan). Prick the pastry all over with a fork and support the sides with foil. Bake for 12–15 minutes, until lightly coloured.

5 Remove the foil and spread the onions evenly over the base of the pastry. Add the fontina and pepper. Drizzle over the remaining oil, then bake for 15–20 minutes, until the filling is piping hot and the cheese is beginning to bubble. Garnish the tart with thyme and serve immediately.

Cheese and Bacon Quiche

Perfect for parties or family suppers, this celebrates the timeless combination of cheese and onion.

Serves 6–8

25g/1oz/2 tbsp butter
1 large onion, thinly sliced
4 rindless streaky (fatty) bacon rashers (strips), chopped
3 eggs
300ml/½ pint/1¼ cups single (light) cream or milk
1.5ml/¼ tsp grated nutmeg
90g/3½oz Cheddar, grated
salt and ground black pepper

For the pastry

200g/7oz/1¾ cups plain (all-purpose) flour
pinch of salt
90g/3½oz/scant ½ cup butter

1 To make the pastry, sift the flour and salt into a small bowl. Dice and rub in the butter until the mixture resembles fine breadcrumbs. Add 45ml/3 tbsp water and mix to a firm dough, adding more water if required. Knead until smooth, wrap in clear film (plastic wrap) and chill for 20 minutes.

2 Roll out the dough on a clean, lightly floured work surface and use to line a 23cm/9in loose-based flan tin (pan). Press firmly into the sides and base of the tin and let it rise above the rim by about 1cm/½in to allow for a little shrinkage during cooking. Prick the pastry base all over with a fork.

3 Line with foil and baking beans and chill for 15 minutes. Preheat the oven to 200°C/ 400°F/Gas 6 with a baking sheet placed in it. Stand the flan tin on the baking sheet and bake blind for 15 minutes. Remove the foil and beans from the pastry case (pie shell) and return it to the oven for 5 minutes.

4 To make the filling, melt the butter in a large frying pan. Add the onion and chopped bacon and sauté for about 10 minutes until the onion is soft and golden. Beat the eggs and the cream or milk together in a bowl. Add the grated nutmeg and season well. Preheat the oven to 180°C/350°F/Gas 4.

5 Spoon the filling into the cooked pastry case and sprinkle over the cheese. Pour the egg and cream mixture over the filling. Bake for 35–40 minutes, until just set. Serve warm.

Red Onion Tart Energy 621kcal/2581kJ; Protein 18.1g; Carbohydrate 45.6g, of which sugars 12.5g; Fat 40.6g, of which saturates 20.7g; Cholesterol 122mg; Calcium 424mg; Fibre 3.8g; Sodium 443mg.
Cheese and Bacon Energy 670kcal/2775kJ; Protein 13g; Carbohydrate 23.7g, of which sugars 1.4g; Fat 58.9g, of which saturates 32.9g; Cholesterol 302mg; Calcium 94mg; Fibre 0.9g; Sodium 611mg.

Quiche Lorraine

This classic quiche from eastern France has some traditional characteristics that are often forgotten in modern recipes, namely a very egg-rich, creamy filling and no cheese or onion.

Serves 4–6

175g/6oz/1½ cups plain (all-purpose) flour, sifted, plus extra for dusting
pinch of salt
115g/4oz/½ cup unsalted (sweet) butter, at room temperature, diced
3 eggs, plus 3 yolks
6 smoked streaky (fatty) bacon rashers (strips), rinds removed
300ml/½ pint/1¼ cups double (heavy) cream
25g/1oz/2 tbsp unsalted (sweet) butter
salt and ground black pepper

1 Place the flour, salt, butter and 1 egg yolk in a food processor and process until blended. Place on to a lightly floured surface and form into a ball. Leave to rest for 20 minutes.

2 Lightly flour a deep 20cm/8in round flan tin (pan), and place it on a baking tray. Roll out the pastry and use to line the tin, trimming off any overhang. Press the pastry into the corners of the tin. If the pastry breaks up, gently push it into shape. Chill for 20 minutes. Preheat the oven to 200°C/400°F/Gas 6.

3 Cut the bacon into strips and grill (broil). Arrange the bacon in the pastry case (pie shell). Mix the cream, remaining eggs and yolks and seasoning, and pour into the pastry case.

4 Bake in the oven for 15 minutes, then reduce the heat to 180°C/350°F/Gas 4 and bake for a further 15–20 minutes. When the filling is puffed up and golden brown and the pastry edges are crisp, remove from the oven and top with knobs of butter. Stand for 5 minutes before serving.

Cook's Tip

To prepare the quiche in advance, bake for 5–10 minutes less than recommended, until the filling is just set. Reheat later at 190°C/375°F/Gas 5 for about 10 minutes.

Wild Mushroom and Fontina Tart

This tart makes a tasty vegetarian main course, when served with a green salad and fresh crusty bread. Consider using any types of wild mushrooms you like – chanterelles, morels, horns of plenty and ceps all have wonderful flavours from earthy to very delicate.

Serves 6

225g/8oz ready-made shortcrust pastry, thawed if frozen
50g/2oz/¼ cup butter
350g/12oz/5 cups mixed wild mushrooms, sliced if large
150g/5oz fontina cheese, sliced
salt and ground black pepper

1 Preheat the oven to 190°C/375°F/Gas 5. Roll out the pastry on a lightly floured surface.

2 Use the rolled dough to a line a 23cm/9in loose-bottomed flan tin (pan). Chill the pastry for 30 minutes, then line the pastry case (pie shell) with baking parchment, add a layer of baking beans and bake in the oven for 15 minutes. Remove the beans and parchment, and bake for a further 5 minutes, until light golden brown on the edges. Set aside.

3 Heat the butter in a large frying pan until foaming. Add the mushrooms and season with salt and ground black pepper. Cook over medium heat for 4–5 minutes, moving the mushrooms about and turning them occasionally with a wooden spoon, until golden.

4 Arrange the mushrooms in the cooked pastry case with the fontina. Return the tart to the oven for 10 minutes, or until the cheese is golden and bubbling. Serve hot.

Cook's Tip

Picking your own wild mushrooms is a rewarding experience. If you are in any doubt as to the variety, then you should not eat them as there are many poisonous mushrooms out there. While picking, you should carry the mushrooms in a basket so they will release their spores back on to the ground.

Quiche Lorraine Energy 670kcal/2775kJ; Protein 13g; Carbohydrate 23.7g, of which sugars 1.4g; Fat 58.9g, of which saturates 32.9g; Cholesterol 302mg; Calcium 94mg; Fibre 0.9g; Sodium 611mg.
Mushroom Tart Energy 409kcal/1701kJ; Protein 10.2g; Carbohydrate 21.9g, of which sugars 2.3g; Fat 31g, of which saturates 13.4g; Cholesterol 143mg; Calcium 121mg; Fibre 2.3g; Sodium 199mg.

Mushroom and Sunflower Seed Flan

The nutritious flan is full of fibre, antioxidents and vitamins, and is also lower in fat than a more traditional tart. It can be prepared in advance and is good warm or cold.

Serves 4

150g/5oz/1 cup (wholemeal) whole-wheat flour
75g/3oz butter
45ml/3 tbsp walnut or sunflower oil
175g/6oz fresh baby corn
50g/2oz sunflower seeds
225g/7oz button (white) mushrooms, wiped
75g/3oz fresh spinach or defrosted frozen leaf spinach
juice 1 lemon or, if you are on a citrus-free diet, 30ml/2 tbsp cider vinegar
salt and ground black pepper

1 Heat the oven to 180°C/350°F/Gas 4. Make the pastry by rubbing the butter into the flour with your fingertips until the mixture resembles fine breadcrumbs. Add enough cold water to make a firm dough.

2 Roll the pastry out and line a 23–25cm/9–10in flan dish. You can press the pastry out into the flan dish rather than rolling it if it is very crumbly.

3 Prick the bottom of the pastry case (pie shell), line it with baking parchment, and weight it with baking beans. Bake for 10 minutes with the paper, then 10 minutes without, so that the pastry case becomes crisp on the base.

4 Heat the oil in a pan and add the corn and sunflower seeds. Fry briskly till they are browned all over. Be careful not to scorch the seeds.

5 Add the mushrooms, reduce the heat slightly and cook for about 3 minutes. Add the chopped spinach, stir well, cover the pan and cook for a further couple of minutes.

6 Add the lemon juice or vinegar and season well. Make sure the ingredients are well amalgamated, then spoon them into the flan case. Serve the flan immediately, or, if you prefer, leave to cool and serve at room temperature.

Wild Mushroom Tart

Alsace is renowned for its abundance of wild mushrooms. This tart is good with a cool white wine.

Serves 4

225g/8oz ready-made shortcrust pastry, thawed if frozen
50g/2oz/4 tbsp unsalted (sweet) butter
3 medium onions, halved and sliced
350g/12oz/3½ cups assorted wild mushrooms, such as ceps, bay boletus, morels, chanterelles, saffron milk-caps, oyster, field and honey mushrooms
leaves of 1 sprig thyme, chopped
salt and ground black pepper
pinch of freshly grated nutmeg
50ml/3½ tbsp full-fat (whole) milk
50ml/3½ tbsp single (light) cream
1 egg and 2 egg yolks

1 Preheat the oven to 190°C/375°F/Gas 5 and lightly grease a 23cm/9in loose-based flan tin (pan) with butter. Roll out the pastry on a lightly floured board and line the tin. Rest in the refrigerator for 1 hour.

2 Place three squares of baking parchment in the tart crust, fill with baking beans, dried pasta or rice, and bake for 25 minutes. Lift out the baking parchment and baking beans, pasta or rice, and leave to cool.

3 Melt the butter in a frying pan, add the onions, cover and cook slowly for 20 minutes. Add the mushrooms and thyme, and continue cooking for another 10 minutes. Season with salt, pepper and nutmeg.

4 Place the milk and cream in a jug (pitcher) and beat in the egg and egg yolks. Place the mushroom mixture in the tart crust and then pour over the egg mixture. Bake for 15–20 minutes until the centre is firm to the touch. Serve immediately, or leave to cool and serve cold as part of a buffet, picnic or as part of a lunch box for school or work.

Cook's Tip
Cultivated mushrooms can be used instead of wild, but use as wide a variety of types as possible for a really rich flavour.

Mushroom Flan Energy 425kcal/1766kJ; Protein 10.2g; Carbohydrate 27.8g, of which sugars 2.1g; Fat 31g, of which saturates 11.8g; Cholesterol 40mg; Calcium 70mg; Fibre 7.7g; Sodium 643mg.
Mushroom Tart Energy 484kcal/2013kJ; Protein 10.4g; Carbohydrate 36.5g, of which sugars 7.9g; Fat 34.1g, of which saturates 14.6g; Cholesterol 202mg; Calcium 130mg; Fibre 4.8g; Sodium 343mg.

Mushroom and Parmesan Quiche

The tangy salty flavour of Parmesan complements the earthy taste of the mushrooms in this tart.

Serves 8

450g/1lb/6 cups mushrooms
30ml/2 tbsp olive oil
15ml/1 tbsp butter
1 clove garlic, finely chopped
15ml/1 tbsp lemon juice
30ml/2 tbsp finely chopped fresh parsley
3 eggs
350ml/12fl oz/1½ cups double (heavy) cream
65g/2½oz/¾ cup freshly grated Parmesan cheese
salt and ground black pepper

For the pastry

200g/7oz/1¾ cups plain (all-purpose) flour
pinch of salt
90g/3½oz/scant ½ cup butter
65g/2½oz/¾ cup freshly grated Parmesan cheese
45–60ml/3–4 tbsp iced water

1 For the pastry, sift the flour and salt. Dice and rub in the butter until it resembles coarse breadcrumbs. Stir in the grated Parmesan, then add in enough water to bind. Gather the pastry into a ball, wrap in clear film (plastic wrap) and chill for 20 minutes. Preheat a baking sheet in a 190°C/375°F/Gas 5 oven.

2 Roll out the dough 3mm/⅛in thick. Transfer to a 23cm/9in quiche tin (pan) and trim. Prick the base all over with a fork. Line with baking parchment and fill with dried beans. Bake for 12 minutes. Remove the paper and beans and continue baking until golden, for about 5 minutes more. Cool on a wire rack.

3 Wipe the mushrooms with damp kitchen paper to remove any dirt. Trim the stalks and slice these thinly.

4 Heat the olive oil and butter in a frying pan. Stir in the mushrooms, garlic and lemon juice. Season with salt and black pepper. Cook until the mushrooms render their liquid, then raise the heat and cook until dry. Stir in the parsley and season.

5 Whisk the eggs and cream together, then stir in the mushrooms. Sprinkle the cheese over the base of the prebaked pastry case (pie shell) and pour the mushroom filling over the top. Bake for 30 minutes until just firm. Serve the quiche warm.

Vegetable Tarte Tatin

This savoury upside-down tart combines Mediterranean vegetables with a medley of rice, garlic, onions and olives.

Serves 2–3

30ml/2 tbsp sunflower oil
25ml/1½ tbsp olive oil
1 aubergine (eggplant), sliced lengthways
1 large red (bell) pepper, cut into long strips
10 tomatoes
2 red shallots, finely chopped
1–2 garlic cloves, crushed
150ml/¼ pint/⅔ cup white wine
10ml/2 tsp chopped fresh basil
225g/8oz/2 cups cooked white or brown long grain rice
40g/1½oz/scant ½ cup stoned (pitted) black olives, chopped
350g/12oz puff pastry, thawed if frozen
ground black pepper
salad leaves, to serve

1 Preheat the oven to 190°C/375°F/Gas 5. Heat the sunflower oil with 15ml/1 tbsp of the olive oil in a frying pan and fry the aubergine slices for 4–5 minutes on each side until golden brown. Drain on several sheets of kitchen paper.

2 Add the pepper strips to the pan, turning them to coat in the oil. Cover and sweat the peppers over a medium high heat for 5–6 minutes, stirring occasionally, until soft and browned.

3 Slice two of the tomatoes and set them aside. Plunge the remaining tomatoes into boiling water for 30 seconds, then drain and peel. Remove the core and seeds and chop roughly.

4 Heat the remaining oil and fry the shallots and garlic for 3–4 minutes. Add the tomatoes and cook for a few minutes. Stir in the wine and basil, with black pepper to taste. Bring to the boil, then remove from the heat. Add the rice and olives.

5 Arrange the tomatos, aubergines and peppers in a single layer in a 30cm/12in shallow ovenproof dish. Spread the rice mixture on top. Roll out the pastry slightly larger than the dish and place it on top of the rice, tucking the overlap down inside the dish. Bake for 25–30 minutes, until golden and risen. Cool slightly, then invert the tart on to a large, warmed serving plate. Serve in slices, with a leafy green salad.

Mushroom Quiche Energy 547kcal/2268kJ; Protein 13g; Carbohydrate 20.7g, of which sugars 1.5g; Fat 46.4g, of which saturates 26g; Cholesterol 190mg; Calcium 249mg; Fibre 2.1g; Sodium 248mg.
Vegetable Tarte Tatin Energy 536kcal/2242kJ; Protein 8.3g; Carbohydrate 59.1g, of which sugars 8.8g; Fat 29.5g, of which saturates 1.2g; Cholesterol 0mg; Calcium 89mg; Fibre 2.6g; Sodium 522mg.

Red Onion and Black Olive Pissaladière

For a taste of the Mediterranean, try this French-style pizza – it makes a delicious and easy snack or appetizer. Cook the sliced red onions slowly until they are caramelized and sweet before piling them into the pastry cases. To prepare this recipe in advance, place the cooled onions on to the pastry round and chill until you are ready to bake it.

Serves 6

75ml/5 tbsp extra virgin olive oil
500g/1¼lb small red onions, thinly sliced
500g/1¼lb puff pastry, thawed if frozen
75g/3oz/¾ cup small pitted black olives
salt and ground black pepper
salad leaves, to serve

1 Preheat the oven to 220°C/425°F/Gas 7. Heat the oil in a large, heavy frying pan and cook the onions gently, stirring frequently, for 15–20 minutes, until they are soft and golden. Season to taste with salt and pepper.

2 Roll out the pastry thinly on a floured surface. Cut out a 33cm/13in round and carefully transfer it to a large, lightly dampened baking sheet.

3 Spread the red onion slices over the pastry round in an even layer. Leave a gap of about 1cm/½in around the edge. Sprinkle the black olives on top.

4 Bake the tart in the oven for about 20–25 minutes, until the pastry is risen and deep golden. Cut into wedges and serve warm or cold with salad leaves.

Variation

Like Italian pizzas, the toppings for a pissaladière can vary depending on your taste. Possible additions include anchovy fillets, sliced tomatoes and a sprinkling of fresh herbs.

Roast Shallot Tart with Thyme

Tarts are perfect for a summer lunch or picnic as they can be eaten with fingers. This is a simple recipe with sheets of ready-rolled puff pastry turning a potentially arduous task into an incredibly easy one.

Serves 4

450g/1lb shallots, peeled and halved
30ml/2 tbsp fresh thyme leaves
375g/13oz packet ready-rolled puff pastry, thawed if frozen
25g/1oz/2 tbsp butter
salt and ground black pepper

1 Preheat the oven to 190°C/375°F/Gas 5. Heat the butter in a large frying pan until foaming, then add the shallots.

2 Season with salt and pepper and cook over low heat for 10–15 minutes, stirring occasionally, until golden. Stir in the thyme, then remove from the heat and set aside.

3 Unroll the puff pastry on to a large baking sheet. Using a small, sharp knife, score a border all the way around, about 2.5cm/1in from the edge, without cutting all the way through the pastry.

4 Spread the halved shallots over the pastry, inside the marked border. Bake in the oven for 20–25 minutes, or until the pastry is golden and risen around the edges. Cut into squares and serve hot or warm.

Cook's Tip

Red onions or even regular white onions could be used in this recipe. They will need to be quartered or possibly cut into smaller wedges if very large.

Variations

- *Try this tart with some chopped cooked sausage added, such as French Toulouse sausages or another flavoursome variety.*
- *Try adding some roasted garlic to the shallots.*

Pissaladière Energy 436kcal/1815kJ; Protein 5.9g; Carbohydrate 37.4g, of which sugars 5.8g; Fat 31.1g, of which saturates 1.5g; Cholesterol 0mg; Calcium 77mg; Fibre 1.5g; Sodium 542mg.
Roast Shallot Tart: Energy 419kcal/1749kJ; Protein 7.1g; Carbohydrate 38.5g, of which sugars 5g; Fat 28.3g, of which saturates 3.3g; Cholesterol 13mg; Calcium 83mg; Fibre 1.6g; Sodium 340mg.

Caramelized Shallot and Garlic Tarte Tatin

In this recipe, shallots are caramelized in butter, sugar and vinegar before being baked beneath a layer of Parmesan pastry. Serve with spring vegetables for the perfect seasonal feast.

Serves 4–6

300g/11oz puff pastry, thawed if frozen
50g/2oz/¼ cup butter
75g/3oz/1 cup freshly grated Parmesan cheese

For the topping

40g/1½oz/3 tbsp butter
500g/1¼lb shallots
12–16 large garlic cloves, peeled but left whole
15ml/1 tbsp golden caster (superfine) sugar
15ml/1 tbsp balsamic or sherry vinegar
45ml/3 tbsp water
5ml/1 tsp chopped fresh thyme, plus a few extra sprigs, to garnish (optional)
salt and ground black pepper

1 Roll out the pastry into a rectangle. Spread the butter over it, leaving a 2.5cm/1in border. Sprinkle the Parmesan on top. Fold the bottom third of the pastry up to cover the middle and the top third down. Seal the edges, give a quarter turn and roll out to a rectangle, then fold as before. Chill for 30 minutes.

2 For the topping, melt the butter in a 23–25cm/9–10in heavy pan that will go in the oven. Add the shallots and garlic, and cook until lightly browned. Sprinkle the sugar over the top and increase the heat a little. Cook until the sugar begins to caramelize, then turn the shallots and garlic in the buttery juices.

3 Add the vinegar, water, thyme and seasoning. Cook gently, with the pan partly covered, for 5–8 minutes, until the garlic is just tender. Leave to cool.

4 Preheat the oven to 190°C/375°F/Gas 5. Roll out the pastry to the diameter of the pan and lay it over the shallots and garlic. Prick the pastry with a sharp knife, then bake for 25–35 minutes, or until the pastry is risen and golden. Set aside to cool for 5–10 minutes, then invert the tart on to a serving platter. Sprinkle with thyme sprigs, if you like, and serve.

Onion Tart

This is a beautifully simple tart in which onions are allowed to take central place. Traditionally served in small slices as a first course, it also makes a delicious main course when served warm with a green salad.

Serves 4–6

175g/6oz/1½ cups plain (all-purpose) flour
75g/3oz/6 tbsp butter, chilled
30–45ml/2–3 tbsp iced water

For the filling

50g/2oz/¼ cup butter
900g/2lb Spanish (Bermuda) onions, thinly sliced
1 egg, plus 2 egg yolks
250ml/8fl oz/1 cup double (heavy) cream
1.5ml/¼ tsp freshly grated nutmeg
salt and ground black pepper

1 Process the flour, a pinch of salt and the chilled butter in a food processor until reduced to fine crumbs. Add the iced water and process briefly to form a dough. Wrap in clear film (plastic wrap) and chill for 40 minutes.

2 Melt the butter in a large pan and add the onions and a pinch of salt. Turn them in the butter. Cover and cook very gently, stirring frequently, for 30–40 minutes. Cool slightly.

3 Preheat the oven to 190°C/375°F/Gas 5. Roll out the dough thinly and use to line a 23–25cm/9–10in loose-based flan tin (pan). Line with foil or baking parchment and baking beans, then bake blind for 10 minutes.

4 Remove the foil or parchment and baking beans, and bake for another 4–5 minutes, until the pastry is lightly cooked to a pale brown colour (blonde is a good description). Reduce the oven temperature to 180°C/350°F/Gas 4.

5 Beat the egg, yolks and cream together. Season with salt, black pepper and grated nutmeg. Place half the onions in the pastry shell and add half the egg mixture. Add the remaining onions, then pour in as much of the remaining custard as you can.

6 Place on a baking sheet and bake on the middle shelf for 40–50 minutes, or until the custard is risen, browned and set.

Shallot Tarte Tatin Energy 618kcal/2567kJ; Protein 12.8g; Carbohydrate 35.5g, of which sugars 9.6g; Fat 48.2g, of which saturates 22.8g; Cholesterol 79mg; Calcium 313mg; Fibre 3g; Sodium 605mg.
Onion Tart Energy 905kcal/3748kJ; Protein 15g; Carbohydrate 36.7g, of which sugars 3g; Fat 78.2g, of which saturates 47.1g; Cholesterol 384mg; Calcium 272mg; Fibre 1.6g; Sodium 383mg.

Caramelized Onion Tart

Served warm with a mixed leaf salad, this classic and elegant French tart makes a perfect light summer lunch.

Serves 6

15ml/1 tbsp unsalted butter
15ml/1 tbsp olive oil
500g/1¼lb onions, sliced
large pinch of ground nutmeg
5ml/1 tsp soft dark brown sugar
150ml/¼ pint/⅔ cup single (light) cream
2 eggs
50g/2oz/½ cup Gruyère cheese, grated
salt and ground black pepper

For the pastry

75g/3oz/⅔ cup plain (all-purpose) flour
75g/3oz/⅔ cup wholemeal (whole-wheat) flour
75g/3oz/6 tbsp unsalted (sweet) butter
1 egg yolk

1 To make the pastry, rub together the plain and wholemeal flours and butter in a large bowl, until the mixture resembles fine breadcrumbs. Mix in the egg yolk and enough cold water to form a dough. Turn out the dough on to a lightly floured work surface and form into a smooth ball, then wrap in clear film (plastic wrap) and chill for about 30 minutes.

2 Meanwhile, make the filling. Heat the butter and oil in a large, heavy frying pan. Cook the onions over a low heat for 30 minutes until very soft and translucent, stirring often. Stir in the nutmeg, sugar and seasoning, and cook for a further 5 minutes until the onions are golden and caramelized.

3 Preheat the oven to 220°C/425°F/Gas 7. Lightly grease a loose-based 35 x 12cm/14 x 4½in fluted tin (pan). Roll out the pastry and use to line the tin. Trim, then chill for 20 minutes.

4 Prick the pastry base with a fork, then line with baking parchment and baking beans and bake blind for 10 minutes until lightly golden. Remove the paper and beans, then spoon the onions into the pastry case (pie shell).

5 Beat the eggs with the cream, then add the cheese and season to taste. Pour the mixture over the onions and bake for 30 minutes until set and golden.

Cheese and Asparagus Flan

The distinctive taste of fresh asparagus comes through in this tasty flan.

Serves 5–6

300g/11oz small asparagus spears weighed after trimming, cooked until tender
75g/3oz mature (sharp) Cheddar cheese, grated
3 spring onions (scallions), sliced
2 eggs
300ml/½ pint/1¼ cups double (heavy) cream
freshly grated nutmeg
salt and ground black pepper

For the pastry

175g/6oz/1½ cups plain (all-purpose) flour
pinch of salt
40g/1½oz/3 tbsp lard or white cooking fat, diced
40g/1½oz/3 tbsp butter, diced

1 To make the pastry, sift the flour and salt into a bowl and rub in the lard or fat and butter until the mixture resembles fine breadcrumbs. Stir in about 45ml/3 tbsp cold water and gather together into a ball. Wrap the pastry and chill for 30 minutes.

2 Put a flat baking sheet in the oven and preheat to 200°C/400°F/Gas 6. Roll out the pastry on a lightly floured work surface and use it to line a 20cm/8in flan tin (pan). Line the pastry case (pie shell) with baking parchment and add a layer of baking beans. Bake on the sheet for 10–15 minutes.

3 Remove the beans and parchment, and bake for a further 5 minutes, until light golden brown on the edges. Remove the flan and reduce the temperature to 180°C/350°F/Gas 4.

4 Cut the cooked asparagus spears into 2.5cm/1in lengths, leaving the tips whole. Sprinkle half the cheese in the base of the pastry case and add the asparagus and the spring onions.

5 Beat the eggs with the cream and season with salt, black pepper and nutmeg. Pour over the asparagus and top with the remaining cheese.

6 Return the flan to the hot baking sheet in the oven and cook for about 30 minutes or until just set. Leave the flan to settle for 5 minutes before cutting and serving.

Caramelized Onion Energy 905kcal/3748kJ; Protein 15g; Carbohydrate 36.7g, of which sugars 3g; Fat 78.2g, of which saturates 47.1g; Cholesterol 384mg; Calcium 272mg; Fibre 1.6g; Sodium 383mg.
Asparagus Flan Energy 547kcal/2266kJ; Protein 10.4g; Carbohydrate 24.7g, of which sugars 2.4g; Fat 45.6g, of which saturates 26.2g; Cholesterol 165mg; Calcium 184mg; Fibre 1.8g; Sodium 167mg.

Chervil Tart

Chervil tart is a long-established country recipe, popular in several north European countries. This is an updated version of one from a Dutch cookbook written in the 16th century. Chervil looks like a more delicate version of flat-leafed parsley, and has a fragrant slightly aniseed flavour.

Serves 4

40g/1½oz/3 tbsp butter, softened, plus extra for greasing
100g/3¾oz/scant 1 cup plain (all-purpose) flour
100g/3¾oz/scant 1 cup self-raising (self-rising) flour
2.5ml/½ tsp salt
100ml/3½fl oz/scant ½ cup white wine
beaten egg, for brushing

For the filling
300g/11oz/1⅓ cups fresh cream cheese
2.5ml/½ tsp salt
4 large (US extra large) eggs
90g/3½oz/scant 2 cups chopped fresh chervil
15ml/1 tbsp chopped fresh chives
15ml/1 tbsp chopped fresh tarragon

1 Preheat the oven to 200°C/400°F/Gas 6. Grease a 28cm/11in loose-based fluted flan tin (pan) with butter.

2 Sift both types of flour and the salt into a bowl. Stir in the butter and wine with a knife and knead quickly to form a smooth and elastic dough. (You may need to add a little more wine or flour.)

3 Roll out the dough on a lightly floured surface until you have a 33cm/13in round.

4 Line the tin with the dough and trim the edge, so that the pastry case (pie shell) is no deeper than 3cm/1¼in. Brush with beaten egg. Place the flan tin on a baking sheet.

5 For the filling, beat the cream cheese in a bowl until smooth, then whisk in the salt and eggs, one at a time.

6 Stir in the chopped chervil, chives and tarragon and spoon the filling into the pastry case. Bake for about 45 minutes, until golden and the filling has set.

Leek, Cheese and Hazelnut Tart

This delicious and tangy tart is best served hot. If your cheese is particularly strong, use the smaller quantity listed in the ingredients.

Serves 6

75g/3oz/¾ cup hazelnuts, skinned
175g/6oz/1½ cups plain (all-purpose) flour
115g/4oz/½ cup butter, chilled and cut into small cubes
15ml/1 tbsp olive oil
350g/12oz leeks, thinly sliced
5 eggs, lightly beaten
450ml/¾ pint single (light) cream
2.5ml/½ tbsp wholegrain mustard
175–225g/6–8oz/1½–2 cups hard goat's cheese, grated
salt and ground black pepper

1 Toast the hazelnuts in a dry frying pan until golden. Leave to cool, roughly chop half and finely chop the rest.

2 Sift the flour and seasoning into a large bowl and stir in the finely chopped nuts. Add the butter. Using your fingertips, rub the butter into the flour until it resembles fine breadcrumbs. Sprinkle over about 45ml/3 tbsp cold water, mix until the crumbs stick together and then gather the mixture into a ball.

3 Roll out the pastry and line a 25cm/10in flan tin (pan). Chill for 10–25 minutes to rest (or leave it there until required). Put a baking sheet in the oven and preheat to 200°C/400°F/Gas 6.

4 Put the oil and leeks into a pan and cook until soft, stirring occasionally. Meanwhile, prick the base of the pastry case (pie shell) and line with baking parchment and dried beans. Put on to the hot baking sheet and cook for 10 minutes. Remove the paper and beans and brush the pastry with beaten egg. Return to the oven for 3–4 minutes.

5 Meanwhile, mix together the remaining eggs with the cream, mustard, half the cheese and a little seasoning. Stir the mixture into the leeks and pour into the hot pastry case. Sprinkle the rest of the cheese on top and sprinkle the remaining (roughly chopped) hazelnuts over the top or around the edges.

6 Put into the hot oven and cook for about 30 minutes until set and golden. Serve hot or at room temperature.

Chervil Tart Energy 672kcal/2793kJ; Protein 14.1g; Carbohydrate 39.4g, of which sugars 1.6g; Fat 50.4g, of which saturates 29.1g; Cholesterol 283mg; Calcium 289mg; Fibre 3.1g; Sodium 703mg.
Leek Tart Energy 683kcal/2835kJ; Protein 20.7g; Carbohydrate 26.9g, of which sugars 4g; Fat 55g, of which saturates 27.3g; Cholesterol 267mg; Calcium 381mg; Fibre 3.1g; Sodium 409mg.

Courgette and Ricotta Tart

This lovely recipe comes from Italy. It makes a perfect appetizer as part of an antipasti selection.

Serves 4

200g/7oz/1¾ cups plain (all-purpose) flour
115g/4oz/½ cup ricotta cheese
115g/4oz/½ cup unsalted (sweet) butter, softened and cubed
1 egg yolk, beaten
sea salt and ground black pepper
flour, for dusting
butter, for greasing

For the filling

500g/1¼lb courgettes (zucchini)
40g/1½oz/3 tbsp unsalted (sweet) butter
2 eggs, beaten
200g/7oz mozzarella cheese, diced
75g/3oz/1 cup freshly grated Parmesan cheese

1 Put the flour into a wide bowl and make a hollow in the centre with your fist. Add the ricotta cheese, the butter and a pinch of salt. Rub the mixture together with your fingertips to make a soft ball of dough, adding a little water, if necessary. Cover and chill for 30 minutes, or until required.

2 To make the filling, cut the courgettes into 1cm/½in discs. Put them in a pan of lightly salted water, bring to the boil and simmer for about 3 minutes. Drain, return them to the pan, add the butter and toss the courgettes in the melting butter to coat.

3 Preheat the oven to 180°C/350°F/Gas 4. Grease and flour a 24cm/9½in flan tin (pan).

4 Mix the courgettes with the beaten eggs, mozzarella and Parmesan cheese, and season with salt and ground black pepper.

5 Roll out the pastry on a floured surface to a thickness of about 3mm/⅛in and use to line the flan tin. Pour the filling into the pastry, spreading it out evenly with a fork.

6 Roll out the remaining pastry to a thickness of about 3mm/⅛in thick, then cut into 1cm/½in wide strips, long enough to cover the full length of the flan tin. Arrange the strips in a lattice on top of the filling and brush with the beaten egg yolk. Bake for 40–45 minutes, or until set and golden brown.

Courgette and Dill Tart

The subtle flavour of courgettes is lifted by the addition of fresh dill in this tasty tart. Take time to arrange the courgette layers and you will have an eye-catching dish.

Serves 4

15ml/1 tbsp sunflower oil
3 courgettes (zucchini), thinly sliced
2 egg yolks
150ml/¼ pint/⅔ cup double (heavy) cream
1 garlic clove, crushed
15ml/1 tbsp finely chopped fresh dill
salt and ground black pepper

For the pastry

115g/4oz/1 cup wholemeal (whole-wheat) flour
115g/4oz/1 cup self-raising (self-rising) flour
pinch of salt
115g/4oz/½ cup butter, chilled and diced
75ml/5 tbsp chilled water

1 To make the pastry, sift the flours into a bowl, tipping the bran into the bowl, then place in a food processor. Add the salt and diced butter and process using the pulse button until the mixture resembles fine breadcrumbs.

2 With the motor running, gradually add the water until the mixture forms a dough. Do not over-process. Wrap the pastry and chill for 30 minutes.

3 Preheat the oven to 200°C/400°F/Gas 6 and grease a 20cm/8in flan tin (pan) with butter.

4 Roll out the pastry and ease it into the tin. Prick the base, trim the edges and bake blind for 10–15 minutes.

5 Meanwhile, heat the oil in a frying pan, add the courgettes and fry for 2–3 minutes until lightly browned, turning occasionally. Mix the egg yolks, cream, garlic and dill in a small bowl. Season with salt and pepper.

6 Line the pastry case (pie shell) with courgettes and pour over the cream mixture. Bake for 25–30 minutes until firm. Cool the pie in the tin, then remove and serve.

Courgette and Ricotta Energy 790kcal/3308kJ; Protein 31g; Carbohydrate 42g, of which sugars 4g; Fat 57g, of which saturates 35g; Cholesterol 316mg; Calcium 573mg; Fibre 2.7g; Sodium 420mg.
Courgette and Dill Energy 666kcal/2767kJ; Protein 11.1g; Carbohydrate 43.6g, of which sugars 4.3g; Fat 50.9g, of which saturates 28.9g; Cholesterol 214mg; Calcium 184mg; Fibre 4.8g; Sodium 293mg.

Leek and Roquefort Tart with Walnut Pastry

Mild leeks go exceptionally well with the salty flavour of the Roquefort cheese. Serve with a green salad of rocket, mizuna or watercress.

Serves 4–6

25g/1oz/2 tbsp butter
450g/1lb leeks, sliced
175g/6oz Roquefort cheese, sliced
2 large (US extra large) eggs
250ml/8fl oz/1 cup double (heavy) cream
10ml/2 tsp chopped fresh tarragon
salt and ground black pepper

For the pastry

175g/6oz/1½ cups plain (all-purpose) flour
5ml/1 tsp soft dark brown sugar
50g/2oz/¼ cup butter
75g/3oz walnuts, ground
15ml/1 tbsp lemon juice
30ml/2 tbsp iced water

1 First make the pastry. Sift the flour and 2.5ml/½ tsp salt into a bowl. Add some black pepper and the sugar. Rub in the butter until the mixture looks like breadcrumbs, then stir in the walnuts. Bind with the lemon juice and iced water. Gather into a ball, wrap in clear film (plastic wrap)and chill for 30 minutes.

2 Preheat the oven to 190°C/375°F/Gas 5. Roll out the pastry and use to line a 21–23cm/8½–9in loose-based flan tin (pan). Protect the sides of the pastry with foil, prick the base with a fork and bake for 15 minutes. Remove the foil and bake for a further 5–10 minutes, until just firm to the touch. Reduce the oven temperature to 180°C/350°F/Gas 4.

3 Meanwhile, make the filling. Melt the butter in a pan, add the leeks, cover and cook for 10 minutes. Season and cook for a further 10 minutes. Leave to cool a little, then spoon into the pastry and arrange the Roquefort on top. Beat the eggs with the cream and season with pepper. Beat in the tarragon and carefully pour the mixture into the tart.

4 Bake the tart in the oven for 30–40 minutes, until the filling has risen and browned and become firm to a gentle touch. Allow to cool for 10 minutes before serving.

Aubergine, Spinach and Feta Pie

Aubergines layered with spinach, feta cheese and rice make a flavoursome and dramatic filling for a spring pie. It can be served warm or cold in elegant slices.

Serves 12

375g/13oz shortcrust pastry, thawed if frozen
45–60ml/3–4 tbsp olive oil
1 large aubergine (eggplant), sliced into rounds
1 onion, chopped
1 garlic clove, crushed
175g/6oz spinach, washed
4 eggs
75g/3oz/½ cup crumbled feta cheese
40g/1½oz/½ cup freshly grated Parmesan cheese
60ml/4 tbsp natural (plain) yogurt
90ml/6 tbsp creamy milk
225g/8oz/2 cups cooked white or brown long grain rice
salt and ground black pepper

1 Preheat the oven to 180°C/350°F/Gas 4. Roll out the pastry thinly and use to line a 25cm/10in flan tin (pan). Prick the base all over and bake in the oven for 10–12 minutes until the pastry is pale golden.

2 Heat 30–45ml/2–3 tbsp of the oil in a frying pan and fry the aubergine slices for 6–8 minutes on each side until golden. Lift out and drain well on kitchen paper.

3 Add the onion and garlic to the oil remaining in the pan, then fry over a low heat for 4–5 minutes until soft, adding a little extra oil if necessary.

4 Chop the spinach finely, by hand or in a food processor. Beat the eggs in a large mixing bowl, then add the spinach, feta, Parmesan, yogurt, milk and the onion mixture. Season well with salt and ground black pepper and stir thoroughly to mix.

5 Spread the rice in an even layer over the base of the part-baked pastry case (pie shell). Reserve a few aubergine slices for the top, and arrange the rest in an even layer over the rice.

6 Spoon the spinach and feta mixture over the aubergines and place the remaining slices on top. Bake for 30–40 minutes until lightly browned. Serve the pie while warm, or leave it to cool.

Leek Tart Energy 683kcal/2835kJ; Protein 20.7g; Carbohydrate 26.9g, of which sugars 4g; Fat 55g, of which saturates 27.3g; Cholesterol 267mg; Calcium 381mg; Fibre 3.1g; Sodium 409mg.
Aubergine Pie Energy 554kcal/2309kJ; Protein 16.6g; Carbohydrate 53.3g, of which sugars 4.3g; Fat 31.4g, of which saturates 15.5g; Cholesterol 185mg; Calcium 299mg; Fibre 2.7g; Sodium 473mg.

Tomato Quiche

The strong Mediterranean flavours of tomatoes, peppers and anchovies complement beautifully the cheesy pastry in this tart.

Serves 8

For the pastry

225g/8 oz/2 cups plain (all-purpose flour
pinch of salt
pinch of dry mustard
115g/4 oz/½ cup butter, chilled and cubed
50g/2 oz Gruyère cheese, grated
basil leaves, to garnish

For the filling

50g/2 oz can of anchovies in oil, drained
50ml/2fl oz/¼ cup milk
30ml/2 tbsp French mustard
45ml/3 tbsp olive oil
2 large Spanish onions, sliced
1 red pepper, very finely sliced
3 egg yolks
350ml/12fl oz/1½ cups double cream
1 garlic clove, crushed
175g/6 oz mature Cheddar cheese, grated
2 large tomatoes, thickly sliced
salt and ground black pepper

1 First make the pastry. Place the flour, salt and mustard powder in a food processor, add the butter and process the mixture until it resembles breadcrumbs.

2 Add the cheese and process again briefly. Add enough iced water to make a stiff dough: it will be ready when the dough forms a ball. Wrap with cling film and chill for 30 minutes.

3 Meanwhile, make the filling. Soak the anchovies in the milk for 20 minutes. Drain away the milk. Heat the oil in a frying pan and cook the onions and red pepper until soft, then set aside to cool. In a separate bowl, beat the egg yolks, cream, garlic and Cheddar cheese together; season well.

4 Roll out the chilled pastry and line a 23cm /9 in loose-based flan tin. Spread over the mustard and chill for a further 15 minutes. Preheat the oven to 200°C / 400°F / Gas Mark 6.

5 Arrange the tomatoes in a single layer in the pastry case (pie shell). Top with the onion and pepper mixture and then the anchovy fillets. Pour over the egg mixture. Bake for 30–35 minutes until firm. Sprinkle over the basil and serve warm in slices.

Tomato and Black Olive Tart

This delicious tart has a fresh, rich Mediterranean flavour and is perfect for summer picnics or buffet celebrations. If you are taking this tart on an al fresco lunch, use a rectangular tin or pan, which makes it easier to transport and cut into portions at the picnic destination.

Serves 8

375g/13oz shortcrust pastry, at room temperature
3 eggs, beaten
300ml/½ pint/1¼ cups milk
30ml/2 tbsp chopped fresh herbs, such as parsley, thyme or basil
6 firm plum tomatoes
75g/3oz ripe Brie cheese
about 16 black olives, pitted
salt and ground black pepper

1 Preheat the oven to 190°C/375°F/Gas 5. Roll out the pastry thinly on a lightly floured surface. Line a 28 x 18cm/11 x 7in loose-based rectangular flan tin (pan), trimming off any overhanging edges.

2 Line the pastry case (pie shell) with baking parchment and baking beans, and bake blind in the oven for 15 minutes. Remove the baking parchment and beans and bake for a further 5 minutes until the base is crisp.

3 Meanwhile, in a large bowl, mix together the eggs, milk, seasoning and herbs until well combined. Slice the tomatoes, cube the cheese, and slice the olives.

4 Place the prepared flan case on a baking sheet, arrange the tomatoes, cheese and olives in the bottom of the case, then pour in the egg mixture. Transfer carefully to the oven and bake for about 40 minutes until just firm and turning golden. Slice hot or cool in the tin, then serve.

Variations

• *This tart is delicious made with other cheeses. Try slices of Gorgonzola or Camembert for a slightly stronger flavour.*
• *Alternatively, sprinkle a few strips of anchovy fillet over the tart before baking.*

Tomato Quiche Energy 406kcal/1869kJ; Protein 12g; Carbohydrate 26g, of which sugars 4g; Fat 29g, of which saturates 17g; Cholesterol 100mg; Calcium 263mg; Fibre 3g; Sodium 498mg.
Tomato and Olive Tart Energy 315kcal/1316kJ; Protein 9.3g; Carbohydrate 26.1g, of which sugars 4.6g; Fat 19.9g, of which saturates 7.2g; Cholesterol 90mg; Calcium 151mg; Fibre 1.7g; Sodium 505mg.

Tomato and Basil Tart

This is a very simple yet extremely tasty tart made with rich shortcrust pastry, topped with mozzarella cheese and tomatoes, drizzled with olive oil and dotted with fresh basil leaves. It tastes best served while it is hot.

Serves 4

150g/5oz mozzarella cheese, thinly sliced
4 large tomatoes, thickly sliced
about 10 fresh basil leaves
30ml/2 tbsp olive oil
2 garlic cloves, thinly sliced
salt and ground black pepper

For the pastry

115g/4oz/1 cup plain (all-purpose) flour, plus extra for dusting
pinch of salt
50g/2oz/¼ cup butter, at room temperature
1 egg yolk

1 To prepare the pastry, sift the flour and salt into a bowl. Rub in the butter until the mixture resembles fine breadcrumbs. Beat the egg yolk and add to the mixture. Add a little water at a time, and mix together until the dough is smooth. Knead lightly on a floured work surface for a few minutes. Place in a plastic bag and chill for about 1 hour.

2 Preheat the oven to 190°C/375°F/Gas 5. Remove the pastry from the refrigerator, allow about 10 minutes for it to return to room temperature and then roll out into a 20cm/8in round. The pastry should be an even thickness all over.

3 Press the pastry into a 20cm/8in flan tin (pan). Bake in the oven for 10 minutes. Allow to cool. Reduce the oven temperature to 180°C/350°F/Gas 4.

4 Lay the mozzarella slices over the pastry. Arrange the sliced tomatoes on top. Dip the basil leaves in olive oil and sprinkle them over the tomatoes.

5 Sprinkle the slices of garlic on top, drizzle the surface with the remaining oil and season. Bake the tart for 45 minutes, or until the pastry case (pie shell) is golden brown and the tomatoes are well cooked. Serve hot.

Spinach and Ricotta Tart

This lovely tart is a perfect summer lunchtime dish when served with a crisp green salad. It can be made in advance and served cold, so it would also be ideal for a picnic or al fresco eating.

Serves 4

250g/9oz ready-made shortcrust pastry
30ml/2 tbsp sunflower oil
1 onion, chopped
1 garlic clove, crushed
125g/4¼oz baby spinach leaves
250g/9oz/generous 1 cup ricotta cheese
2 eggs
60ml/4 tbsp milk or single (light) cream
2.5ml/½ tsp grated nutmeg
50g/2oz feta cheese, crumbled
15ml/1 tbsp pine nuts
salt and ground black pepper

1 Roll out the pastry on a lightly floured surface and use it to line a 20cm/8in round fluted flan tin (pan).

2 Prick the base with a fork. Line with baking parchment and fill with a layer of baking beans, then chill in the refrigerator for 10 minutes or until needed.

3 Preheat the oven to 190°C/375°F/Gas 5. Place the flan tin on a baking tray and cook for 10–15 minutes. Remove the beans and paper, then return to the oven and cook the pastry case (pie shell) for a further 5 minutes, until pale golden.

4 Meanwhile, heat the sunflower oil in a large frying pan, add the onion and garlic, and cook, stirring, for 5 minutes. Add the spinach and cook for 2–3 minutes more, until wilted. Remove the pan from the heat.

5 In a large bowl, mix the ricotta, eggs, milk and nutmeg together with a whisk, then season well. Spoon the spinach mixture into the pastry case and pour the ricotta mixture evenly over the top.

6 Sprinkle the feta cheese and pine nuts over the top of the tart, and bake in the oven for about 30 minutes, until just set. Allow to cool slightly, then serve warm or cold.

Tomato Tart Energy 307kcal/1280kJ; Protein 9.6g; Carbohydrate 19.1g, of which sugars 2.4g; Fat 22g, of which saturates 12.6g; Cholesterol 51mg; Calcium 207mg; Fibre 1.3g; Sodium 262mg.
Spinach Tart Energy 592kcal/2463kJ; Protein 35g; Carbohydrate 35g, of which sugars 4g; Fat 44g, of which saturates 15g; Cholesterol 173mg; Calcium 343mg; Fibre 3.2g; Sodium 683mg.

Ricotta and Basil Tart

The soft, mild taste of ricotta is perked up by the slightly astringent, peppery flavour of fresh basil.

Serves 8–10

50g/2oz/2 cups basil leaves
25g/1oz/1 cup flat-leaf parsley
120ml/4fl oz/½ cup olive oil
2 eggs
1 egg yolk
800g/1¾lb/3½ cups ricotta cheese
90g/3½oz/scant 1 cup black olives, pitted
65g/2½oz/¾ cup freshly grated Parmesan cheese
salt and ground black pepper

For the crust

190g/6½oz/1⅔ cups plain (all-purpose) flour
2.5ml/½ tsp salt
75g/3oz/6 tbsp cold butter, cut into pieces
40g/1½oz/3 tbsp cold margarine, cut into pieces
45–60ml/3–4 tbsp iced water

1 For the crust, combine the flour and salt in a bowl. Add the butter and margarine. Rub in with your fingertips until the mixture resembles coarse breadcrumbs. With a fork, stir in just enough water to bind the dough. Gather into a ball, wrap in clear film (plastic wrap), and chill for 20 minutes.

2 Preheat a baking sheet in a 190°C/375°F/Gas 5 oven. Roll out the dough 3mm/⅛in thick and transfer to a 25cm/10in quiche tin (pan). Prick the base of the pastry with a fork and line with baking parchment. Fill with dried beans and bake in the oven for 12 minutes.

3 Remove the paper and beans and bake until golden, about 3–5 minutes more. Lower the heat to 180°C/350°F/Gas 4.

4 In a food processor or blender, combine the basil, parsley and olive oil. Season well with salt and pepper and pulse to a paste.

5 In a bowl, whisk the eggs and yolk to blend. Gently fold in the ricotta. Fold in the basil mixture and olives until well combined. Stir in the Parmesan and adjust the seasoning.

6 Pour into the pastry case (pie shell) and bake until set, about 30–35 minutes. Serve warm.

Onion and Anchovy Tart

Eggs and anchovies complement each other well, and this is a Mediterranean style recipe that adds the distinctive flavour of sun-dried tomatoes. You can also use slices of bottled or canned pimiento instead.

Serves 8

60ml/4 tbsp olive oil
900g/2lb onions, sliced
5ml/1 tsp dried thyme
2–3 tomatoes, sliced
24 small black olives, pitted
1 x 50g/2oz can anchovy fillets, drained and sliced
6 sun-dried tomatoes, cut into slivers
salt and ground black pepper

For the crust

190g/6½oz/1⅔ cups plain (all-purpose) flour
2.5ml/½ tsp salt
115g/4oz/½ cup cold butter, cut into pieces
1 egg yolk
30–45ml/2–3 tbsp iced water

1 For the crust, sift the flour and salt into a bowl. Rub in the butter with your fingertips until the mixture resembles coarse breadcrumbs. Stir in the yolk and enough water to bind.

2 Roll out the dough to a thickness of about 3mm/⅛in. Transfer to a 23cm/9in flan tin (pan) and trim the edge. Chill in the refrigerator until needed.

3 Heat the oil in a frying pan. Add the onions, thyme and seasoning. Cook over low heat, covered, for 25 minutes. Uncover and continue cooking until soft. Leave to cool. Preheat the oven to 200°C/400°F/Gas 6.

4 Spoon the onions into the pastry case (pie shell) and top with the tomato slices. Arrange the olives in rows. Make a lattice pattern, alternating lines of anchovies and sun-dried tomatoes. Bake until golden, about 20–25 minutes.

Variation
For added piquancy, sprinkle a few baby capers over the top of the tart, if you wish.

Ricotta and Basil Tart Energy 333kcal/1380kJ; Protein 6g; Carbohydrate 14g, of which sugars 0g; Fat 28g, of which saturates 10g; Cholesterol 91mg; Calcium 124mg; Fibre 1g; Sodium 368mg.
Onion and Anchovy Tart Energy 334kcal/1391kJ; Protein 6g; Carbohydrate 29g, of which sugars 10g; Fat 22g, of which saturates 9g; Cholesterol 58mg; Calcium 92mg; Fibre 4g; Sodium 623mg.

Pale Smoked Haddock Flan

The classic combination of potatoes and smoked fish is here reworked in pastry for a delicious flan.

Serves 4

For the pastry

225g/8oz/2 cups plain (all-purpose) flour
pinch of salt
115g/4oz/1½ cup cold butter, cut into chunks
cold water, to mix

For the filling

2 undyed smoked haddock fillets, approximately 200g/7oz
600ml/1 pint/2½ cups full-fat (whole) milk
3–4 black peppercorns
sprig of fresh thyme
150ml/¼ pint/⅔ cup double (heavy) cream
2 eggs
200g/7oz potatoes, peeled and diced
ground black pepper

1 Preheat the oven to 200°C/400°F/Gas 6. Use a food processor to make the pastry. Put the flour, salt and butter into the food processor bowl and process until the mixture resembles fine breadcrumbs. Pour in a little cold water (you will need about 45ml/3 tbsp) and continue to process until the mixture forms a ball. If this takes longer than 30 seconds, add a dash or two more water. Take the pastry ball out of the food processor, wrap in clear film (plastic wrap) and leave to rest in a cool place for about 30 minutes.

2 Roll out the dough and use to line a 20cm/8in flan tin (pan). Prick the base of the pastry all over with a fork, then bake blind in the preheated oven for 20 minutes.

3 Put the haddock in a pan with the milk, peppercorns and thyme. Poach for 10 minutes. Remove the fish from the pan and flake into small chunks. Allow the poaching liquid to cool.

4 Whisk the cream and eggs together thoroughly, then whisk in the cooled poaching liquid.

5 Layer the pastry case (pie shell) with the flaked fish and diced potato, seasoning with black pepper. Pour the cream mixture over the top. Put the flan in the oven and bake for 40 minutes, until lightly browned on top and set. Serve hot.

Smoked Salmon Quiche

The ingredients in this light quiche perfectly complement the melt-in-the-mouth pastry made with potatoes.

Serves 6

For the pastry

115g/4oz floury maincrop potatoes, diced
225g/8oz/2 cups plain (all-purpose) flour, sifted
115g/4oz/½ cup butter, diced
½ egg, beaten
10ml/2 tsp chilled water
salad leaves and chopped fresh dill, to serve

For the filling

275g/10oz smoked salmon
6 eggs, beaten
150ml/¼ pint/⅔ cup full-cream (whole) milk
300ml/½ pint/1¼ cups double (heavy) cream
30–45ml/2–3 tbsp chopped fresh dill
30ml/2 tbsp capers, chopped
salt and ground black pepper

1 Boil the potatoes in a pan of salted water for 15 minutes or until tender. Drain well and return to the pan. Mash the potatoes until smooth and set aside to cool completely.

2 Place the flour in a bowl and rub in the butter to form fine crumbs. Beat in the potatoes and egg. Bring the mixture together, adding chilled water if needed.

3 Roll the pastry out on a floured surface and use to line a deep 23cm/9in round, loose-based, fluted flan tin (pan). Chill in the refrigerator for 1 hour.

4 Preheat the oven to 200°C/400°F/Gas 6. Place a baking sheet in the oven to preheat it.

5 For the filling, chop the salmon into bitesize pieces and set aside. Beat the eggs, milk and cream together. Then stir in the dill and capers and season with black pepper. Add in the salmon and stir to combine.

6 Prick the base of the pastry case (pie shell) with a fork and pour the mixture into it. Bake on a baking sheet for about 35–45 minutes until cooked through. Serve warm with fresh salad leaves and some dill.

Haddock Flan Energy 734kcal/3064kJ; Protein 23.8g; Carbohydrate 58.4g, of which sugars 8.2g; Fat 46.8g, of which saturates 27.9g; Cholesterol 225mg; Calcium 280mg; Fibre 2.3g; Sodium 636mg.
Salmon Quiche Energy 338kcal/1413kJ; Protein 24.3g; Carbohydrate 17.9g, of which sugars 10.2g; Fat 19.4g, of which saturates 7g; Cholesterol 199mg; Calcium 167mg; Fibre 0.7g; Sodium 665mg.

Salmon and Prawn Flan

This flan is unusual because it is made with raw salmon, which means that the fish stays moist. Cooking it this way gives a lovely succulent result. This versatile dish may be served hot with vegetables or cooled with mixed salad leaves and tomato wedges.

Serves 6

350g/12oz shortcrust pastry, thawed if frozen
225g/8oz salmon fillet, skinned
225g/8oz cooked peeled prawns (shrimp)
2 eggs, plus 2 egg yolks
150ml/¼ pint/⅔ cup whipping cream
200ml/7fl oz/scant 1 cup milk
15ml/1 tbsp chopped fresh dill
salt, ground black pepper and paprika
lime slices, tomato wedges and sprigs of dill, to garnish

1 Roll out the pastry on a floured work surface and use it to line a 20cm/8in flan tin (pan). Prick the base all over and mark the edges with the tines of the fork. It need not be too neat. Chill in the refrigerator for about 30 minutes.

2 Meanwhile, preheat the oven to 180°C/350°F/Gas 4. Bake the pastry case (pie shell) for about 30 minutes, until golden brown. Reduce the oven temperature to 160°C/325°F/Gas 3.

3 Cut the salmon fillet into 2cm/¾in cubes. Arrange the salmon and prawns evenly in the pastry case. Dust lightly with paprika.

4 In a bowl, beat together the eggs and yolks, cream, milk and dill and season to tasten with salt and ground black pepper. Pour over the salmon and prawns. Bake for about 30 minutes, until the filling is just set. Serve hot or at room temperature, garnished with lime slices, tomato wedges and dill.

Variation
For a more economical version of this flan, omit the prawns (shrimp) and use some extra salmon fillet instead, or use a mixture of salmon and trout fillet, or salmon and white fish.

Crab and Prawn Filo Tart

This rich tart makes an impressive dinner party main course and is very easy to make as it involves no pre-cooking of either the pastry case or the filling. Pastis is an anise-flavoured liqueur and apéritif from France. You can substitute ouzo or Pernod, or even dry vermouth.

Serves 4–6

2 eggs, beaten
150ml/¼ pint/⅔ cup milk
30ml/2 tbsp pastis
200g/7oz crab meat
200g/7oz cooked prawns (shrimp), peeled and deveined
225g/8oz/1 cup curd (farmers') cheese
115g/4oz/2 cups mushrooms, chopped
10 filo pastry sheets
50g/2oz/¼ cup butter, melted
salt and ground black pepper
50g/2oz/⅔ cup Parmesan cheese shavings, to garnish

1 Preheat the oven to 190°C/375°F/Gas 5. Grease a deep 18cm/7in flan tin (pan). In a large bowl, mix together the eggs, milk, pastis, crab meat, prawns, curd cheese and mushrooms. Season to taste with salt and pepper.

2 Line the flan tin with the filo pastry. Place the pastry sheets at alternate angles, and brush each one with a little of the melted butter. Leave the excess pastry hanging over the sides of the flan tin.

3 Spoon the crab and prawn mixture into the filo-lined tin. Fold the excess pastry over, crumpling it slightly to make a decorative edge. Brush with melted butter.

4 Bake the tart in the oven for around 35–40 minutes. Remove from the oven and sprinkle the Parmesan cheese over. Serve warm.

Cook's Tip
Work quickly with filo pastry as it soon becomes dry and brittle. Cover any filo not actually being used with a damp, clean dish towel to ensure it stays moist.

Salmon Flan Energy 496kcal/2063kJ; Protein 20.6g; Carbohydrate 26.7g, of which sugars 1.3g; Fat 34.8g, of which saturates 8.1g; Cholesterol 249mg; Calcium 111mg; Fibre 1.5g; Sodium 217mg.
Crab Tart Energy 364kcal/1524kJ; Protein 27.1g; Carbohydrate 23.3g, of which sugars 4.3g; Fat 17.5g, of which saturates 9.1g; Cholesterol 202mg; Calcium 234mg; Fibre 1.3g; Sodium 522mg.

Leek and Bacon Tart

This dish makes an ideal savoury first course served in individual portions. It can also be served in larger proportions with a mixed leaf salad as a light main course for lunch or supper.

Makes 6–8 tartlets or 1 large tart serving 8–10

275g/10oz/2½ cups plain (all-purpose) flour
pinch of salt
175g/6oz/¾ cup butter
2 egg yolks
about 45ml/3 tbsp very cold water
lettuce leaves and tomatoes, to garnish

For the filling
225g/8oz streaky (fatty) bacon, diced
4 leeks, sliced
6 eggs
115g/4oz/½ cup cream cheese
15ml/1 tbsp mild mustard
pinch of cayenne pepper
salt and ground black pepper

1 Sift the flour and salt into a bowl, and rub in the butter until it resembles fine breadcrumbs. Add the egg yolks and just enough water to combine the dough. Wrap the dough in clear film (plastic wrap) and place in the refrigerator for 30 minutes.

2 Meanwhile, preheat the oven to 200°C/400°F/Gas 6. Roll out the pastry thinly and use to line six to eight tartlet cases or a 28cm/11in tart dish. Remove any air pockets and prick the base with a fork. Line the pastry loosely with baking parchment, weigh down with baking beans and bake the pastry shell blind for 15–20 minutes, or until golden.

3 To make the filling, cook the bacon in a hot pan until crisp. Add the leeks and continue to cook for 3–4 minutes until just softening. Remove from the heat. In a bowl, beat the eggs, cream cheese, mustard, cayenne pepper and seasoning together, then add the leeks and bacon.

4 Remove the paper and baking beans from the tartlet or tart case, pour in the filling and bake for 35–40 minutes.

5 To serve, plate the tartlets on to individual serving plates or cut the tart into narrow wedges and serve warm, with a small, fresh salad garnish.

Cheese and Spinach Flan

The decorative pastry topping for this flan is made using a lattice cutter. If you don't have one, cut the pastry into fine strips and weave them into a lattice.

Serves 8

450g/1lb frozen spinach
1 onion, chopped
pinch of grated nutmeg
225g/8oz/1 cup cottage cheese
2 large eggs
50g/2oz Parmesan cheese, grated
150ml/¼ pint/⅔ cup single (light) cream
1 egg, beaten
salt and ground black pepper

For the pastry
225g/8oz/2 cups plain (all-purpose) flour
115g/4oz/½ cup butter
2.5ml/½ tsp English (hot) mustard
2.5ml/½ tsp paprika
115g/4oz Cheddar cheese, finely grated
45–60ml/3–4 tbsp chilled water

1 To make the pastry, sift the flour into a large mixing bowl and rub or cut in the butter until the mixture resembles fine breadcrumbs. Stir in the mustard powder, paprika, salt and cheese. Bind to a soft, pliable dough with the chilled water. Wrap in clear film (plastic wrap) and chill for 30 minutes.

2 Put the spinach and onion in a pan, and cook until the onion has softened. Increase the heat to evaporate any liquid in the pan. Season with salt, pepper and nutmeg. Transfer to a bowl and mix in the cottage cheese, eggs, Parmesan and cream.

3 Preheat the oven to 200°C/400°F/Gas 6. Put a baking sheet in the oven to preheat. Roll out two-thirds of the pastry on a lightly floured surface and use to line a 23cm/9in loose-based flan tin (pan). Press the pastry into the edges and make a narrow lip around the top edge. Spoon the filling into the case.

4 Roll out the remaining pastry and cut it with a lattice pastry cutter. Carefully open the lattice and, with the help of a rolling pin, lay it over the flan. Lightly brush the edges with beaten egg, press together and trim off the excess pastry.

5 Brush the top with beaten egg and bake for 35–40 minutes, or until golden brown. Serve hot or cold.

Leek Tart Energy 487kcal/2026kJ; Protein 15.4g; Carbohydrate 28.2g, of which sugars 1.6g; Fat 35.7g, of which saturates 19.1g; Cholesterol 265mg; Calcium 107mg; Fibre 2.1g; Sodium 681mg.
Spinach Flan Energy 401kcal/1674kJ; Protein 17.5g; Carbohydrate 24.1g, of which sugars 2.4g; Fat 26.4g, of which saturates 15.6g; Cholesterol 147mg; Calcium 374mg; Fibre 2.2g; Sodium 389mg.

Swiss Chard Pie

This is a popular recipe from Peru, where the pies are sold in bakeries and often bought as a mid-morning snack.

Serves 8

45ml/3 tbsp vegetable oil
1 small red onion, finely chopped
2 garlic cloves, chopped
1kg/2¼lb Swiss chard, thickly sliced, blanched for 5 minutes then drained
2.5ml/½ tsp grated nutmeg
2.5ml/½ tsp salt
1.5ml/½ tsp black pepper
4 eggs
3 hard-boiled eggs

For the pastry

500g/1¼lb self-raising (self-rising) flour
5ml/1 tsp salt
130g/4½oz butter
75ml/5 tbsp water
1 egg yolk, lightly beaten

1 Heat the oil in a pan over medium heat and fry the onion and garlic for 5 minutes until softened and starting to brown. Stir in the Swiss chard, nutmeg, salt and pepper and continue to cook for 3 minutes, then set aside to cool.

2 To make the pastry, sift the flour and salt into a bowl, then rub in the butter using your fingers. Add the water and draw the pastry together. Knead lightly to form a smooth dough and leave to rest in a cool place for 10 minutes.

3 Preheat the oven to 180°C/350°F/Gas 4 and oil a rectangular baking tray, 25x15cm/10x6in. Divide the dough into two pieces, one larger than the other. On a floured surface, thinly roll out the larger piece of pastry and use to line the tray, leaving the edges of the pastry hanging over the sides.

4 Beat the eggs lightly together and stir them into the cooled filling. Pour the mixture into the pastry-lined tray. Cut the hard-boiled eggs in half and press them into the filling, distributing them evenly. Dampen the edges of the pastry.

5 Roll out the remaining dough and cover the pie, pressing the edges together to seal. Trim the edges and brush with the egg yolk. Bake for about 45 minutes until the pastry is golden. Leave to cool before slicing and serving as an appetizer.

Heart of Palm Pie

This pie originated in Brazil, where the filling is also often used to make empanadas.

Serves 8

25g/1oz/2 tbsp butter
1 large onion, finely chopped
4 garlic cloves, crushed
15ml/1 tbsp plain (all-purpose) flour
200ml/7fl oz/scant 1 cup full-fat (whole) milk
2 hard-boiled eggs, chopped
1 large tomato, peeled and cubed
1 red chilli, seeded and chopped
2 x 400g/14oz cans heart of palm, drained and sliced
15ml/1 tbsp parsley, chopped
salt and ground black pepper

For the pastry

500g/1¼lb/5 cups plain (all-purpose) flour
5ml/1 tsp salt
175g/6oz/¾ cup butter
75g/3oz/6 tbsp lard
1 egg yolk
45ml/3 tbsp cold water

1 Place the flour, salt, butter and lard in a food processor and process until the mixture resembles fine breadcrumbs. With the motor still running, add the egg yolk and enough water to make a firm dough. Divide the pastry into two rounds, one slightly larger, wrap both in clear film (plastic wrap) and chill.

2 Melt the butter in a frying pan over low heat. Stir in the chopped onion and cook for 5 minutes until soft. Add the garlic and cook for a further 2 minutes. Stir the flour into the pan and cook, stirring, for 1 minute. Remove from the heat and stir in the milk, a little at a time.

3 Return to the pan to the heat and cook, stirring, for about 2 minutes to make a thin sauce. Remove from the heat and stir in the chopped hard-boiled eggs, cubed tomato, chilli, palm hearts and parsley. Season with salt and pepper.

4 Preheat the oven to 190°C/375°F/Gas 5. Place a large baking On a floured surface, roll out the larger piece of pastry and line the base and sides of a 23cm/9in loose-based pie pan.

5 Add the filling, then roll out the remaining pastry and use to top the pie. Glaze with a little milk then bake for 45 minutes until golden. Serve warm or at room temperature.

Swiss Chard Pie Energy 274kcal/1138kJ; Protein 9g; Carbohydrate 11g, of which sugars 1.7g; Fat 21.9g, of which saturates 13.4g; Cholesterol 95mg; Calcium 83mg; Fibre 0.6g; Sodium 131mg.
Heart of Palm Pie Energy 710kcal/2955kJ; Protein 9.9g; Carbohydrate 54.8g, of which sugars 6g; Fat 51.7g, of which saturates 30.5g; Cholesterol 193mg; Calcium 178mg; Fibre 3.6g; Sodium 434mg.

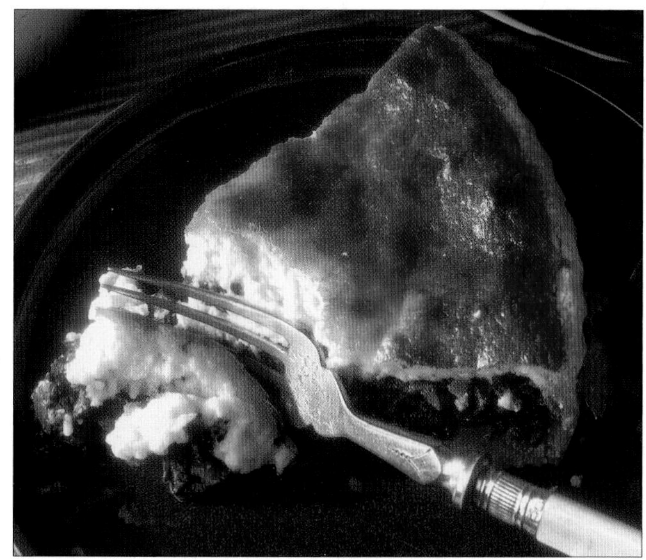

Vegetarian Christmas Pie

This one crust pie is a lovely addition to a Christmas feast.

Serves 8

225g/8oz/2 cups plain (all-purpose) flour
175g/6oz/¾ cup butter
115g/4oz Parmesan cheese, grated
1 egg
15ml/1 tbsp Dijon mustard

For the filling

25g/1oz/2 tbsp butter
1 onion, finely chopped
1–2 garlic cloves, crushed
350g/12oz/5 cups mushrooms, chopped
10ml/2 tsp mixed dried herbs
15ml/1 tbsp chopped fresh parsley
50g/2oz/1 cup fresh white breadcrumbs
salt and ground black pepper

For the cheese topping

25g/1oz/2 tbsp butter
25g/1oz/2 tbsp plain (all-purpose) flour
300ml/½ pint/1¼ cups milk
25g/1oz Parmesan cheese, grated
75g/3oz mature (sharp) Cheddar cheese, grated
1 egg, separated

1 For the pastry, rub the butter into the flour. Add the Parmesan cheese. Bind to a dough with the egg and 15ml/1 tbsp water. Knead, wrap in clear film (plastic wrap) and chill.

2 For the filling, melt the butter and cook the onion until tender. Add the garlic and mushrooms and cook, uncovered, for 5 minutes until there is no liquid left. Remove from the heat and add the dried herbs, parsley, breadcrumbs and seasoning.

3 Preheat the oven to 190°C/375°F/Gas 5. Put a baking tray in the oven. On a floured surface, roll out the pastry and use it to line a 23cm/9in loose-based flan tin (pan). Chill for 20 minutes.

4 For the topping, melt the butter, add the flour and cook for 2 minutes. Blend in the milk. Bring to the boil and simmer for 2–3 minutes. Remove from the heat and add the cheeses and egg yolk. Beat until smooth and season. Whisk the egg white until softly peaking, then fold into the topping. Spread the Dijon mustard over the flan base. Spoon in the mushroom filling. Add the cheese topping and bake the pie for about 35–45 minutes until set and golden. Serve immediately.

Sauerkraut Pie

This winter pie uses shortcrust pastry, and is filled with a mixture of sauerkraut, two types of cabbage and chunks of ham.

Serves 4

300g/11oz sauerkraut
20g/¾oz/1½ tbsp butter
5ml/1 tsp sugar
100ml/3½fl oz/scant ½ cup white wine
150g/5oz white cabbage, shredded
150g/5oz Savoy cabbage, shredded
150g/5oz boiled ham, cubed
1 egg yolk
5ml/1 tsp water

For the pastry

275g/10oz/2½ cups plain (all-purpose) flour
5ml/1 tsp salt
150g/5oz/10 tbsp unsalted butter
45ml/3 tbsp vegetable oil
25ml/1½ tbsp water

1 To make the pastry, put the flour and salt in a large bowl. Cut the butter into small pieces, add to the flour and rub in until the mixture resembles fine breadcrumbs. Alternatively, put the flour and salt in a food processor, add the butter and, using a pulsing action, blend to form fine breadcrumbs. Add the oil and water and mix to form a dough. Shape into a ball, cover with a clean dish towel, then leave to rest in the refrigerator for 1 hour.

2 Rinse the sauerkraut in cold running water if necessary, then put in a pan with the butter and sugar and heat for 1–2 minutes. Add the wine, cover the pan, bring the mixture to the boil, then remove from the heat.

3 Cook the shredded white and the Savoy cabbage in boiling salted water for about 5 minutes until tender, then drain, refresh under cold running water, and drain again. Put in a bowl and add the sauerkraut and ham. Mix together well and transfer to a deep, ovenproof pie dish.

4 Preheat the oven to 180°C/350°F/Gas 4. Roll out the pastry on a lightly floured surface so that it is large enough to cover the dish, and place it over the dish. Combine the egg yolk and water and brush over the pie to glaze. Bake in the oven for 20 minutes or until the pastry is golden brown. Serve hot.

Christmas Pie Energy 513kcal/2135kJ; Protein 17.4g; Carbohydrate 31.9g, of which sugars 3.1g; Fat 35.8g, of which saturates 22.7g; Cholesterol 123mg; Calcium 437mg; Fibre 2g; Sodium 586mg.
Sauerkraut Pie Energy 728kcal/3032kJ; Protein 16.3g; Carbohydrate 59.8g, of which sugars 7.4g; Fat 46.8g, of which saturates 24.1g; Cholesterol 163mg; Calcium 190mg; Fibre 5.4g; Sodium 1652mg.

Potato and Leek Filo Pie

This filo pastry pie makes an attractive and unusual centrepiece for a vegetarian buffet. Serve it cool, with a choice of salads.

Serves 8

800g/1¾lb new potatoes, sliced
400g/14oz leeks (trimmed weight), thinly sliced
75g/3oz/6 tbsp butter
15g/½oz parsley, finely chopped
60ml/4 tbsp chopped mixed fresh herbs (such as chervil, chives, a little tarragon and basil)
12 sheets filo pastry
150g/5oz white Cheshire, Lancashire or Cantal cheese, sliced
2 garlic cloves, finely chopped
250ml/8fl oz/1 cup double (heavy) cream
2 large egg yolks
salt and ground black pepper

1 Preheat the oven to 190°C/375°F/Gas 5. Cook the potatoes in boiling, lightly salted water for 3–4 minutes, then drain well and set aside.

2 Melt 25g/1oz/2 tbsp of the butter and fry the leeks gently, stirring, until softened. Remove from the heat, season with pepper and stir in half the parsley and half the mixed herbs.

3 Melt the remaining butter. Line a 23cm/9in loose-based metal cake tin (pan) with 6–7 sheets of filo pastry, brushing each sheet with butter. Let the edges of the pastry overhang the tin. Layer the potatoes, leeks and cheese in the tin, sprinkling a few herbs and the garlic between the layers. Season.

4 Flip the overhanging pastry over the filling and cover with two sheets of filo, tucking in the sides to fit and brushing with melted butter. Cover loosely with foil and bake for 35 minutes. (Keep the remaining pastry covered with a damp cloth.)

5 Meanwhile beat the cream, egg yolks and remaining herbs together. Make a hole in the centre of the pie and gradually pour in the eggs and cream. Arrange the remaining pastry on top, teasing it into swirls and folds, then brush with melted butter. Reduce the oven temperature to 180°C/350°F/Gas 4 and bake the pie for another 25–30 minutes, until the top is golden and crisp. Allow to cool before serving.

Picnic Pie with Ginger

This version of the elaborate Moroccan bastilla makes a delightful meal.

Serves 6

30ml/2 tbsp olive oil
115g/4oz/½ cup butter
8 spring onions (scallions), chopped
2 garlic cloves, chopped
25g/1oz fresh root ginger, peeled and chopped
225g/8oz/2 cups cashew nuts, roughly chopped
5–10ml/1–2 tsp ground cinnamon, plus extra to garnish
5ml/1 tsp paprika
2.5ml/½ tsp ground coriander, plus extra for dusting
6 eggs, beaten
bunch of flat leaf parsley, finely chopped
large bunch of fresh coriander (cilantro), finely chopped
8 sheets of filo pastry
salt and ground black pepper

1 Preheat the oven to 200°C/400°F/Gas 6. Heat the olive oil with a little of the butter in a heavy pan and stir in the spring onions, garlic and ginger. Add the cashew nuts and cook for a few minutes, then stir in the cinnamon, paprika and ground coriander. Season well, then add the eggs. Cook, stirring, until the eggs begin to scramble but remain moist. Remove from the heat, add the parsley and fresh coriander, and leave to cool.

2 Melt the remaining butter. Separate the sheets of filo and keep them under a slightly damp cloth. Brush an ovenproof dish with a little of the melted butter and cover with a sheet of pastry, allowing the sides to flop over the rim.

3 Brush the pastry with a little more melted butter and place another sheet on top. Repeat with another two sheets to make four layers. Spread the nut mixture over the pastry and fold the pastry edges over the filling.

4 Cover with the remaining sheets of pastry, brushing each one with melted butter and tucking the edges under the pie, as though making a bed.

5 Brush the top of the pie with the remaining melted butter and bake for 25 minutes, or until the pastry is crisp and golden. Dust the top of the pie with a little cinnamon before serving.

Potato Filo Pie Energy 468kcal/1948kJ; Protein 10.7g; Carbohydrate 33g, of which sugars 3.5g; Fat 33.1g, of which saturates 20g; Cholesterol 137mg; Calcium 225mg; Fibre 3.2g; Sodium 218mg.
Picnic Pie Energy 528kcal/2190kJ; Protein 15.9g; Carbohydrate 17.6g, of which sugars 3.1g; Fat 44.5g, of which saturates 15.9g; Cholesterol 231mg; Calcium 93mg; Fibre 2.4g; Sodium 300mg.

Filo and Feta Cheese Pie

This Bulgarian cheese pie is traditionally made in a distinctive spiral shape. You can also make small individual portions in the same coil shapes.

Serves 8

400g/14oz filo pastry, thawed if frozen
65g/2½oz/5 tbsp butter, melted

For the filling
10ml/2 tsp olive oil
8 spring onions (scallions), diced
800g/1¾lb spinach, stalks removed
200g/7oz feta cheese, crumbled
115g/4oz/1 cup grated mild Cheddar cheese
2 eggs, beaten
1 bunch mint, finely chopped
salt and ground black pepper

1 Preheat the oven to 180°C/350°F/Gas 4. Grease a large, round baking dish, about 20–23cm/8–9in in diameter.

2 To make the filling, heat the olive oil in a large, deep pan, add the onions and spinach, and cook for 1–2 minutes, or until the spinach leaves have wilted. Season to taste with salt and pepper.

3 Remove the onions and spinach with a slotted spoon and transfer to a large bowl. Add the feta cheese, Cheddar cheese, eggs and mint. Mix well.

4 To arrange the banitsa, lay a filo sheet on a work surface. (Cover the remaining filo pastry with a damp dish towel to prevent it from drying out.) Brush the filo sheet with melted butter, then top with another filo sheet.

5 Spoon about 30ml/2 tbsp of filling along the long edge of the filo sheet, leaving 2cm/¾in on each side. Fold in the ends and roll the pastry up over the filling. Repeat with the remaining filo sheets and filling.

6 To form the banitsa, shape the rolls into a large spiral shape by firmly coiling them around each other in the baking dish. Brush the tops generously with melted butter.

7 Bake for 30–35 minutes, or until the top is golden. Serve as an appetizer, snack or side dish, hot, warm or cold.

Egg and Spinach Pie

This pie makes an excellent and attractive picnic dish as it is delicious cold. It can also be made in advance and travels well.

Serves 10–12

oil, for greasing
115g/4oz/½ cup butter, melted
1 bunch spring onions (scallions), finely chopped
675g/1½lb fresh or frozen spinach, cooked and chopped
30ml/2 tbsp fresh marjoram or oregano, chopped, or 10ml/2 tsp dried
350g/12oz ricotta cheese
45ml/3 tbsp freshly grated Parmesan cheese
60ml/4 tbsp double (heavy) cream, whipped
5ml/1 tsp grated fresh nutmeg
450g/1lb filo pastry
2 egg whites, stiffly whisked
8 eggs, hard-boiled and peeled
salt and ground black pepper

1 Lightly grease a deep 20 x 25cm/8 x 10in roasting pan. Preheat the oven to 190°C/375°F/Gas 5.

2 Heat 30ml/2 tbsp butter in a large pan and fry the onions until softened. Stir in the spinach and herb, and season with salt and pepper to taste. Mix until well blended and the spinach is quite soft and smooth. In a bowl, beat the ricotta cheese with the Parmesan, cream, nutmeg and seasoning until really smooth.

3 Use just over half the sheets of filo pastry for the base: brush each sheet with melted butter, and layer neatly in the pan, allowing any excess pastry to hang over the edges. Keep the rest of the pastry covered with a damp cloth.

4 Whisk the egg whites, then fold them gently into the cheese. Fold in the spinach until evenly combined. Spoon half the mixture into the pan and arrange the peeled eggs on top. Cover the eggs with the rest of the filling and fold over any excess pastry edges.

5 Brush the remaining sheets of pastry with butter and place over the top. Brush with more butter, then bake for 1 hour until the pastry is golden and the pie feels quite firm. Allow the pie to cool slightly, then carefully invert it on to a clean surface, and serve warm or leave to cool completely and serve cold.

Feta Cheese Pie Energy 394kcal/1645kJ; Protein 17g; Carbohydrate 33.4g, of which sugars 2.8g; Fat 22g, of which saturates 12g; Cholesterol 132mg; Calcium 440mg; Fibre 3.5g; Sodium 697mg.
Egg and Spinach Energy 378kcal/1580kJ; Protein 16.1g; Carbohydrate 25.4g, of which sugars 1.2g; Fat 24.5g, of which saturates 13.6g; Cholesterol 204mg; Calcium 265mg; Fibre 2.5g; Sodium 322mg.

Chestnut, Stilton and Ale Pie

This hearty dish has a rich gravy and a herb pastry top.

Serves 4
30ml/2 tbsp sunflower oil
2 large onions, chopped
500g/1¼lb/8 cups button (white) mushrooms, halved
3 carrots, sliced
1 parsnip, cut into thick slices
15ml/1 tbsp fresh thyme or 5ml/1 tsp dried
2 bay leaves
250ml/8fl oz/1 cup Guinness
120ml/4fl oz/½ cup vegetable stock
5ml/1 tsp Worcestershire sauce
5ml/1 tsp soft dark brown sugar
350g/12oz/3 cups canned chestnuts, halved
30ml/2 tbsp unbleached plain (all-purpose) flour
150g/5oz/1½ cups Stilton, cubed
1 egg, beaten, or milk, to glaze
salt and ground black pepper

For the pastry
115g/4oz/1 cup wholemeal (whole-wheat) flour
a pinch of salt
50g/2oz/4 tbsp butter
15ml/1 tbsp fresh thyme or 5ml/1 tsp dried

1 To make the pastry, rub the flour, salt and butter until it resembles fine breadcrumbs. Add the thyme and enough water to form a soft dough. Turn out on to a floured surface and knead to a smooth dough. Wrap and chill for 30 minutes.

2 Make the filling. Heat the oil in a heavy pan and fry the onions for 5 minutes until softened. Add the mushrooms and cook for 3 minutes, then add the carrots, parsnip and herbs. Cover and cook for 3 minutes, then pour in the Guinness, stock and Worcestershire sauce. Add the sugar and seasoning. Simmer, covered, for 5 minutes, then add the chestnuts.

3 Mix the flour to a paste with 30ml/2 tbsp water. Add to the pan and cook, uncovered, for 5 minutes until the sauce thickens. Stir in the cheese and heat until melted, stirring constantly.

4 Preheat the oven to 220°C/425°F/Gas 7. Roll out the pastry to fit the top of a 1.5 litre/2½ pint/6¼ cup pie dish. Spoon in the filling, dampen the edges of the dish and cover with the pastry. Seal, trim and crimp the edges. Cut a slit in the top, brush with egg or milk and bake for 30 minutes until golden.

Spinach and Cottage Cheese Pie

Inspired by the famous Greek pie, spanakopita, this version uses cottage cheese for a milder flavour. It is equally delicious served hot or at room temperature.

Serves 8
1.3kg/3lb fresh spinach leaves, washed and coarse stems removed
30ml/2 tbsp olive oil
1 medium onion, finely chopped
30ml/2 tbsp chopped fresh oregano, or 5ml/1 tsp dried oregano
4 eggs
450g/1lb cottage cheese
90ml/6 tbsp freshly grated Parmesan cheese
grated nutmeg
50g/2oz butter, melted
12 small sheets of frozen filo pastry, thawed
salt and ground black pepper

1 Preheat the oven to 190°C/375°F/Gas 5. Stack handfuls of the spinach leaves, roll them loosely and cut across the leaves into thin ribbons.

2 Heat the oil in a large pan. Add the onion and cook until softened, about 5 minutes. Add the spinach and oregano and cook over high heat until most of liquid from the spinach evaporates, about 5 minutes, stirring frequently. Remove from the heat and leave to cool.

3 Break the eggs into a bowl and beat. Stir in the cottage cheese and Parmesan cheese, and season generously with nutmeg, salt and pepper. Stir in the spinach mixture.

4 Brush a 33 x 23cm/13 x 9in baking dish with a little butter or margarine. Arrange half the filo sheets in the bottom of the dish to cover evenly and extend about 2.5 cm/1in up the sides. Brush with butter.

5 Ladle in the spinach and cheese filling. Cover with the remaining filo pastry, tucking under the edges neatly. Brush the top with the remaining butter.

6 Score the top with diamond shapes. Bake until the pastry is golden, about 30 minutes. Cut into squares and serve hot.

Chestnut Pie Energy 666kcal/2782kJ; Protein 18.9g; Carbohydrate 70.3g, of which sugars 22.6g; Fat 32.7g, of which saturates 16.6g; Cholesterol 62mg; Calcium 238mg; Fibre 11g; Sodium 415mg.
Spinach Pie Energy 303kcal/1261kJ; Protein 19.8g; Carbohydrate 16.1g, of which sugars 5.6g; Fat 18g, of which saturates 7.9g; Cholesterol 146mg; Calcium 487mg; Fibre 5.6g; Sodium 546mg.

Salmon and Ginger Pie

This exceptional pie is highly recommended. This recipe uses salmon's special flavour to the full. It is very easy to make, but the end result looks and tastes like it has taken much more time and effort. Use all-butter puff pastry for the best taste. Stem ginger is often used in Chinese cooking, but can be found in most supermarkets.

Serves 4

800g/1¾lb middle cut of salmon
45ml/3 tbsp walnut oil
15ml/1 tbsp lime juice
10ml/2 tsp chopped fresh lemon thyme
30ml/2 tbsp white wine
400g/14oz puff pastry
50g/2oz/½ cup flaked (sliced) almonds
3–4 pieces stem ginger in syrup, chopped

1 If the salmon isn't already filleted, split it in half, remove all the bones and skin, and divide into four.

2 In wide dish big, enough to hold the fillets in a single layer, mix the oil, lime juice, thyme, wine and white pepper together. Add the fish, turning to coat in the marinade, then cover, and chill overnight, or for at least two hours, in the refrigerator.

3 Divide the pastry into two pieces, one slightly larger than the other, and roll out – the smaller piece should be large enough to take two of the salmon fillets and the second piece about 5cm/2in larger all round. Drain the fillets. Discard the marinade.

4 Preheat the oven to 190°C/350°F/Gas 5. Place two of the fillets on the smaller piece of pastry, and season. Add the almonds and ginger and cover with the other two fillets.

5 Season again, cover with the second piece of pastry and seal well. Brush with beaten egg and decorate with any leftover pastry. Bake for 40 minutes. Serve warm.

Cook's Tip
White pepper is lovely in this pie, but if you only have black pepper that will also work well.

Golden Filo Fish Pie

This is another pie that would be perfect when entertaining, but is deceptively easy to make.

Serves 4–6

675g/1½lb white fish fillets
300ml/½ pint/1¼ cups milk
flavouring ingredients (onion slices, bay leaf and black peppercorns)
115g/4oz cooked, peeled prawns (shrimp), defrosted if frozen
115g/4oz/½ cup butter
50g/2oz/½ cup plain (all-purpose) flour
300ml/½ pint/1¼ cups single (light) cream
75g/3oz Gruyère cheese, grated
1 bunch watercress, leaves only, chopped
5ml/1 tsp Dijon mustard
5 sheets filo pastry
salt and ground black pepper

1 Place the fish fillets in a pan, pour over the milk and add the flavouring ingredients. Bring just to the boil, then cover and simmer for 10–12 minutes, until the fish is almost tender.

2 Skin and bone the fish, then roughly flake into a shallow ovenproof dish. Sprinkle the prawns over the fish. Strain the milk and reserve.

3 Melt 50g/2oz/4 tbsp of the butter in a pan. Stir in the flour and cook for 1 minute. Stir in the reserved milk and cream. Bring to the boil, stirring, then simmer for 2–3 minutes, until the sauce has thickened.

4 Remove the pan from the heat and stir in the Gruyère, watercress, mustard and seasoning to taste. Pour over the fish and leave to cool.

5 Preheat the oven to 190°C/375°F/Gas 5. Melt the remaining butter. Brush one sheet of filo pastry with a little butter, then crumple up loosely and place on top of the filling. Repeat with the remaining filo sheets and butter until they are all used up and the pie is completely covered.

6 Bake in the oven for 25–30 minutes, until the pastry is golden and crisp. Eat hot, accompanied with a green salad or some fresh green vegetables.

Salmon Pie Energy 905kcal/3768kJ; Protein 48.9g; Carbohydrate 41.8g, of which sugars 5.1g; Fat 60.8g, of which saturates 16.3g; Cholesterol 157mg; Calcium 134mg; Fibre 0g; Sodium 414mg.
Golden Filo Pie Energy 478kcal/1991kJ; Protein 32.8g; Carbohydrate 16.6g, of which sugars 3.9g; Fat 31.6g, of which saturates 19.4g; Cholesterol 173mg; Calcium 297mg; Fibre 0.9g; Sodium 356mg.

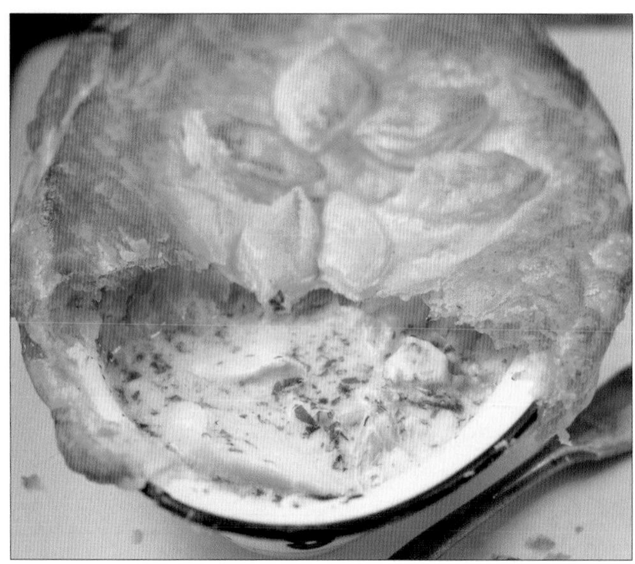

Welsh Fish and Laverbread Pie

This traditional fish pie from Wales uses laverbread, which is made by boiling a type of seaweed, laver, to make a glutinous paste.

Serves 4

225g/8oz skinless white fish,
450ml/¾ pint/scant 2 cups milk
25g/1oz/2 tbsp butter
25g/1oz/¼ cup flour
good pinch of freshly grated nutmeg
1 leek, thinly sliced
200g/7oz shelled cooked cockles (small clam)
30ml/2 tbsp laverbread (optional)
30ml/2 tbsp finely chopped fresh parsley
1 sheet ready-rolled puff pastry
salt and ground black pepper

1 Preheat the oven to 200°C/400°F/Gas 6. Put the white and smoked fish in a pan with the milk. Heat until the milk barely comes to the boil, then cover and poach gently for about 8 minutes or until the fish is just cooked. Lift the fish out, reserving the liquid. Break into flakes, discarding any bones.

2 Melt the butter, stir in the flour and cook for 1–2 minutes. Remove and stir in the reserved cooking liquid. Stir over medium heat until the sauce thickens.

3 Stir in the fish flakes and their juices. Add nutmeg and season to taste. Add the leek, cockles, laverbread and parsley to the sauce and spoon into a 1.2 litre/2 pint/5 cup ovenproof dish.

4 Brush the edges of the dish with water. Unroll the pastry and lay it over the top of the dish, trimming it to fit.

5 Use the pastry off-cuts to make decorative fish or leaves for the top, brushing each one with a little water to help them stick. Put into the hot oven and cook for about 30 minutes, or until the pastry is puffed and golden brown.

Cook's Tip

If you don't have laverbread, add some shredded sorrel or spinach with some finely grated lemon rind instead.

Fish and Pork Pie

This pie from Finland is unusual, but actually the pork belly gives a wonderful flavour to the fish.

Serves 4

1kg/2¼lb perch, cleaned, gutted and heads removed
150g/5oz sliced belly pork
15ml/1 tbsp salt
a little melted butter, to glaze

For the dough

25g/1oz fresh yeast
25ml/1½ tbsp milk, warmed
50g/2oz/¼ cup butter
450g/1lb/4 cups rye flour
5ml/1 tsp salt
500ml/17fl oz/generous 2 cups cold water
50g/2oz/½ cup plain (all-purpose) flour, plus extra for dusting

1 To make the pastry, put the yeast in a small bowl, and pour the warm milk over the yeast. Blend together, then leave for 15 minutes until the yeast bubbles. Melt the butter in a pan and leave to cool. Put 400g/14oz/3½ cups of the rye flour in a large bowl, add the salt, milk and yeast mixture, water and butter and mix together to form a soft dough. Cover the bowl and leave at room temperature for 30 minutes until doubled in size.

2 Preheat the oven to 240°C/475°F/Gas 9. Add the remaining rye flour and the plain flour to the risen mixture to make a stiff dough. Turn on to a lightly floured surface and knead until smooth and elastic. Turn on to baking parchment and roll out to a 20cm/8in rectangle. Place on a baking sheet.

3 Arrange the fish in layers in the middle of the pastry, alternating with the slices of pork. Season each layer with salt. Lift the edges of the dough up and over the filling, overlapping them. Brush the edges of the pastry with water to moisten, then pinch together firmly to seal. Bake in the oven for 30 minutes.

4 Lower the oven to 150°C/300°F/Gas 2. Brush with the cooled, melted butter and cover with baking parchment and then with foil. Bake for a further 3 hours.

5 Remove from the oven and cover with a damp dish towel to soften the crust. Leave for 15 minutes before serving. If serving cold, chill overnight so that the filling sets.

Welsh Fish Pie Energy 573kcal/2401kJ; Protein 36.8g; Carbohydrate 41g, of which sugars 7.3g; Fat 31.2g, of which saturates 4.7g; Cholesterol 92mg; Calcium 270mg; Fibre 1.2g; Sodium 1084mg.
Fish & Pork Energy 862kcal/3634kJ; Protein 55.2g; Carbohydrate 95.5g, of which sugars 0.6g; Fat 31.6g, of which saturates 12.3g; Cholesterol 209mg; Calcium 126mg; Fibre 13.6g; Sodium 1711mg.

Salmon and Chanterelle Cream Pie

This fish shaped pie looks magnificent and tastes superb.

Serves 6

450g/1lb puff pastry
1 egg, beaten, to glaze
2 large salmon fillets, total weight about 900g/2lb, skinned
375ml/13fl oz/generous 1½ cups dry white wine
1 small carrot
1 small onion, halved
½ celery stick, chopped
1 fresh thyme sprig

For the chanterelle cream
25g/1oz/2 tbsp butter
2 shallots, chopped
225g/8oz/3 cups chanterelle mushrooms, trimmed and sliced
75ml/5 tbsp white wine
150ml/¼ pint/⅔ cup double (heavy) cream
bunch of chopped fresh chervil

1 Roll out the pastry on a floured surface to a rectangle 10cm/4in longer and 5cm/2in wider than the salmon fillets. Cut into a fish shape, transfer to a large baking sheet, decorate with a pastry cutter and glaze with beaten egg. Chill for 1 hour.

2 Preheat the oven to 200°C/400°F/Gas 6. Bake the pastry for 30–35 minutes until well risen and golden. Remove from the oven and split in half horizontally to provide two matching fish shapes. Reduce the oven temperature to 160°C/325°F/Gas 3.

3 Make the chanterelle cream. Melt the butter in a heavy pan and fry the shallots gently until soft but not coloured. Add the mushrooms and cook until their juices begin to run. Pour in the wine, increase the heat and cook until dry. Stir in the cream and herbs and bring to a simmer. Season, cover, and keep warm.

4 Place the salmon fillets in a roasting pan. Add the wine, carrot, onion, celery, thyme and cover with water. Bring to the boil slowly, then remove from the heat, cover with a tight-fitting lid or foil and set aside for 30 minutes. The fish will continue to cook. Carefully lift out the salmon fillets, draining them well.

5 Put the base of the pastry on a baking sheet and lay a salmon fillet on top. Spread with the chanterelle cream and cover with a second salmon fillet. Cover with the top of the pastry 'fish' and warm through in the oven for 10–15 minutes.

Trout and Asparagus Pie

Crisp filo pastry filled with layers of trout, ricotta cheese, asparagus and mushrooms makes a dramatic-looking dish.

Serves 6–8

115g/4oz asparagus
75g/3oz/6 tbsp butter
1 small onion, chopped
115g/4oz/1½ cups button (white) mushrooms, sliced
30ml/2 tbsp chopped fresh flat leaf parsley
250g/9oz/generous 1 cup ricotta cheese
115g/4oz/½ cup mascarpone cheese
450g/1lb trout fillet, skinned and any pin bones removed
8 filo pastry sheets
salt and ground black pepper
butter, for greasing

1 Preheat the oven to 200°C/400°F/Gas 6. Grease a 23cm/9in springform cake tin (pan). Bring a pan of water to the boil, add the asparagus and blanch for 3 minutes. Drain, refresh under cold water and drain again.

2 Heat 25g/1oz/2 tbsp of the butter in a frying pan and add the onion. Cook for 3–5 minutes to soften. Add the mushrooms and cook for 2 minutes more. Stir in the parsley and season.

3 In a mixing bowl combine the ricotta and mascarpone cheeses. Stir in the onion mixture. Melt the remaining butter.

4 Line the cake tin with the filo pastry sheets, brushing each layer with melted butter and leaving the edges hanging over the sides of the tin. Keep the rest of the pastry covered with a damp, clean dishtowel so that it does not dry out.

5 Place half the ricotta mixture in the base of the filo-lined tin. Arrange the trout in a single layer over the ricotta. Season well. Top with the asparagus and the remaining ricotta mixture. Bring the overhanging edges of the pastry over the top, and brush the layers with the remaining butter.

6 Bake the pie for 25 minutes or until golden brown. Cover loosely with foil and cook for a further 15 minutes. To serve, remove the pie from the tin and serve in slices.

Salmon Pie Energy 911kcal/3792kJ; Protein 38.5g; Carbohydrate 44.7g, of which sugars 2.9g; Fat 61.1g, of which saturates 26.4g; Cholesterol 185mg; Calcium 139mg; Fibre 1.3g; Sodium 468mg.
Trout Pie Energy 310kcal/1293kJ; Protein 17g; Carbohydrate 13g, of which sugars 3g; Fat 21g, of which saturates 12g; Cholesterol 87mg; Calcium 109mg; Fibre 1g; Sodium 236mg.

Chicken and Ham Pie

This pie has a pastry top and bottom. It is best served cold.

Serves 6

For the pastry

275g/10oz/2½ cups plain (all-purpose) flour
150g/5oz/⅔ cup butter, diced

For the filling

800g/1¾lb skinless chicken breast fillets
350g/12oz smoked or cured ham
6 spring onions (scallions), chopped
15ml/1 tbsp chopped fresh tarragon
10ml/2 tsp chopped fresh thyme
grated rind and juice of ½ lemon
60ml/4 tbsp double (heavy) cream
5ml/1 tsp ground mace or nutmeg
beaten egg, to glaze
salt and ground black pepper

1 Sift the flour into a bowl with the salt and rub in the butter until the mixture resembles fine crumbs. Mix in just enough cold water to bind the mixture, gathering it together with your fingertips. Chill for 30 minutes.

2 Preheat the oven to 190°C/375°F/Gas 5. Roll out one-third of the pastry. Line a 20cm/8in pie dish 5cm/2in deep with the pastry and place on a baking (cookie) sheet.

3 Blitz 115g/4oz of the chicken in a food processor with the gammon. Place the meat in a bowl and mix in the spring onions, tarragon and thyme, lemon rind, 15ml/1 tbsp lemon juice and seasoning, adding enough cream to make a soft mixture.

4 Cut the remaining chicken into 1cm/½in pieces and mix with the remaining lemon juice, the mace or nutmeg and seasoning.

5 Put one-third of the gammon mixture in the pastry base and cover with half the chopped chicken. Repeat the layers, then top with the remaining gammon. Dampen the edges of the pastry base. Roll out the remaining pastry and cover the pie, sealing the edges firmly. Use the trimmings to decorate the top.

6 Make a small hole in the centre and brush with beaten egg. Cook for 20 minutes then turn the oven down to 160°C/325°F/Gas 3 and cook for a further 1–1¼ hours.

Turkish Pilaff Pie

This Anatolian wedding dish, is made with rice baked within a sheet of pastry.

Serves 6–8

45ml/3 tbsp olive oil
25g/1oz/2 tbsp butter
175g/6oz/1 cup blanched almonds
115g/4oz/⅔ cup pistachio nuts
350g/12oz/1¾ cups medium grain rice, rinsed thoroughly
10ml/2 tsp sugar
900ml/1½ pints/3¾ cups chicken stock
225g/8oz puff pastry
500g/1¼lb cooked chicken, cut into pieces or shredded
1 egg yolk, mixed with a little water
10ml/2 tsp nigella seeds
salt and ground black pepper
30ml/2 tbsp pistachio nuts and 15ml/1 tbsp butter, to garnish

1 Preheat the oven to 180°C/350°F/Gas 4 and lightly grease a round baking tin (pan). Heat 15ml/1 tbsp of the olive oil and butter in a large, heavy pan and stir in the blanched almonds and pistachio nuts for 3 minutes, until they begin to colour.

2 Add the rice and the sugar to the pan, making sure the rice grains are coated in the butter. Pour in the stock and bring to the boil. Season with salt and pepper, reduce the heat, and simmer for 10–12 minutes, or until the stock is absorbed.

3 On a floured surface roll out the puff pastry into a circle, about 2mm/¹⁄₁₀in thick (reserve a small, apricot-sized piece for the top). Press into the tin with the edges overlapping the sides.

4 Form the rice into a dome in the middle and arrange the chicken over the top and around the edges. Pull the pastry over the rice and chicken, overlapping the edges to seal. Roll out the reserved pastry into a square. Cut six thin strips. Brush the top of the dome with egg yolk and water and place the pastry square on the top. Place the pastry strips on top and glaze.

5 Sprinkle a few nigella seeds over the top and bake for about 25–30 minutes, or until it is golden brown. Remove from the tin and place on a serving dish. For the garnish, melt the butter in a frying pan and toss in the pistachio nuts, until they begin to brown. Pour over the pastry dome and serve immediately.

Chicken Pie Energy 431kcal/1804kJ; Protein 34.8g; Carbohydrate 23.8g, of which sugars 0.8g; Fat 22.5g, of which saturates 8.3g; Cholesterol 98mg; Calcium 57mg; Fibre 1.1g; Sodium 648mg.
Turkish Pilaff Pie Energy 617kcal/2567kJ; Protein 27.4g; Carbohydrate 48g, of which sugars 2.1g; Fat 35.3g, of which saturates 4.6g; Cholesterol 76mg; Calcium 100mg; Fibre 2.5g; Sodium 224mg.

Chicken Cinnamon Pie

This is a very old recipe from southern Italy and may have been inspired by the Moroccan pastilla.

Serves 4–6

500g/1¼lb/5 cups plain (all-purpose) flour
pinch of salt
2 eggs, beaten
90ml/6 tbsp dry white wine
90ml/6 tbsp extra virgin olive oil

For the filling

1 Italian sausage
275g/10oz cooked chicken
275g/10oz mozzarella cheese
2 eggs
large pinch of ground cinnamon, pinch of salt

1 Put the flour and salt in a large bowl and make a well in the centre. Mix the eggs, wine and oil in a jug (pitcher).

2 Add the mixture to the well in the flour with about 30ml/2 tbsp warm water. Mix with your hands, gradually incorporating the surrounding flour and adding more water if needed, to make a smooth, elastic dough. Cover the bowl and leave the dough to rest while you prepare the filling.

3 Skin the sausage and crumble the meat into a bowl. Cut the chicken and cheese into small pieces. Add these to the sausage meat, then add the eggs and flavour with the cinnamon and a pinch of salt. Preheat the oven to 200°C/400°F/Gas 6. Grease a shallow 20cm/8in pie dish.

4 On a lightly floured surface, roll out the pastry thinly and then cut out two rounds, the first one large enough to line the baking dish and the other, slightly smaller, for the top crust.

5 Use the first piece of pastry to line the dish and then trim the edges with a small, sharp knife. Fill the lined dish with the chicken mixture and cover with the pastry lid. Seal the edges securely by pressing down on the rim with the tines of a fork. Trim away any excess pastry.

6 Pierce the surface of the pie in several places to let the steam escape during cooking. Sprinkle with cinnamon. Bake for about 30 minutes, until the crust is golden. Serve warm.

Chicken Charter Pie

This traditional pie from Cornwall, in England uses whole chicken pieces.

Serves 4

50g/2oz/¼ cup butter
4 chicken legs
1 onion, finely chopped
150ml/¼ pint/⅔ cup milk
150ml/¼ pint/⅔ cup sour cream
4 spring onions (scallions), quartered
20g/¾oz/¾ cup fresh parsley leaves, finely chopped
225g/8oz puff pastry
2 eggs, beaten, plus extra for glazing
120ml/4fl oz/½ cup double (heavy) cream
salt and ground black pepper

1 Melt the butter in a heavy, shallow pan, then brown the chicken legs on all sides. Transfer to a plate. Add the chopped onion to the pan and cook until just softened but not browned. Stir in the milk, sour cream, spring onions, parsley and seasoning. Bring to the boil, then simmer for 2 minutes.

2 Return the chicken to the pan with any juices, cover and cook gently for about 30 minutes. Transfer the chicken and sauce to a 1.2 litre/2 pint/5 cup pie dish and leave to cool.

3 Meanwhile, roll out the pastry until about 2cm/¾in larger all round than the top of the pie dish. Leave the pastry to relax while the chicken is cooling.

4 Preheat the oven to 220°C/425°F/Gas 7. Cut off a narrow strip around the edge of the pastry, then place the strip on the edge of the pie dish. Moisten the strip with a little water, then cover the dish with the pastry. Press the edges together to seal. Trim and neatly crimp the edge all round.

5 Make a hole in the centre of the pastry and insert a small funnel of foil. Brush the pastry with beaten egg, then bake for 15–20 minutes. Reduce the oven temperature to 180°C/350°F/Gas 4. Mix the cream and eggs together, then pour into the pie through the funnel. Gently shake to evenly distribute the cream mixture, then return the pie to the oven for 7 minutes more. Let the pie cool for 5–10 minutes before serving warm, or serve it cold.

Cinnamon Pie Energy 670kcal/2808kJ; Protein 27g; Carbohydrate 66.3g, of which sugars 1.6g; Fat 33.9g, of which saturates 13g; Cholesterol 191mg; Calcium 196mg; Fibre 2.7g; Sodium 329mg.
Charter Pie Energy 588kcal/2459kJ; Protein 23.4g; Carbohydrate 48.4g, of which sugars 2.1g; Fat 34.9g, of which saturates 11.7g; Cholesterol 157mg; Calcium 133mg; Fibre 3.4g; Sodium 496mg.

Chicken and Leek Pie

The chicken and leek filling of this pie is a classic combination, Serve with mashed potatoes for a hearty warming supper.

Serves 4

400g/14oz shortcrust pastry, thawed if frozen
15g/½oz/1 tbsp butter
1 leek, thinly sliced
2 eggs
225g/8oz skinless chicken breast fillets, finely chopped
small handful of fresh parsley or mint, finely chopped
salt and ground black pepper
beaten egg, to glaze
mashed potato, to serve

1 Preheat the oven to 200°C/400°F/Gas 6. Divide the pastry into two, one piece slightly larger. Roll out the larger piece on a lightly floured surface to a thickness of about 3mm/⅛in and line a 20cm/8in pie dish. Roll out the smaller piece ready for the lid.

2 Melt the butter in a large pan, add the sliced leek and cook gently for about 5 minutes, stirring occasionally, until soft but not allowing it to brown.

3 Beat the eggs in a bowl and stir in the chicken, herbs and seasoning. Add the leek and its buttery juices from the pan.

4 Spoon the mixture into the pastry case (pie shell), filling generously. Brush the edges of the pastry with beaten egg and place the pastry for the lid on top, pressing the edges together to seal them. Trim any excess pastry with a knife and then crimp the edges all the way round. Brush the top with beaten egg and make a slit in the centre to allow steam to escape.

5 Place into the hot oven and cook for about 30 minutes, until golden brown and cooked through. Serve warm with creamy mashed potato.

Variation
This pie tastes just as delicious made with puff pastry instead of the shortcrust pastry.

Chicken and Mushroom Pie

A classic pie that goes down well with diners of all ages. Porcini mushrooms intensify the flavour of the chicken.

Serves 6

15g/½oz/¼ cup dried porcini mushrooms, soaked in hot water for 30 minutes
50g/2oz/¼ cup butter
30ml/2 tbsp flour
250ml/8fl oz/1 cup hot chicken stock
60ml/4 tbsp single (light) cream
1 onion, coarsely chopped
2 carrots, sliced
2 celery sticks, coarsely chopped
50g/2oz/¾ cup fresh mushrooms, quartered
450g/1lb cooked chicken, cubed
50g/2oz/½ cup peas
salt and ground black pepper
beaten egg, to glaze

For the pastry

225g/8oz/2 cups plain (all-purpose) flour
1.5ml/¼ tsp salt
115g/4oz/½ cup cold butter, diced
65g/2½oz/⅓ cup lard, diced

1 To make the pastry, sift the flour and salt into a bowl. Rub in the butter and lard until the mixture resembles breadcrumbs. Sprinkle with enough chilled water to make a firm dough. Wrap and chill for at least 30 minutes. Drain the porcini mushrooms and pat dry. Preheat the oven to 190°C/375°F/Gas 5.

2 Melt half the butter in a pan. Whisk in the flour then gradually add the hot stock over a medium heat until the mixture boils. Whisk in the cream. Season and set aside.

3 Heat the remaining butter in a large, frying pan and cook the onion and carrots over a low heat for about 5 minutes. Add the celery and fresh mushrooms and cook for 5 minutes more. Stir in the cooked chicken, peas and drained porcini mushrooms.

4 Add the chicken mixture to the sauce. Adjust the seasoning if necessary. Spoon the mixture into a 2.5 litre/4 pint/2½ quart oval baking dish. Roll out the pastry to a thickness of about 3mm/⅛in. Cut out an oval 2.5cm/1in larger all around than the dish. Lay the pastry over the filling, seal and trim the edges. Crimp all round the pastry edge. Decorate the top with pastry cut outs, then glaze the lid with beaten egg and cut slits in the top. Bake for 30 minutes until golden and serve hot.

Chicken & Leek Energy 588kcal/2459kJ; Protein 23.4g; Carbohydrate 48.4g, of which sugars 2.1g; Fat 34.9g, of which saturates 11.7g; Cholesterol 157mg; Calcium 133mg; Fibre 3.4g; Sodium 496mg.
Chicken & Mushroom Energy 982kcal/4093kJ; Protein 39.5g; Carbohydrate 65g, of which sugars 3.8g; Fat 64g, of which saturates 32g; Cholesterol 245mg; Calcium 184mg; Fibre 3.1g; Sodium 699mg.

Spiced Chicken and Egg Filo Pie

This recipe is based on pastilla, but uses chicken and egg instead of pigeon.

Serves 4

30ml/2 tbsp sunflower oil
25g/1oz/2 tbsp butter
3 chicken quarters
1½ onions, finely chopped
generous pinch of ground ginger
generous pinch of saffron powder
10ml/2 tsp ground cinnamon
40g/1½oz/⅓ cup flaked (sliced) almonds
1 large bunch fresh coriander (cilantro), finely chopped
3 eggs, beaten
about 175g/6oz filo pastry, thawed if frozen
5–10ml/1–2 tsp icing (confectioners') sugar, plus extra for dusting (optional)
salt and ground black pepper

1 Heat the oil and butter in a large pan, add the chicken pieces and brown on all sides. Add the onions, ginger, saffron, 2.5ml/½ tsp of the cinnamon and 300ml/½ pint/1¼ cups water. Season, bring to the boil, cover and simmer gently for about 45–55 minutes. Dry-fry the almonds until golden and set aside.

2 Remove the skin and bones from the chicken, cut the flesh into pieces. Stir the coriander and parsley into the pan and simmer the sauce until thickened. Add the eggs and cook over a low heat, stirring, until the eggs are scrambled.

3 Preheat the oven to 180°C/350°F/Gas 4. Oil a shallow 25cm/10in round ovenproof dish. Place one or two sheets of filo pastry in the dish, so the edges hang over the sides. Brush with oil and add two more layers of filo, brushing each with oil.

4 Place the chicken in the pastry case (pie shell) then pour in the sauce. Place a layer of filo on top and sprinkle with the dry-fried almonds. Lightly sprinkle with the remaining cinnamon and the icing sugar, if using. Fold the edges of the filo over the almonds and then make four further layers, brushing with a little oil. Tuck the filo edges down the side and brush the top with oil.

5 Bake for 40–45 minutes until golden brown. Dust the top of the pie with icing sugar and cinnamon, making a geometrical pattern if you wish. Serve the pie immediately.

Chicken and Apricot Filo Pie

The filling for this pie includes nuts and spices and has a Middle Eastern flavour.

Serves 6

75g/3oz/½ cup bulgur wheat
50g/2oz/¼ cup butter
1 onion, chopped
450g/1lb minced (ground) chicken breast fillets
50g/2oz/¼ cup ready-to-eat dried apricots, finely chopped
25g/1oz/¼ cup blanched almonds, chopped
5ml/1 tsp ground cinnamon
2.5ml/½ tsp ground allspice
50ml/2fl oz/¼ cup Greek natural (plain) yogurt
15ml/1 tbsp chopped fresh chives
30ml/2 tbsp chopped fresh parsley
6 large sheets filo pastry
salt and ground black pepper
fresh chives, to garnish

1 Preheat the oven to 200°C/400°F/Gas 6. Put the bulgur wheat in a bowl with 120ml/4fl oz/½ cup boiling water. Leave to soak for 5–10 minutes, or until the water is absorbed.

2 Heat 15g/½oz/1 tbsp of the butter in a non-stick pan, add the onion and minced chicken and cook gently, stirring occasionally, until pale golden. Stir in the apricots, almonds and bulgur wheat and cook for a further 2 minutes. Remove from the heat and stir in the cinnamon, allspice, yogurt, chives and parsley. Season to taste with salt and pepper.

3 Melt the remaining butter. Unroll the filo pastry and cut into 25cm/10in rounds. Keep the pastry rounds covered with a clean, damp dish towel to prevent them from drying out.

4 Line a 23cm/9in loose-based flan tin (pan) with three of the pastry rounds, lightly brushing each one with melted butter as you layer them. Spoon in the chicken mixture and cover with three more pastry rounds, lightly brushed with melted butter, as before.

5 Crumple the remaining pastry rounds and place them on top of the pie, then brush over any remaining melted butter. Bake the pie in the oven for about 30 minutes, or until the pastry is golden brown and crisp. Serve hot or cold, cut into wedges and garnished with chives.

Spiced Chicken Energy 497kcal/2081kJ; Protein 46.8g; Carbohydrate 28.4g, of which sugars 6.7g; Fat 22.7g, of which saturates 6g; Cholesterol 261mg; Calcium 139mg; Fibre 3.6g; Sodium 190mg.
Chicken & Apricot Energy 263kcal/1104kJ; Protein 21.9g; Carbohydrate 19.9g, of which sugars 3.8g; Fat 11.3g, of which saturates 5.2g, Cholesterol 70mg; Calcium 69mg; Fibre 1.6g; Sodium 106mg.

Chicken and Palm Hearts Pie

Palm hearts are difficult to obtain fresh, so this dish is usually made with canned.

Serves 6

For the filling

700g/1½lb chicken fillets, cubed
4 cloves garlic, crushed
60ml/4 tbsp vegetable oil
1 onion, chopped
4 tomatoes, peeled and seeded
300g/11oz drained canned palm hearts, chopped
30ml/2 tbsp parsley, chopped
4 spring onions (scallions), sliced
salt and ground black pepper

For the shortcrust pastry

850g/1lb 14oz/7½ cups plain (all-purpose) flour
10ml/2 tsp salt
300g/11oz butter
2 egg yolks
1 egg yolk and 5ml/1 tsp olive oil, to glaze

1 Place the chicken in a bowl. Add the crushed garlic, season with salt and pepper, and leave to marinate for 20 minutes. To make the pastry, sift the flour and salt into a large bowl. Rub in the butter until the mixture resembles fine breadcrumbs. Mix in the egg yolks, and enough water to form a dough. Wrap in clear film (plastic wrap) and chill for 30 minutes.

2 Heat the oil in a frying pan and fry the onion for 5 minutes. Add the chicken and fry for 4–5 minutes, stirring. Add the tomatoes, palm hearts, parsley, spring onions, salt and pepper and cook for a further 5 minutes. Remove from the heat.

3 Preheat the oven to 190°C/375°F/Gas 5. Remove the pastry from the refrigerator and cut into two pieces, one slightly larger than the other. Roll out the bigger piece to line a 23cm/9in square cake tin (pan). Ease the pastry in gently, leaving a small amount overhanging the edges. Line with baking parchment and ceramic baking beads. Bake for 20 minutes.

4 Remove the pastry case (pie shell) from the oven and lift out the baking parchment and beans. Allow the pastry to cool for 5 minutes. Then add the filling. Roll out the second piece of pastry and place on top of the filling. Trim the excess pastry with a knife, and seal the edges to seal. Glaze with egg yolk mixture and bake for 30 minutes. Serve in slices, warm or cold.

Chicken Bouche

A spectacular centrepiece, this light pastry contains a delicious chicken and mushroom filling.

Serves 4

450g/1lb prepared puff pastry
beaten egg

For the filling

15ml/1 tbsp oil
450g/1lb/4 cups minced (ground) chicken
25g/1oz/2 tbsp plain (all-purpose) flour
150ml/¼ pint/⅔ cup milk
150ml/¼ pint/⅔ cup hot chicken stock
4 spring onions (scallions), chopped
25g/1oz/¼ cup redcurrants
75g/3oz button (pearl) mushrooms, sliced
15ml/1 tbsp chopped fresh tarragon
salt and ground black pepper

1 Preheat the oven to 200°C/400°F/Gas 6. Roll half the pastry out on a lightly floured work surface to a 25cm/10in oval. Roll out the remainder to an oval of the same size and draw a smaller 20cm/8in oval in the centre.

2 Brush the edge of the first pastry shape with the beaten egg and place the smaller oval on top. Place on a dampened baking sheet and cook for 30 minutes in the preheated oven.

3 For the filling, heat the oil in a large pan. Fry the minced chicken for 5 minutes. Add the flour and cook for a further 1 minute. Stir in the milk and stock and bring to the boil.

4 Add the spring onions, redcurrants and mushrooms. Cook for 20 minutes. Stir in the fresh tarragon and season to taste.

5 Place the pastry bouche on a serving plate, remove the oval centre and spoon in the filling. Place the oval lid on top. Serve with freshly cooked vegetables.

Variation

You can also use shortcrust pastry for this dish and cook as a traditional chicken pie.

Chicken & Palm Energy 1167kcal/4885kJ; Protein 44.3g; Carbohydrate 114.2g, of which sugars 5g; Fat 62.4g, of which saturates 25.9g; Cholesterol 259mg; Calcium 244mg; Fibre 7g; Sodium 954mg.
Chicken Bouche Energy 610kcal/2557kJ; Protein 36g; Carbohydrate 49.1g, of which sugars 3.9g; Fat 31.3g, of which saturates 13.8g; Cholesterol 145mg; Calcium 138mg; Fibre 1g; Sodium 435mg.

Turkey and Cranberry Pie

Cranberries add a tart layer to this classic raised pie.

Serves 8

450g/1lb pork sausage meat (bulk sausage)
450g/1lb minced (ground) pork
15ml/1 tbsp ground coriander
15ml/1 tbsp dried mixed herbs
finely grated rind of 2 large oranges
10ml/2 tsp grated fresh ginger
450g/1lb skinless turkey breast fillets, flattened with rolling pin
115g/4oz/1 cup fresh cranberries
ground black pepper
1 egg, beaten
300ml/½ pint/1¼ cups aspic jelly, made according to instructions

For the pastry

450g/1lb/4 cups plain (all-purpose) flour
5ml/1 tsp salt
150g/5oz/⅔ cup lard
150ml/¼ pint/⅔ cup mixed milk and water

1 Preheat the oven to 180°C/350°F/Gas 4. Place a baking sheet in the oven to preheat. In a bowl, mix the sausage meat, pork, coriander, herbs, orange rind, ginger 10ml/2 tsp salt and pepper.

2 To make the pastry, sift the flour into a large bowl with the salt. Heat the lard in a pan with the milk and water until just beginning to boil. Remove from the heat and allow to cool.

3 Quickly stir the liquid into the flour until a stiff dough forms. Place on a work surface and knead until smooth. Cut one-third off the dough, wrap in clear film (plastic wrap) and keep warm.

4 Roll out the large piece of dough on a floured surface and use to line a greased 20cm/8in loose-based, springform cake tin. Thinly slice the turkey breast fillets. Spoon half the pork mixture into the tin, pressing it well into the edges. Cover it with half the turkey slices and then the cranberries, followed by the remaining turkey and finally the rest of the pork mixture.

5 Roll out the reserved dough and use to cover the filling, trim off any excess and seal the edges with a little beaten egg. Make a steam hole in the centre of the lid. Brush with beaten egg and bake for 2 hours. Place the pie on a wire rack to cool. When cold, use a funnel to fill the pie with liquid aspic jelly. Leave the jelly to set overnight, before unmoulding the pie to serve it.

Turkey Borek

This is a delicious version of the Turkish pie.

Serves 8

50g/2oz/⅓ cup couscous
45ml/3 tbsp olive oil
1 onion, chopped
115g/4oz/1⅔ cups mushrooms
1 garlic clove, crushed
115g/4oz cooked turkey, diced
30ml/2 tbsp walnuts, chopped
30ml/2 tbsp raisins
60ml/4 tbsp chopped parsley
5ml/1 tsp chopped thyme
2 eggs, hard-boiled and peeled
salt and ground black pepper
natural (plain) yogurt, to serve

For the pastry

400g/14oz/3½ cups self-raising (self-rising) flour
5ml/1 tsp salt
1 egg, plus extra for glazing
150ml/¼ pint/⅔ cup natural (plain) yogurt
150ml/¼ pint/⅔ cup olive oil
grated rind of ½ lemon

1 Preheat the oven to 190°C/375°F/Gas 5. Just cover the couscous with boiling water and soak for 10 minutes or until all the liquid is absorbed.

2 Heat the oil in a frying pan and soften the chopped onion without letting it colour. Add the mushrooms and garlic, and cook until the juices begin to run. Increase the heat to boil off the juices.

3 Transfer the mushroom and onion mixture to a mixing bowl, add the turkey, walnuts, raisins, parsley, thyme and couscous, and stir well. Chop the eggs roughly and stir them into the mixture with seasoning to taste.

4 To make the pastry, sift the flour and salt into a bowl. Make a well in the centre, add the egg, yogurt, olive oil and lemon rind, and mix together with a round-bladed knife.

5 Turn out on to a floured surface and roll into a 30cm/12in round. Pile the filling into the centre and bring the edges over to enclose the filling. Turn upside down on to a baking sheet and press out flat with your hand. Glaze with beaten egg and bake in the oven for 25 minutes. Serve the pie warm, in slices, topped with a little yogurt.

Turkey Pie Energy 670kcal/2801kJ; Protein 38.1g; Carbohydrate 50.8g, of which sugars 4.1g; Fat 36.2g, of which saturates 13.9g; Cholesterol 119mg; Calcium 155mg; Fibre 2.5g; Sodium 558mg.
Turkey Borek Energy 238kcal/996kJ; Protein 6g; Carbohydrate 27.4g, of which sugars 4.4g; Fat 12.4g, of which saturates 1.9g; Cholesterol 40mg; Calcium 102mg; Fibre 1.3g; Sodium 174mg.

Lamb and Pork Pie

This traditional meaty pie from the countryside of the Italy can also be made with other kinds of meat. In all cases, the meat tends to remain quite chewy, so make sure it is cut into small cubes. The pie is good served cold.

Serves 8
45ml/3 tbsp olive oil
500g/1¼lb lamb, trimmed of fat and cut into small cubes
200g/7oz pork, trimmed of fat and cut into small cubes
300g/11oz plain (all-purpose) flour, plus extra for dusting
50g/2oz/⅓ cup pork dripping or lard
5 ripe tomatoes, peeled, seeded and chopped
1 garlic clove, finely chopped
45ml/3 tbsp chopped fresh flat leaf parsley
sea salt and ground black pepper

1 Heat 30ml/2 tbsp of the oil in a wide frying pan, add the meat and fry until well browned all over. Put the meat into a sieve (strainer) to drain until required. Preheat the oven to 200°C/400°F/Gas 6.

2 Put the flour on to a work surface, make a hollow in the centre with your fist and put the dripping into the hollow.

3 Knead together gently with your fingers to make a smooth ball of dough, adding a little tepid water if necessary. Rest the dough, wrapped in clear film (plastic wrap), for 10 minutes in the refrigerator.

4 Roll out the dough on a floured surface as thinly as possible. Use two-thirds of it to line a 25cm/10in cake tin (pan) or oval pie dish. Re-roll out the remaining dough to make a lid.

5 Lay the browned meat in the tin or dish and cover with the tomatoes, garlic and parsley. Season, sprinkle with the remaining oil and cover with the prepared dough lid.

6 Moisten the edges of the pie and pinch to seal. Pierce the top in several places with a skewer to allow the steam to escape during cooking. Bake for 1½ hours, or until golden.

Dutch Ham and Apple Pie

A great combination of sweet and savoury flavours makes this pie from Holland an unusual and tasty treat.

Serves 6–8
5 tart cooking apples
60ml/4 tbsp soft light brown sugar
15ml/1 tbsp flour
pinch of ground cloves
pinch of ground black pepper
175g/6oz sliced cooked ham
25g/1oz/2 tbsp butter
60ml/4 tbsp whipping cream
1 egg yolk

For the pastry
225g/8oz/2 cups plain (all-purpose) flour
2.5ml/½ tsp salt
125g/6oz/1 cup cold butter, cut into pieces
60–120ml/4–8 tbsp iced water

1 For the pastry, sift the flour and salt into a large bowl. Rub in the butter until the mixture resembles coarse crumbs. Stir in enough water to bind together, gather into two balls, and wrap in clear film (plastic wrap). Chill for 20 minutes. Preheat the oven to 220°C/425°F/Gas 7.

2 Quarter, core, peel and thinly slice the apples. Place the slices in a bowl and toss with the sugar, flour, cloves and pepper to coat evenly. Set aside.

3 Roll out one dough ball thinly and line a 25cm/10in pie tin (pan), letting the excess pastry hang over the edge. Arrange half the ham slices in the bottom of the pastry case (pie shell). Top with a ring of spiced apple slices, then dot with half the butter. Repeat the layers, finishing with apples. Dot with butter. Pour over 45ml/3 tbsp of the cream.

4 Roll out the remaining pastry to make a lid. Place it on top, fold the top edge under the bottom and press. Roll out the pastry scraps and cut out shapes. Arrange on top of the pie.

5 Scallop the edge, using your fingers and a fork. Cut steam vents. Mix the egg yolk and remaining cream and brush on top to glaze. Bake for 10 minutes. Reduce the heat to 180°C/350°F/Gas 4 and bake until golden, 30–35 minutes more. Serve hot.

Lamb & Pork Pie Energy 374kcal/1566kJ; Protein 21.6g; Carbohydrate 31.1g, of which sugars 2.5g; Fat 19g, of which saturates 7.7g; Cholesterol 69mg; Calcium 64mg; Fibre 1.8g; Sodium 78mg.
Dutch Ham Pie Energy 331kcal/1383kJ; Protein 7.5g; Carbohydrate 31.7g, of which sugars 8.8g; Fat 20.2g, of which saturates 12.2g; Cholesterol 86mg; Calcium 56mg; Fibre 1.2g; Sodium 380mg.

Squab Pie

This is an old English recipe that comes from the south of the country. The name suggests it is made from pigeon, the old word for which is 'squab', but it has always been made from lamb. It is incredibly simple to make, as it needs no baking blind or precooking for the meat.

Serves 4

675g/1½lb lamb neck fillets, cut into 12 pieces
115g/4oz gammon (smoked or cured ham), diced
1 onion, thinly sliced
350g/12oz leeks, sliced
1 large cooking apple, peeled, cored and sliced
1.5–2.5ml/¼–½ tsp ground allspice
1.5–2.5ml/¼–½ tsp freshly grated nutmeg
150ml/¼ pint/⅔ cup lamb, beef or vegetable stock
225g/8oz ready-made shortcrust (pie) pastry
beaten egg or milk, to glaze
salt and ground black pepper

1 Preheat the oven to 200°C/400°F/Gas 6. Layer the lamb and gammon, onion, leeks and apple in a 900ml/1½ pint/3¾ cup pie dish, sprinkling in the spices and seasoning as you go. Pour in the stock.

2 Roll out the pastry to 2cm/¾in larger than the top of the pie dish. Cut a narrow strip from around the pastry, fit it around the dampened rim of the dish, then brush with water.

3 Lay the rolled pastry over the dish, and press the edges together to seal them. Brush the top with beaten egg or milk, and make a hole in the centre.

4 Bake the pie for 20 minutes, then reduce the oven temperature to 180°C/350°F/Gas 4 and continue to bake for 1–1¼ hours, covering the pie with foil if the pastry begins to become too brown.

Cook's Tip

Because the lamb isn't precooked, it is important to cut it in to fairly small pieces, otherwise it won't tenderize.

Shropshire Bacon and Potato Pie

Potatoes, onions, apples and bacon are packed inside a pastry crust for a thrifty and filling pie that was fed to farm workers in rural England at the end of a long hard day in the fields.

Serves 4–5

15ml/1 tbsp oil
225g/8oz lean bacon, cut into small strips
2 medium onions, thinly sliced
450g/1lb potatoes, thinly sliced
10ml/2 tsp sugar
2 medium cooking apples, peeled cored and sliced
4 fresh sage leaves, finely chopped
salt and ground black pepper
300ml/½ pint/1¼ cups vegetable stock or dry (hard) cider
beaten egg or milk, to glaze

For the pastry

75g/3oz plain (all-purpose) flour
75g/3oz plain wholemeal (whole-wheat) flour
pinch of salt
40g/1½oz/3 tbsp lard, diced
40g/1½oz/3 tbsp butter, diced

1 Sift the two flours and salt into a bowl and rub in the fats until the mixture resembles fine crumbs. Mix in enough cold water to bind the mixture, gathering it into a ball of dough. Chill for 30 minutes.

2 Preheat the oven to 180°C/350°F/Gas 4. Heat the oil in a pan and cook the bacon until crisp. Transfer to a mixing bowl.

3 Add the onions, potatoes and sugar to the hot pan and brown until beginning to soften. Add to the bowl.

4 Add the apple slices to the bowl. Stir in the sage, season with salt and pepper and mix well. Transfer the mixture into a 1.5 litre/2½ pint/6¼ cup pie dish, level the surface and pour the stock or cider over.

5 Roll out the pastry on a lightly floured surface until large enough to cover the dish. Brush the edges of the dish with milk or beaten egg. Lay the pastry lid over the top, trim the edges and make a slit in the centre. Brush with beaten egg or milk.

6 Put into the hot oven and cook for about 1 hour, until the crust is golden brown and the filling is cooked through.

Squab Pie Energy 682kcal/2845kJ; Protein 43g; Carbohydrate 35.2g, of which sugars 7.9g; Fat 42.1g, of which saturates 16.6g; Cholesterol 141mg; Calcium 97mg; Fibre 5.5g; Sodium 586mg.
Shropshire Pie Energy 436kcal/1824kJ; Protein 12.7g; Carbohydrate 42.7g, of which sugars 8.2g; Fat 25g, of which saturates 10.7g; Cholesterol 48mg; Calcium 43mg; Fibre 4g; Sodium 754mg.

Pork Pie with Cornmeal Crust

This two-crust pie is famous because it is served at nearly all Spanish special occasions. It is good hot or cold.

Serves 8

75ml/5 tbsp olive oil
2 onions, chopped
4 garlic cloves, finely chopped
1kg/2¼lb boned pork loin, diced
175g/6oz smoked gammon (smoked or cured ham), diced
3 red chorizo about 300g/11oz
3 (bell) peppers,chopped
175ml/6fl oz/¾ cup white wine
200g/7oz can tomatoes
pinch of saffron threads
5ml/1 tsp paprika
30ml/2 tbsp chopped parsley
salt and ground black pepper

For the cornmeal crust

250g/9oz/1½ cups cornmeal
7g/2 tsp easy-blend (rapid-rise) dried yeast
5ml/1 tsp caster (superfine) sugar
250g/9oz plain (all-purpose) flour, plus extra for dusting
5ml/1 tsp salt
200ml/7fl oz/scant 1 cup warm water
30ml/2 tbsp oil
2 eggs, beaten, plus 1 for the glaze

1 Heat 60ml/4 tbsp oil in a pan and fry the onions, adding the garlic when they begin to colour. Transfer the cooked onions to a flameproof casserole. Fry the pork and gammon then add to the casserole. Add 15ml/1 tbsp oil to the pan, fry the sausages and peppers and add to the dish. Deglaze the pan with the wine, and add to the casserole. Add the tomatoes, saffron, paprika and parsley. Season and cook for 20–30 minutes. Leave to cool.

2 Meanwhile, put the cornmeal into a food processor. Add the dried yeast with the sugar. Gradually add the flour, salt, water, oil and 2 eggs and beat to a smooth dough. Put into a bowl, cover with a cloth and leave in a warm place for 40–50 minutes.

3 Preheat the oven to 200°C/400°F/Gas 6. Grease a baking dish 30 x 20cm/12 x 8in. Line with half the dough, leaving the border hanging over the edge. Spoon in the filling. Roll out the lid and lay it in place.

4 Fold the outside edges over the lid and seal. Prick and brush with beaten egg. Bake for 30–35 minutes, covering the edges if they brown too much. Cool and serve at room temperature.

Leek, Bacon and Egg Pie

In this dish, leeks are used to make a sauce that is teamed with bacon and eggs to make a delicious family meal. Serve with fresh seasonal vegetables or salad.

Serves 4–6

15ml/1 tbsp olive oil
200g/7oz lean back bacon rashers (strips), trimmed of rinds and cut into thin strips
250g/9oz/2 cups leeks, thinly sliced
40g/1½oz/⅓ cup plain (all-purpose) flour
1.5ml/¼ tsp freshly grated nutmeg
425ml/¾ pint/scant 2 cups milk, plus extra for brushing
4 eggs
1 sheet ready-rolled puff pastry
salt and ground black pepper

1 Preheat the oven to 200°C/400°F/Gas 6. Put the oil and bacon in a pan and cook for 5 minutes, stirring occasionally, until the bacon is golden brown.

2 Add the sliced leeks to the pan. Stir to combine with the bacon and oil, cover and cook over medium heat for 5 minutes until softened, stirring once or twice.

3 Stir in the flour and nutmeg. Remove from the heat and gradually stir in the milk. Return the pan to the heat and cook, stirring, until the sauce thickens and boils. Season lightly.

4 Transfer the mixture into a shallow ovenproof pie dish, measuring about 25cm/10in in diameter. Using the back of a spoon, make four wells in the sauce and then break an egg into each one.

5 Brush the edges of the dish with milk. Lay the pastry over the dish. Trim off the excess pastry and use it to make the trimmings. Brush the backs with a little milk and stick them on the top of the pie.

6 Brush the pastry with milk and make a small central slit to allow steam to escape. Put into the oven and cook for about 40 minutes until the pastry is puffed up and golden brown, and the eggs have set. Serve hot.

Pork Pie Energy 704kcal/2944kJ; Protein 35.5g; Carbohydrate 58.6g, of which sugars 6.5g; Fat 35.6g, of which saturates 12.2g; Cholesterol 129mg; Calcium 97mg; Fibre 3.2g; Sodium 592mg.
Leek Pie Energy 202kcal/842kJ; Protein 13.4g; Carbohydrate 9.7g, of which sugars 4.4g; Fat 12.5g, of which saturates 4.2g; Cholesterol 149mg; Calcium 125mg; Fibre 1.1g; Sodium 592mg.

Bacon and Egg Pie

Whole eggs are broken over smoked bacon and onions before being covered in pastry in a double-crust pie.

Serves 4

30ml/2 tbsp sunflower oil
4 smoked bacon rashers (strips), cut into 4cm/1½in pieces
1 small onion, finely chopped
5 eggs
25ml/1½ tbsp chopped parsley
salt and ground black pepper
a little milk, to glaze

For the pastry

350g/12oz/3 cups plain (all-purpose) flour
pinch of salt
115g/4oz/½ cup butter, diced
50g/2oz/¼ cup lard
75–90ml/5–6 tbsp chilled water

1 To make the pastry, sift the flour and salt into a large bowl and rub in the fat until the mixture resembles fine breadcrumbs. Sprinkle over most of the water and mix to a pliable dough, adding more water if required. Knead until smooth, then wrap in clear film (plastic wrap) and chill for 30 minutes.

2 Butter a deep 20cm/8in flan tin (pan). Roll out two-thirds of the pastry and use to line the flan tin. Cover the pastry case (pie shell). Chill for 30 minutes.

3 Preheat the oven to 200°C/400°F/Gas 6. Heat the oil in a pan, add the bacon and cook for a few minutes, then add the onion and cook until soft. Remove from the pan to cool.

4 Cover the base of the pastry case with the bacon mixture, then break the eggs on to the bacon, spacing them evenly apart. Carefully tilt the flan tin so the egg whites flow together. Sprinkle the eggs with the chopped parsley, a little salt and plenty of black pepper. Place a baking sheet in the oven to heat.

5 Roll out the remaining pastry, dampen the edges and place over the pie. Trim the edges. Cut curved lines from the centre of the lid to within 2cm/¾in of the edge and brush the pie with the milk to glaze. Bake for 10 minutes, then lower the oven temperature to 180°C/350°F/Gas 4 and bake for a further 20 minutes. Remove from the oven and leave to cool for a few minutes before cutting and serving.

Lamb Currant Pie

This delicious sweet-savoury pie uses a crisp shortcrust pastry made with lard and butter. Serve with a salad of watercress, baby spinach leaves and red onion.

Serves 6

300g/11oz lean minced (ground) lamb, such as shoulder
75g/3oz/⅓ cup currants
75g/3oz/6 tbsp dark muscovado (molasses) sugar
salt and ground black pepper
milk for brushing

For the pastry

250g/9oz/2¼ cups plain (all-purpose) flour
75g/3oz/6 tbsp chilled lard, cut into small cubes
75g/3oz/6 tbsp chilled butter, cubed

1 To make the pastry, sift the flour and salt into a bowl. Add the lard and butter. With the fingertips, rub the fat into the flour until the mixture resembles fine breadcrumbs. Alternatively, you can process the mixture in a food processor.

2 Stir in about 60–75ml/4–5 tbsp cold water until the mixture can be gathered together into a smooth dough. Then wrap and refrigerate the dough for about 20–30 minutes.

3 Preheat the oven to 190°C/375°F/Gas 5. In a large bowl, mix together the lamb, currants and sugar with a little salt and ground black pepper.

4 On a lightly floured surface, roll out two-thirds of the dough into a circle. Use the rolled-out dough to line a 20–23cm/8–9in tart tin (pan).

5 Spread the lamb mixture over the pastry. Roll out the remaining pastry to make a lid and lay this on top of the lamb filling. Then trim off the excess pastry and pinch the edges together to seal them. Make a small slit in the centre of the pastry, and then brush the top with milk.

6 Place the pie into the preheated oven and bake for about 40 minutes, until the pastry is crisp and golden brown and the filling is cooked through. Serve the pie warm or leave to cool and serve at room temperature.

Bacon & Egg Energy 202kcal/843kJ; Protein 13.4g; Carbohydrate 9.7g, of which sugars 4.4g; Fat 12.5g, of which saturates 4.2g; Cholesterol 149mg; Calcium 125mg; Fibre 1.1g; Sodium 592mg.
Lamb Pie Energy 527kcal/2206kJ; Protein 13.9g; Carbohydrate 54g, of which sugars 22.2g; Fat 29.9g, of which saturates 14.7g; Cholesterol 77mg; Calcium 88mg; Fibre 1.5g; Sodium 114mg.

Goulash Puff Pies

Beef fillet is used in this Hungarian recipe, but cheaper cuts of meat can be used. You will need six single-portion pie dishes to make these mouthwatering pies.

Serves 6

200g/7oz puff pastry
800g/1¾lb fillet steak (beef tenderloin), cut into 2.5cm/1in cubes
15ml/1 tbsp cornflour (cornstarch)
60ml/4 tbsp olive oil
1 onion, thinly sliced
2 garlic cloves, crushed
2.5ml/½ tsp caraway seeds
10ml/2 tsp sweet paprika
100ml/3½fl oz/scant ½ cup beef stock
400g/14oz can chopped tomatoes
30ml/2 tbsp chopped fresh oregano leaves
salt and ground black pepper
1 egg yolk, beaten, to glaze
sour cream, to serve

1 Preheat the oven to 200°C/400°F/Gas 6. To make the filling, put the beef and cornflour in a large bowl and mix well to coat the beef pieces. Season with salt and pepper.

2 Heat half the oil in a large, heavy frying pan and sauté the coated beef, a few cubes at a time, so that they can be browned evenly without being crowded in the pan. When all the meat has been browned, remove to one side.

3 Add the remaining oil to the pan with the onion, garlic and caraway seeds, stirring. Stir in the paprika, beef, stock and tomatoes, and simmer uncovered for about 50 minutes, or until the cooking juices have reduced by half. Add the oregano and leave it to cool completely.

4 Roll the pastry to 5mm/¼in thick and cut out six large circles about 12–15cm/4½–6in in diameter, or to cover the tops of your individual pie dishes.

5 Spoon the goulash into six individual pie dishes and put the pastry rounds over each, pressing the sides down to seal well. Cut a cross in the top of each topping and brush with egg yolk.

6 Bake the pies for 30 minutes, or until the tops are golden in colour. Serve with sour cream.

Lamb and Coriander Pie

Ready-made filo pastry is easy to use and very effective in appearance. Thin sheets of folded pastry encase a lightly spiced, fruity lamb filling to make a tasty and attractive pie.

Serves 4

15ml/1 tbsp oil
450g/1lb/4 cups minced (ground) lamb
1 red onion, sliced
30ml/2 tbsp chopped fresh coriander (cilantro)
25g/1oz/2 tbsp plain (all-purpose) flour
300ml/½ pint/1¼ cups lamb stock
50g/1oz/½ cup canned chickpeas, drained
5ml/1 tsp ground cumin
225g/8oz filo pastry
115g/4oz/1¼ cups ready-to-eat dried apricots
1 courgette (zucchini), sliced
25g/1oz/2 tbsp melted butter
salt and ground black pepper

1 Preheat the oven to 190°C/375°F/Gas 5. Heat the oil in a large pan. Add the minced lamb and cook, stirring regularly, for about 5 minutes. Stir in the onion, fresh coriander and flour and cook for a further 1 minute.

2 Pour in the lamb stock and chickpeas. Season to taste with salt and pepper and stir in the cumin. Cook for 20 minutes.

3 Line a deep ovenproof dish with four sheets of filo pastry.

4 Spoon in the mince mixture. Sprinkle with dried apricots and finish with a layer of courgette slices.

5 Lay two sheets of filo pastry on top of the filling and brush with the melted butter. Fold the remaining sheets on top. Pour on the remainder of the butter and cook in the oven for 40 minutes. Serve with freshly cooked vegetables.

Cook's Tip

Filo pastry dries out quickly and cracks easily, so always cover it with baking parchment or a clean tea towel, then a damp dish towel, to keep it flexible.

Goulash Puff Pies Energy 444kcal/1852kJ; Protein 32g; Carbohydrate 19g, of which sugars 4g; Fat 28g, of which saturates 5g; Cholesterol 155mg; Calcium 48mg; Fibre 1.7g; Sodium 285mg.
Lamb Pie Energy 587kcal/2467kJ; Protein 30.8g; Carbohydrate 65g, of which sugars 14.5g; Fat 24.5g, of which saturates 10.8g; Cholesterol 100mg; Calcium 162mg; Fibre 7.2g; Sodium 152mg.

Haggis, Potato and Apple Pie

Here is a tasty way to serve your haggis, with the extra sumptuousness of puff pastry. The tart apple helps cut through the rich meat.

Serves 4

450g/1lb peeled potatoes, sliced
1 garlic clove, crushed with 5ml/1 tsp salt
freshly grated nutmeg
400g/14oz ready-made puff pastry
300g/11oz haggis
2 cooking apples, cored
1 egg, beaten
salt and ground black pepper

1 Preheat the oven to 220°C/425°F/Gas 7. Slice the potatoes and mix with the crushed garlic. Season with a little freshly grated nutmeg and salt and ground black pepper.

2 Roll out the puff pastry into two discs, one about 25cm/10in in diameter and the other a little larger.

3 Place the smaller pastry disc on a baking tray and spread half the potatoes over it, leaving a rim of about 2cm/¾in all the way round the outside.

4 Cut the haggis open and crumble the meat on top. Slice the apple into circles and spread all over the haggis. Then top with the rest of the potatoes.

5 Brush the egg all around the exposed pastry rim then place the other pastry circle on top, pushing down on the rim to seal all round the edge. Use a fork to tidy up the edges and then press down around the edge again to create a firm seal. Leave to rest for 10 minutes.

6 Brush over the pastry with a little more egg and then bake the tart in the preheated oven for about 10 minutes until the pastry is just set.

7 Reduce the oven temperature to 200°C/400°F/Gas 6 and bake the tart for a further 40 minutes until evenly browned and cooked. Serve in slices.

Layered Beef and Pine Nut Pie

This pie, originally from Turkey has a wonderful spiced filling from the cinnamon and herbs.

Serves 4–6

2 eggs
300ml/½ pint/1¼ cups milk
150ml/¼ pint/⅔ cup sunflower oil, plus 15ml/1 tbsp extra
10–12 sheets of filo pastry

For the filling
15ml/1 tbsp olive oil
15g/½oz/1 tbsp butter
1 onion, finely chopped
2–3 garlic cloves, crushed
30–45ml/2–3 tbsp pine nuts
250g/9oz minced (ground) beef
10ml/2 tsp ground cinnamon
10ml/2 tsp dried oregano
1 small bunch parsley, chopped
salt and ground black pepper

1 Preheat the oven to 200°C/400°F/Gas 6 and grease an ovenproof dish. For the filling, heat the olive oil and butter in a heavy pan and stir in the onion. Cook for 1–2 minutes until softened. Add the garlic and pine nuts. Once the pine nuts begin to turn golden, add the meat. Cook the meat for 3–4 minutes, then stir in the cinnamon and herbs. Season with salt and pepper. Leave to cool.

2 In a bowl, beat the eggs with the milk and the oil. Place a layer of filo in the base of the dish, with the sides overlapping the edge. Pour a little of the milk mixture into the centre and spread it to the sides.

3 Tear three to four sheets of filo into wide strips and layer them in the dish, brushing each layer with the milk mixture. Leave the last layer dry and spread the meat mixture over it.

4 Tear the remaining sheets filo and layer them up in the same way with the milk mixture. Reserve 15ml/1 tbsp of the mixture in the bowl and beat in the 15ml/1 tbsp of the oil.

5 Pull up the edges of filo and fold them over the top of the pie, sticking them down with the milk and oil mixture. Bake for 45 minutes. The pie should puff up and turn golden brown.

6 Remove the pie from the oven (it will sink back down quite quickly) and cut it into rectangular, square or triangular wedges.

Haggis Pie Energy 698kcal/2919kJ; Protein 15.8g; Carbohydrate 72.9g, of which sugars 6.1g; Fat 41.2g, of which saturates 5.8g; Cholesterol 68mg; Calcium 88mg; Fibre 1.9g; Sodium 901mg.
Beef Pie Energy 463kcal/1920kJ; Protein 15.1g; Carbohydrate 16.5g, of which sugars 3.6g; Fat 37.9g, of which saturates 8.1g; Cholesterol 97mg; Calcium 101mg; Fibre 0.9g; Sodium 94mg.

Beef, Mushroom and Rice Pasties

A tasty layer of rice and juicy wild mushrooms tops each fillet steak before it is wrapped in puff pastry.

Serves 4

20g/¾oz/¼ cup dried wild mushrooms, soaked for 10 minutes in warm water to cover
115g/4oz/1½–1¾ cups morel mushrooms
about 45ml/3 tbsp olive oil
4 shallots, finely chopped
1 garlic clove, crushed
20g/¾oz/1½ tbsp butter
175g/6oz/1½ cups cooked white long grain rice
10ml/2 tsp chopped marjoram
15ml/1 tbsp chopped parsley
275g/10oz puff pastry
4 fillet steaks (beef tenderloins), each about 90g/3½oz and 2.5cm/1in thick
10ml/2 tsp Dijon mustard
1 egg, beaten with about 15ml/1 tbsp water
salt and ground black pepper
roast potatoes and patty pan

1 Preheat the oven to 220°C/425°F/Gas 7. Drain the dried mushrooms, reserving the liquid, and chop finely. Trim the morels and chop them.

2 Heat 15ml/1 tbsp of the olive oil in a frying pan and fry the shallots and garlic for 2–3 minutes until soft, stirring occasionally.

3 Add the butter to the pan. When it begins to foam, add the mushrooms and cook for 3–4 minutes more, stirring.

4 Scrape the mixture into the bowl of rice and stir in the marjoram and parsley. Season to taste. Cut the pastry into four and roll out each piece into an 18cm/7in circle.

5 Heat the remaining olive oil in the pan and brown the steaks for about 30 seconds on each side. Spread a little mustard over each steak, then place on one side of a piece of pastry. Spoon a quarter of the mushroom and rice mixture on top.

6 Fold the pastry over to make a pasty, sealing the join with a little of the egg wash. Repeat to make four pasties, then place them on an oiled baking sheet. Slit the top of each pasty, decorate with the pastry trimmings, and glaze with more egg wash. Bake in the oven for about 15 minutes, until golden.

Mince Wellington

Making use of a popular recipe, this variation retains all the flavours of the original, but an expensive fillet of beef is replaced with a savoury minced beef filling.

Serves 4

For the filling
15ml/1 tbsp oil
900 g/2 lb/8 cups minced (ground) beef
1 red onion, chopped
2 garlic cloves, crushed
25g/1oz/2 tbsp plain (all-purpose) flour
150ml/¼ pint/⅔ cup red wine
30ml/2 tbsp chopped fresh oregano
75g/3 oz/¾ cup wild and long grain rice
1 egg, beaten
salt and ground black pepper

For the pastry case
450g/1lb prepared puff pastry
225g/8oz Ardennes pâté
50g/2oz/½ cup mixed chopped nuts
beaten egg to glaze

1 Preheat the oven to 200°C/400°F/Gas 6. For the filling, heat the oil in a pan. Add the minced beef, onion and garlic, and fry for 10 minutes. Stir in the flour and cook for a further 1 minute. Stir in the wine and bring to the boil. Add the oregano and cook for 20 minutes.

2 Cook the rice in boiling salted water for 10 minutes or until al dente. Drain well and stir into the mince mixture with the egg. Season to taste and cool.

3 Roll out the pastry to a 35 x 25cm/14 x 10in rectangle. Trim the edges and reserve the offcuts of pastry. Place the mince mixture in the centre of the pastry rectangle, along its length. Top with the pâté and nuts.

4 Brush the edges of the pastry with egg and fold around to encase the filling. Turn over and arrange the pastry trimmings in a lattice pattern on top.

5 Brush with the beaten egg and place on a dampened baking sheet. Cook in the preheated oven for 45 minutes. Serve with freshly cooked vegetables.

Beef Pasties Energy 576kcal/2401kJ; Protein 26.3g; Carbohydrate 50.2g, of which sugars 2.2g; Fat 31.2g, of which saturates 3.8g; Cholesterol 55mg; Calcium 72mg; Fibre 1g; Sodium 331mg.
Wellington Energy 1256kcal/5236kJ; Protein 68.5g; Carbohydrate 62.7g, of which sugars 2.2g; Fat 79.6g, of which saturates 30.4g; Cholesterol 344mg; Calcium 153mg; Fibre 1g; Sodium 998mg.

Steak and Oyster Pie

Oysters are a luxury today, but they add a wonderful flavour to this tasty pie.

Serves 6
30ml/2 tbsp flour
1kg/2¼lb beef steak, diced
45ml/3 tbsp oil
25g/1oz/2 tbsp butter
1 large onion, chopped
300ml/½ pint/1¼ cups beef stock
300ml/½ pint/1¼ cups brown ale
30ml/2 tbsp fresh thyme leaves
225g/8oz brown cap (cremini) mushrooms, halved if large
12 shelled oysters
375g/13oz puff pastry
beaten egg, to glaze
salt and ground black pepper

1 Preheat the oven to 150°C/300°F/Gas 2. Season the flour and toss the pieces of steak in it until well coated. Heat half the oil with half the butter in a flameproof casserole and quickly brown the meat in batches. Set it to one side.

2 Add the remaining oil and butter to the hot pan, stir in the onion and cook over medium heat, stirring occasionally, until golden brown and beginning to soften. Return the meat and any juices to the pan and stir in the stock, ale or wine and thyme.

3 Bring to the boil, then cover the pan and cook in the oven for about 1½ hours, or until the beef is tender.

4 Using a slotted spoon, lift the meat and onion out of the liquid and put it into a 1.75 litre/3 pint/7½ cup pie dish. Bring the liquid to the boil and reduce to about 600ml/1 pint/2½ cups. Season to taste and stir in the mushrooms, then pour the mixture over the meat. Leave to cool. Add the oysters to the cooled meat, pushing them down into the mixture.

5 Roll out the pastry on a floured surface to 2.5cm/1in larger than the dish. Trim off a 1cm/½in strip all around the edge. Brush the rim of the dish with egg and lay the strip on it.

6 Brush the strip with egg, lay the pastry sheet over the top, trim to fit and press the edges together to seal. Brush the top with egg. Bake in the hot oven for about 40 minutes, until the pastry is crisp and golden brown and the filling is piping hot.

Steak, Mushroom and Ale Pie

This recipe is a favourite at any traditional restaurant.

Serves 4
25g/1oz/2 tbsp butter
1 large onion, finely chopped
115g/4oz/1½ cups brown cap (cremini) or button (white) mushrooms, halved
900g/2lb lean beef in one piece, such as rump or braising steak
30ml/2 tbsp plain (all-purpose) flour
45ml/3 tbsp sunflower oil
300ml/½ pint/1¼ cups stout or brown ale
300ml/½ pint/1¼ cups beef stock or consommé
500g/1¼lb puff pastry
beaten egg, to glaze
salt and ground black pepper

1 Melt the butter in a large, flameproof casserole, add the onion and cook gently for about 5 minutes. Add the mushrooms and continue cooking for a further 5 minutes, stirring occasionally. Remove the onion mixture from the casserole and set aside.

2 Trim the meat and cut it into 2.5cm/1in cubes. Season the flour and toss the meat in it. Heat the oil in the casserole, then brown the steak in batches over a high heat to seal in the juices.

3 Replace the vegetables, then stir in the stout or ale and stock or consommé. Simmer for about 1 hour until the meat is tender. Season to taste and transfer to a 1.5 litre/2½ pint/6¼ cup pie dish. Preheat the oven to 230°C/450°F/Gas 8.

4 Roll out the pastry about 4cm/1½in larger all around than the dish. Cut a 2.5cm/1in strip from the edge of the pastry. Brush the rim of the dish with water and press the pastry strip on it. Brush the strip with beaten egg and cover the pie with the pastry lid. Press the lid in place and trim the excess from around the edge. Pinch the pastry between your fingers to flute the edge.

5 Make a hole in the middle of the pie, brush the top carefully with beaten egg and chill for 10 minutes to rest the pastry.

6 Bake the pie for 15 minutes, then reduce the oven temperature to 200°C/400°F/Gas 6 and bake for a further 15–20 minutes, or until the pastry is risen and golden.

Steak & Oyster Energy 689kcal/2874kJ; Protein 49.4g; Carbohydrate 29.8g, of which sugars 1g; Fat 39g, of which saturates 9.1g; Cholesterol 144mg; Calcium 145mg; Fibre 0.4g; Sodium 674mg.
Steak & Ale Energy 1061kcal/4423kJ; Protein 58.8g; Carbohydrate 59.3g, of which sugars 7.6g; Fat 65.3g, of which saturates 24g; Cholesterol 164mg; Calcium 129mg; Fibre 3.2g; Sodium 622mg.

Dingle Pies

These pies are eaten in Ireland on special occasions, and in the past were eaten on the first day of the harvest. The original pies used to make a handy portable meal for farmers.

Makes 6 small pies

450g/1lb boneless mutton or lamb
1 large onion, diced
2 carrots, diced
1 potato, diced
2 celery sticks, diced
1 egg, beaten
salt and ground black pepper

For the shortcrust pastry
500g/1¼lb/5 cups plain (all-purpose) flour
250g/9oz/generous 1 cup butter
120ml/4fl oz/½ cup cold water

1 To make the pastry, sieve the flour into a large bowl and add the butter. Rub the butter into the flour with the fingertips. Add enough chilled water to make a firm dough. Wrap in clear film (plastic wrap) or foil and leave in the refrigerator to relax for 20 minutes before using.

2 Trim any fat or gristle from the meat and cut it up into very small pieces. Place in a large bowl and add the diced onion, carrots, potato and celery. Mix well and season with salt and freshly ground black pepper.

3 Preheat the oven to 180°C/350°F/Gas 4. Cut a third off the ball of pastry and reserve to make the lids of the pies. Roll out the rest and, using a small plate as a guide and re-rolling the pastry as necessary, cut out six circles.

4 Divide the meat and vegetable mixture between the circles, piling it in the middle of each.

5 Roll out the remaining pastry and cut out six smaller circles, about 10cm/4in across. Lay these on top. Dampen the edges of the pastry bases, bring the pastry up around the meat, pleat it to fit the lid and pinch the edges together.

6 Make a small hole in the top of each pie to let out the steam, brush them with beaten egg and slide the pies on to baking sheets. Bake for an hour. Serve warm or cold.

Greek Kleftiko

For this Greek recipe, the pastry crust is unusual. The marinated lamb steaks or chops are slow-cooked to develop an unbeatable, meltingly tender flavour, and the dish is sealed with a flour dough lid to trap succulence and flavour. This is a throwback to the very earliest type of pastry dish, where the crust was part of the cooking process rather than part of the dish.

Serves 4

juice of 1 lemon
15ml/1 tbsp chopped fresh oregano
4 lamb leg steaks or chump chops with bones
30ml/2 tbsp olive oil
2 large onions, thinly sliced
2 bay leaves
150ml/¼ pint/⅔ cup dry white wine
225g/8oz/2 cups plain (all-purpose) flour
salt and ground black pepper
boiled potatoes, to serve

1 Mix together the lemon juice, oregano and salt and pepper, and brush over both sides of the lamb steaks or chops. Leave to marinate in the refrigerator for at least 4 hours or preferably overnight if possible.

2 Preheat the oven to 160°C/325°F/Gas 3. Drain the lamb, reserving the marinade, and dry the lamb with kitchen paper.

3 Heat the olive oil in a large frying pan or sauté pan and fry the lamb over a high heat until browned on both sides

4 Transfer the lamb to a shallow pie dish. Sprinkle the sliced onions and bay leaves around the lamb, then pour over the white wine and the reserved marinade.

5 To make the dough crust, mix the flour with enough water to make a firm dough, adding it a little at a time. Moisten the rim of the pie dish with water.

6 Roll out the dough on a lightly floured surface and use to cover the dish. Press down so that it is tightly sealed.

7 Bake the pie for 2 hours, then break away the dough crust and serve the lamb hot with boiled potatoes.

Dingle Pies Energy 784Kcal/3275kJ; Protein 25.1g; Carbohydrate 74.6g, of which sugars 5.2g; Fat 44.9g, of which saturates 26.1g; Cholesterol 178mg; Calcium 155mg; Fibre 4g; Sodium 345mg.
Kleftiko Energy 658kcal/2760kJ; Protein 57.9g; Carbohydrate 53.8g, of which sugars 8.1g; Fat 22.2g, of which saturates 7.2g; Cholesterol 184mg; Calcium 148mg; Fibre 3.5g; Sodium 130mg.

Steak Pie with Mustard Gravy

The fragrant mustard, bay and parsley gravy is a delicious complement to this traditional pie.

Serves 4

450g/1lb puff pastry
40ml/2½ tbsp plain (all-purpose) flour
675g/1½lb rump (round) steak, cubed
175g/6oz lamb's kidneys
25g/1oz/2 tbsp butter
1 onion, chopped
15ml/1 tbsp English (hot) mustard
2 bay leaves
15ml/1 tbsp chopped fresh parsley
150ml/¼ pint/⅔ cup beef stock
1 egg, beaten
salt and ground black pepper

1 Roll out two-thirds of the pastry on a floured surface to a thickness of 3mm/⅛in. Use to line the base and sides of a 1.5 litre/2½ pint/6¼ cup pie dish. Place a pie funnel in the centre of the dish.

2 Put the flour, salt and pepper in a bowl and toss the steak in the mixture. Remove the fat, skin and tough central core from the kidneys, and slice them thickly. Add the slices to the steak and toss well.

3 Melt the butter in a pan, add the onion and fry over low heat, stirring occasionally, until soft and translucent. Add the mustard, bay leaves, parsley and stock and stir well.

4 Preheat the oven to 190°C/375°F/Gas 5. Place the steak and kidney in the pie dish and add the stock mixture.

5 Roll out the remaining puff pastry to a thickness of 3mm/⅛in to use for the pie lid. Brush the edges of the pastry case (pie shell) with beaten egg and cover with the lid. Press the edges firmly together to seal, then trim. Use the trimmings to decorate the top with pastry leaves.

6 Brush the pie with a little beaten egg and make a small hole in the pastry lid for the funnel. Bake for about 1 hour until the pastry is well risen and golden brown all over. Serve the pie hot, straight from the pie dish.

Veal and Ham Pie

The mixture of veal and ham is usually a filling for a cold raised pie, but this is a lovely aromatic hot version.

Serves 4

450g/1lb boneless shoulder of veal, cut into cubes
225g/8oz gammon (smoked or cured ham), cut into cubes
15ml/1 tbsp plain (all-purpose) flour
large pinch each of dry mustard and ground black pepper
25g/1oz/2 tbsp butter
15ml/1 tbsp oil
1 onion, chopped
600ml/1 pint/2½ cups chicken or veal stock
2 eggs, hard-boiled and sliced
30ml/2 tbsp chopped fresh parsley

For the pastry

175g/6oz/1½ cups plain (all-purpose) flour
pinch of salt
85g/3oz/6 tbsp butter, diced
beaten egg, to glaze

1 Preheat the oven to 180°C/350°F/Gas 4. Mix the veal and gammon in a bowl. Season the flour with the mustard and black pepper, then add it to the meat and toss well.

2 Heat the butter and oil in a large, flameproof casserole until sizzling, then cook the meat mixture in batches until golden on all sides. Use a slotted spoon to remove the meat and set aside. Cook the onion in the fat remaining in the casserole until softened but not coloured. Stir in the stock and the meat. Cover and cook in the hot oven for 1½ hours or until the veal is tender. Adjust the seasoning and leave to cool.

3 To make the pastry, sift the flour into a bowl with the salt and rub in the butter until the mixture resembles fine crumbs. Mix in just enough cold water to bind the mixture. Wrap in clear film (plastic wrap), and chill for at least 30 minutes. Spoon the veal mixture into a 1.5 litre/2½ pint/6¼ cup pie dish. Arrange the egg slices on top and sprinkle with the parsley.

4 On a floured surface, roll out the pastry to about 4cm/1½in larger than the top of the pie dish. Cut a strip from around the edge, dampen the rim of the dish and press the pastry strip on to it. Brush the pastry rim with beaten egg and top with the lid. Trim, brush with beaten egg and bake for 30–40 minutes.

Steak Pie Energy 845kcal/3530kJ; Protein 53.7g; Carbohydrate 51g, of which sugars 2.8g; Fat 49.9g, of which saturates 10.1g; Cholesterol 249mg; Calcium 121mg; Fibre 1.2g; Sodium 565mg.
Veal & Ham Pie Energy 621kcal/2595kJ; Protein 42.4g; Carbohydrate 39.2g, of which sugars 2.6g; Fat 33.8g, of which saturates 17.2g; Cholesterol 281mg; Calcium 128mg; Fibre 2.3g; Sodium 1007mg.

Hare Pot Pies

This winter pie filling is simmered in the slow cooker until tender before being topped with pastry and baked in the oven.

Serves 4

45ml/3 tbsp olive oil
1 leek, sliced
225g/8oz parsnips, sliced
225g/8oz carrots, sliced
1 fennel bulb, sliced
675g/1½lb boneless hare, diced
30ml/2 tbsp plain (all-purpose) flour
60ml/4 tbsp Madeira
300ml/½ pint/1¼ cups game or chicken stock
45ml/3 tbsp chopped fresh parsley
450g/1lb puff pastry, thawed if frozen
beaten egg yolk, to glaze

1 Heat 30ml/2 tbsp of the oil in a pan. Add the leek, parsnips, carrots and fennel and cook for 10 minutes until soft. With a slotted spoon, transfer the vegetables to a ceramic cooking pot. Cover and switch on the slow cooker to high or auto.

2 Heat the remaining oil in the pan and fry the hare in batches until well browned. When all the meat is browned, return it to the pan. Add the flour and cook, stirring, for a few seconds, then gradually add the Madeira and stock and bring to the boil.

3 Transfer the hare mixture to the ceramic cooking pot and cook for 1 hour. Switch the slow cooker to low or leave on auto and cook for 5–6 hours, until the meat and vegetables are tender. Stir in the chopped parsley, then set aside to cool.

4 To make the pies, preheat the oven to 220°C/425°F/Gas 7. Spoon the filling into four small pie dishes. Cut the pastry into quarters and roll out to make the lids, making them larger than the dishes. Trim any excess pastry and use to line the dish rims.

5 Dampen the pastry rims with cold water and cover with the lids. Pinch the edges together to seal. Brush with beaten egg yolk and make a small hole in the top of each one.

6 Stand the pies on a baking tray and bake for 25 minutes, or until the pastry is golden. If necessary, cover the pies with foil to prevent them becoming too brown. Serve immediately.

Rabbit and Game Pie

A quintessential element of the English buffet table has to be a hot water pastry pie.

Serves 10–12

1kg/2¼lb rabbit flesh, diced
600g/1lb 6oz partridge flesh, diced
300g/11oz pork belly, minced
grated rind of 1 lemon
15ml/1 tbsp chopped sage
15ml/1 tbsp chopped thyme
2.5ml/½ tsp grated nutmeg
15ml/1 tbsp English (hot) mustard powder
60ml/4 tbsp ruby port
sea salt and ground black pepper

For the jellied stock

2 pig's trotters (feet), split lengthways
rabbit and game bones
1 carrot, peeled
1 small onion, peeled
1 bay leaf

For the pastry

150g/5oz/⅔ cup lard
150g/5oz/⅔ cup butter
350ml/12fl oz/1½ cups water
850g/1lb 14oz/7½ cups plain (all-purpose) flour
good pinch of sea salt
1 egg, beaten, to glaze

1 The jelly must be made in advance. Place the ingredients in a pan, cover with plenty of water, bring to the boil and skim off any scum and fat. Reduce the heat to a simmer and cook for 6 hours, skimming and topping up with water as necessary.

2 At the end of the cooking time, strain the liquid and discard the meat. Return the stock to the pan and reduce to 600ml/1 pint/2½ cups. Cool and store in the refrigerator: when cold it should be a stiff jelly.

3 To make the pastry, place the fats and water in a pan and heat gently to melt – do not boil. Sift the flour and salt into a bowl, make a well in the centre, pour in the liquid and mix. Knead with your hands to form a soft, pliable dough.

4 Roll out three-quarters of the pastry to a circle 8mm/⅓in thick and line a 20cm/8in springform cake tin (pan). Cover the remaining pastry and keep warm.

5 To make the pie filling, combine all the ingredients in a bowl and mix thoroughly using your hands. Spoon the pie filling into the pastry case (pie shell), gently pushing the mixture into the corners and flattening the top. It should come to just below the top of the pastry case. Preheat the oven to 180°C/350°F/Gas 4.

6 Roll out the remaining pastry into a circle slightly smaller than the diameter of the pan and lower it on to the meat. Dampen the edge with water, fold over the top of the pastry case and crimp the edges together with your fingertips. Make a 1cm/½in hole in the centre of the lid and brush with the beaten egg.

7 Bake the pie in the preheated oven for 40 minutes to set the pastry, then reduce the heat to 140°C/275°F/Gas 1 and continue to cook for 2 hours. Remove from the oven and leave to cool to room temperature.

8 To finish the pie, warm the jellied stock gently until it is liquid, transfer it to a jug (pitcher) and, using a funnel, carefully pour it into the pie through the hole in the top, a little at a time, until the pie will accept no more. Refrigerate overnight. Serve the pie cold, or at room temperature, in slices, accompanied by pickles.

Hare Pot Pies Energy 906kcal/3784kJ; Protein 45g; Carbohydrate 60.4g, of which sugars 10g; Fat 53.7g, of which saturates 15.9g; Cholesterol 107mg; Calcium 180mg; Fibre 7.6g; Sodium 553mg.
Rabbit Pie Energy 728kcal/3045kJ; Protein 42.3g; Carbohydrate 55.7g, of which sugars 1.7g; Fat 38.2g, of which saturates 17.1g; Cholesterol 118mg; Calcium 135mg; Fibre 2.2g; Sodium 215mg.

Game Pie with Port

A good game pie is one of the triumphs of British food.

Serves 8–10

450g/1lb/4 cups plain (all-purpose) flour
10ml/2 tsp salt
175g/6oz/¾ cup lard
175ml/6fl oz/¾ cup milk
10ml/2 tsp powdered gelatine
30ml/2 tbsp cold water
salt and ground black pepper

For the filling
675g/1½lb lean boneless game, such as pheasant, grouse, partridge and rabbit, diced
115g/4oz rindless streaky (fatty) bacon rashers (strips), chopped
115g/4oz minced (ground) pork
30ml/2 tbsp port
10ml/2 tsp grated orange rind
2 juniper berries, crushed
2.5ml/½ tsp dried sage
beaten egg, to glaze

1 Preheat the oven to 200°C/400°F/Gas 6. Grease a 20cm/8in springform cake tin (pan). Sift the flour and salt into a bowl and make a well in the centre.

2 Melt the lard in the milk. Bring to the boil, pour into the well in the flour, and mix until cool enough to handle. Knead until smooth, then wrap in clear film (plastic wrap).

3 Mix the game, bacon and pork in a bowl. Add the port, orange rind, juniper berries and sage. Season with plenty of salt and pepper. Roll out two-thirds of the dough and fit it into the tin, taking care not to stretch it. Do not trim the edge.

4 Fill the pastry case (pie shell) with the meat mixture. Brush the edge of the pastry with beaten egg. Roll the remaining pastry into a round to fit the top of the pie. Make a hole in the middle and crimp the edge. Brush the lid with beaten egg.

5 Bake for 30 minutes, then lower the oven temperature to 180°C/350°F/Gas 4 and bake for 1¼ hours. About 20 minutes before the end of the cooking time, remove the sides of the tin. Brush the sides with beaten egg and return it to the oven.

6 Sprinkle the gelatine over the water in a heatproof bowl, stir over simmering water until dissolved. Pour through a funnel into the pie and leave to cool.

Pigeon Pie

This is a delicious verison of the Moroccan pastilla.

Serves 4

225g/8oz/1 cup butter
1 medium onion, finely chopped
5cm/2in cinnamon stick
2.5ml/½ tsp ground ginger
2.5ml/½ tsp ground coriander
4 plump pigeons
115g/4oz/⅔ cup whole almonds
10ml/2 tsp ground cinnamon
15ml/1 tbsp icing (confectioner's) sugar
5 eggs, beaten
bunch of fresh coriander (cilantro), finely chopped
bunch of parsley, finely chopped
12 sheets filo pastry
sea salt and ground black pepper

1 In a large pan put 50g/2oz/¼ cup of the butter, the onion and spices and place the pigeons on top. Add water to just cover and season generously. Bring the water to a simmer, cover, and braise for 35–45 minutes. Remove the pigeons from the pan, drain and leave to cool. Discard the cinnamon stick and leave the cooking liquid to bubble until reduced to a syrup. When the pigeons have cooled, strip the meat from the bones, chop and set aside. Preheat the oven to 180°C/350°F/Gas 4.

2 Melt 25g/1oz of the butter in a pan and fry the almonds until golden, add the ground cinnamon and icing sugar and mix. Leave to cool, then chop roughly. Add the beaten eggs and chopped herbs to the reduced pigeon stock and cook, stirring, for about 5 minutes until the eggs are scrambled, then set aside.

3 Melt the remaining butter in a pan and generously brush a 23cm/9in cake tin (pan) with some of it. Line with a sheet of filo, brush with butter and add another sheet, edges hanging over the sides of the tin, repeat with five other sheets. Sprinkle cinnamon and icing sugar in the base of the tin, pour in half the egg mixture and spread it out. Layer half the almonds, all the meat, the remaining almonds and the rest of the eggs. Butter a sheet of filo, fold it in half, place it on top of the pie and dust with more cinnamon and icing sugar. Fold the overlapping pastry edges over the pie and press down. Butter the two remaining sheets of filo together, lay them over the pie and tuck the edges down to create a smooth top. Bake for 45 minutes, until golden. Remove from the oven, dust with icing sugar and cinnamon.

Game Pie Energy 469kcal/1961kJ; Protein 24.5g; Carbohydrate 36.2g, of which sugars 1.9g; Fat 25.8g, of which saturates 10.1g; Cholesterol 68mg; Calcium 104mg; Fibre 1.9g; Sodium 407mg.
Pigeon Pie Energy 980kcal/4066kJ; Protein 44.2g; Carbohydrate 19.2g, of which sugars 2.8g; Fat 81.5g, of which saturates 33.7g; Cholesterol 384mg; Calcium 204mg; Fibre 3.9g; Sodium 632mg.

Orange Pastries

Also known as hojaldras, these delicious pastries are popular treats in many Latin American countries. In Colombia and Venezuela they are made particulalry thin and covered with a sprinkling of sugar – in the coastal region this is usually granulated sugar, while cooks in the Andes prefer a dusting of icing, or confectioners' sugar.

Makes about 48

250g/9oz/2¼ cups plain (all-purpose) flour, plus extra for dusting
150ml/¼ pint/⅔ cup orange juice
30ml/2 tbsp butter
15ml/1 tbsp caster (superfine) sugar
2.5ml/½ tsp salt
1.5ml/¼ tsp baking powder
450ml/¾ pint/scant 2 cups oil, for frying
50g/2oz/½ cup icing (confectioner's) sugar, for dusting

1 Place the flour, orange juice, butter, caster sugar, salt and baking powder in a food processor and process until it leaves the sides of the bowl and forms a smooth ball of dough.

2 Wrap the dough in clear film (plastic wrap) and chill in the refrigerator for 30–45 minutes.

3 On a lightly floured surface, roll out the dough to a thickness of 5mm/¼ in (you can use a pasta machine). Cut into strips about 2.5cm/1in wide, then cut diagonally across the strips to form diamond shapes.

4 Heat the oil in a deep pan to 180°C/350°F. Pick up a diamond, lay it on the work surface and roll it again to about 2mm/¹⁄₁₆in thick. It will stick to the rolling pin. Peel it off and fry for 30 seconds per side while you roll the next diamond.

5 As the hojaldras are done, lift them out of the oil and drain on kitchen paper. Dust them with icing sugar and serve.

Cook's Tip

Hojaldras can be stored for up to a week in an airtight container before dusting with icing sugar.

Angel's Wings

These deep-fried pastry strips dusted with sugar, are traditionally made on the last Thursday before Lent.

Serves 4–6

50g/2oz/¼ cup butter, softened
50g/2oz/¼ cup caster (superfine) sugar
3 egg yolks, plus 1 whole egg
250g/9oz/2¼ cups plain (all-purpose) flour
2.5ml/½ tsp bicarbonate of soda (baking soda)
120ml/4fl oz/½ cup sour cream
pinch of salt
30ml/2 tbsp clear honey
45ml/3 tbsp 95 per cent proof Polish spirit or vodka, or rum
15ml/1 tbsp vinegar
vegetable oil, for deep-frying
icing (confectioner's) sugar, for dusting

1 Beat the butter and sugar in a large bowl. Add the eggs, flour, bicarbonate of soda, sour cream, salt, honey, spirit, vodka or rum, and the vinegar. Beat to combine thoroughly and to form a smooth dough.

2 Transfer the dough to a lightly floured surface and roll out in to a long, thin rectangle, about 10cm/4in across, to a thickness of 3mm/⅛in.

3 Cut the dough lengthways into four 2.5cm/1in strips, then cut each of these horizontally, on a slight slant, into pieces about 10cm/4in long.

4 Make a 4cm/1½in lengthways slit in the middle of each strip. Lift the lower end of the pastry and pass it through the slit.

5 Gently pull it through the other side and downwards to create a twist in the pastry.

6 Heat enough oil for deep-frying to 180°C/350°F/Gas 4, then add the pastry strips in batches of two and fry for 5–8 seconds, until they rise to the surface and are golden brown. Remove from the oil immediately, using a slotted spoon, and drain on kitchen paper. Repeat the process with the remaining pastry.

7 Transfer to a serving dish and dust with icing sugar.

Orange Pastries Energy 72kcal/298kJ; Protein 0g; Carbohydrate 5g, of which sugars 2g; Fat 6g, of which saturates 1g; Cholesterol 1mg; Calcium 7mg; Fibre 0.1g; Sodium 23mg.
Angel's Wings Energy 364kcal/1527kJ; Protein 7.7g; Carbohydrate 45.7g, of which sugars 14g; Fat 16.2g, of which saturates 8.3g; Cholesterol 203mg; Calcium 104mg; Fibre 1.3g; Sodium 79mg.

Rugelach

These crisp, flaky cookies, rolled around a sweet filling, resemble a croissant. They are thought to have come from Poland, where they are a traditional sweet treat. Chocolate chip rugelach are very popular in the US.

Makes 48–60

115g/4oz/½ cup unsalted (sweet) butter
115g/4oz/½ cup full-fat soft white (farmer's) cheese
15ml/1 tbsp sugar
1 egg
pinch of salt
about 250g/9oz/2¼ cups plain (all-purpose) flour, plus extra for dusting
about 250g/9oz/generous 1 cup butter, melted
250g/9oz/scant 2 cups sultanas (golden raisins)
130g/4½oz/generous 1 cup chopped walnuts
about 225g/8oz/generous 1 cup caster (superfine) sugar
10–15ml/1–2 tsp ground cinnamon

1 To make the pastry, put the butter and cheese in a bowl and beat until creamy. Beat in the sugar, egg and salt.

2 Fold the flour into the mixture, a little at a time, until the dough can be worked with the hands. Continue adding the flour, kneading with the hands, until it is a consistency that can be rolled out. (Add only as much flour as needed.)

3 Shape the dough into a ball, then cover with clear film (plastic wrap) and chill in the refrigerator for at least 2 hours or overnight. Preheat the oven to 180°C/350°F/Gas 4.

4 Divide the dough into six equal pieces. On a lightly floured surface, roll out each piece into a round about 3mm/⅛in thick, then brush with a little of the melted butter and sprinkle over the sultanas, chopped walnuts, a little sugar and the cinnamon.

5 Cut the rounds into eight to ten wedges and roll the large side of each wedge towards the tip. (Some filling will fall out.)

6 Arrange on baking sheets, brush with a little butter and sprinkle with the sugar. Bake for 15–30 minutes, until lightly browned. Leave to cool before serving.

Carnival Fritters

These Italian pastries are eaten on Shrove Tuesday and during carnival parades through the Easter period.

Serves 8

450g/1lb/4 cups plain (all-purpose) flour, plus extra for dusting
50g/2oz/¼ cup unsalted (sweet) butter, lard or white cooking fat
2 egg yolks
1 egg
15ml/1 tbsp caster (superfine) sugar
pinch of salt
a few drops of lemon juice
30ml/2 tbsp Mistra liqueur (optional)
dry white wine, if needed
sunflower oil, for deep-frying
icing (confectioners') sugar, for dusting
Alchermes liqueur, for sprinkling (optional)
chilled dessert wine, to serve

1 In a large bowl, mix together the flour, butter, lard or white cooking fat, egg yolks and whole egg, sugar, salt, lemon juice and Mistra, if using.

2 Gently knead the ingredients to make a soft ball of dough, not dissimilar to fresh pasta dough. If dry, add a little dry white wine. Leave the dough to rest, covered with a clean dish towel, for about 30 minutes.

3 Place the dough on a lightly floured surface and roll it out thinly, then cut it into long, wide ribbons, using a pastry wheel or sharp knife.

4 Heat the sunflower oil for deep-frying in a large pan until a small cube of bread dropped into it sizzles instantly. Carefully drop a batch of a few fritters into the hot oil, about six or seven in every batch.

5 As soon as they become golden and puffed up and are floating on the surface of the oil, scoop them out with a slotted spoon and drain thoroughly on kitchen paper.

6 Dust the fritters with icing sugar, sprinkle with Alchermes, if using, and serve warm with chilled dessert wine.

Rugelach Energy 143kcal/596kJ; Protein 1.9g; Carbohydrate 13.2g, of which sugars 5.3g; Fat 9.5g, of which saturates 4.7g; Cholesterol 18mg; Calcium 32mg; Fibre 0.6g; Sodium 48mg.
Carnival Fritters Energy 359kcal/1506kJ; Protein 6.1g; Carbohydrate 45.7g, of which sugars 2.8g; Fat 18.2g, of which saturates 5.2g; Cholesterol 65mg; Calcium 87mg; Fibre 1.7g; Sodium 51mg.

Chicken Neck Pastries

These delicious caramel-filled fried pastries from Peru don't have a very appealing name, but it is what they look like. They are sold in bakeries, and street stalls.

Makes 16

30ml/2 tbsp self-raising (self-rising) flour
5ml/1 tsp baking powder
2 egg yolks
50g/2oz/¼ cup margarine
30ml/2 tbsp pisco or grappa
vegetable oil, for frying
1 egg white, lightly beaten
400g/14oz can dulce de leche or sweetened condensed milk
45ml/3 tbsp icing (confectioners') sugar for dusting

1 Sift the flour and baking powder into a bowl, make a well in the centre and add the egg yolks and margarine.

2 Mix the flour, egg and margarine together, gradually adding the pisco or grappa. Knead the dough until smooth, then cover and leave to rest for 1 hour.

3 Dust the work surface with flour and roll the dough out very thinly (about 2mm/ 1/12in). Cut the dough into small triangles about 7.5cm/3in across.

4 Heat the vegetable oil in a frying pan. When it is hot, start rolling up the triangles into cylinders, beginning at a long side and securing the apex with a little egg white. Work quickly, and drop each one into the pan as soon as it is formed so that it keeps its shape.

5 Fry the pastries over medium heat for about 3 minutes, turning them carefully, until they are crisp and golden.

6 As the pastries are done, remove them from the pan with a slotted spoon and drain on kitchen paper. Leave the pastries to cool completely.

7 Fill the pastries with dulce de leche, spooning or piping it from both ends, and dust them with sifted icing sugar before serving. If not serving immediately, keep in an airtight container, then fill and dust just before serving.

Date-filled Pastries

If you are short of time, and need a quick sweet treat to hand round after a meal or for afternoon tea, try these sweet little pastries packed with dates. Made in the microwave they just take 5 minutes to cook, and so a batch can be whizzed up in less than 15 minutes.

Makes about 25

75g/3oz/6 tbsp butter, softened
175g/6oz/1½ cups plain (all-purpose) flour
5ml/1 tsp rose water
5ml/1 tsp orange flower water
45ml/3 tbsp water
20ml/4 tsp icing (confectioners') sugar, sifted, for sprinkling

For the filling

115g/4oz/⅔ cup stoned (pitted) dried dates
50ml/2fl oz/¼ cup boiling water
2.5ml/½ tsp orange flower water

1 To make the filling, chop the dates finely and place in a bowl. Add the boiling water and orange flower water, then beat the mixture vigorously with a wooden spoon. Set aside and leave to cool.

2 For the pastries, rub the butter into the flour with your fingertips. Mix in the rose and orange flower waters and the water to make a firm dough. Shape the dough into about 25 small balls.

3 Press your finger into a ball of dough to make a small container, pressing the sides round and round to make the sides thinner.

4 Put 1.5ml/¼ tsp of the date mixture into the dough. Seal by pressing the pastry together. Repeat with the remaining dough and filling. Arrange the date pastries, seam side down, on lightly greased baking parchment and prick each one with a fork.

5 Microwave on high (100 per cent) power for 3–5 minutes, rearranging twice during cooking. Leave to stand for 5 minutes before transferring to a rack to cool.

6 Put the cooled pastries on a plate and sprinkle over the icing sugar. Shake lightly to make sure they are covered.

Chicken Neck Energy 169kcal/708kJ; Protein 2.9g; Carbohydrate 18.3g, of which sugars 16.8g; Fat 9.5g, of which saturates 2.4g; Cholesterol 34mg; Calcium 80mg; Fibre 0.1g; Sodium 40mg.
Date-filled Energy 59kcal/246kJ; Protein 0.8g; Carbohydrate 8.6g, of which sugars 3.3g; Fat 2.6g, of which saturates 1.6g; Cholesterol 6mg; Calcium 12mg; Fibre 0.4g; Sodium 19mg.

Apricot and Vanilla Triangles

These quite substantial pastries have a luscious filling of dried apricots poached with cinnamon. If serving them as snacks, you can make the pastry cases smaller and more delicate.

Makes about 24

115g/4oz/½ cup unsalted (sweet) butter, softened
250g/9oz/generous 1 cup sugar
30ml/2 tbsp milk
1 egg, beaten
5ml/1 tsp vanilla extract
pinch of salt
200–250g/7–9oz/1¼–2¼ cups plain (all-purpose) flour, plus extra for dusting
icing (confectioners') sugar, for dusting (optional)

For the filling

250g/9oz/generous 1 cup dried apricots
1 cinnamon stick
45ml/3 tbsp sugar

1 Beat the butter and sugar until pale and fluffy. In another bowl mix together the milk, egg, vanilla extract and salt.

2 Add one-third of the flour, stir, then add the rest in batches, alternating with the milk mixture. Cover and chill for 1 hour.

3 To make the filling, put the ingredients in a pan and add enough water to cover. Heat gently, then simmer for about 15 minutes, until the apricots are tender and most of the liquid has evaporated.

4 Remove the cinnamon stick, then purée the apricots in a food processor or blender with a little of the cooking liquid until they form a consistency like thick jam.

5 Preheat the oven to 180°C/350°F/Gas 4. On a lightly floured surface, roll out the dough to 5mm/¼in thick, then cut into 7.5cm/3in rounds using a cookie cutter.

6 Place 15–30ml/1–2 tbsp of filling in the centre of each round, then pinch the pastry together to form three corners.

7 Place on a baking sheet and bake for 15 minutes, or until pale golden. Serve warm or cold, dusted with icing sugar.

Fig Pastries with Nuts and Honey

To make these traditional Italian pastries, the filling must be left for 12 hours before baking, to allow the flavours to develop.

Makes about 20

500g/1lb/ 2½ cups plain (all-purpose) white flour
2 small (US medium) egg yolks
75g/2oz/¼ cup lard or white cooking fat (shortening), diced
115g/4oz/generous ½ cup sugar
40ml/2½ tbsp sweet vermouth
3.5ml/¾ tsp baking powder
7.5ml/1½ tsp olive oil

For the filling

400g/14oz/2⅓ cups dried figs
400g/14oz/2⅓ cups blanched almonds, halved
400g/14oz/2⅓ cups walnut halves
400g/14oz/1¾ cups clear honey
2.5ml/½ tsp ground cinnamon
2.5ml/½ tsp ground cloves
50ml/2fl oz/¼ cup sweet dessert wine
icing (confectioners') sugar

1 To make the filling, cut the figs into quarters and put in a pan.with the almond and walnut halves, honey, spices and wine. Stir over low heat for 10 minutes. Remove the pan from the heat, cover and set aside for 12 hours.

2 To make the dough, put the flour on to a clean work top and make a hollow in the centre with your fist.

3 Put the egg yolks, lard or cooking fat, sugar, vermouth, baking powder and olive oil into the hollow. Mix these ingredients together, gradually incorporating the surrounding flour to make a dough. Knead briefly. Cover with clear film (plastic wrap) and leave to rest for 30 minutes.

4 Roll out the dough on to a thickness of 5mm/¼in. Using a 10–12cm/4–5in pastry cutter or upturned glass, cut it into rounds. Preheat the oven to 180°C/350°F/Gas 4.

5 Spoon a little of the filling on to one half of each round and fold over to make miniature pasties. Seal the edges by pressing together with a fork. Alternatively, top a round with the filling, and cover with a pastry lattice. Arrange on lightly oiled baking sheets. Bake for 10–15 minutes, until pale golden all over. Leave to cool and dust with icing sugar.

Apricot Triangles Energy 125kcal/528kJ; Protein 1.6g; Carbohydrate 21.3g, of which sugars 14.9g; Fat 4.4g, of which saturates 2.6g; Cholesterol 18mg; Calcium 28mg; Fibre 0.9g; Sodium 35mg.
Fig Pastries Energy 541kcal/2267kJ; Protein 10.7g; Carbohydrate 60.1g, of which sugars 40.4g; Fat 30g, of which saturates 3.8g; Cholesterol 24mg; Calcium 162mg; Fibre 4.5g; Sodium 22mg.

Almond Pastries

These simple almond cookies from Puglia seem incredibly hard when you first attempt to bite into them, but once in your mouth they crumble beautifully. They can also be dunked in dessert wine.

Makes about 25

250g/9oz/2¼ cups whole blanched almonds
250g/9oz/generous 1 cup sugar
75ml/5 tbsp cold water
350g/12oz/3 cups plain (all-purpose) white flour, sifted twice

1 Preheat the oven to 200°C/400°F/Gas 6. Sprinkle the almonds evenly over 1 or 2 baking sheets and toast them in the oven for about 5 minutes, or until golden brown. Take the almonds out of the oven, but leave the oven switched on.

2 Put the sugar into a small pan. Add the water and stir over low heat until the sugar has dissolved and the mixture has formed a smooth syrup. Cool slightly.

3 Grind the almonds to a fine powder in a food processor or nut mill. Put three-quarters of the flour on to a clean work surface. Make a hollow in the centre with your fist. Pour the ground almonds into the hollow and add the syrup. Mix the syrup into the flour and almonds with your hands, working quickly to achieve a smooth and elastic dough.

4 Sprinkle half the remaining flour on the work surface. Shape the dough into a cylinder with a diameter of about 4cm/1½in. Using a sharp knife, cut the cylinder into about 20 even discs, then flatten each one with the palm of your hand, lightly floured, so that you reduce its thickness to about 5mm/¼in.

5 Cut each disc into a roughly square shape then reshape the excess dough. Use the remaining flour to dust one or more baking sheets. Arrange the cookies in rows on the baking sheet(s). Bake for 10–15 minutes, until golden.

6 Leave on the baking sheets for 1–2 minutes to firm up, then, using a spatula, transfer them to wire racks to cool completely. Stored in airtight containers, they will keep for up to 1 month.

Almond Cream Puffs

These sweet little pies consist of crisp, flaky layers of pastry surrounding a delicious, creamy filling. They are best served warm straight out of the oven. If needed, reheat any that become cold before eating.

Makes 10

275g/10oz ready-made puff pastry, thawed if frozen
2 egg yolks
15ml/1 tbsp plain (all-purpose) flour
30ml/2 tbsp ground almonds
30ml/2 tbsp caster (superfine) sugar
a few drops of vanilla or almond extract
150ml/¼ pint/⅔ cup double (heavy) cream, whipped
milk, to glaze
icing (confectioners') sugar, for dusting

1 Preheat the oven to 200°C/400°F/Gas 6. Lightly grease a patty or cupcake tin (pan).

2 Roll out the pastry thinly on a lightly floured surface, and stamp out ten 7.5cm/3in plain rounds and ten 6.5cm/2½in fluted rounds. Keep the smaller fluted rounds for the lids and use the larger ones to line the tin. Chill in the refrigerator for about 10 minutes.

3 Whisk the egg yolks with the flour, almonds, sugar and vanilla extract. Fold in the cream and spoon into the pastry cases.

4 Brush the rims with milk, add the lids and press the edges to seal. Glaze the top with milk.

5 Bake for 20–25 minutes, until puffed up and golden. Using a metal spatula carefully transfer the puffs to a wire rack to cool slightly. Dust with icing sugar.

Variations

Other tasty options are to use desiccated (dry unsweetened shredded) coconut or ground hazelnuts instead of ground almonds in the filling.

Almond Pastries Energy 148kcal/625kJ; Protein 3.5g; Carbohydrate 22g, of which sugars 11.1g; Fat 5.8g, of which saturates 0.5g; Cholesterol 0mg; Calcium 49mg; Fibre 1.2g; Sodium 2mg.
Almond Cream Puffs Energy 225kcal/933kJ; Protein 3.2g; Carbohydrate 14.9g, of which sugars 3.9g; Fat 17.6g, of which saturates 5.5g; Cholesterol 61mg; Calcium 39mg; Fibre 0.3g; Sodium 91mg.

Italian Sweetmeat Pastries

Not much of this Sicilian filling will be used to fill the pastries but it keeps for up to a year in the refrigerator. It just needs to be fed every month with a little sweet dessert wine.

Makes about 24

200g/7oz/scant 1 cup soft butter
400g/14oz/2 cups caster (superfine) sugar
2 eggs, well beaten
30ml/2 tbsp milk
5ml/1 tsp vanilla extract
500g/1¼lb/4½ cups plain (all-purpose) white flour
10ml/2 tsp baking powder

For the sweetmeat

450g/1lb/2⅔ cups hard dried figs
450g/1lb/2⅔ cups sultanas (golden raisins) or raisins
115g/4oz/1 cup shelled walnuts
115g/4oz/1 cup blanched almonds
500g/1¼lb/2 cups clear honey
300ml/½ pint/1¼ cups sweet dessert wine
finely grated rind of 1 lemon
finely grated rind of 1 orange

1 First make the sweetmeat. Put the figs and sultanas or raisins in a pan with water to cover. Bring to simmering point and cook for 3–4 minutes. Allow to cool.

2 Chop the walnuts and almonds finely in a food processor. Scrape into a bowl and set aside. Drain the figs and sultanas and pulse them briefly in a food processor until chopped. Add the honey, half the wine. grated lemon and orange rind and process until smooth. Add the chopped nuts and mix. Set aside 90–120ml/6–8 tbsp of the mixture and spoon the rest into a plastic container, and store in the refrigerator.

3 Preheat the oven to 180°C/350°F/Gas 4. Process the butter, sugar, eggs, milk and vanilla extract. Sift in the flour, baking powder and salt. Mix to a soft dough. Chill for at least 1 hour.

4 Roll a teaspoon of dough into a ball and place on a greased baking sheet, press the top to flatten. Repeat with the remaining mixture, leaving room for spreading. Spoon a little filling on to each round and pull up the edges to partially cover.

5 Bake for 10 minutes. Leave for 5 minutes, then transfer to wire racks and sprinkle with caster sugar. Leave to cool.

Baked Cashew Diamonds

An extremely popular sweet dish found all over India, these tasty morsels, called Kaju Burfi, are flavoured with cardamom. The dough is very simple to make, and is formed from a mixture of ground cashew nuts, sugar and ghee, then flattened and baked in the oven.

Makes 16

225g/8oz raw unsalted cashew nuts
100g/3¾oz/½ cup caster (superfine) sugar
15ml/1 tbsp ghee or unsalted (sweet) butter
2.5ml/½ tsp ground cardamom

1 Put the cashew nuts in a small heatproof bowl and pour over enough boiling water to cover. Soak for 20 minutes, then drain them and place in a food processor or blender.

2 Blend the nuts until a smooth paste forms, then transfer the paste to a large mixing bowl.

3 Add the remaining ingredients to the cashew nut paste in the bowl, and knead the mixture carefully, until it becomes smooth and buttery in texture.

4 Preheat the oven to 160°C/325°F/Gas 3. Line a baking sheet with a well-greased baking parchment and spread the mixture on it to form a 20cm/8in square. Bake in the centre of the oven for 35–40 minutes until lightly browned.

5 Remove the baking sheet from the oven and allow the mixture cool to 15 minutes. Remove from the baking sheet and cut into diamonds or squares. These are delicious served at tea time or after dinner with coffee or tea.

Cook's tip
Ghee is the Indian version of clarified butter with a nuttier flavour and a higher burning point. It is available in tins or jars and should be stored in the refrigerator, where it will keep for up to six months.

Sweetmeat Pastries Energy 423kcal/1783kJ; Protein 5.5g; Carbohydrate 70g, of which sugars 54g; Fat 13.9g, of which saturates 5.2g; Cholesterol 35mg; Calcium 117mg; Fibre 2.9g; Sodium 90mg.
Cashew Diamonds Energy 117kcal/490kJ; Protein 2.9g; Carbohydrate 9.2g, of which sugars 7.3g; Fat 7.9g, of which saturates 1.9g; Cholesterol 2mg; Calcium 8mg; Fibre 0.5g; Sodium 48mg.

Fruit-filled Empanadas

Imagine biting through crisp buttery pastry to discover a rich fruity filling flavoured with oranges and cinnamon.

Makes 12

275g/10oz/2½ cups plain (all-purpose) flour, plus extra for dusting
25g/1oz/2 tbsp sugar
90g/3½oz/scant ½ cup butter, chilled and diced
1 egg yolk
iced water
milk, to glaze
caster (superfine) sugar, for sprinkling
whole almonds and orange wedges, to serve

For the filling
25g/1oz/2 tbsp butter
3 ripe plantains, peeled and mashed
2.5ml/½ tsp ground cloves
5ml/1 tsp ground cinnamon
225g/8oz/1⅓ cups raisins
grated rind and juice of 2 oranges

1 Combine the flour and sugar in a mixing bowl. Add the butter and rub in with your fingertips until the mixture resembles fine breadcrumbs.

2 Beat the egg yolk and add to the flour mixture. Add iced water to make a smooth dough. Shape it into a ball.

3 For the filling, melt the butter in a pan. Add the plantains, cloves and cinnamon and cook over a medium heat for 2–3 minutes. Stir in the raisins, with the orange rind and juice. Lower the heat so that the mixture barely simmers. Cook for about 15 minutes, until the raisins are plump and the juice has evaporated. Set aside to cool.

4 Preheat the oven to 200°C/400°F/Gas 6. Roll out the dough on a lightly floured surface. Stamp out 10cm/4in rounds using a cookie cutter. Place on a baking sheet and spoon on a little of the filling. Dampen the rim of the dough rounds with water, fold the dough over the filling and crimp the edges to seal.

5 Brush with milk. Bake in batches if necessary, for about 15 minutes, or until they are golden. Leave to cool a little, sprinkle with caster sugar and serve warm, with whole almonds and orange wedges.

Apple Turnovers

A sweet product associated with New Year celebrations in the Netherlands is the appelflap or 'apple turnover'.

Makes 12

250g/9oz/2¼ cups plain (all-purpose) flour, plus extra for dusting
2.5ml/½ tsp salt
90g/3½oz/scant ½ cup cold butter
5ml/1 tsp white wine vinegar
500g/1¼lb tart apples, such as Goudrenet or Granny Smith
45ml/3 tbsp soft brown sugar
5ml/1 tsp ground cinnamon
2.5ml/½ tsp crushed fennel seeds
beaten egg, to glaze
icing (confectioners') sugar, for sprinkling

1 Sift the flour and salt into a bowl, coarsely grate in the butter and rub in with your fingertips. Using the blade of a knife, gradually stir in 100ml/3½fl oz/scant ½ cup water and the vinegar. Gather the dough together and shape into a ball.

2 Roll out the dough on a lightly floured surface, then fold the top edge down to the centre and the bottom edge up to the centre and roll out again to form a rectangle. Fold the dough in three again, cover with clear film (plastic wrap) and chill in the refrigerator until needed.

3 Peel the apples and grate them coarsely into a bowl. Stir in the sugar, cinnamon and fennel seeds.

4 Preheat the oven to 200°C/400°F/Gas 6. Line a 30 × 40cm/12 × 16in baking sheet with baking parchment.

5 Roll out the dough on a lightly floured surface to 36 × 48cm/14¼ × 19in rectangle, then cut into 12 squares.

6 Cover the centre of each square with some grated apple and fold over to make a triangle. Press the edges together with a fork. Transfer to the prepared baking sheet and brush with beaten egg.

7 Prick the tops several times with a fork. Bake for about 35 minutes. Remove from the oven and leave to cool, then sprinkle generously with icing sugar.

Fruit Empanadas Energy 276kcal/1161kJ; Protein 4g; Carbohydrate 45.4g, of which sugars 15.7g; Fat 9.9g, of which saturates 5.9g; Cholesterol 40mg; Calcium 59mg; Fibre 1.7g; Sodium 80mg.
Apple Turnovers Energy 156kcal/658kJ; Protein 2.2g; Carbohydrate 23.9g, of which sugars 8g; Fat 6.5g, of which saturates 4g; Cholesterol 16mg; Calcium 34mg; Fibre 1.3g; Sodium 47mg.

Apricot Turnovers

These sweet and succulent pastries are delicious served with a big cup of milky coffee for a late breakfast or mid-morning treat.

Serves 4

225g/8oz ready-made puff pastry, thawed if frozen
60ml/4 tbsp apricot conserve
30ml/2 tbsp icing (confectioners') sugar

1 Preheat the oven to 190°C/375°F/Gas 5. Roll out the pastry on a lightly floured surface to a 25cm/10in square. Using a sharp knife, cut the pastry into four 13cm/5in squares.

2 Place a tablespoon of the apricot conserve in the middle of each square of pastry.

3 Using a pastry brush, brush the edges of the pastry with a little cold water and fold each square over to form a triangle. Gently press the edges together to seal.

4 Carefully transfer the turnovers to a baking sheet and bake for 15–20 minutes, or until risen and golden. Using a metal spatula, remove the pastries to a wire rack to cool, then dust generously with icing sugar and serve.

Variations

- *Use any other fruit conserve to ring the changes, for example, black cherry or damson would be delicious and give a gorgeous colour contrast, too.*
- *For a bitter-sweet alternative use a spoonful of marmalade instead of apricot conserve. A Bramley apple purée would make a comforting option.*
- *Try a coffee filling to complement your cup of milky coffee. Just pour 45ml/3 tbsp of near-boiling water over 30ml/2 tbsp of ground coffee and infuse for 4 minutes. Strain through a fine sieve. Cream 40g/1½oz/3 tbsp butter and 115g/4oz/½ cup caster (superfine) sugar together. Beat in 1 egg yolk, 115g/4oz/1 cup ground almonds and 15ml/1tbsp of the infused coffee. Place a spoonful in the middle of each square of pastry.*

Greek Fruit and Nut Pastries

These aromatic Greek pastries are packed with candied citrus peel and walnuts, and then soaked in a coffee syrup.

Makes 16

450g/1lb/4 cups plain (all-purpose) flour, plus extra for dusting
2.5ml/½ tsp ground cinnamon
2.5ml/½ tsp baking powder
pinch of salt
150g/5oz/10 tbsp unsalted (sweet) butter
30ml/2 tbsp caster (superfine) sugar
1 egg
120ml/4fl oz/½ cup milk, chilled

For the filling

60ml/4 tbsp clear honey
60ml/4 tbsp strong freshly brewed coffee
75g/3oz/½ cup mixed candied citrus peel, finely chopped
175g/6oz/1½ cups walnuts, chopped
1.5ml/¼ tsp freshly grated nutmeg
milk, to glaze
caster (superfine) sugar, for sprinkling

1 Preheat the oven to 180°C/350°F/Gas 4. To make the dough, sift the flour, ground cinnamon, baking powder and salt into a bowl. Rub in the butter until the mixture resembles fine breadcrumbs. Stir in the sugar. Make a well in the middle.

2 Beat the egg and milk together and add to the well in the dry ingredients. Mix to a soft dough. Divide the dough into two and wrap in clear film (plastic wrap). Chill for 30 minutes.

3 To make the filling, mix the honey and coffee. Add the peel, walnuts and nutmeg. Stir well and leave to soak for 20 minutes.

4 Roll out a portion of dough on a lightly floured surface to about 3mm/⅛in thick. Stamp out 10cm/4in rounds.

5 Place a heaped teaspoonful of filling on one side of each round. Brush the edges with milk, then fold over and press the edges together to seal. Repeat until all the filling is used.

6 Put the pastries on non-stick baking sheets, brush with milk and sprinkle with caster sugar. Prick each with a fork and bake for 35 minutes. Cool on a wire rack. Transfer to a serving dish and serve warm with a cup of coffee.

Apricot Turnovers Energy 279kcal/1170kJ; Protein 3.3g; Carbohydrate 39.1g, of which sugars 19g; Fat 13.8g, of which saturates 0g; Cholesterol 0mg; Calcium 38mg; Fibre 0g; Sodium 182mg.
Greek Pastries Energy 6106kcal/26,049kJ; Protein 13.2g; Carbohydrate 1612.4g, of which sugars 1612.4g; Fat 0.6g, of which saturates 0g; Cholesterol 0mg; Calcium 1020mg; Fibre 8.9g; Sodium 115mg.

Fruit Turnovers

This recipe uses plums, but you could also use apples, rhubarb or a jar of ready-made fruit compote. Butter gives the pastry a good flavour, while the lard makes it crisp.

Makes 8

450g/1lb plums, stones (pits) removed and chopped
25–40g/1–1½oz/2–3 tbsp sugar
350g/12oz/3 cups plain (all-purpose) flour
75g/3oz/6 tbsp lard or white cooking fat, cut into pieces
75g/3oz/6 tbsp butter, cut into pieces
milk and sugar, for brushing and sprinkling
pinch of salt

1 Bring the fruit and the sugar to the boil with 15ml/1tbsp water, then cover and simmer for 5–10 minutes, stirring frequently, until the fruit is soft. You can reduce the liquid by bubbling uncovered and stirring until thick. Leave to cool.

2 Sift the flour and salt into a bowl, add the lard or cooking fat and butter and rub them into the flour until the mixture resembles fine crumbs (alternatively, process in a food processor). Stir in enough cold water until the mixture forms clumps, then gather together to make a smooth dough. Wrap the pastry and chill for 20–30 minutes to allow it to relax.

3 Preheat the oven to 190°C/375°F/Gas 5. Then line a baking sheet with baking parchment. On a lightly floured surface, roll out the dough to 3–5mm/⅛–¼in thick. Using a small upturned bowl or plate as a guide, cut out eight 15cm/6in circles, re-rolling the pastry offcuts as necessary.

4 Place a spoonful of cooled fruit on to each pastry circle and brush the edges with water. Fold the pastry over the fruit, pinching the edges to seal them well. Arrange the pastries on the baking sheet, brush with milk, sprinkle some sugar over and make a small slit in each.

5 Put into the hot oven and cook for 20–30 minutes until golden brown. Sprinkle with a little extra sugar and transfer to a wire rack to cool.

Fruit and Nut Turnovers

A tasty mixture of dried fruit and nuts is enclosed in crisp little pastry crescents.

Makes 16

225g/8oz/2 cups plain (all-purpose) flour
1.5ml/¼ tsp baking powder
pinch of salt
10ml/2 tsp caster (superfine) sugar
50g/2oz/4 tbsp unsalted (sweet) butter, chilled
25g/1oz/2 tbsp white cooking fat
120–175ml/4–6fl oz/½–¾ cup iced water

For the filling
350g/12oz/2 cups mixed dried fruit, such as apricots and prunes
75g/3oz/generous ½ cup raisins
115g/4oz/½ cup soft light brown sugar
65g/2½oz/generous ½ cup pine nuts or chopped almonds
2.5ml/½ tsp ground cinnamon
oil, for frying
45ml/3 tbsp caster (superfine) sugar mixed with 5ml/1 tsp ground cinnamon, for sprinkling

1 For the dough, sift the flour, baking powder, salt and sugar into a bowl and rub in the fats until the mixture resembles fine breadcrumbs. Mix in enough iced water to form a dough. Shape into a ball, cover and chill for 30 minutes.

2 Place the dried fruit in a pan and add cold water to cover. Bring to the boil, then simmer for 30 minutes, until the fruit is soft enough to purée.

3 Drain and place in a food processor or blender. Process until smooth, then return the purée to the pan.

4 Add the brown sugar and cook for 5 minutes, stirring, until thick. Stir in the nuts and cinnamon, then leave to cool.

5 Roll out the dough to 3mm/⅛in thick. Stamp out rounds with a 10cm/4in cookie cutter. Put a spoonful of fruit in the centre of each round. Brush the edges of the rounds with water, fold in half and crimp the edges with a fork.

6 Heat a 1cm/½in depth of oil in a frying pan. Fry the pastries, in batches, for 1½ minutes on each side, until golden. Drain, sprinkle with cinnamon sugar and serve.

Fruit Turnovers Energy 340kcal/1420kJ; Protein 4.2g; Carbohydrate 38.5g, of which sugars 5.1g; Fat 19.8g, of which saturates 9.9g; Cholesterol 33mg; Calcium 66mg; Fibre 1.5g; Sodium 66mg.
Fruit & Nut Turnovers Energy 199kcal/840kJ; Protein 3.2g; Carbohydrate 33.6g, of which sugars 22.7g; Fat 6.7g, of which saturates 2.5g; Cholesterol 8mg; Calcium 54mg; Fibre 2.2g; Sodium 27mg.

Creole Calas Fritters

These sweet rice fritters are a Creole speciality, sold by female vendors called 'Calas' women on the streets of the French quarter of New Orleans. They are very popular with residents and office workers, for whom they make a tasty breakfast.

Makes about 40

115g/4oz/generous ½ cup short grain pudding rice
900ml/1½ pints/3¾ cups mixed milk and water
30ml/2 tbsp caster (superfine) sugar
50g/2oz/½ cup plain (all-purpose) flour
7.5ml/1½ tsp baking powder
5ml/1 tsp grated lemon rind
2.5ml/½ tsp ground cinnamon
1.5ml/¼ tsp ground ginger
generous pinch of grated nutmeg
2 eggs
sunflower oil, for deep-frying
salt
icing (confectioner's) sugar, for dusting
fruit jam and cream, to serve

1 Put the rice in a pan and pour in the milk and water. Add a pinch of salt and bring the liquid to the boil. Stir, then cover and simmer over very low heat for about 15–20 minutes until the rice is tender.

2 Switch off the heat under the pan, then add the sugar. Stir well, cover and leave until completely cool, by which time the rice should have absorbed all the liquid and become very soft.

3 Put the rice in a food processor or blender and add the flour, baking powder, lemon rind, spices and eggs.

4 Process for about 20–30 seconds so that the mixture is like a thick batter. Heat the oil in a wok or deep-fryer to 160°C/325°F.

5 Scoop up a generous teaspoon of the rice batter and, using a second spoon, push this off carefully into the hot oil. Add four or five more and fry for 3–4 minutes, turning them occasionally, until the calas are a deep golden brown. Drain on kitchen paper and keep warm while cooking successive batches.

6 Dust the calas generously with icing sugar and serve warm with fruit jam and thick cream.

Honey-coated Fritters

The ingredients for these sticky, honey-coated Italian pastries, called Zeppole, could not be simpler, yet they are transformed into something that is pretty to look at and delicious to eat. They are traditionally made on La Festa di San Giuseppe (Saint Joseph's Day) on March 19. In Rome, Naples and Sicily, these little pastries are sometimes sold on street corners and are given away as gifts. In certain parts of Calabria, savoury anchovy zeppole are eaten on New Year's Eve and New Year's Day.

Makes about 30

500ml/17fl oz/generous 2 cups cold water
500g/1¼lb/5 cups very fine plain (all-purpose) white flour or cake flour, sifted twice
light olive oil for deep-frying
90ml/6 tbsp clear honey

1 Pour the cold water into a heavy pan and bring it to the boil. Gradually trickle the flour into the pan, stirring constantly. Continue to stir until the mixture forms a dough and comes away from the sides of the pan. Turn the dough into a bowl and leave to cool.

2 Pinch off small pieces of dough and roll them into small sausage shapes, each about 5cm/2in long and 5mm/¼in wide. Squeeze each sausage in the middle to make a bow shape.

3 Heat the oil in a large pan until a small piece of bread dropped into it sizzles instantly.

4 Add the dough shapes, in batches, and fry until they rise to the surface of the oil and turn golden and crisp.

5 As each batch cooks, lift the bows out with a slotted spoon and drain on kitchen paper. Place them on a warmed heatproof platter and keep them warm while cooking the remaining shapes.

6 Heat the honey in a small pan. When it bubbles, pour it all over the fritters. Allow to cool slightly, then serve while warm.

Calas Fritters Energy 50kcal/206kJ; Protein 0.9g; Carbohydrate 3.5g, of which sugars 1.3g; Fat 3.6g, of which saturates 0.6g; Cholesterol 10mg; Calcium 16mg; Fibre 0g; Sodium 8mg.
Honey Fritters Energy 103kcal/431kJ; Protein 1.6g; Carbohydrate 13g, of which sugars 0.3g; Fat 5.3g, of which saturates 0.8g; Cholesterol 0mg; Calcium 23mg; Fibre 0.5g; Sodium 1mg.

Potato Fritters

These little fritters are a traditional sweet treat of the Italian port city of Trieste. They are sometimes called chifeletti. They are especially delicious when served at the end of a meal with a glass of chilled sweet dessert wine.

Serves 4

1kg/2¼lb floury potatoes, unpeeled
200g/7oz/1¾ cups plain (all-purpose) flour
115g/4oz/generous ½ cup caster (superfine) sugar
2 eggs, beaten
20g/¾oz/1½ tbsp butter, melted
1 litre/1¾ pints/4 cups sunflower oil
30ml/2 tbsp icing (confectioners') sugar, sifted, for dusting
5ml/1 tsp ground cinnamon, for dusting

1 Boil the potatoes in plenty of water until they are tender. Drain the potatoes, remove the skin, then immediately push them through a food mill into a large mixing bowl.

2 Stir the flour into the mashed potatoes with the sugar, eggs, and melted butter.

3 Using a little at a time, shape the mixture into tiny crescent shapes, using extra flour to stop them sticking to your hands or the work surface.

4 Heat the oil in a pan to 180°C/350°F, or until a cube of bread sizzles instantly and browns in about 45 seconds.

5 Fry the crescents, in batches, until they are crisp and golden. Drain them thoroughly on kitchen paper.

6 Serve the fritters hot, dusted with the icing sugar and cinnamon, with cups of hot chocolate, if you like.

Cook's Tip
The dough can be made in advance, if you like. Cover and put in the refrigerator, then form into crescent shapes and deep-fry when needed.

Venetian Pastries

When making these very traditional Venetian biscuits, you will find you need to work with an extremely stiff, hard dough. If necessary, use a food processor to help you. These pastries, called pevarini, keep very well for up to two months in an airtight container. Many recipes from the Veneto region, and Venice in particular, seem to reflect the need for making foods that will store for a while, presumably with the idea of sea voyaging in mind. The marine shapes of these biscuits continue this theme.

Makes about 18 biscuits

300g/11oz/2¾ cups plain (all-purpose) flour
5ml/1 tsp baking powder
25g/1oz/2 tbsp unsalted butter, lard or vegetable oil
50g/2oz/4 tbsp soft dark brown sugar
15ml/1 tbsp mixed spices, including cinnamon, nutmeg and white pepper

1 Preheat the oven to 190°C/375°F/Gas 5 and line a baking tray with baking parchment.

2 Sift the flour on to a work surface with the baking powder. Add the butter, lard or oil, the sugar, and the spices. Knead everything together thoroughly. Roll the dough out to a thickness of 5mm/¼in.

3 With a sharp, pointed knife, cut biscuits (cookies) out of the dough in your desired shapes (traditionally these are fish or seahorse shapes).

4 Arrange on the prepared baking tray and bake in the preheated oven for about 20 minutes, until golden brown.

5 Remove from the baking tray and cool on wire racks, then serve with ice cream or dessert wine.

Cook's Tip
Use mixed (apple pie) spice, if you wish, for these pastries.

Potato Fritters Energy 757kcal/3182kJ; Protein 12.3g; Carbohydrate 109.2g, of which sugars 34.1g; Fat 33.2g, of which saturates 6.8g; Cholesterol 107mg; Calcium 115mg; Fibre 4.1g; Sodium 103mg.
Venetian Pastries Energy 78kcal/330kJ; Protein 1.6g; Carbohydrate 15.9g, of which sugars 3.2g; Fat 1.4g, of which saturates 0.8g; Cholesterol 3mg; Calcium 25mg; Fibre 0.5g; Sodium 11mg.

Sardinian Honey Fritters

These sticky and sweet ravioli fritters are a classic dessert from Sardinia.

Serves 8

500g/1¼lb plain (all-purpose) flour
45ml/3 tbsp white cooking fat
a pinch of salt
sunflower oil, for deep-frying
60ml/4 tbsp clear honey
grated rind of 1 lemon

For the filling

500g/1¼lb/5 cups cream cheese
250ml/8fl oz/1 cup boiling water
a pinch of salt
grated rind of 1 lemon
30ml/2 tbsp fine semolina

1 To make the filling, put the cream cheese in a pan and mix with the boiling water, salt and lemon rind. Simmer gently, stirring with a whisk, until the mixture is smooth and creamy. Add the semolina and whisk until it has become a thick paste. Remove from the heat and leave to cool.

2 Line a baking tray with baking parchment. With damp hands, shape the mixture into little flat discs about 6cm/2½in in diameter and about 1cm/½in thick. Lay the discs out in one layer on the tray, well spaced out. You can lay a sheet of baking parchment on top and arrange another layer of discs on top, if you are short of space.

3 To make the pastry, pile all the flour on to the work surface and make a hole in the centre. Add the white cooking fat and salt. Knead together, adding enough tepid water to make a smooth, elastic dough. Put the dough in a plastic bag and rest it in the refrigerator for about 15 minutes.

4 Divide the dough in half. On a floured surface, roll out each piece very thinly to make two even sheets. Lay the filling discs on one sheet of dough in even rows. Lay the other sheet of dough on top and gently press around the edges to seal. Using a 7.5cm/3in pastry (cookie) cutter, cut around each disc shape, leaving a narrow edge of pastry.

5 Heat the oil in a large pan or deep-fryer and fry the pastries in batches until golden. Sprinkle with lemon rind, drizzle with honey and serve hot.

Sardinian Iced Pastry Cookies

These deliciously nutty, fruity little biscuits are another speciality of picturesque Sardinia and go perfectly with a glass or two of local Moscato wine.

Serves 10 to 12

500g/1¼lb/4¼ cups plain (all-purpose) flour
5ml/1 tsp baking powder
4 eggs, beaten
150g/5oz caster (superfine) sugar
200g/7oz/generous 1 cup lard or white cooking fat, softened
250g/9oz/2¼ cups chopped walnuts
250g/9oz/2¼ cups blanched chopped almonds
250g/9oz/scant 2 cups raisins or sultanas (golden raisins), soaked for 20 minutes in warm water and drained
200g/7oz/scant 2 cups pine nuts
115g/4oz/⅔ cup finely chopped candied orange peel

For the icing

300g/11oz/generous 1½ cups caster (superfine) sugar
2 egg whites
15ml/1 tbsp coloured sugar sprinkles

1 First, begin to make the icing. Place the caster sugar in a heatproof bowl with 45ml/3 tbsp cold water, and set over a pan of simmering water. Stir continuously until the sugar has dissolved, then remove from the heat and set aside.

2 Preheat the oven to 180°C/350°F/Gas 4, and line a baking sheet with baking parchment. Sift the flour and baking powder into a large bowl and stir in the eggs and the sugar until smooth. Gradually mix in the lard or white cooking fat, nuts, raisins or sultanas, pine nuts and candied orange peel. Work this dough with your hands until it is compact and even.

3 Shape the dough into sticks 1cm/½in wide and 6cm/2½in long and arrange on the baking sheet. Bake for 10 minutes, or until they are lightly golden. Transfer to a cooling rack.

4 To finish the icing, whisk the egg whites in a bowl until they form stiff peaks. Gently fold them into the cooled sugar syrup until you have created a shiny, glassy icing. When the biscuits are cool, brush with the icing, then sprinkle them with the sugar sprinkles. Allow to set, before serving.

Honey Fritters Energy 672kcal/2796kJ; Protein 8.3g; Carbohydrate 57.2g, of which sugars 6.6g; Fat 47.2g, of which saturates 22.3g; Cholesterol 65mg; Calcium 150mg; Fibre 2g; Sodium 191mg.
Iced Cookies Energy 881kcal/3676kJ; Protein 17g; Carbohydrate 81g, of which sugars 48.9g; Fat 56.4, of which saturates 10.3g; Cholesterol 79mg; Calcium 191mg; Fibre 4.7g; Sodium 72mg.

Ring Cookies

Designed specifically to be dunked, these unusual ring-shaped pastries are hard in texture so that they won't disintegrate when dipped into wine at the end of a meal. They are especially delicious dunked into milky coffee for breakfast.

Serves 6–8

115g/4oz/generous ½ cup caster (superfine) sugar
100ml/3½fl oz/scant ½ cup red wine
100ml/3½fl oz/scant ½ cup olive oil
about 250g/9oz/2¼ cups plain (all-purpose) flour
15ml/1 tbsp lard or white cooking fat

1 In a large mixing bowl, mix the sugar, wine and oil together using a whisk. Gradually beat in the flour until you have a pliable, kneadable dough. You may not need all of the flour so just add it a little at a time.

2 Transfer the ball of dough to a bowl, cover with a clean dish cloth, and leave the dough to rest in the refrigerator for at least 30 minutes.

3 Preheat the oven to 160°C/325°F/Gas 3 and grease a baking sheet with the lard or fat.

4 Roll the dough into 10cm/4in long sausage shapes on a lightly floured surface. Bend them round to form rings. Arrange on the baking sheet.

5 Bake for 20 minutes, then cool on a wire rack. Serve with a cup of frothy milky coffee or hot chocolate.

Cook's Tip

These simple little biscuits are designed to keep for a long time and will last for up to two weeks as long as they are stored in an airtight container.

Baked Sweet Ravioli

These rich pastries, attractively formed like little pasta ravioli, are flavoured with tangy lemon and filled with a delicious mixture of ricotta cheese, fruit and chocolate. Serve with coffee as a snack or as a sweet treat after a meal.

Serves 4

225g/8oz/2 cups plain (all-purpose) flour
65g/2½oz/⅓ cup caster (superfine) sugar
90g/3½oz/7 tbsp butter, diced
2 eggs
5ml/1 tsp finely grated lemon rind, plus extra for sprinkling

For the filling

175g/6oz/¾ cup ricotta cheese
50g/2oz/¼ cup caster (superfine) sugar
4ml/¾ tsp vanilla extract
1 egg yolk, beaten
15ml/1 tbsp mixed candied fruits
25g/1oz dark (bittersweet) chocolate, finely chopped
icing (confectioners') sugar, for sprinkling
grated dark (bittersweet) chocolate, for sprinkling

1 For the dough, process the flour, sugar and butter in a food processor. Add one egg and the lemon rind and process to form a dough. Wrap in clear film (plastic wrap) and chill.

2 Press the cheese through a sieve (strainer) into a bowl. Stir in the sugar, vanilla, egg yolk, fruits and chocolate.

3 Halve the dough and roll out each half between sheets of clear film to a 15 x 56cm/6 x 22in rectangle.

4 Preheat the oven to 180°C/350°F/Gas 4. Lightly grease a baking sheet.

5 Place mounds of filling, 2.5cm/1in apart, in two rows on one dough strip. Beat the remaining egg and brush between the mounds. Top with the second dough strip and press to seal. Stamp out ravioli around each mound with a 6cm/2½in cookie cutter. Gently pinch to seal the edges.

6 Place on the baking sheet and bake for 15 minutes, until golden. Sprinkle with lemon rind, icing sugar and chocolate.

Ring Cookies Energy 275kcal/1155kJ; Protein 3g; Carbohydrate 39.3g, of which sugars 15.5g; Fat 11.9g, of which saturates 2.2g; Cholesterol 1.7mg; Calcium 52mg; Fibre 0.9g; Sodium 3.1mg.
Baked Ravioli Energy 628kcal/2636kJ; Protein 13.1g; Carbohydrate 81.4g, of which sugars 38.5g; Fat 30.1g, of which saturates 17.7g; Cholesterol 162mg; Calcium 119mg; Fibre 2.1g; Sodium 186mg.

Gazelles' Horns

These Moroccan pastries are a stylish accompaniment to light fruit dishes.

Makes about 16

200g/7oz/scant 2 cups ground almonds
115g/4oz/1 cup icing (confectioners') sugar, plus extra for dusting
30ml/2 tbsp orange flower water
25g/1oz/2 tbsp butter, melted
2 egg yolks, beaten
2.5ml/½ tsp ground cinnamon

For the pastry
200g/7oz/1¾ cups plain (all-purpose) flour
pinch of salt
25g/1oz/2 tbsp butter, melted
about 30ml/2 tbsp orange flower water
1 egg yolk, beaten
60–90ml/4–6 tbsp chilled water

1 Mix the almonds, icing sugar, orange flower water, butter, egg yolks and cinnamon in a mixing bowl to make a smooth paste.

2 Make the pastry. Sift the flour and salt into a large bowl, then stir in the melted butter, orange flower water and about three-quarters of the egg yolk. Stir in enough chilled water to make a fairly soft dough.

3 Quickly and lightly, knead the pastry until it is smooth and elastic, then place on a lightly floured surface and roll out as thinly as possible. With a sharp knife, cut the dough into long strips about 7.5cm/3in wide.

4 Preheat the oven to 180°C/350°F/Gas 4. Roll small pieces of the almond paste into thin sausages about 7.5cm/3in long with tapering ends. Place these in a line along one side of the strips of pastry, about 3cm/1¼in apart.

5 Dampen the pastry edges with water, then fold the other half of the strip over the filling and press the edges together firmly.

6 Using a pastry wheel, cut around each pastry sausage to make a crescent shape. Pinch the edges firmly together. Prick the crescents with a fork and place on a buttered baking sheet. Brush with the remaining egg yolk and bake for 12–16 minutes until lightly coloured. Allow to cool, then dust with icing sugar.

Christmas Stars

These pretty pastries are a delicious twist on the usual mince pies, although the prune filling is less sweet than mincemeat and does not include any alcohol.

Makes 9

200g/7oz/1¾ cups plain (all-purpose) flour
5ml/1 tsp baking powder
130g/4½oz/½ cup butter, softened
150ml/¼ pint/⅔ cup cold water, or enough to bind
200g/7oz/scant 1 cup ready-to-eat prunes
1 egg, beaten, to glaze

1 Preheat the oven to 200°C/400°F/Gas 6. Sift the flour and baking powder into a large bowl.

2 Cut the butter into small pieces, add to the flour and rub in until the mixture resembles fine breadcrumbs. Alternatively, put the flour and baking powder in a food processor, add the butter and, using a pulsating action, blend to form fine breadcrumbs. Gradually add cold water and mix until it forms a dough.

3 On a lightly floured surface, roll out the pastry to a square about 3mm/⅛in thick, then cut the square into a further nine equal squares. Make a diagonal cut from each corner of the squares towards the centre.

4 Chop the prunes into small pieces. Put a spoonful of the chopped prunes in the centre of each square of pastry, then lift each corner of the pastry and fold it over to the centre to form a rough star shape.

5 Place the stars on a baking sheet and brush with beaten egg. Bake in the preheated oven for about 15 minutes, or until golden brown. Serve warm.

Cook's Tip
A little brandy, mixed into the prunes, adds an extra delicious dimension to these tasty treats.

Gazelles' Horns Energy 182Kcal/762kJ; Protein 4.4g; Carbohydrate 18.1g, of which sugars 8.2g; Fat 10.7g, of which saturates 2.5g; Cholesterol 44mg; Calcium 56mg; Fibre 1.3g; Sodium 23mg.
Christmas Stars Energy 140kcal/583kJ; Protein 1.3g; Carbohydrate 13g, of which sugars 6g; Fat 9.5g, of which saturates 5.9g; Cholesterol 24mg; Calcium 21mg; Fibre 1.3g; Sodium 70mg.

English Eccles Cakes

These traditional dried fruit-filled pastry rounds taste fabulous when home-made.

Makes 16

225g/8oz/2 cups plain (all-purpose) flour, plus extra for dusting
200g/7oz/scant 1 cup butter, diced
5ml/1 tsp lemon juice
100ml/3½fl oz/scant ½ cup water
1 egg, beaten
caster (superfine) sugar, for dusting

For the filling

2.5ml/½ tsp mixed (apple pie) spice
50g/2oz/¼ cup muscovado (molasses) sugar
175g/6oz/⅔ cup currants
50g/2oz/⅓ cup mixed chopped (candied) peel
5ml/1 tsp lemon juice
finely grated rind of 1 lemon

1 To make the pastry, sift the flour and salt into a bowl. Add the butter, lemon juice and iced water. Mix to a soft dough using a flat-bladed knife. Add 5–10ml/1–2 tsp extra water if it is too dry. Gently shape the pastry into a rectangle 28 x 13cm/11 x 5in. (The pastry will just hold together and will contain noticeable pieces of diced butter.)

2 Fold up the lower third of pastry and bring the top third down over it. Turn with the fold on the left, and press three times with the rolling pin to flatten. Roll out into a rectangle and fold and roll again. Wrap in a plastic bag and chill for 20 minutes.

3 Repeat the rolling, folding and chilling four more times. Wrap and chill for 20 minutes, or until needed. Preheat the oven to 220°C/425°F/Gas 7 and lightly grease two baking sheets. Put all the filling ingredients in a bowl and stir together.

4 Roll the pastry to 5mm/¼in thick. Using a 10cm/4in round pastry (cookie) cutter, stamp out 16 rounds and place a heaped teaspoonful of the filling in the centre of each.

5 Damp the edges with water, gather up the pastry over the filling and press to seal. Turn so the seal is underneath and roll each gently. Put on a baking sheet. Cut three slits across the top of each. Brush with beaten egg and sprinkle with sugar. Bake for 20 minutes, then cool on a wire rack.

Almond Mincemeat Tarts

These little tartlets are a welcome change from traditional mince pies. Serve them warm with brandy butter. They freeze well and can be reheated for serving.

Makes 36

275g/10oz/2½ cups plain (all-purpose) flour, plus extra for dusting
75g/3oz/generous ¾ cup icing (confectioners') sugar
5ml/1tsp ground cinnamon
175g/6oz/¾ cup butter
50g/2oz/½ cup ground almonds
1 egg yolk
45ml/3 tbsp milk
450g/1lb mincemeat
15ml/1 tbsp brandy or rum

For the filling

115g/4oz/½ cup butter
115g/4oz/generous ½ cup caster (superfine) sugar
175g/6oz/1½ cups self-raising (self-rising) flour
2 large (US extra large) eggs
finely grated rind of 1 large lemon

For the icing

115g/4oz/1 cup icing (confectioners') sugar
15ml/1 tbsp lemon juice

1 Sift the flour, icing sugar and cinnamon into a bowl or a food processor and rub in the butter until it resembles fine breadcrumbs. Add the ground almonds and bind with the egg yolk and milk to a soft dough. Knead the dough until smooth, wrap in clear film (plastic wrap) and chill for 30 minutes. Preheat the oven to 190°C/375°F/Gas 5.

2 On a lightly floured surface, roll out the pastry and stamp out 36 rounds with a cookie cutter. Mix the mincemeat with the brandy or rum and put a teaspoonful in the bottom of each pastry case (pie shell). Chill.

3 For the filling, whisk all the ingredients together until smooth. Spoon on top of the mincemeat, dividing it evenly, and level the tops. Bake for 20–30 minutes, or until golden brown and springy to the touch. Remove and leave to cool on a wire rack.

4 For the icing, sift the icing sugar and mix with the lemon juice to a smooth, thick, coating consistency. Spoon into a piping (pastry) bag and drizzle a zig-zag pattern over each tart.

Eccles Cakes Energy 201kcal/842kJ; Protein 1.7g; Carbohydrate 23.5g, of which sugars 12.8g; Fat 11.8g, of which saturates 7.4g; Cholesterol 30mg; Calcium 38mg; Fibre 0.8g; Sodium 96mg.
Mincemeat Tarts Energy 177kcal/746kJ; Protein 1.8g; Carbohydrate 26.4g, of which sugars 16.9g; Fat 7.8g, of which saturates 4.4g; Cholesterol 34mg; Calcium 32mg; Fibre 0.6g; Sodium 57mg.

Mince Tarts

Taste the difference in these luxurious pies filled with homemade mincemeat.

Makes 36

425g/15oz/3¾ cups plain (all-purpose) flour
150g/5oz/1¼ cups icing (confectioners') sugar
350g/12oz/1½ cups butter, chilled and diced
grated rind and juice of 1 orange
milk, for glazing

For the filling

175g/6oz/1½ cups finely chopped blanched almonds
150g/5oz/⅔ cup ready-to-eat dried apricots, chopped
175g/6oz/generous 1 cup raisins
150g/5oz/⅔ cup currants
150g/5oz/scant 1 cup glacé (candied) cherries, chopped
150g/5oz/scant 1 cup cut mixed (candied) peel, chopped
115g/4oz/⅔ cup chopped suet
grated rind and juice of 2 lemons
grated rind and juice of 1 orange
200g/7oz/scant 1 cup soft dark brown sugar
4 cooking apples, peeled, cored and chopped
10ml/2 tsp ground allspice
250ml/8fl oz/1 cup brandy
225g/8oz/1 cup cream cheese
30ml/2 tbsp caster (superfine) sugar
icing (confectioners') sugar, for dusting

1 Mix the first 13 filling ingredients together. Cover and leave in a cool place for 2 days.

2 For the pastry, sift the flour and icing sugar into a bowl. Rub in the butter. Stir in the orange rind and enough juice to bind. Chill for 20 minutes.

3 Preheat the oven to 220°C/425°F/Gas 7. Lightly grease two or three bun trays (muffin pans).

4 Roll out the dough, stamp out 36 8cm/3in rounds and put into the trays. Half fill with mincemeat. Beat the cream cheese and sugar and add a teaspoonful to each pie. Roll out the trimmings and stamp out 36 5cm/2in rounds. Brush the edges with milk and cover the pies. Cut a slit in each.

5 Brush lightly with milk. Bake for 15–20 minutes, then leave to cool. Dust with icing suga before serving.

Mince Pies with Spiced Pastry

Home-made mince pies are so much nicer than shop bought ones, especially with this tasty pastry. Serve with whipped cream, flavoured with liqueur, for a special festive treat.

Makes 18

225g/8oz/2 cups plain (all-purpose) flour
40g/1½oz/⅓ cup icing (confectioners') sugar
10ml/2 tsp ground cinnamon
150g/5oz/10 tbsp butter
grated rind of 1 orange
60ml/4 tbsp chilled water
225g/8oz/⅔ cup mincemeat
1 beaten egg, to glaze
icing (confectioners') sugar, for dusting

1 Make the pastry. Sift together the flour, icing sugar and cinnamon in a mixing bowl, then rub in the butter until it resembles breadcrumbs. (This can be done in a food processor.) Stir in the grated orange rind.

2 Mix to a firm dough with the chilled water. Knead lightly, then roll out to 5mm/¼in thick.

3 Using a 6cm/2½in round cutter, cut out 18 circles, re-rolling as necessary. Then cut out 18 smaller 5cm/2in circles.

4 Line two bun tins (muffin pans) with the 18 larger circles – they will fill one and a half tins. Spoon a small spoonful of mincemeat into each and top with the smaller pastry circles, pressing the edges lightly together to seal.

5 Glaze the tops of the pies with egg and chill for 30 minutes. Preheat the oven to 200°C/400°F/Gas 6.

6 Bake the pies for 15–20 minutes until they are golden. Cool on wire racks. Serve warm, dusted with icing sugar.

Cook's Tip

Use store-bought mincemeat if you wish, or make the mincemeat filling from the recipe for Mince Tarts on the left.

Mince Tarts Energy 301kcal/1258kJ; Protein 2.9g; Carbohydrate 33g, of which sugars 23.5g; Fat 16.8g, of which saturates 8.8g; Cholesterol 29mg; Calcium 58mg; Fibre 1.6g; Sodium 96mg.
Mince Pies Energy 145kcal/610kJ; Protein 1.3g; Carbohydrate 19.3g, of which sugars 9.7g; Fat 7.6g, of which saturates 4.4g; Cholesterol 18mg; Calcium 24mg; Fibre 0.6g; Sodium 53mg.

Whiskey-laced Mince Pies

A luxury version of the festive favourite, with added fruit and whisky giving them even more of a Christmas flavour.

Makes 12–15

225g/8oz/⅔ cup mincemeat
50g/2oz/⅓ mixed chopped (candied) peel
50g/2oz/¼ cup glacé (candied) cherries, chopped
30ml/2 tbsp whisky
1 egg, beaten or a little milk
icing (confectioners') sugar, for dusting
double (heavy) cream, to serve

For the pastry

1 egg yolk
5ml/1 tsp grated orange rind
15ml/1 tbsp caster (superfine) sugar
10ml/2 tsp chilled water
225g/8oz/2 cups plain (all-purpose) flour
150g/5oz/10 tbsp butter, diced

1 Make the pastry. Lightly beat the egg yolk in a bowl, then add the grated orange rind, caster sugar and water and mix together. Cover and set aside. Sift the flour into a separate mixing bowl.

2 Rub the butter into the flour until the mixture resembles fine breadcrumbs. Stir in the egg mixture and mix to a dough. Wrap in clear film (plastic wrap) and chill for 30 minutes.

3 Mix together the mincemeat, mixed peel and glacé cherries, then add the whisky.

4 Roll out three-quarters of the pastry. With a fluted pastry (cookie) cutter, stamp out rounds and line 12–15 patty tin (muffin pan) holes. Gather the trimmings, re-roll, and stamp out star shapes.

5 Preheat the oven to 200°C/400°F/Gas 6. Spoon a little filling into each pastry case (pie shell) and top with a star shape. Brush with a little beaten egg or milk and bake for 20–25 minutes, or until golden. Leave to cool.

6 If you like, lift the pastry star off each mince pie and place a dollop of thick cream on top of the filling before replacing the star. Lightly dust the mince pies with a little icing sugar.

Fruit and Almond Pastries

These Polish pastries are eaten at Easter. This version has a rich vanilla cream filling.

Serves 6

300g/11oz/2⅔ cups plain (all-purpose) flour
115g/4oz/1 cup icing (confectioners') sugar
250g/9oz/1 cup butter, softened
4 egg yolks

For the filling

500ml/17fl oz/2¼ cups double (heavy) cream
400g/14oz/2 cups caster (superfine) sugar
1 vanilla pod (bean)
400g/14oz/1¾ cups unsalted (sweet) butter
50g/5oz each of almonds and dried fruits, to decorate

1 Sift the flour and icing sugar into a large bowl. Add the softened butter and egg yolks, and mix to make a smooth dough. Form into a ball, wrap and chill in the for 45 minutes.

2 Preheat the oven to 220°C/425°F/Gas 7. Grease a rectangular baking tray. Roll out the pastry and cut a piece that is the same size as the tray. Place on the tray.

3 Cut the remaining pastry into strips about 1cm/½in wide and join to make one long strip. Brush a little water around the edge of the pastry rectangle. Twist the pastry strip around the edge.

4 Bake the pastry in the oven for about 20 minutes, or until golden brown. Leave to cool slightly, then carefully lift it out on to a large serving dish and cool completely.

5 To make the filling, pour the cream into a heavy pan, then add the sugar and vanilla pod. Gently bring to the boil, then boil for about 5 minutes, stirring, until the mixture is thick. Spoon a small amount on to a cold plate. It should set quickly. Remove from the heat and leave to cool slightly.

6 Remove the vanilla pod, then beat in the butter while the cream mixture is still warm. Spread the mixture inside the pastry case (pie shell), smoothing the top. While the filling is still warm, decorate the top with almonds and dried fruits. Sprinkle the nuts and fruit over, or create a pattern.

Mince Pies Energy 195Kcal/818kJ; Protein 1.8g; Carbohydrate 26.3g, of which sugars 14.8g; Fat 9.5g, of which saturates 5.3g; Cholesterol 35mg; Calcium 36mg; Fibre 0.9g; Sodium 75mg.
Fruit Pastries Energy 1989kcal/8270kJ; Protein 14.9g; Carbohydrate 149.4g, of which sugars 110.6g; Fat 152.2g, of which saturates 86.5g; Cholesterol 480mg; Calcium 270mg; Fibre 4g; Sodium 703mg.

Pecan Tassies

Cream cheese pastry has a rich flavour that goes well with the pecan filling in these tiny tartlets, which take their name from a Scottish word meaning 'a small cup'.

Makes 24

2 eggs
175g/6oz/¾ cup firmly packed soft dark brown sugar
5ml/1 tsp vanilla extract
large pinch of salt
25g/1oz/2 tbsp butter, melted
115g/4oz/1 cup pecan nuts

For the pastry

115g/4oz/½ cup butter
400g/14oz/1¾ cups cream cheese
115g/4oz/1 cup plain (all-purpose) flour

1 Place a baking sheet in the oven and preheat to 180°C/350°F/Gas 4. Grease two 12-cup mini muffin or cupcake tins (pans). To make the pastry, cut the butter and cream cheese into pieces and place in a mixing bowl. Sift over the flour and rub with your fingertips to from a smooth dough.

2 Roll out the dough thinly, then, using a 6cm/2½in fluted pastry (cookie) cutter, stamp out 24 rounds. Line the mini muffin cups with the rounds and chill.

3 To make the filling, whisk the eggs in a bowl. Whisk in the brown sugar, a few tablespoons at a time, then add the vanilla, salt and butter. Set aside.

4 Reserve 24 undamaged pecan halves for the decoration and chop the rest.

5 Place a spoonful of chopped nuts in each mini muffin cup and cover with the filling. Set a pecan half on the top of each.

6 Bake on the hot sheet for about 20 minutes, until puffed and set. Cool on a wire rack. Serve at room temperature.

Variation
Walnuts can be used in this recipe instead of the pecans.

Dutch Sugar Slice

These pastries from Holland originally consisted of small drops of dough baked together. In the 19th century, a baker added a layer of almonds and sugar.

Makes about 32

150g/5oz/10 tbsp butter, plus extra for greasing
breadcrumbs, for sprinkling (optional)
250g/9oz/2¼ cups plain (all-purpose) flour, plus extra for dusting
75g/3oz/scant ½ cup caster (superfine) sugar
75g/3oz/⅓ cup muscovado (molasses) sugar
2.5ml/½ tsp tartaric acid
1.5ml/¼ tsp bicarbonate of soda (baking soda)
2.5ml/½ tsp vanilla seeds
2.5ml/½ tsp aniseed
2.5ml/½ tsp ground cinnamon
1 egg

To decorate

45ml/3 tbsp flaked (sliced) almonds
45ml/3 tbsp small pearl sugar

1 Preheat the oven to 160°C/325°F/Gas 3. Grease a 40 x 35cm/16 x 14in baking sheet. Sprinkle with breadcrumbs or line with baking parchment.

2 Sift the flour, sugar, tartaric acid and soda into a bowl. Stir in the vanilla seeds, aniseed and cinnamon. Add the egg, then the butter. Cut with two knives into very small lumps.

3 Knead the mixture to form an elastic dough then, with floured fingers, press it on to the baking sheet, spreading it out to within 2cm/¾in of the rim.

4 Sprinkle with the almonds and sugar, pressing them in well. Bake for 25–30 minutes, until golden brown. Remove the baking sheet from the oven and cut the pastry into bars.

5 Using a spatula, transfer them to a flat, dry surface to cool. If the undersides of the bars are still soft and pale, turn them upside down on the baking sheet and return to the oven for a few minutes. These can be stored for several weeks in an airtight container.

Pecan Tassies Energy 121kcal/502kJ; Protein 2g; Carbohydrate 4g, of which sugars 0g; Fat 11g, of which saturates 5g; Cholesterol 36mg; Calcium 18mg; Fibre 0g; Sodium 57mg.
Sugar Slice Energy 96kcal/400kJ; Protein 1.2g; Carbohydrate 12.7g, of which sugars 6.6g; Fat 4.8g, of which saturates 2.5g; Cholesterol 10mg; Calcium 19mg; Fibre 0.3g; Sodium 29mg.

Almond and Raspberry Slices

A light pastry base is spread with raspberry jam, topped with almond cake and a layer of flaked almonds to make elegant old-fashioned pastry slices. They are the quintessential summer tea-party cake. These slices keep for up to three days in an airtight container.

Makes 16

butter, for greasing
225g/8oz shortcrust or sweet shortcrust pastry, thawed if frozen
flour, for dusting
60ml/4 tbsp raspberry jam
4 egg whites
175g/6oz/1½ cups ground almonds
175g/6oz/scant 1 cup golden caster (superfine) sugar
a few drops of almond extract
75g/3oz/¾ cup flaked (sliced) almonds
15ml/1 tbsp icing (confectioners') sugar, for dusting (optional)

1 Preheat the oven to 180°C/350°F/Gas 4. Grease a 28 x 18cm/11 x 7in shallow tin (pan).

2 Roll out the pastry on a lightly floured surface to a rectangle large enough to line the base and sides of the tin. Lower the pastry into the tin, using a rolling pin. Press into all the corners, then trim the edges.

3 Spread the raspberry jam over the pastry. Place the egg whites into a clean, grease-free bowl and whisk until they have formed stiff peaks.

4 Fold in the ground almonds, sugar and almond extract. Spoon into the tin, then spread the top level with a flat knife. Sprinkle over the flaked almonds.

5 Bake for 30–35 minutes, or until the pastry is crisp and the topping is golden and firm to the touch. Leave to cool completely in the tin.

6 Mark into 16 slices, then cut these out with a sharp knife. Dust with icing sugar, if you like.

Apple Crumble and Custard Slices

These luscious apple slices are easy to make using ready-made sweet pastry and custard. This is a clever way to make a handy portable pastry treat out of one of the world's most favourite desserts.

Makes 16

350g/12oz ready-made sweet pastry dough
1 cooking apple, about 250g/9oz
30ml/2 tbsp caster (superfine) sugar
60ml/4 tbsp ready-made thick custard

For the crumble topping

115g/4oz/1 cup plain (all-purpose) flour
2.5ml/½ tsp ground cinnamon
60ml/4 tbsp sugar
90g/3½oz/7 tbsp unsalted (sweet) butter, melted

1 Preheat the oven to 190°C/375°F/Gas 5. Lightly grease a 28 x 18cm/11 x 7in shallow cake tin (pan).

2 Roll out the dough and use to line the base of the tin. Prick the dough with a fork, line with foil and baking beans and bake blind for about 10–15 minutes. Remove the foil and baking beans and return the pastry to the oven for another 5 minutes, until cooked and golden brown.

3 Meanwhile, peel, core and chop the apple. Place in a pan with the sugar. Heat gently until the sugar dissolves, then cover with a lid and cook gently for 5–7 minutes, until a thick purée is formed. Beat with a wooden spoon and set aside to cool.

4 Mix the cold apple with the custard. Spread over the pastry base in an even layer.

5 To make the crumble topping, put the flour, cinnamon and sugar into a bowl and pour over the melted butter. Stir thoroughly until the mixture forms small clumps. Sprinkle the crumble over the filling.

6 Return to the oven and bake for about 10–15 minutes, until the crumble topping is cooked and golden brown. Leave to cool in the tin, then slice into bars to serve.

Almond Slices Energy 204kcal/850kJ; Protein 4.7g; Carbohydrate 18.7g, of which sugars 12.2g; Fat 12.7g, of which saturates 0.7g; Cholesterol 0mg; Calcium 50mg; Fibre 1.4g; Sodium 41mg.
Apple Crumble Slices Energy 196kcal/822kJ; Protein 2.1g; Carbohydrate 23.7g, of which sugars 8.1g; Fat 11g, of which saturates 4.9g; Cholesterol 15mg; Calcium 37mg; Fibre 0.9g; Sodium 124mg.

Walnut and Coffee Slice

This two-layered slice has a rich walnut base and a creamy light coffee topping. Serve with a complementary drink such as a sour cherry liqueur.

Serves 8–12
4 sheets of filo pastry
50g/2oz/4 tbsp unsalted (sweeet) butter, melted
4 eggs, separated
175g/6oz/scant 1 cup caster (superfine) sugar
90g/3½oz/scant 1 cup walnuts, finely ground
walnut pieces and sifted icing (confectioners') sugar, to decorate

For the topping
200g/7oz/scant 1 cup unsalted (sweet) butter, at room temperature
1 egg yolk
150g/5oz/¾ cup caster (superfine) sugar
45ml/3 tbsp cold strong coffee

1 Preheat the oven to 180°C/350°F/Gas 4. Grease and line a deep 20cm/8in square cake tin (pan). Brush the sheets of filo pastry with the butter, fold them over and place in the base of the prepared tin.

2 Whisk the egg yolks and sugar in a mixing bowl until thick and pale, and the whisk leaves a trail.

3 Whisk the egg whites until stiff. Fold in the ground nuts.

4 Fold the egg white into the egg yolk mixture. Spoon into the prepared tin. Bake in the oven for about 25–30 minutes, until firm. Allow to cool.

5 Meanwhile, for the topping, cream the ingredients well. Spread on the cake with a round-bladed knife. Sprinkle over the walnut pieces. Chill for at least 3–4 hours or overnight. Sprinkle with icing sugar and cut into fingers, triangles or squares.

Cook's Tip
Please note this recipe contains raw egg yolk. Use pistachios in place of the walnuts if preferred, grinding them in a processor.

Grated Berry Bake

Pastry layers envelop a delicious and sticky fruit filling for this traybake. If your pastry skills are zero, never fear, as the pastry is grated into the tin, so you'll still be able to make this a success. Serve this with a spoonful of cream, if you like, and keep for two days in an airtight container.

Makes 12
275g/10oz/2½ cups plain (all-purpose) flour
2.5ml/½ tsp ground cinnamon
175g/6oz/¾ cup butter, diced, plus extra for greasing
115g/4oz/generous ½ cup golden caster (superfine) sugar
1 egg, beaten
icing (confectioners') sugar, for dusting

For the filling
350g/12oz/3 cups fresh or frozen fruits of the forest (mixed blackcurrants, redcurrants, raspberries, blackberries)
150g/5oz/¾ cup sugar

1 Sift the flour and cinnamon into a bowl or food processor, add the butter, then rub together.

2 Stir in the sugar and beaten egg, and mix together to form a firm dough. Put in a plastic bag and chill for 2 hours or freeze for 20 minutes, or until the pastry forms a firm block.

3 To make the filling, put the fruit in a pan with 30ml/2 tbsp water and simmer for 5 minutes to soften. Add the sugar and stir until it dissolves, then boil for 5 minutes, or until syrupy and thick. Leave to cool.

4 Preheat the oven to 200°C/400°F/Gas 6. Grease and line a 28 x 18cm/11 x 7in shallow tin (pan) with baking parchment.

5 Cut the chilled dough in half and, using a coarse grater, grate one half into the tin. Spread out evenly and press down lightly.

6 Spoon the cooled fruit over the pastry. Coarsely grate the rest of the pastry over the fruit to cover completely, but do not flatten it. Bake for 35 minutes, or until golden brown and firm. When cool, remove the lining paper and cut into 12 bars. Dust with icing sugar.

Walnut Slice Energy 377kcal/1573kJ; Protein 4.9g; Carbohydrate 35.2g, of which sugars 28.8g; Fat 25.1g, of which saturates 12.2g; Cholesterol 138mg; Calcium 44mg; Fibre 0.7g; Sodium 157mg.
Grated Berry Bake Energy 286kcal/1203kJ; Protein 3.3g; Carbohydrate 42.2g, of which sugars 24.8g; Fat 12.8g, of which saturates 8.1g; Cholesterol 49mg; Calcium 56mg; Fibre 1.4g; Sodium 118mg.

Spiced Nut Palmiers

Created at the beginning of the last century, these dainty French pastries, with their rich spicy filling, are designed to be served with afternoon tea. The name is said to refer to their similarity to the foliage of palm trees.

Makes 40

75g/3oz/¾ cup chopped almonds, walnuts or hazelnuts
30ml/2 tbsp caster (superfine) sugar, plus extra for sprinkling
2.5ml/½ tsp ground cinnamon
225g/8oz ready-made rough-puff or puff pastry dough, thawed if frozen
1 egg, lightly beaten

1 Lightly butter two large baking sheets, preferably non-stick. In a food processor fitted with a metal blade, process the nuts, sugar and cinnamon until finely ground.

2 Sprinkle the work surface with caster sugar and roll out the dough to a rectangle 50 x 20cm/20 x 8in and about 3mm/⅛in thick. Lightly brush the dough all over with beaten egg and sprinkle evenly with about half of the nut mixture.

3 Fold in the long edges of the dough to meet in the centre and flatten with the rolling pin. Brush with egg and sprinkle with most of the remaining nut mixture. Fold in the folded edges to meet in the centre, brush with egg and sprinkle with the remaining nut mixture. Fold one side of the dough over the other.

4 Cut the dough crossways into 8mm/⅜in slices and place 2.5cm/1in apart on the baking sheets.

5 Spread the dough edges apart to form dough wedges. Chill the palmiers for at least 15 minutes. Preheat the oven to 220°C/425°F/Gas 7.

6 Bake the palmiers for about 8–10 minutes, until the pastry is crisp and golden. Carefully turn them over halfway through the cooking time using a metal spatula. Keep a watchful eye on them as the sugar can easily scorch. Carefully transfer to a wire rack to cool, but eat while fresh before the pastry softens.

Chocolate and Strawberry Palmiers

These traditional little pastries are easy to make, and they look delightful.

Makes 8

butter, for greasing
15g/½oz/2 tbsp unsweetened cocoa powder
375g/13oz puff pastry, thawed, if frozen
25g/1oz/2 tbsp golden caster (superfine) sugar

For the filling

300ml/½ pint/1¼ cups whipping cream, whipped
45ml/3 tbsp dark (bittersweet) chocolate spread
175g/6oz/generous 1 cup sliced strawberries
icing (confectioners') sugar, for dusting

1 Preheat the oven to 220°C/425°F/Gas 7. Grease two large baking sheets. Dust a clean, dry working surface lightly with 15ml/1 tbsp cocoa powder.

2 Keeping the long side of pastry towards you, roll it out on half the cocoa powder to a rectangle 35 x 23cm/14 x 9in. Lightly brush the top of the pastry with cold water, then sprinkle over the caster sugar and remaining cocoa.

3 Measure and mark the centre of the pastry. Roll up each of the short sides like a Swiss roll (jelly roll) so that they both meet in the centre. Brush the join with a little water and press the rolls together to secure.

4 Mark and then cut the roll into 16 slices. Arrange on the baking sheets, spacing them well apart. Bake for 8–10 minutes, or until risen, puffy and golden brown. Transfer to a wire rack.

5 When completely cool, lightly spread half the pastries with the chocolate spread. To make the filling, put the cream in a piping (pastry) bag fitted with a small plain nozzle. Pipe the cream on top of the chocolate spread, then top with a few strawberry slices.

6 Top each chocolate spread cream and strawberry layer with a pastry. Dust lightly with icing sugar and serve immediately.

Spiced Nut Palmiers Energy 37kcal/155kJ; Protein 0.9g; Carbohydrate 3g, of which sugars 0.9g; Fat 2.6g, of which saturates 0.1g; Cholesterol 5mg; Calcium 9mg; Fibre 0.1g; Sodium 20mg.
Strawberry Palmiers Energy 368kcal/1533kJ; Protein 4.2g; Carbohydrate 27g, of which sugars 9.7g; Fat 28.3g, of which saturates 10.4g; Cholesterol 40mg; Calcium 60mg; Fibre 0.5g; Sodium 180mg.

Walnut and Ice Cream Palmiers

These walnut pastries can be served freshly baked, but for convenience, make them ahead and recrisp them in a moderate oven for 5 minutes. Leave to cool before filling with ice cream. They are perfect for a festive winter dessert.

Makes 6

75g/3oz/¾ cup walnut pieces
350g/12oz puff pastry, thawed if frozen
beaten egg, to glaze
45ml/3 tbsp caster (superfine) sugar
about 200ml/7fl oz/scant 1 cup vanilla ice cream

1 Preheat the oven to 200°C/400°F/Gas 6. Lightly grease a large baking sheet with butter. Chop the walnuts finely.

2 On a lightly floured surface roll the pastry to a thin rectangle 30 x 20cm/12 x 8in.

3 Trim the edges of the pastry, then brush with the egg. Sprinkle over all but 45ml/3 tbsp of the walnuts and 30ml/2 tbsp of the sugar. Run the rolling pin over the walnuts to press them into the pastry.

4 Roll up the pastry from one short side to the centre, then roll up the other side until the two rolls meet. Brush the points where the rolls meet with a little beaten egg.

5 Using a sharp knife, cut the pastry into even slices, approximately 1cm/½in thick.

6 Lay the slices of pastry on the work surface and flatten them evenly with a rolling pin.

7 Transfer to the baking sheet. Brush with more of the beaten egg and sprinkle with the reserved walnuts and sugar.

8 Bake in the preheated oven for about 15 minutes until pale golden and crisp all over.

9 Serve the palmiers while still warm, in pairs with a scoop or two of vanilla ice cream sandwiched between the pastry layers.

Maids of Honour Cakes

These little delicacies were allegedly being enjoyed by Anne Boleyn's maids of honour when the English king Henry VIII first met her in Richmond Palace in Surrey, and he is said to have named them. Originally they would have been made with strained curds, which was made in medieval times by adding rennet to milk.

Makes 12

250g/9oz ready-made puff pastry, thawed if frozen
250g/9oz/generous 1 cup curd (farmer's) cheese
60ml/4 tbsp ground almonds
45ml/3 tbsp caster (superfine) sugar
finely grated rind of 1 small lemon
2 eggs
15g/½oz/1 tbsp butter, melted
icing (confectioners') sugar, for dusting

1 Preheat the oven to 200°C/400°F/Gas 6. Lightly grease a 12-cup bun tray (muffin pan).

2 Roll out the dough very thinly on a lightly floured surface and, using a 7.5cm/3in cookie cutter, stamp out 12 rounds. Press the dough rounds into the prepared tray and prick well with a fork. Chill while you make the filling.

3 Put the curd cheese into a bowl and add the almonds, sugar and lemon rind. Lightly beat the eggs with the butter and add to the cheese mixture. Mix well.

4 Spoon the mixture into the pastry cases (pie shells). Bake for about 20 minutes, until the pastry is well risen and the filling is puffed up, golden brown and just firm to the touch.

5 Transfer to a wire rack (the filling will sink down a little as it cools). Serve warm or at room temperature, dusted with a little sifted icing sugar.

Variation
You can sprinkle the filling with a little freshly grated nutmeg at the end of step 4, if you like.

Walnut Palmiers Energy 398kcal/1661kJ; Protein 6.4g; Carbohydrate 38g, of which sugars 16.3g; Fat 25.7g, of which saturates 2.8g; Cholesterol 10mg; Calcium 93mg; Fibre 0.4g; Sodium 205mg.
Maids of Honour Energy 182kcal/758kJ; Protein 5.2g; Carbohydrate 12.6g, of which sugars 5.1g; Fat 12.9g, of which saturates 3g; Cholesterol 43mg; Calcium 31mg; Fibre 0.4g; Sodium 85mg.

Ricotta and Marsala Tarts

These sweet, melt-in-the-mouth tarts have a crisp puff pastry base. The light cheese filling is flavoured in the Italian way with Marsala, which gives them a lovely mellow sweetness.

Makes 12

375g/13oz ready-made puff pastry, thawed if frozen
250g/9oz/generous 1 cup ricotta cheese
1 egg, plus 2 egg yolks
45–60ml/3–4 tbsp caster (superfine) sugar
30ml/2 tbsp Marsala
grated rind of 1 lemon
50g/2oz/scant ½ cup sultanas (golden raisins)

1 Preheat the oven to 190°C/375°F/Gas 5. Lightly grease a muffin tin (pan).

2 Roll out the pastry. Stamp out twelve 9cm/3½in rounds of pastry and line the prepared tin. Leave the pastry rounds to rest in the refrigerator for 20 minutes.

3 Put the ricotta cheese in a bowl and add the egg, extra yolks, sugar, Marsala and lemon rind. Whisk until smooth, then stir in the sultanas.

4 Spoon the mixture into the lined tins. Bake in the oven for about 20 minutes, or until the filling has risen and the pastry is golden and crisp.

5 Cool the tarts slightly before easing each one out with a metal spatula. Serve warm.

Variations

- *Instead of Marsala, you could use Madeira or sweet sherry, but if you prefer a non-alcoholic version, substitute 5ml/1 tsp vanilla extract.*
- *You can substitute curd (farmer's) cheese, strained cottage cheese or mascarpone for the ricotta but neither the texture nor the flavour will be quite the same.*

Little Nutmeg Custard Tarts

These luxurious little tarts are a real treat to eat with afternoon tea.

Serves 8

600ml/1 pint/2½ cups full-cream (whole) milk
6 egg yolks
75g/3oz/6 tbsp caster (superfine) sugar
a whole nutmeg

For the rich butter pastry

175g/6oz/1½ cups plain (all-purpose) flour
a good pinch of salt
75g/3oz/6 tbsp unsalted (sweet) butter, at room temperature
75g/3oz/6 tbsp caster (superfine) sugar
3 egg yolks, at room temperature
2.5ml/½ tsp vanilla extract

1 Make the pastry first. Sift the flour and salt on to a sheet of baking parchment. Put the butter, sugar, egg yolks and vanilla extract in a food processor and process until the mixture resembles scrambled eggs. Add in the flour and combine.

2 Transfer the dough to a floured surface and knead gently until smooth. Form into a ball, flatten and wrap in clear film (plastic wrap). Chill for at least 30 minutes.

3 Roll out the pastry thinly and use to line eight individual 10cm/4in loose-based tart pans. (You can use smaller, deeper pans, but remember they will need slightly longer cooking.) Place the pans on a baking sheet and chill for 30 minutes.

4 Preheat the oven to 200°C/400°F/Gas 6. To make the filling, heat the milk in a pan until just warmed but not boiling. Beat the egg yolks and sugar together in a bowl until pale and creamy. Pour the milk on to the yolks and stir well to mix. Do not whisk as this will produce too many bubbles. Strain the milk mixture into a jug (pitcher) and pour into the tart cases.

5 Liberally grate fresh nutmeg over the surface of the tartlets. Bake for about 10 minutes, then lower the heat to 180°C/350°F/Gas 4 and bake for another 10 minutes, or until the filling has set and is just turning golden. Don't overbake as the filling should be a bit wobbly when the tartlets come out of the oven. Remove from the pans to cool slightly but serve warm.

Ricotta Tarts Energy 222kcal/928kJ; Protein 29g; Carbohydrate 27.3g, of which sugars 10.1g; Fat 11.4g, of which saturates 3.4g; Cholesterol 16mg; Calcium 64mg; Fibre 1.7g; Sodium 119mg.
Custard Tarts Energy 336kcal/1409kJ; Protein 7.9g; Carbohydrate 40g, of which sugars 23.4g; Fat 17.1g, of which saturates 8.6g; Cholesterol 257mg; Calcium 157mg; Fibre 0.7g; Sodium 101mg.

Jam Tarts

Jam tarts probably have their origins in the middle ages, when sugar first became widely available and sweets and desserts became part of any respectable banquet. In more modern times these little pastry treats have long been served at birthday parties and are often a child's first attempt at baking.

Makes 12

175g/6oz/1½ cups plain (all purpose) flour, plus extra for dusting
pinch of salt
30ml/2 tbsp caster (superfine) sugar
75g/3oz/6 tbsp butter, diced
1 egg, lightly beaten
strawberry or raspberry jam

1 Sift together the flour and salt into a large bowl and stir in the sugar. Add the butter and rub it in with your fingertips until the mixture resembles fine breadcrumbs. Stir in the beaten egg and gather the mixture together into a smooth ball of dough.

2 Wrap the dough in clear film (plastic wrap) and chill in the refrigerator for about 30 minutes.

3 Meanwhile, preheat the oven to 220°C/425°F/Gas 7 and lightly grease a 12-cup bun tin (muffin pan).

4 Roll out the dough on a lightly floured surface to about 3mm/⅛in thick. Using a 7.5cm/3in fluted cookie cutter, stamp out rounds. Re-roll the scraps and stamp out more rounds to make a total of 12. Gently press the dough rounds into the prepared tray. Put a teaspoon of jam into each.

5 Bake for 15–20 minutes, until the pastry is firm and light golden brown and the jam has spread to fill the tarts. Using a metal spatula with a flexible blade, carefully transfer the tarts to a wire rack and leave to cool completely.

Cook's Tip
Take care not to overfill the tarts with jam or it will boil over, spoiling the pastry and making a sticky mess.

Raspberry and Lemon Tartlets

Fresh raspberries and popular lemon curd are teamed up to create colourful, tangy tartlets. If you don't make your own, do buy the best lemon curd you can find.

Serves 4

175g/6oz ready-made shortcrust pastry, thawed if frozen
120ml/8 tbsp good quality lemon curd
115g/4oz/⅔ cup fresh raspberries
whipped cream, to serve

1 Preheat the oven to 190°C/375°F/Gas 5. Roll out the pastry and use to line four 9cm/3½in tartlet tins (muffin pans).

2 Line each tin with a circle of baking parchment and fill with baking beans or uncooked rice.

3 Bake for 15–20 minutes, or until golden and cooked through. Remove the baking beans or rice and paper and take the pastry cases (pie shells) out of the tins. Leave the cases to cool completely on a wire rack.

4 Set aside 12 raspberries for decoration and fold the remaining ones into the lemon curd.

5 Spoon the mixture into the pastry cases and top with the reserved raspberries. Serve immediately with whipped cream.

Cook's Tips
- *To save on last-minute preparation, you can make the pastry cases (pie shells) for these little tartlets in advance and store them in an airtight container until ready to serve.*
- *For an attractive finish, dust the raspberry topping with sifted icing (confectioners') sugar and decorate with mint sprigs or finely shredded lemon rind.*

Variation
Stir a little whipped cream into the lemon for a luxurious touch.

Jam Tarts Energy 114kcal/479kJ; Protein 1.1g; Carbohydrate 18.8g, of which sugars 12.5g; Fat 4.3g, of which saturates 2.6g; Cholesterol 18mg; Calcium 16mg; Fibre 0.3g; Sodium 39mg.
Raspberry Tartlets Energy 289Kcal/1214kJ; Protein 3.1g; Carbohydrate 40.6g, of which sugars 13.8g; Fat 13.9g, of which saturates 4.3g; Cholesterol 13mg; Calcium 47mg; Fibre 1.6g; Sodium 195mg.

Red Grape and Cheese Tartlets

The natural partnership of fruit and cheese is the hallmark of this simple recipe. Look out for small, pale, mauve-coloured or red grapes. These are often seedless, and sweeter than large black varieties.

Makes 6

225g/8oz/1 cup curd (farmer's) cheese
150ml/¼ pint/⅔ cup double (heavy) cream
2.5ml/½ tsp vanilla extract
30ml/2 tbsp icing (confectioners') sugar
200g/7oz/2 cups red grapes, halved, seeded if necessary
60ml/4 tbsp apricot jam
15ml/1 tbsp water

For the pastry

200g/7oz/1¾ cups plain (all-purpose) flour
15ml/1 tbsp caster (superfine) sugar
150g/5oz/10 tbsp butter
2 egg yolks
15ml/1 tbsp chilled water

1 Make the pastry. Sift the flour and sugar into a mixing bowl. Rub or cut in the butter until the mixture resembles fine breadcrumbs. Add the egg yolks and water and mix to a dough. Knead lightly until smooth. Wrap in clear film (plastic wrap) and chill for 30 minutes.

2 Preheat the oven to 200°C/400°F/Gas 6. Roll out the pastry and use to line six deep 10cm/4in fluted tartlet tins (muffin pans). Prick the bases, line with foil and fill with baking beans.

3 Bake for 10 minutes, remove the foil and beans, then bake for a further 5 minutes until golden. Remove the pastry cases (pie shells) from the tins and leave to cool.

4 Meanwhile, beat the curd cheese with the double cream, vanilla extract and icing sugar in a small bowl. Divide the mixture among the pastry cases. Smooth the surface and arrange the halved grapes attractively on top.

5 Press the apricot jam through a sieve (strainer) into a small pan. Add the water and heat, stirring constantly, until smooth and glossy. Generously spoon the apricot glaze over the grapes. Leave to cool, then chill before serving.

Orange Curd Tarts with Cointreau

These traditional English tarts combine a creamy filling with a hint of the delicious orange liqueur, Cointreau.

Serves 6

175g/6oz/1½ cups plain (all-purpose) flour
40g/1½oz/3 tbsp butter
40g/1½oz/3 tbsp white cooking fat, diced
30ml/2 tbsp caster (superfine) sugar
1 egg yolk
2.5ml/½ tsp ground nutmeg
orange segments and thinly pared orange rind, to decorate

For the filling

25g/1oz/2 tbsp butter, melted
50g/2oz/¼ cup caster (superfine) sugar
1 egg
175g/6oz/¾ cup curd (farmer's) cheese
30ml/2 tbsp double (heavy) cream
50g/2oz/¼ cup currants
15ml/1 tbsp grated lemon rind
15ml/1 tbsp grated orange rind
15ml/1 tbsp Cointreau

1 Make the pastry. Sift the flour into a large mixing bowl and rub in the butter and fat until the mixture resembles fine breadcrumbs. Stir in the sugar and egg yolk and add enough cold water to make a firm dough.

2 Wrap the pastry in clear film (plastic wrap) and chill for 30 minutes. Preheat the oven to 190°C/375°F/Gas 5.

3 Roll out the dough on a lightly floured surface and line six 10cm/4in fluted flan tins (pans).

4 Make the filling. Combine the melted butter, sugar, egg, curd cheese, cream, currants, grated rind and Cointreau in a bowl. Mix well. Spoon into the pastry cases (pie shells), sprinkle over the nutmeg and bake for 30–35 minutes until golden. Serve decorated with orange segments and pared rind.

Cook's Tips
Curd (farmer's) cheese is a soft unripened cheese with a milky, tangy flavour. To make a large tart, line an 18cm/7in flan tin with the pastry. Spoon in the filling and bake for 45–55 minutes.

Grape Tart Energy 559Kcal/2330kJ; Protein 10.4g; Carbohydrate 45.1g, of which sugars 19.7g; Fat 39.3g, of which saturates 23.9g; Cholesterol 164mg; Calcium 123mg; Fibre 1.3g; Sodium 331mg.
Curd Tarts Energy 638kcal/2666kJ; Protein 7g; Carbohydrate 38g, of which sugars 16g; Fat 52g, of which saturates 29g; Cholesterol 197mg; Calcium 100mg; Fibre 4.3g; Sodium 29mg.

Tia Maria Berry Tarts

The ideal dessert for a tea or coffee break, these mini coffee pastry cases are filled with a chocolate liqueur truffle centre and topped with fresh ripe berries.

Serves 6

300ml/½ pint/1¼ cups double (heavy) cream
225g/8oz/generous ¾ cup seedless bramble or raspberry jam
150g/5oz plain (semisweet) chocolate, broken into squares
45ml/3 tbsp Tia Maria liqueur
450g/1lb mixed berries, such as raspberries, small strawberries or blackberries

For the pastry

225g/8oz/2 cups plain (all-purpose) flour
15ml/1 tbsp caster (superfine) sugar
150g/5oz/10 tbsp butter, cubed
1 egg yolk
30ml/2 tbsp very strong brewed coffee, chilled

1 Preheat the oven to 200°C/400°F/Gas 6. Put a baking sheet in the oven to heat. To make the pastry, sift the flour and sugar into a large bowl. Rub in the butter. Stir the egg yolk and coffee together, add to the bowl and mix to a stiff dough. Knead lightly on a floured surface for a few seconds until smooth. Wrap in clear film (plastic wrap) and chill for about 20 minutes.

2 Use the pastry to line six 10cm/4in fluted tartlet tins (muffin pans). Prick the bases with a fork and line with baking parchment and baking beans. Put on the hot baking sheet and bake for 10 minutes. Remove paper and beans and bake for 8–10 minutes longer, until cooked. Cool on a wire rack.

3 To make the filling, slowly bring the cream and 175g/6oz/generous ½ cup of the jam to the boil, stirring continuously until dissolved.

4 Remove from the heat, add the chocolate and 30ml/2 tbsp of the liqueur. Stir until melted. Cool, then spoon into the pastry cases (pie shells), and smooth the tops. Chill for 40 minutes.

5 Heat the remaining jam and liqueur until smooth. Arrange the fruit on top of the tarts, then brush the jam glaze over it. Chill until ready to serve.

Summer Fruit Brulée Tartlets

This quantity of pastry is enough for eight tartlets, so freeze half.

Makes 4

4 egg yolks
15ml/1 tbsp cornflour (cornstarch)
50g/2oz/¼ cup caster (superfine) sugar
2.5ml/1 tsp vanilla extract
300ml/½ pint/¼ cups milk
225g/8oz/2 cups summer fruits
50g/2oz/½ cup icing (confectioners') sugar

For the pastry

250g/9oz/2¼ cups plain (all-purpose) flour
25g/1oz/¼ cup ground almonds
15ml/1 tbsp icing (confectioners') sugar
150g/5oz/⅔ cup butter, diced
1 egg yolk
about 45ml/3 tbsp chilled water

1 Mix the flour, ground almonds and icing sugar in a bowl. Rub in the butter until the mixture resembles fine breadcrumbs. Add the egg yolk and enough chilled water to form a soft dough. Wrap half in cling film (plastic wrap) and freeze for use later. Cut the remaining half of the pastry into four pieces, roll out and use to line four tartlet tins (muffin pans). Chill.

2 Preheat the oven to 200°C/400°F/Gas 6. Line the pastry cases (pie shells) with baking parchment and baking beans. Bake blind for 10 minutes. Remove the paper and beans, and return to the oven for 5 minutes until golden. Allow to cool.

3 To make the custard filling, beat the egg yolks, cornflour, caster sugar and vanilla extract together in a bowl. Warm the milk in a small pan, pour it on to the egg yolk mixture, whisking, then return the mixture to the cleaned pan. Heat the custard until it thickens, stirring all the time, but do not let it boil. Remove from the heat, cover, and leave to cool.

4 Sprinkle the fruits in the tartlet cases and spoon over the cooled custard. Chill the tartlets for 2 hours.

5 Preheat the grill (broiler) to the highest setting. Sift the icing sugar over the tops of the tartlets. Place the tartlets under the hot grill until the sugar caramelizes. Allow the topping to cool and harden for about 10 minutes before serving.

Tia Maria Tarts Energy 846kcal/357kJ; Protein 7g; Carbohydrate 81g, of which sugars 52g; Fat 56g, of which saturates 34g; Cholesterol 157mg; Calcium 119mg; Fibre 5.5g; Sodium 180mg.
Brulée Tarts Energy 743kcal/3099kJ; Protein 13.6g; Carbohydrate 75.2g, of which sugars 20.7g; Fat 45g, of which saturates 23.8g; Cholesterol 342mg; Calcium 250mg; Fibre 4g; Sodium 282mg.

Curd Tarts

This is a variation of the classic Yorkshire Curd Tart, a tangy sweet tart made from curd cheese, giving the same combination of salty and sweet flavour as you get from a cheesecake. These little tarts make a great treat when cold for children's lunch boxes. Using bought shortcrust pastry makes this a quick and easy baking task.

Makes 24

450g/1lb shortcrust pastry
225g/8oz curd cheese
2 eggs, beaten
75g/3oz/generous ⅓ cup caster (superfine) sugar
5ml/1 tsp finely grated lemon rind
50g/2oz/¼ cup currants
60ml/4 tbsp lemon curd
thick cream or crème fraîche, to serve

1 Preheat the oven to 180°C/350°F/Gas 4. Roll out the shortcrust pastry thinly, stamp out 24 rounds using a 7.5cm/3in plain cutter and use to line patty or tartlet tins (muffin pans). Chill or set aside in a cool place until required.

2 Cream the curd cheese with the eggs, sugar and lemon rind. Stir in the currants.

3 Place 2.5ml/½ tsp of the lemon curd in the base of each tartlet case. Spoon on the filling, flatten the tops and bake for 35–40 minutes, until just turning golden.

4 Serve warm, topped with thick cream or crème fraîche.

Cook's Tip

Pastry freezes very well, so save time by lining the tartlet tins (muffin pans) with pastry, wrapping them tightly and storing them in the freezer. When ready to cook, simply remove from the freezer and allow to defrost for 1 hour, then fill and bake.

Variation

For special occasions, add a drop of brandy to the filling.

Small Blueberry Pies

Delicious little blueberry pies are perfect as a dessert after a Sunday lunch.

Makes 10

For the pastry
50g/2oz/¼ cup butter
200ml/7fl oz/scant 1 cup milk
45ml/3 tbsp water
2.5ml/½ tsp salt
7.5ml/1½ tsp sugar
1 small (US medium) egg
400g/14oz/3½ cups plain white (all-purpose) flour
large pinch of rapid-rise dried yeast

For the filling
300–350g/11–12oz/2¾–3 cups blueberries, fresh or frozen
25g/1oz/2 tbsp caster (superfine) sugar
15ml/1 tbsp cornflour (cornstarch)

For the glaze
150ml/¼ pint/⅔ cup crème fraîche
45ml/3 tbsp caster (superfine) sugar
icing (confectioners') sugar, for dusting

1 To make the dough, melt the butter in a small pan. Add the milk, water, salt and sugar and heat until warm to the finger. Pour the mixture into a large bowl. Add the egg and mix together.

2 Put the flour and yeast in a large bowl and mix together. Stir in the butter mixture, a little at a time, until combined. Knead the dough in the bowl for at least 5 minutes. Cover the bowl with a dish towel and leave the dough to rise in a warm place for 30 minutes until it has doubled in size.

3 Turn the dough on to a lightly floured surface. Cut into 24 pieces and form each into a ball. Leave to rest for 5–10 minutes. Mix the blueberries in a bowl, with the sugar and cornflour.

4 Preheat the oven to 200°C/400°F/Gas 6. Grease a large baking tray. Flatten each ball to a round measuring about 15cm/6in in diameter. Place on the baking tray. Place 45ml/3 tbsp of the mixture in the centre of each round then fold an edge up around the mixture. Bake for 10–15 minutes.

5 Meanwhile, put the crème fraîche and the sugar in a bowl and mix together. When the pies are baked, spoon a little of the glaze over each pie. Dust with icing sugar. Serve hot or cold.

Curd Tarts Energy 125kcal/526kJ; Protein 3.1g; Carbohydrate 15.8g, of which sugars 6.5g; Fat 6.1g, of which saturates 3.1g; Cholesterol 27mg; Calcium 34mg; Fibre 0.4g; Sodium 68mg.
Blueberry Pies Energy 371kcal/1559kJ; Protein 4.4g; Carbohydrate 55.8g, of which sugars 25.7g; Fat 16g, of which saturates 4.9g; Cholesterol 8mg; Calcium 93mg; Fibre 3.2g; Sodium 228mg.

Peach and Redcurrant Tartlets

Tart redcurrants and sweet peaches make a winning combination in these simple tartlets. They look really pretty and make a great end to a dinner party where you just want a sweet little finish that isn't too rich. Small bunches of redcurrants make easy ornaments, dusted with a little icing sugar.

Makes 4

25g/1oz/2 tbsp butter, melted
16 sheets of filo pastry, each measuring 15cm/6in square, thawed if frozen
150ml/¼ pint/⅔ cup double (heavy) cream
130g/4½oz peach and mango fromage frais or yogurt
vanilla extract
15ml/1 tbsp icing (confectioners') sugar, sifted, plus extra for dusting
2 peaches, halved and stoned (pitted)
50g/2oz/½ cup redcurrants, plus redcurrant sprigs, to decorate

1 Preheat the oven to 190°C/375°F/Gas 5. Use a little of the butter to lightly grease four individual tartlet tins (muffin pans). Brush the pastry squares with a little more butter, stack them in fours, then place in the tartlet tins to make four cases.

2 Bake for about 15 minutes until golden. Cool the filo cases on a wire rack before removing them from the tins.

3 To make the filling, whip the cream to soft peaks, then lightly fold in the fromage frais or yogurt with a few drops of the vanilla extract and icing sugar. Divide among the pastry cases.

4 Slice the peaches and arrange the slices on top of the filling, with a few redcurrants. Decorate with redcurrant sprigs and dust with icing sugar.

Cook's Tip
To strip redcurrants from their stalks, pull the stalks through the tines of a fork so that they drop into a bowl.

Nectarine and Physalis Tartlets

These tartlets are so pretty filled with golden nectarines and physalis. Make sure you use really ripe nectarines, the fruit needs to be soft and sweet for the best result. You can also fill these tarts with thinly sliced fresh figs and seeded green grapes.

Makes 4

200g/7oz/1¾ cups plain (all-purpose) flour
15ml/1 tbsp caster (superfine) sugar
150g/5oz/10 tbsp butter
2 egg yolks
15ml/1 tbsp chilled water

For the filling
60ml/4 tbsp apple jelly or raspberry jam
15–30ml/1–2 tbsp Kirsch or fruit juice
450g/1lb nectarines and physalis (cape gooseberries), washed, pitted and sliced as necessary

1 Make the pastry. Sift the plain flour and sugar into a mixing bowl. Rub or cut in the butter until the mixture resembles fine breadcrumbs. Add the egg yolks and water and mix to a dough.

2 Knead lightly then wrap in clear film (plastic wrap) and chill for 30 minutes. Preheat the oven to 200°C/400°F/Gas 6.

3 Roll out the pastry and use to line six deep 10cm/4in fluted tartlet tins (muffin pans). Prick the bases, line with baking parchment and fill with baking beans.

4 Bake for 10 minutes, remove the baking parchment and beans, then bake for a further 5 minutes until golden.

5 Remove the pastry cases from the tins and cool on a wire tray until ready to fill.

6 Shortly before serving, melt the jam in a small pan over a low heat with the Kirsch or fruit juice until melted.

7 Arrange the sliced nectarines and physalis in the tartlet shells and brush the tops liberally with the glaze. Allow to set for 10–15 minutes and the serve.

Peach Tartlets Energy 411kcal/1715kJ; Protein 6g; Carbohydrate 34g, of which sugars 14g; Fat 28g, of which saturates 17g; Cholesterol 71mg; Calcium 56mg; Fibre 4g; Sodium 58mg.
Nectarine Tartlets Energy 559Kcal/2330kJ; Protein 10.4g; Carbohydrate 45.1g, of which sugars 19.7g; Fat 39.3g, of which saturates 23.9g; Cholesterol 164mg; Calcium 123mg; Fibre 1.3g; Sodium 331mg.

Plum and Marzipan Pastries

These Danish pastries can be made with any stoned fruit. Try apricots, cherries, damsons or greengages, adding a glaze made from clear honey or a complementary jam.

Makes 6

375g/13oz ready-made puff pastry, thawed if frozen
90ml/6 tbsp plum jam
115g/4oz/¾ cup white marzipan, coarsely grated
3 red plums, halved and stoned (pitted)
1 egg, beaten
50g/2oz/½ cup flaked (sliced) almonds

For the glaze

30ml/2 tbsp plum jam
15ml/1 tbsp water

1 Preheat the oven to 220°C/425°F/Gas 7. Roll out the pastry, cut it into six equal squares and place on one or two dampened baking sheets.

2 Spoon 15ml/1 tbsp jam into the centre of each pastry square. Divide the marzipan among them. Place half a plum, hollow side down, on top of each marzipan mound.

3 Brush the edges of the pastry with beaten egg. Bring up the corners and press them together lightly, then open out the pastry corners at the top.

4 Brush the pastries all over with a little beaten egg to glaze. Divide the flaked almonds between the six pastries and press all over the tops and sides.

5 Bake the pastries for 20–25 minutes, until crisp and golden brown. Keep a close eye on them towards the end of the cooking time as the almonds can scorch quite quickly, spoiling the appearance and flavour of the pastries.

6 To make the glaze, heat the jam and water in a small pan, stirring until smooth. Press the mixture through a sieve (strainer) into a small bowl, then brush it over the tops of the pastries while they are still hot. Leave to cool a little on a wire rack, but eat while still warm.

Almond Tartlets

Food items don't often make it on to postage stamps, but these delicious double-crust curd tartlets are so famous in Belgium that that they did just that in 1985.

Makes 6

1 litre/1¾ pints/4 cups milk
500ml/17fl oz/generous 2 cups buttermilk
15ml/1 tbsp lemon juice
butter and flour for greasing and dusting
3 eggs, separated
5ml/1 tsp vanilla extract
5ml/1 tsp almond extract
25g/1oz/¼ cup ground almonds
115g/4oz/1 cup icing (confectioners') sugar
675g/1½lb puff pastry, thawed if frozen
1 egg yolk mixed with 30ml/2 tbsp water, to glaze

1 Make the milk curd for the filling the day before. Pour the milk into a pan and bring it to the boil. Remove from the heat and stir in the buttermilk and lemon juice. Leave to stand for 10–15 minutes, to curdle. Pour into a fine sieve (strainer) lined with muslin (cheesecloth). Stand in the sink to drain overnight.

2 Preheat the oven to 220°C/425°F/Gas 7. Grease six 7.5cm/3in loose-bottomed tartlet tins (muffin pans) and dust with flour. Process the curds in a food processor until smooth. Scrape into a bowl and stir in the egg yolks, vanilla extract, almond extract and ground almonds. Add half the sugar and mix well.

3 Roll out the pastry and cut out six 7.5cm/3in rounds as lids for the tartlets and six slightly larger rounds for the cases. Fit the larger rounds into the tins and prick the bases with a fork.

4 Beat the egg whites to stiff peaks, gradually adding the remaining icing sugar. Fold the beaten egg whites into the curd mixture, then divide the filling among the pastry cases (pie shells). Fit the lids on top, and press edges together to seal.

5 Glaze the pastry lids by brushing them with the egg yolk mixture. Using sharp kitchen scissors, cut two slashes in the top of each lid, so steam can escape. Bake for 30–40 minutes or until the pastry is golden. Leave to cool for about 10 minutes, then carefully remove the tartlets from the tins and serve.

Plum Pastries Energy 416kcal/1746kJ; Protein 6.6g; Carbohydrate 51.8g, of which sugars 29.2g; Fat 22.4g, of which saturates 0.6g; Cholesterol 0mg; Calcium 73mg; Fibre 1.2g; Sodium 205mg.
Almond Tartlets Energy 704kcal/2946kJ; Protein 19.3g; Carbohydrate 73.1g, of which sugars 32.8g; Fat 40.3g, of which saturates 5.5g; Cholesterol 155mg; Calcium 402mg; Fibre 0.3g; Sodium 495mg.

Mango and Tamarillo Pastries

These fruit-topped little pastries go down a treat at the end of a spicy meal. Exotic mango and tamarillos provide a refreshing taste, while the marzipan adds a delectable sweetness.

Makes 8

225g/8oz ready-rolled puff pastry (30 x 25cm/12 x 10in rectangle)
1 egg yolk, lightly beaten
115g/4oz/½ cup white marzipan
40ml/8 tsp ginger or apricot conserve
1 mango, peeled and thinly sliced off the stone (pit)
2 tamarillos, halved and sliced
caster (superfine) sugar, for sprinkling

1 Preheat the oven to 200°C/400°F/Gas 6. Unroll the pastry and cut it into 8 rectangles. Carefully transfer to a couple of baking sheets.

2 Using a sharp knife, score the surface of each rectangle of pastry into a diamond pattern, then brush each piece with the egg yolk to glaze.

3 Cut eight thin slices of marzipan slightly smaller than the rectangles of pastry, and lay one slice on each pastry rectangle. Top each with a teaspoon of the ginger or apricot conserve and spread over evenly.

4 Top each pastry rectangle with alternate slices of mango and tamarillo. Sprinkle the fruit with some of the caster sugar.

5 Bake in the preheated oven for 15–20 minutes until the pastry is well puffed up and golden.

6 Transfer the pastries to a wire rack to cool. Sprinkle with more caster sugar before serving.

Variation
If you have difficulty finding tamarillos, use thin apricot or peach slices instead – or a mixture of the two.

Pear and Amaretti Tarts

Crumbled amaretti cover the pastry case for these delectable little tarts, which are topped with pears and pine nuts.

Makes 6 individual tarts

250g/9oz/2¼ cups plain (all-purpose) flour
10ml/2 tsp baking powder
150g/5oz/¾ cup caster (superfine) sugar
115g/4oz/½ cup butter, softened
1 egg, plus 1 egg yolk
5ml/1 tsp vanilla extract
fine breadcrumbs, for dusting
45ml/3 tbsp apricot conserve
75g/3oz amaretti, crumbled
6 small ripe pears, halved, peeled and cored
50g/2oz/½ cup pine nuts
25g/1oz/2 tbsp caster (superfine) sugar
45–60ml/3–4 tbsp milk
icing (confectioners') sugar, for dusting

1 Preheat the oven to 180°C/350°F/Gas 4. Sift the flour and baking powder into a pile on the work surface and make a hollow in the centre with your fist. Add 115g/4oz/generous ½ cup of caster sugar, the butter, egg and yolk, vanilla and salt to the hollow, then knead together to make a soft ball of dough.

2 Divide the dough into two balls, one of a third, the other of two thirds, wrap both and set aside. Generously grease six individual tart tins (pans) with butter, then dust each tin first with plain flour, then with breadcrumbs.

3 Roll out the larger ball of dough on a lightly floured work surface, to about 1cm/½in thick. Cut out circles and use to line each of the greased tart tins.

4 Cover the base of each lined case with a layer of conserve, then arrange a thick layer of the amaretti crumbs on top. Arrange the pears on top of the amaretti crumbs, cutting them to fit, then sprinkle over the pine nuts and remaining sugar.

5 Use the smaller ball of dough to line the edges of the top of each tart, and create a lattice pattern for the tops. Bake in the oven for about 20–30 minutes then brush generously with milk, and bake for a further 8–10 minutes. Remove the tarts from the tins dust with icing sugar, and serve warm.

Mango Pastries Energy 202Kcal/847kJ; Protein 3.2g; Carbohydrate 28.4g, of which sugars 18.3g; Fat 9.5g, of which saturates 0.4g; Cholesterol 25mg; Calcium 43mg; Fibre 1.2g; Sodium 95mg.
Pear Amaretti Energy 521kcal/2192kJ; Protein 6.7g; Carbohydrate 83.5g, of which sugars 46.4g; Fat 19.8g, of which saturates 11.9g; Cholesterol 109mg; Calcium 112mg; Fibre 4g; Sodium 205mg.

Nectarine Puff Pastry Tarts

These simple, fresh fruit pastries are easy to put together, but the puff pastry gives them an elegant look. You could use peaches, apples or pears instead of the nectarines.

Serves 6

15g/½oz/1 tbsp butter, plus extra for greasing
225g/8oz rough puff or puff pastry
30ml/2 tbsp apricot preserve
450g/1lb nectarines
25g/1oz/2 tbsp caster (superfine) sugar
freshly grated nutmeg
crème fraîche or lightly whipped cream, to serve (optional)

1 Lightly grease a large baking sheet and line with baking parchment. Sprinkle very lightly with water.

2 On a lightly floured surface, roll out the rough puff pastry to a large rectangle, measuring about 40 x 25cm/16 x 10in, and cut into six smaller rectangles.

3 Transfer the pastry to the baking sheet. Using the back of a small knife, scallop the edges of each piece of pastry. Then, using the tip of the knife, score a line 1cm/½in from the edge of each rectangle to form a border.

4 Chill the shapes for 30 minutes. Meanwhile, preheat the oven to 200°C/400°F/Gas 6. Halve the nectarines and remove the stones (pits), then cut the fruit into thin slices.

5 Spread a little of the apricot preserve on each of the pastry shapes, then arrange the nectarine slices neatly in the centre of the rectangles, leaving the border uncovered.

6 Sprinkle the fruit with the caster sugar and a little freshly grated nutmeg. Bake in the oven for about 12–15 minutes until the edges of each pastry case (pie shell) are puffed up and golden brown, and the fruit is tender.

7 Transfer the tarts to a wire rack to cool slightly, then serve warm with crème fraîche or whipped cream, if you like.

Danish Pastry

Buttery, flaky Danish pastries are unrivalled in the baking universe. Keep the pastry as cold as you can while using it. See page 1 for image.

Makes 16 pastries

For the pastry

40g/1½oz fresh yeast
150ml/¼ pint/⅔ cup milk
120ml/4fl oz/½ cup double (heavy) cream
50g/2oz/¼ cup caster (superfine) sugar
2 eggs
5ml/1 tsp ground cardamom
5ml/1 tsp salt
5ml/1 tsp vanilla sugar
400g/14oz/3½ cups white bread flour
340g/12oz/1½ cups unsalted (sweet) butter, chilled
1 egg mixed with 30ml/2 tbsp milk, to glaze
flaked (sliced) almonds, to decorate

For the almond filling

115g/4oz/½ cup butter
90g/3½oz/½ cup caster (superfine) sugar
50g/2oz/½ cup ground almonds
45ml/3 tbsp double (heavy) cream
2.5ml/½ tsp almond extract
75g/2½oz/½ cup sultanas (golden raisins)

1 Dissolve the yeast in the milk in a small bowl. Heat the cream gently in a pan to barely lukewarm, 40°C/104°F. Stir the yeast mixture into the cream and leave to stand for 5 minutes.

2 Beat the sugar with the eggs in a large bowl until light and frothy. Stir in the cardamom, salt and vanilla sugar. Mix in the yeast mixture, then stir in the bread flour to make a soft dough. Knead for 2–3 minutes. Cover and chill for at least 2 hours.

3 Turn the dough out on to a lightly floured surface and roll out to a 40cm/16in square about 1cm/½in thick.

4 Cut the butter into thin slices and place side by side down the middle of the pastry square, ending about 2.5cm/1in from the edge of the dough. Fold over one side of the pastry to cover the butter, then the other side. Seal the ends. Wrap and chill for 15 minutes.

5 Unwrap the dough and roll out again to form a 40cm/16in square. Give the dough a quarter turn, then fold in thirds again, at right angles to the first folds. Wrap and refrigerate for another 15 minutes. Repeat the rolling, folding and chilling steps twice more, then cover and leave to rest in the refrigerator for 15 minutes.

6 Meanwhile, preheat the oven to 200°C/400°F/Gas 6. Prepare the filling by combining the butter, sugar, and almonds in a bowl. Stir in the cream, almond extract and sultanas. Set aside. Line a baking sheet with baking parchment.

7 Roll out the dough and cut into 10cm/4in squares. Spoon about 15ml/1tbsp of the filling into the centre of each square. Fold opposite corners over to partially cover the filling.

8 Place the squares on the prepared baking tray, then cover with a clean towel and leave for 15–30 minutes for the pastry to rise slightly. Brush liberally with the milk and egg glaze, sprinkle with flaked almonds and bake for about 15 minutes, until golden brown. Cool on a wire rack, and eat while warm.

Nectarine Tarts Energy 208Kcal/873kJ; Protein 3.2g; Carbohydrate 25.9g, of which sugars 12.5g; Fat 11.3g, of which saturates 1.3g; Cholesterol 5mg; Calcium 30mg; Fibre 0.9g; Sodium 133mg.
Danish Pastry Energy 436kcal/1814kJ; Protein 5.1g; Carbohydrate 32.8g, of which sugars 13.7g; Fat 32.5g, of which saturates 18.9g; Cholesterol 111mg; Calcium 78mg; Fibre 1.1g; Sodium 194mg.

Baked Lattice Peaches

You could use nectarines for this recipe, left unpeeled.

Makes 6
3 peaches
juice of ½ lemon
75g/3oz/scant ½ cup white marzipan
375g/13oz ready-rolled puff pastry, thawed if frozen
a large pinch of ground cinnamon
beaten egg, to glaze
caster (superfine) sugar, for sprinkling

For the sauce
50g/2oz/¼ cup caster (superfine) sugar
30ml/2 tbsp cold water
150ml/¼ pint/⅔ cup double (heavy) cream

1 Preheat the oven to 190°C/375°F/Gas 5. Place the peaches in a bowl and pour over boiling water. Leave for 60 seconds, drain, then peel off the skins. Toss the fruit in the lemon juice.

2 Divide the marzipan into six pieces and shape each to form a small round. Cut the peaches in half and remove their stones. Fill the stone cavity in each with a marzipan round.

3 Unroll the puff pastry and cut it in half. Set one half aside, then cut out six rounds from the rest, making each round slightly larger than a peach half. Sprinkle a little cinnamon on each pastry round, then place a peach half, marzipan side down, on the pastry. Cut small slits in rows all over the remaining pastry, starting each row lower than the last. Cut the lattice pastry into six equal squares.

4 Dampen the edges of the pastry rounds with water, then drape a lattice pastry square over each peach half. Press around the edge to seal, then trim off the excess pastry and decorate with peach leaves made from the trimmings. Transfer the peach pastries to a baking sheet. Brush with the beaten egg and sprinkle with the caster sugar. Bake for 20 minutes, until golden.

5 Meanwhile, make the caramel sauce. Heat the sugar with the water in a small pan until it dissolves. Bring to the boil and continue to boil until the syrup turns a dark golden brown. Stand back and add the cream. Heat gently, stirring until smooth. Serve the peach pastries with the sauce.

Plum Dumpling

These Polish dumplings are made with a potato dough, and contain a plum, stuffed with cinnamon sugar.

Serves 4–6
675g/1½lb potatoes, peeled
250ml/8fl oz/1 cup sour cream
75g/3oz/6 tbsp butter
2 eggs, beaten
250g/9oz/2¼ cups plain (all-purpose) flour
8–12 plums
90g/3½oz/¾ cup icing (confectioners') sugar
30ml/2 tbsp ground cinnamon
45ml/3 tbsp breadcrumbs
icing (confectioners') sugar and cinnamon, for dusting

1 Cut the potatoes into even-sized pieces and cook in a pan of lightly salted boiling water for 10–15 minutes, or until soft. Drain, leave to cool, then mash in a large bowl. Add the sour cream, 25g/1oz/2 tbsp butter, eggs and flour to the mashed potato and stir to combine thoroughly.

2 Turn the dough out on to a lightly floured surface and knead lightly until the dough comes together and is firm. Add a little more flour if necessary – it should not be sticky.

3 Cut a slit down one side of each plum so that you can remove the stone (pit). Mix together the icing sugar and cinnamon, then push a teaspoonful into each of the plums.

4 Roll out the dough to 5mm/¼ in thick and cut into eight or twelve 10cm/4in squares (depending on how many plums you have). Place a plum in the centre of each square, then bring up the dough and pinch the edges together to seal completely.

5 Bring a large pan of water to the boil, and add the dumplings in batches of about six at a time. Cook for about 8 minutes, or until they rise to the surface. Remove with a slotted spoon, transfer to a bowl and keep warm while you cook the rest.

6 Heat the remaining butter in a large frying pan, and fry the breadcrumbs until golden brown. Add the dumplings and gently turn in the breadcrumbs to coat. Transfer to a serving plate and dust with icing sugar and cinnamon. Serve immediately.

Lattice Peaches Energy 472kcal/1971kJ; Protein 6g; Carbohydrate 45g, of which sugars 23g; Fat 31g, of which saturates 9g; Cholesterol 73mg; Calcium 70mg; Fibre 3.1g; Sodium 217mg.
Plum Dumpling Energy 510kcal/2147kJ; Protein 11.1g; Carbohydrate 72.6g, of which sugars 18.6g; Fat 21.6g, of which saturates 12.4g; Cholesterol 115mg; Calcium 147mg; Fibre 5.3g; Sodium 190mg.

Apple, Raisin and Maple Pies

Calvados accentuates the apple flavour of these elegant puff pastry pies.

Serves 4

350g/12oz puff pastry
beaten egg or milk, to glaze
whipped cream, flavoured with orange liqueur and sprinkled with grated orange rind, to serve

For the filling

75g/3oz/6 tbsp soft light brown sugar
30ml/2 tbsp lemon juice
45ml/3 tbsp maple syrup
150ml/¼ pint/⅔ cup water
45ml/3 tbsp Calvados
6 small eating apples, halved, peeled and cored
75g/3oz/½ cup raisins

1 Make the filling. Mix the sugar, lemon juice, maple syrup and water in a pan. Heat over medium heat until the sugar has dissolved, then bring to the boil and cook until reduced by half. Stir in the Calvados.

2 Cut four of the apples into eight even segments. Add the apple pieces to the syrup and simmer for 5–8 minutes until just tender. Lift the apple pieces out of the syrup using a slotted spoon and set them aside.

3 Chop the remaining apples and add to the syrup with the raisins. Simmer until the mixture is thick, then cool.

4 Preheat the oven to 200°C/400°F/Gas 6. Roll out the pastry on a floured surface and stamp out eight 15cm/6in rounds with a fluted cutter. Use half the pastry to line four 10cm/4in individual flan tins (pans). Spoon in the raisin mixture and level the surface.

5 Arrange the apple segments on top of the raisin mixture. Brush the edge of each pastry case (pie shell) with egg or milk and cover with a pastry lid. Trim, seal and flute the edges.

6 Cut attractive shapes from the pastry trimmings and use to decorate the pies. Brush over the tops with beaten egg or milk, then bake for 30–35 minutes until golden. Serve hot, with the liqueur-flavoured cream.

Mini Mille Feuilles

This pâtisserie classic is a delectable combination of crisp puff pastry with luscious pastry cream. As a large one is difficult to cut, making individual servings is a great solution.

Serves 4

450g/1lb ready-made puff pastry, thawed if frozen
6 egg yolks
65g/2½oz/⅓ cup caster (superfine) sugar
45ml/3 tbsp plain (all-purpose) flour
350ml/12fl oz/1½ cups milk
30ml/2 tbsp Kirsch or cherry liqueur
450g/1lb/2⅔ cups raspberries
icing (confectioners') sugar, for dusting

1 Lightly grease two large baking sheets and sprinkle them with a little very cold water.

2 On a lightly floured surface, roll out the pastry to a thickness of 3mm/⅛in. Using a 10cm/4in cookie cutter, stamp out 12 rounds. Place on the baking sheets and prick each with a fork. Chill for 30 minutes. Preheat the oven to 200°C/400°F/Gas 6.

3 Bake the pastry rounds for 15–20 minutes, until golden, then transfer to wire racks to cool.

4 Whisk the egg yolks and sugar for 2 minutes until light and creamy, then whisk in the flour until just blended. Bring the milk to the boil over a medium heat and pour it over the egg mixture, whisking to blend. Return to the pan, bring to the boil and boil for 2 minutes, whisking constantly.

5 Remove from the heat and whisk in the Kirsch or liqueur. Pour into a bowl and press a piece of clear film (plastic wrap) on to the surface to prevent a skin from forming. Set aside.

6 To assemble, carefully split the pastry rounds in half. Spread each round with a little pastry cream. Arrange a layer of raspberries over the cream and top with a second pastry round. Spread with a little more cream and a few more raspberries. Top with a third pastry round and dust with icing sugar.

Apple Pies Energy 545Kcal/2294kJ; Protein 5.8g; Carbohydrate 82.8g, of which sugars 51.6g; Fat 21.6g, of which saturates 0g; Cholesterol 0mg; Calcium 75mg; Fibre 2g; Sodium 316mg.
Mille Feuilles Energy 702kcal/2943kJ; Protein 16.5g; Carbohydrate 79.1g, of which sugars 30.4g; Fat 37.8g, of which saturates 3.4g; Cholesterol 308mg; Calcium 258mg; Fibre 3.2g; Sodium 406mg.

Hungarian Poppy Seed Pastry

The Hungarians like contrasts in their food, and the combination of salty and sweet is as common as the flavours of sweet and sour. This salty–sweet partnership works best by using creamy home-made cottage cheese, which in this recipe is combined with the natural sweetness of honey. These filo pastries are often served in Hungary for breakfast, but also make a lovely dessert.

Makes 20

250g/9oz/generous 1 cup cottage cheese
200g/7oz/scant 1 cup curd (farmer's) cheese
butter, for greasing
5ml/1 tsp ground black pepper
1 large egg yolk
20 sheets filo pastry, thawed if frozen
150g/5oz/10 tbsp butter, melted
30ml/2 tbsp poppy seeds
75–90ml/5–6 tbsp clear honey, to serve

1 Preheat the oven to 180°C/350°F/Gas 4 Combine the cottage cheese and curd cheese in a bowl, then stir in the black pepper and egg yolk. Lightly butter a baking tray.

2 Take a sheet of filo pastry and cover the remaining pastry sheets with a damp cloth.

3 Lightly brush the sheet of filo with some melted butter and fold in half lengthways. Brush with butter and fold it in half again.

4 Put some cheese mixture on the pastry along the shorter edge and roll the pastry over the filling to form a small Swiss roll (jelly roll). Make sure you fold the sides of the pastry inward at the same time, to enclose the filling, and make sure you do not roll too tightly.

5 Place the pastries on to the prepared baking sheet. Continue with the remaining filo sheets and cheese mixture.

6 Brush the pastries with melted butter, then sprinkle with poppy seeds. Bake the pastries in the oven for 20 minutes, or until golden brown. Cool slightly on the baking tray before removing,and then serve warm with a little honey to drizzle over the pastry.

Almond Cigars

These light-as-air pastries are filled with flavoured marzipan, and are sure to delight your guests.

Makes 8–12

250g/9oz marzipan
1 egg, lightly beaten
15ml/1 tbsp rose water or orange flower water
5ml/1 tsp ground cinnamon
1.5ml/¼ tsp almond extract
8–12 sheets filo pastry, thawed if frozen
melted butter, for brushing
icing (confectioners') sugar and ground cinnamon, for dusting

1 Knead the almond paste until soft, then put in a bowl and mix in the egg, flower water, cinnamon and almond extract. Chill for 1–2 hours.

2 Preheat the oven to 190°C/375°F/Gas 5. Lightly grease a baking sheet.

3 Place a sheet of filo pastry on a piece of baking parchment, keeping the remaining pastry covered with a damp cloth, and brush with the melted butter.

4 Shape 30–45ml/2–3 tbsp of the filling into a cylinder and place at one end of the pastry. Fold the pastry over to enclose the ends of the filling, then roll up to form a cigar. Place on the baking sheet and make 7–11 more cigars in the same way.

5 Bake for about 15 minutes, or until golden brown. Leave to cool completely, then serve, dusted with icing sugar and a little ground cinnamon.

Variation

Instead of dusting with sugar, drench the pastries in syrup. In a pan, dissolve 250g/9oz/generous 1 cup sugar in 250ml/8fl oz/1 cup water and boil until thickened. Stir in a squeeze of lemon juice and a few drops of rose water and pour over the pastries. Leave the syrup to soak in before serving.

Poppy Seed Pastries Energy 101kcal/428kJ; Protein 15g; Carbohydrate 8g, of which sugars 6g; Fat 3g, of which saturates 1g; Cholesterol 15mg; Calcium 63mg; Fibre 0.5g; Sodium 118mg.
Almond Cigars Energy 109kcal/458kJ; Protein 2.2g; Carbohydrate 18.9g, of which sugars 14.2g; Fat 3.2g, of which saturates 0.4g; Cholesterol 16mg; Calcium 25mg; Fibre 0.6g; Sodium 10mg.

Almond and Date Filo Parcels

These sweet Moroccan pastries, or briouates, are made with filo or the local equivalent, ouarka, and coated in honey.

Makes 30

15ml/1 tbsp sunflower oil
225g/8oz/1 1/3 cups blanched almonds
115g/4oz/2/3 cup stoned (pitted) dried dates
25g/1oz/2 tbsp butter, softened
5ml/1 tsp ground cinnamon
1.5ml/1/4 tsp almond extract
40g/1 1/2oz/1/3 cup icing (confectioners') sugar
30ml/2 tbsp orange flower water or rose water
10 sheets of filo pastry
50g/2oz/1/4 cup butter, melted
120ml/4fl oz/1/2 cup clear honey
dates, to serve (optional)

1 Heat the oil in a small pan and fry the almonds for a few minutes until golden, stirring all the time. Drain on kitchen paper. When cool, grind the almonds in a coffee or spice mill. Process the dates in a blender or food processor.

2 Spoon the ground almonds into the blender or food processor with the dates, and blend with the softened butter, cinnamon, almond essence, icing sugar and a little flower water to make a soft paste.

3 Preheat the oven to 180°C/350°F/Gas 4. Brush a sheet of filo pastry with melted butter and cut into three equal strips. Place a walnut-size piece of almond paste at the bottom of each strip. Fold one corner over the filling to make a triangle and then fold up, in triangles, to make a neat packet. Brush with melted butter.

4 Repeat to make 30 pastries. Arrange on baking sheets and bake for 20–25 minutes, until golden and crisp.

5 Meanwhile, pour the honey and a little orange flower or rose water into a pan and heat very gently. When the pastries are cooked, lower them one by one into the pan and turn them in the honey so that they are thoroughly coated all over.

6 Transfer the parcels to a plate and cool a little before serving, with dates if you wish.

Filo Crackers

These can be prepared a day in advance, brushed with melted butter and kept covered with clear film in the refrigerator or freezer before baking.

Makes 24

2 x 275g/10oz packets frozen filo pastry, thawed
115g/4oz/1/2 cup butter, melted
thin foil ribbon, to decorate
sifted icing (confectioners') sugar, to decorate

For the filling

450g/1lb eating apples, peeled, cored and finely chopped
5ml/1tsp ground cinnamon
25g/1oz/2 tbsp soft light brown sugar
50g/2oz/1/2 cup pecan nuts, chopped
50g/2oz/1 cup fresh white breadcrumbs
25g/1oz/3 tbsp sultanas (golden raisins)
25g/1oz/2 tbsp currants

For the lemon sauce

115g/4oz/ generous 1/2 cup caster (superfine) sugar
finely grated rind of 1 lemon
juice of 2 lemons

1 Unwrap the filo pastry and cover it with clear film (plastic wrap) and a damp cloth to prevent it from drying out. Mix all the filling ingredients together in a bowl.

2 Take one sheet of pastry at a time and cut it into 115 x 30cm/ 6 x 12in strips. Brush with butter. Place a spoonful of the filling at one end and fold in the sides, so the pastry measures 13cm/5in across. Brush the edges with butter and roll up. Pinch the 'frill' at each end and tie with ribbon. Brush with butter.

3 Place the crackers on baking trays, cover and chill for 10 minutes. Preheat the oven to 190°C/375°F/Gas 5. Brush each cracker with melted butter. Bake the crackers for 30–35 minutes, or until they are golden brown. Let them cool slightly on the baking trays and then transfer them to a wire rack to cool completely.

4 To make the lemon sauce, put all the ingredients in a small pan and heat gently to dissolve the sugar. Serve the sauce warm. Finally, dust the crackers with sifted icing sugar.

Almond Pastries Energy 95kcal/396kJ; Protein 1.8g; Carbohydrate 7.5g, of which sugars 6g; Fat 6.6g, of which saturates 1.7g; Cholesterol 5mg; Calcium 23mg; Fibre 0.7g; Sodium 17mg.
Filo Crackers Energy 149kcal/629kJ; Protein 2.2g; Carbohydrate 23.9g, of which sugars 9.6g; Fat 5.7g, of which saturates 2.7g; Cholesterol 10mg; Calcium 34mg; Fibre 1g; Sodium 46mg.

Truffle-filled Filo Tulips

These cups can be prepared a day ahead and stored in an airtight container.

Makes about 24

3–6 sheets filo pastry
45g/1½oz/3 tbsp unsalted (sweet) butter, melted
sugar for sprinkling
lemon rind, to decorate

For the truffles

250ml/8fl oz/1 cup double (heavy) cream
225g/8oz dark (bittersweet) or plain (semisweet) chocolate, chopped
55g/2oz/4 tbsp unsalted (sweet) butter, diced
30ml/2 tbsp brandy or other liqueur

1 In a pan over medium heat, bring the cream to the boil. Remove from the heat and add the chocolate, stirring until melted. Beat in the butter and add the brandy. Strain into a bowl. Chill for 1 hour until thick.

2 Preheat the oven to 200°C/400°F/Gas 6. Grease a bun tray (muffin pan) with 24 x 4cm/1½in cups.

3 Place the filo sheets on a work surface. Cut each sheet into 6cm/2½in squares. Cover the sheets with a damp dish towel to prevent them from drying out while you are working. Keeping the filo squares covered, place one square on a work surface. Brush lightly with melted butter, turn over and brush the other side in the same way. Sprinkle with sugar.

4 Brush melted butter on another square, place it over the first at an angle and sprinkle with sugar. Butter a third square and place it over the first two squares, so that the corners form an uneven edge. Press the layered square into the tray. Continue to fill the tray with filo squares in this way.

5 Bake the filo cups for 4–6 minutes, until golden. Cool for 10 minutes on a wire rack in the tray. Remove from the tray and leave to cool completely.

6 Stir the chocolate mixture; it should be just thick enough to pipe. Spoon it into a piping (pastry) bag with a star nozzle and pipe a swirl into each cup. Decorate with lemon rind.

Filo Fruit Baskets

Almost too pretty to eat, these crisp filo baskets are filled with fresh fruit set on a rich creamy base with a surprise flavour.

Serves 6

4 large or 8 small sheets of frozen filo pastry, thawed
65g/2½oz/5 tbsp butter, melted
250ml/8fl oz/1 cup double (heavy) or whipping cream
45ml/3 tbsp strawberry jam
15ml/1 tbsp Cointreau or other orange-flavoured liqueur

For the topping

115g/4oz seedless black grapes, halved
115g/4oz seedless white grapes, halved
150g/5oz fresh pineapple, cubed, or drained canned pineapple chunks
115g/4 oz/⅔ cup raspberries
30ml/2 tbsp icing (confectioners') sugar
6 sprigs of fresh mint, to decorate

1 Preheat the oven to 350°F/180°C/Gas 4. Lightly grease six cups of a bun tray (muffin pan).

2 Stack the filo sheets and cut with a sharp knife or scissors into 24 squares each 11cm/4¼in.

3 Place four squares of pastry in each of the six greased cups. Press the pastry firmly into the cups, rotating slightly to make star-shaped baskets.

4 Lightly brush the pastry baskets with melted butter. Bake for about 5–7 minutes, until the pastry is crisp and golden brown. Using a metal spatula, carefully transfer the baskets to a wire rack to cool.

5 In a bowl, lightly whip the cream until soft peaks form. Gently fold the strawberry jam and Cointreau into the cream with a flexible spatula.

6 Just before serving, spoon a little of the cream mixture into each pastry basket. Top with the grapes, pineapple and raspberries. Sprinkle with icing sugar and decorate each basket with a small sprig of mint.

Filo Tulips Energy 147kcal/612kJ; Protein 1.1g; Carbohydrate 9.4g, of which sugars 6.1g; Fat 11.7g, of which saturates 7.2g; Cholesterol 24mg; Calcium 15mg; Fibre 0.4g; Sodium 28mg.
Fruit Baskets Energy 619kcal/2569kJ; Protein 3.9g; Carbohydrate 37.9g, of which sugars 15.6g; Fat 50.9g, of which saturates 20.9g; Cholesterol 80mg; Calcium 76mg; Fibre 1.6g; Sodium 80mg.

Apricot Filo Purses

These little filo parcels contain a special apricot and mincemeat filling. A good way to use up any mincemeat and marzipan that might have been in your cupboard since Christmas.

Makes 8

350g/12oz filo pastry, thawed if frozen
50g/2oz/¼ cup butter, melted
8 apricots, halved and stoned (pitted)
60ml/4 tbsp luxury mincemeat
12 ratafia biscuits (almond macaroons), crushed
30ml/2 tbsp grated marzipan
icing (confectioners') sugar, for dusting

1 Preheat the oven to 200°C/400°F/Gas 6. Cut the filo pastry into 32 x 18cm/7in squares. Brush four of the squares with a little melted butter and stack them, giving each layer a quarter turn so that the stack acquires a star shape. Repeat this stacking process to make eight stars.

2 Place an apricot half, hollow up, in the centre of each pastry star. Mix together the mincemeat, crushed ratafias and marzipan and spoon a little of the mixture into the hollow of each apricot.

3 Top with another apricot half, then bring the corners of each pastry star together and squeeze to make a gathered purse.

4 Place the purses on a baking sheet and brush each one with a little melted butter.

5 Bake for 15–20 minutes or until the pastry is golden and crisp. Lightly dust with icing sugar to serve.

Cook's Tips

- *Whipped cream, flavoured with a little brandy, makes an ideal accompaniment to the delicious parcels.*
- *If ratafias are not available, use amaretti instead or simply leave them out, as the mincemeat adds lots of flavour.*

Plum Filo Pockets

Delicate sugar-dusted layers of filo pastry surround warm plums and soft cheese in these delightful fruit-filled parcels. They make a very elegant summer dessert for a special occasion, when plums are plentiful. This is a very easy way to quickly produce a quite delicious dessert for guests.

Serves 4

115g/4oz/½ cup skimmed milk soft cheese
15ml/1 tbsp light muscovado (brown) sugar
2.5ml/½ tsp ground cloves
8 large, firm plums, halved and stoned (pitted)
8 sheets of filo pastry
sunflower oil, for brushing
icing (confectioners') sugar, to sprinkle

1 Preheat the oven to 220°C/425°F/Gas 7. Mix together the cheese, sugar and cloves.

2 Sandwich the plum halves back together in twos with a spoonful of the cheese mixture.

3 Spread out the pastry and cut into 16 pieces, each about 23cm/9in square. Brush one lightly with oil and place a second at a diagonal on top. Repeat with the remaining pastry to make eight double-layer squares.

4 Place a plum on each pastry square, and pinch the corners together. Place on baking sheet. Bake for 15–18 minutes.

5 Remove from the oven and, while still hot, dust with icing sugar. Serve warm.

Cook's Tips

- *In the summer use small peaches or nectarines in place of the plums – make sure that any fruit you choose is just ripe.*
- *To remove the stones (pits) from plums, first slice all the way around the outside of the fruit, then twist the two halves to break them apart. Give the plum a shake and the stone should fall out easily.*

Apricot Purses Energy 62kcal/263kJ; Protein 0.9g; Carbohydrate 11.3g, of which sugars 7.1g; Fat 1.8g, of which saturates 0.2g; Cholesterol 0mg; Calcium 17mg; Fibre 0.8g; Sodium 24mg.
Plum Pockets Energy 281kcal/1180kJ; Protein 6g; Carbohydrate 37g, of which sugars 15g; Fat 12g, of which saturates 3g; Cholesterol 0mg; Calcium 15 mg; Fibre 2.4g; Sodium 216mg.

Neuris

These melt-in-the-mouth sweet and spicy samosas from India are traditionally eaten during the Hindu festival of Diwali and are given as little gifts to friends.

Makes 12

75g/3oz/1 cup desiccated (dry unsweetened shredded) coconut
50g/2oz/¼ cup light muscovado (brown) sugar
25g/1oz/¼ cup cashew nuts, chopped
50g/2oz/⅓ cup seedless raisins
250ml/8fl oz/1 cup evaporated (unsweetened condensed) milk
large pinch grated nutmeg
2.5ml/½ tsp ground cinnamon
12 sheets filo pastry, about 28 x 18cm/11 x 7in each
sunflower oil, for brushing

For the topping

15ml/1 tbsp evaporated (unsweetened condensed) milk
15ml/1 tbsp caster (superfine) sugar

1 To make the filling, put the coconut, muscovado sugar, cashews, raisins and evaporated milk into a small pan. Bring to the boil, stirring occasionally. Reduce the heat to very low and cook for about 10 minutes, stirring, until the milk has been absorbed. Stir in the nutmeg and cinnamon, then set aside to cool.

2 Preheat the oven to 180°C/350°F/Gas 4. Line two baking sheets with baking parchment.

3 Brush one sheet of filo pastry with a little sunflower oil. Fold the sheet in half lengthways, then brush with more oil and fold widthways. Brush the edges of the folded pastry with water.

4 Place a spoonful of the cooled filling on one half of the folded pastry sheet. Fold the other half of the sheet over the filling, then press together the edges to seal. Trim off the rough edges and place on the baking sheet. Continue making neuris in this way until all the pastry and filling has been used up.

5 To make the topping, put the evaporated milk and sugar into a small pan and heat gently, stirring constantly until the sugar has completely dissolved. Brush the topping over the neuris and sprinkle them with the coconut. Bake for about 20 minutes, until crisp and golden brown. Cool on a wire rack before serving.

Sweet Samosas

These small triangular filo parcels have a wonderful sweet fruit-and-nut filling, moistened with evaporated milk and sugar.

Makes 12

50g/2oz/½ cup desiccated (dry unsweetened shredded) coconut
25g/1oz/¼ cup ground almonds
25g/1oz/¼ cup unsalted cashew nuts, chopped
25g/1oz/⅙ cup seedless raisins
250ml/8fl oz/1 cup evaporated milk
50g/2oz/¼ cup light muscovado (brown) sugar
2.5ml/½ tsp grated nutmeg
2.5ml/½ tsp ground cinnamon
12 sheets of filo pastry
50g/2oz/¼ cup butter, melted, for brushing
icing (confectioners') sugar, for dusting

1 Put the desiccated coconut, almonds, cashew nuts, raisins, evaporated milk and sugar into a small, heavy pan and stir gently over medium heat. After about 5 minutes, when the sugar has dissolved, reduce the heat to low and cook until all the milk has been absorbed, stirring frequently to prevent the mixture sticking and burning. This will take 8–10 minutes.

2 Remove the pan from the heat and stir in the nutmeg and cinnamon. Leave the mixture to cool completely, then divide into 12 equal balls. Preheat the oven to 180°C/350°F/Gas 4. Line a baking sheet with baking parchment.

3 Fold the pastry in half lengthways, brush the surface with butter, then fold it widthways to form a rough square. Place a portion of the filling on to the filo, 5cm/2in from the edge.

4 Turn one corner of the pastry over to make a triangle. Fold the triangle over on itself to make a triangle half the size, fully enclosing the filling. You may need to squash down the filling a little. Seal the edges with melted butter, pressing down well.

5 Place the samosas on the prepared baking sheet and brush with butter. Bake in the centre of the oven for 20–25 minutes or until the samosas are crisp and golden brown. 10 Lightly dust the baked samosas with icing sugar. Arrange on a serving dish and serve warm or cold.

Neuris Energy 164kcal/689kJ; Protein 4.2g; Carbohydrate 24.6g, of which sugars 11.6g; Fat 6.1g, of which saturates 4.1g; Cholesterol 4mg; Calcium 88mg; Fibre 1.5g; Sodium 37mg.
Sweet Samosas Energy 147kcal/614kJ; Protein 3g; Carbohydrate 11g, of which sugars 8g; Fat 10g, of which saturates 6g; Cholesterol 16mg; Calcium 79mg; Fibre 1.0g; Sodium 67mg.

Indian Coconut Parcels

These pretty pastry parcels from India are held together with a whole clove.

Makes about 12

For the pastry

225g/8oz/2 cups plain (all-purpose) flour
40g/1½oz/3 tbsp ghee or butter
125ml/4fl oz/½ cup cold water
12 whole cloves
sunflower oil, for deep-frying

For the filling

50g/2oz/⅔ cup desiccated (dry unsweetened shredded) coconut
75ml/3fl oz/5 tbsp hot milk
50g/2oz seedless raisins
50g/2oz raw cashew nuts, chopped
5ml/1 tsp ground cardamom

For the syrup

175g/6oz/scant 1 cup sugar
5 cardamom pods, bruised
300ml/½ pint/1¼ cups water

1 First make the pastry. Sift the flour into a bowl and rub in the ghee or butter until the flour looks crumbly. Gradually add the water to the flour mixture until a soft dough is formed.

2 Knead for about 1 minute, until it is smooth and pliable. Cover with clear film (plastic wrap) and allow to rest for 30 minutes.

3 Meanwhile, mix all the ingredients for the filling together in a large bowl until thoroughly combined. Set aside.

4 Put all the syrup ingredients into a pan and place over high heat. Bring to the boil, then reduce the heat to low. Simmer the mixture for 10–12 minutes, then switch off the heat.

5 Divide the dough into 12 equal parts and roll each one into a 7.5cm/3in circle. Divide the filling into 12 and place one portion in the centre of each pastry circle. Enclose the filling by folding over the edges to form a square. Secure with a clove.

6 Heat the oil for deep-frying until it reaches 180°C/350°F. Fry the parcels in batches, until crisp and golden brown, then immerse in the hot syrup. Remove the first batch from the syrup and place them in a serving dish, then immerse the second batch in the syrup. When you have taken the last batch out of the syrup, boil the syrup to reduce by half. Spoon over the parcels. Serve at room temperature.

Oznei Haman

These little cookies, shaped like tricorns – three-cornered hats – are eaten at the Jewish feast called Purim, which celebrates the Jews' deliverance from the scheming Haman.

Makes about 20

115g/4oz/½ cup unsalted (sweet) butter, at room temperature, diced
115g/4oz/generous ½ cup caster (superfine) sugar
2.5ml/½ tsp vanilla extract
3 egg yolks
250g/9oz/2¼ cups plain (all-purpose) flour
beaten egg to seal and glaze

For the filling

40g/1½oz/3 tbsp poppy seeds
15ml/1 tbsp clear honey
25g/1oz/2 tbsp caster (superfine) sugar
finely grated rind of 1 lemon
15ml/1 tbsp lemon juice
40g/1½oz/⅓ cup ground almonds
1 small (US medium) egg, beaten
25g/1oz/scant ¼ cup raisins

1 Beat the butter with the sugar until light and creamy. Beat in the vanilla and egg yolks. Sift over the flour, stir in, then work into a dough with your hands. Knead until smooth. Wrap in clear film (plastic wrap) and chill.

2 For the filling, put the poppy seeds, honey, sugar, lemon rind and juice into a pan with 60ml/4 tbsp water and bring to the boil, stirring. Remove from the heat and beat in the almonds, egg and raisins. Cool.

3 Preheat the oven to 180°C/350°F/Gas 4. Line two large baking sheets with baking parchment. Roll out the dough on a lightly floured surface to 3mm/⅛in thickness.

4 Using a plain round 7.5cm/3in cutter, stamp out rounds. Place a heaped teaspoon of filling on each round. Brush the edges with beaten egg, then bring the sides to the centre to form a tricorne shape. Seal the edges well together and place on the prepared baking sheets, spaced slightly apart.

5 Brush with beaten egg and bake for 20–30 minutes, or until golden brown. Transfer to a wire rack and leave to cool.

Coconut Parcels Energy 267kcal/1118kJ; Protein 3.2g; Carbohydrate 34.1g, of which sugars 19.2g; Fat 14g, of which saturates 5g; Cholesterol 1mg; Calcium 46mg; Fibre 1.4g; Sodium 21mg.
Oznei Haman Energy 156kcal/653kJ; Protein 2.8g; Carbohydrate 18.7g, of which sugars 9.1g; Fat 8.3g, of which saturates 3.6g; Cholesterol 52mg; Calcium 46mg; Fibre 0.7g; Sodium 42mg.

Filo Pastry, Ice Cream and Mincemeat Parcels

Looking rather like crispy fried pancakes, these golden parcels reveal hot chunky mincemeat and melting ice cream. They can be made days in advance, ready for easy, last-minute frying.

Makes 12

1 firm pear
225g/8oz/1 cup mincemeat
finely grated rind of 1 lemon
12 sheets of filo pastry, thawed if frozen
a little beaten egg
250ml/8 fl oz/1 cup vanilla ice cream
oil, for deep-frying
caster (superfine) sugar, for dusting

1 Peel, core and chop the pear. Put it in a small bowl and then stir in the mincemeat and lemon rind.

2 Lay one filo sheet on the work surface and cut it into two 20cm/8in squares. Brush one square lightly with beaten egg, then cover with the second square.

3 Lay 10ml/2 tsp mincemeat on the filo, placing it 2.5cm/1in away from one edge and spreading it slightly to cover a 7.5cm/3in area. Lay 10ml/2 tsp of the ice cream over the mincemeat. Brush around the edges of the filo with beaten egg.

4 Fold over the two opposite sides of the pastry to cover the filling. Roll up the strip, starting from the filled end. Transfer to a baking sheet and freeze. Make 11 more rolls in the same way.

5 When you are ready to serve, pour oil into a heavy pan to a depth of 7.5cm/3in. Heat it to 185°C/365°F or until a cube of bread added to the oil browns in 30 seconds.

6 Fry several parcels at a time for 1–2 minutes until pale golden, turning them over during cooking.

7 Drain on kitchen paper while frying the remainder. Dust with caster sugar and serve immediately.

Filo Fruit Scrunchies

Quick and easy to make, these pastries are ideal to serve at tea time.

Makes 6

5 apricots or plums
4 sheets filo pastry, thawed if frozen
20ml/4 tsp butter, melted
50g/2oz/¼ cup demerara (raw) sugar
30ml/2 tbsp flaked (sliced) almonds
icing (confectioners') sugar, for dusting

1 Preheat the oven to 190°C/375°F/Gas 5. Halve the apricots or plums, remove the stones (pits) and slice the fruit.

2 Cut the filo pastry into twelve 18cm/7in squares. Pile the squares on top of each other and cover with a clean dishtowel to prevent the pastry from drying out.

3 Remove one square of filo and brush it with melted margarine. Lay a second filo square on top, then, using your fingers, mould the pastry into folds.

4 Make five more scrunchies in the same way, working quickly so that the pastry does not dry out.

5 Arrange a few slices of fruit in the folds of each scrunchie, then sprinkle each one generously with the demerara sugar and flaked almonds.

6 Place the scrunchies on a baking sheet. Bake for about 8–10 minutes until golden brown.

7 Loosen the scrunchies from the baking sheet with a metal spatula and transfer to a wire rack. Dust with icing sugar and serve immediately.

Variation
For an extra almond flavour, add a few drops of almond extract to the melted butter for brushing.

Filo Parcels Energy 183kcal/764kJ; Protein 1.6g; Carbohydrate 23.3g, of which sugars 16.8g; Fat 9.9g, of which saturates 1.9g; Cholesterol 2mg; Calcium 35mg; Fibre 0.8g; Sodium 17mg.
Fruit Scrunchies Energy 127kcal/534kJ; Protein 2.2g; Carbohydrate 18g, of which sugars 11.5g; Fat 5.7g, of which saturates 0.2g; Cholesterol 0mg; Calcium 33mg; Fibre 1.2g; Sodium 29mg.

Brittany Butter Cookies

These lightly glazed little cookies are similar to shortbread, but are richer. Traditionally, they are made with lightly salted butter.

Makes 18–20

6 egg yolks, lightly beaten
15ml/1 tbsp milk
250g/9oz/2¼ cups plain (all-purpose) flour
175g/6oz/¾ cup caster (superfine) sugar
200g/7oz/scant 1 cup butter at room temperature, diced

1 Preheat the oven to 180°C/350°F/Gas 4. Lightly grease two heavy baking sheets.

2 Mix 15ml/1 tbsp of the egg yolks with the milk to make a glaze. Set aside.

3 In a bowl, beat together the sugar and butter until light and creamy. Add the egg yolks and mix to combine.

4 Add the flour in batches and stir well. Use your fingertips until it is all incorporated and the mixture forms a slightly sticky dough. Gather it together.

5 Using floured hands, pat out the dough to about 5mm/¼in thick and stamp out rounds using a 7.5cm/3in cutter. Transfer the rounds to the prepared baking sheet, brush each with a little of the reserved egg and milk glaze, then, using the back of a knife, score gently with lines to create a lattice pattern.

6 Bake for about 12 minutes or until golden. Cool on the baking sheet to firm up, then transfer to a wire rack and leave to cool completely.

Variation

To make a large Brittany butter cake, pat the dough with well-floured hands into a 23cm/9in loose-based cake tin (pan). Brush with the glaze and score the lattice pattern on top. Bake for 45–60 minutes until firm to the touch and golden brown.

Vanilla Crescents

These attractively shaped cookies are sweet and delicate, ideal to serve with creamy ice cream or a light and fluffy fruit fool for dessert. Kids love them with chocolate ice cream.

Makes 36

175g/6oz/1¼ cups unblanched almonds
115g/4oz/1 cup plain (all-purpose) flour
pinch of salt
225g/8oz/1 cup unsalted (sweet) butter at room temperature, diced
115g/4oz/½ cup sugar
5ml/1 tsp vanilla extract
icing (confectioners') sugar, for dusting

1 Place the almonds in a food processor, blender or nut grinder, with a few tablespoons of the flour. Process gradually in short pulses until finely ground.

2 Sift the remaining flour with the salt into a bowl. Set aside. In a second large bowl, beat together the butter and sugar until light and fluffy.

3 Stir in the almonds, vanilla extract together with the sifted flour and salt. Stir to mix well. Gather the dough into a ball, wrap in baking parchment, and chill in the refrigerator for at least 30 minutes.

4 Preheat the oven to 160°C/325°F/Gas 3. Lightly grease two baking sheets and line with baking parchment.

5 Break off walnut-size pieces of dough and roll them into small cylinders about 1cm/½in in diameter. Bend theminto crescent shapes and place on the baking sheets, spaced well apart.

6 Bake for about 20 minutes until dry but not brown. Transfer to a wire rack to cool only slightly. Set the rack over a baking sheet and dust with an even layer of icing sugar.

7 Leave to cool completely so that they crisp up. These cookies will keep in an airtight container for more than 1 week.

Brittany Butter Cookies Energy 170kcal/711kJ; Protein 2.2g; Carbohydrate 19g, of which sugars 9.4g; Fat 10g, of which saturates 5.7g; Cholesterol 82mg; Calcium 32mg; Fibre 0.4g; Sodium 65mg.
Vanilla Crescents Energy 62kcal/258kJ; Protein 2.5g; Carbohydrate 6.3g, of which sugars 3.6g; Fat 3.1g, of which saturates 0.3g; Cholesterol 3mg; Calcium 19mg; Fibre 0.5g; Sodium 4mg.

Sugar-topped Stars

These cookies are great for little ones to help make.

Makes 10
115g/4oz/½ cup butter
175g/6oz/1½ cups plain (all-purpose) flour, plus extra for dusting
50g/2oz/¼ cup caster (superfine) sugar

For the topping
30ml/2 tbsp golden (light corn) syrup
30ml/2 tbsp preserving sugar

1 Put the butter and flour in a bowl and rub together until the mixture looks like breadcrumbs. Stir in the caster sugar and knead together to make a ball. Chill for 30 minutes.

2 Preheat the oven to 180°C/350°F/Gas 4 and lightly grease two baking sheets.

3 Roll out the dough on a lightly floured surface to a 5mm/¼in thickness and use a 7.5cm/3in cookie cutter to stamp out the stars.

4 Arrange the cookies on the baking sheet. Press the trimmings together and keep rolling out and cutting more biscuits until all the mixture has been used.

5 Bake for 10–15 minutes, until they are golden brown. Transfer to a wire rack to cool completely.

6 Heat the golden syrup in a pan over a low heat. Brush over the cookies and sprinkle the sugar on top. Leave to cool.

Quick Vanilla Cookies

Just a few drops of vanilla extract give these cookies their defining flavour. Beware, these treats are very moreish.

Makes 32
150g/5oz/10 tbsp butter, softened
150g/5oz/¾ cup caster (superfine) sugar
1 egg, lightly beaten
2.5ml/½ tsp vanilla extract
225g/8oz/2 cups plain (all-purpose) flour, sifted

1 Put all the ingredients in a bowl and beat together until a smooth, firm dough is formed.

2 Lightly knead on a floured surface then roll the dough into a log shape about 5cm/2in diameter and 20cm/8in long. Wrap the log in clear film (plastic wrap) and chill for at least 1 hour or until firm enough to slice.

3 Preheat the oven to 190°C/375°F/Gas 5. Lightly grease two large baking sheets.

4 Cut the dough into 5mm/¼in slices. Place the cookies about 2.5cm/1in apart on the baking sheets. Bake for 12 minutes, or until just golden around the edges. Leave on the baking sheets for 2–3 minutes, then transfer to a wire rack to cool.

Sablés with Caramel Glaze

These are very buttery cookies with a dark caramel glaze. Eat on the day of baking for the best taste.

Makes about 18
200g/7oz/1¾ cups plain (all-purpose) flour
pinch of salt
75g/3oz/⅔ cup icing (confectioners') sugar
130g/4½oz/generous ½ cup unsalted (sweet) butter, diced
3 egg yolks
2.5ml/½ tsp vanilla extract
1 egg yolk, for glazing

For the caramel syrup
50g/2oz/¼ cup sugar
20ml/4 tsp water
2.5ml/½ tsp lemon juice
50ml/2fl oz/¼ cup water

1 To make the caramel syrup, put the sugar, 20ml/4 tsp water and lemon juice into a pan. Place over low heat and stir until clear. Boil to a rich golden brown. Remove from the heat and immediately plunge the base of the pan into cold water to stop the cooking. Stir in the 50ml/2fl oz/¼ cup water. Cool.

2 Put the cookie ingredients, except the egg yolks and vanilla, into a food processor then process until the mixture resembles breadcrumbs.

3 Add the egg yolks and vanilla and blend until a firm dough forms. Form into a ball, wrap in clear film (plastic wrap) then chill for 15 minutes.

4 Preheat the oven to 180°C/350°F/Gas 4. Lightly grease two baking sheets.

5 Roll the dough out on baking parchment 5mm/1/4in thick. Using a 7.5cm/3in cookie cutter, stamp out rounds and place them on the baking sheets.

6 In a bowl, beat the egg yolk with 15ml/1 tbsp of the glaze. Brush sparingly over the cookies. Leave to dry, then apply a second layer. Make a pattern using the fork tines.

7 Bake for about 10–15 minutes, or until crisp and golden brown. Transfer to a wire rack to cool.

Sugar-topped Stars Energy 186kcal/778kJ; Protein 1.8g; Carbohydrate 24.4g, of which sugars 11.1g; Fat 9.7g, of which saturates 6g; Cholesterol 25mg; Calcium 31mg; Fibre 0.5g; Sodium 79mg.
Quick Vanilla Cookies Energy 80kcal/334kJ; Protein 0.9g; Carbohydrate 10.4g, of which sugars 5g; Fat 4.1g, of which saturates 2.5g; Cholesterol 16mg; Calcium 14mg; Fibre 0.2g; Sodium 31mg.
Sablés with Caramel Glaze Energy 129kcal/541kJ; Protein 1.6g; Carbohydrate 15.9g, of which sugars 7.5g; Fat 7g, of which saturates 4g; Cholesterol 49mg; Calcium 24mg; Fibre 0.3g; Sodium 46mg.

Sugar-topped Cookies

Buttery, crumbly vanilla cookies with an irresistible crunchy sugar topping, these are great with a cup of tea but also delicious served with luxury vanilla ice cream for a quick dessert.

Makes about 24

115g/4oz/½ cup unsalted (sweet) butter, at room temperature, diced
50g/2oz/¼ cup vanilla caster (superfine) sugar
1 egg, beaten
1.5ml/¼ tsp vanilla extract
200g/7oz/1¾ cups self-raising (self-rising) flour, plus extra for dusting
45ml/3 tbsp cornflour (cornstarch)

For the topping

1 egg white
15ml/1 tbsp vanilla caster (superfine) sugar
75g/3oz sugar cubes, crushed

1 Preheat the oven to 180°C/350°F/Gas 4.

2 In a bowl, beat the butter and sugar together until light and fluffy. Beat in the egg and vanilla extract. Sift together the flour and cornflour over the mixture and mix to a soft dough.

3 Roll the mixture out on a lightly floured surface. Using a cookie cutter, stamp out the cookies and place on a lightly greased baking sheet.

4 For the topping, put the egg white in a small bowl and whisk until foamy. Whisk in the vanilla sugar. Using a pastry brush, spread generously on each cookie. Sprinkle with the crushed sugar cubes.

5 Bake for about 15 minutes, or until the topping is just beginning to turn golden brown. Remove from the oven and transfer to a wire rack to cool.

Cook's Tip

To make vanilla sugar, split a vanilla pod (bean) open down one side. Place in a jar of sugar and leave to infuse for a few days.

Almond Shortbread Fingers

This easy all-in-one recipe makes a very light, crisp shortbread with an excellent flavour, and it keeps well. Serve with tea or coffee, or to accompany light desserts.

Makes about 48

225g/8oz/1 cup butter, softened
75g/3oz/6 tbsp caster (superfine) sugar
275g/10oz/2½ cups plain (all-purpose) flour
25g/1oz/¼ cup ground almonds
grated rind of ½ lemon

1 Preheat the oven to 180°C/350°F/Gas 4. Lightly grease a large Swiss roll tin (jelly roll pan).

2 Beat the butter and sugar together in a mixing bowl until light and fluffy. Set aside.

3 Sift the flour and almonds into a clean mixing bowl. Turn the creamed mixture on to the flour and almonds, then work it together first using a wooden spoon and then using your fingers to make a smooth dough.

4 Turn the mixture out on the prepared tray and flatten it out to the edges with the back of a wooden spoon until it is an even thickness all over.

5 Bake for 20 minutes, or until pale golden brown. Remove from the oven and immediately mark the shortbread into fingers or squares with a sharp knife, while the mixture is soft.

6 Leave the shortbread in the tin to cool for a few minutes, and then transfer to a wire rack and leave to cool completely.

7 If stored in an airtight container, the shortbread can be kept for up to two weeks.

Variation

Replace the lemon rind with the grated rind of two oranges in this recipe, if you like.

Sugar-topped Cookies Energy 96kcal/405kJ; Protein 1.2g; Carbohydrate 14.2g, of which sugars 6.2g; Fat 4.3g, of which saturates 2.6g; Cholesterol 18mg; Calcium 35mg; Fibre 0.3g; Sodium 66mg.
Almond Fingers Energy 64kcal/266kJ; Protein 0.7g; Carbohydrate 6.1g, of which sugars 1.8g; Fat 4.2g, of which saturates 2.5g; Cholesterol 10mg; Calcium 11mg; Fibre 0.2g; Sodium 29mg.

Lemon Shortbread Cookies

These are crisp, lemony shortbread cookies with fluted edges, made and sold in the town of Shrewsbury, in England, since the 17th century.

Makes about 20

115g/4oz/½ cup butter, softened
140g/5oz/¾ cup caster (superfine) sugar
2 egg yolks
225g/8oz/2 cups plain (all-purpose) flour, plus extra for dusting
finely grated rind of 1 lemon

1 Preheat the oven to 180°C/350°F/Gas 4. Lightly grease two baking sheets and line with baking parchment.

2 In a mixing bowl, beat together the butter and sugar until pale, light and fluffy. Beat in each egg yolk one at a time, beating thoroughly after each addition.

3 Sift the flour over the top and add the lemon rind. Stir in with a wooden spoon at first and then gather up the mixture with your fingertips to make a stiff dough.

4 Knead the dough lightly on a floured surface then roll it out evenly to about 5mm/¼in thick. Using a 7.5cm/3in fluted cookie cutter, stamp out rounds and arrange on the baking sheets.

5 Gather up the trimmings and roll out again to make more cookies until all the dough has been used up.

6 Bake for about 15 minutes, until firm to the touch and lightly browned. Transfer to a wire rack and leave to cool completely.

Variations
- *Omit the lemon rind and sift 5ml/1 tsp mixed (apple pie) spice with the flour in step 3.*
- *Add 25g/1oz/2 tbsp currants or raisins to the mixture in step 3.*

Butter and Almond Stars

Moist shortbread cookies, flavoured with almonds, are cut into shapes of your choice and given a generous dusting of sugar so that they are pure white.

Makes 20–22

225g/8oz/1 cup unsalted (sweet) butter
150g/5oz/⅔ cup caster (superfine) sugar
2 egg yolks
5ml/1 tsp vanilla extract
2.5ml/½ tsp bicarbonate of soda (baking soda)
45ml/3 tbsp brandy
500g/1¼lb/5 cups plain (all-purpose) flour, plus extra for dusting
pinch of salt
150g/5oz/1¼ cups blanched almonds, toasted and coarsely chopped
350g/12oz/3 cups icing (confectioners') sugar

1 Preheat the oven to 180°C/350°F/Gas 4. Lightly grease two large baking sheets.

2 In a large bowl, beat together the butter and caster sugar until light and fluffy. Beat in the egg yolks one at a time, then add the vanilla extract.

3 In a small bowl, mix the baking soda with the brandy and stir into the butter and sugar mixture.

4 Sift together the flour and salt over the mixture and mix to a firm dough. Knead lightly with your fingertips, add the almonds and knead again.

5 Roll out the dough to 2.5cm/1in thick on a lightly floured surface. Press out shapes, using cookie cutters. Place on the baking sheets and bake for 20–25 minutes, or until pale golden. Do not let the cookies become brown.

6 Sift a quarter of the icing sugar on to a plate. Set aside. As soon as the cookies come out of the oven, dust them generously with sifted icing sugar. Leave to cool for a few minutes, then place them on the sugar-coated plate. Sift the remaining icing sugar over them. The aim is to give them a generous coating, so they are pure white.

Lemon Cookies Energy 115kcal/482kJ; Protein 1.4g; Carbohydrate 16.1g, of which sugars 7.5g; Fat 5.4g, of which saturates 3.2g; Cholesterol 32mg; Calcium 023mg; Fibre 0.4g; Sodium 37mg.
Almond Stars Energy 325kcal/1363kJ; Protein 4.4g; Carbohydrate 46.1g, of which sugars 26.9g; Fat 14.3g, of which saturates 6.4g; Cholesterol 44mg; Calcium 71mg; Fibre 1.3g; Sodium 72mg.

Sweet Almond Cookies

Serve these crisp cookies with ice cream or fruit fool, or more simply with fresh fruit salad, yogurt or a spoonful of thick cream.

Makes about 25

25g/1oz/2 tbsp butter
30ml/2 tbsp milk
1 egg yolk
225g/8oz/2 cups ground almonds, plus extra for rolling out
25g/1oz/2 tbsp caster (superfine) sugar
5ml/1 tsp baking powder
2.5ml/½ tsp vanilla extract

1 Preheat the oven to 190°C/375°F/Gas 5.

2 Melt the butter in a pan and leave to cool until lukewarm. Blend together the milk and egg yolk.

3 Mix the ground almonds, sugar and baking powder in a large bowl then stir in the melted butter, vanilla extract and the milk and egg mixture.

4 Knead the mixture with your hands to form a moist dough and then roll out to about 5mm/¼in thick on a cool surface lightly dusted with extra ground almonds.

5 Cut the dough into rounds using a 6cm/2½in cookie cutter. Gather up the trimmings together and keep re-rolling the dough out and cutting out more cookies until all the dough mixture has been used up.

6 Transfer the dough rounds to a non-stick baking sheet and bake in the preheated for about 10 minutes until lightly browned all over. Transfer the cookies to a wire rack and leave to cool completely.

Variation

The egg yolk is not essential for this recipe but does help to bind the mixture together. If you prefer, you can use an extra 15ml/1 tbsp milk instead of the egg.

Almond Hearts

Fine sugar and butter combine to give these cookies a light, delicate texture. They can be made days ahead, and are delicious with desserts or coffee.

Makes about 25

115g/4oz/1 cup plain (all-purpose) flour, plus extra for dusting
175g/6oz/1½ cups icing (confectioners') sugar
pinch of salt
50g/2oz/½ cup chopped almonds
2.5ml/½ tsp almond extract
115g/4oz/½ cup unsalted (sweet) butter, softened
icing (confectioners') sugar, for dusting
halved almonds, to decorate

1 Preheat the oven to 180°C/350°F/Gas 4. Lightly grease two large baking sheets.

2 Combine the flour, icing sugar, salt and chopped almonds in a bowl. Add the almond extract.

3 Put the softened butter in the centre of the flour mixture and use your fingertips to draw the dry ingredients into the butter until a dough is formed. Knead until smooth. Shape the dough into a ball.

4 Place the dough on a lightly floured surface and roll it out to a thickness of about 3mm/⅛in. Using a 7.5cm/3in cookie cutter, stamp out 25 rounds, re-rolling the dough as necessary to use up any trimmings. Place the rounds on the baking sheets, leaving a little space between them. Decorate the cookies halved almonds.

5 Bake for 25–30 minutes until pale golden. Leave for 10 minutes, then transfer to wire racks to cool. Dust thickly with icing sugar before serving,

Cook's Tip

Use fancy cookie cutters such as hearts and crescents to make these cookies look even more interesting.

Sweet Almond Cookies Energy 69kcal/288kJ; Protein 2.1g; Carbohydrate 1.7g, of which sugars 1.5g; Fat 6.1g, of which saturates 1g; Cholesterol 10mg; Calcium 25mg; Fibre 0.7g; Sodium 8mg.
Almond Hearts Energy 188kcal/788kJ; Protein 3.5g; Carbohydrate 22.5g, of which sugars 10.9g; Fat 10g, of which saturates 4.4g; Cholesterol 45mg; Calcium 44mg; Fibre 0.8g; Sodium 58mg.

Almond Tiles

These cookies are named after the French roof tiles they resemble. Making them can be a little fiddly, so bake a few at a time until you get the knack.

Makes about 24

70g/2½oz/½ cup whole blanched almonds, lightly toasted
70g/2½oz/⅓ cup caster (superfine) sugar
40g/1½oz/3 tbsp unsalted (sweet) butter, softened
2 egg whites
2.5ml/½ tsp almond extract
35g/1¼oz scant ¼ cup plain (all-purpose) flour, sifted
55g/2oz/⅔ cup flaked (sliced) almonds

1 Preheat the oven to 200°C/400°F/Gas 6. Generously grease two baking sheets.

2 Put the almonds and 30ml/2 tbsp of the sugar in a food processor fitted with the metal blade, and pulse until ground.

3 In a large bowl, beat the butter until creamy, then add the remaining sugar and beat until light and fluffy.

4 Gradually beat in the egg whites until well blended, then add the almond extract. Sift in the flour and fold in, then fold in the ground almond mixture.

5 Drop tablespoons of mixture on to the baking sheets about 15cm/6in apart. With the back of a wet spoon, spread each mound into a paper-thin 7.5cm/3in round. Sprinkle each round with a few flaked almonds.

6 Bake one sheet at a time, for 5–6 minutes until the edges are golden and the centres still pale. Working quickly, use a thin metal spatula to loosen the edges of each cookie. Lift on the spatula and place over a rolling pin, then press down the sides of the cookie to curve it.

7 Continue shaping the cookies, transferring them to a wire rack as they cool and crisp. If the cookies become too crisp to shape, return the baking sheet to the oven for 15–30 seconds to soften them, then continue as above.

Almond Ice Cream Sandwiches

These crisp, nutty wafer cookies make perfect ice cream sandwiches for a summer-time treat.

Makes 6

50g/2oz/¼ cup unsalted (sweet) butter
2 egg whites
75g/3oz/scant ½ cup caster (superfine) sugar
50g/2oz/½ cup plain (all-purpose) flour
40g/1½oz/scant ½ cup ground almonds
30ml/2 tbsp flaked (sliced) almonds (optional)
raspberry ripple or vanilla ice cream, to serve
icing (confectioners') sugar, for dusting

1 Preheat the oven to 200°C/400°F/Gas 6. Line two large baking sheets with baking parchment.

2 Put the butter in a small pan and melt over very low heat.

3 Put the egg whites and sugar in a bowl and whisk lightly with a fork until the egg whites are broken up. Add the flour, melted butter and ground almonds and mix until evenly combined.

4 Drop six level tablespoonfuls of mixture on to each baking sheet, spacing them well apart. Spread each tablespoonful of mixture into circles about 7cm/2¾in in diameter. Sprinkle with almonds, if using, and bake for 10–12 minutes until golden around the edges.

5 Remove from the oven, peel away the paper and transfer to a wire rack to cool.

6 Place a scoop of slightly softened ice cream on to one cookie and top with another, gently pressing them together. Dust with sugar and serve.

Cook's Tip

Don't be tempted to use greaseproof (waxed) paper instead of baking parchment as the cookies may stick to it.

Almond Tiles Energy 59kcal/246kJ; Protein 1.4g; Carbohydrate 4.5g, of which sugars 3.1g; Fat 4.1g, of which saturates 1.1g; Cholesterol 4mg; Calcium 16mg; Fibre 0.4g; Sodium 16mg.
Almond Sandwiches Energy 184kcal/771kJ; Protein 3.3g; Carbohydrate 20.1g, of which sugars 13.5g; Fat 10.7g, of which saturates 4.7g; Cholesterol 18mg; Calcium 36mg; Fibre 0.8g; Sodium 73mg.

Apple Strudel

Originally from Austria, this dessert is so good that it is now an absolute classic.

Serves 4

100g/3½oz strong white (bread) flour, plus extra for dusting
5ml/1 tsp sunflower oil, plus extra for brushing
30–35ml/6–7 tsp lukewarm water
50g/2oz/4 tbsp butter, melted
icing (confectioners') sugar, to dust
custard, to serve

For the filling

10ml/2 tsp raisins
10ml/2 tsp brandy
400g/14oz apples, peeled and cored
juice of 1 lemon
5ml/1 tsp vanilla sugar (about) or 2.5ml/½ tsp vanilla extract
100g/3¾oz caster (superfine) sugar
25g/1oz/¼ cup hazelnuts, finely chopped
50g/2oz/1 cup breadcrumbs

1 Mix the flour with the oil and water to make a smooth dough. Put it in an oiled bowl, cover and leave for 30 minutes in a warm place.

2 To make the filling, soak the raisins in the brandy for about 20 minutes. In the meantime, slice the apples thinly, put them in a bowl and mix with the lemon juice. Add the vanilla sugar, sugar, chopped hazelnuts and breadcrumbs.

3 Preheat the oven to 160°C/325°F/Gas 3. Spread a clean dish towel on the work surface and dust it with flour. Roll out the dough on the towel, then stretch it on all sides with your hands, until it is the same size as the cloth. It should now be very thin.

4 Spoon the apple filling along the lower part of the dough, leaving a space of 4cm/1½in on each side. Brush all the edges with melted butter. Turn in the sides of the dough, then use the towel to help you roll up the strudel around the filling. Brush with the rest of the melted butter and transfer it carefully to a baking tray lined with baking parchment.

5 Bake for 20–30 minutes, until the pastry is golden brown and crisp. Remove the strudel from the oven and leave it to cool for a few minutes. When ready to serve, dust the strudel with icing sugar. Serve warm, cut into slices, and serve with custard.

Poppy Seed and Apple Strudel

Ready-made strudel or filo pastry gives excellent results in this recipe from Hungary, flecked with poppy seeds.

Serves 6–8

12 large sheets fresh filo pastry, thawed if frozen
50g/2oz/¼ cup butter, melted, plus extra for greasing
75ml/5 tbsp ground almonds
10ml/2 tsp poppy seeds
10ml/2 tsp icing (confectioners') sugar

For the filling

60ml/4 tbsp caster (superfine) sugar
60ml/4 tbsp sultanas (golden raisins)
30ml/2 tbsp ground poppy seeds
3 eating apples, peeled and thinly sliced

1 To make the filling, put 100ml/3½fl oz/scant ½ cup water into a pan with the sugar. Bring to the boil and simmer for 2 minutes to dissolve the sugar. Stir in the sultanas and poppy seeds, then set aside to cool. Preheat the oven to 180°C/350°F/Gas 4 and brush a baking sheet with butter.

2 Put the apples in a large mixing bowl and add the cooled sugar syrup, mixing together well. Set aside.

3 Lay a sheet of filo pastry on the baking sheet (cover the remaining sheets with a damp cloth to stop them from drying out). Brush the sheet of filo with melted butter. Sprinkle with some ground almonds. Repeat with another two filo sheets.

4 Spread a thin layer of the apple and poppy seed filling over the filo pastry and then continue with three filo layers as before, followed by another apple and poppy seed layer. Continue until all 12 sheets of filo pastry have been used.

5 Roll up from the short end of the filled pastry layers like a Swiss roll (jelly roll) and tuck in the ends. Turn the strudel seam side down and brush all over all twith the remaining butter.

6 Sprinkle with the whole poppy seeds and bake for about 25–30 minutes, or until golden brown. Cool completely and dust with icing sugar before serving.

Apple Strudel Energy 525kcal/2207kJ; Protein 8.9g; Carbohydrate 69.6g, of which sugars 41g; Fat 24.9g, of which saturates 11.6g; Cholesterol 195mg; Calcium 151mg; Fibre 3.1g; Sodium 228mg.
Poppy Seed Strudel Energy 420kcal/1764kJ; Protein 34g; Carbohydrate 42g, of which sugars 35g; Fat 26g, of which saturates 7g; Cholesterol 21mg; Calcium 350mg; Fibre 5.2g; Sodium 191mg.

Cherry and Apple Strudel

Cherries are among the favourite fillings for a strudel in Eastern Europe.

Serves 8

65g/2½oz/5 tbsp butter, melted, plus extra for greasing
750g/1lb 10oz fresh cherries, pitted
15ml/1 tbsp lemon juice
3 cooking apples, cored, peeled and cut into segments
70g/2¾oz/generous ½ cup walnuts, roughly chopped
75g/3oz/6 tbsp caster (superfine) sugar, plus extra for sprinkling
30g/1oz/1½ cups brioche breadcrumbs
60ml/4 tbsp cherry jam
10 large sheets fresh filo pastry, thawed if frozen
caster (superfine) sugar, to sprinkle

1 Preheat the oven to 200°C/400°F/Gas 6. Butter a baking sheet and line with baking parchment. Put the cherries and lemon juice in a pan and cook over medium heat for 2 minutes.

2 In a large bowl, mix together the apples, walnuts, sugar and breadcrumbs. Stir in the cherries. Put the cherry jam in a pan and heat gently until melted.

3 Lay out a damp cloth on the work surface and put a sheet of filo pastry on top (cover the remaining pastry sheets with a damp cloth). Brush generously with melted butter, then cover with another sheet of filo, brushing again with butter.

4 Repeat with another sheet of filo pastry, but this time also brush it with melted cherry jam. Repeat the same process with the remaining filo sheets, brushing every third sheet with jam.

5 Once you have all the filo buttered and stacked in front of you, put the apple, cherry and walnut mixture in the middle of it and roll the pastry up as though it were a Swiss roll (jelly roll).

6 Brush butter over all the sides of the roll, then put on to the prepared tray, seam side down, with the pastry edge beneath the roll. Sprinkle over some caster sugar and curl into a horseshoe shape. Bake in the oven for 20–30 minutes, until golden brown. Leave to cool on a wire rack.

Cherry and Pecan Strudel

Apple is the most common filling for a strudel, but sweet cherries in season mingled with pecan nuts make this fine, crisp and light dessert a real luxury.

Serves 6

65g/2½oz/5 tbsp butter, melted, plus extra for greasing
30ml/2 tbsp cherry jam
500g/1¼lb fresh cherries, pitted
75g/3oz/½ cup pecan nuts, roughly chopped
80g/3¼oz/scant ½ cup caster (superfine) sugar, plus extra for sprinkling
25g/1oz/½ cup brioche breadcrumbs
10 large sheets of filo pastry, thawed if frozen
icing (confectioners') sugar, to decorate

1 Preheat the oven to 200°C/400°F/Gas 6. Butter and line a baking sheet with baking parchment. Put the cherry jam in a small pan and heat slowly until just melted.

2 In a large bowl combine the cherries, pecan nuts, sugar and brioche breadcrumbs.

3 Lay a damp dish towel on your work surface, then take a sheet of filo pastry and lay on top. (Cover the remaining filo pastry with a damp dish towel to prevent it from drying out.)

4 Brush generously with melted butter, then cover with another sheet of filo and brush that with butter. Add a third sheet, and brush with the melted cherry jam as well as the butter. Continue in this way, with the third sheet brushed with jam and butter, until all the filo is used up.

5 Put the cherry and pecan mixture down the centre of the pastry and roll the pastry up.

6 Butter the strudel on all sides, sprinkle on some caster sugar and curl into a horseshoe. Put on the baking sheet and bake for 20–30 minutes, or until golden brown.

7 Serve warm or cold, dusted with icing sugar.

Cherry Strudel Energy 343kcal/1443kJ; Protein 17g; Carbohydrate 44g, of which sugars 38g; Fat 14g, of which saturates 5g; Cholesterol 17mg; Calcium 51mg; Fibre 5.0g; Sodium 147mg.
Pecan Strudel Energy 370kcal/1553kJ; Protein 3.2g; Carbohydrate 51.2g, of which sugars 33.2g; Fat 18.4g, of which saturates 11.4g; Cholesterol 47mg; Calcium 57mg; Fibre 1.2g; Sodium 197mg.

Mango and Amaretti Strudel

Fresh mango and crushed amaretti wrapped in wafer-thin filo pastry make a special treat. The dessert looks impressive, but actually takes very little time to make.

Serves 4

1 large mango
grated rind of 1 lemon
2 amaretti
25g/1oz/2 tbsp demerara (raw) sugar
60ml/4 tbsp wholemeal (whole-wheat) breadcrumbs
2 sheets of filo pastry, each measuring 48 x 28cm/19 x 11in
25g/1oz/2 tbsp butter, melted
15ml/1 tbsp chopped almonds
icing (confectioners') sugar, for dusting

1 Preheat the oven to 190°C/375°F/Gas 5. Lightly grease a baking sheet. Cut the flesh from the mango and chop into small cubes. Place in a bowl and sprinkle with the grated lemon rind.

2 Crush the amaretti and mix them with the sugar and breadcrumbs in a bowl.

3 Lay one sheet of filo pastry on a flat surface and brush with a quarter of the melted butter. Top with the second sheet, brush with one-third of the remaining melted butter, then fold both sheets over, if necessary, to make a rectangle measuring 28 x 24cm/11 x 9½in. Brush with half the remaining butter.

4 Sprinkle the filo with the amaretti mixture, leaving a border on each long side. Arrange the mango over the top.

5 Carefully roll up the filo from one long side, Swiss-roll (jelly-roll) fashion, to enclose the amaretti mixture.

6 Lift the strudel on to the baking sheet, seam side down. Brush with the remaining melted butter and sprinkle with the chopped almonds.

7 Bake for 20–25 minutes until light golden brown, then transfer to a board. Dust with the icing sugar, slice and serve.

Hungarian Christmas Loaf

This is a loaf that every Hungarian family will prepare for the Christmas celebrations. It is a little like a strudel but is instead made with shortcrust pastry. Walnuts and dried fruits are always used for the filling.

Serves 8

300g/11oz shortcrust pastry, thawed if frozen
flour, for dusting
1 egg yolk, beaten
15ml/1 tbsp icing (confectioners') sugar

For the walnut filling

300g/11oz/2¾ cups walnuts, roughly chopped
200g/7oz/1 cup caster (superfine) sugar
75ml/5 tbsp single (light) cream
1.5ml/¼ tsp ground cinnamon
45ml/3 tbsp raisins
10ml/2 tsp vanilla extract
grated rind of 1 lemon
15ml/1 tbsp orange marmalade

1 Preheat the oven to 180°C/350°F/Gas 4 and line a baking sheet with baking parchment. To make the walnut filling, put the chopped walnuts and sugar into a large bowl and mix together until well combined.

2 Put the cream and the walnut mixture into a heavy pan and simmer over medium heat until it becomes the consistency of a thick purée.

3 Remove from the heat. Add the cinnamon, raisins, vanilla extract, lemon rind and marmalade and mix.

4 Roll out the pastry on a floured board to a large rectangle about 3mm/⅛in thick.

5 Spread the walnut filling over the rectangle, leaving a border of 1cm/½in around the edges.

6 Roll up the dough sheet, starting from the longer side, then lay it seam side down on the baking sheet.

7 Brush the top with the egg yolk and bake for 15–20 minutes, or until golden brown. Leave to cool then sprinkle with icing sugar before serving.

Mango Strudel Energy 222Kcal/937kJ; Protein 4.2g; Carbohydrate 35.4g, of which sugars 13.4g; Fat 8.1g, of which saturates 3.6g; Cholesterol 13mg; Calcium 58mg; Fibre 2g; Sodium 162mg.
Christmas Loaf Energy 584kcal/2437kJ; Protein 9g; Carbohydrate 54g, of which sugars 36g; Fat 39g, of which saturates 7g; Cholesterol 36mg; Calcium 87mg; Fibre 5.2g; Sodium 191mg

Filo Chiffon Pie

Filo pastry is low in fat and is very easy to use. Keep a pack in the freezer, ready to make impressive desserts like this one. Rhubarb can be quite sour, so check the pie filling before you serve, and if it needs sweetening, serve a little bowl of sugar alongside.

Serves 3

500g/1¼lb pink rhubarb
5ml/1 tsp mixed (apple pie) spice
finely grated rind and juice of 1 orange
15ml/1 tbsp caster (superfine) sugar
15g/½oz/1 tbsp butter
3 sheets filo pastry

1 Preheat the oven to 200°C/400°F/Gas 6. Trim the leaves and ends from the rhubarb sticks and chop them in to 2.5cm/1in pieces. Place in a bowl.

2 Add the mixed spice, orange rind and juice and sugar and toss well to coat evenly. Transfer the rhubarb to a 1 litre/1¾ pint/4 cup pie dish.

3 Melt the butter and brush it over the pastry sheets. Lift the pastry sheets on to the pie dish, butter side up, and crumple to form a chiffon effect, covering the pie completely.

4 Place the dish on a baking sheet and bake in the oven for 20 minutes, until golden brown. Reduce the heat to 180°C/350°F/Gas 4 and bake for a further 10–15 minutes, until the rhubarb is tender. Serve warm.

Cook's Tip

When buying rhubarb, choose young, slender, pink stems, as these will be the most tender.

Variation

Other fruit, such as apples, pears or peaches, can be used in this pie – try it with whatever is in season.

Crispy Mango Stacks

This makes an extremely healthy yet impressively attractive dessert – it is low in fat and also contains no added sugar. However, if the fresh raspberries prove to be a little sharp to the taste, then you may prefer to add a pinch of sugar to the fruit purée.

Serves 4

3 filo pastry sheets
2 small ripe mangoes
115g/4oz/⅔ cup raspberries, thawed if frozen
45ml/3 tbsp water
50g/2oz/¼ cup butter, melted

1 Preheat the oven to 200°C/400°F/Gas 6. Lay the filo sheets on a clean work surface and cut out four 10cm/4in rounds from each sheet.

2 Brush each round with the melted butter and carefully lay them out on two baking sheets.

3 Bake the filo rounds for 5 minutes, or until they are crisp and golden in colour. Place on wire racks to cool.

4 Peel the mangoes, then remove the stones (pits) and cut the flesh into thin slices.

5 Put the fresh raspberries in a food processor along with the water and process until the mixture has formed a purée; press the raspberry purée through a sieve (strainer).

6 Place a filo pastry round on each of four individual plates. Top with a quarter of the mango and drizzle with a little of the raspberry purée.

7 Repeat layering in this way until all of the ingredients have been used, finishing off with a layer of mango and a drizzle of the raspberry purée.

8 Serve immediately; this dessert is best served straight away as if it is left to stand for too long the fruit will seep into the pastry rounds and make them soggy.

Chiffon Pie Energy 109Kcal/461kJ; Protein 2.6g; Carbohydrate 15.8g, of which sugars 8.2g; Fat 4.4g, of which saturates 2.6g; Cholesterol 11mg; Calcium 174mg; Fibre 2.7g; Sodium 38mg.
Mango Stacks Energy 194Kcal/815kJ; Protein 2.4g; Carbohydrate 23.6g, of which sugars 12g; Fat 10.7g, of which saturates 6.7g; Cholesterol 27mg; Calcium 40mg; Fibre 3.1g; Sodium 79mg.

Walnut Baklava

This version of the delectable and popular Middle Eastern sweet is made with walnuts.

Serves 12

400g/14oz/scant 2 cups clarified butter, or ordinary butter, melted
500g/1¼lb/3⅓ cups walnuts, roughly chopped
200g/7oz/1 cup caster (superfine) sugar
150g/5oz/1¼ cups ground almonds
25 sheets filo pastry

For the syrup
500g/1¼lb/2¾ cups caster (superfine) sugar
75ml/5 tbsp rose water
juice and grated rind of 2 lemons

1 Preheat the oven to 180°C/350°F/Gas 4. Brush a roasting pan, 30 x 20cm/12 x 8in, with butter. Set aside. Combine the walnuts and caster sugar in a bowl. Put the ground almonds in a separate bowl and stir in all but 30ml/2 tbsp of clarified butter.

2 Lay a sheet of filo pastry in the roasting pan. Sprinkle with 30ml/2 tbsp of the almond and butter mixture. Cover with another sheet of filo pastry and sprinkle over 30ml/2 tbsp of the almond mixture. Continue until you have eight layers.

3 Using about half the walnut mixture, spread a layer over the top layer of filo. Cover with eight more layers of filo and ground almonds, alternating as before. Follow with the remainder of the walnut mixture and press down gently.

4 Finish off with eight more filo sheets layered with the ground almond and butter mixture. Butter the top layer with clarified butter. With a sharp knife, cut into small diamond shapes. Spray the baklava lightly with water and bake for 30 minutes. Reduce the temperature to 140°C/275°F/Gas 1 and cook for 2 hours more. Remove from the oven. Leave to cool in the tin.

5 To make the syrup, put the sugar and 500ml/17fl oz/2 cups water in a pan and bring to the boil. Reduce the heat to low, add the rose water and simmer for about 15 minutes. Stir in the lemon juice and rind. When the baklava is cool, spoon over the hot syrup, making sure that it covers all the pastry. Cover with a clean dish towel, and leave for 48 hours before serving.

Coffee and Pistachio Baklava

In this version of the famous pastry confection, strong coffee flavours the pouring syrup, and the filling is made with pistachio nuts.

Serves 12

50g/2oz/½ cup blanched almonds, chopped
50g/2oz/½ cup pistachio nuts, chopped
75g/3oz/scant ½ cup caster (superfine) sugar
115g/4oz filo pastry
75g/3oz/6 tbsp unsalted (sweet) butter, melted and cooled

For the syrup
115g/4oz/generous ½ cup caster (superfine) sugar
7.5cm/3in piece cinnamon stick
1 whole clove
2 cardamom pods, crushed
75ml/5 tbsp strong brewed coffee

1 Preheat the oven to 180°C/350°F/Gas 4. Mix the almonds and pistachio with the and sugar in a bowl. Cut the pastry to fit a tin (pan) measuring 18 x 28cm/7 x 11in.

2 Brush the tin with a little melted butter. Lay a sheet of pastry in the bottom of the tin and brush with more melted butter. Repeat with three more sheets and spread with half the nut and sugar mixture.

3 Layer up three more sheets of pastry, lightly brushing butter between the layers, then spread the remaining nut and sugar mixture over them, smoothing it over the entire surface. Top with the remaining pastry and butter. Gently press down the edges to seal.

4 With a sharp knife, mark the top into diamonds. Bake for 20–25 minutes until golden brown and crisp.

5 Meanwhile, put the syrup ingredients in a small pan and heat gently until the sugar has dissolved. Cover the pan with a lid and leave to infuse for 20 minutes.

6 Remove the baklava from the oven. Reheat the syrup and strain over the pastry. Leave to cool in the tin and then cut into diamonds, remove from the tin and serve.

Baklava Energy 839kcal/3490kJ; Protein 9.2g; Carbohydrate 63.2g, of which sugars 62.6g; Fat 62.8g, of which saturates 20.9g; Cholesterol 77mg; Calcium 105mg; Fibre 2.4g; Sodium 258mg.
Coffee Baklava Energy 776kcal/3247kJ; Protein 10g; Carbohydrate 91g, of which sugars 62g; Fat 44g, of which saturates 12g; Cholesterol 31mg; Calcium 99mg; Fibre 3.2g; Sodium 272mg.

Choux Custard Pastries

These sweetly scented Italian pastry treats have two contrasting custards – chocolate and vanilla.

Makes about 48

200ml/7fl oz/scant 1 cup water
115g/4oz/½ cup butter
2cm/1in piece vanilla pod (bean)
pinch of salt
150g/5oz/1¼ cups plain (all-purpose) flour
5 eggs

For the custard fillings
50g/2oz cooking chocolate
300ml/½ pint/1¼ cups milk
4 egg yolks
65g/2½ oz/scant ⅓ cup sugar
40g/1½oz/⅓ cup plain (all-purpose) flour
5ml/1 tsp pure vanilla extract
300ml/½ pint/1¼ cups whipping cream
unsweetened cocoa powder and icing (confectioners') sugar, to garnish

1 Preheat the oven to 190°C/375°F/Gas 5. Heat the water with the butter, vanilla and salt. When melted, beat in the flour. Cook over low heat, stirring, for 10 minutes. Remove from the heat. Mix in the eggs one at a time. Remove the vanilla pod.

2 Butter a flat baking tray. Using a piping (pastry) bag fitted with a round nozzle, pipe walnut-size balls on to the tray. Bake for 20–25 minutes, or until golden brown. Cool before filling.

3 Prepare the custard fillings. Melt the chocolate in the top half of a double boiler, or in a bowl set over a pan of simmering water. Heat the milk in a small pan, taking care not to let it boil.

4 Whisk the egg yolks. Add the sugar, and beat until pale. Beat in the flour. Slowly pour in the hot milk, stirring until combined. Pour into a pan, and bring to a boil. Simmer for 5–6 minutes, stirring constantly. Remove from the heat and divide the custard between two bowls. Add the chocolate to one, and stir the vanilla extract into the other. Allow to cool completely.

5 Whip the cream. Fold half into each custard. Fill two pastry bags fitted with round nozzles with each custard. Fill half the pastries with chocolate custard, and the rest with vanilla custard, through a little hole in the side. Dust the chocolate pastries with cocoa powder, and the rest with sugar. Serve immediately.

Coffee Profiteroles

Irresistible coffee-flavoured choux puffs, with a liqueur-laced white chocolate sauce.

Serves 6

65g/2½oz/9 tbsp plain (all-purpose) flour
pinch of salt
50g/2oz/4 tbsp butter, diced
150ml/¼ pint/⅔ cup freshly brewed coffee
2 eggs, lightly beaten
250ml/8fl oz/1 cup double (heavy) cream, whipped

For the white chocolate sauce
50g/2oz/¼ cup granulated sugar
120ml/4fl oz/½ cup water
150g/5oz white chocolate, broken into pieces
25g/1oz/2 tbsp unsalted (sweet) butter
45ml/3 tbsp double (heavy) cream
30ml/2 tbsp coffee liqueur

1 Preheat the oven to 220°C/425°F/Gas 7. Sift the flour and salt on to a piece of baking parchment.

2 Place the butter in a pan with the coffee. Bring to a rolling boil, then remove from the heat and pour in the sifted flour in one go. Beat hard until the mixture leaves the side of the pan, forming a ball of thick paste. Leave to cool for 5 minutes.

3 Gradually add the eggs, beating well after each addition, until the mixture forms a stiff dropping consistency. Spoon into a piping (pastry) bag fitted with a 1cm/½in plain nozzle.

4 Pipe 24 small buns on a dampened baking sheet, leaving plenty of room between them. Bake for 20 minutes, until risen.

5 Remove the buns from the oven and pierce the side of each one with a sharp knife to let out the steam.

6 Make the sauce. Put the sugar and water in a heavy pan, and heat gently until the sugar has completely dissolved. Bring to the boil and simmer for 3 minutes. Remove the pan from the heat, and add the white chocolate and butter, stirring constantly until smooth. Stir in the double cream and liqueur.

7 Spoon the whipped cream into a piping bag and fill the choux buns through the slits. Serve with the sauce poured over.

Choux Pastries Energy 79kcal/331kJ; Protein 1.8g; Carbohydrate 7.3g, of which sugars 3.3g; Fat 5g, of which saturates 3g; Cholesterol 44mg; Calcium 24mg; Fibre 0.2g; Sodium 32mg.
Profiteroles Energy 577Kcal/2393kJ; Protein 6g; Carbohydrate 34.3g, of which sugars 26g; Fat 46.4g, of which saturates 28.1g; Cholesterol 157mg; Calcium 123mg; Fibre 0.3g; Sodium 139mg.

Croquembouche

This stunning choux pastry tower is served in France for special occasions such as weddings. Be careful when you make the caramel, as it can easily burn.

Serves 10
75g/3oz/6 tbsp unsalted (sweet) butter, plus extra for greasing
115g/4oz/1 cup plain (all-purpose) flour, sifted
3 eggs

For the filling
600ml/1 pint/2¼ cups double (heavy) cream
60ml/4 tbsp caster (superfine) sugar

For the caramel
115g/4oz/generous ½ cup caster (superfine) sugar

1 Preheat the oven to 200°C/400°F/Gas 6. Grease four baking sheets. Melt the butter in a pan with 250ml/8fl oz/1 cup water and bring to the boil. Remove from the heat.

2 Sift the flour on to a paper sheet and immediately pour into the pan. Quickly beat together until the mixture forms a ball. Transfer to a bowl and whisk in the eggs, using an electric whisk, until a smooth, thick paste forms.

3 Fill a piping (pastry) bag fitted with a 1cm/½in plain nozzle and pipe small balls about 2.5cm/1in wide on to the baking sheets, spaced well apart.

4 Bake for 20 minutes, or until golden. Pierce a large hole in the base of each to release the steam, then return to the oven for a further 5 minutes. Cool on a wire rack.

5 To make the filling, whip the cream together with the 60ml/4 tbsp sugar, until it forms soft peaks. Spoon into a piping bag fitted with a 5mm/¼in nozzle and pipe cream into each bun through the hole in the base. Arrange the buns in a pyramid.

6 To make the caramel, slowly heat the sugar until liquid in a pan. Drizzle the hot caramel over the pyramid, allowing it to drizzle down over the buns. Serve immediately.

Gâteau Saint-Honoré

This elaborate French confection is named after the patron saint of bakers.

Serves 10
175g/6oz puff pastry

For the choux pastry
300ml/½ pint/1¼ cups water
115g/4oz/½ cup butter, diced
130g/4½oz/generous 1 cup plain (all-purpose) flour, sifted
2.5ml/½ tsp salt
4 eggs, lightly beaten
beaten egg, to glaze

For the filling
3 egg yolks
50g/2oz/¼ cup caster (superfine) sugar
30ml/2 tbsp plain (all-purpose) flour
30ml/2 tbsp cornflour (cornstarch)
300ml/½ pint/1¼ cups milk
150ml/¼ pint/⅔ cup double (heavy) cream
30ml/2 tbsp orange liqueur

For the caramel
225g/8oz/1 cup granulated (white) sugar
120ml/4fl oz/½ cup water

1 Roll out the puff pastry, cut out a 20cm/8in circle, place on a lined baking sheet, prick all over and chill. Make the choux pastry. Heat the water and butter until the butter melts, bring to the boil, add the flour and salt, remove from the heat and beat until the mixture forms a ball. Beat in the eggs to form a paste.

2 Preheat the oven to 200°C/400°F/Gas 6. Using a piping (pastry) bag with a 1cm/½in nozzle, pipe a choux spiral on the puff pastry base. Pipe 16 choux buns on to a lined baking sheet. Brush with egg. Bake the buns for 20 minutes and the base for 35 minutes. Pierce holes in the spiral, and one in the side of each bun. Return to the oven for 5 minutes to dry out. Cool on a rack.

3 Whisk the yolks and sugar for the filling until creamy. Whisk in the flours, then boil the milk and whisk that in. Transfer to a pan. and simmer for about 3 minutes, until thick, cover and cool. Whip the cream, fold in to the cooled filling with the liqueur and pipe into the buns.

4 To make the caramel, simmer the sugar and water until melted and golden. Dip the buns in the caramel, put around the edge of the pastry case, and pipe the remaining filling into the centre. Drizzle with the remaining caramel and leave to set for 2 hours.

Croquembouche Energy 579kcal/2400kJ; Protein 6g; Carbohydrate 32.6g, of which sugars 24.4g; Fat 46.8g, of which saturates 28.3g; Cholesterol 159mg; Calcium 123mg; Fibre 0.3g; Sodium 138mg.
Saint-Honoré Energy 466Kcal/1952kJ; Protein 7.3g; Carbohydrate 51.9g, of which sugars 30.9g; Fat 26.5g, of which saturates 12.5g; Cholesterol 186mg; Calcium 139mg; Fibre 0.5g; Sodium 136mg.

Strawberry and Kirsch Choux Ring

Another spectacular dessert made from individual balls of choux pastry.

Serves 4–6

350g/12oz/generous 2 cups small whole strawberries
75g/3oz/6 tbsp granulated sugar
150ml/¼ pint/⅔ cup double (heavy) cream
30ml/2 tbsp Kirsch
10ml/2 tsp icing (confectioners') sugar, sifted, plus extra for dusting
whipped cream, to serve

For the pastry

150ml/¼ pint/⅔ cup water
50g/2oz/¼ cup butter
65g/2½oz/9 tbsp plain (all-purpose) flour, sifted
2 eggs, beaten

1 Preheat the oven to 220°C/425°F/Gas 7. Reserve half the strawberries and slice the rest. Draw a 15cm/6in circle on a sheet of parchment. Turn it over and press on to a greased baking sheet.

2 Make the pastry. Heat the water and butter in a pan until the butter melts, bring to the boil, add the flour and remove from the heat. Beat with a wooden spoon until the mixture forms a ball, leaving the pan-sides clean. Gradually beat in the eggs to form a smooth paste. Spoon/pipe the pastry in balls, making a circle on the baking sheet, using the drawn circle. The balls should just touch each other. Bake for 15 minutes, then lower the heat to 190°C/375°F/Gas 5 and cook for 20–25 minutes. Make one or two slits in the pastry to let the hot air escape. Leave to cool.

3 Heat the granulated sugar until it dissolves, then increase the heat and cook the syrup until it turns a gold colour and a spoonful hardens when dropped into a bowl of cold water. Using a fork, half-dip and turn each whole strawberry in the syrup. Leave the strawberries to cool on baking parchment.

4 Make the filling. Whip the cream in a bowl until it just starts to thicken. Stir in the Kirsch and icing sugar and continue whisking until stiff. With a wooden spoon, fold in the sliced strawberries. Slice the choux ring in half horizontally, spoon in the strawberry cream and replace the top. Dust with a little icing sugar. Serve with whipped cream and the dipped strawberries.

St Joseph's Day Choux Buns

These Italian buns are traditionally eaten on St Joseph's Day, which is also Father's Day in Italy.

Makes about 24 buns

130g/4½oz/generous ½ cup unsalted (sweet) butter
250ml/8fl oz/1 cup cold water
150g/5oz/1¼ cups plain (all-purpose) flour
4 eggs, beaten
sunflower oil, for deep-frying
icing (confectioners') sugar and cinnamon, for dusting

1 Put the butter in a pan with the water. Heat until the butter has melted and then bring to the boil. Add the flour all at once and stir constantly with a wooden spoon. Cook for 2 minutes, or until the mixture pulls away from the sides of the pan, forming a ball.

2 Remove from the heat and allow to cool. Wrap the dough in clear film (plastic wrap) and chill in the refrigerator for about 30 minutes. Transfer the dough to a bowl. Using a wooden spoon or the paddle attachment of a food processor or mixer, mix the dough for 1–2 minutes.

3 Gradually add the beaten eggs, mixing the dough until smooth each time. Scrape down the sides of the bowl. The dough should be soft and glossy, but able to hold its shape.

4 Heat the sunflower oil in a large pan or deep-fryer until a cube of bread, dropped into the oil, sizzles instantly. Using two teaspoons, scoop balls of the mixture into the hot oil. Leave until they are puffy and golden.

5 Remove the cooked buns from the pan and drain on kitchen paper. Lightly toss the buns in icing sugar and cinnamon, and serve warm.

Variation
Snip the base of the buns open with scissors and fill (using a clean piping bag) with whipped cream.

Choux Ring Energy 324Kcal/1346kJ; Protein 4.1g; Carbohydrate 25.5g, of which sugars 17.2g; Fat 22.3g, of which saturates 13.2g; Cholesterol 115mg; Calcium 54mg; Fibre 1g; Sodium 84mg.
Choux Buns Energy 106kcal/441kJ; Protein 1.7g; Carbohydrate 4.9g, of which sugars 0.1g; Fat 9.1g, of which saturates 3.6g; Cholesterol 44mg; Calcium 14mg; Fibre 0.2g; Sodium 53mg.

Yorkshire Curd Tart

The distinguishing characteristic of this traditional regional tart is allspice, or 'clove pepper' as it was known locally. This tart tastes superb and does not taste too sweet.

Serves 8

90g/3½oz/scant ½ cup soft light brown sugar
large pinch of ground allspice
3 eggs, beaten
grated rind and juice of 1 lemon
40g/1½oz/3 tbsp butter, melted
450g/1lb/2 cups curd (farmer's) cheese
75g/3oz/½ cup raisins
whipped cream, to serve (optional)

For the pastry

225g/8oz/2 cups plain (all-purpose) flour
115g/4oz/½ cup butter, diced
1 egg yolk
15–30ml/1–2 tbsp chilled water

1 Make the pastry. Place the flour in a large mixing bowl and rub or cut in the butter until the mixture resembles fine breadcrumbs. Stir the egg yolk into the flour and add just enough of the water to bind the mixture to form a dough.

2 Put the dough on a floured surface, knead lightly and briefly, then form into a ball. Roll out the pastry thinly and use to line a 20cm/8in fluted loose-based flan tin (pan). Cover with clear film (plastic wrap) and chill for about 15 minutes.

3 Preheat the oven to 190°C/375°F/Gas 5. Mix the sugar with the ground allspice in a bowl, then stir in the eggs, lemon rind and juice, butter, curd cheese and raisins. Mix well.

4 Pour the filling into the pastry case (pie shell), then bake for 40 minutes, or until the pastry is cooked and the filling is lightly set and golden brown. Cut the tart into wedges while it is still slightly warm, and serve with cream, if you like.

Cook's Tip
Although it is not traditional, mixed spice (apple pie spice) would make a good substitute for the ground allspice.

Coconut Cream Pie

A delicately flavoured tart, suitable for any occasion.

Serves 8

200g/7oz/2½ cups desiccated (dry unsweetened) coconut
115g/4oz/generous ½ cup caster (superfine) sugar
60ml/4 tbsp cornflour (cornstarch)
pinch of salt
600ml/1 pint/2½ cups milk
50ml/2fl oz/¼ cup whipping cream
2 egg yolks
25g/1oz/2 tbsp unsalted (sweet) butter
10ml/2 tsp vanilla extract

For the pastry

115g/4oz/1 cup plain (all-purpose) flour
1.5ml/¼ tsp salt
40g/1½oz/3 tbsp cold butter, cut into pieces
25g/1oz/2 tbsp cold lard
30–45ml/2–3 tbsp chilled water

1 Make the pastry. Sift the flour and salt into a bowl. Add the butter and lard and cut in with a pastry blender or two knives until the mixture resembles coarse breadcrumbs. With a fork, stir in just enough water to bind the dough. Gather into a ball, wrap in baking parchment and chill for at least 20 minutes.

2 Preheat the oven to 220°C/425°F/Gas 7. Roll out the dough to 3mm/⅛in thick. Transfer to a 23cm/9in flan tin (pan). Trim and flute the edges. Prick the base. Line with baking parchment and fill with baking beans. Bake for 10–12 minutes.

3 Remove the paper and beans, reduce the heat to 180°C/350°F/Gas 4 and bake for a further 10–15 minutes until brown. Spread 75g/3oz/1 cup of the coconut on a baking sheet. Toast in the oven for 6–8 minutes, stirring often, until golden. Set aside.

4 Put the sugar, cornflour and salt in a pan. In a bowl, whisk together the milk, cream and egg yolks. Add the egg mixture to the pan. Cook over low heat, stirring constantly, until the mixture comes to the boil. Boil for 1 minute, then remove from the heat. Add the butter, vanilla and remaining coconut.

5 Pour into the pastry case (pie shell). When the filling is cool, sprinkle the toasted coconut in a ring in the centre.

Curd Tart Energy 480kcal/2005kJ; Protein 16.2g; Carbohydrate 48.2g, of which sugars 23.7g; Fat 27g, of which saturates 15.8g; Cholesterol 173mg; Calcium 153mg; Fibre 1.2g; Sodium 451mg.
Coconut Pie Energy 445Kcal/1857kJ; Protein 6.3g; Carbohydrate 38.4g, of which sugars 20.6g; Fat 30.7g, of which saturates 21.7g; Cholesterol 82mg; Calcium 136mg; Fibre 3.9g; Sodium 98mg.

Pecan Pie

Almost an American institution, this classic country pie has a golden crust with a dense maple syrup filling topped with pecans halves. Serve warm with whipped cream.

Serves 8

3 eggs
pinch of salt
200g/7oz/scant 1 cup soft dark brown sugar
120ml/4fl oz/½ cup golden (light corn) syrup
30ml/2 tbsp fresh lemon juice
75g/3oz/6 tbsp butter, melted
150g/5oz/1¼ cups chopped pecan nuts
50g/2oz/½ cup pecan halves

For the pastry
175g/6oz/1½ cups plain (all-purpose) flour
15ml/1 tbsp caster (superfine) sugar
5ml/1 tsp baking powder
2.5ml/½ tsp salt
75g/3oz/6 tbsp cold unsalted (sweet) butter, cut in pieces
1 egg yolk
45–60ml/3–4 tbsp whipping cream

1 For the pastry, sift the flour, sugar, baking powder and salt into a bowl. Add the butter and cut in with a pastry blender until the mixture resembles coarse breadcrumbs.

2 In a mixing bowl, beat together the egg yolk and whipping cream until blended. Pour the mixture into the flour mixture and mix in until well combined.

3 Gather the pastry into a ball. On a lightly floured surface, roll out 3mm/⅛in thick and transfer to a 23cm/9in fluted tin (pan).

4 Trim the overhang and flute the edge with your fingers. Chill in the refrigerator for at least 20 minutes.

5 Preheat a baking sheet in the middle of a 200°C/400°F/Gas 6 oven. In a bowl, lightly whisk the eggs and salt. Add the sugar, syrup, lemon juice and butter. Mix well and stir in the chopped nuts. Pour into the pastry case (pie shell) and arrange the pecan halves in concentric circles on top.

6 Bake for 10 minutes. Reduce the heat to 170°C/325°F/Gas 3 and continue baking for 25 minutes. Serve warm.

Almond and Pine Nut Tart

Strange though it may seem, this traditional tart is an Italian version of the homely Bakewell tart from Derbyshire in England.

Serves 8

115g/4oz/½ cup butter, softened
115g/4oz/generous ½ cup caster (superfine) sugar
1 egg, plus 2 egg yolks
150g/5oz/1¼ cups ground almonds
115g/4oz/1⅓ cups pine nuts
60ml/4 tbsp seedless raspberry jam
icing (confectioners') sugar, for dusting

For the pastry
175g/6oz/1½ cups plain (all-purpose) flour
65g/2½oz/5 tbsp caster (superfine) sugar
1.5ml/¼ tsp baking powder
pinch of salt
115g/4oz/½ cup chilled butter, diced
1 egg yolk

1 Make the pastry. Sift the flour, sugar, baking powder and salt on to a clean, dry cold surface or marble pastry board.

2 Make a well in the centre of the flour mixture and put in the diced butter and egg yolk. Gradually work the flour mixture into the butter and egg yolk, using just your fingertips, until you have a soft, pliable dough.

3 Press the dough into a 23cm/9in loose-based fluted flan tin (pan). Chill for 30 minutes.

4 Cream the butter and sugar with an electric whisk until light, then use a wooden spoon to beat in the egg and egg yolks a little at a time, alternating with the almonds. Beat in the pine nuts.

5 Preheat the oven to 160°C/325°F/Gas 3. Spread the jam evenly over the pastry case (pie shell), then spoon in the filling.

6 Bake for 30–35 minutes until golden, or until a skewer inserted in the centre of the tart comes out clean.

7 Transfer to a wire rack and leave to cool, then carefully remove the side of the tin, leaving the tart on the tin base. Dust with icing sugar and serve with whipped cream.

Pecan Pie Energy 587kcal/2449kJ; Protein 7.5g; Carbohydrate 56.7g, of which sugars 39.6g; Fat 38.3g, of which saturates 13.4g; Cholesterol 142mg; Calcium 82mg; Fibre 1.9g; Sodium 185mg.
Almond Tart Energy 643kcal/2675kJ; Protein 10.2g; Carbohydrate 47.7g, of which sugars 30.5g; Fat 47g, of which saturates 17.3g; Cholesterol 161mg; Calcium 108mg; Fibre 2.3g; Sodium 193mg.

Honey and Pine Nut Tart

Wonderful tarts of all descriptions are to be found throughout France, and this recipe recalls the flavours of the south.

Serves 6

115g/4oz/½ cup butter, diced
115g/4oz/generous ½ cup caster (superfine) sugar
3 eggs, beaten
175g/6oz/⅔ cup sunflower honey
grated rind and juice of 1 lemon
225g/8oz/2⅔ cups pine nuts
pinch of salt
icing (confectioners') sugar, for dusting

For the pastry

225g/8oz/2 cups plain (all-purpose) flour
115g/4oz/½ cup butter, diced
30ml/2 tbsp icing (confectioners') sugar
1 egg
15ml/1 tbsp chilled water
crème fraîche or vanilla ice cream, to serve (optional)

1 Preheat the oven to 180°C/350°F/Gas 4. Make the pastry. Sift the flour into a large mixing bowl and rub or cut in the butter until the mixture resembles fine breadcrumbs.

2 Stir in the icing sugar. Add the egg and water and mix to form a soft dough. Knead lightly until smooth.

3 Roll out the pastry on a lightly floured surface and use to line a 23cm/9in flan tin (pan). Prick the base with a fork, then chill for 10 minutes. Line with baking parchment and fill with baking beans. Bake for 10 minutes. Remove the paper and beans and set the pastry case (pie shell) aside.

4 Cream the butter and caster sugar together until light and fluffy. Beat in the eggs one at a time. In a small pan, gently heat the honey until it melts, then add it to the butter mixture with the lemon rind and juice. Mix well. Stir in the pine nuts and salt, blending well, then pour the filling evenly into the pastry case.

5 Bake for about 45 minutes, or until the filling is lightly set. Leave to cool slightly in the tin, then dust with icing sugar.

6 Serve warm, or at room temperature, with crème fraîche or vanilla ice cream, if you like.

Rustic Walnut and Honey Tart

Serve this simple tart with plenty of whipped cream.

Serves 4

90g/3½oz sweet shortcrust pastry
6 sugar cubes
200g/7oz/1¾ cups walnuts
75ml/5 tbsp good honey
45ml/3 tbsp double (heavy) cream

1 Preheat the oven to 200°C/400°F/Gas 6. Roll the pastry out to a round measuring about 25cm/10in across and allow to rest. Place on a baking sheet and bake for 15 minutes.

2 Put the sugar and 60ml/4 tbsp water in a pan and heat until it caramelizes. Add the walnuts and coat, toasting lightly in the pan. Remove from the heat and cool slightly. Mix in the honey and cream, and spread the walnut mixture over the pastry base.

Lattice Jam Tart

Jam tarts are a popular treat in Italy, where they are often eaten with a coffee. They are traditionally decorated with pastry strips as with the attractive lattice covering on this fruit tart.

Serves 6–8

350g/12oz sweet shortcrust pastry
350g/12oz/1¼ cups fruit jam, such as raspberry or strawberry
1 egg, lightly beaten with 30ml/2 tbsp whipping cream

1 Divide the pastry into two, one larger than the other. Lightly grease a shallow 23cm/9in flan tin (pan). Roll out the larger ball of pastry on a lightly floured surface to about 3mm/⅛in thick and line the prepared tin. Trim the edges, prick the bottom and chill for at least 30 minutes.

2 Preheat the oven to 190°C/375°F/Gas 5. Spread jam thickly over the base of the pastry. Roll out the remaining pastry. Cut into strips and arrange over the jam in a lattice pattern.

3 Brush the pastry with the egg and cream mix. Bake for about 35 minutes, or until the pastry is golden. Cool before serving.

Honey Tart Energy 563kcal/2338kJ; Protein 9.1g; Carbohydrate 35.9g, of which sugars 30.8g; Fat 43.5g, of which saturates 6.6g; Cholesterol 15mg; Calcium 70mg; Fibre 2g; Sodium 67mg.
Walnut Tart Energy 573kcal/2378kJ; Protein 8.9g; Carbohydrate 31.4g, of which sugars 20.7g; Fat 46.6g, of which saturates 9.5g; Cholesterol 19mg; Calcium 74mg; Fibre 2.9g; Sodium 98mg.
Jam Tart Energy 340Kcal/1434kJ; Protein 3.4g; Carbohydrate 56.4g, of which sugars 37.3g; Fat 12.8g, of which saturates 7.7g; Cholesterol 54mg; Calcium 49mg; Fibre 0.8g; Sodium 117mg.

Maple Walnut Tart

The distinctive taste of maple syrups goes particularly well with nuts.

Serves 8

3 eggs
pinch of salt
50g/2oz/¼ cup caster (superfine) sugar
50g/2oz/¼ cup butter, melted
250ml/8fl oz/1 cup maple syrup
115g/4oz/1 cup chopped walnuts
whipped cream, for decorating

For the pastry

65g/2½oz/9 tbsp plain (all-purpose) flour
65g/2½oz/9 tbsp wholemeal (whole-wheat) flour
pinch of salt
50g/2oz/¼ cup cold butter, cut in pieces
40g/1½oz/3 tbsp cold white vegetable fat (shortening), cut in pieces
1 egg yolk
30–45ml/2–3 tbsp iced water

1 For the pastry, mix the flours and salt in a bowl. Add the butter and fat and cut in with a pastry blender until the mixture resembles coarse breadcrumbs. With a fork, stir in the egg yolk and just enough water to bind the pastry. Form into a ball. Wrap in baking parchment and chill for 20 minutes. Preheat oven to 220°C/425°F/Gas 7.

2 On a lightly floured surface, roll out the pastry about 3mm/⅛in thick and transfer to a 23cm/9in pie dish. Trim the edge. To decorate, roll out the trimmings. With a small heart-shaped cutter, stamp out enough hearts to go around the rim of the pie. Brush the edge with water, then arrange the pastry hearts all around.

3 Prick the bottom with a fork. Line with crumpled baking parchment and fill with baking beans. Bake for 10 minutes. Remove the paper and beans and continue baking until golden brown, 3–6 minutes more.

4 In a bowl, whisk the eggs, salt and sugar together. Stir in the butter and maple syrup. Pour the filling into the pastry case (pie shell), then sprinkle the nuts over the top.

5 Bake until just set, about 35 minutes. Cool on a rack. Decorate with whipped cream, if you like.

Raspberry and Almond Tart

Raspberries have a short season but are often available in large amounts during that time. This tart is a good way of using a glut, and juicy freshly picked raspberries and almonds go very well together. This is a rich tart, ideal for serving at the end of a special lunch or at a dinner party.

Serves 4

200g/7oz sweet shortcrust pastry
2 large (US extra large) eggs
75ml/2½fl oz/⅓ cup double (heavy) cream
50g/2oz/¼ cup caster (superfine) sugar
50g/2oz/½ cup ground almonds
20g/¾oz/4 tsp butter
350g/12oz/2 cups fresh raspberries, rinsed and drained on kitchen paper

1 Line a 20cm/8in flan tin (pan) with the pastry. Prick the base all over and leave to rest for at least 30 minutes. Preheat the oven to 200°C/400°F/Gas 6.

2 Put the eggs, cream, sugar and ground almonds in a large bowl and whisk together briskly. Melt the butter and pour into the mixture, stirring to combine thoroughly.

3 Sprinkle the raspberries evenly over the pastry case (pie shell). The ones at the top will appear through the surface, so keep them evenly spaced and sitting on their sides. You can also create a pattern with them if you wish.

4 Pour the egg and almond mixture over the top. Once again ensure that it is spread evenly throughout the tart.

5 Bake the tart in the preheated oven for about 25 minutes until just set but still soft. Serve warm or cold.

Variation

Peaches make a very attractive and tasty alternative filling to the raspberries. Use six large, ripe peaches and remove the skin and stone (pit). Cut into slices and use in the same way as the raspberries above.

Maple Tart Energy 442kcal/1846kJ; Protein 6.8g; Carbohydrate 43.3g, of which sugars 32g; Fat 28.1g, of which saturates 10.2g; Cholesterol 128mg; Calcium 52mg; Fibre 1.5g; Sodium 190mg.
Raspberry Tart Energy 548kcal/2284kJ; Protein 10.9g; Carbohydrate 41.7g, of which sugars 18.4g; Fat 38.8g, of which saturates 14.8g; Cholesterol 158mg; Calcium 128mg; Fibre 4.1g; Sodium 282mg.

Boston Banoffee Pie

Simply press this wonderfully biscuity pastry into the tin, rather than rolling it out. Add the fudge-toffee filling and it will prove irresistible.

Serves 6

115g/4oz/½ cup butter, diced
200g/7oz can skimmed, sweetened condensed milk
115g/4oz/½ cup soft brown sugar
30ml/2 tbsp golden (light corn) syrup
2 small bananas, sliced
a little lemon juice
whipped cream, to decorate
5ml/1 tsp grated plain (semisweet) chocolate

For the pastry

150g/5oz/1¼ cups plain (all-purpose) flour
115g/4oz/½ cup butter, diced
50g/2oz/¼ cup caster (superfine) sugar

1 Preheat the oven to 160°C/325°F/Gas 3. In a food processor, process the flour and diced butter until crumbed. Stir in the caster sugar and add just enough cold water to mix to form a soft, pliable dough.

2 Press into a 20cm/8in loose-based flan tin (pan). Bake in the oven for 30 minutes.

3 To make the filling, place the butter in a pan with the condensed milk, brown sugar and syrup. Heat gently, stirring all the time, until the butter has melted and the sugar has completely dissolved.

4 Bring the pan to a gentle boil and cook for 7–10 minutes, stirring constantly, until the mixture thickens and turns a light caramel colour.

5 Pour the hot caramel filling into the pastry case (pie shell) and leave until completely cold. Gently toss the banana slices in lemon juice and arrange in overlapping circles on top of the filling, leaving a gap in the centre.

6 Pipe a generous swirl of whipped cream in the centre and sprinkle with the grated chocolate before serving.

Chocolate-topped Candied Fruit Pie

Use good quality candied fruits for the best flavour with this pie. For the crust, try half digestive biscuits and half ginger nut biscuits.

Serves 10

15ml/1 tbsp rum
50g/2oz/¼ cup mixed glacé (candied) fruit, chopped
475ml/16fl oz/2 cups milk
20ml/4 tsp powdered gelatine
90g/3½oz/½ cup caster (superfine) sugar
2.5ml/½ tsp salt
3 eggs, separated
250ml/8fl oz/1 cup whipping cream, whipped
chocolate curls, to decorate

For the crust

175g/6oz/2 cups crushed digestive biscuits (graham crackers)
75g/3oz/6 tbsp butter, melted
15ml/1 tbsp caster (superfine) sugar

1 To make the crust, mix the digestive biscuits, melted butter and sugar together in a bowl. Press evenly over the base and sides of a 23cm/9in flan tin (pan). Chill in the refrigerator. Stir together the rum and glacé fruit. Set aside.

2 Pour 120ml/4fl oz/½ cup of the milk into a small bowl. Sprinkle over the gelatine and leave for 5 minutes to soften.

3 In the top of a double boiler, or in a heatproof bowl over a pan of simmering water, combine 50g/2oz/¼ cup of the sugar, the remaining milk and the salt. Stir in the gelatine mixture.

4 Cook, stirring, until the gelatine dissolves. Whisk in the egg yolks and cook, stirring, until thick enough to coat the back of the spoon. Pour the custard over the glacé fruit mixture, set in a bowl of iced water.

5 Beat the egg whites until they form soft peaks. Add the remaining sugar and beat until just blended. Fold a large dollop of the egg whites into the cooled gelatine mixture. Pour into the remaining egg whites and fold together. Fold in the cream.

6 Pour the filling into the pie crust and chill in the refrigerator until firm. Decorate with chocolate curls.

Boston Banoffee Energy 672kcal2810 kJ; Protein 7g; Carbohydrate 80g, of which sugars 60g; Fat 39g, of which saturates 24g; Cholesterol 106mg; Calcium 176mg; Fibre 1.9g; Sodium 307mg.
Fruit Pie Energy 333kcal/1388kJ; Protein 5.2g; Carbohydrate 28.9g, of which sugars 19.3g; Fat 22.3g, of which saturates 12.8g; Cholesterol 109mg; Calcium 110mg; Fibre 0.6g; Sodium 213mg.

Sticky Nut Pie

Drambuie is a liqueur which combines the flavours of whisky and heather honey – a delicious combination in this sticky pecan and macadamia nut filling.

Serves 6–8
225g/8oz/2 cups plain (all-purpose) flour
115g/4oz/½ cup butter, diced
30ml/2 tbsp strong black coffee
75g/3oz/¾ cup pecan nut halves
75g/3oz/¾ cup macadamia nuts, halved
ice cream, to serve

For the filling
3 eggs
50g/2oz/5 tbsp molasses
50g/2oz/⅓ cup soft dark brown sugar
30ml/2 tbsp clear honey
30ml/2 tbsp Drambuie
25g/1oz/2 tbsp butter, melted
115g/4oz/1 cup pecan nuts, chopped
115g/4oz/1 cup macadamia nuts, chopped

1 Sift the flour into a bowl and rub in the butter until the mixture resembles fine breadcrumbs. Stir in the coffee to make a soft dough. Add a little water if extra liquid is needed. Wrap the dough in clear film (plastic wrap) and chill for 30 minutes. Preheat the oven to 200°C/400°F/Gas 6.

2 Roll out the pastry on a lightly floured surface to a long rectangle 40 x 16cm/16 x 6½in. Use it to line a 35 x 11.5cm/14 x 4½in oblong flan tin (pan).

3 Make the filling by mixing all the ingredients in a bowl. Stir thoroughly, then spoon the filling into the pastry case (pie shell).

4 Gently place the pecan and macadamia halves in a pattern on top of the tart. Bake for 35–40 minutes until the pastry is golden. Serve warm with ice cream.

Variation
Use hazelnuts instead of macadamia nuts, or walnuts instead of the pecans if you wish, and if you don't have any Drambuie, whiskey can be substituted.

Cider Pie

Few can resist this pie, with its cider-enriched filling, decorated with pastry apples.

Serves six
600ml/1 pint/2½ cups dry (hard) cider
15g/½oz/1 tbsp butter
250ml/8fl oz/1 cup maple syrup
60ml/4 tbsp water
2 eggs, at room temperature, separated and yolks beaten
5ml/1 tsp grated nutmeg
icing (confectioners') sugar, for dusting

For the pastry
175g/6oz/1½ cups plain (all-purpose) flour
1.5ml/¼ tsp salt
10ml/2 tsp granulated sugar
115g/4oz/½ cup cold butter, diced
about 60ml/4 tbsp chilled water

1 To make the pastry, sift the flour, salt and sugar into a mixing bowl. Rub or cut in the butter until the mixture resembles fine breadcrumbs. Add enough chilled water to make the dough hold together. Gather the dough into a ball and flatten into a round. Wrap in clear film (plastic wrap) and chill for 30 minutes.

2 Pour the cider into a pan and boil until 175ml/6fl oz/¾ cup remains, or approximately one-third, then set aside to cool.

3 Roll out the pastry to a thickness of 3mm/⅛in. Use to line a 23cm/9in flan tin (pan). Trim the edge, leaving a 1cm/½in overhang. Fold the overhang under to form a rim. Using a fork, press the rim down and scallop the edge. Chill for at least 20 minutes. Preheat the oven to 180°C/350°F/Gas 4.

4 Place the butter, maple syrup, water and reduced cider in a pan and simmer gently for 5–6 minutes. Leave to cool slightly, then whisk in the egg yolks.

5 Place the egg whites in a large bowl, and whisk vigorously until they form stiff peaks. Using a metal spoon, gently fold in the cider mixture.

6 Pour the filling into the pastry case (pie shell). Lightly dust with the grated nutmeg. Bake for 30–35 minutes, until the filling is set and golden. Dust with icing sugar and serve immediately.

Cider Pie Energy 452Kcal/1897kJ; Protein 5.1g; Carbohydrate 60.1g, of which sugars 37.8g; Fat 20g, of which saturates 11.9g; Cholesterol 110mg; Calcium 70mg; Fibre 0.9g; Sodium 275mg.
Sticky Nut Pie Energy 650kcal/2701kJ; Protein 10.6g; Carbohydrate 39g, of which sugars 16.9g; Fat 50.4g, of which saturates 13.7g; Cholesterol 124mg; Calcium 131mg; Fibre 4.1g; Sodium 151mg.

Thanksgiving Pumpkin Pie

A version of this dish was baked by the earliest American settlers, and now Thanksgiving would not be complete without it. Using canned pumpkin makes it a very easy pie to make.

Serves 8

450g/1lb cooked or canned pumpkin
250ml/8fl oz/1 cup whipping cream
2 eggs
115g/4oz/½ cup soft dark brown sugar
60ml/4 tbsp golden (light corn) syrup
7.5ml/1½ tsp ground cinnamon
5ml/1 tsp ground ginger
1.5ml/¼ tsp ground cloves
2.5ml/½ tsp salt

For the pastry

175g/6oz/1½ cups plain (all-purpose) flour
2.5ml/½ tsp salt
75g/3oz/6 tbsp cold butter, cut into pieces
40g/1½oz/3 tbsp cold white vegetable fat (shortening), cut into pieces
45–60ml/3–4 tbsp iced water
1 egg, beaten

1 For the pastry, sift the flour and salt into a bowl. Cut in the butter and fat until it resembles coarse crumbs. Bind with iced water. Wrap in clear film (plastic wrap) and chill for 20 minutes.

2 Roll out the dough on a lightly floured surface and use it to line a 23cm/9in fluted flan tin (pan). Trim off the overhang. Roll out the trimmings and cut out leaf shapes.

3 Chill the dough in the refrigerator for about 20 minutes. Preheat the oven to 200°C/400°F/Gas 6.

4 Line the pastry case (pie shell) with baking parchment. Fill with baking beans and bake for 12 minutes.

5 Remove the paper and beans and bake until golden, 6–8 minutes more. Reduce the heat to 190°C/375°F/Gas 5.

6 Beat together the pumpkin, cream, eggs, sugar, syrup, spices and salt. Pour into the case and bake for about 25 minutes.

7 Brush the pastry leaves with egg and place around the top of the pie. Bake for 10–15 minutes more.

Vegan Pumpkin Pie

This vegan version of the traditional Thanksgiving celebration dessert means that everyone can enjoy the festive treat. This version has a wholemeal crust for additional nutty crunch and healthy fibre.

Serves 6–8

350g/12oz silken tofu
450g/1lb stewed mashed pumpkin
7.5ml/1½ tsp ground cinnamon
2.5ml/½ tsp ground ginger
2.5ml/½ tsp ground nutmeg
5ml/1 tsp sea salt
5ml/1 tsp vanilla extract
15ml/1 tbsp carob molasses or agave syrup
260g/9½oz/generous 1 cup soft light brown sugar
75ml/2½fl oz/⅓ cup rapeseed (canola) oil

For the pastry

250g/9oz/2¼ cups wholemeal (whole-wheat) flour
7.5ml/1½ tsp ground cinnamon
75ml/2½fl oz/⅓ cup pumpkin seed oil or rapeseed (canola) oil
15ml/1 tbsp pumpkin seed or peanut butter
75ml/2½fl oz/⅓ cup sweetened soya milk

1 Make the pastry. Rub together the flour, cinnamon, oil and butter until the mixture resembles breadcrumbs. Add enough soya milk to form a soft dough.

2 Roll out dough and line an oiled 20cm/8in pie dish. Preheat the oven to 180°C/350°F/Gas 4.

3 Mix all the ingredients for the filling in a food processor or blender until smooth and creamy.

4 Pour the filling into the unbaked pastry case (pie shell), and bake in the preheated oven for about 50 minutes to 1 hour until golden brown.

5 Carefully transfer the pie on to a plate. Leave to cool, then chill in the refrigerator before serving.

Cook's Tip
You can use canned pumpkin if you can't find fresh.

Thanksgiving Pie Energy 434kcal/1809kJ; Protein 6.2g; Carbohydrate 35.3g, of which sugars 19.4g; Fat 30.8g, of which saturates 13.8g; Cholesterol 94mg; Calcium 108mg; Fibre 1.2g; Sodium 60mg.
Pumpkin Pie Energy 434kcal/1809kJ; Protein 6.2g; Carbohydrate 35.3g, of which sugars 19.4g; Fat 30.8g, of which saturates 13.8g; Cholesterol 94mg; Calcium 108mg; Fibre 1.2g; Sodium 60mg.

Bakewell Tart

This traditional sweet almond tart is always the first to go at traditional food fairs and events. It is often attributed to Mrs Greaves, landlady of a pub in the English town of Bakewell in 1820. References have, however, been found to similar tarts dating back to medieval times.

Serves 4

225g/8oz puff pastry
30ml/2 tbsp raspberry jam
2 eggs, plus 2 egg yolks
115g/4oz/generous ½ cup caster (superfine) sugar
115g/4oz/½ cup butter, melted
50g/2oz/⅔ cup ground almonds
a few drops of almond extract
icing (confectioners') sugar, for dusting

1 Preheat the oven to 200°C/400°F/Gas 6. Roll out the pastry on a lightly floured surface and use to line an 18cm/7in pie plate. Trim the edge.

2 Re-roll the pastry trimmings and cut out wide strips of pastry. Use these to decorate the edge of the pastry case (pie shell) by gently twisting them around the rim, joining the strips together as necessary. Prick the pastry case all over with a fork, then spread the jam over the base.

3 Whisk the eggs, egg yolks and sugar together in a bowl until the mixture is thick and pale.

4 Gently stir the melted butter, ground almonds and almond extract into the whisked egg mixture.

5 Pour the mixture into the pastry case and bake for about 30 minutes, or until the filling is just set and is lightly browned. Dust with icing sugar before serving hot, warm or cold.

Cook's Tip

Since this pastry case (pie shell) is not baked blind before being filled, put a baking sheet in the oven while it preheats, then place the tart on the hot sheet. This will ensure that the base of the pastry case cooks right through.

Vegan Bakewell Tart

The jam in a true Bakewell tart is usually raspberry, but you can use strawberry if you wish. This vegan version of a classic tart will be enjoyed by everyone.

Serves 8

60ml/4 tbsp raspberry or strawberry jam
225g/8oz/2 cups wholemeal (whole-wheat) flour
50g/2oz/½ cup ground almonds
175g/6oz/¾ cup soft light brown sugar
5ml/1 tsp finely grated lemon rind
10ml/2 tsp baking powder
150ml/¼ pint/⅔ cup vegetable oil
200ml/7fl oz/scant 1 cup soya milk
5ml/1 tsp vanilla extract
5ml/1 tsp almond extract
25g/1oz flaked (sliced) almonds

For the pastry

250g/9oz/2¼ cups wholemeal (whole-wheat) flour
75ml/2½fl oz/⅓ cup rapeseed (canola) oil
15ml/1 tbsp sesame tahini
75ml/2½fl oz/⅓ cup sweetened soya milk

1 Preheat the oven to 190°C/375°F/Gas 5. Make the pastry. In a bowl, rub together the flour, oil and tahini until the mixture resembles breadcrumbs. Gradually add the soya milk to the bowl and mix to form a soft dough.

2 Roll out the dough on a lightly floured surface into a circle that will line a 20cm/8in oiled pie dish. Prick the dough all over with a fork and bake it in the oven for about 10–15 minutes. Set aside to cool.

3 Spread a layer of the raspberry jam over the base of the pastry case (pie shell).

4 In a bowl, mix together the flour, ground almonds, sugar, lemon rind and baking powder. Add the oil, soya milk and extracts and mix again.

5 Pour the mixture over the jammy pastry base. Sprinkle with flaked almonds on top. Bake for 35 minutes.

6 Serve the tart warm, cut into slices, with hot oat milk custard or soya ice cream.

Bakewell Tart Energy 700Kcal/2919kJ; Protein 10.8g; Carbohydrate 57.1g, of which sugars 36.7g; Fat 49.9g, of which saturates 17.1g; Cholesterol 257mg; Calcium 110mg; Fibre 0.9g; Sodium 394mg.
Vegan Bakewell Energy 538kcal/2257kJ; Protein 11g; Carbohydrate 66.9g, of which sugars 30g; Fat 26.9g, of which saturates 2.8g; Cholesterol 0mg; Calcium 76mg; Fibre 6.2g; Sodium 17mg.

Treacle Tart

An old-fashioned favourite, with its sticky filling and twisted lattice topping, this tart is perfect with custard.

Serves 4–6

260g/9½oz/generous ¾ cup golden (light corn) syrup
75g/3oz/1½ cups fresh white breadcrumbs
grated rind of 1 lemon
30ml/2 tbsp lemon juice

For the pastry

150g/5oz/1¼ cups plain (all-purpose) flour
2.5ml/½ tsp salt
130g/4½oz/9 tbsp chilled butter, diced
45–60ml/3–4 tbsp chilled water

1 Make the pastry. Combine the flour and salt in a bowl. Rub or cut in the butter until the mixture resembles breadcrumbs.

2 With a fork, stir in just enough water to bind the dough. Gather into a smooth ball, knead lightly until smooth then wrap in clear film (plastic wrap) and chill for at least 20 minutes.

3 On a lightly floured surface, roll out the pastry to a thickness of 3mm/⅛in. Transfer to a 20cm/8in fluted flan tin (pan) and trim off the overhang. Chill the pastry case (pie shell) for 20 minutes. Reserve the pastry trimmings.

4 Put a baking sheet in the oven and preheat to 200°C/400°F/Gas 6. To make the filling, warm the syrup in a pan until it melts.

5 Remove the syrup from the heat and stir in the breadcrumbs and lemon rind. Leave to stand for 10 minutes, then add more breadcrumbs if the mixture is too thin and moist. Stir in the lemon juice, then spread the mixture evenly in the pastry case.

6 Roll out the pastry trimmings and cut into 10–12 thin strips. Twist the strips into spirals, then lay half of them on the filling. Arrange the remaining strips at right angles to form a lattice. Press the ends on to the rim.

7 Place the tart on the hot baking sheet and bake for 10 minutes. Lower the oven temperature to 190°C/375°F/Gas 5. Bake for 15 minutes more, until golden. Serve warm.

Marsala Custard Tart

The unmistakable flavour of Marsala transforms this tart.

Serves 6–8

200g/7oz sweet shortcrust pastry
3 eggs
30ml/2 tbsp soft light brown sugar
250ml/8fl oz/1 cup creamy milk
60ml/4 tbsp Marsala
freshly grated nutmeg

1 Roll out the pastry on a lightly floured surface to a 25cm/10in round and use it to line a 20cm/8in flan tin (pan) Line with baking parchment and baking beans and bake for 12 minutes.

2 Whisk the eggs and sugar lightly in a bowl. Heat the milk to just below boiling point, stir in the Marsala and whisk into the eggs and sugar. Remove the paper and baking beans from the flan case, pour in the custard mixture and grate nutmeg over the surface. Bake for 25–35 minutes until the custard has set.

Ricotta Tart

This tart has a ricotta cheese filling flavoured with tangy orange.

Serves 4–6

200g/7oz shortcrust pastry
450g/1lb/2 cups ricotta cheese
120ml/4fl oz/½ cup double (heavy) cream
2 eggs and 1 egg yolk
75g/3oz/⅓ cup caster (superfine) sugar
finely grated rind of 1 orange
finely grated rind of 1 lemon

1 Preheat the oven to 200°C/400°F/Gas 6. Roll out the pastry and line a 20cm/8in flan tin (pan). Line with baking parchment, fill with baking beans and bake for 10 minutes. Set the pastry case (pie shell) aside.

2 Beat together the ricotta, cream, eggs, egg yolk, sugar and orange and lemon rinds in a large bowl. Spoon the cheese and cream filling into the pastry case. Re-roll the pastry trimmings and cut into strips. Arrange on top in a lattice pattern. Bake for 30–35 minutes until golden and set. Transfer to a wire rack and leave to cool slightly before removing from the tin. Serve warm.

Treacle Tart Energy 420Kcal/1764kJ; Protein 4.1g; Carbohydrate 63.5g, of which sugars 35.1g; Fat 18.4g, of which saturates 11.3g; Cholesterol 46mg; Calcium 62mg; Fibre 1.1g; Sodium 344mg.
Marsala Tart Energy 201kcal/838kJ; Protein 5.3g; Carbohydrate 19.4g, of which sugars 7.9g; Fat 10.8g, of which saturates 3.7g; Cholesterol 95mg; Calcium 73mg; Fibre 0.6g; Sodium 147mg.
Ricotta Tart Energy 453kcal/1894kJ; Protein 15.7g; Carbohydrate 38.1g, of which sugars 16.7g; Fat 27.6g, of which saturates 16.9g; Cholesterol 170mg; Calcium 287mg; Fibre 0.9g; Sodium 1024mg.

Vanilla Cream Cheese Tart

This light, creamy tart from Finland is perfect as an accompaniment to coffee but, when topped with any of the many berries that appear in late spring, it can also be served as a fine dessert.

Serves 6–8

150g/5oz/10 tbsp unsalted (sweet) butter, softened, plus extra for greasing
150g/5oz/¾ cup caster (superfine) sugar
2 eggs, beaten
5ml/1 tsp vanilla extract
grated rind of 1 lemon and 15ml/1 tbsp lemon juice
250g/9oz/generous ¾ cup cream cheese
mixed berries, to decorate (optional)

For the pastry

500g/1¼lb/4½ cups plain (all-purpose) flour
5ml/1 tsp baking powder
30ml/2 tbsp caster (superfine) sugar
150g/5oz/10 tbsp unsalted butter
1 egg, beaten

1 Preheat the oven to 180°C/350°F/Gas 4. Grease a deep, loose-bottomed 23cm/9in cake tin (pan) with butter.

2 To make the pastry, sift the flour and baking powder into a large bowl and add the sugar. Cut the butter into small pieces, add to the flour and rub in until the mixture resembles fine breadcrumbs. Alternatively, put the flour, baking powder and sugar in a food processor, add the butter and, using a pulsating action, blend to form fine breadcrumbs.

3 Add the beaten egg to the flour mixture and mix lightly together to form a dough. Pat the dough into the bottom and up the sides of the tin.

4 Cream the butter and sugar in a large mixing bowl, then add the eggs, one at a time, and beat until smooth. Add the vanilla extract, lemon juice and rind, and the cream cheese, and mix gently to combine.

5 Pour the mixture into the pastry-lined cake tin and bake in the oven for about 40 minutes, until set. Leave to cool in the tin before serving and decorating with mixed berries, if liked.

Cheese and Honey Tart

This is Mediterranean cheesecake from the Aegean, made with fragrant Greek honey and the fresh, unsalted local cheese, called myzithra. It is similar to Italian ricotta, which makes a good substitute if necessary.

Serves 6–8

225g/8oz/2 cups plain (all-purpose) flour sifted with a pinch of salt
30ml/2 tbsp caster (superfine) sugar
115g/4oz/½ cup unsalted (sweet) butter, cubed
45–60ml/3–4 tbsp cold water

For the filling

4 eggs
50g/2oz/¼ cup caster (superfine) sugar
15ml/1 tbsp plain (all-purpose) flour
500g/1¼lb/2½ cups fresh myzithra or ricotta cheese
60ml/4 tbsp Greek thyme-scented honey
2.5ml/½ tsp ground cinnamon

1 Mix the flour and sugar in a bowl, then rub in the butter until the mixture resembles breadcrumbs. Add the water, a little at a time, until the mixture clings together and forms a dough. It should not be too wet. Draw it into a ball, wrap it in clear film (plastic wrap) and chill for 30 minutes.

2 Preheat the oven to 180°C/350°F/Gas 4. Put a baking sheet in the oven to heat. Roll out the pastry thinly on a lightly floured surface and use to line a 25cm/10in round springform tin (pan). Carefully trim off any excess pastry.

3 To make the filling, beat the eggs in a bowl, add the sugar and flour and beat until fluffy. Add the cheese, honey and half the cinnamon and beat until well mixed. Pour into the pastry case (pie shell) and level the surface. Place the tart on the hot baking sheet and cook for 50–60 minutes, until light golden. Sprinkle with the remaining cinnamon while still hot.

Cook's Tip

Save time by using a 500g/1¼lb packet of ready-made shortcrust pastry instead of making your own.

Vanilla Energy 5891kcal/24582kJ; Protein 70g; Carbohydrate 578.4g, of which sugars 197.4g; Fat 382.9g,of which saturates 234.6g; Cholesterol 1258mg; Calcium 1151mg; Fibre 15.5g; Sodium 2734mg.
Cheese Tart Energy 399kcal/1670kJ; Protein 12.4g; Carbohydrate 39.4g, of which sugars 17.9g; Fat 22.4g, of which saturates 12.8g; Cholesterol 177mg; Calcium 212mg; Fibre 1.2g; Sodium 194mg.

Raisin Cheesecake

Cheesecakes were originally baked rather than set with gelatine. This East European dessert has a lovely sweet almond pastry base.

Serves 8

115g/4oz/1 cup plain (all-purpose) flour
50g/2oz/4 tbsp butter
15ml/1 tbsp caster (superfine) sugar
25g/1oz/¼ cup almonds, very finely chopped
30ml/2 tbsp cold water
15ml/1 tbsp icing (confectioners') sugar, for dusting

For the filling

115g/4oz/8 tbsp butter
150g/5oz/¾ cup caster (superfine) sugar
5ml/1 tsp vanilla extract
3 eggs, beaten
25g/1oz/¼ cup plain (all-purpose) flour, sifted
400g/14oz/1¾ cups curd (farmer's) cheese
grated rind and juice of 2 lemons
65g/2½oz/½ cup raisins

1 Sift the flour into a bowl. Rub in the butter, until the mixture resembles fine breadcrumbs. Stir in the sugar and almonds. Add the water and mix to a dough. Lightly knead on a floured surface for a few seconds. Wrap in clear film (plastic wrap) and chill for 30 minutes.

2 Preheat the oven to 200°C/400°F/Gas 6. Roll out the pastry on a lightly floured surface to a 25cm/10in circle and use it to line the base and sides of a 20cm/8in tart tin (pan). Trim the edges of the pastry with a sharp knife.

3 Prick with a fork, cover with oiled foil and bake for 6 minutes. Remove the foil and bake for 6 more minutes. Allow to cool and reduce the temperature to 150°C/300°F/Gas 2.

4 For the filling, cream the butter, sugar and vanilla extract together. Beat in one egg, then stir in the flour. Beat the cheese until soft, then gradually mix in the remaining eggs. Blend this into the butter mixture. Stir in the lemon rind, juice and raisins.

5 Pour the filling over the pastry base. Bake in the oven for 1½ hours, until firm. Turn off the oven, leave the door ajar and allow to cool before removing. Dust with icing sugar.

Buckwheat Cheesecake

This light cheesecake, made with a butter-rich pastry crust, is a classic Eastern European version.

Serves 8

For the pastry

100g/3¾oz/scant 1 cup buckwheat flour
100g/3¾oz/scant 1 cup plain (all-purpose) flour
115g/4oz/½ cup butter, diced
1 egg yolk
15–30ml/1–2 tbsp chilled water
icing (confectioner's) sugar for dusting, and mixed red fruit, to serve, if you wish

For the filling

500g/1¼lb curd (farmer's) cheese
115g/4oz/⅔ cup caster (superfine) sugar
3 eggs, lightly beaten
150ml/¼ pint/⅔ cup sour cream
30ml/2 tbsp plain (all-purpose) flour

1 Place a baking sheet in the oven and preheat to 190°C/375°F/Gas 5. Sift the flours into a bowl and rub in the butter until the mixture takes on the texture of fine breadcrumbs.

2 Stir the egg yolk into the flour and add just enough of the water to bind the mixture together to make a dough. Wrap the pastry in clear film (plastic wrap). Chill for 20 minutes.

3 Roll out the pastry on a floured surface and line a 20cm/8in fluted loose-based flan tin (pan). Add baking parchment, add dried beans or rice and blind bake for 10 minutes.

4 For the filling, beat the curd cheese and sugar together, then beat in the eggs, a little at a time. Stir in two-thirds of the sour cream. Sift the flour over the surface and gently fold it in.

5 Spoon the cheese mixture on to the pastry and spread evenly. Spread the remaining sour cream evenly over the top.

6 Bake the cheesecake for about 40 minutes, until the filling is lightly set (it will firm more as it cools) and the top is pale golden-brown.

7 Leave to cool in the pan and serve while still slightly warm, or cold topped with fruit and with extra sour cream, if you like.

Raisin Energy 480kcal/2005kJ; Protein 16.2g; Carbohydrate 48.2g, of which sugars 23.7g; Fat 27g, of which saturates 15.8g; Cholesterol 173mg; Calcium 153mg; Fibre 1.2g; Sodium 451mg.
Buckwheat Energy 403kcal/1685kJ; Protein 14.9g; Carbohydrate 37.1g, of which sugars 18.1g; Fat 23.7g, of which saturates 14.2g; Cholesterol 156mg; Calcium 135mg; Fibre 1.9g; Sodium 418mg.

Lemon Cheesecake

This simple German cheesecake is baked in a rich shortcrust pastry case flavoured with lemon.

Serves 8–10

675g/1½lb/3 cups cream cheese
4 eggs, separated
150g/5oz/⅔ cup caster (superfine) sugar
45ml/3 tbsp cornflour (cornstarch)
150ml/¼ pint/⅔ cup sour cream
grated rind and juice of ½ lemon
5ml/1 tsp vanilla extract
poached red berries, to serve

For the pastry
225g/8oz/2 cups plain (all-purpose) flour
115g/4oz/½ cup butter, diced
15ml/1 tbsp caster (superfine) sugar
finely grated rind of ½ lemon
1 egg, beaten

1 To make the pastry, sift the flour into a large mixing bowl. Rub or cut in the butter until the mixture resembles fine breadcrumbs. Stir in the sugar and lemon rind, then add the beaten egg and mix to a dough. Wrap in clear film (plastic wrap) and chill for 30 minutes.

2 Roll out the pastry and use to line a 25cm/10in loose-based fluted flan tin (pan). Chill for 1 hour. Preheat the oven to 200°C/400°F/Gas 6. Prick the base of the chilled pastry case (pie shell) all over with a fork, line it with baking parchment bake for about 5 minutes. Remove the paper and bake for a further 5 minutes. Remove from the oven and lower the oven temperature to 180°C/350°F/Gas 4.

3 Put the cream cheese in a bowl with the egg yolks and caster sugar and mix together. Blend the cornflour with a little of the sour cream, then mix in to the cheese mixture along with the remaining sour cream, lemon rind and juice and vanilla extract.

4 Whisk the egg whites until stiff, then fold into the cheese mixture, one-third at a time. Pour the filling into the pastry case and bake for 1–1¼ hours, or until golden and firm. Let the cheesecake cool, then chill for 2 hours.

5 Serve the well-chilled cheesecake in slices, with poached red berries, or fresh fruit if you prefer.

Coffee Custard Tart

For sheer decadence, this creamy coffee-flavoured tart is hard to beat. It is perfect for serving with a cup of espresso coffee.

Serves 6–8

1 vanilla pod (bean)
30ml/2 tbsp very strong, freshly made coffee
300ml/½ pint/1¼ cups single (light) cream
150ml/¼ pint/⅔ cup milk
2 eggs, plus 2 egg yolks
50g/2oz/¼ cup caster (superfine) sugar
whipped cream, to serve

For the pastry
175g/6oz/1½ cups plain (all-purpose) flour
30ml/2 tbsp icing (confectioners') sugar
115g/4oz/½ cup butter, diced
75g/3oz/¾ cup walnuts, chopped
1 egg yolk
5ml/1 tsp vanilla extract
10ml/2 tsp chilled water

1 Make the pastry. Sift the flour and sugar into a mixing bowl. Rub or cut in the butter until the mixture resembles fine breadcrumbs. Stir in the walnuts then the egg yolk, vanilla and water to make a smooth dough. Wrap in clear film (plastic wrap); chill for 20 minutes. Put a heavy baking sheet in the oven and preheat the oven to 200°C/400°F/Gas 6.

2 Roll out the pastry and use to line a 20cm/8in loose-based flan tin (pan). Trim the edges. Chill for 20 minutes.

3 Prick the pastry base all over with a fork. Line with baking parchment and fill with baking beans. Place on the baking sheet and bake for 10 minutes. Remove the paper and beans, bake for 10 minutes more, then remove from the oven and reduce the temperature to 150°C/300°F/Gas 2.

4 Meanwhile, split the vanilla pod and scrape out the seeds. Put both in a pan with the coffee, cream and milk. Heat until almost boiling, remove from the heat, cover and infuse for 10 minutes. Whisk the eggs, egg yolks and caster sugar together in a bowl.

5 Bring the coffee mixture back to the boil, then pour on to the egg mixture, stirring. Strain into the tin. Bake for 40–45 minutes until lightly set, then cool. Top with whirls of cream to serve.

Lemon Cheesecake Energy 296kcal/1238kJ; Protein 7.6g; Carbohydrate 27.1g, of which sugars 19g; Fat 18g, of which saturates 9g; Cholesterol 83mg; Calcium 56mg; Fibre 1.1g; Sodium 139mg.
Coffee Tart Energy 408kcal/1698kJ; Protein 8.1g; Carbohydrate 29.6g, of which sugars 12.8g; Fat 29.5g, of which saturates 13.8g; Cholesterol 176mg; Calcium 119mg; Fibre 1g; Sodium 129mg.

Key Lime Pie

This American classic is ideal for a festive treat.

Serves 10

225g/8oz/2 cups plain (all-purpose) flour
115g/4oz/½ cup chilled butter, diced
30ml/2 tbsp caster (superfine) sugar
2 egg yolks
pinch of salt
30ml/2 tbsp cold water
thinly pared lime rind and mint leaves, to decorate

For the filling

4 eggs, separated
400g/14oz can sweetened condensed milk
grated rind and juice of 3 limes
a few drops of green food colouring (optional)
30ml/2 tbsp caster (superfine) sugar

For the topping

300ml/½ pint/1¼ cups double (heavy) cream
2–3 limes, thinly sliced

1 Sift the flour and rub in the butter until the mixture resembles breadcrumbs. Add the sugar, egg yolks, salt and water. Mix to a soft dough. Roll out the pastry and use to line a deep 21cm/8½in fluted flan tin (pan), allowing the excess pastry to hang over the edge. Prick the pastry base and chill for 30 minutes.

2 Preheat the oven to 200°C/400°F/Gas 6. Trim off the excess pastry from the edge of the pastry case (pie shell) and line the pastry case with baking parchment and baking beans. Bake the pastry case blind for 10 minutes. Remove the paper and beans and return the case to the oven for 10 minutes.

3 Meanwhile, make the filling. Beat the egg yolks in a bowl until light and creamy, then beat in the condensed milk, with the lime rind and juice. Add the food colouring, if using, and beat until the mixture is thick. In a grease-free bowl, whisk the egg whites to stiff peaks. Whisk in the caster sugar, then fold into the filling.

4 Lower the oven to 160°C/325°F/Gas 3. Pour the filling into the pastry case. Bake for 20–25 minutes or until it has set and is browned. Cool, then chill. Before serving, whip the cream and spoon around the edge. Twist the lime slices and arrange between the cream. Decorate with lime rind and mint leaves.

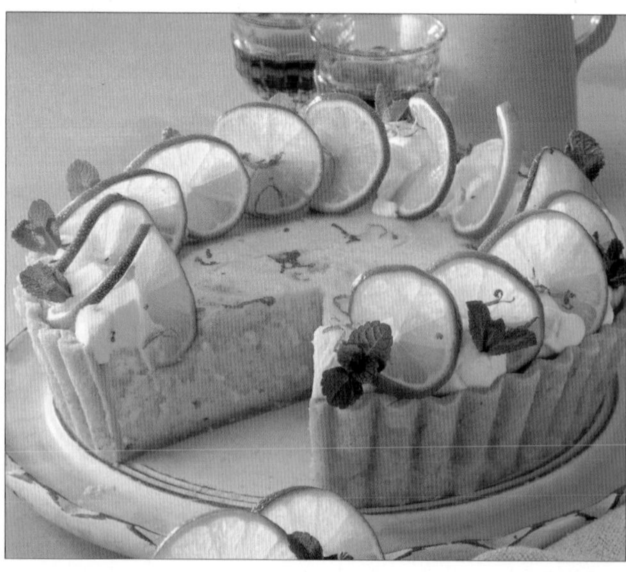

Shoofly Pie

A wonderful sweet pie from the American Deep South.

Serves 8

115g/4oz/1 cup plain (all-purpose) flour
115g/4oz/scant ½ cup soft dark brown sugar
1.5ml/¼ tsp each salt, ground ginger, cinnamon, mace, and nutmeg
75g/3oz/6 tbsp cold butter, diced
2 eggs
185g/6½oz/½ cup black treacle (molasses)
120ml/4fl oz/½ cup boiling water
1.5ml/½ tsp bicarbonate of soda (baking soda)

For the pastry

115g/4oz/½ cup cream cheese
115g/4oz/½ cup butter, diced
115g/4oz/1 cup plain (all-purpose) flour

1 Preheat the oven to 190°C/375°F/Gas 5. Meanwhile make the pastry. Put the cream cheese and butter in a mixing bowl. Sift over the flour. Rub in with your fingertips or cut in with a pastry blender to bind the dough together. Wrap in clear film (plastic wrap) and chill for at least 30 minutes.

2 Make the filling. Mix the flour, brown sugar, salt, spices and butter in a bowl. Rub in with your fingertips until the mixture resembles coarse breadcrumbs, then set aside.

3 Roll out the dough thinly on a lightly floured surface to a thickness of about 3mm/⅛in and use to line a 23cm/9in pie plate. Trim and flute the pastry edges. Spoon one-third of the filling mixture into the pastry case (pie shell).

4 Whisk the eggs with the treacle in a large bowl. Put a baking sheet in the oven to preheat.

5 Pour the boiling water into a small bowl and stir in the bicarbonate of soda; it will foam. Pour it immediately into the egg mixture and whisk to blend fully. Pour the filling into the pastry case and sprinkle any remaining mixture over the top in an even layer.

6 Place the pie on the hot baking sheet and bake for about 35 minutes, or until browned. Leave to cool and serve warm.

Key Lime Pie Energy 510kcal/2126kJ; Protein 9.2g; Carbohydrate 46.6g, of which sugars 29.4g; Fat 33.2g, of which saturates 19.5g; Cholesterol 196mg; Calcium 182mg; Fibre 0.7g; Sodium 163mg.
Shoofly Pie Energy 472Kcal/1975kJ; Protein 5.2g; Carbohydrate 53g, of which sugars 31g; Fat 28.1g, of which saturates 17.1g; Cholesterol 112mg; Calcium 201mg; Fibre 0.9g; Sodium 248mg.

Chess Pie

A classic recipe from the Southern States of America, this pie is thought of one of their signature dishes. The name may have come from 'pie chest', where freshly baked pies were kept in American kitchens.

Serves 8
2 eggs
45ml/3 tbsp whipping cream
115g/4oz/½ cup soft dark brown sugar
30ml/2 tbsp sugar
30ml/2 tbsp plain (all-purpose) flour
15ml/1 tbsp whisky
40g/1½oz/3 tbsp butter, melted
50g/2oz/½ cup chopped walnuts
75g/3oz/½ cup pitted dates, chopped
whipped cream, for serving

For the pastry
75g/3oz/6 tbsp cold butter
40g/1½oz/3 tbsp cold vegetable fat
175g/6oz/1½ cups plain (all-purpose) flour
2.5ml/½ tsp salt
45–60ml/3–4 tbsp iced water

1 For the pastry, cut the butter and fat into small pieces. Sift the flour and salt into a bowl. With a pastry blender, cut in the butter and fat until the mixture resembles coarse crumbs. Stir in just enough water to bind. Gather into a ball, wrap in baking parchment and chill for at least 20 minutes.

2 Place a baking sheet in the oven and preheat it to 190°C/375°F/Gas 5. Roll out the dough thinly and line a 23cm/9in pie tin (pan). Trim the edge. Roll out the trimmings, cut thin strips and braid them. Brush the edge of the pastry case (pie shell) with water and fit the pastry braids around the rim.

3 In a mixing bowl, whisk together the eggs and cream. Add both sugars and beat until well combined. Sift over 15ml/1 tbsp of the flour and stir in. Add the whisky, the melted butter and the walnuts. Stir to combine.

4 Mix the dates with the remaining flour and stir into the walnut mixture. Pour the mixture into the pastry case and bake in the oven until the pastry is golden and the filling has puffed up, about 35 minutes. Serve at room temperature, with whipped cream, if you like.

Linzertorte

Use a good quality high fruit content jam or conserve to fill the cinnamon and almond pastry case in this traditional Austrian speciality, and dust it with icing sugar before serving it.

Serves 8–10
200g/7oz/scant 1 cup butter
200g/7oz/scant 1 cup caster (superfine) sugar
3 eggs, plus 2 egg yolks
2.5ml/½ tsp ground cinnamon
grated rind of ½ lemon
115g/4oz/2 cups fine sweet biscuit (cookie) crumbs
150g/5oz/1¼ cups ground almonds
225g/8oz/2 cups plain (all-purpose) flour, sifted
225g/8oz/¾ cup raspberry jam
icing (confectioners') sugar, for dusting

1 Preheat the oven to 190°C/375°F/Gas 5. Cream the butter and sugar together until light. Slowly add the eggs and 1 of the egg yolks, beating all the time, then add the cinnamon and rind.

2 Stir the crumbs and ground almonds into the mixture. Mix well, then add the sifted flour. Knead the mixture to form a dough, then wrap in clear film (plastic wrap) and chill in the refrigerator for about 30 minutes.

3 Roll out two-thirds of the pastry on a lightly floured surface and use to line a deep 25cm/10in loose-based flan tin (pan). Press the pastry into the sides and trim the edge.

4 Spread the raspberry jam generously and evenly over the base of the pastry case. Roll out the remaining pastry into a long rectangle. Cut this into even strips with a sharp knife and arrange in a lattice pattern over the jam filling.

5 Lightly beat the remaining egg yolk in a small bowl, then brush it evenly over the pastry rim and lattice. Bake the flan for 45 minutes, or until golden brown.

6 Leave to cool slightly in the tin before turning out on to a wire rack. Just before serving, still warm for the best flavour, sift a little icing sugar over the top of the Linzertorte. Serve with custard, if you like.

Chess Pie Energy 423kcal/1767kJ; Protein 5.8g; Carbohydrate 44.7g, of which sugars 25.1g; Fat 25.4g, of which saturates 11.9g; Cholesterol 99mg; Calcium 65mg; Fibre 1.8g; Sodium 113mg.
Linzertorte Energy 537kcal/2247kJ; Protein 8.5g; Carbohydrate 63g, of which sugars 39.1g; Fat 29.7g, of which saturates 12.8g; Cholesterol 125mg; Calcium 106mg; Fibre 2.1g; Sodium 223mg.

Mincemeat Tart

Fruity home-made mincemeat is the perfect partner here to the crumbly, nutty pastry. This very special pie is a rich treat during the festive season and other celebrations.

Serves 8

225g/8oz/2 cups plain (all-purpose) flour
10ml/2 tsp ground cinnamon
50g/2oz/½ cup finely ground walnuts
115g/4oz/½ cup butter
50g/2oz/¼ cup caster (superfine) sugar, plus extra for dusting
1 egg
2 drops vanilla extract
15ml/1 tbsp cold water

For the mincemeat
2 eating apples, peeled, cored and grated
225g/8oz/generous 1½ cups raisins
115g/4oz/½ cup ready-to-eat dried apricots, chopped
115g/4oz/⅔ cup ready-to-eat dried figs or prunes, chopped
225g/8oz/2 cups green grapes, halved and seeded
50g/2oz/½ cup chopped almonds
finely grated rind of 1 lemon
30ml/2 tbsp lemon juice
30ml/2 tbsp brandy or port
1.5ml/¼ tsp mixed (apple pie) spice
115g/4oz/½ cup soft light brown sugar
25g/1oz/2 tbsp butter, melted

1 Process the flour, cinnamon, nuts and butter in a food processor or blender to make fine crumbs. Turn into a bowl and stir in the sugar. Beat the egg with the vanilla extract and water, and stir into the dry ingredients. Form a soft dough, knead until smooth, then wrap and chill for 30 minutes.

2 Mix the mincemeat ingredients together. Use two-thirds of the pastry to line a 23cm/9in, loose-based flan tin (pan). Trim and fill with the mincemeat.

3 Roll out the remaining pastry and cut into 1cm/½in strips. Arrange the strips in a lattice over the top of the pastry, wet the joins and press them together. Chill for 30 minutes.

4 Preheat a baking sheet in the oven at 190°C/375°F/Gas 5. Brush the pastry with water and dust with caster sugar. Bake the tart on the baking sheet for 30–40 minutes. Cool in the tin on a wire rack for 15 minutes, then remove the tin.

Fresh Lemon Tart

Serve this prettily decorated tart at room temperature to enjoy the zesty lemon flavour to the full.

Serves 6–8

350g/12oz ready-made rich sweet shortcrust pastry

For the filling
3 eggs
115g/4oz/½ cup caster (superfine) sugar
115g/4oz/1 cup ground almonds
105ml/7 tbsp double (heavy) cream
grated rind and juice of 2 lemons

For the topping
2 thin-skinned unwaxed lemons, thinly sliced
200g/7oz/1 cup caster (superfine) sugar
105ml/7 tbsp water

1 Roll out the pastry and line a deep 23cm/9in fluted flan tin (pan). Prick the base and chill for 30 minutes.

2 Preheat the oven to 200°C/400°F/Gas 6. Line the pastry with baking parchment and baking beans and bake blind for 10 minutes. Remove the paper and beans and return the pastry case (pie shell) to the oven for 5 minutes more.

3 Meanwhile, make the filling. Beat the eggs, caster sugar, almonds and cream in a bowl until smooth. Beat in the lemon rind and juice. Pour the filling into the pastry case. Lower the oven temperature to 190°C/375°F/Gas 5 and bake for 20 minutes or until the filling has set and the pastry is golden.

4 Make the topping. Place the lemon slices in a pan and pour over water to cover. Simmer for 15–20 minutes or until the skins are tender, then drain. Place the sugar in a pan and stir in the measured water. Heat gently until the sugar has dissolved, stirring constantly, then boil for 2 minutes. Add the lemon slices and cook for 10–15 minutes until the skins become candied.

5 Lift out the candied lemon slices and arrange them over the top of the tart. Return the syrup to the heat and boil until reduced to a thick glaze. Brush this over the tart and allow to cool completely before serving.

Mincemeat Tart Energy 434kcal/1822kJ; Protein 4.8g; Carbohydrate 63.6g, of which sugars 42.1g; Fat 19.6g, of which saturates 8.1g; Cholesterol 57mg; Calcium 74mg; Fibre 1.8g; Sodium 108mg.
Fresh Lemon Energy 528Kcal/2212kJ; Protein 7.8g; Carbohydrate 61.7g, of which sugars 42.3g; Fat 29.6g, of which saturates 5.6g; Cholesterol 89mg; Calcium 91mg; Fibre 1.9g; Sodium 104mg.

Lemon and Ricotta Tart

Citrus fruits come into their own under the baking hot Calabrian sun in southern Italy. This deliciously tangy lemon tart uses lots of freshly grated lemon rind to give the filling a really intense flavour. Serve this tart cold accompanied by small glass of Limoncello for a delicious grown-up dessert.

Serves 6

250g/9oz/2¼ cups plain (all-purpose) flour, plus extra for dusting
125g/4¼oz/generous ½ cup cold unsalted (sweet) butter, diced
115g/4oz/½ cup caster (superfine) sugar
1 egg, plus 1 egg yolk
icing (confectioners') sugar, for dusting

For the filling

250ml/8fl oz/generous 1 cup custard
115g/4oz/½ cup sugar
250g/9oz/generous 1 cup ricotta cheese
1 egg, beaten
finely grated rind of 3–4 unwaxed lemons

1 Put the plain flour in a bowl. Add the chopped butter and rub it in until the mixture resembles fine breadcrumbs.

2 Stir in the sugar and add the egg and egg yolk. Mix to a soft dough. Knead lightly, wrap in clear film (plastic wrap) and chill in the refrigerator until required.

3 While the pastry is resting, make the filling. Heat the custard and stir in the sugar and lemon rind until the sugar is dissolved, then cover the surface of the custard with baking parchment and leave it to cool.

4 Preheat the oven to 180°C/350°F/Gas 4. Grease a 20cm/8in tart tin (pan) with butter. Beat the ricotta into the custard, then add the beaten egg. Mix thoroughly.

5 On a large sheet of baking parchment, roll out the pastry using a lightly floured rolling pin. Line the tart tin and trim. Pour the lemon filling into the tart case and bake in the oven for 30 minutes. Leave to cool, then dust with icing sugar. Serve at room temperature or cold.

Lemon and Passion Fruit Tart

This is a twist on the traditional lemon tart. It still has a tangy lemon flavour but is laced with fresh passion fruit, which, along with the ground almonds, gives added texture.

Serves 4–6

225g/8oz ready-made shortcrust pastry
2 eggs, plus 1 egg yolk
125g/4¼oz/generous 1 cup icing (confectioners') sugar, plus extra
2 passion fruit, halved, insides scooped out with a teaspoon, skins discarded
finely grated rind of 1 lemon and the juice of 3 lemons
50g/2oz/¼ cup butter, melted
75g/3oz/¼ cup ground almonds

1 Roll out the pastry on a lightly floured surface and use it to line a 20cm/8in round fluted tart tin (pan). Prick the base with a fork. Line with baking parchment and fill with a layer of baking beans, then chill in the refrigerator for 10 minutes.

2 Preheat the oven to 200°C/400°F/Gas 6. Line the pastry with baking parchment and baking beans and bake blind for 10 minutes. Remove the paper and beans and return the pastry case to the oven for 5 minutes more. Remove from the oven and lower the temperature to 190°C/375°F/Gas 5.

3 Meanwhile, whisk the eggs, egg yolk and icing sugar together in a large mixing bowl. Stir in the passion fruit pulp, together with the lemon rind and juice.

4 Stir in the melted butter and ground almonds, and pour evenly into the pastry case. Bake for 20 minutes or until the filling has set and the pastry is golden.

5 Remove the tart from the oven, and leave to cool on a wire rack. Remove from the tin on to a serving plate and dust with icing sugar before serving.

Cook's Tip
Select passion fruit with a hard skin as this means they are ripe.

Lemon Tart Energy 605kcal/2539kJ; Protein 12.2g; Carbohydrate 80.5g, of which sugars 46.7g; Fat 28.3g, of which saturates 15.9g; Cholesterol 162mg; Calcium 149mg; Fibre 1.3g; Sodium 218mg.
Lemon & Passion Fruit Tart Energy 418kcal/1747kJ; Protein 7g; Carbohydrate 41g, of which sugars 23g; Fat 26g, of which saturates 9g; Cholesterol 95mg; Calcium 76mg; Fibre 2.5g; Sodium 222mg.

Fresh Orange Tart

Orange zest gives this rich pastry its wonderful flavour. A creamy custard filling and fresh oranges turn it into a sophisticated dessert.

Serves 9

2 eggs, plus 2 egg yolks
150g/5oz/⅔ cup caster (superfine) sugar
150ml/¼ pint/⅔ cup single (light) cream
grated rind and juice of 1 orange
6–8 oranges
fresh mint sprigs, to decorate

For the pastry

175g/6oz/1½ cups plain (all-purpose) flour
90g/3½oz/scant ½ cup butter, diced
15ml/1 tbsp caster (superfine) sugar
finely grated rind of 1 orange
1 egg yolk
about 10ml/2 tsp orange juice

1 To make the pastry, sift the flour and rub or cut in the butter. Stir in the sugar and orange rind. Beat the egg yolk with the orange juice, then add to the dry ingredients and mix to a until a firm dough forms.

2 Lightly and quickly knead the dough until smooth. Roll out and use to line a 20cm/8in square fluted tin (pan). Wrap in clear film (plastic wrap) and chill for 30 minutes.

3 Put a baking sheet in the oven and preheat to 200°C/400°F/Gas 6. Prick the pastry case (pie shell) all over with a fork and line with foil and baking beans. Place on the hot baking sheet and bake blind for 12 minutes. Remove the foil and beans and bake the pastry for a further 5 minutes.

4 Whisk the eggs, yolks and sugar in a bowl until foamy. Whisk in the cream, followed by the orange rind and juice. Pour into the pastry case and bake for 30–35 minutes until firm. Remove from the oven and leave to cool on a wire rack still in the tin.

5 Peel the oranges, removing all the white pith and separate the segments by cutting between the membranes. Arrange the segments in rows on top of the tart. Chill until ready to serve, then carefully remove the tart from the tin and decorate with sprigs of fresh mint.

Orange Sweetheart Tart

This tart is filled with frangipane, and topped with orange slices.

Serves 8

200g/7oz/1 cup sugar
250ml/8fl oz/1 cup fresh orange juice, strained
2 large oranges, cut in thin slices
75g/3oz/½ cup blanched almonds
50g/2oz/¼ cup butter
1 egg
15ml/1 tbsp plain (all-purpose) flour
45ml/3 tbsp apricot jam

For the pastry

175g/6oz/1½ cups plain (all-purpose) flour
2.5ml/½ tsp salt
75g/3oz/6 tbsp butter, diced
45ml/3 tbsp chilled water

1 Sift the flour and salt into a mixing bowl. Add the butter and rub in with your fingertips until the mixture resembles fine breadcrumbs. Add the water and mix to a dough. Chill for at least 30 minutes. Roll out on a floured surface and line a 20cm/8in heart-shaped tart tin (pan). Trim and chill again for a further 30 minutes. Preheat the oven to 200°C/400°F/Gas 6.

2 Line the pastry case (pie shell) with baking parchment and fill with baking beans. Bake blind for 10 minutes. Remove the parchment and beans and cook for 5 minutes more.

3 Meanwhile put 150g/5oz/¾ cup of the sugar into a heavy pan and pour in the orange juice. Bring to the boil, stirring until the sugar has dissolved, then boil steadily for 10 minutes.

4 Add the orange slices to the syrup. Simmer for 10 minutes. Transfer the slices to a wire rack placed over a plate to dry. Reserve the syrup. When the orange slices are cool, cut in half.

5 Grind the almonds in a food processor. Cream the butter and remaining sugar until light. Beat in the egg and 30ml/2 tbsp of the orange syrup. Stir in the almonds, then add the flour.

6 Melt the jam over low heat, then brush over the pastry. Pour in the ground almond mixture. Bake for 20 minutes until set. Leave to cool in the tin. Decorate with the orange slices and brush the top with the remaining syrup.

Fresh Orange Tart Energy 500kcal/2093kJ; Protein 8.6g; Carbohydrate 59.4g, of which sugars 37.4g; Fat 27g, of which saturates 7.7g; Cholesterol 50mg; Calcium 129mg; Fibre 3.1g; Sodium 137mg.
Orange Sweetheart Energy 405Kcal/1699kJ; Protein 6.4g; Carbohydrate 53.7g, of which sugars 36.8g; Fat 19.8g, of which saturates 9g; Cholesterol 81mg; Calcium 98mg; Fibre 2g; Sodium 123mg.

Rustic Apple Tart

This easy apple tart looks as though it has come straight from the kitchen of a French farmhouse. Cooking the apples before putting them on the pastry prevents a soggy crust.

Serves 6

900g/2lb cooking apples, peeled, quartered and cored
15ml/1 tbsp lemon juice
50g/2oz/¼ cup caster (superfine) sugar
40g/1½oz/3 tbsp butter
crème fraîche or lightly whipped cream, to serve

For the pastry

225g/8oz/2 cups plain (all-purpose) flour
pinch of salt
15ml/1 tbsp caster (superfine) sugar
150g/5oz/⅔ cup butter, diced
1 egg yolk
30ml/2 tbsp chilled water

1 To make the pastry, sift the flour, salt and sugar into a bowl. Rub or cut in the butter until the mixture resembles fine breadcrumbs. Combine the egg and water, sprinkle over the dry ingredients and mix to a dough. Wrap in clear film (plastic wrap) and chill for 30 minutes.

2 Slice the apple quarters and place in a bowl. Sprinkle with the lemon juice and sugar, and toss to combine.

3 Melt the butter in a large heavy frying pan over medium heat and add the apples. Cook, stirring frequently, for about 12 minutes until the apples are just turning golden brown. Remove the frying pan from the heat and set aside. Preheat the oven to 190°C/375°F/Gas 5.

4 On a lightly floured work surface, roll out the pastry to a 30cm/12in round and trim the edge if uneven. Transfer the pastry to a baking sheet. Heap the apple slices on the pastry, leaving a 5cm/2in border all round the edge of the pastry.

5 Gather the pastry border around the apple slices, enclosing those closest to the rim and leaving the centre open. Bake the tart for 35–40 minutes until the pastry is crisp and golden brown. Serve warm, with crème fraîche or whipped cream.

French Apple Tart

This glorious tart makes a truly indulgent dessert. For an early morning treat, try a slice for breakfast with a cup of strong black coffee.

Serves 8

350g/12oz sweet shortcrust pastry

For the filling

115g/4oz/½ cup butter, softened
115g/4oz/½ cup caster (superfine) sugar
2 large (US extra large) eggs, beaten
115g/4oz/1 cup ground almonds
25g/1oz/¼ cup plain (all-purpose) flour

For the topping

3 Braeburn apples
60ml/4 tbsp apricot jam
15ml/1 tbsp water

1 Preheat the oven to 190°C/375°F/Gas 5. Place a baking sheet in the oven to heat up. Roll out the shortcrust pastry on a lightly floured surface and line a 23cm/9in fluted flan tin (pan).

2 Beat all the ingredients for the filling together until light and fluffy. Spoon into the pastry case (pie shell) and level the surface.

3 Make the topping. Peel the apples, remove the cores, and cut them in half. Place each half, cut side down, on a board. Using a sharp, fine knife, slice the apples thinly, keeping the shape, then press down lightly to fan each apple half in a row.

4 Using a palette knife or metal spatula, carefully transfer each row of apple slices to the tart, arranging them on the filling so that they resemble the spokes of a wheel. You may need to overlap the slices in the middle slightly to fit. Press the slices down well into the filling.

5 Warm the apricot jam with the water, then press the mixture through a sieve (strainer) into a small bowl.

6 Using a pastry brush, brush half this jam glaze over the apples. Place the tin on the hot baking sheet and bake the tart for 45 minutes or until the pastry is golden and the apples have started to singe slightly. Warm the remaining jam glaze and brush it over the apples. Let the tart cool slightly before serving warm.

Rustic Apple Tart Energy 372kcal/1560kJ; Protein 5.1g; Carbohydrate 49.1g, of which sugars 23.7g; Fat 18.7g, of which saturates 11.2g; Cholesterol 76mg; Calcium 86mg; Fibre 3.9g; Sodium 142mg.
French Apple Tart Energy 638kcal/2666kJ; Protein 7g; Carbohydrate 38g, of which sugars 16g; Fat 52g, of which saturates 29g; Cholesterol 197mg; Calcium 100mg; Fibre 4.3g; Sodium 29mg.

Crunchy Apple and Almond Flan

Don't put sugar with the apples, as this produces too much liquid. The sweetness is in the pastry and topping.

Serves 8

75g/3oz/6 tbsp butter
175g/6oz/1½ cups plain (all-purpose) flour
25g/1oz/¼ cup ground almonds
25g/1oz/2 tbsp caster (superfine) sugar
1 egg yolk
15ml/1 tbsp cold water
1.5ml/¼ tsp almond extract
675g/1½lb cooking apples
25g/1oz/2 tbsp raisins

For the topping

115g/4oz/1 cup plain (all-purpose) flour
1.5ml/¼ tsp mixed (apple pie) spice
50g/2oz/¼ cup butter, cut into small cubes
50g/2oz/4¼ cup demerara (raw) sugar
50g/2oz/½ cup flaked (sliced) almonds

1 To make the pastry, rub the butter into the flour using your fingertips or a pastry cutter until it resembles breadcrumbs. Stir in the almonds and sugar.

2 Whisk the egg yolk, water and almond extract together and mix into the dry ingredients to form a soft dough. Knead until smooth, wrap, and leave to rest for 20 minutes.

3 To make the topping, sift the flour and spice into a bowl and rub in the butter. Stir in the sugar and almonds.

4 Roll out the pastry and use to line a 23cm/9in loose-based flan tin (pan). Trim the top and chill for 15 minutes.

5 Preheat a baking sheet in the oven at 190°C/375°F/Gas 5. Peel, core and slice the apples thinly. Arrange over the pastry in overlapping, concentric circles, doming the centre. Sprinkle with the raisins.

6 Cover with the topping mixture, pressing it on lightly. Bake on the hot baking sheet for 25–30 minutes, or until the top is golden brown and the apples are tender (test them with a fine skewer). Leave the flan to cool in the tin for 10 minutes before serving.

Tarte Tatin

This upside-down apple tart was first made by two sisters at their restaurant in the Loire Valley in France.

Serves 8–10

225g/8oz puff or shortcrust pastry
10–12 large eating apples
lemon juice
115g/4oz/½ cup butter, cut into pieces
90g/3½oz/½ cup caster (superfine) sugar
1.5ml/½ tsp ground cinnamon
crème fraîche or whipped cream, to serve

1 On a lightly floured surface, roll out the pastry into a 28cm/11in round, less than 5mm/¼in thick. Transfer to a lightly floured baking sheet and chill.

2 Peel the apples, cut them in half lengthways and core. Sprinkle them generously with lemon juice.

3 Preheat the oven to 230°C/450°F/Gas 8. In a 25cm/10in tarte tatin tin (pan), cook the butter, sugar and cinnamon over medium heat until the sugar has dissolved, stirring occasionally. Continue cooking for 6–8 minutes, until the mixture turns a caramel colour. Remove from the heat and arrange the apple halves in the tin, fitting them in tightly since they will shrink.

4 Return the apple-filled tin to the heat and bring to a simmer over medium heat for 20–25 minutes until the apples are tender and coloured. Remove the tin from the heat and leave to cool slightly.

5 Place the pastry on top of the apple-filled pan and tuck the edges of the pastry inside the edge of the tin around the apples.

6 Pierce the pastry in two or three places, then bake for 25–30 minutes until golden. Cool for 10–15 minutes.

7 To serve, run a sharp knife around edge of the tin to loosen the pastry. Cover with a serving plate and, holding them tightly, carefully invert the tin and plate together (do this over the sink in case any caramel drips). Lift off the tin and loosen any apples that stick with a spatula. Serve the tart warm with cream.

Crunchy Apple Flan Energy 358kcal/1499kJ; Protein 6.2g; Carbohydrate 42.5g, of which sugars 14.6g; Fat 19.3g, of which saturates 8.8g; Cholesterol 59mg; Calcium 86mg; Fibre 3.2g; Sodium 102mg.
Tarte Tatin Energy 237kcal/990kJ; Protein 2g; Carbohydrate 26g, of which sugars 15g; Fat 15g, of which saturates 6g; Cholesterol 18mg; Calcium 24mg; Fibre 1g; Sodium 144mg.

Fruit Tart with Cranberry Sauce

Berries abound in this medley of fruit flavours, given a special lift with a little gin.

Serves 6–8

225g/8oz/2 cups plain (all-purpose) flour
115g/4oz/½ cup butter, diced
10ml/2 tsp grated lime rind
egg or milk, to glaze

For the filling

225g/8oz cooking apples, peeled, cored and grated
175g/6oz/1½ cups cranberries
115g/4oz/1 cup blueberries
50g/2oz/⅓ cup soft light brown sugar
grated rind and juice of 1 lime
15ml/1 tbsp gin
150ml/¼ pint/⅔ cup water

For the sauce

175g/6oz/1½ cups cranberries
30ml/2 tbsp clear honey
30ml/2 tbsp gin
300ml/½ pint/1¼ cups fresh orange juice

1 Sift the flour into a bowl. Rub in the butter, then stir in the grated lime rind. Add enough cold water to make a soft dough. Wrap in clear film (plastic wrap) and chill for 30 minutes.

2 Make the filling. Put the grated apples, cranberries, blueberries, sugar, lime rind and juice, gin and water in a large saucepan and bring to the boil. Lower the heat and simmer, stirring, until the fruit begins to pulp down and thicken. Set aside to cool. Preheat the oven to 200°C/400°F/Gas 6.

3 Roll out three-quarters of the pastry on a lightly floured surface to a 25cm/10in round and use it to line a deep-sided 18cm/7in flan tin (pan). Roll out the remaining pastry and cut thin strips for a lattice and small flower shapes for the decoration.

4 Spoon the filling into the pastry case (pie shell). Make a lattice top with the pastry strips, brush with a little egg or milk and attach the flower shapes. Bake for 30–35 minutes. Remove from the oven and leave to cool in the tin for 15 minutes.

5 Meanwhile, make the sauce by mixing the cranberries, honey, gin and orange juice in a pan. Bring to the boil, then lower the heat and simmer for 10 minutes. Process in a blender or food processor until smooth. Serve hot or cold with slices of the tart.

Custard Tart with Plums

When this tart is made with really ripe, sweet plums, it makes a wonderful hot or cold weekend dessert. It is delicious served with thick cream or ice cream.

Serves 4–6

175g/6oz/1½ cups plain (all-purpose) flour
pinch of salt
45ml/3 tbsp caster (superfine) sugar
115g/4oz/½ cup unsalted (sweet) butter
2 eggs, plus 2 yolks
350g/12oz ripe plums
300ml/½ pint/1¼ cups milk
few drops of vanilla extract
thick cream or ice cream, to serve
toasted flaked (sliced) almonds and sifted icing (confectioners') sugar, to decorate

1 Place the flour, salt, 15ml/1 tbsp of the sugar, the butter and one of the eggs in a food processor or blender and process until thoroughly combined. Turn out the mixture on to a clean, lightly floured surface and bring it together into a ball. Cover the pastry and leave for 10 minutes to rest.

2 Flour a deep 18cm/7in square or 20cm/8in round loose-bottomed tin (pan). Roll out the pastry and use to line the tin. This pastry is soft at this stage, so don't worry if you have to push it into shape. Chill for another 10–20 minutes.

3 Preheat the oven to 200°C/400°F/Gas 6. Line the pastry case (pie shell) with baking parchment and fill with baking beans, then bake for 15 minutes. Remove the paper and beans, reduce the heat to 180°C/350°F/Gas 4 and bake the case for a further 5–10 minutes until the base is dry.

4 Halve and stone (pit) the plums, and arrange them neatly in the pastry case. Whisk together the remaining egg and egg yolks with the sugar, the milk and vanilla extract and pour the mixture over the fruit in the case.

5 Return the tart to the oven and bake for 25–30 minutes. When the custard is just firm to the touch, remove the tart from the oven and allow to cool. Sprinkle with flaked almonds and dredge with icing sugar before serving. Add a generous dollop of cream or ice cream to each portion.

Fruit Tart Energy 283kcal/1189kJ; Protein 3.3g; Carbohydrate 39.2g, of which sugars 17.8g; Fat 12.3g, of which saturates 7.6g; Cholesterol 31mg; Calcium 56mg; Fibre 4.1g; Sodium 94mg.
Custard Tart Energy 396kcal/1652kJ; Protein 5.5g; Carbohydrate 37.2g, of which sugars 18.2g; Fat 25.2g, of which saturates 14.7g; Cholesterol 155mg; Calcium 74mg; Fibre 1.7g; Sodium 104mg.

Alsatian Plum Tart

Fruit and custard tarts, similar to a fruit flan, are typical in Alsace, in the east of France. Sometimes they have a yeast dough base instead of pastry. You can use other seasonal fruits in this tart, or a mixture of fruit, if you like.

Serves 6–8

450g/1lb ripe plums, halved and stoned (pitted)
30ml/2 tbsp Kirsch or plum brandy
350g/12oz shortcrust or sweet shortcrust pastry, thawed if frozen
30ml/2 tbsp seedless raspberry jam

For the custard filling

2 eggs
25g/1oz/4 tbsp icing (confectioners') sugar
175ml/6fl oz/¾ cup double (heavy) cream
grated rind of ½ lemon
1.5ml/¼ tsp vanilla extract

1 Preheat the oven to 200°C/400°F/Gas 6. Mix the plums with the Kirsch or brandy and set aside for about 30 minutes.

2 Roll out the pastry thinly and use to line a 23cm/9in flan tin (pan). Prick the base of the pastry case (pie shell) all over with a fork, and line with foil. Add a layer of baking beans and bake for 15 minutes, or until slightly dry and set. Remove the foil and the baking beans.

3 Brush the base of the pastry case with a thin layer of jam, then bake for a further 5 minutes.

4 Remove the pastry case from the oven and transfer to a wire rack. Reduce the oven temperature to 180°C/350°F/Gas 4.

5 To make the custard filling, beat the eggs and sugar until well combined, then beat in the cream, lemon rind, vanilla extract and any juice from the plums.

6 Arrange the plums, cut side down, in the pastry case and pour over the custard mixture. Bake for about 30–35 minutes, or until a knife inserted into the centre comes out clean. Serve the tart warm or at room temperature.

Plum and Marzipan Puff

Plums and marzipan are terrific together and here they are used as a delicious topping for light puff pastry. Simplicity itself to make, this tart is the perfect dessert for an informal gathering.

Serves 4

375g/13oz ready-rolled puff pastry, thawed if frozen
115g/4oz marzipan
6–8 plums, stoned (pitted) and sliced
icing (confectioners') sugar, for dusting
crème fraîche, to serve

1 Preheat the oven to 190°C/375°F/Gas 5. Unroll the pastry on to a large baking sheet lined with baking parchment.

2 Using a small, sharp knife, score a border 5cm/2in from the edge of the pastry, without cutting all the way through.

3 Roll out the marzipan into a rectangle, to fit just within the pastry border, then lay it on top of the pastry, pressing down lightly with the tips of your fingers.

4 Sprinkle the sliced plums on top of the marzipan in an even layer and bake for 20–25 minutes, or until the pastry is risen and golden brown.

5 Carefully transfer the tart to a wire rack and leave to cool slightly. Dust lightly with icing sugar.

6 To serve the tart, cut it into squares, or wedges if you prefer, and serve with crème fraîche.

Variation

Apricots and peaches also have a natural affinity with almonds, so they can be successfully substituted for the plums in this tart. Using slightly underripe fruit is fine in this recipe, as baking them increases their flavour.

Alsatian Tart Energy 375kcal/1563kJ; Protein 4.8g; Carbohydrate 31.7g, of which sugars 11.6g; Fat 25.5g, of which saturates 11.5g; Cholesterol 84mg; Calcium 65mg; Fibre 1.7g; Sodium 200mg.
Marzipan Puff Energy 478Kcal/2003kJ; Protein 7.1g; Carbohydrate 58.1g, of which sugars 24.6g; Fat 26.7g, of which saturates 0.3g; Cholesterol 0mg; Calcium 79mg; Fibre 1.3g; Sodium 297mg.

Yellow Plum Tart

This lovely tart consists of glazed yellow plums arranged on top of a delectable almond filling.

Serves 8

175g/6oz/1½ cups plain (all-purpose) flour
pinch of salt
75g/3oz/6 tbsp butter, chilled
30ml/2 tbsp caster (superfine) sugar
a few drops of pure vanilla extract
45ml/3 tbsp iced water
45ml/3 tbsp apricot jam, sieved
cream or custard, to serve

For the filling

75g/3oz/6 tbsp caster (superfine) sugar
75g/3oz/6 tbsp butter, softened
75g/3oz/¾ cup ground almonds
1 egg, beaten
30ml/2 tbsp plain (all-purpose) flour
450g/1lb yellow plums or greengages, halved and stoned (pitted)

1 Sift the flour and salt into a bowl, then rub in the butter until the mixture resembles fine breadcrumbs. Stir in the sugar, vanilla extract and enough of the iced water to form a soft dough.

2 Knead the dough gently on a lightly floured surface until smooth. Wrap in clear film (plastic wrap); chill for 10 minutes.

3 Preheat the oven to 200°C/400°F/Gas 6. Roll out the pastry and line a 23cm/9in fluted flan tin (pan), allowing any excess pastry to overhang the top. Prick the base with a fork and line with non-stick baking parchment and baking beans.

4 Bake blind for 10 minutes, remove the paper and beans, then return the pastry case (pie shell) to the oven for 10 minutes. Remove and allow to cool. Trim off any excess pastry.

5 To make the filling, beat together all the ingredients except the plums. Spread on the base of the pastry case. Arrange the plums on top, cut side down. To make a glaze, heat the jam with 15ml/1 tbsp water, then brush a little over the fruit.

6 Bake the plum tart for about 50 minutes, until the almond filling is cooked and the plums are tender. Warm any remaining jam glaze and brush over the top. Serve with cream or custard.

Plum and Kirsch Tart

This tart is made from yeast dough, and can be open-faced, covered or latticed.

Serves 6–8

250g/9oz/2¼ cups plain (all-purpose) flour
50g/2oz/¼ cup sugar
15ml/1 tbsp easy-blend (rapid-rise) dried yeast
2.5ml/½ tsp salt
1 egg, beaten
100ml/3½fl oz/scant ½ cup milk
50–75g/2–3oz/4–6 tbsp unsalted (sweet) butter, softened

For the filling

675g/1½lb fresh ripe plums, quartered
60ml/4 tbsp soft light brown sugar
15ml/1 tbsp ground cinnamon
15ml/1 tbsp kirsch or rum
5ml/1 tsp cornflour (cornstarch)

1 Place the flour, sugar, dried yeast and salt in a food processor and pulse. With the motor running, pour in the beaten egg, milk and butter and pulse until the dough forms a ball.

2 On a lightly floured surface, knead the dough lightly, form it into a ball and place in a large, lightly oiled bowl. Cover with clear film (plastic wrap) and leave to rise for 30 minutes.

3 Put the plums in a bowl. Sprinkle with 45ml/3 tbsp of the brown sugar and two-thirds of the cinnamon. Add the kirsch or rum, stir and leave to stand. Preheat the oven to 220°C/425°F/Gas 7 and place a baking sheet inside to heat.

4 Grease a 23cm/9in loose-bottomed tart or flan tin (pan) and dust it lightly with flour. Knock back (punch down) the dough. Roll out on a lightly floured surface and line the tart or flan pan without stretching the dough. Prick the base with a fork. Sprinkle with the remaining brown sugar and cinnamon. Leave to stand for 15 minutes.

5 Sift the cornflour over the plums, then layer them in the pastry case (pie shell). Place the tin on the hot baking sheet in the oven. Bake for 30–45 minutes or until the pie is cooked and the pastry is golden brown. Leave to cool on a wire rack for about 15 minutes then remove from the tin and put it on a plate. Serve immediately, in slices.

Yellow Plum Tart Energy 361kcal/1510kJ; Protein 6g; Carbohydrate 38g, of which sugars 18g; Fat 22g, of which saturates 10g; Cholesterol 69mg; Calcium 72mg; Fibre 2.1g; Sodium 177mg.
Plum & Kirsch Tart Energy 304kcal/1285kJ; Protein 5.9g; Carbohydrate 57.5g, of which sugars 23.6g; Fat 6.7g, of which saturates 3.7g; Cholesterol 38mg; Calcium 100mg; Fibre 2.7g; Sodium 56mg.

Pear and Almond Cream Tart

In this sweet tart recipe, fanned pears glazed with brandy rest on a light almond filling. This dish is equally successful made with other orchard fruits, such as nectarines, peaches, apricots or apples.

Serves 6

350g/12oz shortcrust or sweet shortcrust pastry, thawed if frozen
3 firm pears
lemon juice
15ml/1 tbsp peach brandy or cold water
60ml/4 tbsp peach jam, sieved

For the filling

90g/3½oz/generous ½ cup blanched whole almonds
50g/2oz/¼ cup caster (superfine) sugar
65g/2½oz/5 tbsp butter
1 egg, plus 1 egg white
a few drops of almond extract

1 Roll out the pastry and use to line a 23cm/9in flan tin (pan). Chill in the refrigerator while you make the filling.

2 For the filling, put the almonds and sugar in a food processor or blender and pulse until finely ground but not pasty. Add the butter and process until creamy, then add the egg, egg white and almond extract, and mix well.

3 Preheat a baking sheet in the oven at 190°C/375°F/Gas 5.

4 Peel the pears, halve them, remove the cores and rub with lemon juice. Put the pear halves, cut side down, on a board and slice thinly crossways, keeping the slices together.

5 Pour the filling into the pastry case. Slide a metal spatula under one pear half and press the top to fan out the slices. Transfer to the tart, placing the fruit on top of the filling like the spokes of a wheel.

6 Bake the tart on the baking sheet for 50–55 minutes, or until the filling is set and well browned. Cool on a wire rack.

7 Heat the brandy or water with the jam. Brush over the top of the hot tart to glaze. Serve at room temperature.

Pear Tarte Tatin with Cardamom

Cardamom is a spice that is equally at home in sweet and savoury dishes. It is delicious with pears, and brings out their flavour beautifully in this easy-to-make tart.

Serves 4–6

50g/2oz/¼ cup butter, softened
50g/2oz/¼ cup caster (superfine) sugar
seeds from 10 green cardamom pods
225g/8oz fresh ready-made puff pastry
3 ripe, large round pears
single (light) cream, to serve

1 Preheat the oven to 220°C/425°F/Gas 7. Spread the butter over the base of an 18cm/7in heavy ovenproof omelette pan. Sprinkle the butter with the sugar, then sprinkle the cardamom seeds evenly over the top.

2 On a lightly floured work surface, roll out the pastry to a circle slightly larger than the pan. Prick the pastry all over with a fork, place on a baking sheet and chill.

3 Peel the pears, cut in half lengthways and remove the cores. Arrange the pears, rounded side down, in the pan. Place over medium heat and cook until the sugar melts and begins to bubble with the juice from the pears.

4 Once the sugar has caramelized, remove the pan from the heat. Carefully place the pastry on top, tucking in the edges with a knife. Bake for 25 minutes.

5 Leave the tart in the pan for about 2 minutes until the juices have stopped bubbling.

6 Invert a serving plate over the pan then, wearing oven gloves to protect your hands, firmly hold the pan and plate together and quickly turn over, gently shaking them to release the tart. It may be necessary to slide a spatula underneath the pears to loosen them.

7 Allow the tart to cool slightly, then serve while warm, with a dollop of single cream.

Pear Cream Tart Energy 544kcal/2271kJ; Protein 8.4g; Carbohydrate 51.5g, of which sugars 24.4g; Fat 34.7g, of which saturates 11.7g; Cholesterol 63mg; Calcium 106mg; Fibre 3.9g; Sodium 330mg.
Pear Tarte Tatin Energy 265Kcal/1106kJ; Protein 2.5g; Carbohydrate 30.1g, of which sugars 16.8g; Fat 16.1g, of which saturates 4.3g; Cholesterol 18mg; Calcium 36mg; Fibre 1.7g; Sodium 170mg.

Pear and Hazelnut Flan

A delicious fruit flan for Sunday lunch. Grind the hazelnuts yourself if you prefer, or use ground almonds instead.

Serves 6–8

115g/4oz/1 cup plain (all-purpose) flour
115g/4oz/1 cup plain wholemeal (whole-wheat) flour
115g/4oz/½ cup sunflower margarine
45ml/3 tbsp cold water

For the filling

50g/2oz/½ cup self-raising (self-rising) flour
115g/4oz/1 cup ground hazelnuts
5ml/1 tsp vanilla extract
50g/2oz/¼ cup caster (superfine) sugar
50g/2oz/¼ cup butter, softened
2 eggs, beaten
400g/14oz can pears in natural juice
45ml/3 tbsp raspberry jam
a few chopped hazelnuts, to decorate

1 For the pastry, stir the flours together, then rub in the margarine using your fingertips or a pastry (cookie) cutter, until the mixture resembles fine breadcrumbs. Mix to a firm dough with the water.

2 Roll out the dough and use to line a 23–25cm/9–10in flan tin (pan), pressing it up the sides after trimming, so that the pastry sits a little above the tin. Prick the base with a fork, line with baking parchment and fill with baking beans. Chill for 30 minutes.

3 Preheat the oven to 200°C/400°F/Gas 6. Place the flan tin on a baking sheet and bake blind for 20 minutes. Remove the paper and beans after 15 minutes.

4 To make the filling beat together the flour, hazelnuts, vanilla extract, sugar and eggs. If the mixture is too thick, stir in some of the juice from the canned pears.

5 Reduce the oven temperature to 180°C/350°F/Gas 4. Spread the jam over the base of the pastry case (pie shell) and spoon over the filling.

6 Drain the pears and arrange them, cut side down, in the filling. Sprinkle over the nuts for decoration. Bake for 30 minutes, or until risen, firm and golden brown.

Apricot Frangipane Tart

Take a light lime-flavoured pastry case, fill it with moist almond sponge generously laced with Kirsch and topped with fresh apricots and crushed macaroons, and the result is simply sensational. It is delicious warm or cold, served with yogurt or cream.

Serves 6

225g/8oz/2 cups plain (all-purpose) flour
115g/4oz/½ cup butter
10ml/2 tsp finely grated lime rind
12 fresh apricots, stoned (pitted), some halved, and some thickly sliced
75g/3oz macaroons, crushed
natural (plain) yogurt or single (light) cream, to serve

For the filling

25g/1oz/2 tbsp butter, softened
30ml/2 tbsp soft light brown sugar
15ml/1 tbsp plain flour
50g/2oz/½ cup ground almonds
1 egg, beaten
45ml/3 tbsp Kirsch

1 Sift the flour into a mixing bowl, then rub in the butter until the mixture resembles breadcrumbs. Stir in the grated lime rind and add enough cold water to make a soft dough. Wrap in clear film (plastic wrap) and chill for 30 minutes.

2 Meanwhile, make the filling. Cream the butter with the soft brown sugar, then stir in the flour, ground almonds, egg and Kirsch. Preheat the oven to 200°C/400°F/Gas 6.

3 Roll out the pastry on a lightly floured surface to a 40 x 16cm/16 x 6½in rectangle and use it to line a 35 x 11.5cm/14 x 4½in rectangular flan tin (pan).

4 Spread the filling in the pastry case (pie shell) and arrange the apricot halves and slices, cut side down, on top. Sprinkle over the crushed macaroons. Bake for 35–40 minutes until the pastry is golden. Serve warm or cold, with yogurt or cream.

Cook's Tip

If you find the pastry difficult to handle, roll it out between sheets of baking parchment or clear film (plastic wrap).

Pear Flan Energy 389kcal/1626kJ; Protein 7.6g; Carbohydrate 40.9g, of which sugars 16g; Fat 22.8g, of which saturates 3.5g; Cholesterol 49mg; Calcium 69mg; Fibre 3.6g; Sodium 138mg.
Apricot Tart Energy 350Kcal/1459kJ; Protein 5.9g; Carbohydrate 31.5g, of which sugars 17.5g; Fat 23.1g, of which saturates 10.4g; Cholesterol 98mg; Calcium 73mg; Fibre 2g; Sodium 121mg.

Rice Custard Tart with Apricots

This Belgian favourite with a yeast pastry case is filled with sweet apricot preserve and creamy rice custard.

Serves 6–8

250g/9oz/2¼ cups plain (all-purpose) flour
50g/2oz/¼ cup sugar
15ml/1 tbsp easy-blend (rapid-rise) dried yeast
1 egg, beaten
100ml/3½fl oz/scant ½ cup milk
50–75g/2–3oz/4–6 tbsp butter, softened

For the filling
500ml/17fl oz/2 cups milk
150g/5oz/⅔ cup short grain rice
50g/2oz/¼ cup caster (superfine) sugar
pinch of salt
5ml/1 tsp vanilla extract
2 eggs, separated, plus 2 yolks
60ml/4 tbsp apricot preserve
400g/14oz can apricot halves

1 Place the flour, sugar, dried yeast and salt in a food processor and pulse. With the motor running, pour in the beaten egg, milk and butter and pulse until the dough forms a ball. On a lightly floured surface, knead the mixture lightly, form into a ball and place in a lightly oiled bowl. Cover with clear film (plastic wrap) and leave to rise in a warm, for about 30 minutes.

2 Pour the milk into a pan. Bring to the boil, then stir in the rice. Reduce the heat to low, cover the pan and simmer for about 30 minutes, stirring frequently, until all the milk has been absorbed. Stir in the sugar and salt. Set aside to cool.

3 Preheat the oven to 180°C/350°F/Gas 4 with a baking sheet inside. Grease a 23cm/9in springform tin. Knock back (punch down) the dough. Roll out and line the tin. Prick with a fork.

4 Add the vanilla extract and 1 egg yolk to the cool rice mixture. Stir to mix, then beat in the remaining 3 egg yolks one by one. In a clean bowl, beat the 2 egg whites until stiff, then fold them into the rice custard.

5 Spread a layer of apricot preserve in the pastry case (pie shell). Pour in the rice mixture. Arrange the apricot halves on top, cut-side down. Put the pan on the hot baking sheet in the oven and bake for 35–40 minutes. Serve at room temperature.

Apricot and Almond Tart

This dish has a unique pastry made from brown rice flour and cornmeal, which makes a delicious, light crust.

Serves 6

115g/4oz/½ cup butter
115g/4oz/generous ½ cup caster (superfine) sugar
1 egg, beaten
50g/2oz/⅓ cup ground rice
50g/2oz/½ cup ground almonds
few drops of almond extract
450g/1lb fresh apricots, halved and stoned (pitted)
sifted icing (confectioners') sugar, for dusting (optional)

For the pastry
115g/4oz/1 cup brown rice flour
115g/4oz/1 cup cornmeal
115g/4oz/½ cup butter
25g/1oz/2 tbsp caster (superfine) sugar
1 egg yolk

1 Make the pastry. Place the rice flour and cornmeal in a large mixing bowl and stir to mix. Lightly rub in the butter until the mixture resembles fine breadcrumbs. Add the sugar, the egg yolk and enough chilled water to make a smooth, soft but not sticky dough. Wrap the dough in clear film (plastic wrap) and chill for about 30 minutes.

2 Preheat the oven to 180°C/350°F/Gas 4. Line a 24cm/9½in loose-based flan tin (pan) with the pastry by pressing it gently over the base and up the sides, making sure that there are no holes in the pastry. Trim any excess from the edge of the pastry with a sharp knife.

3 Make the almond filling. Place the butter or margarine and sugar in a large mixing bowl and cream together with a wooden spoon until the mixture is light and fluffy. Gradually add the beaten egg to the mix, beating well after each addition. Fold in the ground rice and almonds and the almond extract and mix well to incorporate.

4 Spoon the mixture into the pastry case (pie shell), spreading it evenly, then arrange the apricot halves cut side down on top. Place the tart on a baking sheet and bake for 40–45 minutes until the filling and pastry are cooked and lightly browned. Serve warm or cold, dusted with icing sugar.

Rice Custard Tart Energy 374kcal/1572kJ; Protein 10.2g; Carbohydrate 59.3g, of which sugars 20.5g; Fat 11.8g, of which saturates 6g; Cholesterol 145mg; Calcium 169mg; Fibre 1.4g; Sodium 106mg.
Plum Tart Energy 265kcal/1123kJ; Protein 6g; Carbohydrate 51.6g, of which sugars 20.2g; Fat 5.3g, of which saturates 2.6g; Cholesterol 59.6mg; Calcium 123mg; Fibre 2.2g; Sodium 46mg.

Strawberry Tart

This tart is best assembled just before serving, but you can bake the pastry case and make the filling ahead.

Serves 6
350g/12oz rough-puff or puff pastry, thawed if frozen
225g/8oz/1 cup cream cheese
grated rind of ½ orange
30ml/2 tbsp orange liqueur or orange juice
45–60ml/3–4 tbsp icing (confectioners') sugar, plus extra for dusting (optional)
450g/1lb/4 cups ripe strawberries, hulled

1 Preheat the oven to 200°C/400°F/Gas 6. Roll out the pastry to about a 3mm/⅛in thickness and use to line a 28 x 10cm/11 x 4in rectangular flan tin (pan). Trim the edges, then chill in the refrigerator for 30 minutes.

2 Prick the base of the pastry all over with a fork. Line with foil, fill with baking beans and bake for 15 minutes. Remove the foil and beans and bake for a further 10 minutes, or until the pastry is browned. Gently press down on the pastry base to deflate, then leave to cool on a wire rack.

3 Beat together the cheese, orange rind, liqueur or juice and icing sugar to taste. Spread the filling in the pastry case (pie shell).

4 Halve the strawberries and arrange them on top of the filling. Dust with icing sugar, if you like and serve.

Rough-puff Pastry
Cut 175g/6oz/¾ cup butter into small pieces. Sift 8oz/225g/2 cups plain (all-purpose) flour into a bowl and add the butter, 5ml/1 tsp salt, 5ml/1 tsp lemon juice and 150ml/¼ pint/⅔ cup iced water. Mix together with a knife. Turn on to a work surface and gather it together. Roll into a rectangle. Fold up the bottom third to the centre, fold the top third to meet it and then turn the pastry a quarter turn. Repeat the rolling and folding. Wrap and chill for 20 minutes (or put into the freezer for 5 minutes). Roll, fold and chill twice more.

Raspberry Tart

A lovely, summery dessert, this glazed fruit tart really does taste as good as it looks.

Serves 8
4 egg yolks
65g/2½oz/5 tbsp sugar
45g/1¾oz/3 tbsp plain (all-purpose) flour
300ml/½ pint/1¼ cups milk
pinch of salt
2.5ml/½ tsp vanilla extract
450g/1lb/2½ cups fresh raspberries
75ml/5 tbsp redcurrant jelly
15ml/1 tbsp fresh orange juice

For the pastry
150g/5oz/1¼ cups plain (all-purpose) flour
2.5ml/½ tsp baking powder
1.5ml/¼ tsp salt
15ml/1 tbsp sugar
grated rind of ½ orange
90ml/6 tbsp cold butter, diced
1 egg yolk
45ml/3 tbsp whipping cream

1 Make the pastry. Sift the flour, baking powder and salt into a bowl. Stir in the sugar and orange rind. Add the butter and rub in until the mixture resembles coarse breadcrumbs. With a fork, stir in the egg yolk and just enough cream to bind the dough. Gather into a ball, wrap in clear film (plastic wrap) and chill.

2 Make the custard filling. Beat the egg yolks and sugar until thick and lemon-coloured. Gradually stir in the flour.

3 In a pan, bring the milk and salt just to the boil, and remove from the heat. Whisk into the egg yolk mixture, return to the pan, and continue whisking over medium-high heat until just bubbling for 3 minutes to thicken. Transfer at once to a bowl and stir in the vanilla. Cover closely with baking parchment.

4 Preheat the oven to 200°C/400°F/Gas 6. Roll out the dough on a lightly floured surface to 3mm/⅛in thick. Use to line a 25cm/10in flan tin (pan) and trim the edge. Prick the pastry case (pie shell) all over and line with baking parchment. Fill with baking beans and bake for 15 minutes. Remove the paper and beans. Bake for 6–8 minutes more until golden. Cool.

5 Spread the filling in the pastry case. Top with the raspberries. Melt the jelly and orange juice together and brush on to glaze.

Strawberry Tart Energy 434kcal/1805kJ; Protein 5.2g; Carbohydrate 34.4g, of which sugars 13.5g; Fat 32.2g, of which saturates 11.1g; Cholesterol 36mg; Calcium 87mg; Fibre 0.8g; Sodium 299mg.
Raspberry Tart Energy 322Kcal/1353kJ; Protein 6.5g; Carbohydrate 40.6g, of which sugars 22g; Fat 16.1g, of which saturates 8.8g; Cholesterol 158mg; Calcium 120mg; Fibre 2.2g; Sodium 97mg..

Raspberry and Crème Brûlée Tart

Fresh raspberries and a crunchy caramel topping contrast with a thick vanilla-scented custard filling.

Serves 8

5ml/1 tsp vanilla extract
450ml/¾ pint/scant 2 cups double (heavy) cream
1 whole egg, plus 3 egg yolks
30ml/2 tbsp caster (superfine) sugar
150g/5oz/scant 1 cup fresh raspberries
75ml/5 tbsp icing (confectioners') sugar

For the pastry
150g/5oz/1¼ cups plain (all-purpose) flour
pinch of salt
25g/1oz/¼ cup icing (confectioners') sugar
75g/3oz/6 tbsp butter, diced
2 egg yolks
finely grated rind of 1 orange

1 To make the pastry, sift the flour, salt and icing sugar into a mixing bowl. Rub or cut in the butter until the mixture resembles fine breadcrumbs. Mix the egg yolks and orange rind together, add to the dry ingredients and mix to a soft dough. Wrap in clear film (plastic wrap) and chill for 30 minutes.

2 Roll out the pastry and use to line a fluted 23cm/9in flan tin (pan). Cover and chill for a further 30 minutes. Preheat the oven, with a baking tray inside, to 200°C/400°F/Gas 6.

3 Prick the base of the pastry all over with a fork and line with baking parchment and baking beans. Bake on the hot baking sheet for 10 minutes. Remove the paper and beans and bake the pastry for 5 minutes more.

4 Mix the vanilla extract and cream in a small pan and slowly bring to the boil. In a mixing bowl, whisk the egg and egg yolks with the sugar until pale. Slowly whisk in the hot cream.

5 Sprinkle the raspberries in the pastry case. Pour the custard in, then bake for 17–20 minutes, or until very lightly set. Cool on a wire rack then chill for at least 4 hours. For the crunchy topping protect the edges of the pastry case (pie shell) with foil. Dredge a layer of icing sugar over top, and place under a hot grill (broiler) until golden. Cool for 10 minutes then serve.

Blackcurrant Tart

Blackcurrants grow in the wild, are cultivated throughout Europe, and are widely available in North America. This tart makes the most of these exquisite summer fruits, and is quick and easy to prepare using ready-made puff pastry. Serve with whipped cream.

Serves 4

500g/1¼lb/5 cups blackcurrants
115g/4oz/generous ½ cup caster (superfine) sugar
250g/9oz ready-made puff pastry
50g/2oz/½ cup icing (confectioners') sugar
whipped cream, to serve

1 Preheat the oven to 220°C/425°F/Gas 7.

2 Trim the blackcurrants, making sure you remove all the stalks and any hard parts in the middle.

3 Add the caster sugar and mix together well.

4 Roll out the pastry to about 3mm/⅛in thick and cut out four discs roughly the size of a side plate or a large cereal bowl.

5 Then, using a smaller plate (or bowl), use the point of a knife to lightly mark a circle about 2cm/¾in inside each disc.

6 Spread the blackcurrants over the discs, keeping them within the marked inner circle. Bake in the oven for 15 minutes.

7 Dust generously with the icing sugar.

8 Serve hot with a large dollop of whipped cream, or alternatively serve cold as a teatime snack.

Cook's Tip

If you are picking wild blackcurrants, look for fruits that are dark, juicy and ripe. Avoid any that are mouldy or have insects or snails on them, and those that are broken. Pick them individually so that you do not squash them.

Crème Brûlée Energy 469kcal/1646kJ; Protein 5g; Carbohydrate 24g, of which sugars 9g; Fat 40g, of which saturates 24g; Cholesterol 171mg; Calcium 70mg; Fibre 1.9g; Sodium 134mg.
Blackcurrant Tart Energy 426kcal/1798kJ; Protein 4.9g; Carbohydrate 73.2g, of which sugars 50.9g; Fat 15.3g, of which saturates 0g; Cholesterol 0mg; Calcium 133mg; Fibre 4.5g; Sodium 200mg.

Border Tart

The borders of Scotland are particularly associated with sweet tarts that make tasty mid-morning snacks, as well as satisfying desserts. This one is delicious served hot or cold with cream. Unusually for a tart this recipe does not require the pastry case to be baked blind, as the filling is both light and dry it allows the pastry to crisp up.

Serves 4
1 egg
75g/3oz/scant ½ cup soft light brown sugar
50g/2oz/¼ cup butter, melted
10ml/2 tsp white wine vinegar
115g/4oz/½ cup currants
25g/1oz/¼ cup chopped walnuts
double (heavy) cream, to serve (optional)

For the sweet pastry
150g/5oz/10 tbsp butter
50g/2oz/¼ cup caster (superfine) sugar
225g/8oz/2 cups plain (all-purpose) flour
1 egg

1 Make the sweet pastry. Cream the butter with the caster sugar together in a food processor. Add the plain flour and egg. Pulse gradually until just combined, being careful not to over-process the mixture.

2 Roll the dough into a ball, and then flatten into a disc, wrap in plastic film and leave in a cool place for an hour before use.

3 Roll the pastry out and line a 20cm/8in flan tin (pan). Preheat the oven to 190°C/375°F/Gas 5.

4 Mix the egg, sugar and melted butter together in a bowl. Stir the vinegar, currants and walnuts into the egg mixture.

5 Pour the mixture into the pastry case (pie shell) and bake in the preheated oven for 30 minutes.

6 Remove from the oven when thoroughly cooked, take out of the flan tin and leave to cool on a wire rack for at least 30 minutes. Serve on its own or with a dollop of fresh cream.

Blackberry Tart

Bake this easy tart when blackberries are in season.

Serves 6
500g/1¼lb/5 cups blackberries
115g/4oz/generous ½ cup caster (superfine) sugar
250g/9oz ready-made puff pastry
50g/2oz/½ cup icing (confectioners') sugar
whipped cream, to serve

1 Preheat the oven to 220°C/425°F/Gas 7. Wash the berries and mix with the caster sugar in a bowl. Roll out the pastry to about 3mm/⅛in thick and trim to a circle.

2 Mark a border about 2cm/1in from the outside of the circle to create a crust. Spread the fruit in the marked inner circle. Bake in the oven for 15 minutes. Dust with the icing sugar and serve hot with a large dollop of whipped cream.

Blueberry and Almond Tart

This is a cheat's version of a sweet almond tart and the result is superb. Whisked egg whites and grated marzipan cook to form a light sponge under a tangy topping of contrasting blueberries.

Serves 6
250g/9oz shortcrust pastry
175g/6oz/generous 1 cup white marzipan
4 large (US extra large) egg whites
130g/4½oz/generous 1 cup blueberries

1 Preheat the oven to 200°C/400°F/Gas 6. Roll out the pastry and use to line a 23cm/9in round, loose-based flan tin (pan). Bake blind for 15 minutes. Reduce the oven temperature to 180°C/350°F/Gas 4.

2 Grate the marzipan. Whisk the egg whites until stiff. Sprinkle half the marzipan over them and fold in. Then fold in the rest. Turn the mixture into the pastry case (pie shell) and spread evenly. Sprinkle the blueberries over and bake for 20–25 minutes, until just set. Cool for 10 minutes before serving.

Border Tart Energy 312kcal/1307kJ; Protein 3.4g; Carbohydrate 41.1g, of which sugars 41g; Fat 16.1g, of which saturates 7.3g; Cholesterol 74mg; Calcium 54mg; Fibre 0.8g; Sodium 99mg.
Blackberry Tart Energy 285kcal/1198kJ; Protein 3.2g; Carbohydrate 48.4g, of which sugars 33.5g; Fat 10g, of which saturates 4.7g; Cholesterol 24mg; Calcium 64mg; Fibre 3.5g; Sodium 133mg.
Blueberry Tart Energy 321kcal/1347kJ; Protein 6g; Carbohydrate 42.3g, of which sugars 22.3g; Fat 15.4g, of which saturates 4g; Cholesterol 6mg; Calcium 56mg; Fibre 1.8g; Sodium 212mg.

Blueberry and Coffee Flan

A lemon pastry case is filled with a sweet filling, dotted with blueberries.

Serves 6
30ml/2 tbsp ground coffee
45ml/3 tbsp milk
50g/2oz/¼ cup unsalted (sweet) butter
50g/2oz/¼ cup caster (superfine) sugar
1 egg
115g/4oz/1 cup ground almonds
15ml/1 tbsp plain (all-purpose) flour, sifted
225g/8oz/2 cups blueberries
30ml/2 tbsp jam
15ml/1 tbsp brandy

For the pastry
175g/6oz/1½ cups plain (all-purpose) flour
115g/4oz/½ cup unsalted (sweet) butter or margarine
25g/1oz/2 tbsp caster (superfine) sugar
finely grated rind of ½ lemon
15ml/1 tbsp chilled water

1 Preheat the oven to 190°C/375°F/Gas 5. To make the pastry, sift the flour into a bowl and rub in the butter. Stir in the sugar and lemon rind, then add the water and mix to a firm dough. Wrap in clear film (plastic wrap) and chill for 20 minutes.

2 Roll out the pastry on a lightly floured work surface and use to line a 23cm/9in loose-based flan tin (pan). Line the pastry with baking parchment and baking beans and bake for about 10 minutes. Remove the paper and beans and bake for a further 10 minutes. Remove from the oven.

3 Meanwhile, make the filling. Put the ground coffee in a bowl. Bring the milk almost to the boil, then pour over the coffee and leave to infuse for 4 minutes. Cream the butter and sugar until pale. Beat in the egg, then add the almonds and flour. Finely strain in the coffee-flavoured milk and fold in.

4 Spread the coffee mixture into the pastry case (pie shell). Sprinkle the blueberries over and push down slightly. Bake for 30 minutes, until firm, covering with foil after 20 minutes.

5 Heat the jam and brandy in a small pan until melted. Brush over the flan and remove from the tin.

Summer Berry Tart

A classic vanilla-flavoured custard tart topped with luscious berry fruits.

Serves 6–8
3 egg yolks
50g/2oz/¼ cup caster (superfine) sugar
30ml/2 tbsp cornflour (cornstarch)
30ml/2 tbsp plain (all-purpose) flour
5ml/1 tsp vanilla extract
300ml/½ pint/1¼ cups milk
150ml/¼ pint/⅔ cup double (heavy) cream
800g/1¾lb/4½–5 cups mixed summer berries, such as raspberries, blueberries, loganberries or boysenberries
60ml/4 tbsp redcurrant jelly
30ml/2 tbsp raspberry liqueur

For the pastry
185g/6½oz/1⅔ cups plain (all-purpose) flour
pinch of salt
115g/4oz/½ cup butter, diced
1 egg yolk
30ml/2 tbsp chilled water

1 Sift the flour and salt into a bowl. Rub in the butter. Mix the egg yolk with the chilled water and sprinkle over the dry ingredients. Mix to a firm dough. Put the dough on to a lightly floured surface and knead for a few seconds. Wrap in clear film (plastic wrap) and chill for 30 minutes. Roll out the pastry and use to line a 25cm/10in petal-shaped flan tin (pan) or a 23cm/9in round pan. Wrap in clear film and chill.

2 Put a baking sheet in the oven and preheat to 200°C/400°F/Gas 6. Prick the base of the pastry, line with foil and baking beans and bake for 15 minutes. Remove the foil and beans and bake for 10 minutes more. Leave to cool.

3 Beat the egg yolks, sugar, cornflour, flour and vanilla together. Bring the milk to the boil in a pan. Pour on to the egg mixture, and whisk. Pour the custard into the cleaned pan and cook over a low heat, stirring. Return to a clean bowl, cover with clear film and set aside. Whip the cream until thick, then fold into the custard. Spoon the custard into the pastry case (pie shell) and spread out.

4 Arrange the fruit on top of the custard. Heat the redcurrant jelly and liqueur together until melted. Allow to cool, then brush over the fruit. Serve the tart within 3 hours of assembling.

Blueberry Tart Energy 523Kcal/2180kJ; Protein 8.9g; Carbohydrate 44.9g, of which sugars 20.2g; Fat 34.8g, of which saturates 15.6g; Cholesterol 91mg; Calcium 132mg; Fibre 3.6g; Sodium 188mg.
Summer Tart Energy 432kcal/1807kJ; Protein 6.7g; Carbohydrate 47.6g, of which sugars 21.8g; Fat 25.7g, of which saturates 14.6g; Cholesterol 160mg; Calcium 130mg; Fibre 2g; Sodium 150mg..

Glazed Prune Tart

Here, plump prunes add a wonderful taste and texture.

Serves 8

225g/8oz/1 cup prunes
60ml/4 tbsp brandy or kirsch
175g/6oz/1½ cups plain (all-purpose) flour
115g/4oz/½ cup butter, diced
25g/1oz/2 tbsp caster (superfine) sugar
2 egg yolks
60ml/4 tbsp apricot jam and 15ml/1 tbsp brandy or kirsch, to glaze

For the filling
150ml/¼ pint/⅔ cup double (heavy) cream
150ml/¼ pint/⅔ cup milk
1 vanilla pod
3 eggs
50g/2oz/¼ cup caster (superfine) sugar

1 Put the prunes in a bowl with the brandy or kirsch and leave for about 4 hours until most of the liqueur has been absorbed. To make the pastry, sift the flour into a bowl. Add the butter, and rub in with the fingertips. Stir in the sugar and egg yolks and mix to a dough. Wrap and chill for 30 minutes.

2 Preheat the oven to 200°C/400°F/Gas 6. Roll out the pastry and use to line a 24–25cm/9½–10in loose-based flan tin. Line with baking parchment and fill with baking beans if you have them. Bake for 15 minutes. Remove the beans and paper and bake for a further 5 minutes. Arrange the prunes in the pastry case (pie shell), reserving any liqueur left in the bowl.

3 For the filling, put the cream and milk in a pan with the vanilla pod and bring to the boil. Turn off the heat and leave the mixture to infuse for 15 minutes.

4 Whisk together the eggs and sugar in a bowl. Remove the vanilla pod from the cream and return the cream to the boil. Pour over the eggs and sugar, whisking to make a smooth custard. Cool slightly then pour the custard over the prunes. Bake for about 25 minutes until the filling is just set.

5 Press the apricot jam through a sieve (strainer) into a small pan. Add the liqueur and heat through gently. Use to glaze the tart. Serve warm or cold, dusted with icing sugar.

Prune and Armagnac Tart

Almond-and-apricot-stuffed prunes paired with armagnac and crisp orange pastry make for a superb sweet.

Serves 4–6

225g/8oz/2 cups plain (all-purpose) flour
115g/4oz/½ cup margarine, diced
10ml/2 tsp grated orange rind

For the filling
75g/3oz almond paste
3 dried apricots, finely chopped
12 ready-to-eat prunes, pitted
2 eggs, beaten
150ml/¼ pint/⅔ cup single (light) cream
175g/6oz/1 cup soft dark brown sugar
45ml/3 tbsp armagnac

1 Sift the flour into a mixing bowl. Rub in the margarine until the mixture resembles fine breadcrumbs, then stir in the grated orange rind. Add enough cold water to make a soft dough. Wrap in clear film (plastic wrap) and chill for 1 hour.

2 Roll out the pastry on a floured surface and use it to line a 20cm/8in flan tin (pan). Line with foil and fill with baking beans, then bake blind for 10 minutes. Set the pastry case (pie shell) aside. Preheat the oven to 200°C/400°F/Gas 6.

3 Make the filling. Knead the almond paste with the chopped apricots on a clean work surface.

4 Press a little of the apricot and almond paste mixture into each pitted prune. When all the prunes have been filled, arrange them in the pastry case.

5 In a small bowl, combine the eggs and cream with half the sugar. Mix well and stir in the armagnac. Pour the mixture over the prunes, sprinkle the remaining sugar over the top and bake for 25–30 minutes. Serve hot or warm.

Cook's Tip

Fill a jar with ready-to-eat dried fruits, cover with armagnac or eau de vie and leave for a few days, to make a sauce that tastes superb with ice cream or yogurt.

Glazed Prune Tart Energy 329kcal1380 kJ; Protein 7g; Carbohydrate 38g, of which sugars 18g; Fat 16g, of which saturates 8g; Cholesterol 148mg; Calcium 110mg; Fibre 4.8g; Sodium 155mg.
Armagnac Tart Energy 525kcal/2206kJ; Protein 5.9g; Carbohydrate 74.8g, of which sugars 46.2g; Fat 22.7g, of which saturates 13.2g; Cholesterol 55mg; Calcium 107mg; Fibre 3g; Sodium 131mg.

Exotic Fruit Tranche

This is a good way to make the most of a small selection of exotic fruit.

Serves 8

175g/6oz/1½ cups plain (all-purpose) flour
50g/2oz/¼ cup butter
25g/1oz/2 tbsp white vegetable fat
50g/2oz/¼ cup caster (superfine) sugar
2 egg yolks
about 15ml/1 tbsp water
double (heavy) cream, to serve

For the filling

150ml/¼ pint/⅔ cup double (heavy) cream
250g/9oz/generous 1 cup mascarpone
25g/1oz/2 tbsp icing (confectioners') sugar, sifted
grated rind of 1 orange
450g/1lb/3 cups prepared fruits, such as fig, mango, papaya, star fruit, kiwi fruit and blackberries
90ml/6 tbsp apricot jam, strained
15ml/1 tbsp white or coconut rum
115g/4oz/scant ½ cup apricot jam, strained and warmed

1 Sift the flour into a bowl and rub in the butter and fat until it resembles fine breadcrumbs. Stir in the caster sugar. Add the egg yolks and enough cold water to make a soft dough.

2 Thinly roll out the pastry between two sheets of clear film (plastic wrap) and use the pastry to line a 35 x 12cm/14 x 4½in fluted tranche tin or a 23cm/9in flan tin (pan). Allow the excess pastry to hang over the edge. Chill for 30 minutes.

3 Preheat the oven to 200°C/400°F/Gas 6. Prick the base of the pastry case (pie shell) and line with baking parchment and baking beans. Bake for 10–12 minutes. Lift out the paper and beans and return the pastry case to the oven for 5 minutes.

4 Trim off the excess pastry and brush the inside of the case with the warmed apricot jam. Cool on a wire rack.

5 Make the filling. Whip the cream to soft peaks, then stir it into the mascarpone with the icing sugar and orange rind. Spread in the cooled pastry case and top with the prepared fruits.

6 Warm the apricot jam with the rum and drizzle or brush over the fruits to make a glaze. Serve with cream.

Fresh Fig Filo Tart

Figs cook wonderfully well and taste superb in this filo pastry tart – the riper the figs, the better.

Serves 6–8

5 sheets of filo pastry, each 35 x 25cm/14 x 10in, thawed if frozen
25g/1oz/2 tbsp butter, melted, plus extra for greasing
6 fresh figs, cut into wedges
75g/3oz/⅔ cup plain (all-purpose) flour
75g/3oz/6 tbsp caster (superfine) sugar
4 eggs
450ml/¾ pint/scant 2 cups milk
2.5ml/½ tsp almond extract
15ml/1 tbsp icing (confectioners') sugar, for dusting
whipped cream or Greek (US strained plain) yogurt, to serve

1 Preheat the oven to 190°C/375°F/Gas 5. Grease a 25 x 16cm/10 x 6¼in baking tin (pan) with butter. Brush each filo sheet in turn with melted butter and use to line the prepared tin.

2 Using scissors, cut off any excess pastry, leaving a little overhanging the edge. Arrange the figs in the filo case.

3 Sift the flour into a large mixing bowl and stir in the caster sugar. Add in the eggs and a little of the milk and whisk until the mixture is smooth.

4 Gradually whisk in the remaining milk and the almond extract. Pour the mixture over the figs; bake for 1 hour or until the batter has set and is golden.

5 Remove the tart from the oven and allow it to cool in the tin on a wire rack for 10 minutes. Dust with the icing sugar and serve with whipped cream or Greek yogurt.

Cook's Tip

Filo pastry dries out quickly, so keep the sheets not currently being used covered under a clean damp dish towel. Also, work as quickly as possible. If the filo should turn dry and brittle, simply brush it with melted butter to moisten.

Fruit Tranche Energy 429Kcal/1801kJ; Protein 6.4g; Carbohydrate 53.3g, of which sugars 36.9g; Fat 22.2g, of which saturates 12.7g; Cholesterol 99mg; Calcium 105mg; Fibre 2.1g; Sodium 136mg.
Fresh Fig Tart Energy 213Kcal/900kJ; Protein 5.8g; Carbohydrate 36.7g, of which sugars 20g; Fat 5.9g, of which saturates 2.5g; Cholesterol 102mg; Calcium 89mg; Fibre 1.8g; Sodium 65mg.

Date and Almond Tart

Fresh dates are delicious in a tart when teamed with a sponge filling.

Serves 6

90g/3½oz/scant ½ cup butter
90g/3½oz/scant ½ cup caster (superfine) sugar
1 egg, beaten
90g/3½oz/scant 1 cup ground almonds
30ml/2 tbsp plain (all-purpose) flour
30ml/2 tbsp orange flower water
12–13 fresh dates, halved and pitted
60ml/4 tbsp apricot jam

For the pastry

175g/6oz/1½ cups plain (all-purpose) flour
75g/3oz/6 tbsp butter, diced
1 egg
15ml/1 tbsp chilled water

1 Preheat the oven to 200°C/400°F/Gas 6 and place a baking sheet in it. To make the pastry, sift the flour into a bowl, then rub or cut in the butter until the mixture resembles fine breadcrumbs. Add the egg and water, then work to a dough. Wrap in clear film (plastic wrap) and chill for 20 minutes.

2 Roll out the pastry on a lightly floured surface and use to line a 20cm/8in flan tin (pan). Prick the base with a fork, then chill in the refrigerator until required.

3 Cream the butter and sugar in a small mixing bowl with a wooden spoon until light, then beat in the egg. Stir in the ground almonds, flour and 15ml/1 tbsp of the orange flower water and mix thoroughly.

4 Spread the almond filling evenly over the base of the pastry case (pie shell). Arrange the dates, cut side down, on the mixture. Bake the tart on the hot baking sheet for about 10–15 minutes, then lower the oven to 180°C/350°F/Gas 4. Bake for 15 minutes more, or until pale golden and set.

5 Transfer the tart to a wire rack to cool. In a small pan, gently heat the apricot jam, then press through a sieve (strainer) into a bowl. Stir the remaining orange flower water into the jam. Lightly brush the apricot glaze over the top of the tart and serve at room temperature.

Baked Fruit Flan

Crisp pastry, juicy baked fruit and a delectable creamy yogurt and almond topping make this flan a family treat.

Serves 6

115g/4oz/1 cup wholemeal (whole-wheat) flour
50g/2oz/½ cup gram flour
50g/2oz/4 tbsp low-fat spread
about 45ml/3 tbsp cold water

For the filling and topping

15ml/1 tbsp liquid pear and apple concentrate
1 Bramley cooking apple
2 large oranges
3 kiwi fruit
300ml/½ pint/1¼ cups creamy Greek (US strained plain) yogurt
15ml/1 tbsp browned flaked (sliced) almonds

1 Preheat the oven to 180°C/350°F/Gas 4. Mix the wholemeal and gram flours in a large mixing bowl and rub in the low-fat spread with fingertips until the mixture resembles coarse breadcrumbs. Add just enough cold water to make a dough.

2 Roll out the pastry on a lightly floured surface and use it to line a 20cm/8in round flan dish. Prick the base of the pastry case with a fork, line it with foil and add a layer of baking beans.

3 Bake blind for 15 minutes, then remove the foil and beans. Bake for 10 minutes more, until crisp. Remove the pastry case (pie shell) from the oven, but leave the oven on.

4 Spread the pear and apple concentrate on the bottom of the pastry case. Peel and slice the apple, oranges and kiwi fruit. Arrange the fruit in the pastry case, cover with foil and bake for 20 minutes more. Leave to cool slightly. Spoon the yogurt over the fruit, sprinkle the flaked almonds over, and serve.

Cook's Tip

To brown the almonds, spread them out in a grill (broiler) pan and place them under medium heat. Cook them until they are golden brown, shaking the pan frequently to make sure they brown on all sides. The process only takes a few minutes at most, so watch them closely in case they burn.

Date Tart Energy 618kcal/2587kJ; Protein 10g; Carbohydrate 73g, of which sugars 47g; Fat 34g, of which saturates 16g; Cholesterol 136mg; Calcium 117mg; Fibre 5.6g; Sodium 208mg.
Baked Fruit Flan Energy 249kcal/1047kJ; Protein 9.8g; Carbohydrate 30.7g, of which sugars 15g; Fat 10.4g, of which saturates 4.3g; Cholesterol 9mg; Calcium 127mg; Fibre 5.3g; Sodium 97mg.

Chocolate and Date Filo Coil

Experience the allure of the Middle East with this delectable dessert. Crisp filo pastry conceals a chocolate and rose water filling studded with delicious dates and almonds.

Serves 6

275g/10oz filo pastry
50g/2oz/¼ cup butter, melted
icing (confectioners') sugar, unsweetened cocoa powder and ground cinnamon, for dusting

For the filling

75g/3oz/6 tbsp butter
115g/4oz dark (bittersweet) chocolate, broken up into pieces
115g/4oz/1⅓ cups ground almonds
115g/4oz/⅔ cup chopped dates
75g/3oz/⅔ cup icing (confectioners') sugar
10ml/2 tsp rose water
2.5ml/½ tsp ground cinnamon

1 Preheat the oven to 180°C/350°F/Gas 4. Grease a 22cm/8½in round cake tin (pan). To make the filling, melt the butter with the chocolate in a heatproof bowl set over a pan of barely simmering water, then remove from the heat and stir in the remaining ingredients to make a thick paste. Leave to cool.

2 Lay one sheet of filo on a clean, flat surface. Brush with melted butter, then lay a second sheet on top and brush with more butter.

3 On a board, roll a handful of the chocolate and almond mixture into a long sausage shape and place along one long edge of the layered filo. Roll up the pastry tightly around the filling to make a roll.

4 Fit the filo roll in the cake tin, in such a way that it sits snugly against the outer edge. Make more filo rolls in the same way, adding them to the tin from the outside towards the centre, until the coil fills the tin.

5 Brush the coil with the remaining melted butter. Bake for 30–35 minutes until the pastry is golden brown and crisp. Transfer the coil to a serving plate. Serve warm, dusted with icing sugar, cocoa and cinnamon.

Chocolate Lemon Tart

In this easy-to-make recipe, the chocolate-flavoured pastry is pressed into the tin rather than rolled out, helping to speed up the preparation. With a simple lemon filling, this is a great dessert for the busy cook.

Serves 8–10

175g/6oz/1½ cups plain (all-purpose) flour
10ml/2 tsp unsweetened cocoa powder
25g/1oz/¼ cup icing (confectioners') sugar
2.5ml/½ tsp salt
115g/4oz/½ cup unsalted (sweet) butter or margarine, plus extra for greasing
15ml/1 tbsp water

For the filling

225g/8oz/1 cup caster (superfine) sugar
6 eggs
grated rind of 2 lemons
175ml/6fl oz/¾ cup freshly squeezed lemon juice
175ml/6fl oz/¾ cup double (heavy) or whipping cream
chocolate curls, to decorate

1 Grease a 25cm/10in loose-based flan tin (pan). Sift the flour, cocoa, icing sugar and salt into a bowl. Set aside.

2 Melt the butter or margarine and water in a pan over low heat. Add the flour mixture and stir until the flour has absorbed all the liquid and the dough is smooth.

3 Press the dough evenly over the base and side of the prepared tin. Chill the pastry case (pie shell).

4 Preheat the oven to 190°C/375°F/Gas 5, and place a baking sheet inside to heat up. Make the filling. Whisk the caster sugar and eggs in a bowl until the sugar has dissolved. Add the lemon rind and juice and mix well. Stir in the cream. Taste and add more lemon juice or sugar if needed, for a sweet taste with a touch of tartness.

5 Pour the filling into the pastry shell and place the tin on the hot baking sheet. Bake for 20–25 minutes or until the filling is set. Cool the tart on a rack, then remove from the tin. Decorate with the chocolate curls and serve.

Chocolate Coil Energy 543Kcal/2267kJ; Protein 8.2g; Carbohydrate 55.4g, of which sugars 32.4g; Fat 33.6g, of which saturates 15g; Cholesterol 46mg; Calcium 108mg; Fibre 3.2g; Sodium 133mg.
Choc Lemon Tart Energy 379Kcal/1585kJ; Protein 6.1g; Carbohydrate 40.5g, of which sugars 27g; Fat 22.6g, of which saturates 12.9g; Cholesterol 163mg; Calcium 68mg; Fibre 0.7g; Sodium 127mg.

Velvety Mocha Tart

A creamy smooth filling tops a dark chocolate but light-textured base in this wondrous dessert, which is attractively decorated with cream and chocolate-coated coffee beans.

Serves 8

10ml/2 tsp instant espresso coffee
175g/6oz plain (semisweet) chocolate
25g/1oz dark (bittersweet) cooking chocolate
350ml/12fl oz/1½ cups whipping cream, slightly warmed
120ml/4fl oz/½ cup whipped cream, to decorate
chocolate-coated coffee beans, to decorate

For the base

150g/5oz/2½ cups crushed chocolate wafers
30ml/2 tbsp caster (superfine) sugar
65g/2½oz/5 tbsp butter

1 To make the base, place the sugar and butter in a large pan and heat until the butter is melted and the sugar has dissolved. Add the crushed chocolate wafers and mix well.

2 Press the mixture over the base and sides of a 23cm/9in pie dish. Place in the refrigerator to chill.

3 Dissolve the instant coffee in 30ml/2 tbsp just boiled water, then set aside to cool.

4 Melt the plain and bitter chocolates in the top of a double boiler or in a heatproof bowl over a pan of simmering water. Once the chocolate has melted, remove from the double boiler and set the base of the pan in cold water to cool.

5 Whip the cream in a large bowl until light and fluffy. Add the coffee and whip again until the cream just holds its shape.

6 When the chocolate has cooled to room temperature, fold it gently into the cream using a metal spoon.

7 Pour the filling into the wafer base and return to the refrigerator until firm. Decorate with piped whipped cream and chocolate-coated coffee beans just before serving.

Chocolate Chiffon Pie

Decorate this rich chocolate tart with chocolate curls for a pretty finish.

Serves 8

175g/6oz plain (semisweet) chocolate squares, chopped
25g/1oz dark (bittersweet) chocolate, chopped
250ml/8fl oz/1 cup milk
15ml/1 tbsp powdered gelatine
130g/4½oz/⅔ cup sugar
2 eggs, separated
5ml/1 tsp vanilla extract
350ml/12fl oz/1½ cups whipping cream
pinch of salt
whipped cream, to decorate

For the crust

75g/3oz/1½ cups digestive biscuit (graham cracker) crumbs
75g/3oz/6 tbsp butter, melted

1 Place a baking sheet in the oven and preheat to 180°C/350°F/Gas 4. Make the crust. Mix the biscuit crumbs and butter in a bowl. Press the crumbs evenly over the base and sides of a 23cm/9in pie tin (pan). Bake for 8 minutes. Allow to cool.

2 Grind the chocolate in a food processor or blender. Set aside. Place the milk in the top of a double boiler or in a heatproof bowl. Sprinkle over the gelatine. Let stand for 5 minutes to soften.

3 Set the top of the double boiler or heatproof bowl over hot water. Add 50g/2oz/¼ cup of the sugar, the chocolate and egg yolks. Stir until dissolved. Add the vanilla extract.

4 Place the top of the double boiler or the heatproof bowl in a bowl of ice and stir until the mixture reaches room temperature. Remove from the ice and set aside.

5 Whip the cream lightly. Set aside. With an electric whisk, beat the egg whites and salt until they hold soft peaks. Add the remaining sugar and beat only enough to blend. Fold a dollop of egg whites into the chocolate mixture, then pour back into the whites and gently fold in.

6 Fold in the cream and pour into the tin. Freeze for about 5 minutes until just set. If the centre sinks, fill with any remaining mixture. Chill for 3–4 hours. Decorate with whipped cream.

Mocha Tart Energy 507kcal/2103kJ; Protein 3.6g; Carbohydrate 30.3g, of which sugars 27g; Fat 42.1g, of which saturates 26.2g; Cholesterol 83mg; Calcium 71mg; Fibre 0.8g; Sodium 83mg.
Chocolate Chiffon Energy 509Kcal/2120kJ; Protein 5.5g; Carbohydrate 43.2g, of which sugars 37.8g; Fat 36.2g, of which saturates 21.7g; Cholesterol 121mg; Calcium 98mg; Fibre 0.8g; Sodium 158mg.

Chocolate Almond Meringue Pie

This dreamy dessert offers a velvety chocolate filling on a light orange pastry case, topped with fluffy meringue.

Serves 6

175g/6oz/1½ cups plain (all-purpose) flour
50g/2oz/⅓ cup ground rice
150g/5oz/10 tbsp unsalted (sweet) butter
finely grated rind of 1 orange
1 egg yolk
flaked almonds and melted chocolate, to decorate

For the filling

150g/5oz plain (semisweet) chocolate, broken into squares
50g/2oz/¼ cup unsalted (sweet) butter, softened
75g/3oz/6 tbsp caster (superfine) sugar
10ml/2 tsp cornflour (cornstarch)
4 egg yolks
75g/3oz/¾ cup ground almonds

For the meringue

3 egg whites
150g/5oz/¾ cup caster (superfine) sugar

1 Sift the flour and ground rice into a bowl. Rub in the butter to resemble breadcrumbs. Stir in the orange rind. Add the egg yolk; bring the dough together. Roll out and use to line a 23cm/9in round flan tin (pan). Chill for 30 minutes.

2 Preheat the oven to 190°C/375°F/Gas 5. Prick the pastry base all over with a fork, cover with baking parchment, weighed down with baking beans, and bake blind for 10 minutes. Remove the pastry case; take out the baking beans and paper.

3 Make the filling. Melt the chocolate in a heatproof bowl over hot water. Cream the butter with the sugar in a bowl, then beat in the cornflour and egg yolks. Fold in the almonds, then the chocolate. Spread in the pastry case. Bake for 10 minutes more.

4 Make the meringue. Whisk the egg whites until stiff, then whisk in half the sugar. Fold in the remaining sugar. Spoon the meringue over the filling, lifting with the spoon to form peaks. Reduce the oven temperature to 180°C/350°F/Gas 4 and bake the pie for 15–20 minutes or until the topping is pale gold.

5 Remove from the oven, cool for 10 minutes then serve sprinkled with almonds and drizzled with melted chocolate.

Chocolate Amaretto Nut Tart

A sophisticated tart, perfect to end a dinner party.

Serves 6–8

200g/7oz/1¾ cups dry amaretti
90g/3½oz/generous ½ cup blanched almonds
50g/2oz/⅓ cup blanched hazelnuts
45ml/3 tbsp caster (superfine) sugar
200g/7oz plain (semisweet) chocolate
45ml/3 tbsp milk
50g/2oz/¼ cup butter
45ml/3 tbsp amaretto liqueur
30ml/2 tbsp single (light) cream

For the pastry

225g/8oz/2 cups plain (all-purpose) flour
30ml/2 tbsp cocoa powder
115g/4oz/½ cup butter, diced
60ml/4 tbsp caster (superfine) sugar

1 Grease a shallow loose-based 23cm/9in flan tin (pan). Make the pastry by rubbing the butter into the flour and cocoa powder until it resembles breadcrumbs. Stir in the sugar, then enough cold water to form a dough. Chill for 30 minutes, then roll out the pastry on a lightly floured surface, and use it to line the tin. Prick the base with a fork and chill for 30 minutes.

2 Grind the amaretti in a blender or food processor. Transfer into a bowl. Set eight whole almonds aside and place the rest in the food processor or blender with the hazelnuts and sugar. Grind to a medium texture. Mix the nuts with the amarett.

3 Preheat the oven to 190°C/375°F/Gas 5. Slowly melt the chocolate with the milk and butter in the top of a double boiler or in a heatproof bowl over a pan of simmering water. Once the chocolate has melted, stir until smooth.

4 Pour the chocolate mixture into the dry ingredients and mix well. Add the liqueur or brandy and the cream.

5 Spread the filling evenly in the pastry case (pie shell). Bake for 35 minutes, or until the crust is golden brown and the filling has puffed up and is beginning to darken. Allow to cool to room temperature. Split the reserved almonds in half and use to decorate the tart.

Meringue Pie Energy 792Kcal/3312kJ; Protein 11.4g; Carbohydrate 87g, of which sugars 56g; Fat 46.4g, of which saturates 23.5g; Cholesterol 241mg; Calcium 128mg; Fibre 2.6g; Sodium 248mg.
Amaretto Tart Energy 644kcal/2685kJ; Protein 9.6g; Carbohydrate 56.4g, of which sugars 32g; Fat 42.4g, of which saturates 13.4g; Cholesterol 21mg; Calcium 122mg; Fibre 3g; Sodium 241mg.

Chocolate and Pine Nut Tart

Orange-flavoured pastry makes this tempting tart a real winner.

Serves 8

200g/7oz/1¾ cups plain (all-purpose) flour
50g/2oz/¼ cup caster (superfine) sugar
pinch of salt
grated rind of ½ orange
115g/4oz/½ cup unsalted (sweet) butter, cut into small pieces
3 egg yolks, lightly beaten
15–30ml/1–2 tbsp chilled water

For the filling
2 eggs
45ml/3 tbsp caster (superfine) sugar
grated rind of 1 orange
15ml/1 tbsp orange liqueur
250ml/8fl oz/1 cup whipping cream
115g/4oz plain (semisweet) chocolate, cut into small pieces
75g/3oz/¾ cup pine nuts, toasted

For the decoration
thinly pared rind of 1 orange
50g/2oz/¼ cup granulated sugar

1 Process the flour, sugar, salt and orange rind in a food processor, add the butter and process for 30 seconds. Add the egg yolks and pulse until the dough sticks together. If it is dry, gradually add the water. Knead, then wrap and chill for 2–3 hours.

2 Grease a 23cm/9in loose-based flan tin (pan). Roll out the dough on a floured surface into a 28cm/11in round. Ease it into the tin and roll a rolling pin over the edge to trim. Prick the base. Chill for 1 hour. Preheat the oven to 200°C/400°F/Gas 6.

3 Line the pastry with foil, fill with baking beans and bake blind for 5 minutes. Remove the foil and beans and bake for 5 minutes more, then cool. Lower the temperature to 180°C/350°F/Gas 4.

4 Beat the eggs, sugar, orange rind and liqueur in a bowl. Stir in the cream. Sprinkle the chocolate and pine nuts over the base. Pour in the filling. Bake for 20–30 minutes, until golden.

5 Make the decoration. Cut the orange rind into strips. Dissolve the sugar in 120ml/4fl oz/½ cup water over a medium heat, add the rind and boil for 5 minutes. Remove from the heat and stir in 15ml/1 tbsp cold water. Brush the orange syrup over the tart and decorate with the caramelized strips. Serve warm.

Chocolate Tiramisu Tart

This tart has an utterly delicious creamy filling.

Serves 12–16

115g/4oz/½ cup butter
15ml/1 tbsp coffee-flavoured liqueur
175g/6oz/1½ cups plain (all-purpose) flour
25g/1oz/¼ cup unsweetened cocoa powder plus extra for dusting
25g/1oz/¼ cup icing (confectioners') sugar
pinch of salt
2.5ml/½ tsp vanilla extract

For the chocolate layer
350ml/12fl oz/1½ cups double (heavy) cream
15ml/1 tbsp golden (light corn) syrup
115g/4oz plain (semisweet) chocolate, chopped into pieces
25g/1oz/2 tbsp unsalted (sweet) butter, cut into small pieces
30ml/2 tbsp coffee-flavoured liqueur

For the filling
250ml/8fl oz/1 cup whipping cream
350g/12oz/1½ cups mascarpone, at room temperature
45ml/3 tbsp icing sugar
45ml/3 tbsp cold espresso or strong black coffee
45ml/3 tbsp coffee-flavoured liqueur
90g/3½oz plain (semisweet) chocolate, grated

1 Grease a 23cm/9in springform tin (pan). To make the base, heat the butter and liqueur until the butter melts. Sift the flour, cocoa, icing sugar and salt into a bowl. Remove the butter from the heat, stir in the vanilla and add into the flour mixture to form a soft dough. Press in to the tin, and chill for 40 minutes.

2 Preheat the oven to 190°C/375°F/Gas 5. Bake the pastry case (pie shell) for 8–10 minutes. If the pastry puffs up, prick it with a fork and bake for 2–3 minutes more. Cool in the tin on a rack.

3 Mix the cream and syrup in a pan. Bring to a boil over medium heat. Off the heat, stir in the chocolate until melted. Beat in the butter and liqueur and pour into the pastry case. Cool and chill in the refrigerator.

4 Make the filling. In one bowl, whip the cream until soft peaks form; in another, beat the cheese until soft, then beat in icing sugar until smooth. Add the coffee, liqueur, cream and chocolate. Spoon into the pastry case, on top of the chocolate layer. Level the surface. Chill until ready to serve, dusted with cocoa.

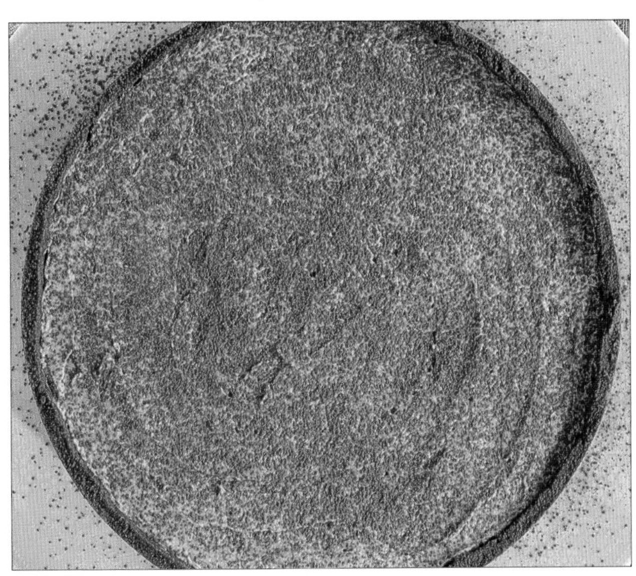

Chocolate Tart Energy 543Kcal/2261kJ; Protein 7.8g; Carbohydrate 42.7g, of which sugars 23.5g; Fat 38.6g, of which saturates 19.2g; Cholesterol 187mg; Calcium 84mg; Fibre 1.3g; Sodium 118mg.
Tiramisu Tart Energy 399Kcal/1657kJ; Protein 4.8g; Carbohydrate 24.4g, of which sugars 15.8g; Fat 30.9g, of which saturates 20.4g; Cholesterol 60mg; Calcium 49mg; Fibre 0.9g; Sodium 86mg.

Mississippi Mud Pie

This famous tart is the ultimate in chocolate desserts.

Serves 6–8

3 eggs, separated
20ml/4 tsp cornflour (cornstarch)
75g/3oz/6 tbsp sugar
400ml/14fl oz/1⅔ cups milk
150g/5oz plain (semisweet) chocolate, melted
5ml/1 tsp vanilla extract
15ml/1 tbsp powdered gelatine
45ml/3 tbsp water
30ml/2 tbsp dark rum
175ml/6fl oz/¾ cup double (heavy) cream, whipped
a few chocolate curls, to decorate

For the pastry

250g/9oz/2¼ cups plain (all-purpose) flour
150g/5oz/10 tbsp butter, diced
2 egg yolks
15–30ml/1–2 tbsp chilled water

1 Make the pastry. Sift the flour into a bowl. Rub in the butter until breadcrumbs form. Stir in the yolks with enough chilled water to make a soft dough. Roll out and use to line a deep 23cm/9in flan tin (pan). Chill for 30 minutes. Preheat the oven to 190°C/375°F/Gas 5. Prick the pastry, line with baking parchment and beans, and bake blind for 10 minutes. Remove the foil and beans, and return to the oven for 5 minutes until crisp and golden. Cool.

2 Mix the yolks, cornflour and 30ml/2 tbsp of the sugar in a bowl. In a pan, bring the milk almost to a boil, then beat into the egg mixture. Return to the cleaned pan and stir over low heat until the custard thickens. Pour half into a bowl.

3 Add the melted chocolate to the custard in the bowl. Mix in the vanilla extract. Spread in the pastry case (pie shell), cover to prevent a skin forming, cool, then chill until set. Add the gelatine to the water in a small bowl, leave until spongy, then place over a pan of simmering water until the gelatine dissolves. Stir into the remaining custard, with the rum.

4 Whisk the egg whites until stiff peaks form, whisk in the rest of the sugar, then fold into the gelatine and custard mix before it sets. Spoon over the chocolate custard to cover. Chill until set, then remove from the tin. Spread whipped cream over the top, decorate with chocolate curls and serve immediately.

Chocolate Truffle Tart

This luxurious tart has a rich choclate truffle filling.

Serves 12

350ml/12fl oz/1½ cups double (heavy) cream
350g/12oz plain (semisweet) chocolate, chopped
50g/2oz/4 tbsp unsalted butter, cut into small pieces
30ml/2 tbsp brandy
25g/1oz fine quality white or milk chocolate, melted
whipped cream for serving

For the pastry

115g/4oz/1 cup plain (all-purpose) flour
30g/1¼oz/⅓ cup unsweetened cocoa powder
50g/2oz/¼ cup caster (superfine) sugar
115g/4oz/½ cup butter, diced
1 egg yolk
15–30ml/1–2 tbsp iced water

1 Prepare the pastry. In a food processor, process the flour and cocoa with the sugar and salt. Add the butter and pulse until the mixture resembles coarse breadcrumbs. In a bowl, lightly beat the yolk with the iced water. Add to the flour mixture and pulse until the dough forms a ball. Turn out the dough on to a sheet of clear film, form into a flat disc. Wrap and chill for 1 hour.

2 Lightly grease a 23 cm/9 in tart tin (pan) with a removable base. Let the dough soften briefly, then roll it out between sheets of waxed paper or clear film and line the prepared tin. Prick with a fork. Chill for 1 hour. Preheat oven to 180°C/350°F/Gas 4. Line the tart with baking parchment and baking beans. Bake for 5–7 minutes, remove the paper and beans, and bake for 5–7 minutes more. Cool completely in the tin on a rack.

3 In a large pan bring the cream to the boil. Remove the pan from the heat and stir in the chocolate until melted. Stir in the butter and brandy. Strain into the cooled tart shell.

4 Spoon the melted chocolate into a paper piping bag and cut off the tip. Drop rounds of chocolate over the surface of the tart and use a skewer or toothpick to draw a point gently through the chocolate to produce a marbled effect. Chill for 2–3 hours, until set. Allow the tart to soften slightly at room temperature before serving with whipped cream.

Mud Pie Energy 571Kcal/2385kJ; Protein 9.4g; Carbohydrate 53.5g, of which sugars 22.7g; Fat 36.2g, of which saturates 21.2g; Cholesterol 196mg; Calcium 160mg; Fibre 1.3g; Sodium 180mg.
Truffle Tart Energy 474kcal/1969kJ; Protein 3.7g; Carbohydrate 32.5g, of which sugars 24.6g; Fat 36.8g, of which saturates 22.6g; Cholesterol 88mg; Calcium 48mg; Fibre 1.4g; Sodium 117mg.

White Chocolate and Mango Tart

Mango and white chocolate make a fabulous combination of flavours.

Serves 8

175g/6oz/1½ cups plain (all-purpose) flour
75g/3oz/1 cup desiccated (dry unsweetened) coconut
115g/4oz/½ cup butter, softened
30ml/2 tbsp caster (superfine) sugar
2 egg yolks
2.5ml/½ tsp almond extract
120ml/4fl oz/½ cup double (heavy) cream, whipped
1 large mango, peeled and sliced
whipped cream and toasted almonds, to decorate

For the filling

150g/5oz good-quality white chocolate, chopped finely
120ml/4fl oz/½ cup double (heavy) cream
75ml/5 tbsp cornflour (cornstarch)
15ml/1 tbsp plain (all-purpose) flour
50g/2oz/¼ cup sugar
350ml/12fl oz/1½ cups milk
5 egg yolks

1 Beat the flour, coconut, butter, sugar, egg yolks and almond extract in a bowl to form a soft dough. Grease a 23cm/9in flan tin (pan) with a removable base and press the pastry into the tin to line. Prick the base with a fork. Chill for 30 minutes.

2 Preheat the oven to 180°C/350°F/Gas 4. Line the pastry case (pie shell) with baking parchment; fill with baking beans and bake blind for 10 minutes. Remove the paper and beans and bake for a further 5–7 minutes. Cool in the tin on a wire rack.

3 Make the filling. In a small pan over low heat, melt the white chocolate with the cream, stirring until smooth. Combine the cornflour, plain flour and sugar in another pan. Gradually stir in the milk and cook gently, stirring constantly, until thickened.

4 Beat the egg yolks in a small bowl. Slowly stir in some of the hot milk mixture. Return the yolk mixture to the rest of the sauce in the pan, stirring. Bring to a gentle boil, stirring, until thickened. Stir in the melted chocolate. Cool, then fold in the whipped cream. Spoon half the custard into the pastry case and arrange the mango on top. Cover with the rest of the custard. Remove from the tin and decorate with piped cream and nuts before serving in slices.

Chocolate, Pear and Pecan Pie

Another great fruit and chocolate combination gives this classic pie a tempting new twist.

Serves 8–10

3 small pears, peeled
150ml/¼ pint/⅔ cup water
165g/5½oz/¾ cup caster (superfine) sugar
pared rind of 1 lemon
50g/2oz plain (semisweet) chocolate, broken into pieces
50g/2oz/¼ cup butter, diced
225g/8oz/scant ¾ cup golden (light corn) syrup
3 eggs, beaten
5ml/1 tsp vanilla extract
150g/5oz/1¼ cups pecan nuts, chopped

For the pastry

175g/6oz/1½ cups plain (all-purpose) flour
115g/4oz/½ cup butter, diced
25g/1oz/2 tbsp caster (superfine) sugar
1 egg yolk

1 Sift the flour into a bowl, rub in the butter and stir in the sugar. Add the egg yolk and enough water to mix to a dough. Knead lightly, wrap and chill for 30 minutes.

2 Roll out the pastry and use to line a 23cm/9in flan tin (pan). Chill for 20 minutes. Preheat the oven to 200°F/400°C/Gas 6. Line the pastry case (pie shell) with foil, fill with baking beans and bake for 10 minutes. Lift out the foil and beans and bake for 5 minutes more. Set aside to cool.

3 Halve and core the pears. Bring the water, 50g/2oz/1⁄4 cup of the sugar and the lemon rind to the boil. Add the pears, cover and simmer for 10 minutes. Remove the pears from the pan.

4 Melt the chocolate over simmering water, beat in the butter and set aside. Heat the remaining sugar and syrup until the sugar has dissolved. Bring to the boil and simmer for 2 minutes. Whisk the eggs into the chocolate mixture until combined, then whisk in the syrup mixture. Stir in the vanilla and nuts.

5 Slice the pear halves lengthways without cutting all the way through. Arrange them in the pastry case and pour in the nut mixture. Bake in the oven for about 25–30 minutes. Leave to cool and then serve sliced.

Mango Tart Energy 802Kcal/3336kJ; Protein 12.3g; Carbohydrate 57.3g, of which sugars 30.3g; Fat 59.8g, of which saturates 41.9g; Cholesterol 217mg; Calcium 256mg; Fibre 3.1g; Sodium 195mg.
Pear & Pecan Pie Energy 499Kcal/2090kJ; Protein 5.8g; Carbohydrate 59.9g, of which sugars 46.3g; Fat 28g, of which saturates 11g; Cholesterol 113mg; Calcium 68mg; Fibre 2.4g; Sodium 186mg.

Dark Chocolate and Hazelnut Tart

The hazelnut pastry tastes wonderful with a luxurious chocolate filling.

Serves 10

300ml/½ pint/1¼ cups double (heavy) cream
150ml/¼ pint/⅔ cup whole milk
150g/5oz dark (bittersweet) chocolate, chopped
4 eggs
50g/2oz/¼ cup caster (superfine) sugar
5ml/1 tsp vanilla extract
15ml/1 tbsp plain (all-purpose) flour
115g/4oz/1 cup hazelnuts, toasted
10ml/2 tsp icing (confectioners') sugar, for dusting

For the pastry

150g/5oz/1¼ cups plain (all-purpose) flour
40g/1½oz/3 tbsp caster (superfine) sugar
50g/2oz/½ cup ground hazelnuts
90g/3½oz/scant ½ cup butter

1 Make the pastry. Sift the flour, salt and sugar into a mixing bowl, then mix in the toasted hazelnuts. Rub in the butter until the mixture resembles breadcrumbs. Add enough water to mix to a firm dough. Wrap in plastic wrap and chill for 30 minutes. Roll out the pastry and line a 23cm/9in loose-based flan tin (pan). Trim the edges. Cover and chill.

2 Re-roll the pastry trimmings into a strip about 30cm/12in long. Cut into six strips, and make two plaits (braids) with three strips in each and form in a circle to fit the pie case. Place on a baking sheet lined with baking parchment, and chill.

3 Preheat to 200°C/400°F/Gas 6. Line the pastry case (pie shell) with baking parchment and baking beans and bake for 10 minutes. Remove the paper and beans and bake for a further 5 minutes. Bake the pastry plait for 10 minutes.

4 Pour the cream and milk into a pan and bring to the boil. Add the chocolate and melt. Whisk the eggs, sugar, vanilla and flour in a bowl. Whisk the hot chocolate cream into the egg mixture. Stir in the hazelnuts. Pour the chocolate and hazelnut mixture into the pastry case and bake for 25 minutes. Cool, remove from the tin, transfer to a serving plate and place the pastry rope on top of the tart, then dust with icing sugar.

Chocolate Cheesecake Tart

This double chocolate variation of the American classic is made with a crunchy cinnamon and chocolate base.

Serves 10–12

175g/6oz plain (semisweet) chocolate, chopped
115g/4oz dark (bittersweet) chocolate, chopped
1.2kg/2½lb/5 cups cream cheese, at room temperature
200g/7oz/1 cup caster (superfine) sugar
10ml/2 tsp vanilla extract
4 eggs, at room temperature
175ml/6fl oz/¾ cup sour cream

For the base

75g/3oz/1½ cups chocolate biscuit (cookie) crumbs
75g/3oz/6 tbsp butter, melted
2.5ml/½ tsp ground cinnamon

1 Preheat the oven to 180°C/350°F/Gas 4. Grease a 23cm/9in springform cake tin (pan).

2 Make the base. Mix the chocolate biscuit crumbs with the butter and cinnamon. Press evenly over the bottom of the tin.

3 Melt the plain and dark chocolate in the top of a double boiler, or in a heatproof bowl set over a pan of simmering water. Set aside.

4 With an electric whisk, beat the cream cheese until smooth, then beat in the sugar and vanilla extract.

5 Add the eggs, one at a time, scraping the bowl with a spatula when necessary.

6 Add the sour cream to the cheese mixture, then stir in the melted chocolate, mixing well. Pour into the tin. Bake for 1 hour. Allow to cool, then remove from the tin. Chill before serving.

Variation
For a chocolate-orange cheesecake, replace the vanilla extract with finely grated orange rind.

Hazelnut Tart Energy 544Kcal/2261kJ; Protein 8.8g; Carbohydrate 35.6g, of which sugars 22.5g; Fat 41.8g, of which saturates 19.2g; Cholesterol 158mg; Calcium 105mg; Fibre 2g; Sodium 106mg.
Cheesecake Energy 717kcal/2972kJ; Protein 5.2g; Carbohydrate 37.5g, of which sugars 34.9g; Fat 61.8g, of which saturates 38.4g; Cholesterol 118mg; Calcium 131mg; Fibre 0.7g; Sodium 362mg.

Baked Chocolate Cheesecake

This rich chocolate cheesecake has a crispy chocolate pastry base and a delicious, creamy filling – perfect for chocolate lovers.

Serves 8–10

75g/3oz/ ¾ cup plain (all-purpose) flour
45ml/3 tbsp unsweetened cocoa powder
75g/3oz/½ cup semolina
50g/2oz/¼ cup caster (superfine) sugar
115g/4oz/½ cup unsalted (sweet) butter, softened

For the filling

225g/8oz/1 cup cream cheese
120ml/4fl oz/½ cup natural (plain) yogurt
2 eggs, beaten
75g/3oz/6 tbsp caster (superfine) sugar
finely grated rind of 1 lemon
75g/3oz/½ cup raisins
45ml/3 tbsp plain (semisweet) chocolate chips

For the topping

75g/3oz plain chocolate, chopped
30ml/2 tbsp golden (light corn) syrup
40g/1½oz/3 tbsp butter

1 Preheat oven to 150°C/300°F/Gas 2. Sift the flour and cocoa powder together and stir in the semolina and sugar. Using your fingertips, rub the butter in until it makes a firm dough.

2 Press the dough into the base of a 22cm/8½in springform tin (pan). Prick all over with a fork and bake in the oven for 15 minutes. Remove the tin but leave the oven on.

3 Make the filling. In a large bowl, beat the cream cheese with the yogurt, eggs and sugar until evenly mixed. Stir in the lemon rind, raisins and chocolate chips.

4 Smooth the cream cheese mixture over the chocolate shortbread base and bake for a further 35–45 minutes or until the filling is pale gold and just set. Cool in the tin on a wire rack.

5 For the topping, combine the chocolate, syrup and butter in a heatproof bowl over a pan of simmering water. Heat gently, stirring, until melted. Pour over the cheesecake and let until set.

6 Remove the sides of the tin and carefully slide the cheesecake on to a serving plate. Serve sliced, with single cream, if you like.

Chocolate Ricotta Pie

This is a chocolate-enriched version of an Italian favourite.

Serves 6

225g/8oz/2 cups plain (all-purpose) flour
30ml/2 tbsp unsweetened cocoa powder
60ml/4 tbsp caster (superfine) sugar
115g/4oz/½ cup unsalted (sweet) butter
60ml/4 tbsp dry sherry

For the filling

2 egg yolks
115g/4oz/½ cup caster (superfine) sugar
500g/1¼lb/2½ cups ricotta cheese
finely grated rind of 1 lemon
90ml/6 tbsp dark chocolate chips
75ml/5 tbsp chopped mixed peel
45ml/3 tbsp chopped angelica

1 Sift the flour and cocoa into a bowl, then stir in the sugar. Rub in the butter using your fingertips, then work in the sherry to make a firm dough.

2 Preheat oven to 200°C/400°F/Gas 6. Roll out three-quarters of the pastry on a lightly floured surface and line a 24cm/9½in loose-based flan tin (pan).

3 Make the filling. Beat the egg yolks and sugar in a bowl, then beat in the ricotta to mix thoroughly. Stir in the lemon rind, chocolate chips, mixed peel and angelica.

4 Scrape the ricotta mixture into the pastry case and level the surface. Roll out the remaining pastry and cut into strips. Arrange these in a lattice over the pie.

5 Bake for 15 minutes. Lower the oven temperature to 180°C/350°F/Gas 4 and cook for a further 30–35 minutes, until golden brown and firm. Cool the pie in the tin, and then serve at room temperature.

Variation

If you don't like mixed peel, replace this and the angelica with the same amount of raisins instead.

Cheesecake Energy 784kcal/3253kJ; Protein 6.2g; Carbohydrate 43.8g, of which sugars 37.1g; Fat 66.2g, of which saturates 40.8g; Cholesterol 127mg; Calcium 145mg; Fibre 1.1g; Sodium 433mg.
Chocolate Pie Energy 701kcal/2938kJ; Protein 14.2g; Carbohydrate 83.4g, of which sugars 54.1g; Fat 35.6g, of which saturates 21.3g; Cholesterol 144mg; Calcium 115mg; Fibre 3g; Sodium 223mg.

Chocolate, Banana and Toffee Pie

As an alternative to the coffee topping, just decorate the pie with whipped cream and extra banana slices.

Serves 6

65g/2½oz/5 tbsp unsalted (sweet) butter, melted
250g/9oz milk chocolate digestive biscuits (graham crackers), crushed
chocolate curls, to decorate

For the filling

400g/14oz can sweetened condensed milk
150g/5oz plain (semisweet) chocolate, chopped
120ml/4fl oz/½ cup crème fraîche
15ml/1 tbsp golden (light corn) syrup

For the topping

2 bananas
250ml/8fl oz/1 cup crème fraîche
10ml/2 tsp strong black coffee

1 Mix the butter with the biscuit crumbs. Press on to the base and sides of a 23cm/9in loose-based flan tin (pan). Chill.

2 Make the filling. Place the unopened can of condensed milk in a deep pan of boiling water, making sure that it is completely covered. Lower the heat and simmer, covered for 2 hours, topping up the water as necessary. The can must remain covered at all times.

3 Remove the pan from the heat and set aside, covered, until the can has cooled down completely in the water. Do not attempt to open the can until it is completely cold.

4 Gently melt the chocolate with the crème fraîche and golden syrup in a heatproof bowl over a pan of simmering water. Stir in the caramelized condensed milk and beat together until thoroughly combined. Pour the chocolate filling into the biscuit crust and spread it evenly.

5 Slice the bananas evenly and arrange them over the chocolate filling in an attractive pattern.

6 Stir the crème fraîche and coffee together in a bowl, then spoon the mixture over the bananas. Sprinkle the chocolate curls on top. Serve at room temperature.

Rich Chocolate-Berry Tart

Berries and chocolate have a natural affinity, showcased in this dense, rich tart.

Serves 10

115g/4oz/½ cup butter, softened
90g/3½oz/½ cup caster (superfine) sugar
50g/2oz/½ cup unsweetened cocoa powder
215g/7½oz/scant 2 cups plain (all-purpose) flour

For the chocolate filling

475ml/16fl oz/2 cups double (heavy) cream
150g/5oz/½ cup seedless blackberry preserve
225g/8oz plain (semisweet) chocolate, chopped
25g/1oz/2 tbsp butter

For the blackberry sauce

225g/8oz blackberries
15ml/1 tbsp lemon juice
25g/1oz/2 tbsp caster (superfine) sugar
30ml/2 tbsp blackberry liqueur
450g/1lb fresh blackberries, for topping

1 Make the pastry. Process the butter and sugar in a food processor. Add the cocoa and flour and blend. Wrap in clear film (plastic wrap), shape into a flat disc and chill for 1 hour.

2 Grease a 23cm/9in loose-based flan tin (pan). Roll the dough between two sheets of clear film. Place in the tin pressing on to the base and sides, then cut off any overhang. Prick the base and chill for 1 hour. Preheat the oven to 180°C/350°F/Gas 4. Line with baking parchment and fill with baking beans. Bake in the oven for 10 minutes, then lift out the paper and beans and bake for 5 minutes more. Place on a wire rack to cool.

3 Make the filling. Place the cream and blackberry preserve in a pan and bring to the boil. Remove from the heat and add the chocolate, stirring until smooth. Stir in the butter then strain into the pastry. Leave to cool completely.

4 Make the sauce. In a food processor, combine the berries, lemon juice and sugar and process until smooth. Strain into a small bowl and add the blackberry-flavour liqueur. To serve, remove the tart from the tin. Place on a serving plate and arrange the berries on top. Serve the sauce separately.

Banana & Toffee Energy 900Kcal/3758kJ; Protein 11.5g; Carbohydrate 90g, of which sugars 73.2g; Fat 57.4g, of which saturates 35.8g; Cholesterol 139mg; Calcium 275mg; Fibre 1.8g; Sodium 368mg.
Rich Berry Tart Energy 653kcal/2722kJ; Protein 6g; Carbohydrate 58.9g, of which sugars 41.8g; Fat 44.9g, of which saturates 27.7g; Cholesterol 96mg; Calcium 95mg; Fibre 3.5g; Sodium 152mg.

Chocolate Apricot Linzer Tart

This makes an excellent dinner party dessert.

Serves 10–12

50g/2oz/⅓ cup blanched almonds
115g/4oz/generous ½ cup caster (superfine) sugar
175g/6oz/1½ cups plain (all-purpose) flour
30ml/2 tbsp unsweetened cocoa powder
5ml/1 tsp ground cinnamon
2.5ml/½ tsp salt
5ml/1 tsp grated orange rind
225g/8oz/1 cup unsalted (sweet) butter, cut into small pieces
75g/3oz/½ cup chocolate chips
icing (confectioners') sugar, for dusting

For the apricot filling

350g/12oz/1½ cups ready-to-eat dried apricots
120ml/4fl oz/½ cup orange juice
40g/1½oz/3 tbsp sugar
50g/2oz/2 tbsp apricot jam
2.5ml/½ tsp almond extract

1 For the filling, simmer the apricots, orange juice and 175ml/6fl oz/¾ cup water, stirring, until the liquid is absorbed. Stir in the remaining ingredients. Strain into a bowl, cool, cover and chill.

2 Grease a 28cm/11in loose-based flan tin (pan). Grind the almonds and half the sugar in a food processor. Sift in the flour, cocoa, cinnamon and salt, add the remaining sugar and process. Add the rind and butter. Process until the mixture resembles breadcrumbs. Add 30ml/2 tbsp iced water and pulse, adding a little more water until the dough holds together.

3 Turn out and knead the dough on a lightly floured surface. Halve and press one piece on to the base and sides of the tin. Prick the base and chill for 20 minutes. Roll out the rest of the dough between sheets of clear film (plastic wrap) to a 28cm/11in round, slide on to a baking sheet and chill for 30 minutes.

4 Preheat the oven to 180°C/350°F/Gas 4. Spread the filling in the pastry case (pie shell) and sprinkle with chocolate chips. Cut the dough round into 1cm/½in strips. Leave to soften, then place the strips over the filling, about 1cm/½in apart, to form a lattice. Press the ends on to the side of the tart and trim of the excess. Bake in the oven for 35–40 minutes, until golden. Cool on a rack and dust with icing sugar.

Pear and Chocolate Tartlets

Puff pastry is topped with spicy poached pears and served with chocolate sauce.

Serves 6

3 firm pears, peeled
450ml/¾ pint/scant 2 cups water
strip of thinly pared orange rind
1 vanilla pod (bean)
1 bay leaf
50g/2oz/¼ cup granulated sugar
350g/12oz puff pastry
40g/1½oz/⅓ cup unsweetened cocoa powder
75ml/5 tbsp double (heavy) cream
15g/½oz/1 tbsp butter, softened
15ml/1 tbsp soft light brown sugar
25g/1oz/¼ cup walnuts, chopped
1 egg, beaten
15g/½ oz/1 tbsp caster (superfine) sugar

1 Cut the pears in half and scoop out the cores. Put the water in a pan with the orange rind, vanilla pod, bay leaf and sugar. Bring to the boil. Add the pears, cover and cook gently for about 15 minutes until just tender. Remove the pears with a slotted spoon and set aside to cool slightly. Reserve the syrup.

2 Roll out the pastry on a lightly floured work surface and cut out six pear shapes, slightly larger than the pear halves. Place the shapes on lined baking sheets and chill for 30 minutes.

3 Remove the spices from the syrup, then it to the heat and boil rapidly for 10 minutes. Blend the cocoa powder with 60ml/4 tbsp cold water in a separate pan.

4 Stir a few spoonfuls of the syrup into the cocoa paste, then whisk the paste into the syrup in the pan. Continue to cook until reduced to about 150ml/¼ pint/⅔ cup. Remove the pan from the heat and stir in the cream.

5 Preheat the oven to 200°C/400°F/Gas 6. In a bowl, mix together the butter, sugar and walnuts. and spoon a little filling into each pear cavity. Put a pear half, filled side down, in the centre of each one and sprinkle with a little sugar.

6 Bake for 12 minutes, or until the pastry has puffed up around the pear and is golden brown. Drizzle over some of the warm chocolate sauce and serve immediately.

Linzer Tart Energy 368Kcal/1539kJ; Protein 4.4g; Carbohydrate 44.3g, of which sugars 32.8g; Fat 20.4g, of which saturates 11.4g; Cholesterol 40mg; Calcium 69mg; Fibre 3.1g; Sodium 147mg.
Pear Tartlets Energy 443kcal/1847kJ; Protein 6.7g; Carbohydrate 44.2g, of which sugars 22.5g; Fat 28.4g, of which saturates 6.8g; Cholesterol 54mg; Calcium 73mg; Fibre 2.6g; Sodium 277mg.

Almond Chocolate Mazarins

These tartlets are from Denmark, where they are called mazarins: crisp pastry shells with an almond paste filling and a chocolate fondant topping.

Makes 12

For the filling

150g/5oz/1¼ cups plain (all-purpose) flour
90g/3½ oz/7 tbsp unsalted (sweet) butter
25g/1oz/¼ cup icing (confectioner's) sugar
1 egg yolk

For the filling

65g/2½oz/5tbsp unsalted (sweet) butter
75g/3oz/⅔ cup icing (confectioners') sugar
2 small eggs
115g/4oz/1 cup ground blanched almonds
1 tiny drop green food colouring (optional)

For the icing

200g/7oz plain (semisweet) chocolate
25g/1oz/2 tbsp unsalted (sweet) butter

1 To make the pastry, sift the flour and icing sugar into bowl, then rub in butter until the mixture resembles breadcrumbs. Stir in the egg yolk and use your fingers to work the mixture into a soft, smooth dough. Gather the dough into a ball, wrap in baking parchment and refrigerate for 1 hour.

2 Roll out the dough to a thickness of 3mm/⅛in and use to line 12 oval-shaped, fluted tartlet tins (muffin pans). Place the tins on a baking sheet and refrigerate while you make the filling. Preheat the oven to 190°C/375°F/Gas 5.

3 To make the filling, cream the butter and sugar until light and fluffy. Add the eggs, one at a time, stirring vigorously to mix after each addition. Stir the almonds into the mixture, and add the green food colouring, if using.

4 Spoon the almond filling into the pastry cases. Bake for about 20 minutes, until the tops are light brown. Cool on a rack.

5 To make the icing, break up the chocolate and melt it with the butter in a pan over low heat. Cool slightly, then spread over the cooled mazarins.

Greek Chocolate Mousse Tartlets

Irresistible Greek-style tartlets with a lightweight chocolate and yogurt filling.

Serves 6

175g/6oz/1½ cups plain (all-purpose) flour
30ml/2 tbsp cocoa powder (unsweetened)
30ml/2 tbsp icing (confectioners') sugar
115g/4oz/½ cup butter
60ml/4 tbsp water
melted dark (bittersweet) chocolate, to decorate

For the filling

200g/7oz white chocolate
120ml/4fl oz/½ cup milk
10ml/2 tsp powdered gelatine
25g/1oz/2 tbsp caster (superfine) sugar
5ml/1 tsp vanilla extract
2 eggs, separated
250g/9oz/generous 1 cup Greek (US strained plain) yogurt

1 Preheat the oven to 190°C/375°F/Gas 5. Sift the flour, cocoa and icing sugar into a large bowl.

2 Place the butter in a pan with the water and heat gently until just melted. Cool, then stir into the flour to make a smooth dough. Chill until firm.

3 Roll out the pastry and line six deep 10cm/4in loose-based flan tins (pans). Prick the base of the pastry cases (pie shells), cover with baking parchment, weigh down with baking beans and bake blind in the oven for 10 minutes. Remove the beans and paper, return to the oven and bake for 15 minutes until firm. Leave to cool.

4 Make the filling. Melt the broken-up chocolate in a heatproof bowl over hot water. Pour the milk into a pan, sprinkle over the gelatine and heat gently, stirring, until the gelatine has dissolved. Remove from the heat and stir in the chocolate.

5 Whisk the sugar, vanilla and egg yolks in a large bowl, then beat in the chocolate mixture. Beat in the yogurt until mixed.

6 Whisk the egg whites in a clean, grease-free bowl until stiff, then fold into the chocolate mixture. Spoon into the pastry cases and leave to set. Drizzle with melted chocolate to serve.

Almond Mazarins Energy 347kcal/1446kJ; Protein 5.3g; Carbohydrate 29.8g, of which sugars 19.8g; Fat 23.8g, of which saturates 11.4g; Cholesterol 78mg; Calcium 59mg; Fibre 1.5g; Sodium 105mg.
Mousse Tartlets Energy 555Kcal/2320kJ; Protein 11.9g; Carbohydrate 55g, of which sugars 32.2g; Fat 34g, of which saturates 19.7g; Cholesterol 105mg; Calcium 242mg; Fibre 1.5g; Sodium 263mg.

Chocolate Whirls

These tempting puff pastry whirls are made with ready-made puff pastry rolled up with a chocolate filling. They're easy to make as a special treat for breakfast.

Serves 20

75g/3oz/⅓ cup golden caster (superfine) sugar
40g/1½oz/6 tbsp unsweetened cocoa powder
2 eggs
500g/1lb 2oz puff pastry
25g/1oz/2 tbsp butter, softened
75g/3oz/generous ½ cup sultanas (golden raisins)
90g/3½oz milk chocolate

1 Preheat the oven to 220°C/425°F/Gas 7. Grease two baking sheets. Put the sugar, cocoa powder and eggs in a large mixing bowl and mix to a paste.

2 Roll out the pastry on a lightly floured surface to make a 30cm/12in square. Trim off any rough edges using a sharp knife.

3 Dot the pastry all over with the softened butter, then spread with the chocolate paste and sprinkle the sultanas over the top.

4 Roll the pastry into a sausage-shape, then cut the roll into 1cm/½in slices. Place the slices on the baking sheets, spacing them well apart. Bake the cookies in the oven for 10 minutes until risen and pale golden.

5 Transfer to a wire rack and leave to cool. Break the milk chocolate into pieces and put in a heatproof bowl set over a pan of gently simmering water. Heat, stirring frequently until melted and smooth.

6 Spoon or pipe lines of melted chocolate over the cookies, taking care not to completely hide the swirls of chocolate filling.

Variation

For extra chocolate, grate 70% dark (bittersweet) chocolate over the top of the paste before you roll up the pastry.

Chocolate Boats

Buttery sweetcrust pastry cases are the perfect vehicle for dark chocolate ganache.

Makes 24

115g/4oz butter, softened
50g/2oz/¼ cup caster (superfine) sugar
175g/6oz/1½ cups plain (all-purpose) flour
½ egg yolk

For the filling

60ml/4 tbsp double (heavy) cream
50ml/2fl oz/¼ cup golden (light corn) syrup or liquid glucose
175g/6oz dark (bittersweet) chocolate (64–70% cocoa solids), finely chopped

1 To make the pastry, cream the butter and sugar until light but not too fluffy. Add the flour and salt and mix until just combined. Add the egg yolk and bring together into a ball. Wrap in clear film (plastic wrap) and press into a disc. Place in the refrigerator to chill for about 30 minutes.

2 Lightly dust a work surface and the dough with flour. Roll out the dough to about 3mm/⅛in thickness. The pastry boats need to be strong enough to stand on their own, but not so thick that they dominate the chocolate.

3 Cut teardrop shapes that are slightly larger than the boat moulds. Use a knife or metal spatula to gently lift them up off the counter and into the moulds. Press into place and trim.

4 Place the moulds on a baking sheet and chill for 15 minutes. Meanwhile, preheat the oven to 180°C/350°F/Gas 4. Bake in the oven for about 7 minutes, until just golden on the edges and cooked through. Leave to cool, then remove them from their moulds and transfer to a serving tray. To make the filling, place the cream and golden syrup or glucose in a small pan and bring to the boil.

5 Put the chopped chocolate in a large, heatproof bowl and pour the hot cream over it. Stir every few minutes until the chocolate is melted. Spoon the ganache into the pastry cases (pie shells). Serve immediately or store in the refrigerator.

Chocolate Whirls Energy 165kcal/689kJ; Protein 2.9g; Carbohydrate 18.6g, of which sugars 9.4g; Fat 9.5g, of which saturates 1.9g; Cholesterol 23mg; Calcium 34mg; Fibre 0.4g; Sodium 117mg.
Chocolate Boats Energy 126kcal/526kJ; Protein 1.2g; Carbohydrate 14.4g, of which sugars 7.5g; Fat 7.6g, of which saturates 4.6g; Cholesterol 19mg; Calcium 17mg; Fibre 0.2g; Sodium 41mg.

Double Chocolate Choux Puffs

These choux puffs are made with double helpings of chocolate and cream.

Makes 12

150g/5oz/1¼ cups plain (all-purpose) flour
25g/1oz/2 tbsp unsweetened cocoa powder
250ml/8fl oz/1 cup water
2.5ml/½ tsp salt
15ml/1 tbsp sugar
115g/4oz/½ cup unsalted (sweet) butter, diced
4–5 eggs

For the cream

150g/5oz plain (semisweet) chocolate, melted
475ml/16fl oz/2 cups milk
6 egg yolks
100g/3½oz/scant ½ cup sugar
50g/2oz/½ cup plain (all-purpose) flour
120ml/4fl oz/½ cup whipping cream

For the glaze

300ml/10fl oz 1¼ cups whipping cream
55g/2oz/4 tbsp unsalted (sweet) butter, diced
225g/8oz plain (semisweet) chocolate, chopped
15ml/1 tbsp golden (light corn) syrup

1 Preheat the oven to 200°C/400°F/Gas 6. Lightly grease a large baking sheet. To make the cream puffs, sift the flour and cocoa powder into a bowl.

2 In a medium pan, bring the water, salt, sugar and butter to a boil. Continue to make and bake the choux puffs following the recipe for Coffee Profiteroles on page 173.

3 To make the cream, melt the chocolate and set it aside. Bring the milk to a boil. In a bowl, beat the egg yolks with the sugar until pale and thick. Stir in the flour. Slowly pour over half of the hot milk, stirring constantly. Return the yolk mixture to the milk pan and cook until boiling. Stir in the melted chocolate. Cool to room temperature. Whip the cream. Fold into the cooled custard mixture. Fill each puff with the pastry cream using a piping (pastry) bag.

4 Melt the glaze ingredients in a medium pan over low heat, stir until smooth. Cool slightly and pour over the cream puffs.

Chocolate Eclairs

A delicious version of a popular French dessert.

Makes 12

300ml/½ pint/1¼ cups double (heavy) cream
10ml/2 tsp icing (confectioners') sugar, sifted
1.5ml/¼ tsp vanilla extract
115g/4oz plain (semisweet) chocolate
30ml/2 tbsp water
25g/1oz/2 tbsp butter

For the pastry

65g/2½oz/9 tbsp plain (all-purpose) flour
pinch of salt
50g/2oz/¼ cup butter, diced
150ml/¼ pint/⅔ cup water
2 eggs, lightly beaten

1 Preheat the oven to 200°C/400°F/Gas 6. Grease a large baking sheet and line with baking parchment. Make the pastry. Sift the flour and salt on to a sheet of parchment. Heat the butter and water in a pan until the butter melts. Increase the heat to a rolling boil. Remove from the heat and beat in the flour with a wooden spoon. Return to low heat, then beat the until it forms a ball. Set aside and allow to cool for 2–3 minutes.

2 Gradually beat in the beaten eggs until you have a smooth paste thick enough to hold its shape. Spoon the pastry into a piping (pastry) bag with a 2.5cm/1in plain nozzle. Pipe 10cm/4in lengths on to the prepared baking sheet. Bake for 25–30 minutes, until the pastries are well risen and golden brown.

3 Remove from the oven and make a slit along the side of each to release steam. Lower the heat to 180°C/350°F/Gas 4 and bake for 5 minutes. Cool on a wire rack.

4 Make the filling. Whip the cream with the icing sugar and vanilla extract until it just holds its shape. Spoon into a piping bag fitted with a 1cm/½in plain nozzle and use to fill the éclairs.

5 Place the chocolate and water in a small bowl set over a pan of hot water. Melt, stirring until smooth. Remove from the heat and gradually stir in the butter. Dip the top of each éclair in the melted chocolate, place on a wire rack and leave in a cool place to set. Ideally, serve within 2 hours of making.

Chocolate Puffs Energy 576kcal/2401kJ; Protein 9.2g; Carbohydrate 46.9g, of which sugars 33.7g; Fat 40.4g, of which saturates 23.5g; Cholesterol 235mg; Calcium 133mg; Fibre 1.6g; Sodium 166mg.
Eclairs Energy 253Kcal/1050kJ; Protein 2.5g; Carbohydrate 11.6g, of which sugars 7.4g; Fat 22.2g, of which saturates 13.5g; Cholesterol 80mg; Calcium 29mg; Fibre 0.4g; Sodium 56mg.

Chickpea Chocolate Pastries

This Christmas Eve speciality comes from Italy where it is traditional to make a wish for the coming year as you make them.

Makes about 30

500g/1¼lb plain (all-purpose) flour, sifted
90ml/6 tbsp olive oil
1.5ml/¼ tsp salt
10ml/2 tsp vanilla extract
60ml/4 tbsp dry white wine
sunflower oil, for deep-frying
45ml/3 tbsp icing (confectioners') sugar
7.5ml/1½ tsp ground cinnamon

For the filling

500g/1¼lb dried chickpeas, soaked overnight and drained
45ml/3 tbsp unsweetened cocoa powder
45ml/3 tbsp caster (superfine) sugar
200g/7oz/generous 1 cup chopped candied citrus peel
45ml/3 tbsp clear honey
30ml/2 tbsp Amaretto liqueur

1 Rinse the soaked chickpeas, then boil rapidly for 5 minutes in fresh water. Drain and rinse again, then cover with fresh water and simmer slowly for 3 hours, until tender and almost pulpy. Drain the chickpeas and process or blend to a purée.

2 In a large mixing bowl, mix the chickpea purée with the cocoa powder, caster sugar, citrus peel, honey and liqueur. Set the filling aside while you make the pastry.

3 To make the pastry, pile all the flour on to the work surface and make a hole in the centre with your fist. Pour the oil into the centre with the salt, vanilla extract and half the wine. Mix the ingredients into the flour, adding wine a little at a time, until you have a shiny, elastic dough. You may not need all the wine.

4 Roll the dough out very thinly and cut it into 7.5cm/ 3in circles using a pastry (cookie) cutter. Put a spoonful of filling on one half of each circle, fold the circles in half and seal them closed using the prongs of a fork. Heat the sunflower oil in a large pan or deep-fryer until a small piece of the pastry, dropped into the oil, sizzles and browns almost immediately.

5 Fry in batches of four or five at a time. As soon as they are puffy, remove from the pan and dust with sugar and cinnamon.

Chocolate Tuiles

Light and crisp, these are the perfect accompaniment to ice cream or chocolate mousse. You can pipe them into shapes or bend them while they are hot, or leave them in long flat strips.

Makes 20–30

125g/4¼oz/generous ½ cup butter, softened, plus extra for greasing
125g/4¼ oz/scant ¾ cup caster (superfine) sugar
3 egg whites
100g/3¾oz/generous ¾ cup plain (all-purpose) flour, plus extra for dusting
25g/1oz/¼ cup unsweetened cocoa powder
poached fruit and single (light) cream or chocolate mousse, to serve

1 Grease a baking sheet and dust it with flour. Preheat the oven to 180°C/350°F/Gas 4.

2 Cream the soft butter and sugar until light and fluffy. Add the egg whites and incorporate fully.

3 Sift the flour and cocoa powder over the mixture and fold it in with a rubber spatula or metal spoon. Try not to overmix the batter or it will become tough.

4 Pour the mixture into a piping (pastry) bag and pipe into shapes or use moulds to create shapes. Bake in the oven for 6–8 minutes, until just golden.

5 Remove from the oven. If you want to shape them at this stage, very quickly wrap them around a rolling pin or the handle of a wooden spoon, then slide them off on to a wire rack and leave to cool. They start to set as soon as you remove them from the oven, so you need to do this quickly. If the become too firm to mould, simply return them to the oven briefly for a few seconds.

6 Leave the tuiles to cool completely, then serve them with poached fruit and cream, or you can accompany them with a rich chocolate mousse if you prefer. The tuiles will keep in an airtight container for up to 3 days.

Chickpea Pastries Energy 131kcal/544kJ; Protein 3.4g; Carbohydrate 5.6g, of which sugars 1.2g; Fat 10.7g, of which saturates 5.5g; Cholesterol 48mg; Calcium 7mg; Fibre 0.4g; Sodium 261mg.
Chocolate Tuiles Energy 62kcal/260kJ; Protein 0.8g; Carbohydrate 7g, of which sugars 4.4g; Fat 3.6g, of which saturates 2.4g; Cholesterol 10mg; Calcium 9mg; Fibre 0.2g; Sodium 46mg.

Dark Chocolate Fingers

With their understated elegance and distinctly grown-up flavour, these deliciously decadent chocolate fingers are ideal for serving with after-dinner coffee and liqueurs.

Makes about 26

115g/4oz/1 cup plain (all-purpose) flour
2.5ml/½ tsp baking powder
30ml/2 tbsp unsweetened cocoa powder
50g/2oz/¼ cup unsalted (sweet) butter, softened
50g/2oz/¼ cup caster (superfine) sugar
20ml/4 tsp golden (light corn) syrup
150g/5oz dark (bittersweet) chocolate
chocolate-flavour mini flakes, for sprinkling

1 Preheat the oven to 160°C/325°F/Gas 3. Line two baking sheets with baking parchment.

2 Put the flour, baking powder, cocoa powder, butter, caster sugar and golden syrup in a large mixing bowl. Work the ingredients together with your fingertips to combine until they form into a dough.

3 Roll the dough out between sheets of baking parchment to an 18 x 24cm/7 x 9½in rectangle. Remove the top sheet. Cut in half lengthways, then into bars 2cm/¾in wide. Place on the baking sheets.

4 Bake in the oven for about 15 minutes, taking care not to allow the bars to brown or they will taste bitter. Transfer to a wire rack to cool completely.

5 Melt the chocolate in a heatproof bowl set over a pan of gently simmering water. Half-dip the cookies, place on baking parchment, sprinkle with chocolate flakes, then leave to set.

Variation
If you're making these cookies for children, dip them in melted plain (semisweet) or milk chocolate.

Chocolate Cinnamon Tuiles

These elegant, crisp French cookies are classically plain – but this special version is delicately flavoured with cocoa and cinnamon.

Makes 12

1 egg white
50g/2oz/¼ cup caster (superfine) sugar
30ml/2 tbsp plain (all-purpose) flour
40g/1½oz/3 tbsp butter, melted
15ml/1 tbsp unsweetened cocoa powder
2.5ml/½ tsp ground cinnamon

1 Preheat the oven to 200°C/400°F/Gas 6. Lightly grease two large baking sheets.

2 Whisk the egg white in a grease-free bowl until it forms soft peaks. Gradually whisk in the sugar.

3 Sift the flour over the mixture and fold in evenly. Stir in the melted butter. Transfer about 45ml/3 tbsp of the mixture to a small bowl and set aside.

4 Sift together the cocoa and ground cinnamon over the flour and butter mixture, in batches, stirring well after each addition.

5 Leaving room for spreading, drop spoonfuls of the chocolate-flavoured mixture on to the prepared baking sheets, then spread each gently with a metal spatula to make a neat round.

6 Using a small spoon, carefully drizzle the reserved unflavoured mixture over the rounds to create a pretty softly marbled effect.

7 Bake for 4–6 minutes, until just set. Using a metal spatula, lift each cookie carefully and quickly drape it over a rolling pin to give a curved shape as it hardens.

8 Leave the tuiles to cool until set, then remove them gently and place on a wire rack to cool completely. Serve on the same day as making them.

Dark Chocolate Fingers Energy 72kcal/303kJ; Protein 0.9g; Carbohydrate 9.9g, of which sugars 6.3g; Fat 3.5g, of which saturates 2.1g; Cholesterol 4mg; Calcium 11mg; Fibre 0.4g; Sodium 25mg.
Chocolate Cinnamon Tuiles Energy 55kcal/229kJ; Protein 0.8g; Carbohydrate 6.5g, of which sugars 4.4g; Fat 3g, of which saturates 1.9g; Cholesterol 7mg; Calcium 8mg; Fibre 0.2g; Sodium 38mg.

Chocolate Pretzels

These scrumptious snacks look so charming twisted into little knots. Sweet pretzels are a speciality of Germany and Austria.

Makes 28

115g/4oz/1 cup plain (all-purpose) flour
pinch of salt
45ml/3 tbsp unsweetened cocoa powder
115g/4oz/½ cup butter
150g/5oz/¾ cup caster (superfine) sugar
1 egg
1 egg white, lightly beaten, for glazing
sugar crystals, for sprinkling

1 Sift together the flour, salt and cocoa powder. Set aside. Lightly grease two baking sheets.

2 In a large bowl, beat the butter until pale and soft. Add the sugar and continue beating until light and fluffy. Beat in the egg.

3 Add the dry ingredients and stir to blend. Gather the dough into a ball, wrap in baking parchment and chill for 1 hour or freeze for 30 minutes.

4 Preheat the oven to 190°C/375°F/Gas 5.

5 Roll the dough into 28 small balls. Roll each ball into a rope about 25cm/10in long. With each rope, form a loop with the two ends facing you. Twist the ends and fold back on to the circle, pressing in, to make a pretzel shape.

6 Place on the prepared baking sheets. Brush with the egg white and sprinkle sugar crystals over the tops to decorate.

7 Bake in the oven for 10–12 minutes, until firm. Transfer to a wire rack to cool.

Cook's Tip
To make mocha-flavoured pretzels, replace 10ml/2 tsp of the unsweetened cocoa powder with instant coffee powder.

Chocolate Churros

Churros, basically a fried choux pastry doughnut, are originally from Spain where they are usually served simply rolled in sugar. This Argentinian version goes one step further and dips the just-cooked churros in melted chocolate. In Argentina they are a served as a breakfast treat for children at weekends.

Serves 4–6

500g/1¼lb/4½ cups strong white flour
5ml/1 tsp salt
500ml/17fl oz/generous 2 cups water
115g/4oz plain (semi-sweet) chocolate
vegetable oil, for deep-frying
caster (superfine) sugar, for sprinkling

1 Sift the flour on to a small sheet of baking parchment. Bring the water and salt to the boil in a pan.

2 Add in the flour and beat vigorously with a wooden spoon until the mixture is smooth. Remove the pan from the heat and let the dough cool a little. Spoon the mixture into a piping (pastry) bag fitted with a large fluted nozzle.

3 Heat the oil in a deep-fat fryer or heavy pan to 180°C/350°C. Squeeze the piping bag over the pan, snipping off the lengths with kitchen scissors. Fry in batches of 4–6 until golden.

4 Remove with a slotted spoon and drain on kitchen paper. Sprinkle one end of each churros generously with sugar while they are still hot.

5 Break the chocolate into pieces and place in a heatproof bowl over a pan of near-boiling water.

6 Leave until melted then stir gently. Holding the sugared end of each churros, dip the plain end into the chocolate.

7 Lift out the churros, and let the excess chocolate drip back into the bowl, then it place on a tray lined with baking parchment. Dip the remaining churros in the chocolate and leave to set before serving.

Chocolate Pretzels Energy 72kcal/303kJ; Protein 1g; Carbohydrate 9.1g, of which sugars 5g; Fat 3.8g, of which saturates 2.3g; Cholesterol 16mg; Calcium 13mg; Fibre 0.3g; Sodium 37mg.
Churros Energy 573kcal/2410kJ; Protein 8.9g; Carbohydrate 86.7g, of which sugars 23g; Fat 23.6g, of which saturates 5.6g; Cholesterol 1mg; Calcium 126mg; Fibre 4.1g; Sodium 332mg.

Deep-dish Apple Pie

Adding a buttery caramel to the apples, coupled with the mixed spice, gives a rich flavour to the juices in this delicious shortcrust pie.

Serves 6

900g/2lb eating apples
75g/3oz/6 tbsp unsalted (sweet) butter
45–60ml/3–4 tbsp demerara (raw) sugar
3 cloves
2.5ml/½ tsp mixed (apple pie) spice

For the pastry

250g/9oz/2¼ cups plain (all-purpose) flour
pinch of salt
50g/2oz/¼ cup lard or white cooking fat, chilled and diced
75g/3oz/6 tbsp unsalted (sweet) butter, chilled and diced
30–45ml/2–3 tbsp chilled water
a little milk, for brushing
caster (superfine) sugar, for dredging
clotted cream, ice cream or double (heavy) cream, to serve

1 Preheat the oven to 200°C/400°F/Gas 6. Make the pastry first. Sift together the flour and salt into a bowl. Rub in the lard or fat and butter until the mixture resembles fine breadcrumbs. Stir in enough chilled water to bring the pastry together. Knead lightly then wrap in clear film (plastic wrap) and chill for 30 minutes.

2 To make the filling, peel, core and thickly slice the apples. Melt the butter in a frying pan, add the sugar and cook for 3–4 minutes allowing it to melt and caramelize. Add the apples and stir around to coat. Cook over medium heat until the apples take on a little colour, add the spices and tip out into a bowl to cool slightly.

3 Divide the pastry in two and, on a lightly floured surface, roll out into two rounds that will easily fit a deep 23cm/9in pie plate. Line the plate with one round of pastry. Spoon in the cooled filling and mound up in the centre. Cover the apples with the remaining pastry, sealing and crimping the edges. Make a 5cm/2in long slit through the top of the pastry to allow the steam to escape. Brush the pie with milk and dredge with caster sugar.

4 Place the pie on a baking sheet and bake in the oven for 25–35 minutes until golden and firm. Serve with clotted cream, ice cream or double cream.

Basque Apple Pie

The pastry for this Spanish pie has a delicious cake-like texture.

Serves 6

215g/7½oz/scant 2 cups plain (all-purpose) flour, plus extra for rolling
5ml/1 tsp baking powder
pinch of salt
115g/4oz/½ cup cold unsalted (sweet) butter, cubed, plus extra for greasing
finely grated rind of ½ lemon
75g/3oz/6 tbsp caster (superfine) sugar, plus extra for sprinkling
2 small (US medium) eggs
3 eating apples, peeled, cored and cubed
ground cinnamon, for sprinkling

1 Sift the flour, baking powder and salt into a food processor. Add the butter and grated lemon rind and process to combine, then add the sugar, 1 whole egg and the yolk of the second egg to the flour mixture and process to make a soft dough.

2 Divide the dough into two pieces, one portion nearly double the size of the other. Pat into two flat cakes. Wrap tightly in clear film (plastic wrap) and chill for at least 2 hours until firm.

3 Preheat the oven to 180°C/350°F/Gas 4. Place a baking sheet in the oven and grease a 20cm/8in loose-based flan tin (pan). Place the larger piece of dough on a lightly floured piece of clear film and cover with another piece of film. Roll out to a 25cm/10in round. Remove the film, transfer to the tin and press into the tin so that it stands just clear of the top.

4 Pack the tin with the apples and sprinkle with cinnamon. Roll out the second piece of dough in the same way, to exactly the same size as the tin. Lay the dough on top of the apples and fold the overlapping edges of the bottom piece of dough inward. Gently press the edges together with a fork, to seal.

5 Prick the dough a few times with a fork, brush with egg white and sprinkle with sugar. Place on the hot baking sheet and bake for about 20 minutes. Reduce the oven temperature to 160°C/325°F/Gas 3 for a further 25–30 minutes until golden. Cool the pie in the tin for 30 minutes, then remove from the tin. Cool on a wire rack.

Deep-dish Apple Energy 610kcal/2566kJ; Protein 8.1g; Carbohydrate 86.1g, of which sugars 40.2g; Fat 28.5g, of which saturates 8.8g; Cholesterol 14mg; Calcium 168mg; Fibre 8.1g; Sodium 413mg.
Basque Apple Pie Energy 232Kcal/984kJ; Protein 5.7g; Carbohydrate 45.4g, of which sugars 18.1g; Fat 4.4g, of which saturates 1.9g; Cholesterol 69mg; Calcium 69mg; Fibre 1.9g; Sodium 41mg.

Plated Apple Pie

Bake this pie in a traditional metal pie plate so that the pastry base will be perfectly cooked. Serve with custard.

Serves 6

225g/8oz/2 cups plain (all-purpose) flour
130g/4½ oz/generous ½ cup butter, or mixed butter and white vegetable fat (shortening)
25g/1oz/2 tbsp caster (superfine) sugar
45ml/3 tbsp very cold milk or water
custard, to serve

For the filling

675g/1½lb cooking apples
75g/3oz/½ cup sultanas (golden raisins) (optional)
a little grated lemon rind
75g/3oz/6 tbsp caster (superfine) sugar
a knob (pat) of butter
a little milk, to glaze

1 Sieve the flour into a large mixing bowl, add the butter and cut it into small pieces. Rub the butter into the flour with your fingertips. Mix the caster sugar with the chilled milk in separate bowl, add to the flour and butter and mix with a knife or fork until the mixture clings together.

2 Turn on to a floured worktop and knead lightly until smooth. Wrap in baking parchment or foil and leave in the refrigerator to relax for 20 minutes before using. Meanwhile, preheat the oven to 200°C/400°F/Gas 6.

3 Roll out one-third of the pastry and use to line a 23cm/9in pie plate. Use any trimmings to make a second layer of pastry around the top edge of the pie plate.

4 Peel, core and slice the apples and arrange half of them on the pastry base, then sprinkle over the sultanas and lemon rind. Top with the sugar, remaining apples and dots of the butter.

5 Roll out the remainder of the pastry to make a circle about 2.5cm/1in larger than the pie plate. Dampen the pastry edging on the rim and lay the top over the apples. Press the rim to seal. Knock up the edge with a knife, and pinch the edges neatly with the fingers to make a fluted edge. Brush with milk and bake for about 30 minutes. Serve hot with custard.

American Apple Pie

A classically decorated apple pie. The pastry uses white vegetable fat, but if you prefer, use half butter.

Serves 8

about 900g/2lb tart eating apples, peeled, cored and sliced
15ml/1 tbsp fresh lemon juice
5ml/1 tsp vanilla extract
115g/4oz caster (superfine) sugar
2.5ml/½ tsp ground cinnamon
45g/1½oz butter
1 egg yolk
10ml/2 tsp whipping cream

For the pastry

225g/8oz plain (all-purpose) flour
5ml/1 tsp salt
115g/4oz white vegetable fat (shortening)
60–75ml/4–5 tbsp iced water
15ml/1 tbsp quick-cooking tapioca

1 Preheat the oven to 200°C/400°F/Gas 6. For the pastry, sift the flour and salt into a bowl. Rub in the butter until the mixture resembles coarse breadcrumbs. Sprinkle in the water, 15ml/1 tbsp at a time, tossing lightly with your fingertips or with a fork until the pastry forms a ball.

2 Divide in half and shape each into a ball. On a floured surface, roll out one of the balls to a circle about 30cm/12in in diameter.

3 Use it to line a 23cm/9in pie tin (pan), easing the dough in and being careful not to stretch it. Trim off the excess pastry. Sprinkle the tapioca over the bottom of the pastry case (pie shell). Roll out the remaining pastry to 3mm/⅛in thickness. With a sharp knife, cut out eight large leaf-shapes. Cut the trimmings into small leaf shapes. Score the leaves with the back of the knife.

4 In a bowl, toss the apples with the lemon juice, vanilla, sugar and cinnamon. Fill the pastry case with the apple mixture and dot with the butter. Arrange the large leaves in a decorative pattern on top. Decorate the edge with small leaves.

5 Mix together the egg yolk and cream and brush over the leaves to glaze them. Bake for 10 minutes, then reduce the heat to 350°F/180°C/Gas 4 and continue baking for 35–45 minutes until the pastry is golden brown. Let the pie cool in the tin, set on a wire rack, then serve.

Apple Pie Energy 393Kcal/1650kJ; Protein 4.1g; Carbohydrate 56.3g, of which sugars 27.7g; Fat 18.4g, of which saturates 11.4g; Cholesterol 46mg; Calcium 68mg; Fibre 2.5g; Sodium 136mg.
American Pie Energy 404kcal/1691kJ; Protein 3.5g; Carbohydrate 47g, of which sugars 25.5g; Fat 23.8g, of which saturates 12g; Cholesterol 42mg; Calcium 54mg; Fibre 3.6g; Sodium 165mg.

Apple Lattice Pie

This Dutch version of apple pie is the first recipe a child in Holland learns to bake.

Serves 8–10

175g/6oz/¾ cup butter, softened
175g/6oz/1½ cups plain (all-purpose) flour
175g/6oz/1½ cups self-raising (self-rising) flour
175g/6oz/scant 1 cup caster (superfine) sugar
1 egg
2.5ml/½ tsp grated lemon rind
pinch of salt
60ml/4 tbsp apricot jam and 30ml/2 tbsp rum, to glaze

For the filling

1kg/2¼lb tart apples, such as Goudrenet or Granny Smith
juice of 1 lemon
60ml/4 tbsp sugar
10ml/2 tsp ground cinnamon
30ml/2 tbsp breadcrumbs
5ml/1 tsp aniseed, crushed

1 Preheat the oven to 200°C/400°F/Gas 6. Grease a 33cm/13in springform tin (pan) with butter. To make the filling, peel and core the apples, then thinly slice them into even pieces and place them in a non-metallic bowl. Mix together the lemon juice, sugar and cinnamon, pour over the apples and set aside.

2 Meanwhile, make the dough. Sift the flour into a bowl, stir in the sugar. butter, egg, lemon rind and salt and knead to a dough. Cut off one-third of the dough and set aside. Roll out the remaining dough on a lightly floured surface to a 37cm/14½in round and use to line the prepared tin. If the dough cracks.

3 Mix together the breadcrumbs and aniseed and sprinkle the mixture evenly over the base of the pastry case (pie shell). Arrange the apple slices in slightly overlapping concentric circles on top of the breadcrumb mixture.

4 Roll out the remaining dough to a 33cm/13in round. Cut into 1cm/½in wide strips and arrange them in a lattice pattern over the apples. Bake for 45–55 minutes, until golden brown.

5 Mix together the jam and rum for the glaze. Remove the pie from the oven and brush the top with the glaze. Remove the sides of the tin, and serve or leave to cool completely. This pie freezes well. Ensure it is well wrapped before freezing.

Filo-topped Apple Pie

With its crisp, melt-in-the-mouth filo topping and minimal butter, this is a really light dessert, making it the perfect choice for those with a healthy eating plan. There's certainly no loss of flavour, so feel free to serve it to family and friends who will soon discover that it tastes as good as it looks.

Serves 6

900g/2lb cooking apples
75g/3oz/6 tbsp caster (superfine) sugar
grated rind of 1 lemon
15ml/1 tbsp lemon juice
75g/3oz/½ cup sultanas (golden raisins)
2.5ml/½ tsp ground cinnamon
4 large sheets of filo pastry, thawed if frozen
25g/1oz/2 tbsp butter, melted
icing (confectioners') sugar, for dusting

1 Peel, core and dice the apples. Place the apples in a pan with the caster sugar and lemon rind. Drizzle the lemon juice over.

2 Bring the mixture to the boil, stir well, then cook for about 5 minutes, until the apples have softened. Stir the sultanas and cinnamon into the apples.

3 Spoon the mixture into a 1.2 litre/2 pint/5 cup pie dish; level the top. Set aside and alow to cool.

4 Preheat the oven to 180°C/350°F/Gas 4. Place a pie funnel in the centre of the fruit in the pie dish. Brush each sheet of filo with the melted butter.

5 Scrunch the filo up loosely and place on the fruit to cover it completely. Bake for 20–30 minutes until the filo is golden. To serve, dust the pie with the icing sugar.

Cook's Tip

For a delightful change of flavour and texture, substitute flaked (sliced) almonds – plain or toasted – for some or all of the sultanas (golden raisins) in the pie.

Lattice Pie Energy 4174kcal/17592kJ; Protein 48.1g; Carbohydrate 672.4g, of which sugars 383.2g; Fat 155.5g, of which saturates 93.4g; Cholesterol 563mg; Calcium 760mg; Fibre 27.5g; Sodium 1431mg.
Filo-topped Pie Energy 198kcal/843kJ; Protein 2.2g; Carbohydrate 44.8g, of which sugars 35.3g; Fat 2.4g, of which saturates 0.6g; Cholesterol 0mg; Calcium 38mg; Fibre 3g; Sodium 44mg.

Apple and Orange Pie

Oranges add an evocative Mediterranean twist to an Anglo-American favourite. You can replace the oranges with tangerines if you wish, for a Christmas pie.

Serves 4–6
3 navel oranges
1kg/2¼lb cooking apples, peeled, cored and thickly sliced
30ml/2 tbsp demerara (raw) sugar
beaten egg, to glaze
caster (superfine) sugar, for sprinkling

For the pastry
275g/10oz/2½ cups plain (all-purpose) flour
2.5ml/½ tsp salt
150g/5oz/10 tbsp chilled butter, diced
45ml/4 tbsp chilled water

1 Make the pastry. Sift the flour and salt into a large bowl. Rub in the butter with your fingertips, until the mixture resembles fine breadcrumbs. Mix in the water and knead lightly to form a firm dough. Wrap the dough in clear film (plastic wrap) and chill for at least 30 minutes.

2 Roll out the pastry on a lightly floured work surface to a shape 2cm/¾in larger than the top of a 1.2 litre/2 pint/5 cup pie dish. Cut off a narrow strip around the edge of the pastry, brush it with a little cold water and firmly attach it to the rim of the pie dish.

3 Preheat the oven to 190°C/375°F/Gas 5. Using a sharp knife, cut a thin slice of peel and pith from both ends of each orange. Place cut side down on a plate and cut off the peel and pith in strips. Remove any bits of remaining pith. Cut out each segment leaving the membrane behind. Squeeze the remaining juice from the membrane.

4 Mix together the orange segments and juice, the apples and sugar in the pie dish. Place a pie funnel in the centre of the dish. Dampen the pastry strip on the rim of the dish and cover with the pastry. Press the edges to the pastry strip.

5 Brush the top with beaten egg to glaze. Bake for 35 minutes, or until golden. Sprinkle with caster sugar before serving.

Apple and Raisin Pie

Russians like to finish the day with vechernij chaj – evening tea. Chocolate confectionary, cookies, berries and spoonfuls of jam may be served to accompany plentiful cups of tea. If something more substantial is required, a large home-baked pie is served with the steaming hot tea.

Serves 4–6
5–6 cooking apples
40–50g/1½–2oz/3–4 tbsp butter
45ml/3 tbsp raisins
1 sheet ready-made chilled puff pastry, measuring about 40 x 20cm/16 x 8in
1 egg yolk
5ml/1 tsp water

1 Slice the apples, discarding the cores. Put the butter in a medium frying pan and heat until melted. Add the apples and stir-fry, over low heat, for 5 minutes, until soft.

2 Remove the pan from the heat, add the raisins and mix together. Set aside and leave to cool.

3 Preheat the oven to 220°C/425°F/Gas 7. Put the sheet of pastry on a dampened baking tray. Distribute the apple filling over the pastry, leaving a 5cm/2in border around the edge.

4 Brush the edges of the pastry with water or milk and fold over to enclose the filling.

5 Whisk the egg yolk and water together. Brush the pastry with the mixture and make some small holes in the top with a fork.

6 Bake the pie in the oven for 12–15 minutes, until golden brown. Allow the pie to rest for 5–10 minutes then cut into slices and serve with a spoonful of smetana or crème fraîche.

Cook's Tip
If your sheets of pastry are smaller than the sheet specified in the recipe, put three smaller sheets together and seal them into one large sheet.

Apple & Orange Pie Energy 444Kcal/1865kJ; Protein 5.7g; Carbohydrate 61.2g, of which sugars 26.3g; Fat 21.4g, of which saturates 13.1g; Cholesterol 53mg; Calcium 108mg; Fibre 5.2g; Sodium 324mg.
Apple & Raisin Pie Energy 393kcal/1650kJ; Protein 4.1g; Carbohydrate 56.3g, of which sugars 27.7g; Fat 18.4g, of which saturates 11.4g; Cholesterol 46mg; Calcium 68mg; Fibre 2.5g; Sodium 136mg.

Peach and Brandy Pie

Slices of juicy, ripe peaches, gently cooked in butter and sugar, are encased in crisp puff pastry to make this fragrant fruit pie.

Serves 8

6 large, firm ripe peaches
40g/1½oz/3 tbsp butter
45ml/3 tbsp brandy
75g/3oz/6 tbsp caster (superfine) sugar
450g/1lb puff pastry
vanilla ice cream, to serve

For the glaze

1 egg
5ml/1 tsp water
15ml/1 tbsp sugar

1 Immerse the peaches in boiling water for about 30 seconds. Lift them out with a slotted spoon, dip in cold water, then peel off the skins. Halve and stone (pit) the peaches, then cut into slices.

2 Melt the butter in a large frying pan. Add the peach slices, then sprinkle with the brandy and sugar. Cook for about 4 minutes, shaking the pan frequently, or until the sugar has dissolved and the peaches are tender. Set the pan aside to cool.

3 Cut the pastry into two pieces, one slightly larger than the other. Roll out on a lightly floured surface and, using plates or cake tins as a guide, cut the larger piece of pastry into a 30cm/12in circle and the smaller one into a 28cm/11in circle. Place on separate baking sheets lined with baking parchment, and chill for 30 minutes. Preheat the oven to 200°C/400°F/Gas 6.

4 Spoon the peaches into the middle of the larger round of pastry to within about 2cm/1in of the edge. Place the smaller pastry round on top. Brush the edge of the larger pastry round with a little water, then fold this over the top pastry round and press to seal. Twist the edges together to make a pattern all the way round the pie.

5 Make the glaze by mixing the egg and water. Lightly brush it over the pastry and sprinkle over the granulated sugar, spreading it evenly over the pastry. Make five or six small cuts on the top of the pastry. Bake for about 45 minutes, or until the pastry is risen and golden brown. Serve warm in slices with vanilla ice cream.

Walnut and Pear Lattice Pie

This attractive lattice topped pie has a delicious autumnal filling, and a nut-enriched pastry case.

Serves 6

225g/8oz/2 cups plain (all-purpose) flour mixed with 30ml/2 tbsp chopped walnuts
130g/4½oz/½ cup butter
30–45ml/3–4 tbsp iced water
900g/2lb pears, peeled, cored and thinly sliced
50g/2oz/2 tbsp caster (superfine) sugar
50g/2oz/2 tbsp plain (all-purpose) flour
2.5ml/½ tsp grated lemon rind
25g/1oz/1 tbsp raisins or sultanas (golden raisins)
25g/1oz/1 tbsp walnuts, chopped
2.5ml/½ tsp ground cinnamon
50g/2oz/2 tbsp icing (confectioner's) sugar
15ml/1 tbsp lemon juice

1 Preheat a 190°C/375°F/Gas 5 oven. In a large bowl rub the butter in to the flour and walnut mixture. Use enough iced water to make a firm dough. Wrap and chill for 30 minutes. Roll out half the dough and use to line a 23cm/9in pie dish.

2 Combine the pears, caster sugar, flour and lemon rind in a bowl. Toss gently until the fruit is evenly coated with the dry ingredients. Mix in the raisins, nuts and cinnamon.

3 Put the pear filling into the pastry case (pie shell) and spread it evenly. Roll out the remaining pastry dough and using a ruler cut into strips 1.5cm/½in wide. Lay half the strips across the pie filling, keeping them neatly parallel and spacing them evenly.

4 Fold back every other strip from the centre. Lay a strip across the centre at right angles, then fold over the strips that aren't already folded over to make a plaited effect. Continue in the same way, folding back alternate strips to overlap the next strip. Once the lattice is complete, brush with a little milk and bake for 55 minutes or until the pastry is golden brown.

5 Combine the icing sugar, lemon juice and water in a bowl and stir until smoothly blended. Remove the pie from the oven. Drizzle the icing sugar glaze evenly over the top of the pie, on pastry and filling. Serve warm.

Peach Pie Energy 353kcal/1480kJ; Protein 5.2g; Carbohydrate 41.8g, of which sugars 21.7g; Fat 18.1g, of which saturates 9.1g; Cholesterol 67mg; Calcium 48mg; Fibre 2.3g; Sodium 215mg.
Walnut Pie Energy 426Kcal/1787kJ; Protein 6.4g; Carbohydrate 60.5g, of which sugars 26.5g; Fat 18.9g, of which saturates 10.2g; Cholesterol 64mg; Calcium 53mg; Fibre 3.2g; Sodium 127mg.

Peach Leaf Pie

Pretty pastry leaves decorate this most attractive spiced summer fruit pie.

Serves 8

1.2kg/2½lb ripe peaches
juice of 1 lemon
90g/3½oz/½ cup caster (superfine) sugar
45ml/3 tbsp cornflour (cornstarch)
1.5ml/¼ tsp freshly grated nutmeg
2.5ml/½ tsp ground cinnamon
1 egg beaten with 15ml/1 tbsp water, to glaze
25g/1oz/2 tbsp cold butter, diced

For the pastry

275g/10oz/2½ cups plain (all-purpose) flour
4ml/¾ tsp salt
115g/4oz/½ cup cold butter, diced
60g/2¼oz/4½ tbsp cold white cooking fat or lard, diced
75–90ml/5–6 tbsp iced water

1 To make the pastry, sift the flour and salt into a bowl. Rub in the butter and fat using your fingertips or a pastry (cookie) cutter until the mixture resembles breadcrumbs. Stir in just enough water to bind the dough. Gather into two balls, one slightly larger than the other. Wrap and chill for at least 20 minutes. Place a baking sheet in the oven and preheat to 220°C/425°F/Gas 7.

2 Drop the peaches into boiling water for 20 seconds, then transfer to a bowl of cold water. When cool, peel off the skins. Slice the flesh and combine with the lemon juice, sugar, cornflour and spices. Set aside.

3 Roll out the larger dough ball to 3mm/⅛in thick. Use to line a 23cm/9in pie plate. Chill. Roll out the remaining dough to 5mm/¼in thick. Cut out leaves 7.5cm/3in long. Mark veins. With the scraps, roll a few balls.

4 Brush the pastry base with egg glaze. Add the peaches and dot with the butter. Starting from the outside edge, cover the peaches with a ring of leaves. Place a second, staggered ring above. Continue until covered. Place the balls in the centre.

5 Brush the top of the pie with glaze. Bake in the oven for 10 minutes. Lower the heat to 180°C/350°F/Gas 4 and bake for 35–40 minutes more.

Plum Polenta Pie

Polenta adds a wonderful golden hue and crunchiness to the rich pastry base for this pie, while the oat crumble topping makes a perfect contrast to the ripe, juicy plum filling. Use red plums if you can't find dark.

Serves 6–8

10ml/2 tsp caster (superfine) sugar
15ml/1 tbsp polenta
450g/1lb purple plums
25g/1oz/¼ cup rolled oats
15ml/1 tbsp demerara (raw) sugar
custard or cream, to serve

For the pastry

115g/4oz/1 cup plain (all-purpose) flour, sifted
115g/4oz/1 cup wholemeal (whole-wheat) flour
150g/5oz/¾ cup caster (superfine) sugar
115g/4oz/1 cup polenta
5ml/1 tsp baking powder
pinch of salt
150g/5oz/10 tbsp butter, diced
1 egg, beaten
15ml/1 tbsp olive oil
about 60ml/4 tbsp chilled water

1 Make the pastry. Mix the dry ingredients in a large bowl. Rub or cut in the butter until the mixture resembles fine breadcrumbs. Stir in the egg, olive oil and chilled water to form a dough.

2 Grease a 23cm/9in springform cake tin (pan). Press two-thirds of the dough evenly over the base and sides of the tin. Wrap the remaining dough in clear film (plastic wrap) and chill.

3 Preheat the oven to 180°C/350°F/Gas 4. Sprinkle the sugar and polenta into the pastry case (pie shell). Cut the plums in half and remove the stones (pits), then place the plums, cut side down, on top of the polenta base.

4 Unwrap the chilled dough, crumble with your fingers into a mixing bowl, then add the oats and mix lightly. Sprinkle the mixture over the plums. Sprinkle the demerara sugar on top.

5 Bake the pie for 50 minutes, or until golden. Leave for about 15 minutes before removing the pie from the tin. Leave to cool for a few minutes before serving in slices with custard or cream.

Peach Leaf Pie Energy 424kcal/1778kJ; Protein 4.8g; Carbohydrate 54.2g, of which sugars 22.8g; Fat 22.4g, of which saturates 12.2g; Cholesterol 44mg; Calcium 68mg; Fibre 3.1g; Sodium 112mg.
Plum Polenta Energy 426Kcal/1787kJ; Protein 6.4g; Carbohydrate 60.5g, of which sugars 26.5g; Fat 18.9g, of which saturates 10.2g; Cholesterol 64mg; Calcium 53mg; Fibre 3.2g; Sodium 127mg.

Plum Pie

English fruit pies are made either in a pie dish with a deep filling or on a plate with a crust both top and bottom, and even sometimes with an extra, third, pastry layer dividing the fruits inside. A range of fruits can be used, such as apples, gooseberries, blackberries, rhubarb or, as here, plums. Serve the pie with whipped cream or custard.

Serves 6

200g/7oz/1¾ cups plain (all-purpose) flour
25g/1oz/4 tbsp icing (confectioner's) sugar
115g/4oz/½ cup butter, diced
1 egg, lightly beaten
800g/1¾lb plums, stoned (pitted)
about 75g/3oz caster (superfine) sugar, plus extra for sprinkling
beaten egg white, to frost

1 Sift the flour and icing sugar into a bowl and rub in the butter until the mixture resembles fine crumbs. Stir in the egg and gather together into a smooth dough. Chill for 30 minutes.

2 Preheat the oven to 190°C/375°F/Gas 5. Place half the plums in a 1 litre/1¾ pint/4 cup pie dish. Sprinkle the caster sugar over them, adjusting the amount according to the sweetness of the fruit, then add the remaining plums.

3 Trim the edges and pinch to make a decorative edging. Brush the top with egg white and sprinkle with a little caster sugar. Make a small slit in the centre to allow steam to escape.

4 Cook in the oven for 35–40 minutes until the pastry is golden brown and the plums are soft (check by inserting a knife through the slit). Sprinkle with extra caster sugar and then serve hot with whipped cream or custard.

Variation
When plums are not in season make this pie with a mixture of apple and soft ready-to-eat dried apricots. Use a crisp, sour apple, such as Bramley, for a good contrast with the sweet apricot, there is no need to soak the apricots first.

German Plum Cake

This kind of cake, with a shortcrust base and a crumble topping makes pastry making easy, as there is no chilling or rolling, The filling can be made with various different fruits, depending on the time of year. Plums are harvested from the end of summer until the middle of autumn, and while they are in season every German bakery sells fresh plum cake.

Makes about 16 pieces

200g/7oz/scant 1 cup butter, softened
150g/5oz/¾ cup caster (superfine) sugar
pinch of salt
1½ tsp vanilla extract or 2 packs vanilla sugar (about 10g/1/4oz)
2 eggs
400g/14oz/3½ cups plain (all-purpose) flour
icing (confectioners') sugar, to dust

For the filling

800g/1¾lb plums, halved and stoned (pitted)
100g/3½oz/½ cup caster sugar
whipped double (heavy) cream, to serve

1 Preheat the oven to 180°C/350°F/Gas 4. Put the butter in a bowl with the sugar, salt, vanilla, eggs and flour. Rub the mixture with your fingertips until it is crumbly.

2 Use half the crumble dough to line a 40 x 30cm/16 x 12in baking tray, pressing it evenly over the base and up the sides.

3 Put in the halved plums and sprinkle the sugar on top. Sprinkle the rest of the crumble on top of the plums.

4 Bake the cake in the preheated oven for 45–60 minutes. Dust with icing sugar and cut into squares to serve with whipped cream.

Variation
For a crunchier topping, sprinkled a layer of sunflower seeds over the top before baking. You could also reduce the amount of flour by 115g/4oz and replace that amount with oats.

Plum Pie Energy 360kcal/1516kJ; Protein 4.1g; Carbohydrate 57g, of which sugars 25.5g; Fat 14.5g, of which saturates 7.5g; Cholesterol 26mg; Calcium 73mg; Fibre 2.9g; Sodium 61mg.
Plum Cake Energy 265kcal/1115kJ; Protein 3.5g; Carbohydrate 39.9g, of which sugars 20.9g; Fat 11.3g, of which saturates 7g; Cholesterol 53mg; Calcium 55mg; Fibre 1.5g; Sodium 105mg.

Pear and Plum Pie

This delectable dish resembles a classic fruit pie, although the sweet pastry is delightfully different from the usual pastry that encases fruit pies.

Serves 6

1kg/2¼lb assorted fresh fruit such as apples, pears, cherries and plums
275g/10oz/2½ cups plain (all-purpose) white flour
2 egg yolks
200g/7oz/scant 1 cup unsalted butter, diced, plus softened butter for greasing
finely grated rind of 1 lemon
200g/7oz/scant 1 cup caster (superfine) sugar
1 beaten egg, for glazing

1 Peel and core or stone (pit) all the fruit as necessary. Slice and poach lightly in a little water until just tender but still holding their shape. Drain and set aside.

2 Pile the flour on a clean work surface and make a hollow in the centre with your fist. Add the egg yolks, butter, lemon rind and half the sugar to the hollow.

3 Mix to a very soft pastry with your hands and knead gently. Wrap in clear film (plastic wrap) and set aside to rest for about 20 minutes.

4 Preheat the oven to 200°C/400°F/Gas 6. Grease a shallow 23cm/9in cake tin (pan) with butter.

5 Roll out half the pastry on a lightly floured surface and use it to line the bottom and sides of the cake tin. Do not worry if the pastry breaks or cracks; just use your fingers to press it back together into shape.

6 Check that the fruit is well drained, then spoon it into the lined tin. Sprinkle the remaining sugar over the top.

7 Roll out the remaining pastry and make a lid for the pie. Fit it over the fruit, pinch the pastry edges together to seal, and brush with beaten egg. Bake for 40 minutes, until the pastry is golden and the filling is cooked. Serve cold.

Passion Fruit Pie

Crisp puff pastry is teamed with a wonderfully creamy passion fruit and orange filling enhanced with Grand Marnier to make an unforgettable dessert.

Serves 4–6

175g/6oz puff pastry, thawed if frozen
icing (confectioners') sugar, for dusting

For the filling

60ml/4 tbsp apricot conserve
6 passion fruits
115g/4oz/½ cup cream cheese
300ml/½ pint/1¼ cup sour cream
2 eggs, beaten
75g/3oz/6 tbsp caster (superfine) sugar
grated rind and juice of 1 orange
30ml/2 tbsp Grand Marnier

1 Preheat the oven to 190°C/375°F/Gas 5. Roll out the pastry on a lightly floured surface and use it to line an 18cm/7in flan tin (pan). Prick the pastry base with a fork, then spread over the apricot conserve.

2 Cut the passion fruits in half. Using a teaspoon, scoop out the pulp and press it through a sieve into a bowl. Discard the seeds.

3 Add the cream cheese to the bowl, together with the soured cream, eggs, caster sugar, orange rind and juice and beat with a wooden spoon to combine. Stir in the Grand Marnier. Spoon the filling into the flan case. Bake in the oven for 25–30 minutes until golden.

4 Carefully heat some metal skewers. Dust the pie with icing sugar. Holding a skewer with oven gloves, press it on to the icing sugar, which will melt and caramelize. Continue to brand the topping, creating a lattice effect.

Cook's Tip

If you don't have time to brand the top of the pie, simply dust it with icing sugar, protect the pastry edge with pieces of foil and put the pie under a hot grill for a few seconds to caramelize the icing sugar.

Pear & Plum Energy 612kcal/2571kJ; Protein 6.1g; Carbohydrate 85.3g, of which sugars 50.4g; Fat 29.8g, of which saturates 18.6g; Cholesterol 144mg; Calcium 101mg; Fibre 4.1g; Sodium 260mg.
Passion Fruit Energy 414kcal/1725kJ; Protein 6.3g; Carbohydrate 34.3g, of which sugars 23.9g; Fat 28.1g, of which saturates 15.8g; Cholesterol 142mg; Calcium 99mg; Fibre 0g; Sodium 202mg.

Apricot Pie

This is a traditional Hungarian pie where apricots are very popular.

Serves 8

250g/9oz/generous 1 cup very cold butter, cubed
500g/1¼lb/5 cups plain (all-purpose) flour
130g/4½oz caster (superfine) sugar
1 egg yolk
30ml/2 tbsp sour cream
1 small egg, beaten, for brushing
60ml/4 tbsp chopped almonds

For the filling

2kg/4½lb apricots, stoned pitted, and cut in quarters
45ml/3 tbsp soft light brown sugar
30ml/2 tbsp ground almonds

1 Put the butter into a bowl and add the flour. Rub the flour into the butter until it resembles fine breadcrumbs. Add the sugar, egg yolk and sour cream, and work the dough until it is completely smooth. Chill, covered, for 2 hours.

2 Preheat the oven to 180°C/350°F/Gas 4 and butter a 20cm/8in, shallow, square cake tin (pan). To make the filling, put the apricots and brown sugar into a large bowl and mix together well.

3 Remove the dough from the refrigerator and divide it in half. Roll each half to about 5mm/¼in thickness.

4 Line the cake tin with one of the rolled dough pieces. Sprinkle with the ground almonds and then spoon in the apricots. Moisten the edge of the pastry with water, then cover with the remaining dough and seal all the edges.

5 Prick the pie top with a fork. Brush with beaten egg and sprinkle with the chopped almonds. Bake the pie for 40 minutes, or until golden brown. Cool completely before serving.

Cook's Tips

When buying apricots, look for plump and juicy ones with an evenly distributed orange colour.

Apricot and Almond Jalousie

Jalousie means 'shutter' in French, and the slatted puff pastry topping of this popular fruit pie, traditionally made in a rectangular shape, looks very much like the shutters used outside the windows of houses across France.

Serves 4

225g/8oz ready-made puff pastry
a little beaten egg
90ml/6 tbsp apricot preserve
30ml/2 tbsp caster (superfine) sugar
30ml/2 tbsp flaked (sliced) almonds
whipped cream, to serve

1 Preheat the oven to 220°C/425°F/Gas 7. Roll out the pastry on a lightly floured surface and cut into a 30cm/12in square. Cut in half to make two rectangles.

2 Place a piece of pastry on a wetted baking sheet and brush round the edges with beat egg. Spread over the apricot preserve.

3 Fold the remaining rectangle in half lengthways and cut about eight diagonal slits from the centre fold to within about 1cm/½in of the edge all the way along.

4 Unfold the pastry and place it on top of the preserve-covered pastry on the baking sheet, matching each edge carefully to the base. Press the pastry edges together well, to seal, and scallop the edges at close intervals with the back of a small knife.

5 Brush the slashed pastry top with a little water and sprinkle evenly with the sugar and the flaked almonds.

6 Bake in the oven for 25–30 minutes, until well risen and golden brown. Remove the jalousie from the oven and leave to cool on a wire rack. Serve the jalousie sliced, with cream or natural yogurt.

Variation

Make the jalousie using plum preserve instead of apricot.

Apricot Pie Energy 599kcal/2515kJ; Protein 11g; Carbohydrate 73g, of which sugars 25g; Fat 32g, of which saturates 18g; Cholesterol 121mg; Calcium 156mg; Fibre 7.6g; Sodium 211mg.
Apricot Jalousie Energy 339kcal/1423kJ; Protein 4.9g; Carbohydrate 43.5g, of which sugars 23.2g; Fat 18g, of which saturates 0.3g; Cholesterol 0mg; Calcium 56mg; Fibre 0.6g; Sodium 186mg.

Moroccan Apricot Coil

This is the most famous, sweet dish in Morocco.

Serves 8–10

115g/4oz/1 cup blanched almonds
300g/11oz/2¾ cups ground almonds
50g/2oz/½ cup icing (confectioners') sugar
115g/4oz/⅔ cup caster (superfine) sugar
115g/4oz/½ cup butter, softened, plus 20g/¾oz for cooking nuts
5–10ml/1–2 tsp ground cinnamon
15ml/1 tbsp orange flower water
3–4 sheets filo pastry
1 egg yolk
icing (confectioners') sugar
ground cinnamon

1 Fry the blanched almonds in a little butter until golden , then process. Place in a bowl and add the ground almonds, icing sugar, caster sugar, butter, cinnamon and orange flower water. Use your hands to form the mixture into a smooth paste. Cover and chill in the refrigerator for about 30 minutes.

2 Preheat the oven to 180°C/350°F/Gas 4. Open out the sheets of filo pastry, keeping them in a pile so they do not dry out, and brush the top one with a little melted butter.

3 Take lumps of the almond paste and roll them into fingers. Place them end to end along the long edge of the top sheet of filo, then roll the filo up into a roll the thickness of your thumb, tucking in the ends to stop the filling oozing out. Repeat with the other sheets of filo, until all the filling is used up.

4 Grease a large round baking pan or the widest baking sheet you can find. Lift one of the filo rolls in both hands and gently push it together from both ends, like an accordion, to relax the pastry before coiling it in the centre of the pan or baking sheet. Do the same with the other rolls, placing them end to end to form a tight coil like a snake.

5 Mix the egg yolk with a little water and brush this over the pastry, then bake for 30–35 minutes, until crisp and lightly browned. Top the freshly cooked pastry with a liberal sprinkling of icing sugar, and add lines of cinnamon like the spokes of a wheel. Serve at room temperature.

Blueberry and Orange Pie

American blueberries or European bilberries can be used for this scrumptious pie. You may need to add a little more sugar if you are lucky enough to find native bilberries.

Serves 6

2 x 225g/8oz ready-rolled shortcrust pastry sheets, thawed if frozen
800g/1¾lb/7 cups blueberries
75g/3oz/6 tbsp caster (superfine) sugar, plus extra for sprinkling
45ml/3 tbsp cornflour (cornstarch)
grated rind and juice of ½ orange
grated rind of ½ lemon
2.5ml/½ tsp ground cinnamon
15g/½oz/1 tbsp unsalted (sweet) butter, diced
beaten egg, to glaze
whipped cream, to serve

1 Preheat the oven to 200°C/400°F/Gas 6. Use one sheet of pastry to line a 23cm/9in pie dish, leaving the excess pastry hanging over the edges.

2 Mix the blueberries, caster sugar, cornflour, orange rind and juice, lemon rind and cinnamon in a large bowl. Spoon into the pastry case and dot with the butter. Dampen the rim of the pastry case (pie shell) with a little water and top with the remaining pastry sheet.

3 Cut the pastry edge at 2.5cm/1in intervals, then fold each section over on itself to form a triangle and create a sunflower edge. Trim off the excess pastry and cut out decorations from the trimmings. Stick them to the pastry lid with a little of the beaten egg.

4 Glaze the pastry with the egg and sprinkle with caster sugar. Bake for 30–35 minutes or until golden.

5 Serve the pie warm or cold with whipped cream.

Variation

Substitute a crumble topping for the pastry lid. The contrast with the juicy blueberry filling is sensational.

Apricot Coil Energy 261kcal/1091kJ; Protein 3.8g; Carbohydrate 25.9g, of which sugars 17.9g; Fat 16.6g, of which saturates 6.7g; Cholesterol 45mg; Calcium 55mg; Fibre 1.2g; Sodium 74mg.
Blueberry Pie Energy 458Kcal/1915kJ; Protein 4.7g; Carbohydrate 60g, of which sugars 20.4g; Fat 23.8g, of which saturates 1.3g; Cholesterol 5mg; Calcium 95mg; Fibre 5.6g; Sodium 143mg.

Peach and Blueberry Lattice Pie

This colourful lattice pie is bursting with fruit flavours.

Serves 8

225g/8oz/2 cups plain (all-purpose) flour
5ml/1 tsp sugar
150g/5oz/10 tbsp cold butter
1 egg yolk
30–45ml/2–3 tbsp iced water
30ml/2 tbsp milk, for glazing

For the filling

6 peaches, peeled, stoned (pitted) and sliced
225g/8oz/2 cups fresh blueberries
150g/5oz/¾ cup sugar
30ml/2 tbsp fresh lemon juice
40g/1½oz/⅓ cup plain (all-purpose) flour
pinch of grated nutmeg
25g/1oz/2 tbsp butter

1 Sift the flour, salt and sugar into a bowl, and rub in the butter. Mix the egg yolk with 30ml/2 tbsp of the iced water and sprinkle over the flour mixture. Combine until the pastry holds together. If the pastry is too crumbly, add a little more water. Gather the pastry into a ball and flatten into a disc. Wrap in clear film (plastic wrap) and chill for at least 20 minutes.

2 Roll out two-thirds of the pastry to a thickness of 3mm/⅛in. Use to line a 23cm/9in fluted tin (pan). Trim all around, leaving a 1cm/½in overhang, then trim the edges. Gather the remaining pastry into a ball, and roll out to a thickness of about 6mm/¼in. Cut strips 1cm/½in wide. Chill the pastry case (pie shell) and the strips for 20 minutes. Preheat the oven to 200°C/400°F/Gas 6.

3 Line the pastry case with baking parchment and fill with dried beans. Bake 12–15 minutes. Remove from the oven and lift out the paper with the beans. Prick the pastry case, then bake for 5 minutes more. Let the pastry case cool slightly before filling.

4 In a bowl, combine the peach slices with the blueberries, sugar, lemon juice, flour and nutmeg. Spoon the fruit mixture evenly into the pastry case. Dot with the pieces of butter.

5 Weave a lattice top with the chilled pastry strips, pressing the ends to the baked pastry-case edge. Brush with the milk. Bake for 15 minutes. Reduce the heat to 180°C/350°F/Gas 4, and continue baking 30 minutes more. Serve the pie warm.

Cherry Pie

This is a favourite dessert from America, it is best eaten slightly warm or at room temperature, on the day of baking, with lots of whipped cream.

Serves 6

225g/8oz/2 cups plain (all-purpose) flour
130g/4½oz/½ cup butter
30–45ml/3–4 tbsp iced water
whipped cream, to serve

For the filling

800g/1¾lb/7 cups fresh cherries, pitted or 2 x 400g/14oz cans or jars, drained
75g/3oz/6 tbsp caster (superfine) sugar, plus extra for sprinkling
45ml/3 tbsp cornflour (cornstarch)
grated rind of ½ lemon
2.5ml/½ tsp almond extract
40g/1½oz/3 tbsp butter
beaten egg, mixed with a little water, to glaze

1 Preheat a 190°C/375°F/Gas 5 oven. In a large bowl rub the butter in to the flour and walnut mixture. Use enough iced water to make a firm dough. Wrap and chill for 30 minutes. Roll out half the dough and use to line a 23cm/9in pie dish.

2 In a mixing bowl, combine the cherries, sugar, cornflour, lemon rind and almond extract. Mix so that all the fruit is coated in the sugar mixture. Spoon the mixture into the pastry case and dot with the butter.

3 Roll out the remaining pastry dough and using a ruler cut into strips 1.5cm/½in wide. Lay half the strips across the pie filling, keeping them neatly parallel and spacing them evenly.

4 Fold back every other strip from the centre. Lay a strip across the centre at right angles, then fold over the strips that aren't already folded over to make a plaited effect.

5 Continue in the same way, folding back alternate strips to overlap the next strip. Once the lattice is complete, brush with a little milk to glaze.

6 Bake the pie for 40–50 minutes or until the pastry is golden brown. Allow to cool slightly on a wire rack, before serving warm in slices with whipped cream.

Peach Lattice Pie Energy 391kcal/1640kJ; Protein 4.7g; Carbohydrate 53g, of which sugars 27.7g; Fat 19.3g, of which saturates 11.7g; Cholesterol 72mg; Calcium 86mg; Fibre 2.9g; Sodium 139mg.
Cherry Pie Energy 420kcal/1754kJ; Protein 4g; Carbohydrate 47g, of which sugars 23g; Fat 25g, of which saturates 11g; Cholesterol 28mg; Calcium 61mg; Fibre 3g; Sodium 271mg.

Dunfillan Bramble Pudding

This warming pudding comes from Dunfillan in Perthshire. It is easy to make, if you have a little time, and is perfect with fresh cream as a tasty dessert or teatime indulgence.

Serves 4

For the pastry

50g/2oz/¼ cup butter
50g/2oz/¼ cup caster (superfine) sugar
1 large egg, well beaten
115g/4oz/1 cup plain (all-purpose) flour, sifted
pinch of baking powder
30ml/2 tbsp milk
grated rind of 2 lemons

For the filling

450g/1lb/4 cups blackberries
75g/3oz/scant ½ cup caster (superfine) sugar
squeeze of lemon juice
sprinkling of cornflour (cornstarch)

1 Preheat the oven to 180°C/350°F/Gas 4. Put the blackberries in a pan and barely cover with water, then add the sugar and lemon juice. Cook until soft, about 5 minutes.

2 Transfer the blackberries to an ovenproof dish in layers, sprinkling each layer with a little cornflour.

3 To make the pastry, cream the butter and sugar then add the beaten egg. Mix the flour and baking powder then add it alternately with the milk to the butter mixture, mixing well after each addition. Finally stir in the lemon rind.

4 Spread the pastry evenly over the fruit, taking small batches from the bowl and spreading carefully. Cook in the preheated oven for 20–30 minutes, or until the top is golden brown. Serve hot or cold.

Variation
Blackberries or brambles grow wild and have a short season, if you can't find enough to make this pie, add sliced apple to make up to the correct weight of fruit, or use frozen fruits of the forest from the supermarket.

Bilberry and Apple Pie

Bilberries, wild blueberries or whortleberries are tiny and take a long time to pick enough fruit for a pie. You can, however, bulk them out with blackberries or frozen berry mixes.

Serves 6

2 cooking apples, total weight about 400g/14oz
10ml/2 tsp cornflour (cornstarch)
350g/12oz/3 cups whinberries
40–50g/3–4 tbsp caster (superfine) sugar, plus extra for sprinkling
milk for brushing

For the pastry

250g/9oz/2¼ cups plain (all-purpose) flour
25g/1oz/2 tbsp caster (superfine) sugar
150g/5oz/10 tbsp butter, chilled and cut into small cubes
1 egg

1 Sift the flour into a bowl and stir in the sugar. Add the butter and rub into the flour until the mixture resembles fine crumbs. Stir in the egg and enough cold water until the mixture forms clumps, then gather it together to make a smooth dough. Wrap the pastry and refrigerate for 20–30 minutes.

2 Preheat the oven to 190°C/375°F/Gas 5. On a lightly floured surface, roll out half the dough to make a circle and use it to line a deep 23cm/9in tart tin (pan) or ovenproof dish. Roll out the remaining pastry to a circle large enough to make a lid.

3 Peel the apples, remove their cores and chop them into small pieces. Toss the apple pieces with the cornflour until evenly coated and arrange them in the bottom of the pastry case. Scatter the whinberries (or blueberries) on top and sprinkle the sugar over. Lightly brush the edges of the pastry with water.

4 Lay the pastry lid over the fruit filling. Trim off the excess pastry and pinch the edges together to seal. Make a slit in the centre, then brush the top with milk and sprinkle with sugar.

5 Put into the hot oven and cook for 30–40 minutes until the pastry is crisp and golden brown and the filling is cooked through. While the pastry is still hot, sprinkle with more caster sugar. Serve warm.

Dunfillan Pudding Energy 366kcal/1539kJ; Protein 6.2g; Carbohydrate 60.2g, of which sugars 39.2g; Fat 12.8g, of which saturates 7.2g; Cholesterol 90mg; Calcium 122mg; Fibre 4.4g; Sodium 107mg.
Whinberry Pie Energy 403kcal/1688kJ; Protein 5.76g; Carbohydrate 51.4g, of which sugars 18.15g; Fat 20.8g, of which saturates 12.5g; Cholesterol 81.5mg; Calcium 98.6mg; Fibre 3.5g; Sodium 157.5mg.

Rhubarb Pie

This pie is as attractive as it is delicious.

Serves 6
175g/6oz/1½ cups plain (all-purpose) flour
2.5ml/½ tsp salt
10ml/2 tsp caster (superfine) sugar
75g/3oz/6 tbsp cold butter
30ml/2 tbsp single (light) cream

For the filling
1kg/2¼lb fresh rhubarb, cut into 2.5cm/1in slices
30ml/2 tbsp cornflour (cornstarch)
1 egg
275g/10oz/1½ cups caster (superfine) sugar
15ml/1 tbsp grated orange rind

1 Make the pastry. Sift the flour, salt and sugar into a bowl. Add the butter and rub in until the mix resembles breadcrumbs. Sprinkle the flour mixture with enough chilled water, about 45ml/3 tbsp, to bind the ingredients into a dough that just holds together. If the dough is too crumbly, mix in a little more chilled water. Gather the dough into a ball, flatten into a round, place in a plastic bag and chill for 20 minutes.

2 Roll out the pastry between two sheets of baking parchment to 3mm/⅛in thick. Use to line a 23cm/9in pie dish or tin (pan). Trim around the edge, leaving a 1cm/½in overhang. Fold the overhang under the edge and flute. Chill the pastry case (pie shell) and trimmings for 30 minutes.

3 Put the rhubarb in a bowl, sprinkle with the cornflour and toss to coat. Preheat the oven to 220°C/425°F/Gas 7.

4 Beat the egg with the sugar in a bowl until blended, then mix in the orange rind. Stir the sugar mixture into the rhubarb and mix well, then spoon the fruit into the prepared pastry case.

5 Roll out the pastry trimmings and make decorative shapes with a cutter. Arrange on top of the pie. Brush the shapes and the edge of the case with cream. Bake for 30 minutes. Reduce the temperature to 160°C/325°F/Gas 3 and bake for 15–20 minutes more, until the pastry is golden brown and the rhubarb is tender.

Rhubarb and Cherry Pie

This pastry is made shorter and more crumbly with a mix of butter and white vegetable fat.

Serves 8
450g/1lb rhubarb, chopped
450g/1lb canned pitted tart red or black cherries, drained
275g/10oz/1½ cups caster (superfine) sugar
25g/1oz quick-cooking tapioca

For the pastry
275g/10oz/2½ cups plain (all-purpose) flour
5ml/1 tsp salt
75g/3oz/6 tbsp cold butter, cut in pieces
50g/2oz/⅓ cup cold white vegetable fat (shortening), cut in pieces
50–120ml/2–4fl oz/¼–½ cup iced water
milk, for glazing

1 For the pastry, sift the flour and salt into a bowl. Add the butter and fat to the dry ingredients and cut in with a pastry blender until the mixture resembles coarse breadcrumbs.

2 With a fork, stir in just enough water to bind the pastry. Gather into two balls, one slightly larger than the other. Wrap the pastry in baking parchment and chill for at least 20 minutes.

3 Preheat a baking sheet in the centre of a 200°C/400°F/Gas 6 oven. On a lightly floured surface, roll out the larger pastry ball to a thickness of about 3mm/⅛in.

4 Roll the pastry around the rolling pin and transfer to a 23cm/9in pie dish. Trim the edge to leave a 1cm/½in overhang. Chill the pastry case (pie shell) while making the filling.

5 In a mixing bowl, combine the rhubarb, cherries, sugar and tapioca, and spoon into the pie shell. Roll out the remaining pastry and cut out leaf shapes.

6 Transfer the pastry lid to the pie and trim to leave a 2cm/¾in overhang. Fold the top edge under the bottom, and flute. Roll small balls from the scraps.

7 Mark veins in the pastry leaves and place on top with the balls. Glaze the top and bake until golden, about 40–50 minutes.

Rhubarb Pie Energy 431Kcal/1823kJ; Protein 5.8g; Carbohydrate 78.4g, of which sugars 51.6g; Fat 12.7g, of which saturates 7.4g; Cholesterol 61mg; Calcium 233mg; Fibre 3.3g; Sodium 100mg.
Rhubarb & Cherry Energy 431Kcal/1823kJ; Protein 5.8g; Carbohydrate 78.4g, of which sugars 51.6g; Fat 12.7g, of which saturates 7.4g; Cholesterol 61mg; Calcium 233mg; Fibre 3.3g; Sodium 100mg.

One-crust Rhubarb & Ginger Pie

The method used for this simple shortcrust pie can be used for all sorts of fruit, and it is completely foolproof. It doesn't matter how rough the pie looks when it goes into the oven; it always comes out looking fantastic.

Serves 6

350g/12oz shortcrust pastry, thawed if frozen
1 egg yolk, beaten
25g/1oz/3 tbsp semolina
25g/1oz/¼ cup hazelnuts, coarsely chopped
30ml/2 tbsp golden sugar

For the filling

450g/1lb rhubarb, cut into 2.5cm/1in pieces
75g/3oz/6 tbsp caster (superfine) sugar
1–2 pieces preserved stem ginger in syrup, drained and finely chopped

1 Preheat the oven to 200°C/400°F/Gas 6. Roll out the pastry to a circle 35cm/14in across. Lay it over the rolling pin and transfer it to a large baking sheet. Brush a little egg yolk over the pastry. Scatter the semolina over the centre, leaving a wide rim all round the edge.

2 Make the filling. Place the rhubarb pieces, caster sugar and chopped ginger in a large bowl and mix well.

3 Pile the rhubarb mixture into the middle of the pastry. Fold the rim roughly over the filling so that it almost covers it. Some of the fruit will remain visible in the centre.

4 Brush the pastry rim with any remaining egg yolk to glaze, then sprinkle the hazelnuts and golden sugar over the top. Bake the pie for 30–35 minutes or until the pastry is golden brown. Serve hot or warm.

Cook's Tip

Egg yolk glaze brushed on to pastry gives it a nice golden sheen. However, be careful not to drip the glaze on the baking sheet, or it will burn and be difficult to remove.

Mango Pie

This recipe captures all the sunshine flavours of the Caribbean. For the tastiest pie, be sure the mangoes are good and ripe.

Serves 6

175g/6oz/1½ cups plain (all-purpose) flour
pinch of salt
75g/3oz/⅓ cup unsalted (sweet) butter, chilled and diced
25g/1oz/2 tbsp white vegetable fat (shortening), chilled and diced
15ml/1 tbsp caster (superfine) sugar, plus extra for sprinkling
about 45ml/3 tbsp cold water
beaten egg, to glaze
vanilla ice cream, to serve

For the filling

2 ripe mangoes
45ml/3 tbsp fresh lime juice
115g/4oz/½ cup caster (superfine) sugar
15ml/1 tbsp arrowroot mixed to a paste with 15ml/1 tbsp water

1 Sift the flour and salt into a mixing bowl. Rub in the butter and white vegetable fat until the mixture resembles fine breadcrumbs, then stir in the caster sugar. Add enough cold water to make a dough. Knead lightly, then roll out two-thirds of the pastry and line a 18cm/7in pie dish. Wrap the remaining pastry in clear film (plastic wrap) and chill both the pastry and the pastry case for 30 minutes.

2 Meanwhile, make the filling. Peel the mangoes and slice the flesh off the stone. Reserve half the sliced mango, and coarsely chop the rest. Place the chopped mango in a pan with the lime juice and caster sugar. Cover and cook for 10 minutes, or until soft. Pour in the arrowroot paste and cook, stirring all the time until thickened. Set the filling aside to cool.

3 Preheat the oven to 190°C/375°F/Gas 5. Pour the cooled mango sauce into the chilled pastry case and top with the reserved slices. Roll out the remaining pastry to make a pie lid. Dampen the rim of the pastry case and add the lid. Crimp the edges to seal, then cut a cross to allow the steam to escape.

4 Glaze the pastry with the beaten egg and sprinkle lightly with caster sugar. Bake for 35–40 minutes until the pastry is golden brown. Cool slightly on a wire rack. Serve warm with a scoop of vanilla ice cream.

Rhubarb Pie Energy 373kcal/1562kJ; Protein 6g; Carbohydrate 45g, of which sugars 15g; Fat 20g, of which saturates 6g; Cholesterol 43mg; Calcium 131mg; Fibre 4g; Sodium 241mg.
Mango Pie Energy 353kcal/1494kJ; Protein 4g; Carbohydrate 55g, of which sugars 30g; Fat 70g, of which saturates 58g; Cholesterol 70mg; Calcium 58mg; Fibre 2.5g; Sodium 84mg.

Lemon Meringue Pie

Crisp on top, soft beneath, and deliciously tangy in the middle, this is a classic dish, the popularity of which never seems to wane.

Serves 8

225g/8oz shortcrust pastry, thawed if frozen
grated rind and juice of 1 large lemon
250ml/8fl oz/1 cup plus 15ml/1 tbsp cold water
115g/4oz/generous ½ cup caster (superfine) sugar plus 90ml/6 tbsp extra
25g/1oz/2 tbsp butter
45ml/3 tbsp cornflour (cornstarch)
3 eggs, separated
a pinch of salt
a pinch of cream of tartar

1 Line a 23cm/9in pie dish with the pastry, folding under a 1cm/½in overhang to give a firm edge. Crimp the edge and chill for 20 minutes.

2 Preheat the oven to 200°C/400°F/Gas 6. Prick the pastry case (pie shell), base line with baking parchment and fill with baking beans.

3 Bake for 12 minutes. Remove the paper and beans and bake until golden, 6–8 minutes more.

4 In a pan, combine the lemon rind and juice with 250ml/8fl oz/1 cup of the water, 115g/4oz/generous ½ cup of the sugar, and the butter. Bring to the boil.

5 Meanwhile, dissolve the cornflour in the remaining water. Add the egg yolks. Beat into the lemon mixture, return to the boil and whisk until thick, about 5 minutes. Cover the surface with baking parchment and leave to cool.

6 For the meringue, beat the egg whites, using an electric hand whisk, with the salt and cream of tartar until stiffly peaking. Add the remaining sugar a spoonful at a time and beat until glossy.

7 Spoon the lemon mixture into the pastry case. Spoon the meringue on top, sealing it with the pastry rim. Bake until golden, 12–15 minutes.

Lime Meringue Pie

This American recipe uses condensed milk to make a sweet filling that offsets the tangy fresh lime.

Serves 6

3 egg yolks
350ml/2fl oz sweetened condensed milk
finely grated rind and juice of 4 limes
7 egg whites
pinch salt
squeeze of fresh lemon juice
115g/4oz/½ cup caster (superfine) sugar
2.5ml/½ tsp vanilla extract

For the pastry
200g/7oz/1¾ cups plain (all-purpose) flour
115g/4oz/½ cup butter, diced
30ml/2 tbsp sugar

1 To make the pastry, sift the flour into a bowl and add the walnuts. Rub in the butter until the mixture resembles very fine breadcrumbs. Stir in the sugar and egg yolk mixture to make a firm dough. Knead lightly, wrap and chill for 30 minutes.

2 Preheat the oven to 190°C/375°F/Gas 5. Roll out the pastry on a lightly floured surface and use to line a 23cm/9in fluted flan tin (pan). Prick the base all over with a fork. Line the pastry with foil and baking beans, then bake for 15 minutes.

3 With an electric mixer on high speed, beat the yolks and condensed milk. Stir in the lime rind and juice.

4 In another clean bowl, beat three of the egg whites until stiff. Fold into the lime mixture. Spread the lime filling in the pastry case. Bake for 10 minutes.

5 Meanwhile, beat the remaining egg whites with the salt and lemon juice until soft peaks form. Beat in the sugar, one tablespoon at a time, until stiff peaks form. Add the vanilla.

6 Remove the pie from the oven. Using a metal spatula, spread the meringue over the lime filling, making a swirled design. Bake for a further 12 minutes until the meringue is lightly browned. Let cool, in the tin, on a wire rack. Serve in slices, slightly warm or at room temperature

Lemon Meringue Energy 357kcal/1497kJ; Protein 6.8g; Carbohydrate 42.8g, of which sugars 25.1g; Fat 18.9g, of which saturates 9g; Cholesterol 129mg; Calcium 108mg; Fibre 0.7g; Sodium 137mg.
Lime Meringue Energy 267kcal/1117kJ; Protein 6g; Carbohydrate 31g, of which sugars 15g; Fat 15g, of which saturates 6g; Cholesterol 78mg; Calcium 41mg; Fibre 1g; Sodium 231mg.

Rhubarb Meringue Pie

Tangy rhubarb contrasts beautifully with meringue.

Serves 6

675g/1½lb rhubarb, chopped
250g/9oz/1¼ cup caster (superfine) sugar
grated rind and juice of 3 oranges
3 eggs, separated
75ml/5 tbsp cornflour (cornstarch)

For the pastry

200g/7oz/1¾ cups plain (all-purpose) flour
25g/1oz/¼ cup ground walnuts
115g/4oz/½ cup butter, diced
30ml/2 tbsp sugar
1 egg yolk, beaten with 15ml/1 tbsp water

1 To make the pastry, sift the flour into a bowl and add the walnuts. Rub in the butter until the mixture resembles very fine breadcrumbs. Stir in the sugar and egg yolk mixture to make a firm dough. Knead lightly, wrap and chill for 30 minutes.

2 Preheat the oven to 190°C/375°F/Gas 5. Roll out the pastry on a lightly floured surface and use to line a 23cm/9in fluted flan tin (pan). Prick the base all over with a fork. Line the pastry with foil and baking beans, then bake for 15 minutes.

3 Meanwhile, to make the filling, put the chopped rhubarb in a large pan with 75g/3oz/6 tbsp of the sugar. Add the orange rind. Cover and cook over low heat until tender.

4 Remove the foil and beans from the pastry case (pie shell), then brush all over with a little egg yolk. Bake the pastry case for about 15 minutes, or until the pastry is crisp and golden.

5 Mix together the cornflour and the orange juice in a mixing bowl. Remove the rhubarb from the heat, stir in the cornflour mixture, then return the pan to the heat and bring to the boil, stirring constantly. Cook for 1–2 minutes more. Cool slightly, then beat in the remaining egg yolks. Pour into the pastry case.

6 Whisk the egg whites until they form soft peaks, then whisk in the remaining sugar, 15ml/1 tbsp at a time. Swirl over the filling and bake for 25 minutes until the meringue is golden.

Crunchy-Topped Coffee Meringue Pie

For a special treat, try this coffee flavoured meringue.

Serves 6

30ml/2 tbsp ground coffee
350ml/12fl oz/1½ cups milk
25g/1oz/¼ cup cornflour (cornstarch)
130g/4½oz/⅔ cup caster (superfine) sugar
4 egg yolks
15g/½oz/1 tbsp butter

For the pastry

175g/6oz/1½ cups plain (all-purpose) flour
15ml/1 tbsp icing (confectioners') sugar
75g/3oz/6 tbsp butter, diced
1 egg yolk
finely grated rind of ½ orange
15ml/1 tbsp orange juice

For the meringue

3 egg whites
1.5ml/¼ tsp cream of tartar
150g/5oz/¾ cup caster (superfine) sugar
15ml/1 tbsp demerara (raw) sugar
25g/1oz/¼ cup skinned hazelnuts

1 Preheat the oven to 200°C/400°F/Gas 6. Make the pastry, following the instructions for Rhubarb Meringue Pie, left, and line a 23cm/9in flan tin (pan). Chill for 30 minutes. Bake blind for 15 minutes, then cool on a wire rack. Lower the oven temperature to 160°C/325°F/Gas 3.

2 Put the coffee in a small bowl. Heat 250ml/8fl oz/1 cup of the milk until near-boiling and pour over the coffee. Leave to infuse (steep) for 4–5 minutes, then strain. Blend the cornflour and sugar with the remaining milk in a small pan, and whisk in the coffee flavoured milk. Bring to the boil, stirring until thick.

3 In a bowl, beat the egg yolks. Stir a little of the coffee mixture into the egg yolks, then add to the remaining coffee mixture in the pan with the butter. Cook over a low heat until very thick. Pour the coffee filling into the pastry case. Whisk the egg whites and cream of tartar in a small bowl until stiff peaks form. Whisk in the caster sugar, a spoonful at a time.

4 Spoon the meringue over the filling and spread to the edge, swirling into peaks. Sprinkle with demerara sugar and hazelnuts. Bake for 30–35 minutes. Serve warm or cold.

Rhubarb Meringue Energy 567Kcal/2388kJ; Protein 8.4g; Carbohydrate 89.5g, of which sugars 52.6g; Fat 22.1g, of which saturates 11.1g; Cholesterol 136mg; Calcium 202mg; Fibre 2.8g; Sodium 68mg.
Coffee Meringue Energy 540Kcal/2274kJ; Protein 9.5g; Carbohydrate 83.6g, of which sugars 57.4g; Fat 21g, of which saturates 10g; Cholesterol 203mg; Calcium 168mg; Fibre 1.2g; Sodium 160mg.

Plum Meringue Pie

A fruit brandy made from Mirabelle plums intensifies the flavour of fresh fruits.

Serves 6–8

175g/6oz/1½ cups plain (all-purpose) flour
40g/1½oz/3 tbsp butter, diced
40g/1½oz/3 tbsp white cooking fat, diced
3 egg whites
75g/3oz/6 tbsp caster (superfine) sugar

For the filling

350g/12oz plums, stoned (pitted) and sliced
10ml/2 tsp sugar
60ml/4 tbsp orange juice
3 egg yolks, beaten
45ml/3 tbsp eau de vie de Mirabelle

1 Make the pastry. Sift the flour into a mixing bowl. Rub in the butter and white fat until the mixture resembles fine breadcrumbs, then stir in enough cold water to give a soft dough. Wrap in clear film (plastic wrap) and chill for 30 minutes. Preheat the oven to 190°C/375°F/Gas 5.

2 Roll out the pastry on a lightly floured surface and line an 18cm/7in flan ring. Line the pastry case (pie shell) with baking parchment, fill with baking beans and bake for 12 minutes. Remove the foil and beans. Bake for 5 minutes more, until golden.

3 Make the filling. Mix the plums, sugar and orange juice in a pan. Bring to the boil, then lower the heat and simmer until the fruit is cooked and the mixture is thick. Cool completely and then mix in the egg yolks and eau de vie de Mirabelle. Spoon the mixture into the flan case.

4 Whisk the egg whites in a clean bowl until stiff peaks form. Whisk in half the caster sugar. When the mixture is stiff again, fold in the remaining sugar. Pipe or spread the meringue over the filling and bake for 15–20 minutes until golden.

Variation
This is equally delicious when made with strawberries and framboise or stoned cherries and Kirsch.

Walnut and Coffee Pie

Sweetened with coffee-flavoured maple syrup, this pie has a rich and sticky texture. The walnuts can be replaced by pecan nuts for an authentic American pie.

Serves 8

30ml/2 tbsp ground coffee
175ml/6fl oz/¾ cup maple syrup
25g/1oz/2 tbsp butter, softened
175g/6oz/¾ cup soft light brown sugar
3 eggs, beaten
5ml/1 tsp vanilla extract
115g/4oz/1 cup walnut halves

For the pastry

150g/5oz/1¼ cups plain (all-purpose) flour
pinch of salt
25g/1oz/¼ cup icing (confectioners') sugar
75g/3oz/6 tbsp butter, diced
2 egg yolks

1 Preheat the oven to 200°C/400°F/Gas 6. To make the pastry, sift the flour, salt and icing sugar into a mixing bowl. Rub or cut in the butter until the mixture resembles fine breadcrumbs. Add the egg yolks and mix well to form a soft dough.

2 Knead the pastry on a lightly floured surface for a few seconds until smooth. Wrap in clear film (plastic wrap) and chill for 30 minutes.

3 Roll out the pastry and use to line a 20cm/8in fluted flan tin (pan). Line with baking parchment and baking beans and bake for about 10 minutes.

4 Remove the paper and beans and bake for a further 5 minutes until brown. Set the pastry case (pie shell) aside. Lower the oven temperature to 180°C/350°F/Gas 4.

5 Heat the coffee and maple syrup in a pan until almost boiling. Set aside to cool slightly. Mix the butter and sugar in a bowl, then gradually beat in the eggs. Strain the reserved maple syrup mixture into the bowl, add the vanilla extract and stir well.

6 Arrange the walnuts in the pastry case, then pour in the filling. Bake for 30–35 minutes until lightly browned. Cool slightly before serving warm with crème fraîche or vanilla ice cream.

Plum Meringue Pie Energy 254kcal/1068kJ; Protein 4.6g; Carbohydrate 34g, of which sugars 17.4g; Fat 10.6g, of which saturates 5.8g; Cholesterol 97mg; Calcium 51mg; Fibre 1.9g; Sodium 90mg.
Walnut Pie Energy 462kcal/1938kJ; Protein 7.2g; Carbohydrate 58.5g, of which sugars 44.1g; Fat 23.8g, of which saturates 8.3g; Cholesterol 148mg; Calcium 75mg; Fibre 1.1g; Sodium 166mg.

Scottish Black Bun

The fruit for this spicy cake is soaked in whisky overnight

Serves 14

115g/4oz/½ cup butter, diced
225g/8oz/2 cups plain (all-purpose) flour
1 egg, beaten, to glaze

For the filling

350g/12oz/generous 1½ cups currants
400g/14oz/3 cups mixed raisins and sultanas (golden raisins)
50g/2oz/½ cup flaked (sliced) almonds
90ml/6 tbsp whisky or brandy
115g/4oz/1 cup plain (all-purpose) flour
5ml/1 tsp ground allspice
5ml/1 tsp ground cinnamon
5ml/1 tsp ground ginger
2.5ml/½ tsp cream of tartar
2.5ml/½ tsp bicarbonate of soda (baking soda)
115g/4oz/½ cup soft dark muscovado (molasses) sugar
1 egg, beaten

1 Put the dried fruits and nuts in a bowl with the alcohol. Soak overnight. Preheat the oven to 180°C/350°F/Gas 4. Grease a 900g/2lb loaf tin (pan).

2 Put the flour in a large bowl or food processor and add the fat. Rub in or process until the mixture resembles fine crumbs. Add 45–60ml/3–4 tbsp cold water and mix to a ball. Knead lightly until smooth, then wrap and chill for 30 minutes.

3 Cut off a third of the pastry and set aside. Roll out the remaining pastry and line the tin, leaving the edges overhanging.

4 Sift the flour, spices, cream of tartar and bicarbonate of soda into a bowl, then add the sugar, the beaten egg, the soaked fruit and nuts, and the liquid from the bowl and mix thoroughly. Spoon the fruit mixture into the pastry case (pie shell) and loosely fold the edges over the filling.

5 Roll out the remaining pastry to a rectangle for the top. Wet the edges and press the rectangle on top. Trim, then crimp.

6 Bake for 2 hours or until an inserted skewer comes out clean. Cool in the tin for 5 minutes, then turn out on a wire rack to cool completely.

Jam Roly Poly

This warming winter pudding, made with suet pastry, appeared on English tables in the 1800s. A savoury version, known as Plough Pudding had a filling of bacon, onion and sage, and was eaten by Victorian stable lads for their supper on chilly days. While steaming is the traditional cooking method for jam roly poly, baking produces a lovely crisp golden crust and a sticky jam filling. Serve it thickly sliced with custard.

Serves 4–6

175g/6oz/1½ cups self-raising (self-rising) flour
pinch of salt
75g/3oz shredded suet (or vegetarian equivalent)
finely grated rind of 1 small lemon
90ml/6 tbsp jam

1 Preheat the oven to 180°C/350°F/Gas 4 and line a baking sheet with baking parchment.

2 Sift the flour and salt into a bowl and stir in the suet and lemon rind. With a round-ended knife, stir in just enough cold water to enable you to gather the mixture into a ball of soft dough, finishing off with your fingers.

3 Remove the ball of dough from the bowl, and on a lightly floured work surface or board, knead it very lightly until smooth.

4 Gently roll out the pastry into a rectangle that measures approximately 30 x 20cm/12 x 8in.

5 Using a palette knife or metal spatula, spread the jam evenly over the pastry, leaving the side edges and ends clear.

6 Brush the edges of the pastry with a little water and, starting at one of the short ends, carefully roll up the pastry. Try to keep the roll fairly loose so that the jam is not squeezed out.

7 Place the roll, seam side down, on the prepared baking sheet. Put into the hot oven and cook for 30–40 minutes until risen, golden brown and cooked through. Leave the pudding to cool for a few minutes before cutting into thick slices to serve.

Black Bun Energy 435kcal/1828kJ; Protein 5.3g; Carbohydrate 67.8g, of which sugars 45.2g; Fat 14.7g, of which saturates 4.5g; Cholesterol 26mg; Calcium 101mg; Fibre 2.1g; Sodium 250mg.
Roly Poly Energy 240kcal/1008kJ; Protein 2.8g; Carbohydrate 33.7g, of which sugars 10.7g; Fat 11.3g, of which saturates 5.7g; Cholesterol 0mg; Calcium 104mg; Fibre 0.9g; Sodium 111mg.

Apple Puffs

Whole crisp apples stuffed with brown cinnamon sugar and baked in pastry are a speciality of the province of Antwerp, traditionally served on the first Monday after Three Kings' Day

Serves 4

500g/1¼lb pack puff pastry, thawed if frozen
50g/2oz/¼ cup sugar
5ml/1 tsp ground cinnamon
4 crisp eating apples, such as Boskoop, Jonagold, Pippin or Granny Smith, peeled and cored
1 egg mixed with 15ml/1 tbsp water
icing (confectioners') sugar, for dusting

For the filling

100g/3½oz/½ cup soft light brown sugar
ground cinnamon, to taste
25ml/1½ tsp cold butter, diced

1 Roll out the pastry on a floured surface and cut it into four squares, each large enough to wrap an apple easily.

2 Mix the sugar and cinnamon in a bowl and roll each apple in it, to coat. Preheat the oven to 200–220°C/400–425°F/Gas 6–7. Place an apple in the centre of each square of pastry.

3 Mix together all the ingredients for the filling and use the mixture to stuff the cavities of the apples.

4 Brush the edges of the pastry with water, then lift the corners and bring them together in the centre. Pinch the edges of the pastry together with wet fingers, to seal the seams.

5 Place on a baking sheet, spacing about 2.5cm/1in apart, and brush with the egg mix. Bake for 20–30 minutes until golden.

6 Remove from the oven, and leave to cool for 5 minutes. Transfer to plates and sift icing sugar over and around them.

Cook's Tip
The dumplings can be made in advance and baked shortly before serving.

Baked Apple Dumplings

The sharpness of the fruit contrasts perfectly with the maple syrup drizzled over this delightful pastry parcel.

Serves 8

8 firm cooking apples, peeled
1 egg white
130g/4½oz/⅔ cup caster (superfine) sugar
45ml/3 tbsp double (heavy) cream, plus extra, to serve
2.5ml/½ tsp vanilla extract
250ml/8fl oz/1 cup maple syrup

For the pastry

475g/1lb 2oz/4½ cups plain (all-purpose) flour
2.5ml/½ tsp salt
350g/12oz/1½ cups butter or white vegetable fat (shortening), diced
175–250ml/6–8fl oz/¾–1 cup chilled water

1 To make the pastry, sift the flour and salt into a large bowl. Rub in the butter or fat until the mixture resembles fine breadcrumbs. Sprinkle over 175ml/6fl oz/¾ cup water and mix until the dough holds together, adding a little more water if necessary. Gather into a ball. Wrap and chill for 20 minutes.

2 Preheat the oven to 220°C/425°F/Gas 7. Cutting from the stem end, core the apples without cutting through the base. Roll out the pastry. Cut squares large enough to enclose the apples; brush with egg white and set an apple in the centre of each.

3 Cut pastry rounds to cover the tops of the apples. Reserve the trimmings. Combine the sugar, cream and vanilla extract in a small bowl. Spoon into the hollow of each apple.

4 Place a pastry circle on top of each apple, then bring up the sides of the pastry square to enclose it, pleating the larger piece of pastry to make a snug fit. Moisten the joins where they meet.

5 Decorate with leaf shapes from the trimmings. Set on a baking dish, 2cm/¾in apart. Bake for 30 minutes, then lower the oven temperature to 180°C/350°F/Gas 4 and continue baking for 20 minutes more until the apples are tender.

6 Mix the maple syrup with the juices in the baking dish and drizzle over the dumplings. Serve hot with whipped cream.

Apple Puffs Energy 659kcal/2768kJ; Protein 9.1g; Carbohydrate 92.1g, of which sugars 47.5g; Fat 32.1g, of which saturates 0.4g; Cholesterol 48mg; Calcium 103mg; Fibre 1.2g; Sodium 409mg.
Apple Dumplings Energy 713kcal/2988kJ; Protein 6.6g; Carbohydrate 94.7g, of which sugars 49.5g; Fat 36.8g, of which saturates 22.9g; Cholesterol 93mg; Calcium 108mg; Fibre 3g; Sodium 361mg.

Snake-shaped Cake

The pastry for this classic Italian speciality is made with olive oil, and has quite a different texture to butter pastry. Serve thinly sliced, with chilled dessert wine.

Serves 6–8

115g/4oz/⅔ cup sultanas (golden raisins)
225g/8oz/2 cups plain (all-purpose) flour
115g/4oz/generous ½ cup caster (superfine) sugar
60ml/4 tbsp extra virgin olive oil, plus extra for greasing
pinch of salt
100–150ml/3½fl oz–¼ pint/ ½–⅔ cup warm water
50g/2oz/⅓ cup blanched almonds, coarsely chopped
8 walnuts, coarsely chopped
3 apples, peeled and sliced
5 dried figs, chopped
5 ready-to-eat prunes, pitted and chopped
30–45ml/2–3 tbsp icing (confectioners') sugar
2 glacé (candied) cherries, 1 blanched almond and 10–20ml/ 2–4 tsp caster (superfine) sugar, to decorate

1 Soak the sultanas in a bowl of warm water for about 20 minutes, until plump and softened.

2 Put the flour and caster sugar on to the work surface and add the oil and the salt. Add a little warm water, then knead gently to make a fairly solid pastry dough. Cover with a clean dish towel and leave to rest for about 20 minutes. Preheat the oven to 180°C/350°F/Gas 4. Grease and flour a baking sheet.

3 Roll out the pastry on a floured surface as thinly as possible. Sprinkle the blanched, chopped almonds over the dough.

4 Drain the sultanas and pat them dry with kitchen paper. Spread them over the almonds, with the walnuts, apples, figs and prunes. Sprinkle with the icing sugar and carefully roll the dough up on itself, to form a long cylinder. Twist the cylinder around to form a coiled snake shape and transfer on to the baking sheet.

5 To make the decoration, press the glacé cherries or coffee beans into place to represent the snake's eyes, and then press in the almond to represent the snake's tongue. Sprinkle with sugar. Bake for 40 minutes. Cool on a wire rack before serving.

Almond & Cinnamon Coil

This famous Moroccan pastry is filled with lightly fragrant almond paste and dusted with cinnamon.

Serves 8

8 sheets of filo pastry
50g/2oz/¼ cup butter, melted
1 egg, beaten
5ml/1 tsp ground cinnamon
icing (confectioners') sugar, for dusting

For the almond paste
about 50g/2oz/¼ cup butter, melted
225g/8oz/2⅔ cups ground almonds
2.5ml/½ tsp almond extract
50g/2oz/½ cup icing (confectioners') sugar
1 egg yolk, beaten
15ml/1 tbsp rose water or orange flower water

1 Make the almond paste. Mix the melted butter with the ground almonds and almond extract in a bowl. Add the sugar, egg yolk and rose or orange flower water, mix well and knead until soft and pliable. Chill for 10 minutes.

2 Break the paste into 10 even balls and, with your hands, roll them into 10cm/4in sausages. Chill again.

3 Preheat the oven to 180°C/350°F/Gas 4. Place two sheets of filo pastry on the work surface so that they overlap slightly to form an 18 x 56cm/7 x 22in rectangle. Brush the overlapping edges with butter to secure and then lightly brush all over. Cover with another two sheets of filo in the same way.

4 Place five almond paste sausages along the lower edge of the filo sheet and roll up tightly, tucking in the ends. Repeat with the remaining filo and almond paste, so that you have two rolls. Shape the first roll into a loose coil, then transfer to a baking sheet brushed with butter. Attach the second roll and continue coiling the filo to make a snake. Tuck the end under.

5 Beat the egg with half the cinnamon; brush over the pastry. Bake in the oven for 25 minutes until golden. Carefully invert the snake on to another baking sheet and return to the oven for 5–10 minutes more. Transfer to a serving plate, dust with icing sugar, then sprinkle with the remaining cinnamon.

Snake-shaped Cake Energy 368kcal/1548kJ; Protein 5.8g; Carbohydrate 57.6g, of which sugars 36g; Fat 14.3g, of which saturates 1.5g; Cholesterol 0mg; Calcium 85mg; Fibre 2.6g; Sodium 8mg.
Cinnamon Coil Energy 341Kcal/1417kJ; Protein 7.7g; Carbohydrate 18.3g, of which sugars 8g; Fat 26.9g, of which saturates 8g; Cholesterol 54mg; Calcium 94mg; Fibre 2.5g; Sodium 83mg.

Garlic Mayonnaise

Make this mayonnaise to accompany savoury tarts served with a crisp salad.

Serves 4–6
2 large egg yolks
pinch of dried mustard
up to 300ml/½ pint/1¼ cups vegetable oil or mild olive oil, or a mixture of the two
15–30ml/1–2 tbsp lemon juice, or white wine vinegar
2–4 garlic cloves, crushed
salt and ground black pepper

1 Bring the egg yolks to room temperature before you start. Place the yolks in a bowl with the mustard and a pinch of salt, and whisk.

2 Gradually whisk in the oil, one drop at a time. When almost half the oil has been fully incorporated, add it in a steady stream, but keep whisking. As the mayonnaise starts to thicken, thin it down with a few drops of lemon juice or vinegar.

3 When the mayonnaise is as thick and soft, stop adding oil. Season to taste adding more lemon juice or vinegar if required.

4 Stir the garlic into the mayonnaise. For a slightly milder flavour, blanch the garlic twice in plenty of boiling water, then purée the cloves before beating them into the mayonnaise.

Variations
• *To make Provençal aioli, crush 3–5 garlic cloves with a pinch of salt in a bowl, then whisk in the egg yolks. Omit the mustard but continue as above, using all olive oil.*
• *For spicy garlic mayonnaise, omit the mustard and stir in 2.5ml/½ tsp harissa or red chilli paste and 5ml/1 tsp sun-dried tomato paste with the garlic.*
• *Use roasted garlic purée or puréed smoked garlic to create a different flavour.*
• *Beat in about 15g/½oz mixed fresh herbs such as tarragon, parsley, chervil and chives. Blanch the herbs in boiling water for 20–30 seconds, then drain and pat them dry on kitchen paper before finely chopping them.*

Pickled Red Onion Relish

A perfect accompaniment to cold raised pies or pasties.

Makes 1 jar
500g/1¼lb red onions, sliced
250ml/8fl oz/1 cup rice wine vinegar or tarragon vinegar
5ml/1 tsp salt
15ml/1 tbsp caster (superfine) sugar
6 juniper berries, lightly crushed
30ml/2 tbsp chopped fresh dill
15ml/1 tbsp coriander seeds, crushed

1 Place the onions in a large bowl and cover with boiling water. Immediately place them into a colander, then set aside and allow to drain completely. Then return the onions to the dried bowl.

2 In another bowl, mix together the vinegar, salt, sugar, juniper berries and chopped dill.

3 Heat the coriander seeds in a dry frying pan until they give off their aroma. Add the toasted seeds to the vinegar mixture and stir. Pour over the onions, toss to mix, then leave to stand at room temperature for 1 hour before serving with cold raised pies or Cornish pasties.

English Pickled Onions

These onions are a great with quiches and cheese tarts.

Makes 3–4 450g/1lb jars
1kg/2¼lb pickling onions
115g/4oz/½ cup salt
750ml/1¼ pints/3 cups malt vinegar
15ml/1 tbsp sugar
2–3 dried red chillies
5ml/1 tsp brown mustard seeds
15ml/1 tbsp coriander seeds
5ml/1 tsp allspice berries
5ml/1 tsp black peppercorns
5cm/2in piece fresh root ginger, sliced
2–3 blades of mace
2–3 fresh bay leaves

1 Trim off the root end, of the onions but leave the onion skin attached. Cut a thin slice off the top (neck) end of the onion. Place the onions in a bowl, cover with boiling water, let stand for 5 minutes, then drain. Peel with a small, sharp knife.

2 Place the peeled onions in a bowl and cover with cold water, then transfer the water to a large pan. Add the salt, heat slightly to dissolve it, cool, then pour the brine over the onions.

3 Cover the bowl with a plate and weigh it down slightly so that it keeps all the onions submerged in the brine. Leave the onions to stand in the salted water for 24 hours.

4 Place the vinegar in a pan. Wrap the remaining ingredients, except the bay leaves, in a piece of muslin (cheesecloth) and add to the vinegar with the bay leaves. Bring to the boil, simmer for 5 minutes, then remove from the heat. Leave to infuse overnight.

5 Drain the onions, rinse and pat dry. Pack into sterilized jars. Add some of the spice from the vinegar, but not the ginger. The pickle will be hotter if you add the chillies. Pour the vinegar over the onions to cover and add the bay leaves. Cover the jars with lids and store in a cool dark place for 6 weeks before eating.

Apple and Sultana Chutney

This is a great chutney to serve with meat pies and little turnovers.

Makes about 900g/2lb

350g/12oz cooking apples
115g/4oz/⅔ cup sultanas (golden raisins)
50g/2oz onion
25g/1oz/¼ cup almonds, blanched
5ml/1 tsp white peppercorns
2.5ml/½ tsp coriander seeds
175g/6oz/scant 1 cup sugar
10ml/2 tsp salt
5ml/1 tsp ground ginger
450ml/¾ pint/scant 2 cups cider vinegar or wine vinegar
1.5ml/¼ tsp cayenne pepper
red chillies (optional)

1 Peel, core and chop the apples. Chop the sultanas, onion and almonds. Tie the peppercorns and coriander seeds together in a piece of muslin (cheesecloth), using a long length of string, and then tie to the handle of a special preserving pan or use a stainless steel pan.

2 Put the sugar, salt, ground ginger and vinegar into the pan, with the cayenne pepper to taste. Heat the mixture gently, stirring, until the sugar has completely dissolved.

3 Add the chopped fruit to the pan. Bring the mixture to the boil and then lower the heat. Simmer for about 1½–2 hours, or until most of the liquid has evaporated.

4 Spoon the chutney into warmed sterilized jars and place one whole fresh chilli in each jar, if using. Leave until cold, then cover and seal the jars and attach a label to each one.

5 Store in a cool, dark place. The chutney is best left for a month to mature before eating and will keep for at least 6 months, if it is correctly stored.

Variation
For a mild chutney, add only a little cayenne pepper. For a spicier one, increase the quantity to taste.

Squash, Apricot and Almond Chutney

Ideal for accompanying spicy vegetable or meat samosas, this chutney is made in the slow cooker and is full of taste and colour.

Makes about 1.8kg/4lb

1 small butternut squash, weighing about 800g/1¾lb
400g/14oz/2 cups golden caster (superfine) sugar
300ml/½ pint/1¼ cups cider vinegar
2 onions, finely chopped
225g/8oz/1 cup ready-to-eat dried apricots, chopped
finely grated rind and juice of 1 orange
2.5ml/½ tsp turmeric
15ml/1 tbsp coriander seeds
15ml/1 tbsp salt
115g/4oz/1 cup flaked (sliced) almonds

1 Halve the butternut squash and scoop out the seeds. Peel off the skin, then cut the flesh into 1cm/½in cubes.

2 Put the sugar and vinegar in the ceramic cooking pot of the cooker and switch to high. Heat for 30 minutes, then stir until the sugar has completely dissolved.

3 Add the butternut squash, onions, apricots, orange rind and juice, turmeric, coriander seeds and salt to the slow cooker pot and stir well until the ingredients are well combined.

4 Cover the slow cooker with the lid and cook for about 5–6 hours, stirring occasionally during that time.

5 After about 5 hours the chutney should be a fairly thick consistency with relatively little liquid. If it is still quite runny at this stage, cook uncovered for the final hour. Stir the flaked almonds into the chutney.

6 Spoon the chutney into warmed sterilized jars, cover and seal. Store in a cool, dark place and allow the chutney to mature for at least 1 month before eating. It should be used within 2 years. Once opened, store jars of the chutney in the refrigerator and use within 2 months.

Onion Gravy

This makes a delicious, intense gravy to go with most hot meat pies. Serve with mashed potatoes and peas for a wonderful traditional meal.

Serves 4

40g/1½oz/3 tbsp butter
450g/1lb onions, thinly sliced
2.5ml/½ tsp soft light brown sugar
45ml/3 tbsp plain (all-purpose) flour
400–500ml/14–17fl oz/1⅔–2 cups hot beef or vegetable stock
1 fresh thyme sprig
10ml/2 tsp dark soy sauce
5ml/1 tsp Worcestershire sauce
salt and ground black pepper

1 Melt the butter over low heat. Add the onions and fry, stirring occasionally, for 15–20 minutes, until soft and beginning to brown. Add the sugar, increase the heat slightly and cook for another 20–30 minutes, until the onions are brown.

2 Stir in the flour, cook for a few minutes, stirring all the time, then gradually stir in 400ml/14fl oz/1⅔ cups of the hot stock. Simmer, stirring, to make a thickened gravy, adding a little more stock if the gravy is too thick.

3 Add the thyme, season with a little salt and pepper, then cook very slowly, stirring frequently, for 10–15 minutes. Stir in the soy sauce, Worcestershire sauce, and seasoning, if necessary. Remove the thyme, and serve immediately.

Variations

• *The onions can be browned in the oven. This is best done in vegetable oil rather than butter or dripping. Place the sliced onions in an ovenproof dish and toss with 45ml/3 tbsp oil. Cook at 190°C/375°F/Gas 5 for 20 minutes, stirring once or twice. Stir in the sugar, then cook at 220°C/425°F/Gas 7 for a further 15–25 minutes, until the onions are dark brown and caramelized.*

• *Part of the beef or vegetable stock may be replaced with red wine or dark beer. You may need to add a little extra sugar to balance the acidity of the wine or beer.*

White Onion Sauce

This is a classic French white onion sauce. It is excellent with veal, chicken, pork or lamb pies.

Serves 4

40g/1½oz/3 tbsp butter
350g/12oz onions, finely chopped
25g/1oz/¼ cup plain (all-purpose) flour
500ml/17fl oz/generous 2 cups mixture of hot milk and stock
1 fresh bay leaf
a few parsley stalks
120ml/4fl oz/½ cup double (heavy) cream
freshly grated nutmeg
salt and ground black pepper

1 Melt the butter in a large heavy pan. Add the onions and fry gently over low heat, stirring occasionally, for 10–12 minutes, until they are soft and golden yellow, but not at all browned.

2 Stir in the flour and cook gently, stirring constantly, for 2–3 minutes. Gradually stir in the hot milk, stock, or milk and stock mixture and bring to the boil. Add the bay leaf and parsley. Part-cover the pan and cook very gently, stirring frequently, for 15–20 minutes.

3 Remove and discard the bay leaf and parsley, then process the sauce in a blender or food processor if you want a smooth sauce, or leave as it is if you prefer.

4 Stir in the cream and reheat the sauce gently. Season to taste with salt and pepper. Add a little more milk or stock if the sauce is very thick. Season with grated nutmeg just before serving.

Variations

• *For leek sauce, substitute leeks for onions, using the white part of the leeks. Cook for just 4–5 minutes in the butter before adding the flour. Omit the nutmeg and stir in 15ml/1 tbsp Dijon mustard just before serving.*

• *Season the sauce with about 30ml/2 tbsp Dijon mustard at the end of cooking to make Sauce Robert. It also goes very well with chicken or ham pies.*

Bread Sauce

Often served with poultry, this English sauce is also delicious with chicken pie.

Serves 6–8

475ml/16fl oz/2 cups milk
1 small onion, stuck with 4 cloves
1 celery stick, chopped
1 fresh bay leaf, torn in half
6 allspice berries
1 blade of mace
90g/3½oz/1¾ cups breadcrumbs
freshly grated nutmeg
30ml/2 tbsp double (heavy) cream
15g/½oz/1 tbsp butter
salt and ground black pepper

1 Place the milk, onion, celery, bay leaf, allspice and mace in a pan and bring to the boil. Take off the heat, half-cover, and set aside to infuse for 30–60 minutes.

2 Remove and discard the cloves from the onion. Process the onion and celery with the milk until smooth, then strain the liquid back into the clean pan. Bring back to the boil and stir in the breadcrumbs. Simmer gently, stirring, until the sauce thickens. Add a little extra milk if the sauce is too thick.

3 Season to taste with salt, pepper and freshly grated nutmeg. Just before serving, whisk in the cream and butter. Serve warm.

Raita

Serve this cool yogurt dip with meat samosas.

Serves 4

15cm/6in piece cucumber, grated
5ml/1 tsp sea salt
300ml/½ pint/1¼ cups Greek (US strained plain) yogurt
3–4 garlic cloves, crushed
15ml/1 tbsp dried mint or 45ml/3 tbsp chopped fresh mint
ground black pepper
chopped fresh mint and ground toasted cumin seeds, to garnish

1 Place the cucumber in a sieve (strainer) and sprinkle with half the salt. Leave on a deep plate for 30 minutes to drip. Rinse the cucumber in cold water, pat dry and mix with the yogurt, garlic and mint. Season. Leave for 30 minutes, then stir and sprinkle with fresh mint and toasted cumin to garnish.

Walnut and Garlic Sauce

This richly flavoured dip is excellent with savoury little pastry appetizers

Serves 4

2 x 1cm/½in slices good white bread, crusts removed
60ml/4 tbsp milk
150g/5oz/1¼ cups shelled walnuts
4 garlic cloves, chopped
120ml/4fl oz/½ cup mild olive oil
15–30ml/1–2 tbsp walnut oil
juice of 1 lemon
salt and ground black pepper
walnut or olive oil, for drizzling

1 Soak the slices of white bread in the milk for about 5 minutes, then process with the walnuts and chopped garlic in a food processor or blender, to make a rough paste. Gradually add the olive oil to the paste with the motor still running, until the mixture forms a smooth thick sauce. Blend in the walnut oil,.

2 Scoop the sauce into a bowl and squeeze in lemon juice to taste, season with salt and pepper and beat well. Transfer to a serving bowl, drizzle over a little more walnut or olive oil, then dust lightly with paprika, if using.

Salsa Verde

Serve this Italian sauce as a dip for pastry snacks.

Serves 4

1–2 garlic cloves, finely chopped
25g/1oz flat leaf parsley leaves
15g/½oz fresh basil, mint or coriander or a mixture of herbs
15ml/1 tbsp chopped chives
15ml/1 tbsp salted capers, rinsed
5 anchovy fillets in olive oil, drained and rinsed
10ml/2 tsp French mustard
120ml/4fl oz/½ cup extra virgin olive oil
a little grated lemon rind and juice
ground black pepper

1 Process the garlic, parsley, basil, mint or coriander, chives, capers, anchovies, mustard and 15ml/1 tbsp of the oil in a blender or food processor. Gradually add the remaining oil in a thin stream with the motor running. Transfer to a bowl, adjust the seasoning, and add a little lemon juice and rind to serve.

Custard

Homemade custard makes a fruit pie into a dessert sensation. Make in advance and reheat, or leave to cool, chill, and serve cold.

Serves 4

500ml/17fl oz/generous 2 cups milk, plus extra to taste
½ vanilla pod (bean)
40g/1½oz/⅓ cup cornflour (cornstarch)
40g/1½oz/scant ¼ cup sugar
2 large (US extra large) egg yolks

1 Rinse out a pan with cold water, pour in 400ml/14fl oz/1⅔ cups of the milk, add the vanilla pod and bring to the boil. Simmer gently over low heat for a few minutes.

2 Meanwhile, mix together the cornflour and sugar in a small bowl, add the egg yolks and stir until very smooth. Stir in the remaining milk and strain into a clean bowl.

3 Bring the vanilla-flavoured milk back to the boil, then remove the pan from the heat. Stir the cornflour mixture into the pan and return to very low heat. Cook, stirring frequently, for about 3 minutes.

4 Remove and discard the vanilla pod. Cover the surface of the custardwith clear film (plastic wrap) to prevent a skin from forming, reheat to serve or leave to cool.

5 If using cold, use a hand-held mixer to whisk the mixture with cold milk to create the required consistency, which is usually a cross between a sauce and a dessert.

Variations

- *For chocolate custard mix 50g/2oz/½ cup unsweetened cocoa powder with 45ml/3 tbsp cornflour (cornstarch) and 115g/4oz/generous ½ cup sugar and omit the eggs.*
- *For a slightly spiced custard mix in a little ground cinnamon and some whipped cream just before serving.*

Dulce de Leche

Dulce de leche is loved in South America and used as a filling in all kinds of pastries.

Makes about 400g/2 cups

1 litre/1¾ pints/4 cups whole milk
350g/12oz/1¾ cups caster (superfine) sugar
150g/5oz glucose
5ml/1 tsp vanilla extract
1.5ml/¼ tsp bicarbonate of soda (baking soda)

1 Put the milk and sugar into a heavy pan on a very low heat. Add the glucose and vanilla and heat, stirring until the sugar dissolves. Simmer for 30–45 minutes, stirring often. Blend the bicarbonate of soda with 15ml/1 tbsp cold water and stir into the mixture. Turn up the heat a little and cook for 20–30 minutes or until it reaches 107°C/225°F on a sugar thermometer, stirring constantly towards the end of cooking.

2 When ready, the mixture should be thick and a brown. To test, drizzle some of the sauce over the surface, if it forms a ribbon that does not disappear after 10 seconds, it is ready. Straight away, plunge the base of the pan into a sink containing cold water, to cool. Transfer to a jar and keep in the fridge.

Chocolate Sauce

This rich, dense sauce is a lovely accompaniment to pear or almond tarts.

Serves 4

250g/9oz good quality dark (bittersweet) chocolate
40g/1½oz unsalted (sweet) butter
5ml/1 tsp vanilla extract
75ml/5 tbsp double (heavy) cream

1 To make the chocolate sauce, break the chocolate into small pieces and put into a pan. Add the butter and 30ml/2 tbsp water. Heat gently over a low heat, without stirring, until the chocolate has melted.

2 Add the vanilla extract and cream, and mix gently to combine. Serve warm with fruit or frangipane tarts and pies.

Blueberry and Lime Jam

The subtle yet fragrant flavour of blueberries can be elusive on its own. Adding a generous quantity of tangy lime juice enhances their flavour. Use the jam for tarts and pies.

Makes about 1.3kg/3lb

1.3kg/3lb/12 cups blueberries
finely pared rind and juice of 4 limes
1kg/2¼lb/5 cups preserving sugar with pectin

1 Put the blueberries, lime juice and half the sugar in a large, non-metallic bowl and lightly crush the berries using a potato masher. Set aside for about 4 hours.

2 Transfer the crushed berry mixture into a pan and stir in the finely pared lime rind together with the remaining preserving sugar. Heat slowly, stirring continuously, until the sugar has completely dissolved.

3 Increase the heat and bring to the boil. Boil rapidly for about 4 minutes, or until the jam reaches setting point (105°C/220°F).

4 Remove the pan from the heat and set aside for 5 minutes. Stir the jam gently, then pour into warmed sterilized jars. Seal the jars, then label when completely cool. Store in a cool, dark place.

Cook's Tip
Blueberries are not naturally high in pectin, so extra pectin is needed for a good set. If you prefer, use granulated (white) sugar, and add pectin according to the instruction on the packet in place of the preserving sugar with pectin.

Variation
You can replace the lime juice with lemon juice or the juice of sharp oranges, such as Seville (Temple) oranges, to give a more citrusy zing.

Cranberry and Claret Jelly

The slight sharpness of cranberries makes this a superb jelly for serving with rich lamb or cold game pies. Together with claret, the cranberries give the jelly a beautifully deep red colour, ideal for Christmas time.

Makes about 1.2kg/2½lb

900g/2lb/8 cups fresh or frozen cranberries, thawed
350ml/12fl oz/1½ cups water
about 900g/2lb/4½ cups preserving or granulated (white) sugar
250ml/8fl oz/1 cup claret

1 Wash the cranberries, if fresh, and put them in a large heavy pan with the water. Cover the pan and bring to the boil.

2 Reduce the heat under the pan and simmer for about 20 minutes, or until the cranberries are soft.

3 Pour the fruit and juices into a sterilized jelly bag suspended over a large bowl. Leave to drain for at least 3 hours or overnight, until the juices stop dripping.

4 Measure the juice and wine into the cleaned preserving pan, adding 400g/14oz/2 cups preserving or granulated sugar for every 600ml/1 pint/2½ cups liquid.

5 Heat the mixture gently, stirring occasionally, until the sugar has dissolved, then bring to the boil and boil rapidly for about 10 minutes until the jelly reaches setting point (105°C/220°F). Remove the pan from the heat.

6 Skim any scum from the surface using a slotted spoon and pour the jelly into warmed sterilized jars. Cover and seal. Store in a cool, dark place and use within 2 years. Once opened, keep in the refrigerator and eat within 3 months.

Cook's Tip
When simmering the cranberries, keep the pan covered until they stop 'popping', as they can occasionally explode and jump out of the pan.

Mincemeat

Unlike many mincemeat recipes, here, slow cooking intensifies the flavour, so that the mincemeat may be used straight away without being left to mature.

Makes about 1.75g/4lb

450g/1lb cooking apples
115g/4oz/¾ cup mixed (candied) citrus peel
115g/4oz/½ cup candied cherries
115g/4oz/½ cup ready-to-eat dried apricots
115g/4oz/1 cup blanched almonds
150ml/¼ pint/⅔ cup brandy
225g/8oz/1 cup currants
225g/8oz/1⅓ cups sultanas (golden raisins)
450g/1lb/3¼ cups seedless raisins
225g/8oz/1 cup soft dark brown sugar
225g/8oz/1⅔ cups suet (US chilled, grated shortening)
10ml/2 tsp ground ginger
5ml/1 tsp ground allspice
5ml/1 tsp ground cinnamon
2.5ml/½ tsp grated nutmeg
grated rind and juice of 1 lemon
grated rind and juice of 1 orange

1 Peel, core and chop the cooking apples, then roughly chop the citrus peel, glacé cherries, apricots and blanched almonds.

2 Reserve half the brandy and put the rest into the ceramic cooking pot with all the other ingredients. Stir well until thoroughly mixed.

3 Cover the ceramic cooking pot with the lid and switch the slow cooker to high. Cook for 1 hour.

4 Stir the mixture well, then re-cover the pot and reduce the temperature to low. Cook for a further 2 hours, stirring halfway through cooking to prevent the mixture from overheating and sticking to the sides of the pot.

5 Remove the lid and leave the mixture to cool completely, stirring occasionally.

6 Stir the reserved brandy into the mincemeat and spoon the mixture into sterilized jars. Cover and store in a cool, dry place for up to six months. Once opened, store in the refrigerator and use within two weeks.

Blackberry and Apple Jam

This richly coloured autumn preserve makes the most of the blackberry season, and is lovely in apple pies.

Makes about 4.5kg/10lb

1.3kg/3lb cooking apples
1.8kg/4lb/16 cups blackberries
2.75kg/6lb/13½ cups sugar, warmed

1 Peel, core and cut the apples roughly. Put into a large pan. Add half of the water, bring to the boil and simmer until soft.

2 Wash and drain the blackberries and place in a preserving pan with 300ml/½ pint/1¼ cups water and simmer until tender.

3 Add the apples and the sugar to the pan. Stir over low heat until the sugar has dissolved, and then bring to the boil. Boil hard for about 15 minutes, or until setting point is reached. To test, put a drop of jam on to a plate. Allow to cool slightly, and then push the surface of the jam. If a skin has formed it is set.

4 Skim if necessary, then pour into warmed, sterilized jars. Cover, seal and store in a cool, dark place until required.

Raspberry Jam

For many people this is the best of jams. It is perfect in a whole range of tarts, large or small. Use firm fruit for the best results.

Makes about 3.1kg/7lb

1.8kg/4lb/10⅔ cups raspberries
juice of 1 large lemon
1.8kg/4lb/9 cups sugar, warmed

1 Put 175g/6oz/1 cup of the raspberries into the preserving pan and crush them. Add the rest of the fruit and the lemon juice, and simmer until soft and pulpy. Add the sugar and stir until dissolved, then bring back to the boil and boil hard until setting point is reached, testing after 3–4 minutes.

2 Pour into warmed, sterilized jars. When cold, cover, seal and store in a cool, dark place until required. The jam will store well for 6 months.

Grapefruit and Cranberry Marmalade

Cranberries give this glorious marmalade an extra tartness and a full fruit flavour, as well as an inimitable vibrant colour. The resulting preserve makes a lively choice for breakfast, but it also makes a brilliant accompaniment for cold raised game or pork pies, during the festive season.

Makes about 2.25kg/5lb

675g/1½lb pink grapefruit, but if you can't find pink, use yellow
2 lemons
225g/8oz/2 cups cranberries, fresh or frozen
1.3kg/3lb/6½ cups granulated (white) sugar, warmed

1 Wash and quarter the grapefruit, then slice them thinly, reserving the pips (seeds) and any juice that runs out. Juice the lemons, reserving the pips.

2 Tie the grapefruit and lemon pips in a muslin (cheesecloth) bag and place in a large pan with the grapefruit slices and lemon juice.

3 Add 900ml/1½ pints/3¾ cups water and bring to the boil. Cover and simmer gently for 1½–2 hours, or until the grapefruit rind is tender. Remove the muslin bag, leave to cool, then squeeze over the pan.

4 Add the cranberries, then bring to the boil. Simmer for 15–20 minutes, or until the berries have popped and softened.

5 Add the sugar to the pan and stir over low heat until the sugar has completely dissolved.

6 Bring to the boil and boil rapidly for about 10 minutes, or until setting point is reached (105°C/220°F).

7 Remove the pan from the heat and skim off any scum from the surface using a slotted spoon.

8 Leave to cool 10 minutes, then stir and pour into warmed sterilized jars. Seal, then label when the marmalade is cold.

Lemon Curd

This classic tangy, creamy curd is still one of the most popular of all the curds. It is delicious spread thickly over freshly baked white bread or served with American-style pancakes, and also makes a wonderfully rich, zesty tart filling, or a sauce spooned over, fresh fruit pies.

Makes about 450g/1lb

3 unwaxed lemons
200g/7oz/1 cup caster (superfine) sugar
115g/4oz/½ cup unsalted (sweet) butter, diced
2 large (US extra large) eggs
2 large (US extra large) egg yolks

1 Wash the lemons, then finely grate the rind and place in a large heatproof bowl. Using a sharp knife, halve the lemons and squeeze the juice into the bowl. Set over a pan of gently simmering water and add the sugar and butter. Stir until the sugar has dissolved and the butter melted.

2 Put the eggs and yolks in a bowl and beat together with a fork. Pour the eggs through a sieve (strainer) into the lemon mixture, and whisk well until thoroughly combined.

3 Stir the mixture constantly in the bowl over the pan of simmering water until the lemon curd thickens and lightly coats the back of a wooden spoon.

4 Remove the pan from the heat and pour the curd into small, warmed sterilized jars. Cover, seal and label. Store in a cool, dark place, ideally in the refrigerator. Use within 3 months. (Once opened, store in the refrigerator.)

Cook's Tip

If you are really impatient when it comes to cooking, it is possible to cook the curd in a heavy pan directly over low heat. However, you really need to watch it like a hawk to avoid the mixture curdling. If the curd looks as though it's beginning to curdle, plunge the base of the pan in cold water and beat vigorously.

Plum and Apple Jelly

Use dark red cooking plums, damsons or wild plums such as bullaces to offset the sweetness of this deep-coloured fruit jelly. Its flavour complements rich meat pies as well as roast poultry.

Makes about 1.3kg/3lb
900g/2lb plums
450g/1lb tart cooking apples
150ml/¼ pint/⅔ cup cider vinegar
about 675g/1½lb/scant 3½ cups preserving or granulated (white) sugar

1 Cut the plums in half along the crease, twist apart, then remove the stones (pits) and roughly chop the flesh. Chop the apples, including the cores and skins. Put the fruit in a large heavy pan with the vinegar and 750ml/1¼ pints/3 cups water.

2 Bring the mixture to the boil, reduce the heat, cover and simmer for 30 minutes, or until the fruit is soft and pulpy.

3 Pour the fruit and juices into a sterilized jelly bag suspended over a large bowl. Leave to drain for at least 3 hours, or until the fruit juices stop dripping.

4 Measure the juice into the cleaned pan, adding 450g/1lb/2¼ cups sugar for every 600ml/1 pint/2½ cups juice.

5 Bring the mixture to the boil, stirring occasionally, until the sugar has dissolved, then boil rapidly for about 10 minutes, or until the jelly reaches setting point (105°C/220°F). Remove the pan from the heat.

6 Skim any scum from the surface, then pour the jelly into warmed sterilized jars. Cover and seal while hot. Store in a cool, dark place and use within 2 years.

Cook's Tip
This jelly can be stored for up to 2 years. However, once opened, it should be stored in the refrigerator and eaten within 3 months.

Strawberry Jam

This is the classic fragrant fruit preserve for English afternoon tea, It makes a delicious filling for all kind of sweet pastry recipes, like jam tarts and Bakewell tart, and is even more enjoyable when you've made your own.

Makes about 1.3kg/3lb
1kg/2¼lb/8 cups small strawberries
900g/2lb/4 cups granulated (white) sugar
juice of 2 lemons

1 Layer the strawberries and sugar in a large bowl. Cover and leave overnight.

2 The next day, scrape the strawberries and their juice into a large, heavy pan. Add the lemon juice. Gradually bring to the boil over low heat, stirring until the sugar has dissolved completely.

3 Boil steadily for 10–15 minutes, or until the jam registers 105°C/220°F on a sugar thermometer. Alternatively, test for setting by spooning a small amount on to a chilled saucer. Chill for 3 minutes, then push the jam with your finger: if wrinkles form on the surface, it is ready. Cool for 10 minutes.

4 Stir the jam before pouring it into warm sterilized jars, filling them right to the top.

5 Cover with waxed paper discs and seal with lids immediately. Label when cool, and store in a cool, dark place.

Blackcurrant Jam

This jam has a rich, fruity flavour and a wonderfully deep colour. It is punchy and delicious with scones for tea or as a filling for Danish pastries or turnovers.

Makes about 1.3kg/3lb
1.3kg/3lb/12 cups blackcurrants
grated rind and juice of 1 orange
1.3kg/3lb/6½ cups granulated (white) sugar, warmed
30ml/2 tbsp cassis (optional)

1 Place the blackcurrants, orange rind and juice and 475ml/16fl oz/2 cups water in a large heavy pan. Bring to the boil, reduce the heat and simmer for 30 minutes.

2 Add the warmed sugar to the pan and stir over low heat until the sugar has dissolved.

3 Bring the mixture to the boil and cook for about 8 minutes, or until the jam reaches setting point (105°C/220°F).

4 Remove the pan from the heat and skim off any scum from the surface using a slotted spoon. Leave to cool for 5 minutes, then stir in the cassis, if using.

5 Pour the jam into warmed sterilized jars and seal. Leave the jars to cool completely to avoid any risk of burning yourself on the hot glass. Write the contents of the jars on the labels and store in a cool, dark place.

Greengage and Almond Jam

This is the perfect preserve to make when greengages are readily available in stores, or if you find you have a glut of the fruit. It has a gloriously rich, golden honey colour. The added texture from the almonds mean that this is adds a special layer to a flan or tart.

Makes about 1.3kg/3lb

1.3kg/3lb greengages, stoned (pitted)
juice of 1 lemon
50g/2oz/½ cup blanched almonds, cut into thin slivers
1.3kg/3lb/6½ cups granulated (white) sugar, warmed

1 Put the greengages and 350ml/12fl oz/1½ cups water in a preserving pan with the lemon juice and almond slivers. Bring to the boil, then cover and simmer for 15–20 minutes, or until the greengages are really soft.

2 Add the sugar to the pan and stir over a low heat until the sugar has dissolved. Bring to the boil and cook for 10–15 minutes, or until the jam reaches setting point (105°C/220°F).

3 Remove the pan from the heat and skim off any scum from the surface using a slotted spoon.

4 Leave to cool for 10 minutes, then stir gently and pour into warmed sterilized jars. Seal, then leave to cool completely before labelling. Store in a cool place.

Cook's Tip
Greengages look like unripened plums. However, despite their appearance, they have a wonderfully aromatic flavour that is captured perfectly in this delicious jam.

Variation
Coarsely chopped almonds work well with dried apricots to make a deliciously rich jam.

Cherries in Eau de Vie

These potent cherries should be consumed with respect, as they pack quite an alcoholic punch. Serve them with a rich, dark chocolate tart, or as a delicious topping for a custard tart.

Makes about 1.3kg/3lb

450g/1lb/generous 3 cups ripe cherries
8 blanched almonds
75g/3oz/6 tbsp granulated (white) sugar
500ml/17fl oz/scant 2¼ cups eau de vie

1 Wash and pit the cherries, then pack them into a sterilized, wide-necked bottle along with the blanched almonds.

2 Spoon the sugar over the fruit, then pour in the eau de vie to cover and seal tightly.

3 Store for at least 1 month before serving, shaking the bottle now and then to help dissolve the sugar.

Cook's Tip
Eau de vie actually refers to all spirits distilled from fermented fruits. It is in fact a fruit brandy. Eau de vie is always colourless, with a high alcohol content (sometimes 45% ABV) and a clean, pure scent and the flavour of the founding fruit. This is due to the fast fermenting process used. Popular eaux de vie are made from cherries and strawberries, which go perfectly with the luscious ripe cherries used in this recipe, producing a heady aroma of summer fruit.

Variation
Strawberries, raspberries and blackcurrants are all excellent preserved in eau de vie. They will all produce fine fruity liqueurs and macerated fruit. Orchard fruits, such as apples, pears and plums, are also used to make eau de vie. Use one of these as a base for a preserve of the same type of fruit. The resulting fruit liqueurs, strained, make fabulous Champagne cocktails.

Index

ale
- chestnut, Stilton and ale pie 100
- steak, mushroom and ale pie 117

almonds
- almond and cinnamon coil 243
- almond and date filo parcels 156
- almond and pine nut tart 177
- almond and raspberry slices 140
- almond chocolate mazarins 218
- almond cigars 155
- almond cream puffs 126
- almond ice cream sandwiches 167
- almond mincemeat tarts 136
- almond pastries 126
- almond pastry 11
- almond shortbread fingers 164
- almond stars 166
- almond tartlets 150
- almond tiles 167
- apricot and almond jalousie 232
- apricot and almond tart 201
- apricot frangipane tart 199
- Bakewell tart 183
- blueberry and almond tart 203
- butter and almond stars 165
- chocolate almond meringue pie 210
- crunchy apple and almond flan 194
- Danish pastry 152
- date and almond tart 207
- fruit and almond pastries 138
- gazelles' horns 135
- greengage and almond jam 253
- maids of honour cakes 143
- oznei haman 160
- pear and almond cream tart 198
- plum and marzipan puff 196
- raspberry and almond tart 179
- squash, apricot and almond chutney 245
- sweet almond cookies 166
- sweet samosas 159
- trout with pastry and almond crust 65

amaretti
- mango and amaretti strudel 170
- pear and amaretti tarts 151

amaretto
- chocolate amaretto nut tart 210

anchovies
- egg and anchovy pies 67
- onion and anchovy tart 92
- sweet pepper choux with anchovies 68

apples
- American apple pie 225
- apple and orange pie 227
- apple and raisin pie 227
- apple and sultana chutney 245
- apple crumble and custard slices 140
- apple lattice pie 226
- apple puffs 242
- apple strudel 168
- apple turnover 128
- apple, raisin and maple pies 154
- baked apple dumplings 242
- Basque apple pie 224
- bilberry and apple pie 235
- blackberry and apple jam 250
- cherry and apple strudel 169
- crunchy apple and almond flan 194
- deep-dish apple pie 224
- Dutch ham and apple pie 110
- filo-topped apple pie 226
- French apple tart 193
- haggis, potato and apple pie 115
- mince tarts 137
- plated apple pie 225
- plum and apple jelly 252
- poppy seed and apple strudel 168
- rustic apple tart 193
- tarte tatin 194

apricots
- apricot and almond jalousie 232
- apricot and almond tart 201
- apricot and vanilla triangles 125
- apricot filo purses 158
- apricot frangipane tart 199
- apricot pie 232
- apricot turnovers 129
- chicken and apricot filo pie 107
- chocolate apricot Linzer tart 217
- Moroccan apricot coil 233
- rice custard tart with apricots 200
- squash, apricot and almond chutney 245

Armagnac
- prune and Armagnac tart 205

asparagus
- trout and asparagus pie 103

aubergine and bean one-crust pie 59
aubergine, spinach and feta pie 89

bacon
- bacon and egg pie 113
- chard and bacon pasties 75
- leek and bacon tart 95
- leeks, bacon and egg pie 112
- mini pork and bacon pies 45
- quiche Lorraine 81
- Shropshire bacon and potato pie 111

Bakewell tart 183
baking blind 9
bamboo shoots
- crystal dumplings 48

bananas
- Boston banoffee pie 180
- chocolate, banana and toffee pie 216

basil
- ricotta and basil tart 92
- tomato and basil tart 91

beancurd skin parcels, braised 48
beans
- aubergine and bean one-crust pie 59

beef
- beef and curd cheese pasties 76
- beef and mushroom pudding 79
- beef turnovers 78
- beef Wellington 74
- beef, leek and cheese tartlets 46
- beef, mushroom and rice patties 116
- Brazilian beef pasties 34
- caraway and beef pastries 36
- Cornish pasties 77
- golden beef and potato puffs 35
- golden beef samosas 33
- goulash puff pies 114
- layered beef and pine nut pie 115
- little Russian beef pies 35
- meat briouates 78
- mince Wellington 116
- mushrooms and meat fritters 47
- Peruvian beef pies 36
- savoury cigars 31
- Siberian beef dumplings 54
- steak and kidney pudding 79
- steak and onion pasties 77
- steak and oyster pie 117
- steak pie with mustard gravy 119
- steak, mushroom and ale pie 117

berries
- grated berry bake 141
- summer berry tart 204
- Tia Maria berry tarts 147

bilberry and apple pie 235
blackberries
- blackberry and apple jam 250
- blackberry tart 203
- Dunfillan bramble pudding 235
- rich chocolate-berry tart 216

blackcurrant jam 252
blackcurrant tart 202
blueberries
- blueberries and lime jam 249
- blueberry and almond tart 203
- blueberry and coffee flan 204 
- blueberry and orange pie 233
- peach and blueberry lattice pie 234
- small blueberry pies 148

brandy
- brandied Roquefort tarts 42
- peach and brandy pie 228

bread sauce 247
buckwheat cheesecake 186
butter
- Brittany butter cookies 162
- butter and almond stars 165
- chicken parcels with herb butter 72

cabbage
- puff pastry cabbage pie 61

caramel
- caramelized onion tart 86
- sablés with caramel glaze 163

caraway and beef pastries 36
cardamom
- pear tarte tatin with cardamom 198

cashew nuts
- baked cashew diamonds 127
- neuris 159

chard
- chard and bacon pasties 75
- Swiss chard pie 96

cheese
- aubergine, spinach and feta pie 89
- baked sweet ravioli 134
- beef and curd cheese pasties 76
- beef, leek and cheese tartlets 46
- brandied Roquefort tarts 42
- cheese aigrettes 14
- cheese and asparagus flan 86
- cheese and dill pastries 18
- cheese and bacon quiche 80
- cheese and pesto triangles 16
- cheese and spinach flan 95
- cheese filo scrolls 14
- cheese straws 12
- cheese, rice and vegetable strudel 60
- chestnut, Stilton and ale pie 100
- chicken, cheese and leek plait 73
- corn and cheese pastries 16
- cottage cheese dumplings 57
- courgette and ricotta tart 88
- crab and ricotta tartlets 42
- creamy Roquefort tartlets 38
- deep-fried pastry with cheese 12
- feta and olive tartlets 40
- filo and feta cheese pie 99
- filo cigars filled with feta 15
- filo purses with creamy leeks 17
- Gouda-filled puffs 13
- half-moon cheese pies 19
- leek and Roquefort tart with walnut pastry 89
- leek, cheese and hazelnut tart 87
- maids of honour cakes 143
- mushroom and Parmesan quiche 83
- onion tarts with goat's cheese 37
- potato and cheese pirozhki, 56
- prosciutto and mozzarella parcels 28
- ratatouille and fontina strudel 60
- ricotta and basil tart 92
- rugelach 123
- Sardinian honey fritters 133
- savoury cigars 31
- spinach and cottage cheese pie 100
- spinach and ricotta tart 91
- tiny cheese puffs 13
- tomato and cheese cups 15
- vegetarian Christmas pie 97
- wild mushroom and fontina tarts 81

cheesecake
- baked chocolate cheesecake 215
- buckwheat cheesecake 186
- cheese and honey tart 185
- chocolate cheesecake tart 214
- chocolate ricotta pie 215
- chocolate truffle tart 212
- curd tarts 148
- lemon cheesecake 187
- lemon and ricotta tart 191
- orange curd tarts with Cointreau 146
- raisin cheesecake 186
- red grape and cheese tartlets 146
- ricotta tart 184
- ricotta and Marsala tarts 144
- vanilla cream cheese tart 185
- Yorkshire curd tart 176

chermoula
- fish and chermoula mini pies 26

cherries
- cherries in eau de vie 253
- cherry and apple strudel 169
- cherry and pecan strudel 169
- cherry pie 234
- rhubarb and cherry pie 236

chervil tart 87
chestnut, Stilton and ale pie 100
chicken
- braised beancurd skin parcels 48
- chicken and apricot filo pie 107
- chicken and asparagus tartlets 45
- chicken and couscous turnover 72
- chicken and ham pie 104
- chicken and leek pie 106
- chicken and mushroom pie 106
- chicken and mushroom vol-au-vents 44
- chicken and onion turnovers 28
- chicken and palm hearts pie 108
- chicken bouche 108
- chicken charter pie 105
- chicken cinnamon pie 105
- chicken parcels with herb butter 72
- chicken, cheese and leek plait 73
- small chicken pies 44
- smoked chicken with peach mayonnaise in filo tartlets 29
- spiced chicken and egg filo pie 107
- Tunisian brik 27
- Turkish pilaff pie 104

chickpeas
- chickpea chocolate pastries 221
- spicy chickpea samosas 20

chive dumplings 49
chocolate
- almond chocolate mazarins 218
- baked chocolate cheesecake 215
- baked sweet ravioli 134
- chickpea chocolate pastries 221
- chocolate almond meringue pie 210
- chocolate amaretto nut tart 210
- chocolate and date filo coil 208
- chocolate and pine nut tart 211
- chocolate and strawberry palmiers 142
- chocolate apricot Linzer tart 217
- chocolate boats 219
- chocolate cheesecake tart 214
- chocolate chiffon pie 209
- chocolate churros 223
- chocolate cinnamon tuiles 222
- chocolate eclairs 220
- chocolate lemon tart 208
- chocolate pretzels 223
- chocolate ricotta pie 215
- chocolate tiramisu tart 211
- chocolate truffle tart 212
- chocolate tuiles 221
- chocolate whirls 219
- chocolate-topped candied fruit pie 180
- chocolate, banana and toffee pie 216
- chocolate, pear and pecan pie 213
- chocolate sauce 248
- dark chocolate and hazelnut tart 214
- dark chocolate fingers 222
- Greek chocolate mousse tartlets 218
- Mississippi mud pie 212
- pear and chocolate tartlets 217
- rich chocolate-berry tart 216
- truffle-filled filo tulips 157
- velvety mocha tart 209
- white chocolate and mango tart 213

chorizo pastry puffs 37
choux pastry 11
- chocolate eclairs 220
- choux custard pastries 105
- coffee profiteroles 105
- croquembouche 174
- double chocolate choux puffs 220
- gâteau Saint-Honoré 174
- mushroom and quail's egg gougère 62
- seafood gougère 69
- St Joseph's Day choux buns 175
- strawberry and Kirsch choux ring 175
- sweet pepper choux with anchovies 68
- trout gougère 70

cider pie 181
cinnamon
almond and cinnamon coil 243
chicken cinnamon pie 105
chocolate cinnamon tuiles 222
mince pies with spiced pastry 137
spiced nut palmiers 142
claret
cranberry and claret jelly 249
cockles
wild mushroom and cockle puff 58
coconut
coconut cream pie 176
Indian coconut parcels 160
cod
filo-wrapped cod 64
fish and prawn vol-au-vents 24
coffee
blueberry and coffee flan 204
coffee and pistachio baklava 172
coffee custard tart 187
coffee profiteroles 105
crunchy-topped coffee meringue pie 239
velvety mocha tart 209
walnut and coffee pie 240
walnut and coffee slice 141
Cointreau
orange curd tarts with Cointreau 146
condensed milk
Boston banoffee pie 180
chicken neck pastries 124
chocolate, banana and toffee pie 216
key lime pie 188
coriander
lamb and coriander pie 114
corn
corn and cheese pastries 16
Thai tung tong 26
Cornish pasties 77
cornmeal
pork pie with cornmeal crust 112
courgette and dill tart 88
courgette and ricotta tart 88
couscous
chicken and couscous turnover 72
crab
crab and prawn filo tart 94
crab and ricotta tartlets 42
pork and crab spring rolls 53
steamed crab dim sum 55
cranberries
cranberry and claret jelly 249
fruit tart with cranberry sauce 195
grapefruit and cranberry marmalade 251
turkey and cranberry parcels 29
turkey and cranberry pie 109
cream
almond cream puffs 126
chocolate tiramisu tart 211
coconut cream pie 176
creamy Roquefort tartlets 38
raspberry and crème brûlée tart 202
salmon and chanterelle cream pie 103
truffle-filled filo tulips 157
currants
Border tart 203
lamb currant pie 113
custard 248
apple crumble and custard slices 140
choux custard pastries 105
coffee custard tart 187
custard tart with plums 195
little nutmeg custard tarts 144
Marsala custard tart 184
rice custard tart with apricots 200

Danish pastry 152 (image on page 1)
dates
almond and date filo parcels 156
chess pie 189
chocolate and date filo coil 208
date and almond tart 207
date-filled pastries 124
dill
cheese and dill pastries 18
courgette and dill tart 88
filo baskets with ginger and dill 17
duck wontons 52
dulce de leche 248

Eccles cakes 136
eggs
bacon and egg pie 113
carnival fritters 123
egg and anchovy pies 67
egg and salmon puff parcels 67
egg and spinach pie 99
Jewish tuna and egg pasties 24
leeks, bacon and egg pie 112
mushroom and quail's egg gougère 62
picnic pie with ginger 98
quail's egg and vermouth tartlets 41
quiche Lorraine 81
spiced chicken and egg filo pie 107
summer fruit brulée tartlets 147
tuna and egg galette 63
Tunisian brik 27

figs
fig pastries with nuts and honey 125
fresh fig filo tart 206
fish
fish and chermoula mini pies 26
fish in a dough jacket 68
golden filo fish pie 101
Welsh fish and laverbread pie 102
flaky pastry 10
food processors 8
fruit
baked fruit flan 207
chocolate-topped candied fruit pie 180
exotic fruit tranche 206
filo fruit baskets 157
filo fruit scrunchies 161
fruit tart with cranberry sauce 195
summer fruit brulée tartlets 147
fruit, dried
English Eccles cakes 136
filo crackers 156
fruit and almond pastries 138
fruit and nut turnovers 130
Greek fruit and nut pastries 129
Italian sweetmeat pastries 127
mince pies with spiced pastry 137
mince tarts 137
Sardinian iced pastry cookies 133
Scottish black bun 241
snake-shaped cake 243
whiskey-laced mince pies 138

game
game pie with port 121
hare pot pies 120
pheasant pasty 76
pigeon pie 121
rabbit and game pie 120
garlic
caramelized shallot and garlic tarte tatin 85
garlic mayonnaise 244
potato, shallot and garlic samosas 20
walnut and garlic sauce 247
ginger
filo baskets with ginger and dill 17
one-crust rhubarb and ginger pie 237
picnic pie with ginger 98
salmon and ginger pie 101
gluten-free pastry 10
grapefruit and cranberry marmalade 251
grapes
red grape and cheese tartlets 146
green curry puffs 54
greengage and almond jam 253

haddock
pale smoked haddock flan 93
haggis cups with neeps and tatties 30
haggis, potato and apple pie 115
ham
chicken and ham pie 104
Dutch ham and apple pie 110
veal and ham pie 119
hare pot pies 120
hazelnuts
dark chocolate and hazelnut tart 214
leek, cheese and hazelnut tart 87
pear and hazelnut flan 199
herbs
chicken parcels with herb butter 72
herbed mini tarts 38
honey
angel's wings 122
cheese and honey tart 185
fig pastries with nuts and honey 125
honey and pine nut tart 178
honey-coated fritters 131
rustic walnut and honey tart 178
Sardinian honey fritters 133

ice cream
almond ice cream sandwiches 167
filo pastry, ice cream and mincemeat parcels 161
walnut and ice cream palmiers 143

jam
Bakewell tart 183
blackberry and apple jam 250
blackcurrant jam 252
cranberry and claret jelly 249
grapefruit and cranberry marmalade 251
greengage and almond jam 253
jam roly poly 241
jam tarts 145
lattice jam tart 178
Linzertorte 189
plum and apple jelly 252
strawberry jam 252
vegan Bakewell tart 183

kasha and mushroom knishes 47
Kirsch
plum and Kirsch tart 197
strawberry and Kirsch choux ring 175

lamb
curried lamb samosas 32
Dingle pies 118
Greek kleftiko 118
lamb and coriander pie 114
lamb and pork pie 110
lamb currant pie 113
leg of lamb in pastry 75
lamb roll with pear stuffing 74
Lebanese meat pastries 33
meat briouates 78
mushrooms and meat fritters 47
squab pie 111
Turkish lamb kebab puffs 32
laverbread
Welsh fish and laverbread pie 102
leeks
beef, leek and cheese tartlets 46
chicken and leek pie 106
chicken, cheese and leek plait 73
filo purses with creamy leeks 17
leek and bacon tart 95
leek and onion tartlets 40
leek and Roquefort tart with walnut pastry 89
leek, cheese and hazelnut tart 87
leek, saffron and mussel tartlets 39
leeks, bacon and egg pie 112
potato and leek filo pie 98

vegetarian Christmas pie 97
lemons
chocolate lemon tart 208
fresh lemon tart 190
lemon and passion fruit tart 191
lemon and ricotta tart 191
lemon cheesecake 187
lemon curd 251
lemon meringue pie 238
lemon shortbread cookies 165
raspberry and lemon tartlets 145
lentils
spiced lentil-filled pasties 23
limes
blueberries and lime jam 249
key lime pie 188
lime meringue pie 238

maids of honour cakes 143
mango
crispy mango stacks 171
mango and amaretti strudel 170
mango and tamarillo pastries 151
mango pie 237
white chocolate and mango tart 213
maple syrup
apple, raisin and maple pies 154
maple and walnut tart 179
Marsala
Marsala custard tart 184
ricotta and Marsala tarts 144
marzipan
plum and marzipan pastries 150
plum and marzipan puff 196
meringue
chocolate almond meringue pie 210
crunchy-topped coffee meringue pie 239
lemon meringue pie 238
lime meringue pie 238
plum meringue pie 240
rhubarb meringue pie 239
mincemeat 250
almond mincemeat tarts 136
filo pastry, ice cream and mincemeat parcels 161
mince pies with spiced pastry 137
mince tarts 137
mincemeat tart 190
whiskey-laced mince pies 138
mushrooms
beef and mushroom pudding 79
beef, mushroom and rice patties 116
braised beancurd skin parcels 48
chicken and mushroom pie 106
filo baskets with ginger and dill 17
kasha and mushroom knishes 47
mushroom and Parmesan quiche 83
mushroom and quail's egg gougère 62
mushroom and sunflower seed flan 82
mushroom börek 58
mushroom, nut and prune jalousie 59
mushrooms and meat fritters 47
mushroom tarts with walnut pastry 39
Polish mushroom dumplings 56
salmon and chanterelle cream pie 103
scallops with wild mushrooms 69
snails with ceps 71
steak, mushroom and ale pie 117
vegetarian Christmas pie 97
wild mushroom and cockle puff 58
wild mushroom and fontina tarts 81
wild mushroom tart 82
mussels
leek, saffron and mussel tartlets 39
mustard
steak pie with mustard gravy 119
mutton
Dingle pies 118
mutton pies 46

nectarine and physalis tartlets 149
nectarine puff pastry tarts 152
nutmeg
little nutmeg custard tarts 144
nuts
chocolate amaretto nut tart 210
fig pastries with nuts and honey 125
fruit and nut turnovers 130
Italian sweetmeat pastries 127
mushroom, nut and prune jalousie 59

picnic pie with ginger 98
Sardinian iced pastry cookies 133
snake-shaped cake 243
spiced nut palmiers 142
sticky nut pie 181

olives
feta and olive tartlets 40
red onion and black olive pissaladière 84
tomato and black olive tart 90
onions
caramelized onion tart 86
cheese and bacon quiche 80
chicken and onion turnovers 28
English pickled onions 244
leek and onion tartlets 40
onion and anchovy tart 92
onion gravy 246
onion tart 85
onion tarts with goat's cheese 37
pickled red onion relish 244
red onion and black olive pissaladière 84
red onion tart 80
steak and onion pasties 77
white onion sauce 246
oranges
apple and orange pie 227
blueberry and orange pie 233
fresh orange tart 192
fruit-filled empanadas 128
orange curd tarts with Cointreau 146
orange pastries 122
orange sweetheart tart 192
spiced orange pastry 11
oysters
steak and oyster pie 117

pastry
almond 11
baking blind 9
choux 11
flaky 10
gluten-free 10
pâte sucrée 9
puff 10
rich shortcrust 8
shortcrust 8
palm hearts
chicken and palm hearts pie 108
heart of palm pie 96
passion fruit
lemon and passion fruit tart 191
passion fruit pie 231
pâte brisée 8
pâte sucrée 9
peaches
baked lattice peaches 153
peach and blueberry lattice pie 234
peach and brandy pie 228
peach and redcurrant tartlets 149
peach leaf pie 229
peanuts
pork and nut dumplings 49
pork and peanut wontons 50
pears
chocolate, pear and pecan pie 213
lamb roll with pear stuffing 74
pear and almond cream tart 198
pear and amaretti tarts 151
pear and chocolate tartlets 217
pear and hazelnut flan 199
pear and plum pie 231
pear tarte tatin with cardamom 198
walnut and pear lattice pie 228
peas
spiced pea samosas 23
pecans
cherry and pecan strudel 169
chocolate, pear and pecan pie 213
pecan pie 177
pecan tassies 139
peppers
grilled pepper tartlets 41
red pepper and watercress parcels 18
sweet pepper choux with anchovies 68
perch
fish and pork pie 102
pesto
cheese and pesto triangles 16
pheasant pasty 76
physalis
nectarine and physalis tartlets 149
pigeon pie 121
pine nuts
honey and pine nut tart 178
layered beef and pine nut pie 115
spinach pastries with pine nuts 21
pistachios
coffee and pistachio baklava 172
Turkish pilaff pie 104
plums
Alsatian plum tart 196
custard tart with plums 195
fruit turnovers 130
German plum cake 230
pear and plum pie 231
plum dumpling 153
plum and marzipan puff 196
plum and apple jelly 252
plum and Kirsch tart 197
plum and marzipan pastries 150
plum filo pockets 158
plum meringue pie 240
plum pie 230
plum polenta pie 229
yellow plum tart 197
polenta
plum polenta pie 229
pork
crackling flat cakes 34
deep-fried wontons 51
minced pork and taro puffs 31
mini pork and bacon pies 45
mushrooms and meat fritters 47
pork and crab spring rolls 53
pork and nut dumplings 49
pork and peanut wontons 50
pork and prawn dumplings 51
pork pie with cornmeal crust 112
pork sausage plait 73
roast pork dumplings 50
port
game pie with port 121
potatoes
golden beef and potato puffs 35
haggis cups with neeps and tatties 30
haggis, potato and apple pie 115
potato and cheese pirozhki 56
potato and leek filo pie 98
potato dumplings 57
potato fritters 132
potato, shallot and garlic samosas 20
Shropshire bacon and potato pie 111
spicy potato strudel 61
prawns
crab and prawn filo tart 94
firecrackers 25
fish and chermoula mini pies 26
fish and prawn vol-au-vents 24
Moroccan prawn packages 25
pork and prawn dumplings 51
prawn tartlets 43
salmon and prawn flan 94
prosciutto and mozzarella parcels 28
prunes
Christmas stars 135
glazed prune tart 205
prune and Armagnac tart 205
puff pastry 10
pumpkin
Thanksgiving pumpkin pie 182
vegan pumpkin pie 182

quiche Lorraine 81
quinoa
salmon and quinoa pie 65

rabbit and game pie 120
raisins
apple and raisin pie 227
apple, raisin and maple pies 154
fruit-filled empanadas 128
neuris 159
oznei haman 160
raisin cheesecake 186
sweet samosas 159
raita 247
raspberries
almond and raspberry slices 140
crispy mango wontons with raspberry drizzle sauce 52
mini mille feuilles 154
raspberry and almond tart 179
raspberry and crème brûlée tart 202
raspberry and lemon tartlets 145
raspberry jam 250
raspberry tart 201
ratatouille and fontina strudel 60
redcurrants
peach and redcurrant tartlets 149
rhubarb
filo chiffon pie 171
one-crust rhubarb and ginger pie 237
rhubarb and cherry pie 236
rhubarb meringue pie 239
rhubarb pie 236
rice
beef, mushroom and rice patties 116
cheese, rice and vegetable strudel 60
Creole Calas fritters 131
rice custard tart with apricots 200
rice pudding pastries 22
Turkish pilaff pie 104

sablés with caramel glaze 163
saffron
leek, saffron and mussel tartlets 39
salmon
salmon and chanterelle cream pie 103
salmon and ginger pie 101
salmon and prawn flan 94
salmon and quinoa pie 65
salmon coulibiac 66
salmon parcels 27
salmon puffs 66
smoked salmon quiche 93
salsa verde 247
sardine and spinach parcels 63
sauerkraut pie 97
sausage rolls 30
scallops with wild mushrooms 69
sea bream
fillets of sea bream in filo pastry 64
seafood gougère 69
seafood puff ring 71
seeds
Hungarian poppy seed pastry 155
mushroom and sunflower seed flan 82
poppy seed and apple strudel 168
shallots
caramelized shallot and garlic tarte tatin 85
potato, shallot and garlic samosas 20
roast shallot tart with thyme 84
shellfish in puff pastry 70
shortcrust pastry 8
rich shortcrust pastry 8
snails with ceps 71
spices
shoofly pie 188
spiced chicken and egg filo pie 107
spiced lentil-filled pasties 23
spiced orange pastry 11
spiced pea samosas 23
spiced sweet potato turnovers 22
Venetian pastries 132
spinach
aubergine, spinach and feta pie 89
cheese and spinach flan 95
egg and spinach pie 99
sardine and spinach parcels 63
savoury cigars 31
spinach and cottage cheese pie 100
spinach and ricotta tart 91
spinach empanadillas 21
spinach pastries with pine nuts 21
squash, apricot and almond chutney 245
steak and kidney pudding 79
steak and onion pasties 77
steak and oyster pie 117
steak pie with mustard gravy 119
steak, mushroom and ale pie 117
strawberries
chocolate and strawberry palmiers 142
strawberry and Kirsch choux ring 175
strawberry jam 252
strawberry tart 201
sugar
Dutch sugar slice 139
shoofly pie 188
sugar-topped cookies 164
sugar-topped stars 163
sultanas
apple and sultana chutney 245
rugelach 123
swede
haggis cups with neeps and tatties 30
sweet potatoes
spiced sweet potato turnovers 22

tamarillo
mango and tamarillo pastries 151
tapenade
tomato and tapenade tartlets 62
taro
minced pork and taro puffs 31
thyme
roast shallot tart with thyme 84
Tia Maria berry tarts 147
tofu
steamed tofu dumplings 55
tomatoes
tomato and basil tart 91
tomato and black olive tart 90
tomato and cheese cups 15
tomato and tapenade tartlets 62
tomato quiche 90
treacle tart 184
trout
smoked trout tartlets 43
trout and asparagus pie 103
trout gougère 70
trout with pastry and almond crust 65
tuna
Jewish tuna and egg pasties 24
tuna and egg galette 63
turkey and cranberry parcels 29
turkey and cranberry pie 109
turkey börek 109

vanilla
apricot and vanilla triangles 125
quick vanilla cookies 163
vanilla cream cheese tart 185
vanilla crescents 162
veal
mushrooms and meat fritters 47
veal and ham pie 119
vegetables
baked vegetable samosas 19
cheese, rice and vegetable strudel 60
crispy vegetable spring rolls 53
ratatouille and fontina strudel 60
vegetable tarte tatin 83
vegetarian Christmas pie 97
vermouth
quail's egg and vermouth tartlets 41

walnuts
Border tart 203
chess pie 189
Greek fruit and nut pastries 129
Hungarian Christmas loaf 170
leek and Roquefort tart with walnut pastry 89
maple and walnut tart 179
rugelach 123
rustic walnut and honey tart 178
walnut and coffee pie 240
walnut and coffee slice 141
walnut and garlic sauce 247
walnut and ice cream palmiers 143
walnut and pear lattice pie 228
walnut baklava 172
watercress
red pepper and watercress parcels 18
whiskey-laced mince pies 138

Yorkshire curd tart 176